BECKET'S CROWN

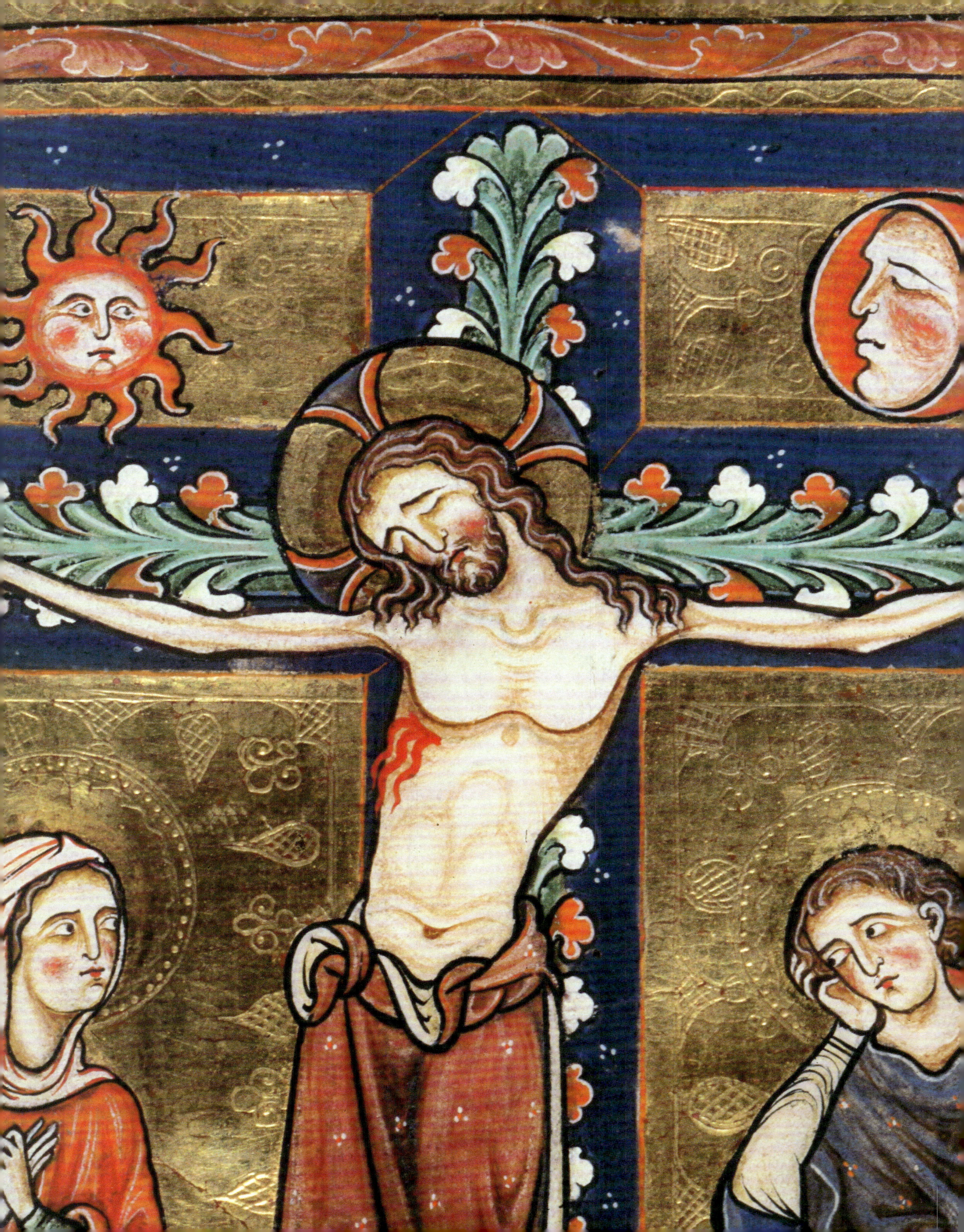

PAUL BINSKI

BECKET'S CROWN

ART AND IMAGINATION IN GOTHIC ENGLAND

1170–1300

Published for
THE PAUL MELLON CENTRE FOR STUDIES IN BRITISH ART
by
YALE UNIVERSITY PRESS
NEW HAVEN AND LONDON

Designed by Gillian Malpass

Printed in Italy

Library of Congress Cataloging-in-Publication Data

Binski, Paul.
Becket's crown: art and imagination in Gothic England, 1170–1350 / Paul Binski.
p. cm.
Includes bibliographical references and index.
ISBN 0-300-10509-6 (cl : alk. paper)
1. Architecture, Gothic – England. 2. Church architecture – England. 3. Liturgy and architecture – England. 4. Architecture and religion – England. 5. England – Church history. I. Title.
NA5463.B45 2004
726.5′0942′0902 – dc22 2004002273

A catalogue record for this book is available from
The British Library

FRONTISPIECE Crucifixion. Psalter of Robert of Lindsey, Society of Antiquaries MS 59, fol. 35v, *c.* 1220 (detail of fig. 169)

PAGE VI Elevation of the Host. Decretals of Gregory IX. Cambridge, Fitzwilliam Museum, Marlay Cutting Fr. 2, *c.* 1340 (detail of fig. 124)

For Anne

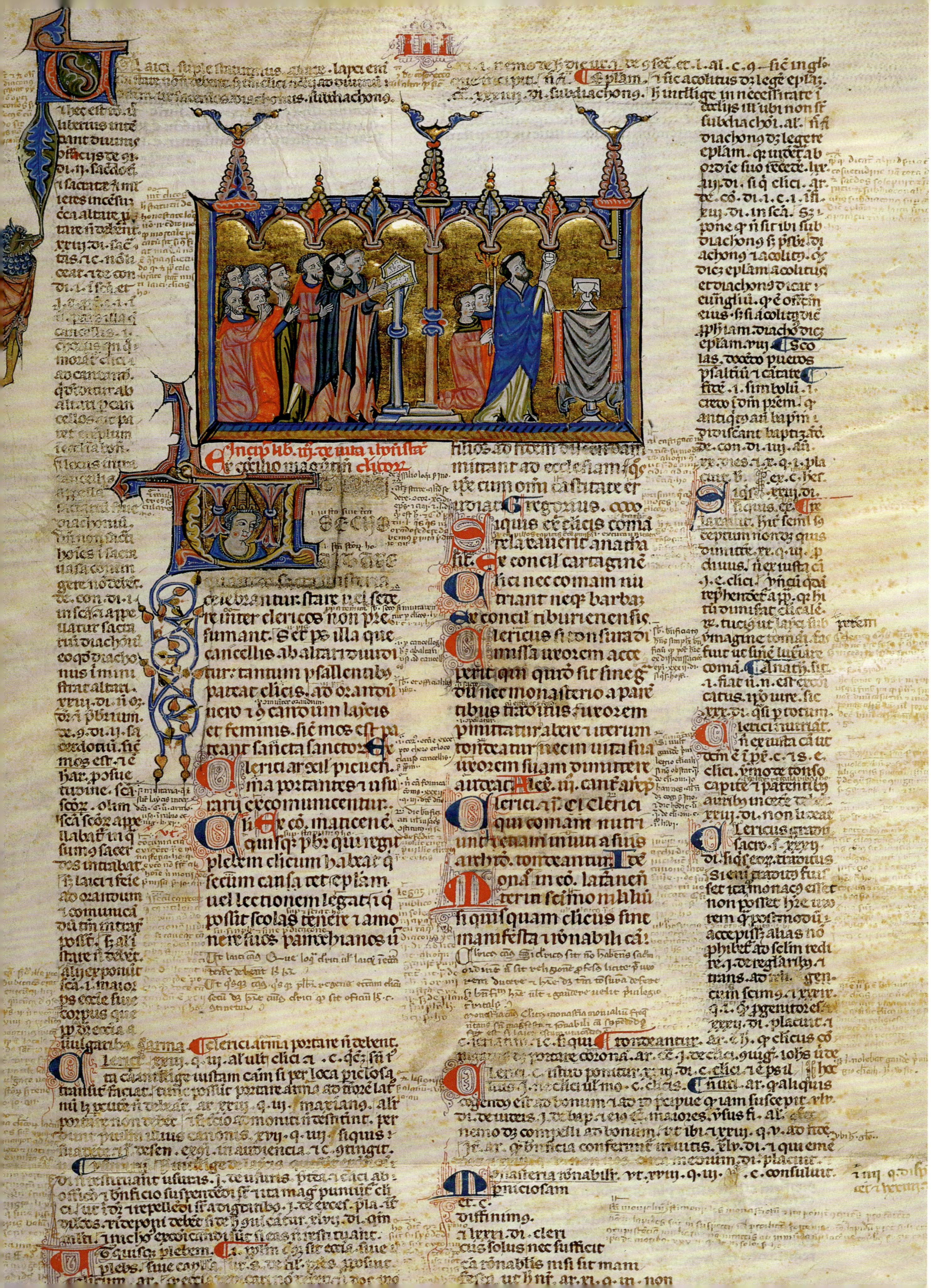
Incipit lib. iii de uita et honestate
clericorum
celebrantur stare uel sedere
inter clericos non pre-
sumant. Sed pars illa que
cancellis ab altari diuidi-
tur tantum psallentibus
pateat clericis. ad orandum
uero et communicandum laicis
et feminis sicut mos est pa-
teant sancta sanctorum.
Siquis ex clericis comam
relaxauerit anathema
sit. Ex concil. cartaginense.
Clerici nec comam nu-
triant neque barbam.
Clericus si tonsuram di-
missa uxorem acce-
perit
Gregorius.

Contents

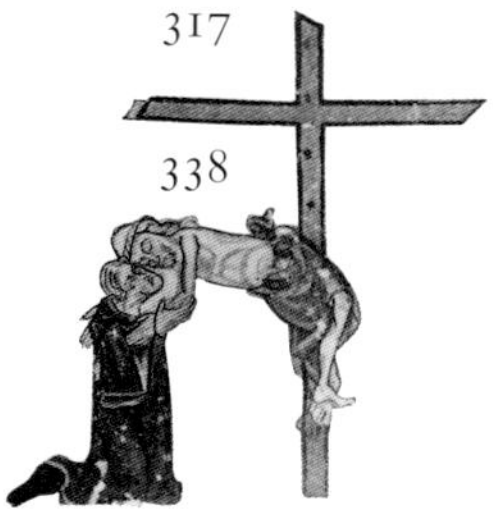

Acknowledgements

Some of the material in this book was first presented to a public audience in the Paul Mellon Lectures which I delivered in 2002–3 at the National Gallery, London, and again at the Yale Center for British Art in New Haven. Since then it has of course been very substantially recast; but I am most grateful for having had the opportunity to share my ideas with quick-witted and surprisingly tenacious audiences on either side of the Atlantic. In particular, I would like to extend my warmest thanks to the staff of the Paul Mellon Centre for Studies in British Art and the Yale Center for British Art for their magnificent hospitality, and for enabling this book to appear in its present form. As well as having the support of the Paul Mellon Centre I must acknowledge the honour extended to me by the award of a British Academy/Leverhulme Trust Senior Research Fellowship for 2003–4, which has allowed me to bring the book satisfactorily to completion. I am extremely grateful to my colleagues in the Department of the History of Art at Cambridge for tolerating my absence on leave, and to the Master and Fellows of Caius College for releasing me from my college duties for the duration.

My debts to my friends and fellow medievalists are many. I owe particular thanks to Paul Crossley, whose positive and trenchant criticisms of a draft of the book were delivered with characteristic cheer and enthusiasm. Julian Luxford was kind enough to offer valuable and detailed notes on the text, and Christopher Wilson offered moral and practical support. All my students have helped in various ways, though I would like to thank especially Matthew Reeve, Christopher Moule and Laura Williams for pointing things out and generally for keeping me on my toes. At Caius, John Casey discussed with me various aspects of Cardinal Newman, Hegel and Sartre, and Peter Stacey offered fresh and perceptive criticism of the discussion of affect in Part IV. Help has also been rendered over the years by Adelaide Bennett, Christopher Brooke, Anne Duggan, Lindy Grant, Sandy Heslop, Håkan Lindberg, Nigel Morgan, Christopher Norton, Unn Plahter, Miri Rubin, Tim Tatton-Brown and Nicholas Vincent. Assistance beyond the call of duty was provided by John Crook, Glyn Davies and Jerry Sampson in providing illustrations, and pictures were also provided by Øystein Ekroll, Elly Miller and Sebastian Strobl. I am also grateful to the staff of the many institutions which have facilitated my research, and particularly to the University Library in Cambridge, an institution almost uniquely suited to the kind of academic legwork involved. Gillian Malpass and Ruth Thackeray made the book as well as it could be made, and Anne Page helped in all sorts of ways. I hope it will not come as a surprise to those who know us that she is the dedicatee of this book.

King's Parade
Cambridge
All Saints Day 2003

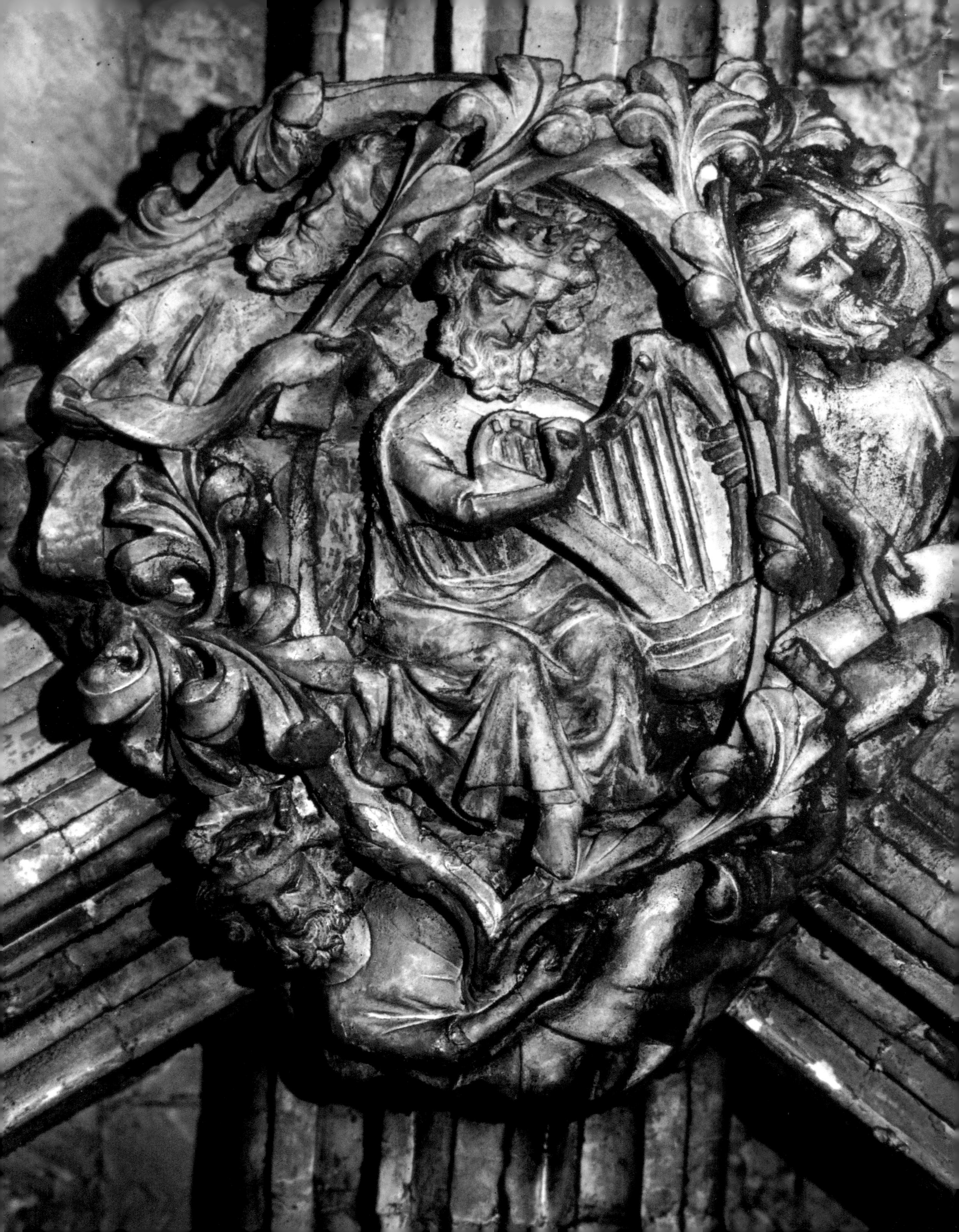

Prologue

Art, Imagination and Authority: Four Paths of Enquiry

The choice of the English thirteenth century as the topic for an extended study of the visual arts has not been a natural one in recent decades. Perhaps two published texts stand out. Peter Brieger's thoroughly sensible and still useful contribution to the Oxford History of Art series entitled *English Art 1216–1307*, the only remotely comprehensive text of its type, was published as long ago as 1957. The exhibition *Age of Chivalry*, held thirty years later at the Royal Academy in London in 1987–8, offered a snapshot of the results of the veritable explosion of specialized studies which have dominated the field as it is understood at present. *Age of Chivalry* was shaped by a progressive interest in the patronage, social history and function of art in the whole period 1200–1400, taking far greater account of various social groups not included by Brieger, and in its sheer range of exhibits and ideas reflecting a more inclusive notion of 'visual culture' than would have been conceivable in the 1940s or 1950s.

My aims in the present book are both narrower and broader than those of the above two very different volumes, for it neither observes the constraints expected of a textbook such as Brieger's, nor enjoys the freedoms of an exceptionally rich and necessarily diverse exhibition such as *Age of Chivalry*. To a greater extent than either, it is preoccupied with religion, ethics and the domain of the aesthetic; also, much more time is spent here in the sustained criticism and discussion of specific works of art and architecture in relation to a few fundamental themes. It is theoretically eclectic in inspiration and practical in its methods. The writings of the 'Cambridge school' of art history that grew up under the tutelage of George Henderson in the 1970s and 1980s exemplified a style – 'style' seems preferable to method or theory – of commentary on works of art, at the heart of which lay an interest in textual, social and cultural exegesis and also a (then unfashionable, but highly productive) disregard for the often institutionally imposed frontiers around the study of the various visual media. Its products have been as diverse as the work of the late and much-lamented Michael Camille, and that of the present writer, both of whom, though pursuing quite different interests, have been significantly shaped too by contact with universities in the United States. My discussion owes much to the English academic tradition, while also taking account of historical and cultural theories developed by American thinkers. An instance is the work of Clifford Geertz at Princeton. The opening chapter of his *Interpretation of Cultures* (1973), entitled 'Thick Description: Toward an Interpretive Theory of Culture', states that 'man is an animal suspended in webs of significance he himself has spun. I take culture to be those webs, and the analysis of it to be therefore not an experimental science in search of law but an interpretative one in search of meaning.' What defines this insight for Geertz is the 'elaborate venture in, to borrow a notion from Gilbert Ryle, "thick description"', which is to say the placement of cultural products or signs within a multiplicity of complex structures – which might be social, economic, religious, ethical, aesthetic, mythological – in such a way as to suggest their fulness of meaning within the public domain. The liberal, holistic and occasionally paradoxical character of this style of analysis is attractive and congenial to the present writer's intention of offering some account of what Geertz, in the same chapter, calls the 'imaginative universe' within which cultural signs operate. If this means anything for the study of English art of the Middle Ages, it is that scholars have a positive duty to explain in a generally educated manner to non-experts why this art should be interesting at all. This aim is not entirely foreign to the nature of specialized study, as the very real debt owed by this work to the many outstanding books, papers and articles produced in the last two or so generations shows; but it is to an extent obscured by it.

FACING PAGE Tree of Jesse, with David tuning his harp. Lincoln Cathedral, Angel Choir, boss in south aisle (detail of fig. 222).

So my question, then, is 'what was the "imaginative universe" of early Gothic art and architecture in England up to about 1300?' It was with some such question in mind that I published a book in 1995 on Westminster Abbey. This (for some) unconventional enquiry, usually called a 'monograph' in virtue of its object domain, proposed that no account of a great church and its art is complete without a properly inclusive or holistic account of the 'webs of significance', human, ideological (or mythological) and artistic within which it was produced in the first place. In Westminster's case the webs were woven from the silver threads of sanctity, royal image-making, royal ritual and state formation. Inserting an object domain into a culture (which culture?) is no more easy than breathing life back into the notion of 'context'. Such exercises are never easy. They irritate specialists. They require both tact and courage, and perhaps above all a certain vigilance, a preparedness in the face of the possibility that the richest insights may come from unexpected quarters, and that in open-minded exegesis nothing should be ruled out on *a priori* grounds. What 'holism' or 'integration' in such study rather emphatically does not imply is the modern or post-modern yearning for lost intactness and shared symbolic order, summoned in criticism of some integrative interpretation by the eminent German scholar Willibald Sauerländer, in an introductory contribution to the essays also published in 1995 under the title *Artistic Integration in Gothic Buildings*. He says: 'If integration is taken to mean [. . .] that all the different parts and images of the Gothic cathedral corresponded to a medieval concept of order, then one can only say that such a holistic assumption is not confirmed by the study of the different cathedrals, of their program, of their performance, and of their context'.[1] In so far as the type of holistic or thick description envisaged by the present study does not actually claim to discover such universal or essential ordering principles, this stricture is uncontroversial. Holism in this sense is not premised upon bourgeois romantic fantasies of lost world-orders, but almost the reverse: the recognition that a really dense and supple analysis of a building or artwork or set of social relations engaged in art production and reception may expose discontinuities and contentions, disorder not order. This book, shunning cut-and-dried interpretative schedules, in fact tries to argue for the simultaneous existence in the thirteenth century of local and more general discourses, while at the same time accepting that some ideas and outlooks were more important than others.

Indeed, the recognition that causation and meaning are vastly complex and intimidating affairs should not lead one to shed all notions of grand narrative, or of order and rationality, in medieval art. Scepticism about the basically philological methods and reconstitutive objectives of much mid-twentieth-century method, while healthy, need not lead to the sort of overreaction that would strip all art works of coherence and rationality for fear of the charge of over-interpretation or romantic delusion. After all, the search for coherent historical, rhetorical and symbolic significance lies at the heart of medieval contemporaries' efforts to comprehend or justify the creation of art and architecture: towards the end of the twelfth century Gervase of Canterbury proposed one style of account of his cathedral which is scarcely nonsensical, even if it fails to satisfy all the demands of modern empirical enquiry; the author of the Metrical Life of St Hugh proposed another in relation to Lincoln which is easy to dismiss merely because of its commonplaces; Abbot Suger had volunteered perhaps the most remarkable in the 1140s; and there were many others. Formulaic and conventional such accounts may be; but in both language and architectural practice, formulas and conventions are used consciously or unconsciously for a reason, and their ethical and interpretative purpose was surely not the celebration of what would now be identified as a post-modern bricolage or a deliberate promotion of the merits of disorder for its own sake.

A second point needs to be made about the idea of grand narrative, which is that relativism, anti-essentialism and the critical privileging of diversity have rendered it unfashionable to speculate about the existence of dominant ethical and aesthetic traits within a pluralistic horizon. Such traits are taken for granted, not least by the history-as-power school of interpretation; but they are less often examined directly. In arguing that one needs to think about their nature precisely in order better to understand marginality and diversity, the present book aims to restore reflection about the category of the 'aesthetic' to the centre of the field of enquiry, not in its eighteenth-century sense as the sphere of disinterested contemplation, but in the older and fuller sense which takes seriously the moral and political conviction that the study of appearances in relation to social existence, of 'form' generally, is of real consequence and capable of practical historical demonstration. This book is not a study of 'styles' in the ordinary sense of art-historical practice, but of styles in relation to the human *habitus* as a whole: styles of being, of acting, creating, moving, expressing, thinking and believing. Its most persistent question is whether, and to what extent, widely held beliefs about the *habitus* can shed light on those things conventionally grouped under style labels such as 'Gothic', or on the ideals and practices of religion. Inevitably then, this book is about people, about role models, ideals and manners, and, from the viewpoint of authority, methods of codification and implementation. The viewpoint is also, in the first instance, necessarily that of the 'centre'. There is no need to apologize for this, since the formation of these ideals and methods can now only be traced downwards and outwards from their point of origination among the intellectual elites (the schoolmen of the twelfth and thirteenth centuries) to public culture more generally, in so far as it can be defined at all. Public culture was not determined by such ideals and models, but it may have been shaped in important regards by them. The role of intellectuals and art – to paraphrase the subtitle of Beryl Smalley's admirable study *The Becket Conflict and the Schools* – was demonstrably important, because that role was not only closely tied in to public power at large, but also became bound up with the pastoral agenda of the Church. Assessing this role entails the examination of ideals that were of ancient derivation and enduring power, and indeed ancestral to many modern notions of art – for example, the ideal of utility. The fact that such concepts were being shaped at a time of unprecedented innovation in bureaucracy and technology between 1100 and 1300 is also germane. In this period the reformist and pastoral Church was engaged in the development of what amounted almost to a legislative aesthetic, the formation, dissemination and 'top-down' enforcement of which cannot be severed from consideration of what is ordinarily called Gothic, even at the grass-roots level of the parish church and local community. One must therefore ask whether the Church, more than any other political institution, developed a rationale or set of rationales that helped it especially to accommodate, and exploit pragmatically, the inevitable developments of the time in the fields of law, bureaucracy, technology and theology. The religious domain in England provides exceptional quantities and qualities of the evidence one might need to tackle this problem; therefore religion, not only for its own sake, but because it and its human institutions instantiated the highest and most ambitious moral, intellectual and aesthetic ideals of the time, plays a far greater role in this account than it appears to have done in earlier general surveys. In saying that, I am not here proposing a social history of religion, so much as a history of ideals and expectations whose principal vehicles were either in the first instance absolutely religious, or significantly so. That the book is largely about religious beliefs therefore needs no emphasis – or at least it would not, were it not for the evident revival of interest in religion as a hot topic, rather than a theoretical embarrassment, over the last decade or so in the English-speaking world. Arguably the practices of formalism have in themselves tended to be secularist by nature and intention. Though not motivated by any particular religious affiliation, the present text seeks ways of escaping from that tendency precisely by reflecting in different ways upon the notion of the aesthetic itself.

In examining these ethical and religious ideals, it is impossible to disregard the enormous contribution made to their form and, sometimes, content by the heritage of the thought of the pre-Christian ancient world. Rhetorical and ethical yardsticks set out in the Latin literature of the period and assimilated routinely by the clerical *literati* are inescapable, so much so that even chivalry might have been regarded, in C. Stephen Jaeger's words, as a 'neo-classical institution'.[2] The image of the classical has long been influential: when Brieger described the 'classical perfection' of the art of the thirteenth century as 'remote in its serenity', he was using a figure of speech which has been taken rather more seriously in recent studies of the aesthetic of great churches such as Salisbury Cathedral.[3] I would not go so far as to propose that the clerical agenda of the reformist Church was actually itself a neo-classical agenda. Nevertheless, I have taken serious account of specific and general derivations from the ancient world in regard (for example) to the use and symbolism of columns, notions of utility, the 'courtly' formation of ideals of conduct based upon classical ethical notions, and the legacy of forensic rhetoric for the understanding of theatre, music and performativity. All these, I suggest, imply the existence of substantial living traditions of moral and aesthetic speculation among 'intellectuals and art' which cannot be separated from Christian speculation. The growing interest in the heritage of ancient Latin art and letters for artistic theory and practice in the period 1170–1300, quite as much as for the 'civilizing process' set out by Norbert Elias and Jaeger,[4] raises important questions about the comparatively recent tendency to split the Middle Ages from both the ancient world and the Renaissance, so detaching them from their classical roots, and converting them into an anthropologized liberal culture of 'images' contrasted with an authoritarian and classicizing Renaissance, in which 'art' starts to enjoy a modern autonomy. Much in this book suggests that this tendency is, to say the least, unhelpful: the *antiqui* and the *moderni* shared many common assumptions and discourses, and had much to teach one another.

In pursuing the idea of the artificial through the domains of the *habitus* construed at its widest, one is obliged to take into account a very wide range of sources: rich insights come from unexpected quarters. Such sources include all forms of historical writings, hagiography, texts on the regulation of conduct, works of pastoral instruction, encomiastic poetry, ecumenical and diocesan legislation, visitation records, curricular literature and, of course, art and architecture. Since my concerns are with the reformist secular Church at the height of its practical power in the thirteenth century, the date limits proposed for the book are provided at the outset by the revolutionary new building and cult at Canterbury and by the ecumenical legislation inaugurated by the Third and Fourth Lateran Councils (1179, 1215); and finally, in the early fourteenth century, by the end of the great age of diocesan legislation and of the creation of new, generally episcopal, saints in England. In essence, then, the text is about a 'long' thirteenth century. It is incontrovertibly true that this was the age of the great church; hence there can be no serious question of imbalance if the focus is on the diocesan agenda, just as there could be no question of imbalance if the later Middle Ages were regarded as the great age of the parish church. It is also important that the evidence and argument should have an international dimension. The values of the clerical regime of the thirteenth century were in important respects formed and recognized internationally by a class of men of similar training, cultural assumptions, tastes and technical language, familiar as much with Rome or Paris as with Canterbury, Lincoln, Oxford or Salisbury. Developments in law, bureaucracy and technology in the era following Gregorian reform were blind to national or regional frontiers: much that is said in this book could also be said about thirteenth-century Spain, or Norway, though probably not Italy. Arguments about 'national' styles are therefore set to one side in this book in favour of a broad range of comparisons with the art and architecture not only of the French territories, but also of Scandinavia and the Holy Roman Empire. The astonishing survivals of figurative art in Norway, Sweden and Denmark alone have quite as much to say about the lost realities of the greater and lesser churches of thirteenth-century England as the heritage of northern France – a fact that Scandinavian scholars have been much quicker than the British to acknowledge.

In pursuit of these very general interpretative goals, I have followed four broad paths of enquiry. As already indicated, no account of this period would be complete without some consideration of the great church, the cathedrals especially. Part I of this book is therefore devoted not to architectural history as such, but to a cluster of ideas grouped under the title 'Edification', because that term captures something of the potential or actual relationship between church building and the formulation and propagation of ideas. The association is of course Panofskian, though the substance of the account is absolutely un-Panofskian in its methods.[5] The key points of focus are allegory and morality. The rebuilding of Canterbury Cathedral in the 1170s is taken as a point of departure, because Canterbury was important not only in regard to its assimilation of various new ideas from northern France, but also because of the real likelihood that striking and unusual aspects of its architecture are explicable in the light of what might be called local knowledge, namely the development of ideas about martyrdom and allegory specific to the cult of St Thomas himself which could be given objective expression in architecture. This local knowledge or hermeneutic is essentially a 'web of significance'. Canterbury has a very high specific gravity that sets it aside from virtually everything that followed it in the thirteenth century. It alone cannot dictate how one should understand the achievements of the next generations at Lincoln and Salisbury, except perhaps in the sense that its allegorical density and undoubted magnificence lent it immense stature. In any event, the discussion that grows out of Canterbury and into the thirteenth century attempts to sketch out some ideas about how utilitarian ethics and allegory played a role in the reception of such buildings; this may or may not shed light on the circumstances in which they were conceived. This is a sensitive matter, since it will be clear not only from architecture, but also from developments in the figurative arts, that hard causal schedules simply cannot be brought to bear upon all the dramatic changes to central signs of Christianity typical of the early Gothic era. My preference here is for much softer styles of explanation, since that is all, for the most part, that the evidence can justify. It is held to be broadly true, for example, that the dominant ethos of thought about the utility or non-utility of church building was of some consequence for the appearance of early Gothic churches. Ascetic critiques failed to gain hold; allegorical reception on the other hand flourished. Ample room has also to be left for the simple fact that artists and architects in this period were themselves significant innovators working within a cultural milieu which was in some respects very tightly regulated, and in other respects astonishingly open. The efforts of commentators on artistic change in the period, whether they concerned rib vaults or three-nail crosses, demonstrate a persistent desire on the part of the commissioning elites to comprehend, legitimize and then deploy sometimes astonishing artistic and technological change, accelerated in England by the great wealth of its diocesan Church and, more generally, by the momentum of the medieval urban economy in general.

Part II, 'Sanctification', sets itself the dual aims of enquiring about various types of English sainthood in the conventional sense, as well as about the way specific communities, elites especially, elected by means of sainthood – specifically the creation of a new group of episcopal saints – to 'sanctify' other ideals: of these the most important were those associated with the class of school-educated *magistri* employed both by the Church and by public power. The debt in this part of the book to the work of Beryl Smalley and André Vauchez is considerable.[6] Again, a belief in the importance of the various moral and aesthetic styles of sainthood and sanctity will be evident: this is neither a functionalist history of shrines and cults, nor a complete overview of English sainthood as a whole, but rather an investigation of the politics and aesthetics of specifically royal and aristocratic sanctity and the ways in which it impinged upon buildings and other artefacts. The initial questions, implied by Vauchez's typology of sainthood, concern traditional royal and aristocratic sanctity and its impact upon such significant great churches as Ely and Wells. The argument focuses especially, however, on the English episcopal saints created in the era of the renewal of the sanctoral in the wake of the canonization of St Thomas of Canterbury, and the rich future of the role model provided by Becket's example. These saints, often *magistri* themselves, may be said to have embodied the ideals and expectations of the clerical class. Though not always aristocratic in origin, the bishop-saints were seen to conform to disciplinary ideals derived ultimately from the ancient world, and whose character was also 'courtly'. This new and perhaps more meritocratic class of scholarly, ascetic clerical saint both provoked and produced a pastoral literature that made the example of such saints widely relevant by embodying a reformed notion of leadership and rulership, and adhering to new styles of spirituality.

In so far as this book contains a social history of images, it does so especially in Part III, entitled 'Regulation', which sets out to examine in a practical way the consequences of reformist and pastoral policies for the Church at large in the course of the thirteenth century. This part of the book can no more tackle the generality of parish church religion than Part II could embrace all aspects of national and local sainthood. Nevertheless, the related issues of how theories of religious belief and conduct were developed, how they were embodied in law, how those laws were administered by the regulatory hierarchy of the Church, what fate universal laws enjoyed at the local parish level, and how the regulation of public conduct stood in relation to personal conduct, are inescapable and of quite fundamental importance to this study. As R. H. Helmholz has recently written of canon law, 'From its inception, the classical canon law had ambitious goals. It provided guidance to right conduct, as well as punishing evil conduct and settling disputes. Its purpose was to lead men to the good.'[7] In studying regulation, my debt to the work of Christopher Cheney is very marked, except that his remarkable efforts in understanding and publishing the English diocesan legislation are pursued into the practical domain of art production in a way that he himself might not have envisaged.[8] These chapters explore especially a paradox of the period: that, while England was indubitably a closely governed country in regard to belief and practice, and generally free of heterodox opinion, the aesthetic theories that are demonstrably implicit or explicit in its most ambitious pastoral legislation enjoyed a very haphazard fate at local level. One cannot understand the arts of the thirteenth-century Church without studying its legislation, yet one cannot fail to notice at the same time that such legislation had a remarkably open texture: very little of importance was actually legislated into existence, so much as legislated about retractively. What might seem like a top-down account of the dissemination of certain ideals cannot in fact be so. Even in this era of growing intolerance, much was left undecided and unregulated, and it is in those spheres especially that the reader is invited to pause and consider the overlapping and conflicting domains of authority and community. In these various interstices, I suggest, lay not an increasingly dull, sclerotic and authoritarian regime of 'public church art' but rather precisely the creative loopholes that enabled the public arts of the Church to flourish as they had never done before, as for example in regard to the art of the sacraments. It may indeed be the case that the mismatches between official expectation and actual practice permitted both lively creativity and experimentation and, no less importantly, the flourishing of a closely related personal or private religious culture in proximity to the daily life of the Church. The recent stress on 'private' religious culture in the late Middle Ages may, therefore, obscure the debt owed by that culture to the antecedent creative chaos of the 'public' Church of the early Gothic era, and its development of what might be termed 'publicly sanctioned inwardness'. Devotion was not separable from public liturgy. The inner regulation of the self was surely inseparable from its outer regulation.

It is for this reason that my study of regulation moves from the sphere of lights, altarpieces and statues to the sphere of inner and outer conduct: the inner adornment not of the Church but of the Christian self, again a key objective of the pastoral movement, as writers such as Caroline Walker Bynum have demonstrated.[9] This is best done by examining the intellectual and aesthetic ideas in some of the more influential pastoral texts produced by the masters, the reformist bishops and members of the new religious orders, texts that prescribed deportment in prayer, methods of contemplation, examination in the confessional, the catechism and curriculum of religion, and lay and clerical behaviour in church during Mass especially. These discourses indisputably emerged from the very heart of the regime. Another often forgotten point is that the Church was capable in the last resort of censoring unsuitable images in the interests of the *cura animarum*. Why certain images were thought unsuitable may help one to understand attitudes to symbolism and the *habitus* more generally. All these factors helped to shape the 'repertoire of inherited and shared beliefs and symbols' of 'traditional religion' of the fourteenth and fifteenth centuries discussed so eloquently by Eamon Duffy.[10]

The rationale of censorship leads to the final path, entitled 'Expression', a modern term with a variety of resonances used here to introduce the issue of affect: intellectual and emotional stances towards religious images, and the embodiment or objectification of such stances in images themselves. In bringing together discussions of allegory, decorum and religious affect and their reciprocity, I begin with the central Christian sign, the Crucifixion. It might be objected, not unfairly, that Marian devotion enjoyed primacy over devotion to the Cross in this period; and indeed, I have aimed to make Mary's a presence to be felt throughout this book. However, this is not a comprehensive study of the patterns of religious devotion of the times, and interest in the Gothic crucifixion is on this occasion vindicated principally by the remarkable lack of sustained study of it in comparison with the impact of the cult of the Virgin on architecture and the figurative arts. The Gothic cross after 1200 underwent a variety of important changes that are hard to account for without resort to notions of artistic freedom on the one hand, and notions of affect on the other. Not all these changes are susceptible to rational explanation in terms of traditional textual discourses of the Passion, because their character was in the first instance not so much symbolic as aesthetic. What did it mean to continue to represent Christ's suffering in a persuasive and affective way, while adhering to traditional doctrinal and symbolic constraints? To what extent was the decorum of the Cross, so to speak, related to the important aesthetic and ethical ideals being worked out in other areas of religious consciousness in the Gothic era? Did the new images speak in the same way to different communities? In suggesting that to understand these new affective images one should examine the theories of 'corporeal style' implicit in their formation, my argument moves on to consider representation of the human body and face more generally, and so into that sphere of the 'rationale of human movement' already very effectively discussed by Jean-Claude Schmitt and others.[11] Gothic images, like Gothic crosses, look different from their precursors because they were animated in ways that implied not only a change in representational language but also in the reciprocal relationship between image and spectator, and hence the social life of images. This will be considered as if it were a phenomenological and imaginative issue quite as much as a functional one. By examining theories of laughter, for instance, one might come to some understanding of some of the more radical traits of the period in Gothic sculpture and painting. I suggest that this was not a matter of 'naturalistic' representation so much as of artificiality: the drawing of images into a wider rationale of codified behaviour in such a way that images gained new constitutive power, a power that is ancestral to many modern notions of how images work. That a particularly dazzling generation of artists was involved in giving outward shape to this process is beyond question. That its work was not wholly alien to currents of moral thinking in the schools is also stressed – and the consequences of this insight for a purely populist view of Gothic art, considered.

The final chapters continue with the domain of the persuasive, by examining the nexus of art, theatre and music. The virtue of this is that it enables the reader to return to the holistic examination of important ensembles produced towards the end of the period, notably the Angel Choir at Lincoln, but in such a way as to bring to the forefront the matter of the Church's attitude to new technologies of communication and persuasion; how it faced up to their inevitability, and how it harnessed them to brilliant effect.

Part I

EDIFICATION

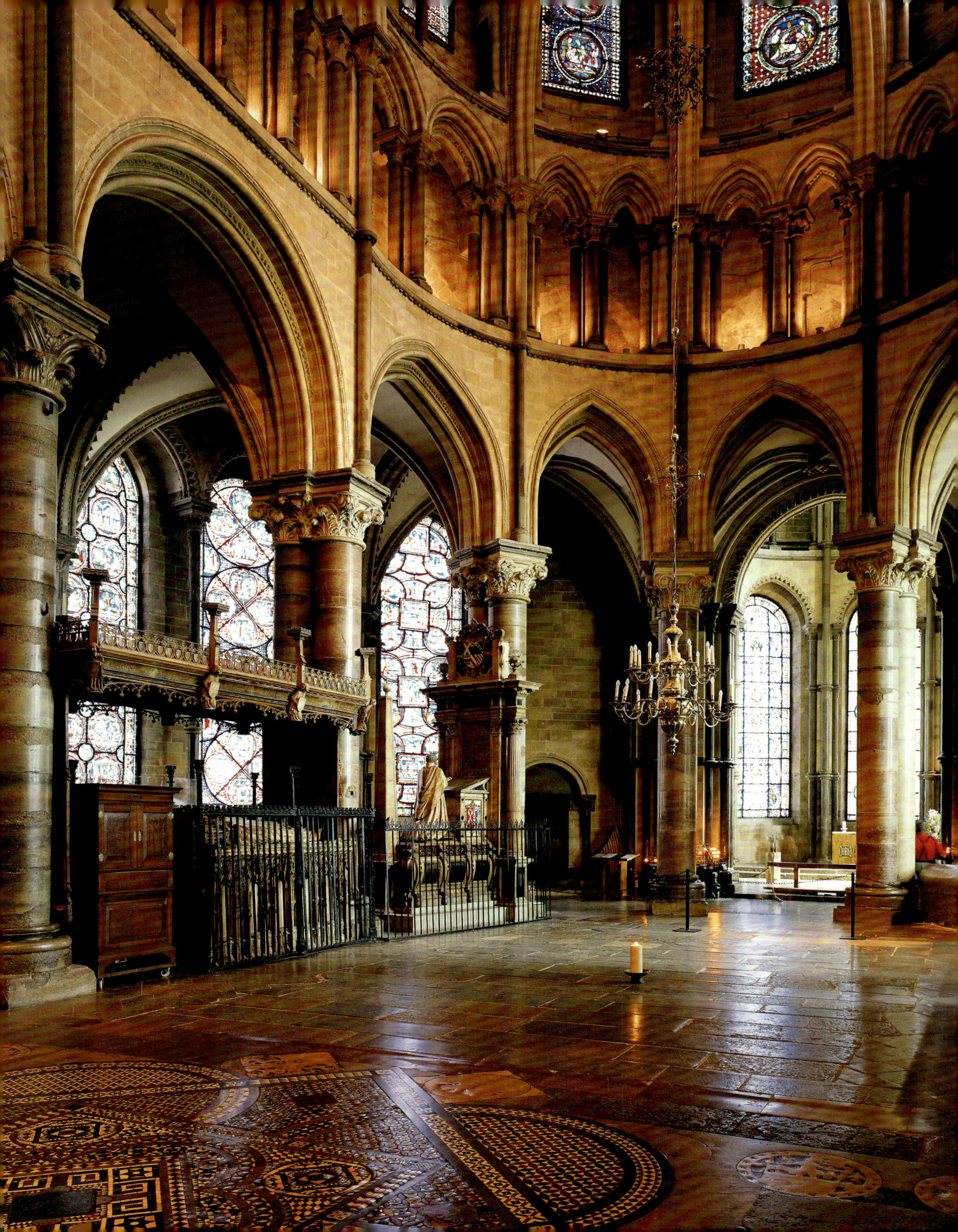

Chapter 1

CANTERBURY: THE AESTHETICS OF MARTYRDOM

My beloved is white and ruddy, the chiefest among ten thousand.

Canticles 5: 10

O far far far far in the past; and I wander in a land of barren boughs; if I break them, they bleed; I wander in a land of dry stones; if I touch them they bleed.

T. S. Eliot, *Murder in the Cathedral*

The Lily and the Rose

On a bright summer morning, the interiors of the Trinity Chapel and Corona at the east end of Canterbury Cathedral can be seen to particular advantage (fig. 1). The Corona and the aisles of the Trinity Chapel have large broad windows with low sills, suffusing the aisles and the outer faces of the coupled pillars of the arcading with a gentle light, qualified by the stained glass and reflected off the polished coloured surfaces of the building itself. This part of the architecture of Christ Church – the Trinity Chapel or Chapel of St Thomas – is famously opulent. The main columns are doubled and topped with ample and dignified capitals, a clever regard for scale marking the transition from the steady generous bulk, smoothness and solemnity of the arcades to the slender subtlety of the glossy shafts and capitals of the outer walls of the aisles. The double columns of the arcades were arranged in such a way as to permit maximum visibility of the aisle windows from the central vessel, and their forms, albeit lacking an entasis, are reminiscent of Corinthian columns. Their 'classicism' is elusive, yet present. This is a self-consciously magnificent building, without stridency or assertive luxuriousness. Though inspired formally by the latest fashions in northern French Gothic, the surface and chromatic effects of the ensemble are unusual. The partly original marble paving and marble columns and shafting lend it sombre variegated warmth. But within this variety lies order, not least in the distribution of colour. A hard, variegated rose-pink marble blankets the pavement area within the apse around the site of the shrine of St Thomas. The coupled columns have a regular scheme of polished stones of counterchanged hues, using the same rose marble, a smooth creamy-white pelletal limestone and a grey-green Purbeck. To the west are pairs of limestone and Purbeck; Purbeck meets rose marble either side of the shrine, with the rose on the inside facing the shrine; Purbeck and limestone are repeated, and then the two easternmost piers couple limestone and rose, white and pink-red.

This use of coloured stones in the context of the most modern French Gothic architecture is peculiar. Its ordering is thoughtful, its columnar grandeur self-evident. It seems especially worthy of the encomiastic poetry of architecture in antiquity, especially those inspired by the so-called 'Augustan marble revolution'.[1] Such poetry, known in the Middle Ages in the works of curriculum authors such as Virgil or Statius, commonly emphasized scale, variety, colour, opulence, improvement and outdoing as signs of magnificence in architecture and patronage.[2] Virgil's *Aeneid* lauds the royal palace of Rome raised on a hundred columns; Statius's account in the *Silvae* of the Palace of Domitian says that it was 'distinguished not by a hundred columns but by as many as could shoulder the gods and the sky', its multi-coloured and many-sourced marble decorations vying with one another for attention; Sidonius marvels at the size of the

1 Canterbury Cathedral, Trinity Chapel looking east. The site of St Thomas's shrine is marked by a candle: in the left foreground is the *Opus alexandrinum* pavement (John Crook).

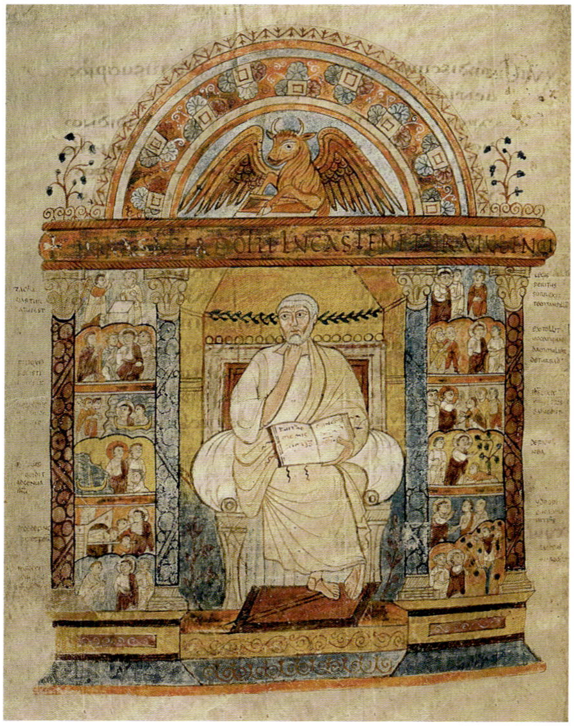

2 St Luke. St Augustine's Gospels, Cambridge, Corpus Christi College MS 286, fol. 129v, sixth century (Master and Fellows of Corpus Christi College, Cambridge).

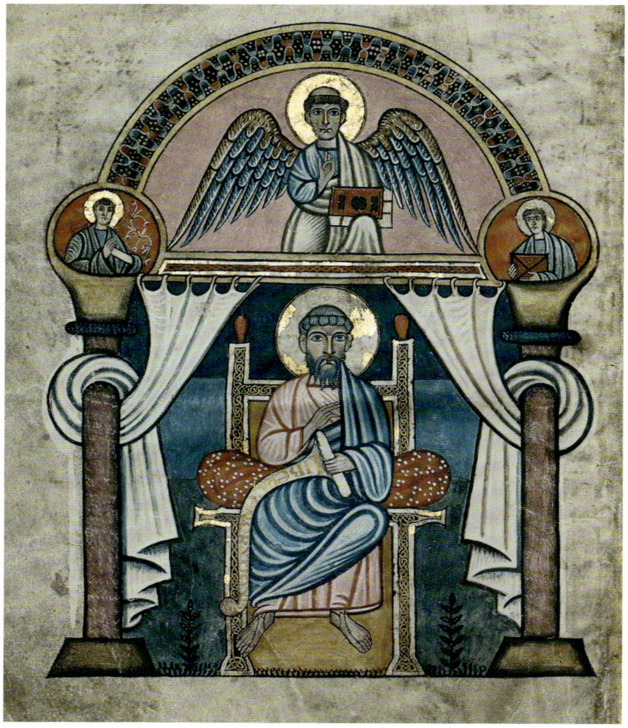

3 St Matthew. Canterbury *Codex aureus*, Stockholm, Kungliga Biblioteket MS A. 135, fol. 9v, eighth century (The Royal Library, National Library of Sweden).

columns supporting Roman baths, and Ovid at those in the Palace of the Sun.[3] The same themes are found in Gallo-Roman Christian writing, as in Gregory of Tours's inventory of the numbers of columns and windows in sixth-century churches in Tours and Clermont-Ferrand; later, marble is an aspect of *venustas* in building, in Isidore of Seville's *Etymologies*.[4] Examples are legion in both Greek and Latin Christian speculation on architecture and fine marbles.

Something of this tradition was still alive at late twelfth-century Canterbury. The monastic chronicler and sacrist of Christ Church, Gervase, in his *De combustione*, written some time after 1188, deploys formal antitheses familiar in Roman poetry in order to underline the scheme of improvement brought about by the architects William of Sens and English William in the rebuilding of the east end of the church after the fire of 1174.[5] Thus, says Gervase, while the capitals of the former Romanesque work were plain, in the new they were exquisite in sculpture and so, implicitly, capable of greater *varietas*; no marble columns were in the old church, but in the new were innumerable ones.[6] Gervase calls William of Sens a 'most subtle' worker in stone.[7] Gervase is sometimes dismissed by modern commentators, not entirely unfairly, as an empiricist uninterested in matters of symbolism. But he was very close indeed to the works at Canterbury, and there is no reason in principle why his account should not have represented local views of architecture preoccupied, as in older Roman poetic models, with notions of outdoing and pre-eminence. His priorities, if not his language, are, loosely speaking, Vitruvian: old fire-damaged piers are replaced because they are unsound, lacking *firmitas*; the design of the new building is useful because its peculiarities of form follow in part from the need to accommodate frequent processions, so demonstrating its *utilitas*; and the building possesses a beauty beyond that of the former one, i.e. *venustas*.[8] Gervase imported into his chronicle exactly those ancient literary conventions that stressed scale, richness of materials and stupendous workmanship to the point of inexpressibility (e.g. 'innumerable' columns).[9] But his immediate source was the post-Conquest monastic historian and hagiographer Eadmer, for like Eadmer, whom he cites extensively, Gervase was concerned to preserve the memory of the great Anglo-Saxon saints of Canterbury and their relics by inventorial recording and topographically precise description.[10] His aim was to demonstrate the monastery's sound custodianship of its extraordinary sacred heritage, of which excellent building was an aspect. From Eadmer's *Opuscula*, and doubtless from other sources, he learned that the oldest church on the site was of Roman workmanship with a crypt, or what the Romans called a *confessio*.[11] It has even been suggested that Gervase was the young industrious monk who was temporary overseer of the masons after the fall of William of Sens, and that he was the author of the plan preserved in the great waterworks drawing in the Eadwine Psalter, a local equivalent of his *Mappa mundi*.[12] This specificity is what makes Gervase an important, and generally very reliable, source for much that was going on at Canterbury in the 1170s and 1180s.

Gervase did not write about colour, but it would clearly be nonsense to claim that Canterbury's use of rich marble columns could not have exemplified thoughts about coloured materials and especially high-grade stones and metals. In this scheme of things one would be perfectly entitled to see in these stones an allusion to the subtle, rich livery of antique marbles, and so to regard the grey-green Purbeck of the Trinity Chapel as a species of green marble, not unlike ineluctable bronze, and the rose marble as a form of noble porphyry.[13] And although these columns are not monoliths, but are composed of drums, their size and splendour might accord them the type of praise accorded to the greatest triumphs of art over nature, the giant columns and blocks in Rome.[14] So much would consort well with the still-living Benedictine tradition of writings about great monastic patrons, and with the actual conduct of patronage in such circles, in the era of Gregorian reform. The pagan Roman ideal of mastery of natural resources by imperial and military might was now Christianized, spiritualized in a miraculous, salvific, drama of divine intervention; Rome's destiny had become the Church's. The solemn, serried ranks of re-used porphyry columns in the ecclesiastical architecture of early Christian and medieval Rome offered to visually articulate visitors to Rome the square meal of experience of the physical heritage of the great age of martyrdom.[15] Much nearer home, substantial romanizing columns (now in the crypt at Canterbury) fronted the apse of the seventh-century minster church founded in the Roman fort at Reculver, in Kent.[16] Important relics of apostolic Christianity at Canterbury, and of which Christ Church and St Augustine's were themselves important and self-conscious representatives, preserved for local scrutiny and admiration examples of the antique taste for coloured columns as the Trinity Chapel piers: russet and grey-blue marbled columns frame the portrait of St Luke in the sixth-century St Augustine's Gospels, and columns of porphyry-like purple flecked with black and white flank the Evangelist portraits in the eighth-century Canterbury *Codex aureus* (figs 2–3).[17] The Trinity Chapel rose marble (fig. 4) is not in fact exactly like imperial porphyry, for it has a wider range of reds and is more softly variegated than the crisply mottled, solid hues of true porphyry, ranging instead from a lightish dusty pink to a dark, offal blood-red, and marbled and clouded with grey-whites. Paulus Silentarius's remarks on the Hagia Sophia's rose-like Phrygian marble mingling with airy white catch very well these effects of dynamic colour.[18] Their glowing nobility notwithstanding, such colours as pink-red rose, purple and amethyst had in fact long been located by such medieval writers as Isidore, Bede and Marbod at the light end of the scale of hues.[19]

Gervase was not a symbolist; although poetically informed, his account of the completion of the Trinity Chapel in the early 1180s is notoriously brief. Nothing is said about the coloured marbles, and indeed nothing about the shrine after the apparently more important

4 Canterbury Cathedral, Trinity Chapel, columns on north-east side (author).

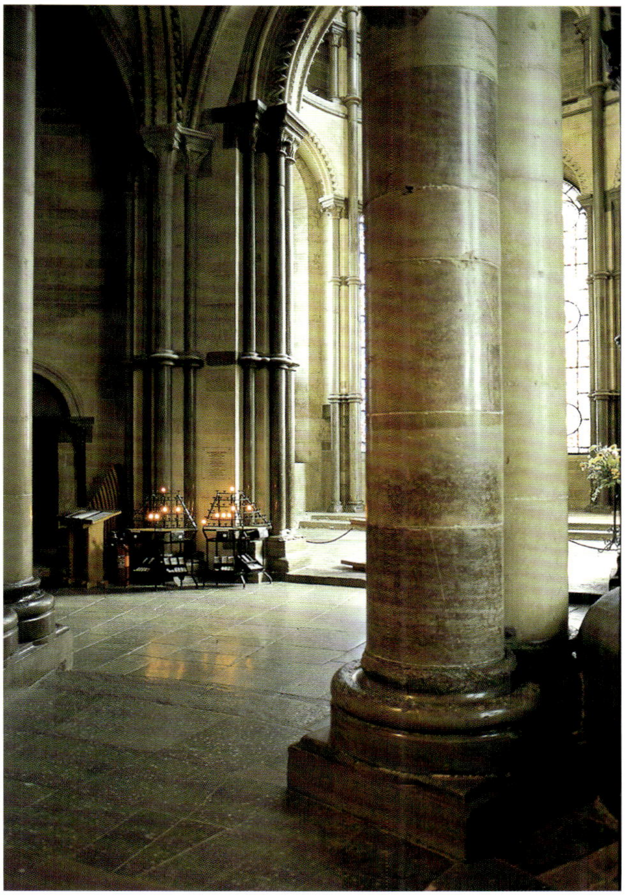

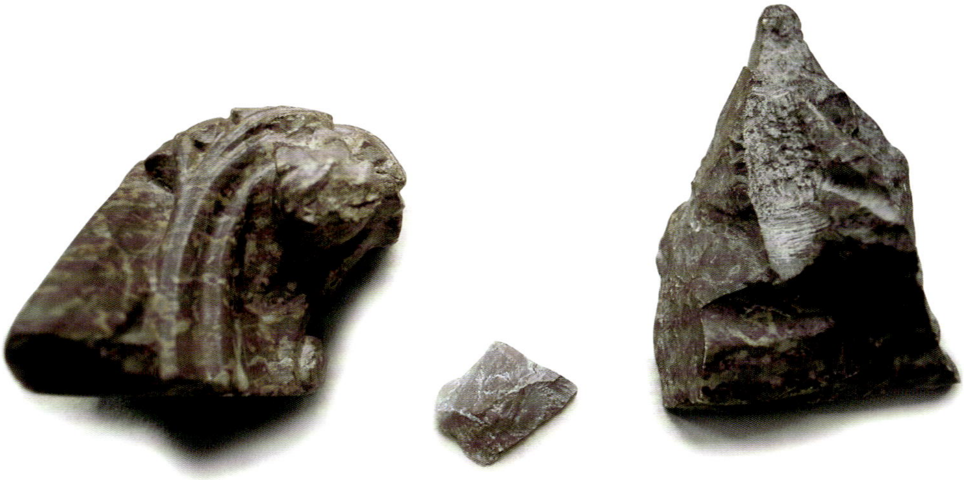

5 Sculpted fragments reputedly from St Thomas's shrine.

regaining by the monks of the Paradise of the choir in April 1180.[20] Yet his account, though in important respects strikingly blank, is still historically invaluable. Under the year 1181 he notes the erection of the exterior aisle walls of the Trinity Chapel as far as their marble capitals.[21] Since the neat bases and some of the rings and capitals of the delicate shafts of the outer walls are made of rose marble, it therefore must have been supplied by 1181. Gervase states next that the eight interior pillars, by which he presumably meant pairs of pillars, were raised in 1182.[22] Because they are not monoliths, it is unlikely that the actual size of the components used in the piers governed the design, or redesign, of the main elevation around 1179 to accommodate the vaulted tomb-space of Becket beneath the Trinity Chapel.[23] There was clearly room for adjustment and compromise, because the two easternmost piers use only rose marble for the drums in their lower halves, being finished above in Purbeck (fig. 1). Such compromise may have been the product of the 'want of funds' mentioned in 1183 by Gervase before the main vault of the Trinity Chapel was closed in 1184, or of a change of design which led to a shortfall of supplies of rose marble.[24] In any event, unless new supplies of rose marble were gained after 1183–4, the marble for the shrine base and surrounding pavement in the Trinity Chapel was presumably ordered and set aside rather earlier. Though much uncertainty prevails as to the actual appearance of Becket's shrine, the detailing of the rose-marble volutes which survive from capitals purportedly from the stone base itself (fig. 5) is so close to that of the main capitals of the chapel, that a start on the base in the 1180s seems probable, under English William's direction, in preparation for the translation first mooted by the strongly pro-Becket Prior Alan of Benevento in the summer of 1185.[25] The choice of such stones for the shrine itself merely reinforces their importance.

But if the plan to have coloured marble decoration for the apse, aisles, shrine and flooring was implemented at the latest by 1181, when was it developed? This issue touches on the relationship between the work of English William, who indubitably raised the fabric of the Trinity Chapel, and that of William of Sens. It is certain from Gervase's account that William of Sens opened the supply lines for stones from overseas used in, and probably throughout, the eastern arm of the church, much as he established its major design premises.[26] Indeed the rose marble has been identified as coming from the Philippeville area of what is now southern Belgium, and so from the area just east of the territories in which it is now agreed that William of Sens conducted some of his architectural researches for the design of his building, including the area of southern Flanders or Hainault as well as Arras, Cambrai, Reims, Laon and Paris.[27] Canterbury volunteers an elaborate commentary, or series of commentaries, on architecture in Paris and the regions to its north and east. It is also now acknowledged that the stimulus to the use of Purbeck, Bethersden and other dark 'marbles' in southern England, including Canterbury, from the mid-twelfth century onwards had come at least in part from Tournai and the region to the east of the Ile-de-France.[28] By 1170 or 1175 the time was ripe for the serious deployment of such materials on a large scale and in a major apostolic church in England. So, if it is correct to suppose that English William was putting into effect one of the plans for the east end of the church generated in 1174–5 by William of Sens (which, as Peter Kidson has shown, may have included a Sens-derived enneagonal geometry for the projected plans of the Trinity Chapel and Corona), the way is then open to believing that coloured stones were factored into the design, or designs, of the main elevations at an early stage, that is to say for all practical purposes in the period 1175–80.[29] The possibility that the paired columns at Sens too were originally painted may also be important.[30] Canterbury was probably intended to have a bright structural polychromy in its Holy of Holies from the start. Yet it also innovated. So far, the tendency had been to select for shafting the dark-toned or even black marbles of the type for which Tournai is famous. The Canterbury designers used a dark Purbeck or Bethersden marble for the choir and presbytery, but for the shrine area alone selected from the Tournai region the brighter-hued rose-pink, which they then matched with Purbeck and with the cream-white pelletal limestone from Caen. This choice of marble was never repeated elsewhere for a Gothic church of the period; given its prestigious context, it is likely to have involved serious thought.

The corroborative reasons for thinking that this was so are entirely local. On almost all such matters Gervase is silent; though he was close to the works at Christ Church, it may be a mistake to assume that he should be the absolute and final arbiter of matters of interpretation. Churchmen had long since developed an exegesis of the coloured sanctuaries of the Christian martyrs. Such interpretations possessed a certain universalism. Red and purple were for obvious reasons dense with symbolism: so, following Cyprian, Bede in his interpretation of the veils of the Mosaic tabernacle in *De tabernaculo* connects purple to blood, and so typologically to martyrdom and baptism in blood.[31] Canterbury's rose marble, though unprecedented in English medieval architecture, can be understood in this general sense, as a token of martyrdom suffusing the east end of the shrine church. But the orderly combination of this blood-coloured stone with creamy white limestone is more particular and seemingly deliberative; and the reason for this is that its meaning was both universal and particular. Indeed red and white, the colours of the rose and the lily respectively, enjoyed a local and very coherent form of attention at late twelfth-century Christ Church.

It has long been noticed that the biographies of Thomas Becket, compiled after his martyrdom in the cathedral in December 1170, commonly employ the idea of the imitation of Christ in relating the passion of the saint (fig. 6). This organizing principle of christomimesis is acknowledged immediately at the start of William

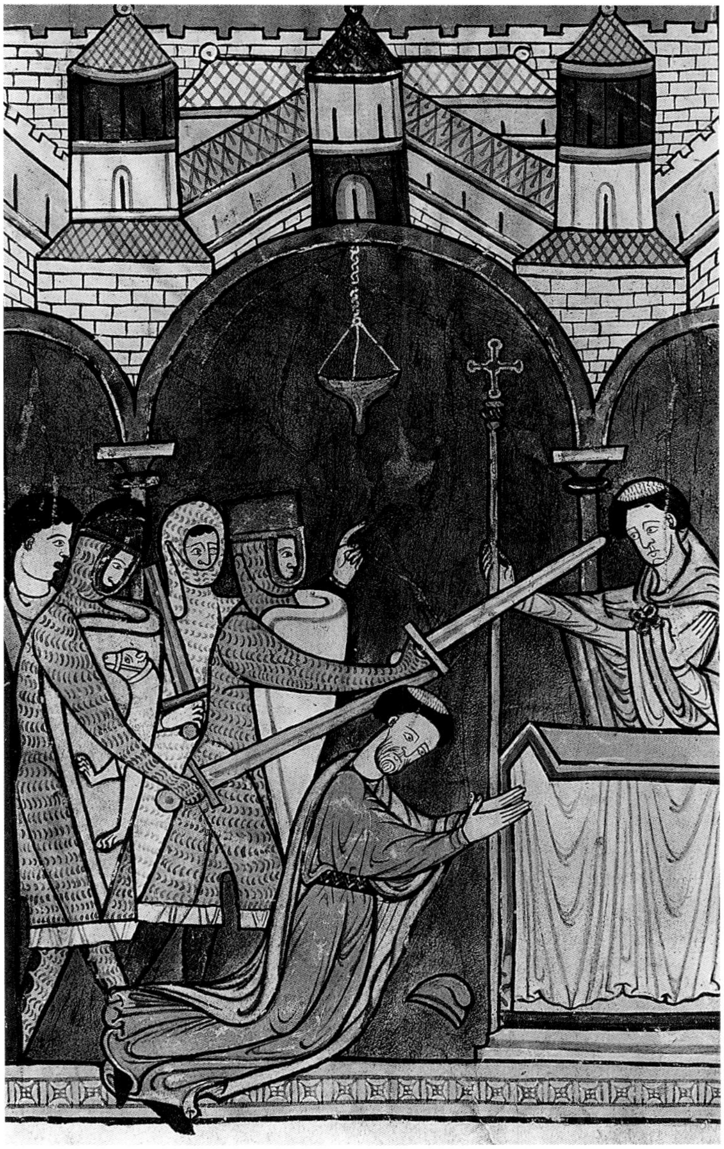

6 Martyrdom of St Thomas. Psalter, BL MS Harley 5102, fol. 32, *c.* 1220 (by permission of the British Library).

of Canterbury's semi-official Life which, having opened with the gold and stone adornments of the Tabernacle in Exodus (*alius auro, alius argento, lapidibus pretiosis, bysso, purpura, cocco, jacinto*), states that Thomas was the martyr alike to the Lord in his suffering (*et martyr qui Domino similis est in passione*): he had foreknowledge of his approaching passion; he staged a final *Adventus*; he held a last supper; his garments were parted; his disciples fled; he gave forth water and blood.[32] Other writers regularly extend the comparisons to Christ's entry into Jerusalem, his carrying of a cross, his five wounds, his last words, his burial in a newly hewn tomb. His martyrdom occurred just after the feasts of St Stephen and the Holy Innocents. John of Salisbury was in accord with this view, as was the *Quadrilogus* of the later 1190s, the four-voiced official compilation about Becket that framed his Life in quasi-evangelical terms.[33] The insistence of early iconographers of the saint that he was martyred sacrilegiously before an altar implied that Christ was crucified again in Thomas's martyrdom.[34] The biographer Benedict daringly connected the bloodied miraculous water of Thomas, the Lamb of Canterbury (*agnus Cantuariensis*), drunk as is the blood of the Lamb of Bethlehem, an image that consorts well with the carved *Agnus Dei* boss with which William of Sens locked his eastern crossing

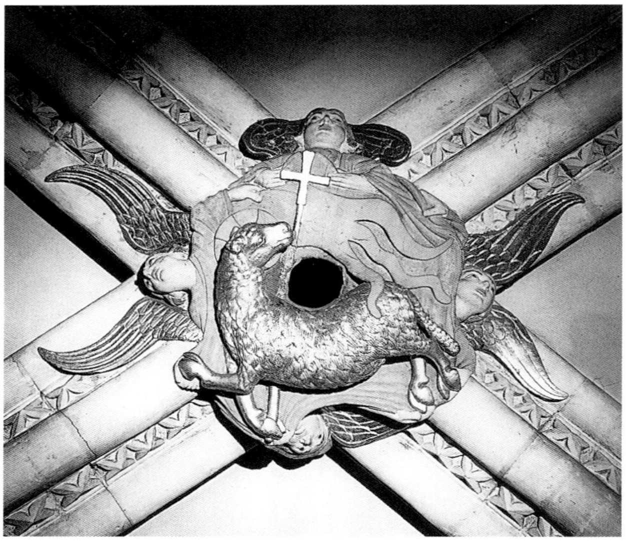

7 Canterbury Cathedral, *Agnus Dei* on keystone of eastern crossing vault (reproduced by permission of English Heritage. NMR).

vault (fig. 7).[35] Also, as is well known, the biographers make much of the harrowing details of the martyrdom itself: its patient and seemingly deliberate acceptance; its dramatic incident; and especially of the final and still shocking outrage committed by Hugh of Horsea, nicknamed Mauclerk, in hoisting Becket's brains out of his skull and scattering them on the pavement of the church. Their lingering and thorough accounts are gripping, and provoke the fascination that attends any vivid account of a great death.

But the verisimilitude of these histories should not lead one to overlook their densely symbolic character, which for some has provided 'an unrivalled illustration of the role of allegorical language'.[36] The gruesome facts of St Thomas's martyrdom illustrate the way in which allegory helped those nearest to Thomas to comprehend and assimilate horror, and also the extent to which such narratives were premised upon liturgical and allegorical thinking. Allegory's purpose was thus both psychological and intellectual, and because of this purpose the specific physical details of the passion, and their significatory potential, mattered especially. The way in which they were interpreted is surprising, but absolutely relevant to the problem of colour in the Trinity Chapel. Edward Grim and William fitz Stephen liken the spilt brains and blood, one reddening and one whitening the other, to the lily and the rose.[37] Indeed this floral image is employed by five of Becket's biographers.[38] The source for this image is specifically Canticles 2: 1 (*ego flos campi et lilium convallium*), also 5: 10 (*dilectus meus candidus et rubicundus*), texts that received frequent comment, as for instance by Richard of Saint-Victor writing within a mystical tradition that regarded Canticles (the Song of Songs) as an anagogic marriage-song consoling the virtuous in their suffering by the promise of the reward of heaven.[39] In her remarkable study of this gloss on Canticles in the Becket Lives, Jennifer O'Reilly shows that the origins of Canterbury interest in the imagery of white and red, lily and rose, are ultimately to be traced to patristic exegesis as it was later developed in medieval works on affective meditation on the Passion, particularly those of Cistercian authors. For example, the eleventh-century *Meditationes* by John of Fécamp see the white breast and red blood of Christ crucified as attributes of Christ in his divine and human aspects.[40] Like St Bernard, Edward Grim and William fitz Stephen think of the lily and rose in terms of virgins, confessors and martyrs.[41] The biographers also noted that the brains and blood suffused each other with their colours. This reddening of the brains and the whitening of the blood noted by Grim, fitz Stephen and 'Anonymous X' exhibits a colour dynamism also found in the miraculous water of St Thomas (in the antiphon for Lauds in his feast in the Sarum Breviary), which changes colour five times, once into milk, four times into blood:

> Aqua Thomae quinquies varians colorem
> in lac semel transiit, quater in cruorem.[42]

This association of blood and milk, Christ and Mary, redemption and doctrine, is closely linked to the new affective piety of the Cistercians, as represented by Aelred of Rievaulx, in this period.[43] A similar line of thought on the lily and the rose and their mutual colouring is found in the Life of Becket by Guernes de Pont-Sainte-Maxence, writing around 1174–7, and in the Icelandic Thomas Saga, compiled from about 1200 onwards.[44] Canticles was not the only point of departure for this comparison of hues. The red-white imagery provoked associations with the two-fold garment imagery of Isaiah 63: 1–3 and with Revelation 7: 14, where those who have come out of great tribulation wash their robes white in the blood of the Lamb. Becket's garments of martyrdom, the bloodied exterior vestments and the verminous underclothing of sackcloth and hair revealed after his death, signified a dual nature, that of inner, private (white) and outer, public (red) martyrdom.[45] Indeed the account in 'Anonymous IV' makes it clear that this nature is sponsorial – Becket's garments were white and red like those of the Beloved in Canticles 5: 10 – and hence mystical, for Becket is not only to be a guest at the heavenly banquet, but is the Spouse.[46] This divine love-mysticism was to find a new context in the apocalyptic tone of Stephen Langton's translation ceremonies for Becket in 1220 and the Sarum lections for the saint's feast.[47] Langton had been consecrated Archbishop of Canterbury in 1207; his sermon on Becket, given in Rome in 1220, takes as its text Canticles 2: 3–4 and Ecclesiasticus 50: 1, 8, the lily symbolizing Becket's suffering, its six leaves his six years of exile and its red seeds his martyrdom; Becket is the High Priest, the martyred rose of Ecclesiasticus, its thorn being England, but the thorn also producing other great saints such as Alphege and Edmund.[48] Colour allegory was also becoming part of the universal language of the Church. In the 1190s Lotario de' Conti, the future Pope Innocent III, a schoolman from the same circle as Langton, and a devotee of Becket, volunteered one of the first and most important codifications of colour symbolism in his thoughts on liturgical colours in *De missarum misteriis* which recorded contemporary Roman practice understood within a broadly Victorine framework of allegory. Drawing on Exodus 28, Canticles 2: 1 and Canticles 5: 10, Innocent states that of the five colours used in the Church (white, red, green, black and violet) white is the colour for the feasts of confessors and virgins, red for the apostles and martyrs.[49]

Seen in the light of this allegorizing, the unusual choice for the Trinity Chapel of rose-red and lily-white stones – stones which, in the case of the clouded rose-pink marble, exhibit exactly the reddening and whitening phenomenon noted in the exegesis of Canticles – falls very satisfactorily into a contemporary milieu of speculation about Becket's Christ-like and sponsorial nature, as revealed in writings about the saint, especially about his passion, dating to the 1170s and 1180s within Becket's own circle of *eruditi*.[50] As Christopher Wilson has observed, 'The presence of the shrine determines not only the subject matter of the glass in the windows [. . .] but also the materials of the inner columns, rare cream and pink stones symbolizing Becket's virginity and martyrdom and also the brains and blood spilt at his death'.[51] This idea, if pursued from the realm of speculation to architecture, might be developed to say that a spiritual allegory derived from the historical circumstances of a great martyrdom became, through built stones, something rhetorically 'present', with humanly recognizable weight.[52] The columns do not so much reflect a series of spiritual meanings as carry or embody them as extremely latent symbols: acknowledgement of their significance as representation, and as something beyond representation – as a form of 'real presence' – more fully integrates an understanding of the building as a total work of art. Coloured marbles are 'symbols' in the sense that symbols serve as the vehicle for conceptions.[53] Becket is embodied in the Church, and the Church in him. Such interpretation is inevitably a delicate matter. Canterbury's new architecture is not so fully propositional as to allow 'Becket' to be deduced from it alone, any more than 'scholasticism' can be deduced from Amiens or 'Use of Sarum' from Salisbury.[54] This should warn against too ready an acceptance of broad and uncorroborated alliances of concept and form.[55] But at Canterbury one is dealing with matters more concrete than a general mentality. Viewed contextually, and with the help of well-attested local allegorical traditions, the building can reasonably be seen to prompt and incorporate thoughts about its subject, Becket, of which it is a memorial.

This is not an especially characteristic insight about Canterbury's architecture, the study of which is dominated, not unfairly, by preoccupations with the introduction and form of early Gothic style in England and not what might be called the 'allegorical mode'. But it is one which sets in train some of the arguments that follow in this study, about architecture, the visual arts and the Church in all its manifestations.

Those who thought through the planning of the Trinity Chapel as a memorial to Becket were, perhaps needless to say, not without precedent. The use of columns to provoke thoughts about persons was a species of anthropomorphism whose origins, as is well known, lay in pagan and Christian antiquity. Specific classical orders and high-grade materials had long been reserved in Christian tradition for the inner sanctum of the Church, to which they lent formal and dramatic expressivity.[56] Canterbury indicates that this sort of formal variation, in a sufficiently important context, could be orderly and theoretically coherent, though not necessarily or solely in a classical way.[57] Christian allegory provided a conventional but important starting-point. The symbolism of building up the Church was

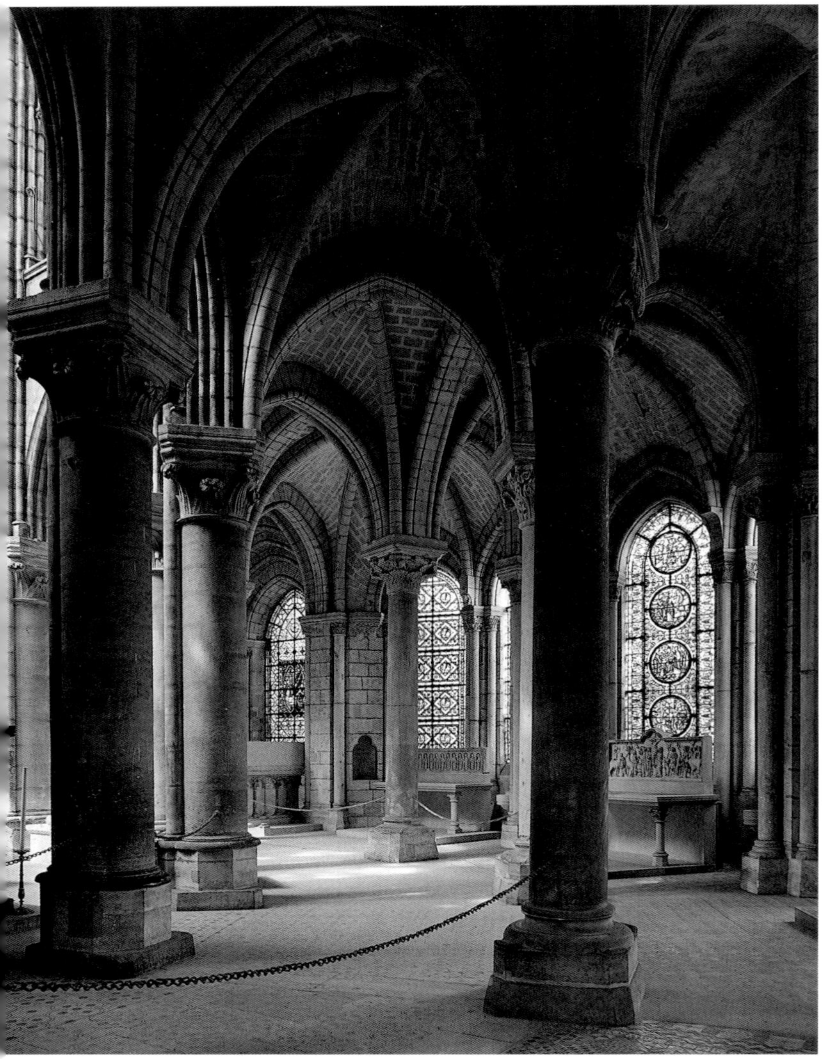

8 Paris, Saint-Denis, eastern ambulatory (James Austin).

established by St Paul in Galatians 2: 9, in which James, Cephas and John are likened to columns, and in Ephesians 2: 19–22, in which the unity of the Church is founded on the Apostles and Prophets, Jesus Christ himself being the chief cornerstone, following Psalm 117: 22. The most celebrated citation of St Paul in this period is that by Abbot Suger in his gloss on the columns of the chevet of Saint-Denis, dedicated in 1144 (fig. 8).[58] Even Gervase of Canterbury discloses some sense of the importance of Ephesians 2: 19–22 in his account of the virtues of the new building, in which the great vault stretching over the eastern crossing is described as being locked by one keystone which rests upon four principal pillars.[59] One is entitled to ask whether these features were thought to signify Christ the keystone and the Evangelists, because the keystone in question is sculpted with the *Agnus Dei* and four angels (fig. 7). Gervase wears his symbolism lightly; his language is suffused with that of the Bible.

The allegory of columns had been familiar to pre-Conquest English writers promoting the cause of virtuous monastic reform. Thus the Winchester Mass for the translation of St Swithun described him as an 'Olympic column of shining glory'; columnar imagery is used of St Oswald in his Life, and also of St Dunstan by his biographer Adelard, who named him 'a most solid cube of faith and truth', a 'cornerstone' and a 'column of light', indeed 'the column of monastic religion' itself.[60] These were more than rhetorical flourishes: Canterbury and Saint-Denis reflected, and possessed texts of, a long-standing and practical Early Christian, Frankish and Anglo-Saxon exegesis as practised by Rhabanus Maurus (*De universo*) and Smaragdus (*Diadema*) in which exactly this sort of image occurs.[61] The same pattern of allegorical reading of columns and other parts of the Church can be recognized in the *De gemma animae* of Honorius of Autun and in Peter of Roissy's later treatise on the liturgy, the *Manuale de mysteriis ecclesiae*.[62] Columnar and lapidary images are used pointedly with reference to Becket himself. Before about 1174, Robert of Cricklade, whose lost Life of Becket formed a basis for the Icelandic Thomas Saga, wrote a homily on Ezekiel in which he added the saint to the list of martyrs who were pillars of the church, including Stephen and Lawrence, so echoing Galatians 2: 9. In his words, 'the palm of martyrdom has added him to the fabric of the church [. . .] he is set up as a great and mighty pillar to hold up the fabric, which was just nigh to ruin'.[63] John of Salisbury's prologue to his Life of the saint opens with the imagery of the choir of apostles and the purpled army of the martyrs, who by their teaching and example join together and reinforce the living stones (*vivi lapides*) of the Body of Christ, echoing I Peter 2: 5.[64] A lection for the feast of St Thomas in the *sanctorale* of the Sarum Breviary likens Becket to the cornerstone of the church, after Ephesians 2: 20.[65] The Sarum texts were following that for the translation drawn up at Canterbury in 1220 by Langton himself, and they have much in common with his translation preaching.[66] His sermon of 1221 on the anniversary of the translation of Becket, perhaps delivered to the Canterbury synod, likens the saint to Judas Maccabeus in his resistance to temporal tyranny. He recalls that the great stone set up by Joshua as a witness (Joshua 24: 26–7) stands for Becket, the *lapis grandis in sanctuario*, raised up from his tomb; the martyrs are represented by stones, Becket being the precious stone (*lapidem preciosum*).[67]

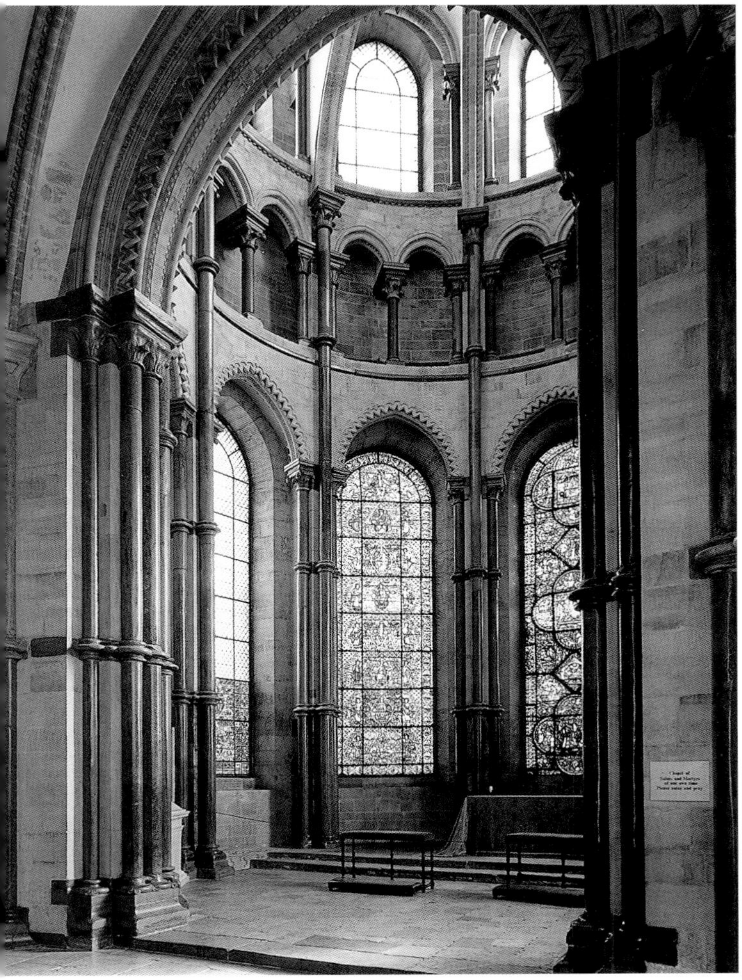

9 Canterbury Cathedral, Corona, from ambulatory (Conway Library, Courtauld Institute of Art).

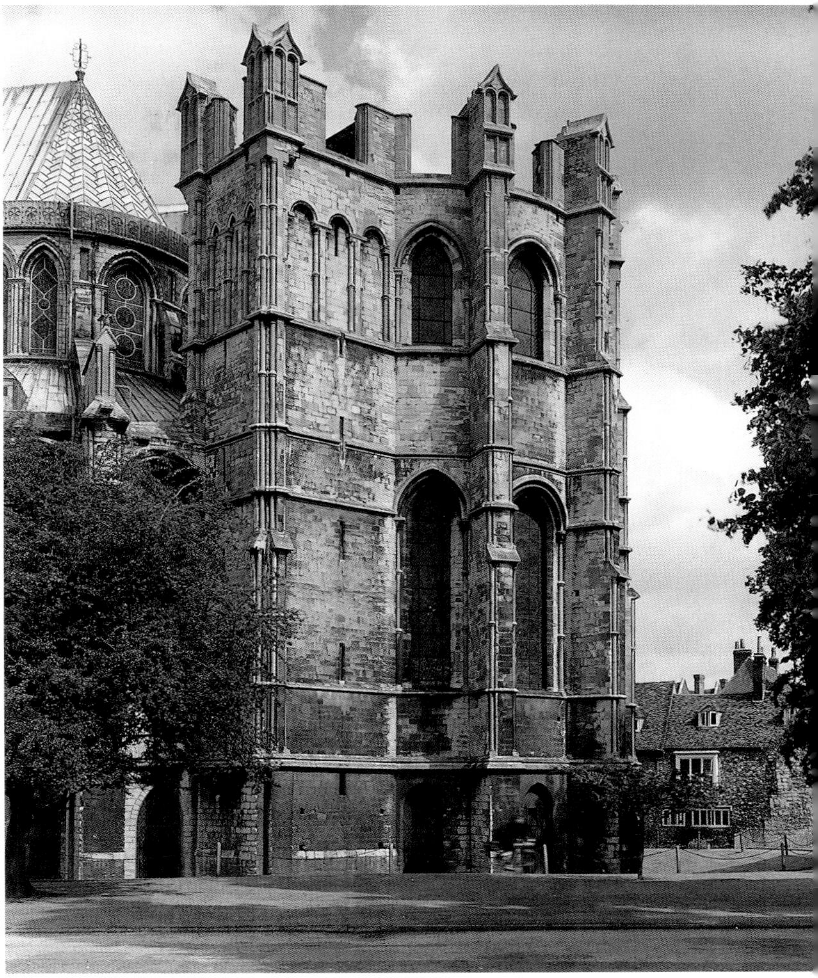

10 Canterbury Cathedral, Corona, from south-east (Conway Library, Courtauld Institute of Art).

Such literal translations of conventional metaphors into physical form in architecture took on particular resonance in the context of the Becket conflict. Besides the columns, there is another aspect of the commemoration of Becket and his martyrdom at Canterbury: the Corona to the east of the Trinity Chapel, the nine-sided polygonal termination to the two-levelled eastern arm of the church which was in effect its *caput*, signifying Christ as in Ephesians 4: 15–16, and probably containing the Trinity altar and the relic of Becket's severed crown (figs 9–11). If, for contemporaries, the columnar supports of the Trinity Chapel might have prompted thoughts about Becket's passion, blood and brains, the Corona embodied an equally studied and perhaps even more obvious synechdochal train of thought about his wounded head, which linked Becket's severed crown to the round crown-like form of the building, laid out as it were *ad staturam humani corporis*.[68] The Corona (the term is early) was almost certainly the intended point of display for the corona relic and the place where donations to it were gathered. Canterbury had several head reliquaries, including St Dunstan's, but Thomas's corona was the proudest.[69] And in regard of this dreadful token of his murder, Canterbury thought was again deliberative, for the corona was his crown of martyrdom and also his tonsure, the corona anointed by the oil of holy chrism and dedicated to God.[70] The narratives of his martyrdom are, once again, carefully staged symbolic accounts of the transgressive character of the lopping-off of this symbol of divinely sanctioned clerical autonomy, which also signal the voluntary character of Becket's martyrdom, his acquiescence in the deed.[71] Later sermons on Becket use the image of the corona in its various senses.[72] By the second quarter of the thirteenth century on the west

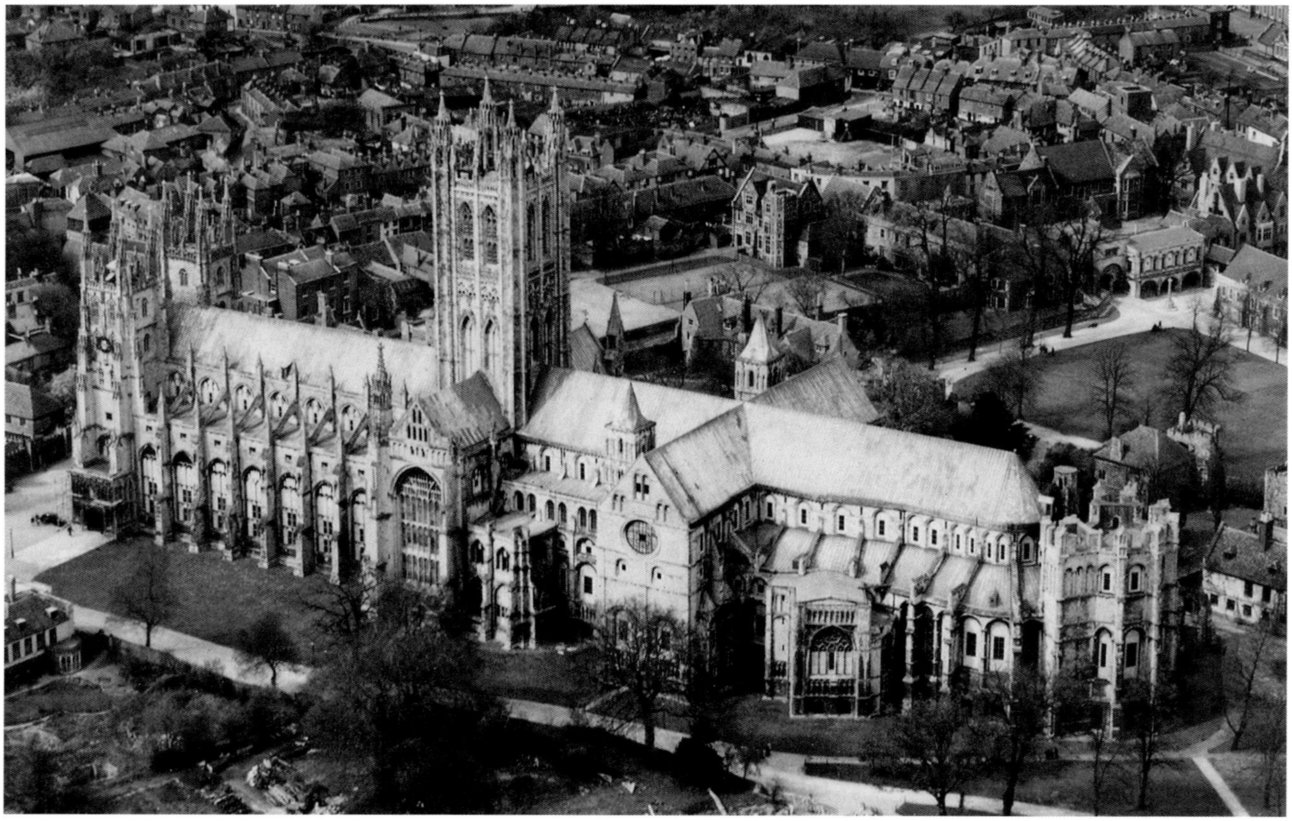

11 Canterbury Cathedral, aerial view from south-east (Simmons Aerofilms Ltd).

front of Wells Cathedral, the sculpted image of Becket was to be shown bearing in his hands the severed tonsure and corona as an attribute, indeed almost as an item of regalia (fig. 12).[73] Again, then, the building deliberately thematizes and embodies Becket imagery: the Corona is a fully up-to-date and articulate memorial to the English St Denis. Early Gothic architecture had arrived at Canterbury, fully formed, as an architecture not only susceptible to allegorical reading, but actively informed by allegory itself.

St Thomas and St Denis

This last analogy with St Denis is chosen deliberately. The various Lives of Becket are absolutely consistent in recording that Becket invoked the name of St Denis the Apostle of France, together with (though the emphasis varies) the Virgin Mary, Alphege and the saints of Canterbury, in commending his soul to God before his martyrdom.[74] Denis plays a much greater role in the biographies than the obvious exemplar, the protomartyr Stephen, though the analogy with Christ outshone any comparison.[75] Thomas's shrine was to be the point of climax in the veritable phalanx of the relics of the holy archbishops of Canterbury whose resting places were carefully noted from the time of Eadmer onwards, and who gathered with other saints in the transepts and around the high altar as his witnesses, contending for the cause: this communion of saints included Wilfrid, Odo, Anselm, Swithun, Aelfric, Alphege and Dunstan.[76] The stained glass of Canterbury gives prominent place to the imagery of Sts Martin, Dunstan, Gregory and Alphege, though nothing survives, if it ever existed, of St Denis.[77] The association with Denis especially was nevertheless explicit. The Canterbury monk William even related that St Denis handed the cure of a possessed Frenchman over to his fellow martyr, Thomas; Guernes de Pont-Sainte-Maxence stated that Thomas is *le martyr* of the *regne saint Denis*.[78]

The style of Becket's death also prompted thought about the great French martyr on the part of a somewhat exclusive circle of men who were also developing an intellectual as well as devotional interest in Denis, and whose culture was strongly French. William presents St Denis as handing cures over to St

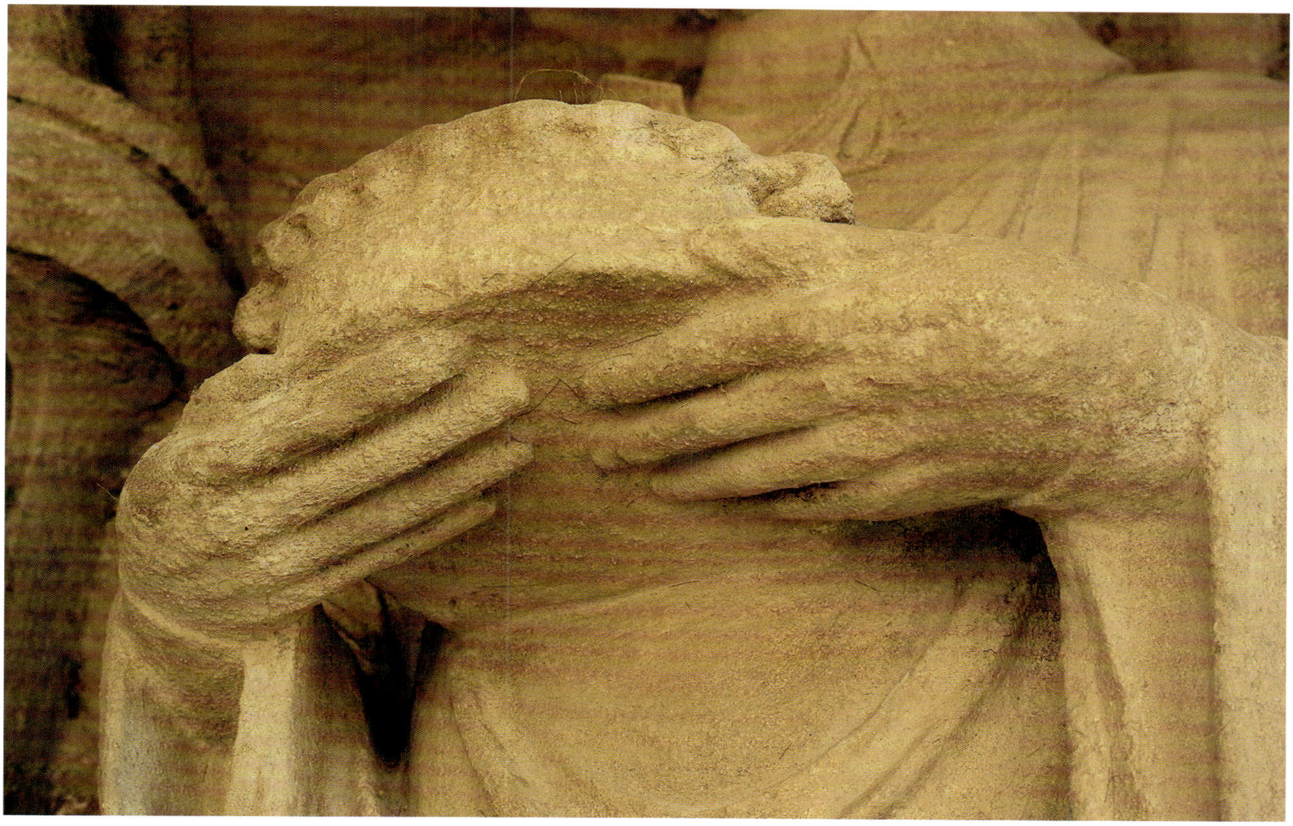

12 Corona in hands of St Thomas, west front, Wells Cathedral (Jerry Sampson).

Thomas while intent upon 'symbolic and anagogic demonstrations, and meditating on the celestial hierarchies'.[79] This new strand of thought by the *eruditi* in Becket's sphere has been explored authoritatively by David Luscombe, though the consequences of it for an understanding of architecture at late twelfth-century Canterbury have been overlooked. Becket's associate John of Salisbury, later Bishop of Chartres, was in close touch with John the Saracen, a student and translator of the works of the man, St Denis, who had long been conflated with the great Pseudo-Dionysius, author of the *Celestial Hierarchy*. It seems that both men were responsible for the circulation of translations of Denis's treatises in France, in association with Odo, Abbot of Saint-Denis (d. *c.* 1169).[80] The Kentishman Ralph of Sarre, later dean of Reims, who emerged with John of Salisbury and Becket from the *familia* of Theobald, Archbishop of Canterbury, and who went into exile in sympathy with Becket, bequeathed a copy of Eriugena's exposition on the *Celestial Hierarchy* and his own translation of Denis's entire works to the library at Christ Church.[81]

A strand of Dionysian thinking is also apparent in the work of one of Becket's biographers, Herbert of Bosham (d. *c.* 1194), Becket's master of the holy page, *major domo* and spiritual advisor, and a brilliant Hebraist.[82] Herbert, who was also close to William, Archbishop of Sens, was one important channel whereby the Becket circle was familiarized with the thinking of the Parisian schools, Saint-Denis and Saint-Victor, since he had worked with Peter Lombard and perhaps with Andrew of Saint-Victor.[83] His dandified dress and one spectacular outburst of cheek to Henry II are celebrated. His later career after the Becket exile was spent almost wholly in France, including Saint-Denis.[84] In view of this it is perhaps not suprising that, of the *eruditi*, Herbert of Bosham, in his somewhat prolix writings on Becket assembled in the mid-1180s and dedicated to Baldwin of Ford, used terminology that is closest to Dionysian.[85] One particular passage has stood out for commentators, the account of Becket's conduct at Mass:[86] when celebrating (often rapidly), Becket commonly used a book of the prayers of his predecessor St Anselm, a reminder that Becket referred to the works and example of his predecessor constantly, and a pointer to the close link between traditions of private affective devotion and the liturgy.[87] The passage goes on to contrast the pure and natural Christian sacrament with the bloody sacrifices of the Synagogue[88] before employing Pauline imagery (*per speculum in enigmate*) and the emphatically Dionysian term *theophania* or mystical experience of the divine, which for Herbert was part of the proof of the existence of God.[89] His account therefore shows familiarity with apophatic or negative theology of the sort identified with Dionysian texts, a theology that emphasized man's incapacity to understand God directly. Though Herbert had a special affection for the monks of Canterbury, he was neither a monk, and nor was he at Canterbury in the key period for this book, the 1170s.[90] Yet his close contacts as a highly educated clerk associated with Saint-Denis and Saint-Victor, his knowledge of Parisian glosses, and the fashionably Dionysian theology that surfaces in his Life of Becket, written in the 1180s, accord exactly with what is known of the northern French and particularly Parisian intellectual and artistic outlook of Becket and his immediate circle during the exile of 1164–70.[91] Becket had preached at Saint-Victor shortly before his martyrdom, and a chapel there was shortly to be dedicated to him.[92] The history of glossed manuscripts copied and illuminated for Becket towards 1170 certainly indicates familiarity with the latest Parisian fashions (fig. 14).[93]

Could the northern French Gothic style have moved to Canterbury in the same way as the glosses, and in a fashion reminiscent of the links between the spread of the Gothic of Paris and the Victorine sequences?[94] It is hard to say. The *eruditi* and William of Sens aside, there is a formidable dearth of positive evidence about agency at Canterbury in these critical years. The obvious hypothetical focus is Becket himself. Yet the suggestion that he was the 'prime mover' in the introduction of Gothic architecture into England, either at Canterbury or in the service of a projected canons' church at Hackington nearby, cannot be without controversy.[95] The terms of reference of the Hackington project belonged to a later generation than Becket's (see p. 35 below); and the extent of his art patronage, if not its quality, is open to question.[96] One should also be wary of notions of posthumous patronage. Gervase's silence on Becket's ambitions contrasts strikingly with his eulogy of the works of Hubert Walter, and Becket's biographers say nothing of interest on the point. This is likely to be significant, given that architectural patronage was a mark of pastoral greatness, proper to hagiography. While this silence is open to interpretation, it may simply indicate that the post-fire rebuilding reflected the interests of a coterie; and the most well-informed coterie on matters French at Canterbury in 1174 seems to have consisted more of Becket's secular clerks than the monks with whom William of Sens had to negotiate – though stating as much proves nothing. Too little is known about any of these groups to eliminate them from consideration. It may be relevant that Gervase, who presents the negotiations about the rebuilding essentially in terms of a dialogue between the architect and the monks, and so the chapter, was chronically suspicious of secular clerks in the archiepiscopal household at the time when he wrote, and might have been disposed to downplay their influence by stressing instead the capability of the monks, with whom he sided, to erect a great building and preserve its heritage of relics.[97] William of Sens is most unlikely to have acted in a vacuum, and it would not be incompatible with the qualities attributed to him by Gervase to suggest that he was close to this immediate clerical circle, and well able to articulate its ideas.

Yet those who presided over the refashioning of the building's eastern limb from west to east in the 1170s were not entirely single minded. As is well known, the evidence of the junction at the ambulatory steps between the presbytery and the Trinity Chapel, showing that there had been an earlier plan to drive the ambulatory forward at the same level as the choir (fig. 13), betrays a certain equivocation as to how the climax of

13 Canterbury Cathedral, steps up to Trinity Chapel showing buried wall arcading, north ambulatory (author).

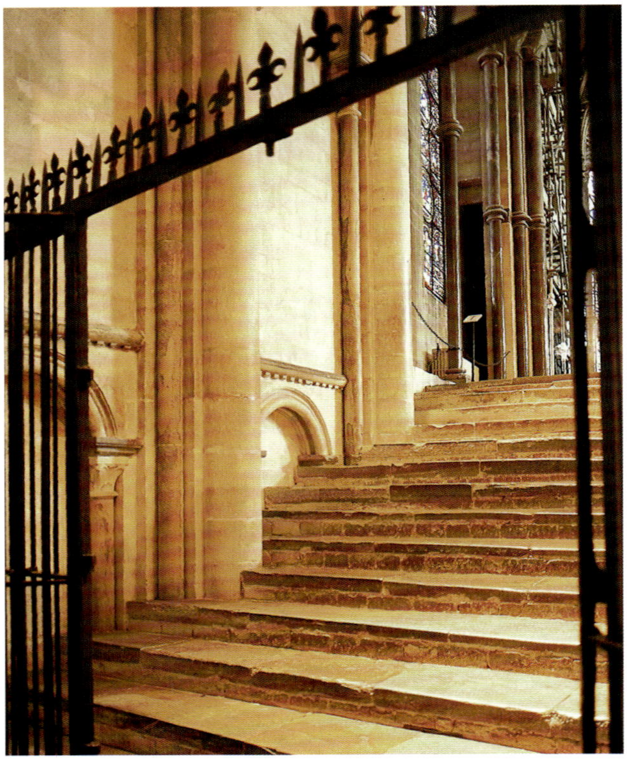

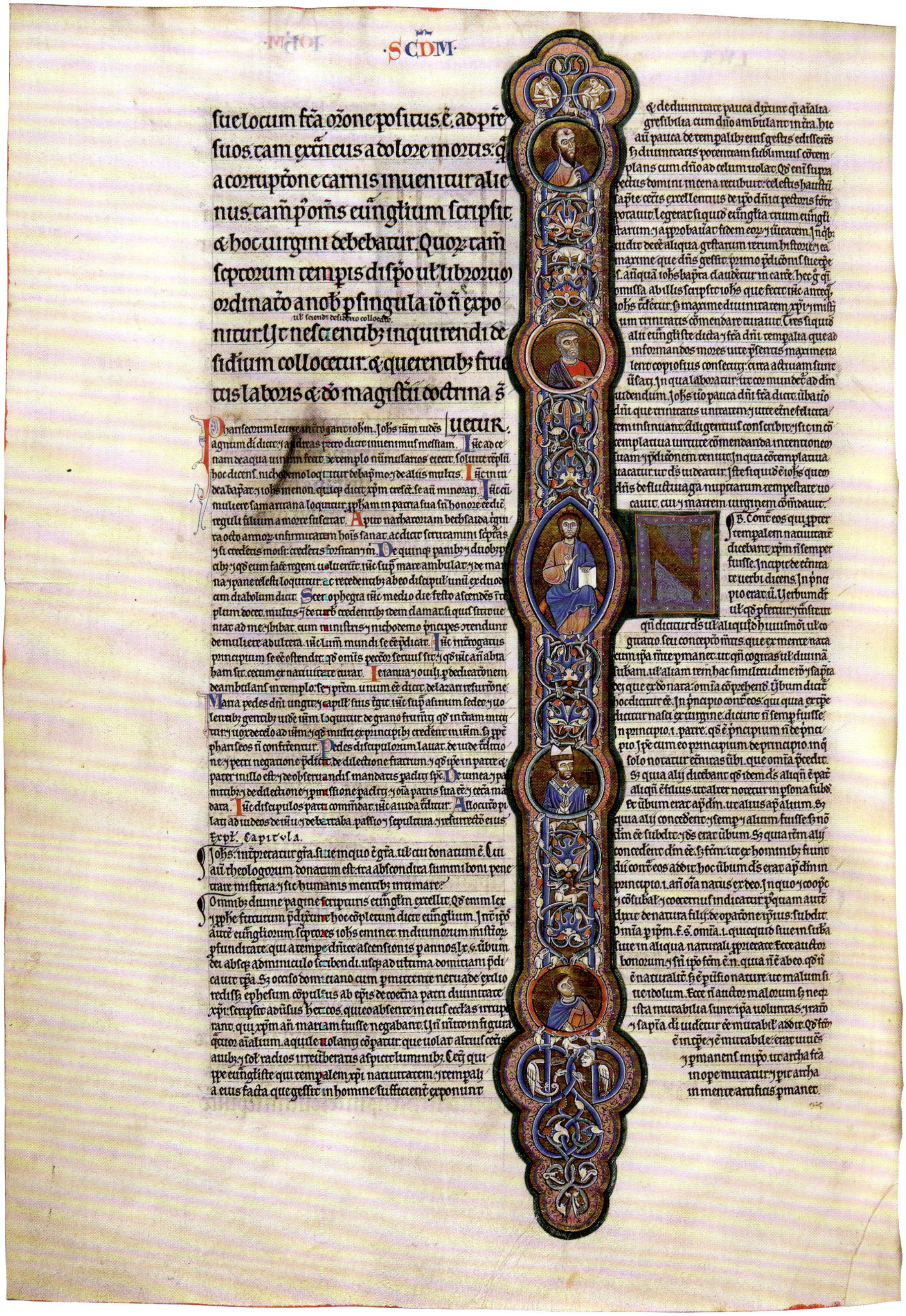

14 Initial I (showing Becket midway down lower half of stem?). Glossed Bible owned by Becket, late 1160s. Cambridge, Trinity College MS B.5.5, fol. 130v (Master and Fellows of Trinity College, Cambridge).

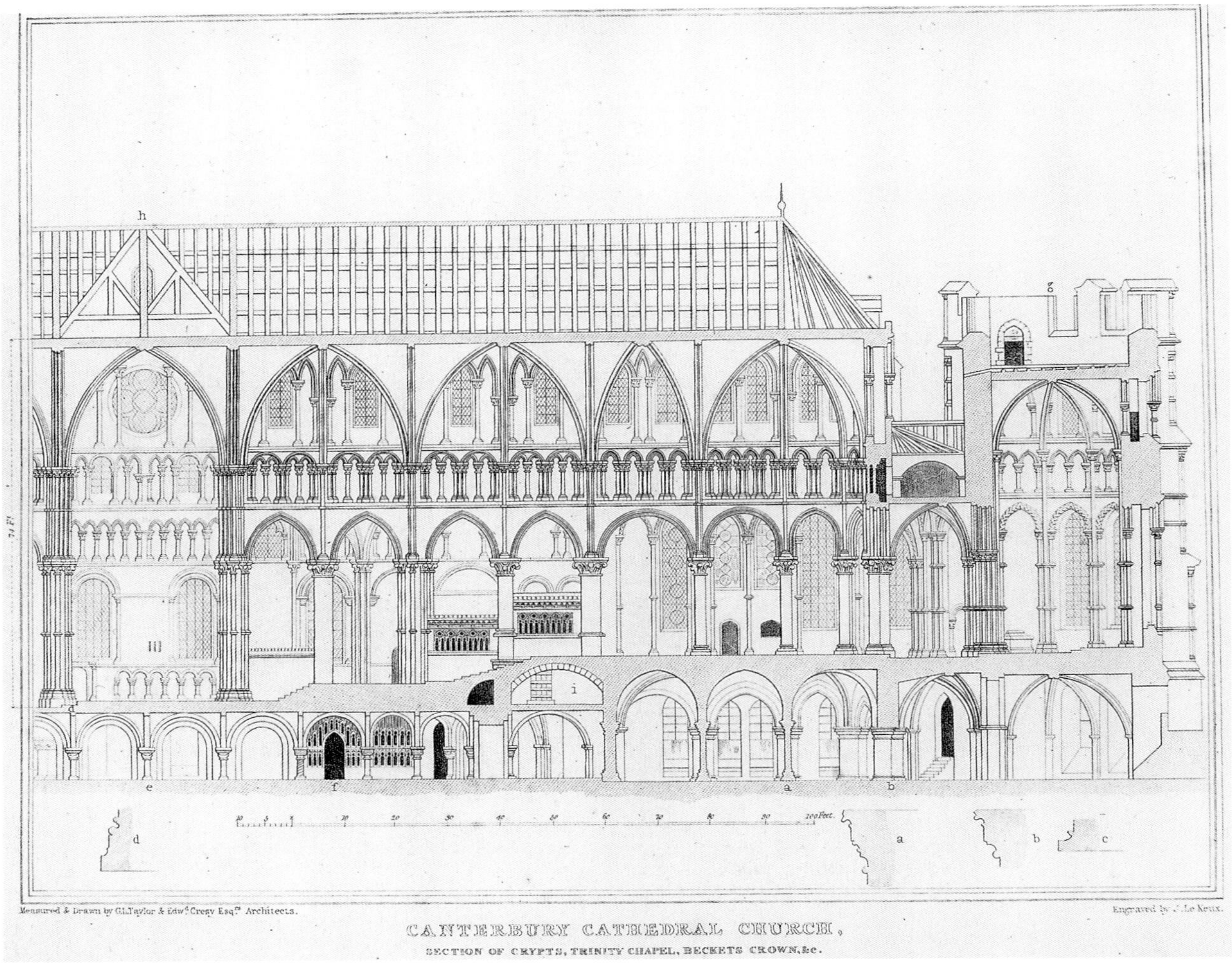

15 Canterbury Cathedral, cross-section of Trinity Chapel and Corona showing crypt (after J. Britton, *History and Antiquities [. . .] of Canterbury* (1821), pl. XI).

the building, its shrine space, should function and appear. There appears to have been some sort of crisis at the time of the transition from William of Sens' to English William's control of the works around 1179, of which the current elevated eastern arrangements were the final, and very satisfying, product. It is possible to offer some very general account of the issues at stake. Contrary to some late twentieth-century accounts of the internal politics of the management of the cult at Canterbury, which place a great deal of faith in the importance of matters of local agency and politics, and an ability to resolve them, the question was not so much the political and symbolic standing of the cult of Becket for Christ Church as the more complex practical implications of its early development.[98]

Here two related issues can be identified: those arising from the nature of St Thomas's passion, and those arising from pilgrimage. The manner and circumstances of Becket's martyrdom possessed not only tremendous imaginative power, but also presented those fashioning the cult spaces with the logistical conundrum posed by a series of disastrous events that had, as it were, fragmented Becket and his narrative into a cluster of objects of devotion. There was not only the site of his martyrdom, but his tomb, his shrine and the *disjecta membra* of the broken sword-point, the corona, the contact relics and so on. As if like a fractured Host, the physical traces of Becket were spread throughout the eastern arm of a church whose aesthetic character took account of their presence. For this reason in the history of buildings devoted to great saints, Canterbury is of revolutionary importance. It aimed consciously, and in a way without obvious English precedent, to concert its ancient relic-cults, those mentioned by Eadmer and Gervase, with

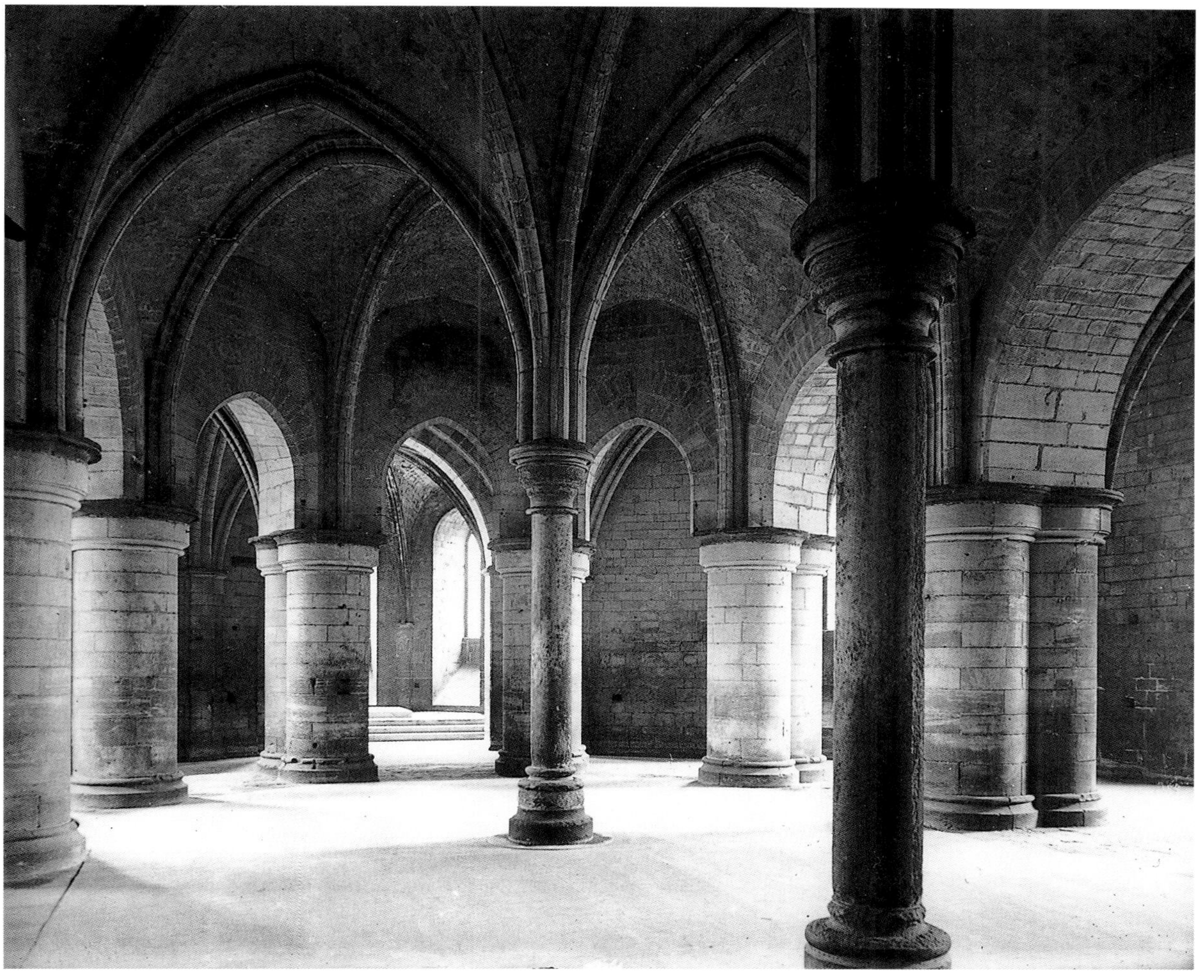

16 Canterbury Cathedral, crypt beneath Trinity Chapel showing site of St Thomas's tomb between the two central columns (Conway Library, Courtauld Institute of Art).

something new and of quite extraordinary scale, complexity and power. The indecisions and perplexities that mark the frontier between the presbytery and the Trinity Chapel seem principally to have concerned one major aspect of this cultic dispersal at Canterbury: the relationship between the crypt and the upper church. The magnificent Romanesque crypt built by Archbishop Anselm had been specifically intended for the reassertion and promotion of the pre-Conquest Canterbury cults as well as that of the Virgin Mary.[99] The old Trinity Chapel at its east end had similarly been a two-storeyed repository of the relics of the archbishops, Becket's being included in view of his pattern of private devotions and first saying of Mass in the chapel. In the first phases of

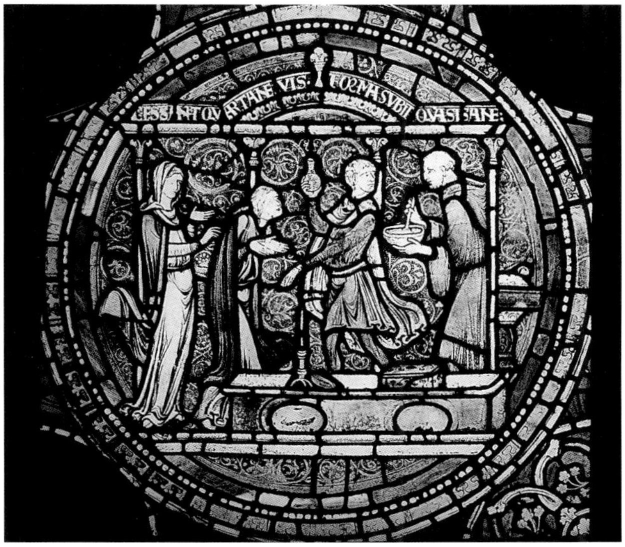

17 Canterbury Cathedral, Trinity Chapel Miracle Windows, showing tomb and donation box (Sebastian Strobl).

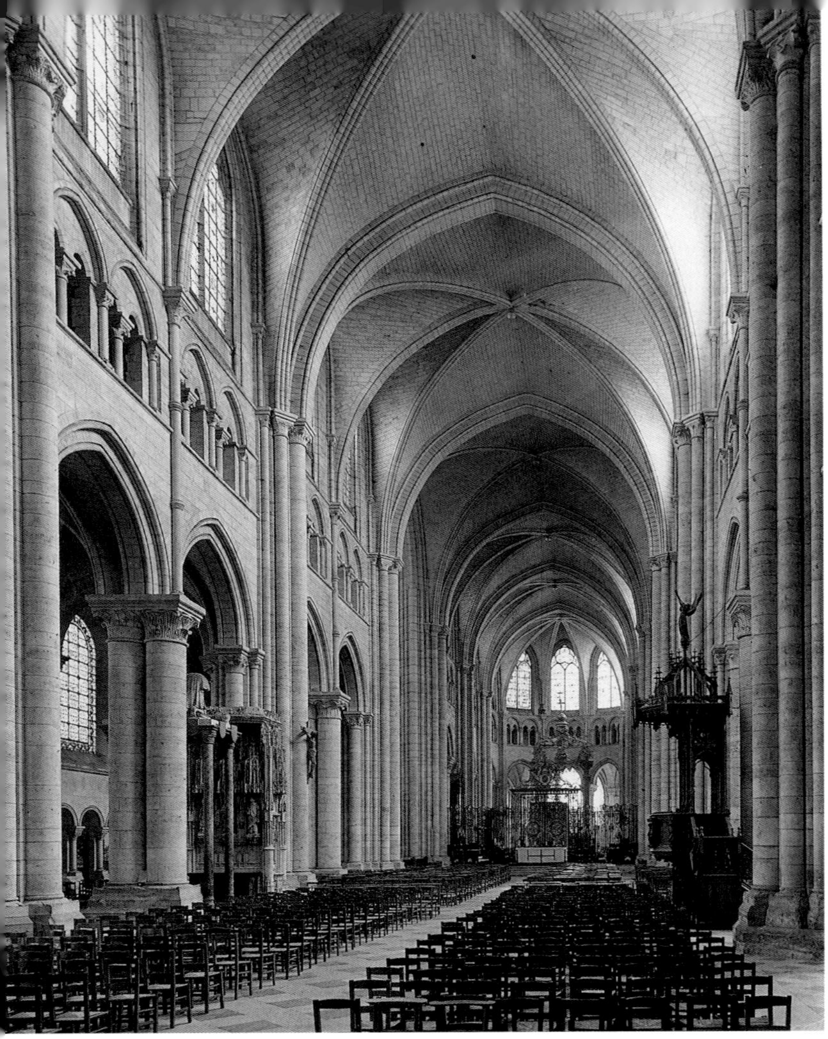

18 Sens Cathedral, nave (James Austin).

the rebuilding after 1174, at least one scheme for the completion of the eastern termination must have envisaged the retention of the lower portion of the old and modestly proportioned Trinity Chapel as a Becket relic, and the design of an upper church of corresponding form with proportions more in line with those of the choir, and with a lower shrine-platform. But another scheme, perhaps one generated among several possibilities by William of Sens, and the one eventually put into effect by English William between 1179–80 and about 1184, took the old Trinity Chapel down entirely and, retaining the burial place of Becket, erected around it an austerely detailed but quite loftily vaulted and aisled vessel, a lower church in all but name, supporting the raised upper chapel dedicated to the Trinity (figs 15–16).[100] The quandary of the eastern arm thus resolved into a dialogue between the lower and upper churches which benefited both, the proportions of the upper church settling into a more satisfactory interrelationship of parts than those found in the earlier work in the choir and presbytery, the lower church gaining enormously in stature.

Aesthetic considerations were certainly at work here, but the governing impetus to this rethinking of the component parts came, above all, from a decision to promote the cult of Becket's tomb as well as his shrine. Becket had been buried between two other archbishops beneath the crypt of the old Trinity Chapel, and a low but strong marble structure with oval openings called either *fenestrae* or *foraminae* was erected over his sarcophagus, the site being regularly visited by pilgrims from Easter 1171.[101] Though it was clearly intended that Becket's body should be translated to the upper church, the tomb, as the site of so many wonders, was a fundamental relic of Becket and a powerful object of veneration. Benedict specifies that the openings in the tomb were intended to permit pilgrims to insert their heads to kiss the sarcophagus within, and the tomb with its openings and a donation box is shown frequently in the Becket glass upstairs (fig. 17).[102] This stress on the cult of an empty saint's tomb was not new in England.[103] But its architectural incorporation at Canterbury into a dual tomb-shrine church on two levels was its most grandiloquent expression, and pointed forward to instances in the next century where the tombs of saints appear to have been separately venerated from their shrines, as in the cases of St Frideswide at Oxford, St Wulfstan at Worcester (can. 1203), St Hugh at Lincoln (can. 1220), St William of York (can. 1227), St John of Beverley and St Kentigern at Glasgow, with longer-standing examples of the tradition at Durham and Winchester.[104] Its objective, as the extraordinary emphasis given to the tomb site in the hagiography and stained glass of Becket shows, was certainly in the first instance devotional. Nevertheless, as is suggested by records for receipts from 1198 onwards, the new arrangements created scope for four different locations and points for offerings associated with Becket: the shrine (after 1220), the Corona, the tomb and the altar of the martyrdom.[105] Though the capacity of separate relic sites to generate increased revenues was not realized as was planned (revenue from the tomb fell off markedly from 1221), a practical endeavour to 'milk' the cult of Becket cannot have been far from the minds of those in charge, particularly if it could be done in a manner congenial to the daily routines of the monastic offices.

If one issue was therefore implicit in the events of Thomas's death and physical remains, the second arose from the understanding – which cannot have been self-evident in the early years of the cult – that Thomas was going to be the permanent focus of mass pilgrimage and not the faddish object of a short-lived if spec-

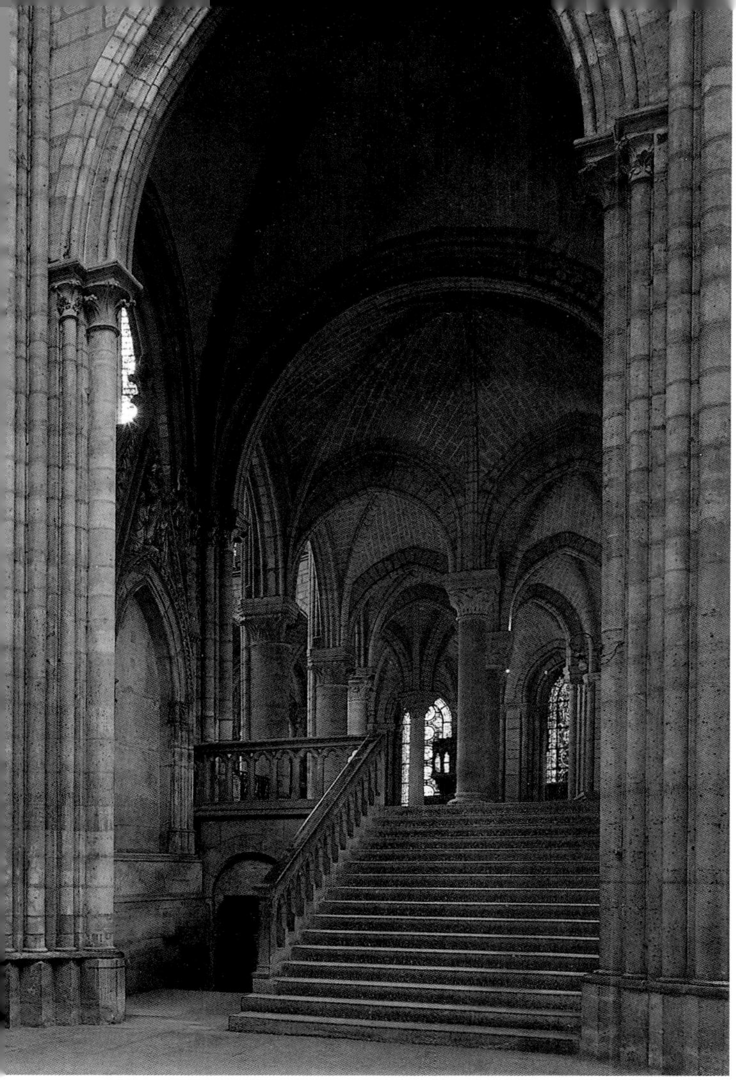

19 Paris, Saint-Denis, steps up to southern ambulatory from crossing (James Austin).

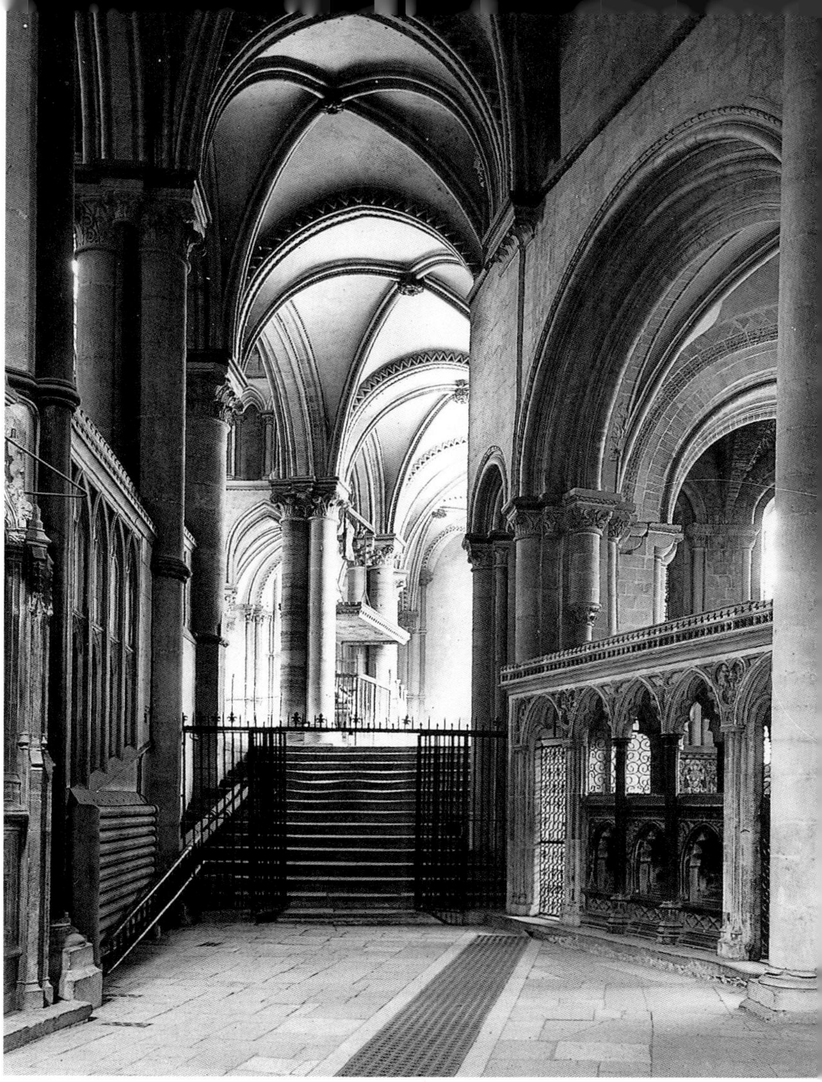

20 Canterbury Cathedral, steps up to Trinity Chapel, south side (reproduced by permission of English Heritage. NMR).

tacular cult. The creation of a double church marked the transition from a cult- to a pilgrimage-centred building; and it is exactly this expansive frame of mind, emerging and consolidating in the 1170s with the burgeoning records of miracles there, encountered in William of Canterbury's triumphalist compilation about the saint, which lends much greater weight to the issue of pilgrimage than Benedict's more cautious and, as it turned out, somewhat less successful, collection.[106] Promoted Prior of Canterbury in 1175, Benedict left to be Abbot of Peterborough in 1177.[107] The signs of restlessness that mark aspects of the development of Christ Church's architecture around its shrine testify not so much to local and inevitable oscillations of political sentiment about Becket's importance within the community at Canterbury, as to utterly unforeseeable external pressures beyond the church's control, which were continuing to form a pattern throughout the 1170s.

That the outcome for the presentation of the main shrine above in the new chapel of St Thomas should have been so entirely and deliberately spectacular is a sign of how successfully these competing forces – cult sites, pilgrimage and the emulation of the best examples of French Gothic architecture, as at Saint-Denis and Sens – were reconciled. Here the drift of analysis of Canterbury's sources away from northern and eastern France (though the links are undeniable), and back to Paris-Sens, is instructive.[108] Although the Trinity Chapel demonstrates detailed knowledge of architecture to the north and east of Paris, whoever steered the project to completion remained intent on a return to the great founding monuments, the cynosures, of the new style in France, Sens Cathedral (fig. 18), but especially Saint-Denis (fig. 19), the consecration of which had been witnessed by Archbishop Theobald in 1144. It is hard – and many commentators agree – to see the steps which mount up from the presbytery aisles to the elevated shrine space as anything other than a conscious dramatization of the new fact of mass pilgrimage at Canterbury (fig. 20), and equally as a conscious invocation of the arrangement of crypt and ambulatories at Saint-Denis, whose comparatively recent rehabilitation as the single most important point of reference for this building has been notable.[109] The formal analogies with Saint-Denis in respect of the columnar supports, greatly enlarged ambulatory windows and even the use of marble shafting are still striking.[110] Benedictine models for the elevated presentation of a major shrine and walkway, such as those established earlier at Saint-Benoît-sur-Loire and Saint-Denis, addressed an obvious practical concern, and the diaphonous, civilized and high-status columnar architecture of the Dionysian building especially, an aesthetic need.[111]

Yet other factors were at work. At Canterbury, pilgrimage was both a commemoration of Becket's passion and a spiritual progress. Arguably the new and singular solution of the shrine-church gained by mountainous steps effected a spiritual allegory of climax: Langton's anniversary sermon of 1221 moved swiftly from Becket as the great stone of the sanctuary, to Isaiah 56: 7: *adducam eos in montem sanctum meum* – 'even them will I bring to my holy mountain'.[112] So the austere mode of tomb-church beneath, with its clean and somewhat antiseptic lines, and its modest and practical thaumaturgical apparatus of empty tomb and foramina for prayer and confession, ceded above to a super-elevated marbled and jewelled sarcophagus on stilts (fig. 21). Wonderful to behold and forming the centrepiece of a veritable theatre of allegory and spiritual enlightenment, this was illuminated with the shining and mystical virtues of precious stones, lustrous marbles, coruscating floors and radiant glass. In this sermon Langton related the elevation of Becket's relics to the rising sun, an image which, though not uncommon in the history of sainthood, resonates throughout the thirteenth century in the history of the placement of major shrines to come.[113] Well might the two Irish friars who witnessed this thoroughly concerted display in 1323 have thought of the glitter of the Heavenly Jerusalem.[114] In one of the Becket windows the saint is shown emerging at night from his shrine (the term used in the glass caption is specifically *feretrum*) as a sort of muse to one of his biographers, asleep at the shrine's foot in the manner of St John on Patmos.[115] The shrine satisfies the longing for God; it is the ultimate point of return for the pilgrim from the other relic-sites, the church's singularity. It is a statement of the sublime, in the service of a charismatic individual, but in the name of the triune God to whom this part of the church was anciently dedicated and to whom the souls of the martyrs and the blessed were to return.

Nothing in this hierarchical arrangement is incompatible with the idea of the Trinity Chapel as itself a 'Dionysian' complex, in the literal sense that its architecture was formulated, or reformulated, to resemble that of Saint-Denis, and in the imaginative sense that its spaces were premised upon an anagogical progress. What this means for an understanding of Saint-Denis itself is open to debate.[116] The coincidence of architectural forms and theological speculation in the two milieux is certainly striking. Canterbury's context was scarcely atheoretical. It was formed of men given to mystical and speculative traditions of thought. In support of this is the evidence of the exegetical manoeuvres outlined above in relation to the mystical signification of the colours that represented Becket's passion, the allegorical potential of his corona, as well as the new wave of specifically Dionysian discourse at Canterbury in Becket's circle. While Canterbury does not vindicate Panofsky's reading of Suger's Saint-Denis as a Dionysian building, any more than it commits one to a definite view of that great Parisian exemplar, it may serve as a reminder that empiricist commentary on early Gothic architecture has recently tended to be critical or dismissive of such speculative links, and has in Canterbury's case seemingly underestimated the richness of its creative milieu.[117] An interest in Dionysian theology is unlikely of itself to have causally determined the aesthetic of the two buildings, but it may have been contributory in the sense that it directed Canterbury patrons as to where to look. The historical links between the two places were sufficiently strong for Canterbury to be seen at the very least as one important element in the reception of Saint-Denis in the twelfth century, and as a dynamic statement of the new style in its own right.

This is not to claim that Canterbury and Saint-Denis were in total agreement. There were important differences between the buildings and their cults. Though Canterbury, like Saint-Denis, has a Tree of Jesse in its *caput*, the Corona, and also uses the typological method in its stained glass, its iconography does not imitate the dense, modish and somewhat obscure allegories found in Saint-Denis's stained glass: nothing survives at Canterbury of the imagery of St Denis or of a specifically 'Dionysian' or Pauline type, and nothing either (perhaps more surprisingly) of Trinitarian imagery, which had certainly preoccupied Suger's Saint-Denis.[118] The 'bookishness' of its glazing does not outweigh the much more frankly demotic aspect of the Becket windows in the Trinity Chapel. Moreover, the two buildings housed principal cults of a very different order and character.

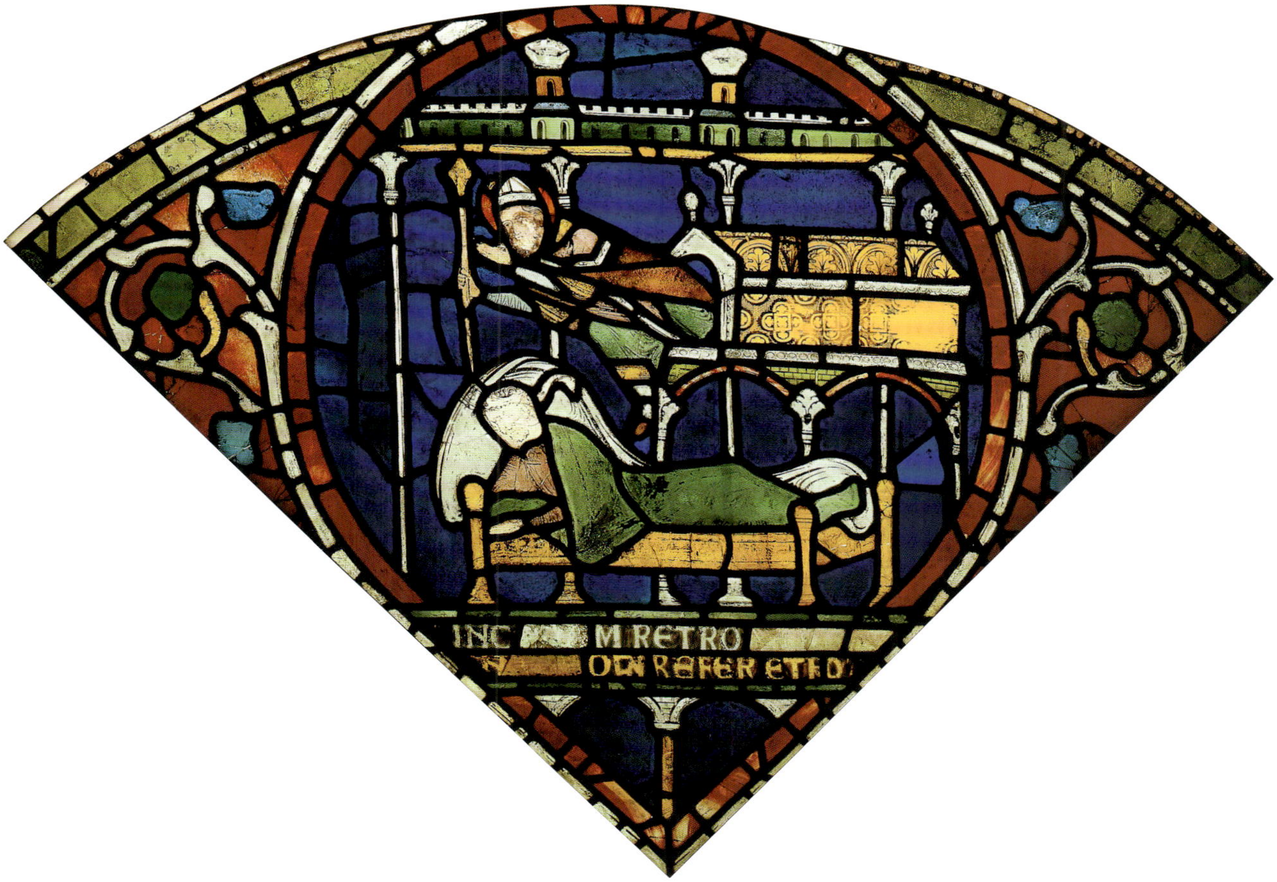

21 Canterbury Cathedral, Trinity Chapel Miracle Windows, showing a vision of St Thomas appearing from his shrine to one of his sleeping biographers (Sonia Halliday and Laura Lushington).

The lively reportage of the miracles, especially the tomb miracles, in the Becket windows conveys little or nothing of the allegorizing and occasionally somewhat esoteric mentality found in contemporary hagiographies. It stresses instead the sheer eventfulness of Becket's miracles, and the wide social acceptance and popular acclaim of his cult. It was fundamentally much more modern. Its public character was, to be sure, much in line with the oldest views of 'red' martyrdom as a public demonstration of sanctity in the era before the process of formal Roman canonization.[119] Becket himself was canonized according to Roman process by Alexander III in 1173, the second major canonization in the juridical sense of the word of an English saint since Edward the Confessor's in 1161.[120] Becket had attended St Edward's translation, though his attitude to the promotion of the saintliness of the royal dynasty is likely to have been complex and calculated.[121] Before this period, the English and particularly the Anglo-Saxon cults had been exactly what Becket's cult in so many ways purported to be, namely popular cults recognized and promulgated locally. This tension between universal and local, or national, recognition is reminiscent of the vision reported early in the miracles related by William of Canterbury. Two priests who sought an antiphon for the new martyr were in a dilemma because he had not yet been declared a saint by Rome (*nondum enim ex apostolica auctoritate catalogo martyrum martyr ascriptus erat*). They therefore improvised a homespun English antiphon:

> Hali Thomas of hevenriche
> Alle postles evenliche [. . .]
> Dhu ert help in Engelande,
> Ure stefne to understande.[122]

By about 1200, to judge from one reliquary of Becket which aligns him both with the great saints of Canterbury and with Sts Edmund and Edward, and certainly by the time of that accomplished and well-connected thirteenth-century monastic hagiographer, Matthew Paris, Thomas had been assimilated fully and

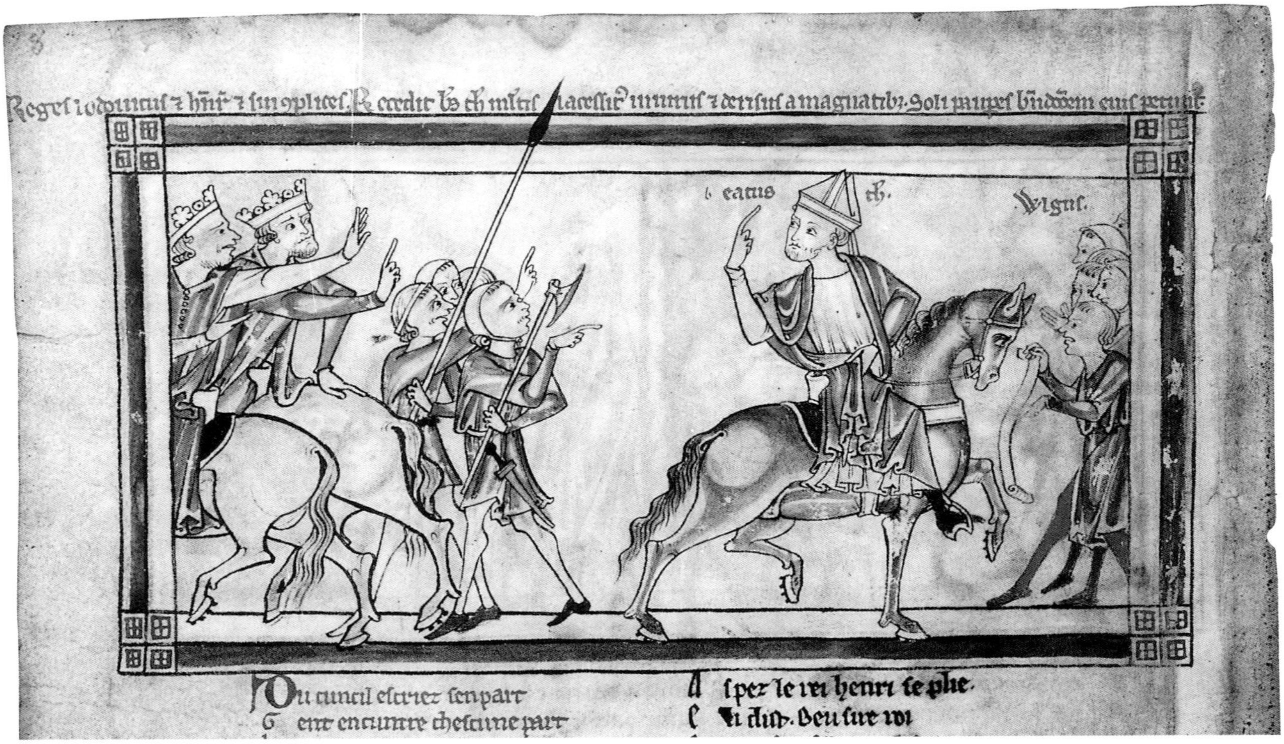

22 St Thomas parts company with Henry II and Louis VII and rides towards the *Vulgus*. Leaf (fol. 2v) from fragmentary Anglo-Norman verse Life of St Thomas, *c.* 1230 (by permission of the British Library and the Estate of the late Sir Paul Getty, K.B.E., Wormsley Library).

routinely into the pantheon of national sainthood.[123] His illustrated Life was coupled with that of Edward the Confessor in manuscripts owned by members of the royal family and read for pastoral purposes (see p. 123 below). Thirteenth-century pictorial hagiographies of the type produced by Matthew, such as that preserved in fragmentary form in the so-called 'Becket leaves' of around 1230, which illustrate a versification of the *Quadrilogus*, continue to stress Becket's role as a popular leader.[124] When Becket parts company with Henry II and Louis VII in the illustration on folio 2v of this Life, one of the most dramatic and telling in the whole corpus of English medieval illustrated hagiography, he moves on towards the crowd of ordinary folk, who petition him and who are labelled the *Vulgus* (fig. 22).[125]

It is absolutely symptomatic of the cult's popular character that one of the earliest English occurrences of the sentiment *Vox populi, vox Dei* should have been attached to Becket himself, in the Life of the 'Anonymous of Lambeth' ('Anonymous II') of around 1172–3.[126] This writer quotes the adage, which had first been used by Alcuin under the influence of Bede in the eighth century, in the context of Thomas's acceptance as a saint before his formal canonization, and the tearful homage paid to his memory by his former enemies before Henry II's reconciliation with the Church at Avranches.[127] Though the sentiment possessed a certain ambiguity, Alcuin appears to have thought of the word *populus* not in a Roman civic sense but a Christian one, of God's elect people, as used in I Samuel 8: 7 in the context of the tyrannical potential of anointed kingship. Significantly it had been used by William of Malmesbury, again under the influence of Alcuin, in connection with the right of free episcopal election of Odo, Archbishop of Canterbury, and also in an early biography of St Edward himself.[128] Becket was well aware of these resonances, and in an absolutely symbolic gesture claimed as his fee for attending the translation of St Edward in 1163 the tombstone of St Edward into which St Wulfstan had rammed his pastoral staff as a sign of resistance to the tyranny of William the Conqueror.[129] Becket's biographers rapidly assimilated his cause to the notion of the ancient communal liberties of the English people, which could be represented by virtuous kingship as manifested in St Edward. His promotion as a saint of the English served to tie him in to, and so refresh and radicalize, the powerful Anglo-Saxon tradition of sanctified rulers and bishops which was central to the formation of the idea of English nationhood and *communitas regni*, and which offered a stark contrast to the contemporary clerical critique of Angevin despotism.[130] In particular, this way of promoting saints was linked to past and future reform. It remained for Stephen Langton, Becket's brilliant and highly organized follower, to give formal shape to this notion of the *communitas regni* in connection with the saint's spectacular translation in 1220: the legacy of these ideas for the next century was to be fundamental, and I return to them in Part II. For the present, it is necessary only to note the possibility that the remarkable elevation of the east end of the cathedral, quite as much as its populist glass, was itself acknowledgement of Becket's embodiment of the *Vox populi*.

Becket was also being presented as a universal saint, as the triumphant representative of a wider conflict. His name and not St Denis's was taken up by the French 'nation' in the schools of Paris; it was spread with phenomenal speed and by aristocratic and clerical agency to France, Scandinavia, Poland, the Holy Roman Empire, the Iberian peninsula, Sicily, Italy and Hungary.[131] The Becket storm, pentecostal in force, was witnessed instantly through remote visions as much as by the infinitely extendable relics of his passion, his blood and water. Thoughts about Becket and his cause impacted on the French schools and in the thirteenth-century *Bibles moralisées* which not only couple Thomas with St Denis, but deploy him as a universal type for the priesthood.[132] As Anne Duggan put it, 'Becket became the hero of the reformed and reforming church, his martyrdom vindicating the dignity and freedom for which it had striven since the days of Gregory VII.'[133] Thomas was universal, as Prior Benedict and Matthew Paris claimed, because his cause was universal.[134]

The Heroic Mode and Canterbury's 'Humanism'

If Becket's cult was positioned between the local and the universal, the architecture and furnishings of Canterbury produced in the early Gothic period are a reminder that Christ Church was itself positioned at a moment of particularly fertile and unpredictable innovation. Its French-trained architects were studiously keeping up with innovations in France at such places at Laon, Reims and Paris, to the point where Gervase's chronological account can be appropriated to shed light on the sheer pace of change in the building history of the rising great churches of northern France.[135] Indeed there is much to be said for Canterbury's positive role in the increasingly homogeneous clerical, intellectual and architectural culture of southern England and northern France, and for seeing that role as having its own special authority and impact.[136] Canterbury's distinguished monastic visual culture was an important aspect of its apostolic standing in general. The legacy of texts, buildings, images and artefacts maintained at its two great religious houses, starting with such works as the St Augustine's Gospels and *Codex aureus* (figs 2–3), was in fact singularly cosmopolitan, and its language and attitudes naturally attuned by dint of circumstances to the heritage of the ancient Christian world. The early cathedral at Christ Church had observed Roman forms.[137] When, earlier in the twelfth century, masons elected to provide the altar of the Virgin Mary in the crypt of the eastern arm with spiral columns of the sort long associated with the high altar of Old St Peter's in Rome, and so used the formal vocabulary of apostolic Rome, they were not 'quoting', any more than the Psalms were 'quoted' in the daily offices; rather they were speaking the authentic language of a wider Roman Church.[138] The same might be said for the enclosure of Conrad's magnificent choir, destroyed in the fire of 1174; it was referred to by Gervase as *tabulis marmoreis compositus*, composed of marble slabs, as though modelled on the chancel walls of the new churches of the Rome of Calixtus II, for example San Clemente.[139] The apostolic character of these furnishings and motifs was evidence of a much easier familiarity with the heritage of Roman Christianity. Canterbury's authoritative visual culture was saluted in the remarkable tradition of copying Frankish illustrated Psalters, culminating in the mid-twelfth-century Eadwine Psalter and the slightly later Great Canterbury Psalter.[140] It is intrinsically likely that contemporary patrons discussed the centrally planned and double-columned fourth-century mausoleum of Santa Costanza in Rome, or something very like it, in their deliberations over the analogous *heroa* for St Thomas at Canterbury, for interest in a model of this type could explain the revitalization of the medieval tradition of centrally planned martyria or mausolea (figs 23–4).[141] It is possible that, when Becket promoted the canonization of his predecessor Anselm in 1163, he had the chapel of Sts Peter and Paul decorated with scenes from the Acts in commemoration of the primitive apostolic church.[142] Garnier states that no less a figure than Henry of Blois had commended Paul's conversion to Thomas as an example of what Thomas's attitude to the Church should become.[143] Thomas's biographers show comfortable familiarity with the ancient language of martyrs, gladiators and athletes of Christ in illuminating the Lives of their spiritual hero. His eulogists made it plain that St Thomas's martyr-

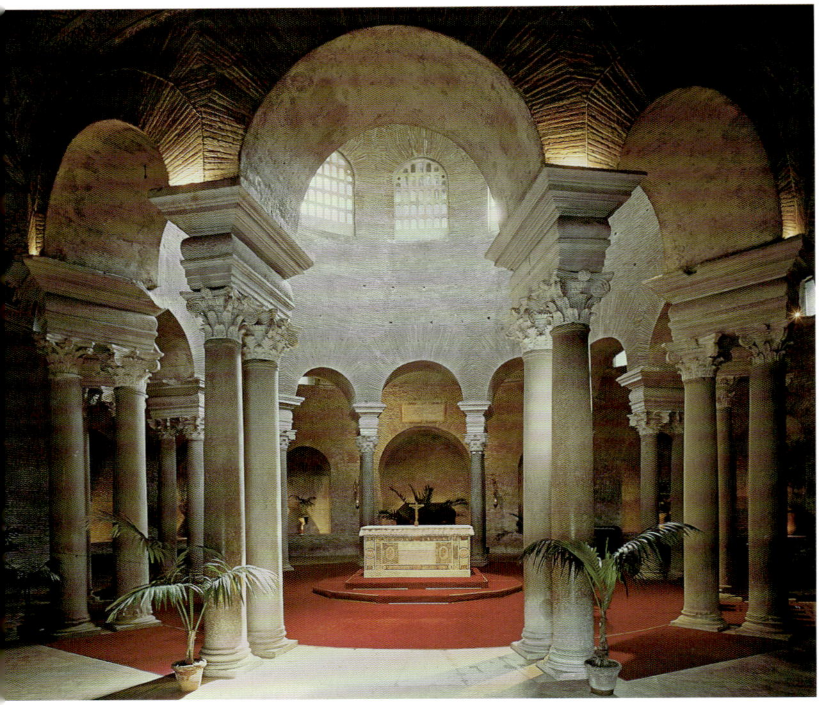

23 Rome, basilica of Santa Costanza (© Photo Scala, Florence).

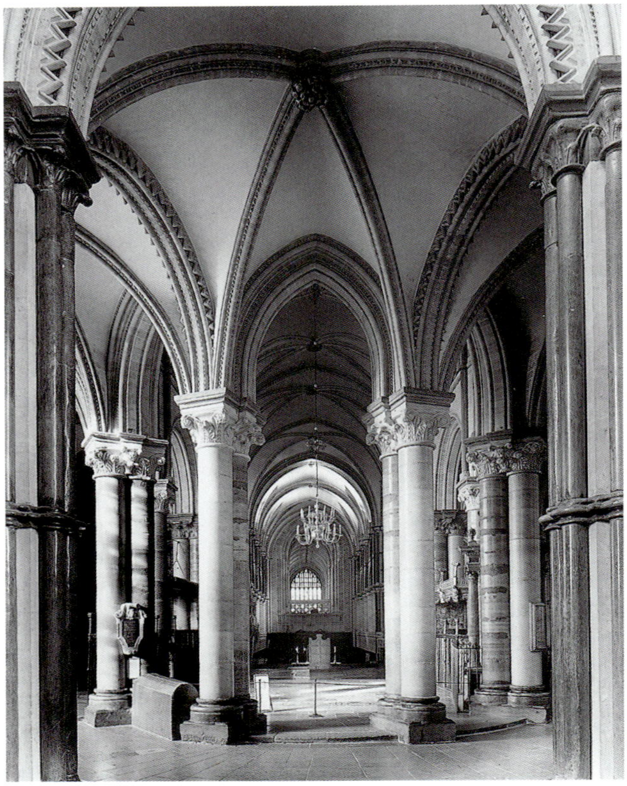

24 Canterbury Cathedral, Trinity Chapel, ambulatory from Corona (Conway Library, Courtauld Institute of Art).

dom, voluntarily undertaken, connected Canterbury to the great early tradition of Christian martyrdom in the primitive church.[144] Canterbury's *romanitas* and Becket's epic standing both demonstrated metropolitan catholicity.

Canterbury's apprehension of its own past as well as of a wider history, which for some might be called its 'antiquarianism', leads one to wonder to what extent the new choir amplified or preserved ideas, materials and artefacts present in the Romanesque 'Glorious Choir' destroyed by fire in 1174.[145] The new choir echoed Conrad's old one in having round and octagonal pillars; stained glass was re-used from the old choir;[146] and materials from its old pavements were very likely recycled in the new church.[147] In such instances salvage after the fire would have concentrated on high-grade materials that possessed the greatest status and significance, stemming too from a desire to preserve that which was best in the old building for which the monks had grieved in 1174. William of Malmesbury, a sharp-eyed and articulate observer, had already praised the glitter of the marbled pavements of the old pre-1174 Romanesque choir in such a way as to bring to mind the rich and various glistering stones, the *lapides onychinos* of Solomon's Temple in I Chronicles 29: 2; onyx was used, unusually, for the claustral buildings of mid-twelfth-century Canterbury.[148] The old choir or presbytery pavements, in view of their association with the resting-place of Becket before the high altar immediately after his martyrdom and before his hasty burial, were in effect relics of his passion.[149] Their salvage and reinclusion in a harmoniously arranged *opus sectile* pavement at the climax of the new church would make sense, and this may explain the origins and salient meaning of the great *Opus alexandrinum* pavement, now much restored, which was laid down before the shrine of St Thomas between about 1184 and 1220 (figs 1, 25).[150] Witnesses may have thought of the *mare vitreum simile cristallo*, the 'sea of glass like unto crystal' of Revelation 4: 6, as evoked by these shiny mosaic-like inlays. Certainly the colossal formal armature of the new pavement brings to mind the grand and various geometry of the *ferramenta* of the contemporary stained glass designed for the church by English William, the old being retained but recast.[151] Yet such costly floors were falling out of fashion, and were reminiscent of an older world.

All this is suggestive of conventional pietas. Magnificently polished and effulgent glass-like pavements and columns, attesting to the fundamental continuity of the Church and to the sacrifice of the athletes of Christ, are exactly the sort of thing to have provoked sentiments that had been articulated by Benedictine observers for generations. This is a theme found in the writings of Abbot Suger. Suger was familar at first hand with Roman basilicas and monuments, and lived at a time in Paris when Roman or Merovingian spolia were being deployed in new royally sponsored churches in Paris, as at Saint-Pierre-de-Montmartre; and Suger himself oversaw the reintegration of the old into the new.[152] He deployed mosaic on his west facade even though it was unfashionable, doubtless because it had figured in the building he was replacing.[153] His treatises bear witness to the mythic stature of the greatest examples of all medieval building beyond the seas, especially Hagia Sophia in Constantinople, which had already received lavish praise from Procopius and Paulus Silentarius in almost Sugerian terms.[154] His range of reference is as wide as that of Canterbury and as heroic in tone, for Suger stresses the difficulty of obtaining suitable materials, columns especially, for his new church, and treats

25 Canterbury Cathedral, Trinity Chapel, view west from triforium showing pavements (Christopher Wilson).

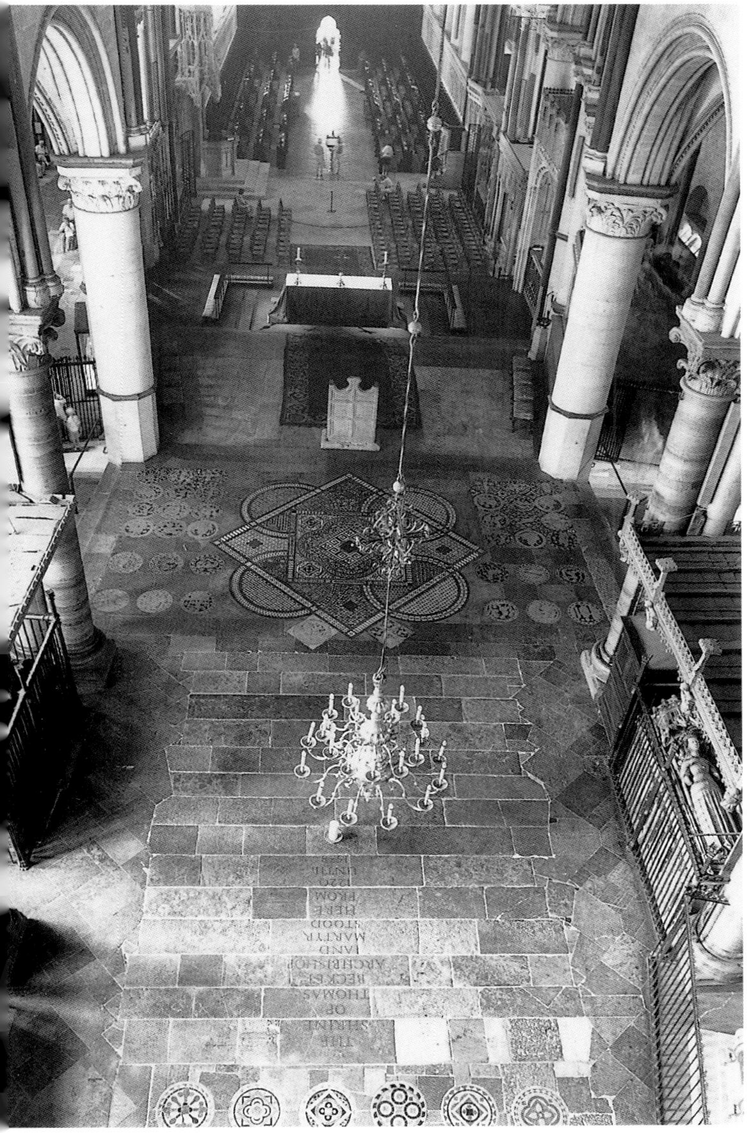

26 Canterbury Cathedral, Trinity Chapel, general view to east (reproduced by permission of English Heritage. NMR).

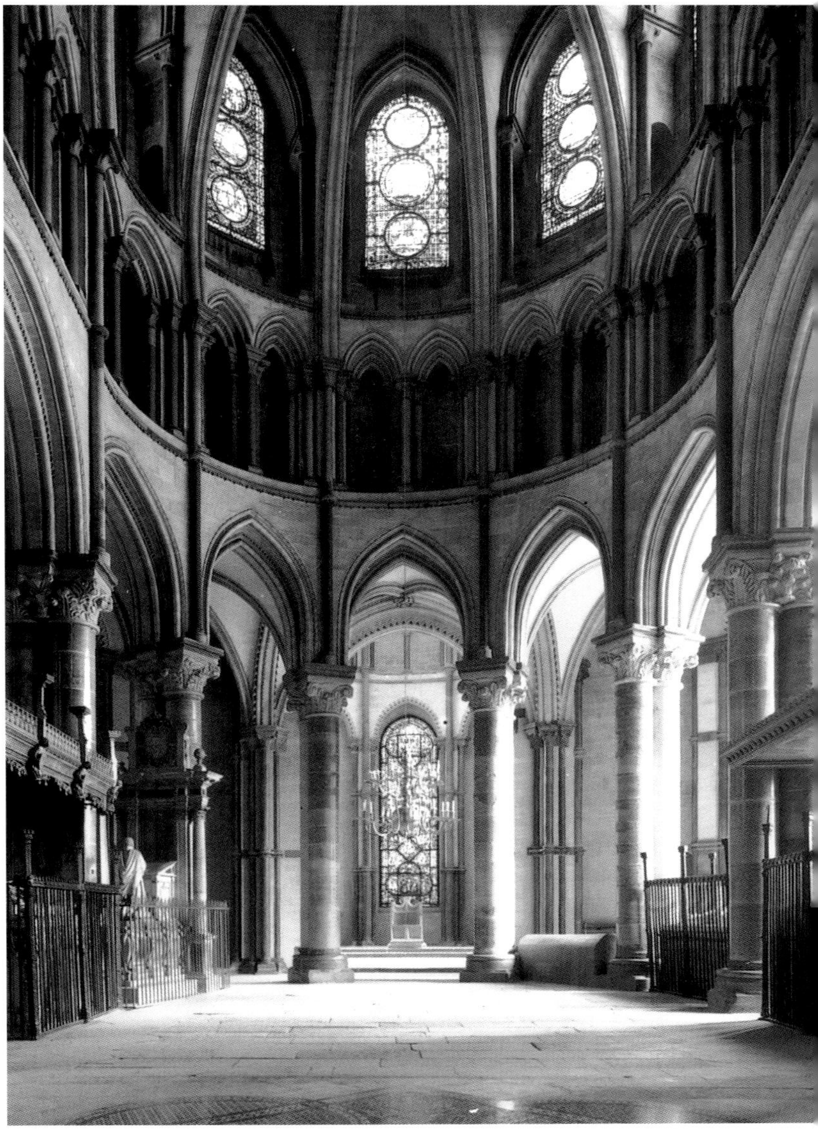

his overcoming of these difficulties as a drama of divine intervention.[155] Rome and Constantinople were his natural yardsticks. In his edition of Suger's writings, Erwin Panofsky astutely noted the 'imaginary Odyssey' in the well-known passage in *De consecratione*, in which Suger reports his wish to obtain marbles from Rome for laborious transportation by sea through the Mediterranean and the English Channel to the Seine.[156] Panofsky rightly likened this to earlier accounts of such importations, notably that by Leo of Ostia of the works of Desiderius (later Pope Victor III), Abbot of Montecassino in the 1060s, who obtained marble and columns in Rome and had them dragged up mountains for the sake of St Benedict.[157] These were commonplaces in much Benedictine encomiastic literature on heroic Christian patronage. The aim of this had been to stress the wealth, tireless energy and imagination of great men and in which, as Michael Greenhalgh observed, following Pliny, 'Difficulties encountered were perhaps part of the game'; indeed the most authoritative source for the miraculous movement of stones was Pope Gregory the Great's Life of St Benedict.[158] Bonus, Abbot of San Michele at Pisa, brought columns from Rome by ship in the 1040s; the Life of the tenth-century St Gerard of Broigne includes a colourful account of the transportation of porphyry and other stones *ab Urbe* and through the perilous straits of the Alps, for the beautification of the church at Broigne.[159] In England, Aldhelm is reported by William of Malmesbury to have brought an altar stone from Rome to England which had broken both itself and the back of the camel carrying it: Aldhelm miraculously restored both.[160] Under Prior Roger of Durham in the late 1130s or 1140s, the provision of grand pavements for St Cuthbert led to the acquisition of a stone of middling size but precious quality from the inevitable source, Rome, but only at enormous inconvenience to a knight, Harpin.[161] Saint-Benoît-sur-Loire is another case in point: the early eleventh-century *Vita Gauzlini* states that around 1026 the choir of either Saint-Pierre or Sainte-Marie at Fleury was adorned with marbles brought from Constantinople and porphyry from Rome.[162] Cluny and St Augustine's were not untouched.[163] Goscelin uses manifestly similar language to Suger's; and in Goscelin's *De miraculis sancti Augustini*, St Augustine rescues a ship laden with stones from Caen and Flanders for use in building his church at Canterbury, calming the storm like Christ.[164]

Had Becket's cause goaded into existence the same sensibility at Christ Church? No one can be sure; but the evidence of the lapidary art of its new shrine-chapel points in that direction. The project was certainly not unlike Suger's Saint-Denis in catering for pilgrimage and in witnessing to the allure of Christian antiquity and of the heroic age of Christian martyrdom and patronage represented by Constantinian Rome, which had been so widely revived in post-investiture Rome under Calixtus II.[165] There was at least one figure at Canterbury in the 1170s and 1180s, Prior Alan of Tewkesbury (1179–86), a former canon of the substantial and important early religious and 'antiquarian' centre of Benevento, who was directly familiar with the southern Italian aftermath of the post-investiture building projects of Calixtine Rome; and the priors of Canterbury had always been influential.[166] Doubtless the great pavement owed something to the *opus sectile* or cosmatesque pavements coming rapidly into fashion in post-investiture central Italy. There is nothing intrinsically improbable in the idea that St Thomas, a charismatic and spiritually heroic individual, was intended to be commemorated in charismatic terms recognizable to the twelfth-century Roman Church – *pro salute fidelium et pace universalis ecclesiae*, as Alexander III put it of Becket in 1173 when admitting him to the sanctoral.[167]

And, as at Saint-Denis, a building particularly constrained by the physical traces of its considerable past, Gothic structural and spatial innovation enjoyed, indeed arguably arose within, a creative symbiosis between the *antiqui* and the *moderni*.[168] The paired columns of the Trinity Chapel with which I began – and many early Gothic buildings are in this sense 'columnar'[169] – have very fairly been compared in their proportions and shape with the classical Corinthian order.[170] Yet whoever designed these columns aimed not to understand their models, and so the rules governing the classical orders, but rather to imitate their surface characteristics. *Imitatio* here testifies to the enduring traditional power of certain forms, generally understood, to speak with absolute conviction to subsequent generations: the sense of the word 'classic' still depends upon this eloquence.[171] Surface imitation of this type is broadly compatible with the medieval understanding of antiquity, and with many of the practices of later humanism. It is essentially a method of assimilation, synthesis and allegory, text and commentary being indistinguishable in a fully contemporary understanding of what was held to be authoritative and good in architecture. Gervase's encomiastic language belongs to the same pattern. But what was being assimilated at Canterbury in the 1170s was the antiquity of Christianity, quite as much as that of the pagan ancients: it was the antiquity of the *veteres*, of the oldest Christian dispensation, which now sustained the *moderni*.[172] In his *Metalogicon* of around 1159, John of Salisbury, the greatest humanist of the period and the grandest of the *eruditi* of Becket, attributed to Bernard of Chartres the remark that 'we are like dwarfs perched on the shoulders of giants so that we can see more and further than they, not by our own sharpness of vision or physical stature, but because we are borne aloft and raised up on their gigantic height' – an image given anthropomorphic expression in the thirteenth-century stained glass of the south transept of Chartres Cathedral in which the prophets sustain the evangelists on their shoulders.[173] As a rib-vaulted and highly articulated building in the best and latest French Gothic style (fig. 26), Canterbury was a novel and subtle building supported, literally, by an ancient, perhaps more obscure, yet still ideal and vital architecture of columns – and perhaps principally in this sense is it a monument to twelfth-century 'humanism' and its (far from settled) anxieties about the relationship of old and new.[174] St Thomas's Canterbury is both a modern and an archetypal building which was intended to stand as cosmopolitan testimony to the highest, most educated and most allegorically rich vision of patronage of its time; and I now turn to the reactions, negative or positive, to this vision by churchmen and other patrons in the dawning thirteenth century.

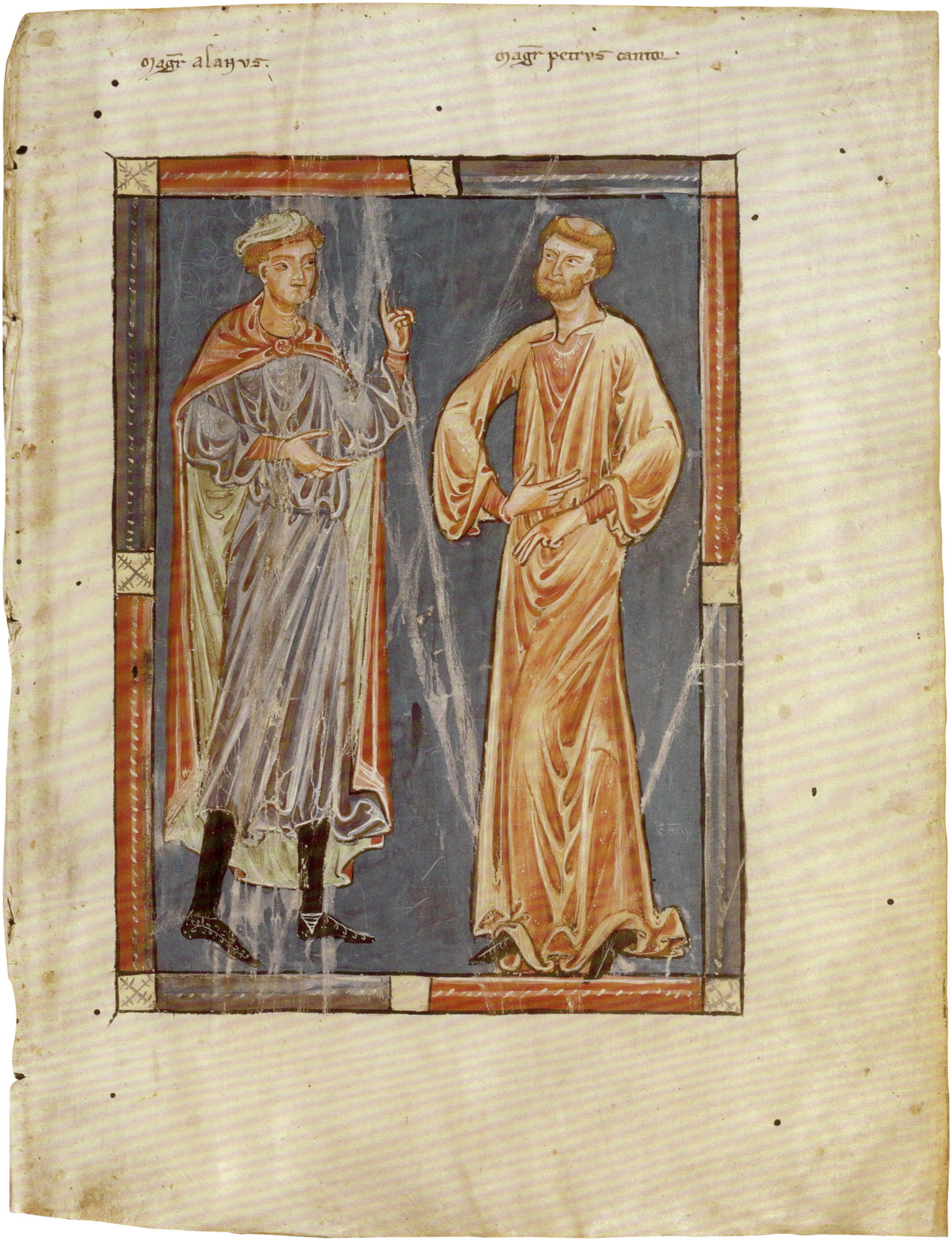

27 Master Alan of Lille and Master Peter the Chanter. BL Add.MS 19767, fol. 217, early thirteenth century (by permission of the British Library).

Chapter 2

THE ASCETICS

The moral laws are simple and few in number.

Le Corbusier, *Towards a New Architecture*

The Masters

Canterbury as rebuilt in the late twelfth century provided a brilliant, and, in the best sense of the word, peculiar, resolution of its special predicament as the shrine-church of a quite exceptional cult. It is a unique building, but in being unique it was also representative of the pattern of English great church building that was to establish itself in the next century or so. As a concerted and assured exemplification of northern French Gothic, its role as a yardstick was guaranteed. It was now almost inconceivable that a great secular church should continue to adhere to the tenets of Romanesque architecture. But it was not so clear what the tenets of the new style should be. Canterbury was not to be the sole source for the new ideas, and it was never to be copied, so much as interpreted; and this process of interpretation began quickly and decisively in the 1180s and 1190s, in the hands of patrons and architects who went on to produce buildings each of which has a quite special and, one is inclined to say, local character. The process of assimilation, commentary and outright rejection involved both English and French buildings and in England was exemplified by a new wave of astonishingly various, precocious and far-flung buildings, including the rebuilding of Wells Cathedral from around 1180 and Lincoln Cathedral a decade or so later.[1] The impression of formidable speed of development is strong, for a series of new and essentially distinct buildings seems to arrive on the scene rapidly and fully formed in the period between Canterbury, the start of work on Salisbury around 1220, and indeed beyond.

This pattern of protean diversity and outbursting of creative and somewhat unpredictable energy was a symptom of rude health. It is not entirely easy to reconcile it with R.W. Southern's stimulating, yet Olympian, observation that England in the twelfth century was merely 'a colony of the French intellectual Empire'.[2] This insight contains a significant grain of truth, but there is a contrary case: Canterbury was hardly a 'colonial' edifice, for it was a part of the mainstream development of northern French Gothic which happened to be on Kentish soil; the next generation of major English buildings challenged and rejected many aspects of this French solution;[3] as far as is known their builders were not, unlike William of Sens, Frenchmen; and the period was also one in which the development of figurative arts occurred, notably painting, whose authority on the European stage was recognized as far away as Navarre.[4] These were not signs of cultural vassalage, any more than they were signs of a nascent nationalistic sensibility. There is on the contrary much to be said for the response to Southern by R. M. Thomson, who noted of England and northern France that they formed a 'homogeneous cultural region' in which the lessons of the French schools were well learned by such men as Robert Pullen, Robert of Melun, Alexander Nequam, Baldwin of Ford, Robert of Courçon, Stephen Langton and Richard Poore precisely because there was already a significant 'scholastic consciousness' in England itself.[5]

This culture of school-trained masters, emerging strongly at the time of the 'Becket controversy' and in its wake, is central to the present chapter on the new wave of English Gothic architecture – and indeed to much of the human activity and thought explored throughout this book.[6] That it should have been an international or supra-regional culture is important. It was not on the whole fostered in English schools, for although a *studium generale* had been formed at Oxford by about 1200, the tendency in England was for the development of local scholastic institutions to be hampered by, among other things, an increasingly powerful royal government and bureaucracy which inhibited the growth of autonomous intellectual centres outside the monasteries, and which drained away talent. School-trained masters had already pervaded the courts of Henry II and John, and this high rate of absorption of clerks by government continued to be a function of England's outstanding administrative precocity.[7] In France – to put the case very generally – royal government was on the whole weaker and less bureaucratized, and the schools in northern France, and Paris especially, correspondingly more lively and independent.[8] As a rule – though not invariably (it could also apply to those who had mastered arts or skills) – the designation 'master' or *magister* applied since at least the twelfth century to someone who had undergone educational preparation of the higher sort in law or theology, typically in France, and who then went into government and the Church as a cathedral canon, i.e. a member of the staff of the cathedral's chapter. Many English canons were not educated in English cathedral schools; by contrast, in, say, Germany, the oblate system in effect tied boys and young men to cathedral establishments from the start.[9] For ambitious and clever young Englishmen this resulted in a greater freedom of movement nationally and internationally; and this freedom was aided by the more highly developed English monetary economy and, most importantly, abetted by the fact that the collation (or appointment) of cathedral prebends (canons with stipends yielded by designated lands) was to a greater extent in England in the hands of bishops who might have come from outside the diocese, and so who were less controlled by local interests. The power to collate friends, family or clerks to prebends was an important aspect of the independence of episcopal patronage, not least in a period that was profoundly affected by a movement to free the chapters of secular churches, in regard to their elective autonomy and conduct, from the influence of older controlling interests represented, especially, by the monasteries.

The product of this was a period of particularly close contact with the French schools and interest in Bible study, already apparent in the circle of Becket's *eruditi*; during the late twelfth century the proportion of English students at Paris amounted to something between 25 and 38 per cent of the student population there.[10] Because it was now vital to be a master before collation to a prebend or further advancement, masters were increasingly prevalent in the cathedral chapters in the late twelfth and early thirteenth centuries: 42 per cent at Lincoln, 47 per cent at London, 66 per cent at Canterbury and nearly 50 per cent at Salisbury by the mid-thirteenth century.[11] The intellectual and practical quality of his chapter became the subject of the mythology of the great saint-bishop, as at Lincoln, where St Hugh's astute appointment of worldly and civilized clerks was held by his hagiographers to be an aspect of his prudence and pastoral care, to be mentioned exactly in tandem with his great work as a patron of church building: just as the great patron and pastor summoned intelligent clerks from far afield so, presumably, did he muster intelligent architects. And intelligent these men certainly were. It is a measure of the training – and the ambitions – of such men as Walter Map, Nigel Longchamp and Gerald of Wales that they were often mordantly articulate, possessed of a powerfully developed (perhaps even priggish) ethical sense and personal *mores*, classical learning, dialectical subtlety, love of allegory, and what Knowles called a 'spirit of polished satire' which found its more satisfying outlet in the critique of both Church and public power.[12] Much of their school education in Latin letters had carried with it the ethical imperatives of the ancient world found in the curriculum authors.[13] The masters figured significantly in shaping reformist sentiments and tended themselves to be reformers; their satire was part of a moral outlook as well as of their position as *literati*.[14] Their training brought them, at least in theory, into contact with the practical objectives of the moral theology taught in the French schools by such men as Peter the Chanter (fig. 27), which in turn carried Gregorian reform forwards in reasoned guise, through pastoral endeavour, to the lay world. They were, perhaps, the class most readily identified with 'modernity' and its acceptance, with the development of the new technologies of government that did so much to give their regime enduring power in the domain of both 'church' or 'state', and with new intolerances.[15] And, at a time when Benedictine historical writing still carried the burden of comment on art patronage of any type, they both commissioned and commented upon, architecture.

But in thinking of a 'culture' of school-trained masters one must be careful not to generalize to excess about the possibility of a collective and fixed moral position on its part about 'group thinking'. It is historically demonstrable, and humanly true, that ethical and political positions change within the lifetime of a single thinker, let alone a group – as occurred during and after the 'Becket controversy'.[16] 'Reform' was a pluralistic phenomenon which took many guises, and its relationship to the ethical and practical art of building often ambivalent. It was not the product of a readily identifiable and narrow mindset. Certainly, the broad tone of clerical thought in this period became more broadly 'reformist', though in England the tendency towards 1200 was for the universal issue of the relationship of the Church to public power to give way to that of internal ecclesiastical discipline: the house had to be put in order first.[17] But there was also a growing and more subtle recognition that, following Becket, an accommodation would have to be reached between the values of the Church and public power, the Crown especially. The clerks had a vested interest in government quite as much as the Church, not least because even the more reformist among them conceded that access to public power – and the necessary compromises it entailed for the purity and integrity of the Church – could be of broader pastoral benefit. Rulers could be improved, but they had first to be reached on terms comprehensible to them. Precisely because the secular church was pastoral in nature its character had to be adaptive and pragmatic; and it will be argued here that this was of long-standing practical consequence for the history of English architecture and art.

One instance of this outlook is provided by an almost totally obscure member of the Becket circle, himself associated with a building receptive to the new Canterbury: Gervase of Chichester. Herbert of Bosham identifies Gervase, a theologian and homilist, as one of the *eruditi* of Becket.[18] He was a master, presumably trained in Paris, and a canon of Chichester by the 1160s, and he flourished until about 1190; Herbert mentions him as being admirable in letters and *mores*, i.e. moral character.[19] Gervase is mentioned by Smalley as an example of the more accommodating and pragmatic attitude among theologians and homilists of the late twelfth century, who had an attitude of 'grudging permissiveness' to the issue of the role of churchmen in civil affairs: thus, says Gervase, one should respect even bad rulers, and service to a prince is acceptable if driven by the motive of love and desire to correct him.[20] The clergy have a role in ethical mentorship at court. On the other hand they must watch their ways. Gervase's views about clerical service to secular princes were put forward in a homily on Malachi; written towards 1190, it proceeds in a reformist spirit to castigate the conduct of the English clergy who, like Malachi's priests, have neglected their covenant and the example of St Thomas. The English clergy are more morally lax than their European counterparts; patronage thinks only of its kinsmen and friends and so promotes the unworthy to the priesthood, and the Church indulges in pointless litigation. Religion is also contaminated by thoughts of external show: and it is in this context that Gervase suddenly holds forth on art and architecture. In his moralized commentary on Malachi 1: 12, Gervase states that foolish opinions assert that to adorn the temple is preferable to the adornment of the mind: variously painted walls, crosses, texts and utensils shining with gems and gold, silken cloths, marble pavements and dressed stonework are thought more important than the internal cultivation of the soul and the spiritual embellishment of the mind (*potius quam internum animae cultum ac spiritualem mentis ornatum*), for the soul is more important than vaults of stone (*lapidei tabulatus*).[21]

Gervase's striking remarks about building echo much older ascetic positions, notably that of St Jerome, who in his own exegetical works had contrasted the splendour of church building with inner spiritual debility.[22] He might also have developed such views as a result of a training in Paris, for such ideas were being reformulated in twelfth-century France. But his critique could also have been provoked by circumstances. It is possible, though unlikely, that it was directed at Canterbury – unlikely given that Gervase would presumably have regarded Canterbury as an appropriate tribute to St Thomas and his example. Events at Chichester itself were more relevant, since Gervase's homily was almost certainly framed at the time when the rebuilding of the cathedral church of Chichester had been undertaken under Bishop Seffrid II (1180–1204) after a fire in 1187, the new retrochoir at the east end being dedicated in 1199 (fig. 28).[23] The retrochoir possesses features that clearly derive from a study of Canterbury's new east end (fig. 29), including flying buttresses, rib vaulting, round-headed and richly moulded arcade arches which harmonized with those in the old church to the west, and two complex intermediate Purbeck marble columnar piers with finely wrought French-style crocket capitals and detached shafts at the cardinal points of the pier. Like Canterbury, the refurbishment of Chichester after 1187 involved the considered deployment of coloured marble shafts throughout the building, veering in hue from dark browns and rust-reds to grey-greens, and with dark red shafts disposed to either side of the high altar, perhaps with Canterbury's use of rose-red stone in mind. Such choices were obviously aesthetic, not functional, since Chichester had no major shrine to which they could be addressed. Much play is made with shaft and arch effects. In the eastern triforium of the retrochoir the front shafts of the triforium arcade are out of alignment with those of the wall arcade behind, an effect to be developed more conspicuously at Lincoln and Beverley.[24] The inner faces of the entrances to the chapels at the east end of the retrochoir aisles have serried ranks of three widely separated slim columns

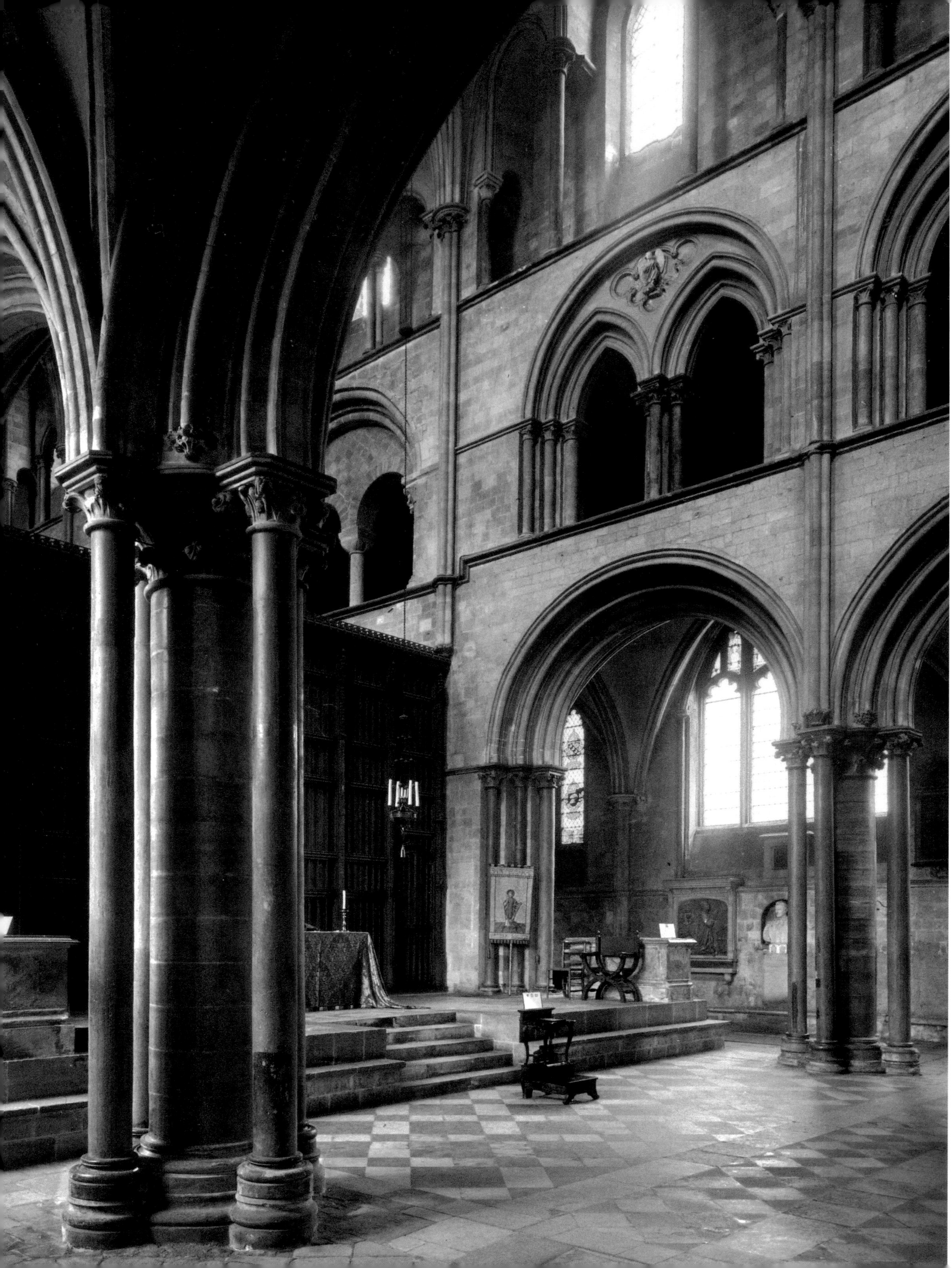

whose capitals sustain prominent moulded string courses which resemble epistyles, producing a classicizing effect. The retrochoir's main intermediate piers are particularly virtuosic, for the perceived relationship of the four rather widely detached shafts to the larger central column changes with the movement of the spectator, now appearing close to the central column, now dynamically separate from it. This almost miraculous apparent contraction and expansion of the piers, now collapsing into a solid dense mass, now opening out as if into thin air, has no direct surviving source at Canterbury, where widely separated shafts had appeared principally in the Trinity Chapel and Corona, but it is reminiscent of the subjectively varying aspects of the towers of the great west facade of Laon Cathedral, a north-eastern French building with which both Canterbury and Chichester evidently had links, and which itself witnessed various experiments in pier design.[25] These piers, smooth, firm and bronze-like, are, like many instances of experimental pier design in England in this period, conspicuous one-offs with few followers (e.g. Boxgrove Priory nearby). That they were capable of being understood in terms of human movement, however, is suggested by a remark about St Hugh's choir at Lincoln, as discussed below.[26]

Whatever the case, these 'sumptuous polishings' (to cite St Bernard's *Apologia*) belonged uncompromisingly to the new decorative language of magnificent great church building.[27] One might have expected ideas from Canterbury to have moved precisely through the human agency of clerks such as Gervase, or Matthew of Chichester, another of Becket's *eruditi* and Dean of Chichester Cathedral.[28] But history, and men's opinions, are not always so predictable or helpful. The *eruditi* were not of fixed views. If his homily is anything to go by, at least one of them, Gervase, may even have taken exception to Chichester's fine effects, or something like them, at exactly the time they are likely to have been debated in chapter around 1187. Yet much of this is hypothetical: from Gervase's reformist homily it can be deduced only that ascetic criticisms tended to arise as part of wider discourses about the role and character of the Church; that they could have been provoked by building activity or projects; and that, even if they were aimed at a particular project, they made little or no difference to its outcome. In this it seems that they were typical.

Another instance of the relationship between 'reform' and architectural patronage, and also within the aesthetic and ideological orbit of Canterbury, is provided by Trondheim Cathedral in Norway, the metropolitan church of the new archdiocese of Nidaros created under the English Pope Adrian IV in 1152–3.[29] Like Canterbury, Trondheim was a shrine-church, because it possessed the relics of the martyr-saint King Olaf (d. 1030), whose miraculous healing well was to be incorporated into the design of the cathedral's east end.[30] The rebuilding of this Romanesque church had been galvanized by Archbishop Øystein Erlendsson (1161–88), and stylistically transformed in the early 1180s following his flight and exile to England during his conflict with King Sverre (1177–1202).[31] Sverre also forced Øystein's successor, Eirik Ivarsson, into exile, and this train of events halted the progress of the cathedral church. As reworked under Øystein after 1183, and as completed in the thirteenth century, Trondheim is indebted to the new works

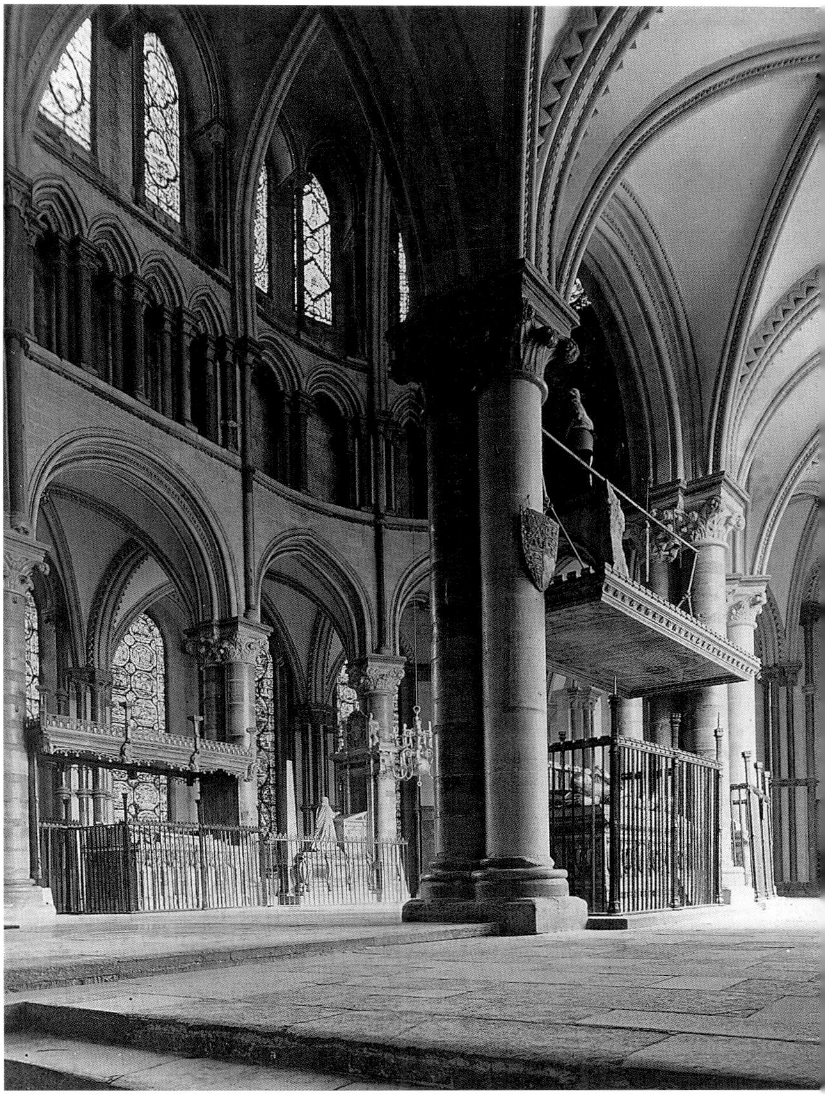

29 Canterbury Cathedral, Trinity Chapel, from south ambulatory (reproduced by permission of English Heritage. NMR).

28 (FACING PAGE) Chichester Cathedral, retrochoir looking north-west (reproduced by permission of English Heritage. NMR).

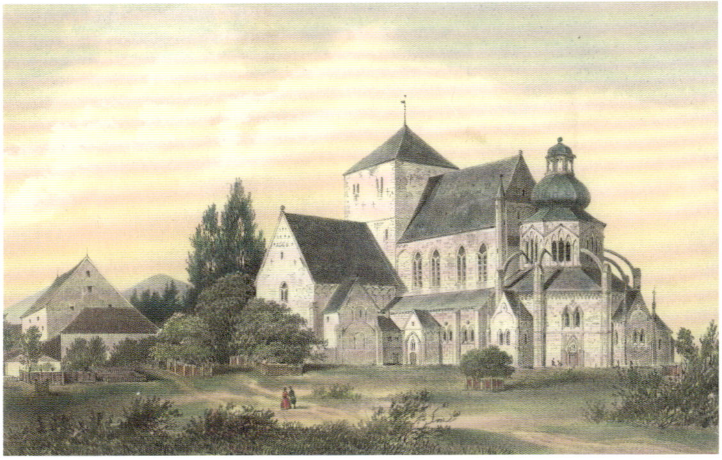

30 Trondheim Cathedral lithograph by M.F. Dalager, *c.* 1830 (The Restoration Workshop of Nidaros Cathedral).

at Canterbury and, subsequently, Lincoln. Canterbury suggested itself on the obvious grounds of its splendour and its politically relevant cult, Lincoln because of its geographical proximity to north-west Norway, and because it had already provided ideas for Øystein's earliest building campaigns.[32] Like Canterbury, and doubtless with reference to it, Lincoln as rebuilt from around 1192 developed a complex form of east end, which consisted of a wedge-shaped *caput* with small polygonal attached chapels, of which the central easternmost one was at first intended for the relics of Bishop Remigius.[33] Canterbury's Corona (figs 9–11), which Øystein or a member of his entourage presumably saw in 1180–83 (and not Lincoln, begun after his death), in turn gave rise to the octagonal chapel for the relics of St Olaf inaugurated by Øystein at the east end of Trondheim Cathedral – a centrally planned martyrium of a type long sanctioned by older models (figs 30, 69).[34] St Thomas's cult enjoyed enormous authority in Scandinavia, second only to Olaf's; as already mentioned, it carried with it a view of the morality, good or bad, of public power.[35] Øystein was staunchly pro-Becket, his flight from King Sverre to England ominously and deliberately reminiscent of Becket's flight from Henry II, as was the contemporary flight of Eskil, Archbishop of Lund, from Valdemar the Great of Denmark, to Sens, where Becket had also been in exile.[36] Øystein was also a zealous reformer ofVictorine bent. He constructed a new liturgy for Trondheim in the 1170s which incorporated the feast for Becket; Becket's translation office was added to it in 1221.[37] This was much in line with the reception accorded Becket by the Parisian Victorines: Becket had preached at Saint-Victor in 1169, an altar to him there was raised rapidly after 1173; and a sequence for him alluding to his exile and stay at Sens before his immolation on the altar may also have been composed there.[38] This again illustrates the variety of attitudes that could be said to shelter beneath the term 'reform'. Øystein's patronage owed nothing to the type of ascetic position set out by Gervase of Chichester, for Trondheim, though eccentrically detailed by the standards of its cynosures at Canterbury and Lincoln, is a richly wrought building conceived together with a new palace which Øystein undertook in 1173. The cathedral as completed in the thirteenth century, presumably in the fashion Øystein intended, indeed stood as a self-consciously magnificent monument to the 'Becket model'. Its generous aesthetic (fig. 31), quite as much as its historically allusive planning, celebrated a just and virtuous Norwegian king

31 Trondheim Cathedral, octagon, ambulatory (The Restoration Workshop of Nidaros Cathedral).

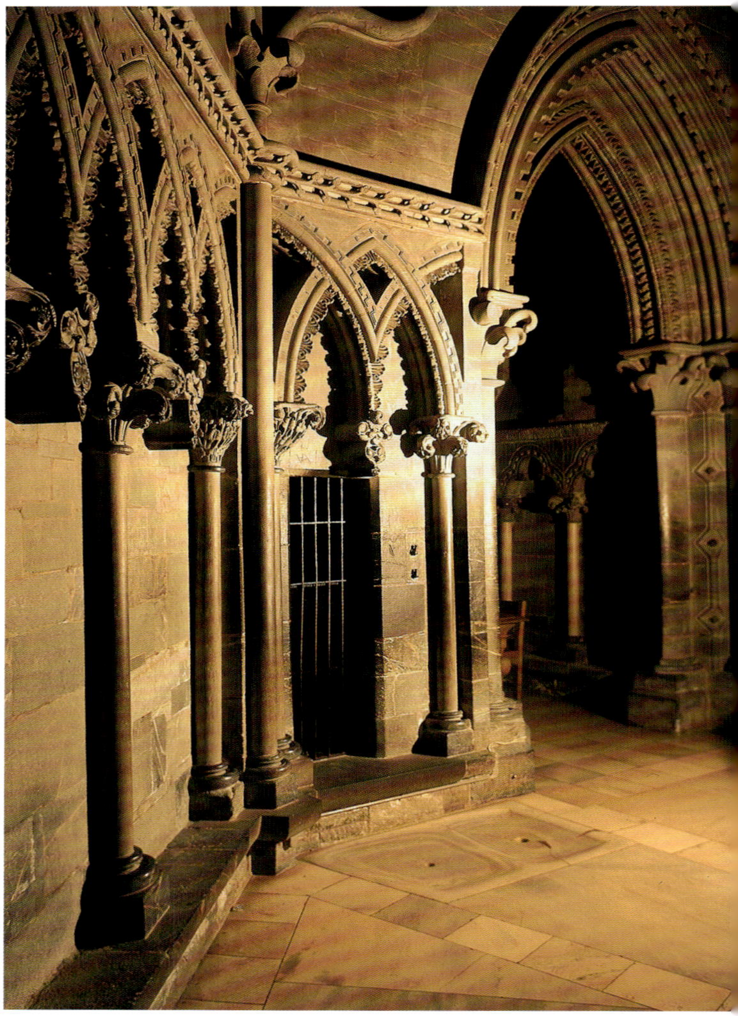

and showed what public power might be when harnessed to the pastoral objectives of the Church as represented by the ideal bishop, Thomas, and arguably by Øystein, himself a candidate for canonization between 1251 and 1254.[39]

The ethical nature of public power and the Church's role in shaping it had been, and continued to be, given a theoretical basis by masters who were somewhat more tolerant of secular values than monastic moralists.[40] Many of them recognized that bishops and their clerks could hold secular power, and it is intrinsically probable that this recognition was to have consequences for the character of the art and architecture those bishops commissioned. The law forbade only specific practices: clerks in holy orders were not to act professionally as lawyers in lawsuits before secular judges, or to hold offices that might make them answerable in lay courts.[41] Monasticism itself was also an important part of this equation. The masters increasingly stressed the need to discipline and then separate the secular clergy from the interests of the powerful and stubborn monastic orders which, towards and around 1200, were at the height of their power in terms of numbers, wealth and presence among the bishops. In the 1180s the dioceses of Canterbury, London and Lincoln were presided over by a Cistercian, a Cluniac and a Carthusian respectively. Yet the age of the monk-bishop was drawing to a close. Monastic houses were tormented by debt and litigation, and the masters had started to adopt a distinctly sceptical tone about the monks; Gerald of Wales thought that secular clergy made better bishops than monks.[42] Conflict arose between monastic houses and local diocesan authority: Bishops Hugh of Nonant, William Longchamp and Savaric of Bath engaged tirelessly in disputes with the monks of Coventry, Ely and Glastonbury; this took place in ways that, as at Wells, could lead to the formation of chapters of secular clergy independent of the local monastic bodies.[43]

At Wells and at Canterbury, to which I now return, such jurisdictional tensions were to have physical consequences in outward show. The battles were not always easy, for the monks were persistent, controlled the writing of history, and periodically enjoyed papal support, while the bishops were distracted by pastoral administration. The disputes dragged on in desultory, and occasionally explosive, fashion well into the thirteenth century. Becket's successors at Canterbury, Richard of Dover and Baldwin of Ford, were at heart church administrators on generally good terms with Henry II.[44] This was reflected by the size of their secretariats. Baldwin of Ford (fig. 32) had a large and capable circle of secular clerks for which he felt a radical sympathy; and, as a Cistercian, he regarded the Canterbury monks as rich, incorrigible and reliant upon the type of local customary understanding of rights and privileges of which a canonist of the period would be suspicious.[45] Gervase of Canterbury, a staunch ally of the convent, also accused these clerks, whom the convent could not support financially, of subverting the monks.[46] The crux of the problem was that Baldwin wanted to establish an independent college of secular canons to provide patronage for his clerks independent of the monastic chapter. In 1186 he gained papal privileges for the establishment of a collegiate church dedicated to St Stephen at Hackington near Canterbury, with the explicit intention of supporting his clerks: it was to be endowed in part from Christ Church property, the king and all Canterbury's suffragans were to have prebendal stalls, and it was to have an 'admirable' church. Because this was essentially a college intended to promote free canonical elections, it posed a serious, indeed possibly terminal, threat to the electoral rights of the monks, to their revenues and to

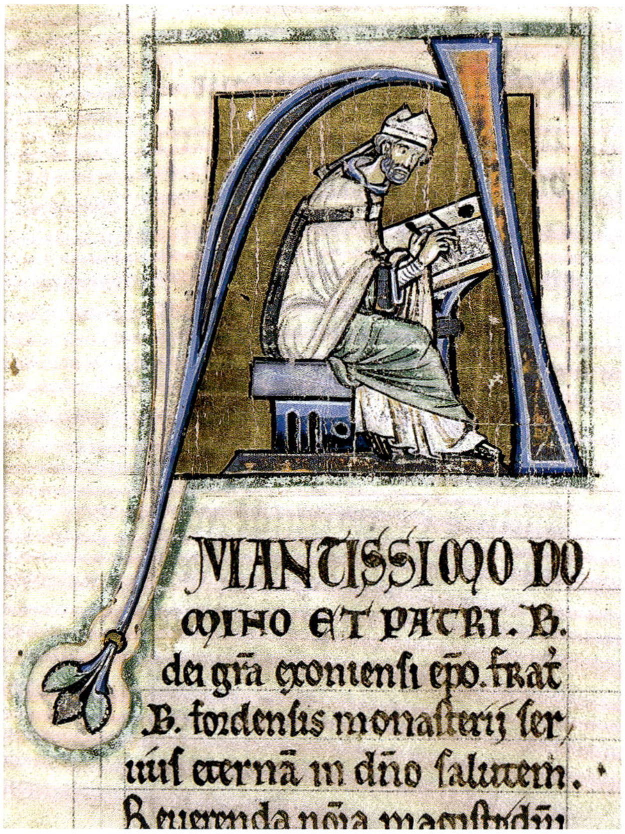

32 Archbishop Baldwin as author of *De sacramento altaris*. Cambridge, Corpus Christi College MS 200, fol. 1, late 12th century (Master and Fellows of Corpus Christi College, Cambridge).

the metropolitan status of Christ Church itself.[47] Anticipating their resistance, Baldwin claimed that the scheme had actually been formulated by St Thomas, but the monks would have none of it, Gervase relating that Becket appeared in a series of visions to the monks warning them that the scheme if implemented would amount to a second severing of his head.[48] It was defeated in its essentials by 1189–90, and technically by a bull issued by Pope Innocent III in 1201.[49]

Hackington failed, and its church of St Stephen remained no more than a twinkle in Baldwin's eye;[50] but in 1189–90, just before his death, Baldwin reopened the issue with a new plan to erect a college and church dedicated to Sts Stephen and Thomas, this time at Lambeth, near to the rising centre of royal power at Westminster.[51] His successor at Canterbury, the remarkable Hubert Walter (1193–1205), who had been Bishop of Salisbury and Baldwin's executor, tried to persist with the Lambeth project between 1197 and 1200 with predictable results for his relations with the monks at Canterbury, who again blamed his clerks.[52] This was consistent with his policy while at Salisbury of trying to regulate the rights of local monasteries, questioning their claims to exemption from diocesan control and favouring the regular canons.[53] The fierce Carthusian Hugh, Bishop of Lincoln, had warned him off the project.[54] Again, this scheme was squashed by Innocent III late in 1199 on the grounds that it was injurious to the monastic house, and in the monks' eyes it was to his credit that Walter submitted gracefully to the point where they could all be 'of one heart and soul'.[55]

Hubert Walter was a brilliant and innovative administrator, a reformer and a patron. He was an outstanding example of a generation in which some twenty of the forty-three bishops promoted between 1170 and 1213 had experience in the royal household or the branches of royal government.[56] He had risen in the service of his uncle Ranulph Glanville, Chief Justiciar, and was himself Justiciar (1193–8) and Chancellor (1199–1205) of England, and transformed pretty well any bureaucratic machinery with which he had to deal, most especially by creating the type of archival memory that formed the basis for the royal administration's record-keeping.[57] He was not a man of school learning, however, and tended to provoke monks and clerks alike, most famously Gerald of Wales, who engaged in a lawsuit with him and who cattily named his school as the Exchequer 'in which he had already grown old [. . .] like a fish out of water, he cannot live without the court and secular care'.[58] The chronicler of St Augustine's snootily dismissed him as *laicus*, *illiteratus* and a legal *ignoramus*, neither school-trained nor versed in traditional monastic humanism.[59]

Yet although he was perceived by some as an upstart, there are positive reasons for seeing Hubert as another important reformer in the so-called 'interconciliar period', i.e. the period between the Third and Fourth Lateran Councils of 1179 and 1215. His first recorded act as archbishop was to don the habit of the Austin canons at Merton, in Surrey, so imitating Becket's practice of wearing both canonical and monastic garb and signalling his support for the regular canons.[60] In 1200 he summoned a provincial council of his suffragans at Westminster, the first such assembly since 1175, with the specific objective of legislating for the province.[61] Cheney called the canons promulgated by the council 'the most elaborate piece of local legislation for the English Church since the Norman Conquest'.[62] Their papal background was significant, for the canons cited nine decrees of the Third Lateran Council at length, but they also resembled contemporary Norman and Parisian church legislation and reflected the sacramental and moral theology of the schools of Paris.[63] Stephen Langton was himself later to take over a large part of Hubert's canons in his own diocesan legislation in 1213–14.[64] And another aspect of reformist zeal, the promotion of new saints, was apparent in Hubert's support for the canonization of two holy Englishmen, Gilbert of Sempringham and Wulfstan of Worcester.[65] Episcopal reformers were interested in the saints, old and new, throughout this period. In short, Hubert was a reformer both of public power and the Church. His pursuit of the Lambeth project had practical and long-lasting consequences, for it was there that the archbishops of Canterbury found permanent physical accommodation near to the principal seat of royal power. The scheme showed a liking for thorough planning, for it included not only an archbishop's residence near the court, but also a close with a collegiate church and canons' houses: in fact much the same sort of total planning that was to produce Salisbury Cathedral and its environs a generation later.[66] It is not impossible that the Salisbury scheme had itself been mooted by Hubert Walter when bishop there in 1189–93.[67] But his role as papal legate in 1195–8 might have prompted another idea: to establish a new metropolitan cathedral at Lambeth, staffed by canons who were part of an electoral college, rather like that of the cardinals in Rome; that much was suspected by the Canterbury monks, who presented this development as a threat to Rome itself.[68] It was, however, Innocent III who brought Hubert's legatine powers to a close and in 1198 ordered the demolition of the works begun at Lambeth.[69]

Nothing specific can be said about the collegiate churches that were planned at Hackington and Lambeth beyond the fact of their ambition, but at least something can be ascertained about the general tenor of Hubert's patronage and that of his milieu from two objects in Canterbury Cathedral intended for his use: St Augustine's Chair and Hubert's tomb; and the Great Hall, which Hubert undertook within the precinct.

The Purbeck marble archiepiscopal throne called St Augustine's Chair fits so snugly into the environment of the Trinity Chapel that of these it is probably the least informative about personal taste (fig. 34). Whoever designed it, first in wood and finally in the newly fashionable Purbeck, had paid close attention to the *ferramenta* or supporting ironwork installed in the windows of the new east end. This is proved by the odd design of the inside top of the back of the throne that introduced two oculi into the fielded panels which were then sliced diagonally to create a central feature with a tau cross-bar and small tufts of foliage at the severed top ends of the arcs, an idiosyncratic formal language virtually identical with the ironwork and glass of one of the window heads in the north choir aisle containing figures of Balaam and Isaiah (fig. 33).[70] Coincidences like this illustrate the imaginative dominance of the new medium of stained glass in the church, and the same liking for large intersected geometrical forms is shown also by the *Opus alexandrinum* pavement (figs 1, 25) before the shrine. The use of simple classical fielded panels on the outside faces of the throne is unusual, but could have been prompted by Roman or Romanesque wooden or bronze doors; it may be relevant that simple marbled rectilinear framing devices were used for at least one of the Gospel narrative pages of the sixth-century St Augustine's Gospels (fol. 125), an outstanding local relic of Canterbury's apostolic authority. This may have influenced anew the layout of pages of other Canterbury illuminated manuscripts of the second half of the twelfth century, namely the

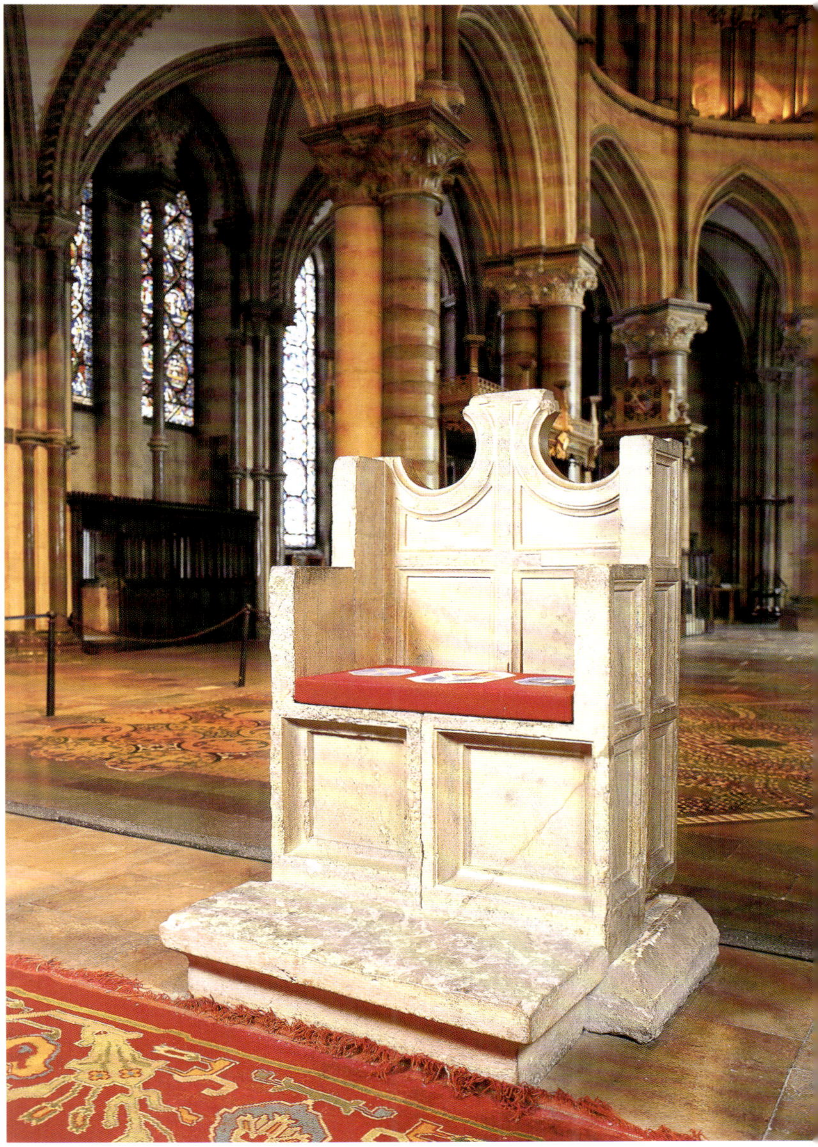

34 Canterbury Cathedral, St Augustine's Chair (John Crook).

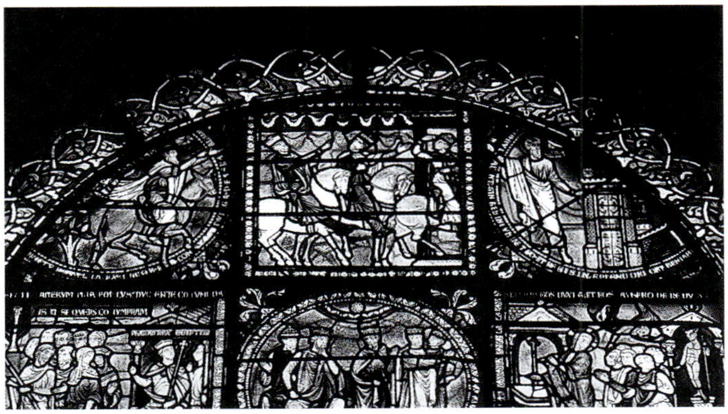

33 Canterbury Cathedral, head of window n: XV, north choir aisle (Sebastian Strobl).

Eadwine and Great Canterbury Psalters.[71] Such works as the St Augustine's Gospels and the *Codex aureus* are cited above in connection with Canterbury's *romanitas*. That some such community of interest existed around 1200 in Canterbury's early heritage is demonstrated conclusively by the allusion in the Becket glass of the Trinity Chapel to classical aedicular forms also found in the St Augustine's Gospels (figs 2, 17), though radically slimmed down rather in the manner of twelfth-century wall paintings in Calixtine Rome.[72]

It is therefore not inconceivable that the throne was itself a conscious homage to Canterbury's apostolic past.

Since the chair has some small points in common with Hubert Walter's tomb, designed in or after 1205, and makes use of motifs in the glazing programme, a date for it much before the end of the twelfth century, and indeed before the monastery undertook to 'perfect' the choir in 1199, is improbable.[73] Another consideration that probably delayed the provision of a new archiepiscopal throne, aside from the fact that churches tend to be furnished only after they have been built, was the fractious relationship between the convent and the archbishops before the Hackington and Lambeth settlement of 1200–01. Only after this were Hubert Walter and the monks of 'one heart and soul'. Attention to the formalized seating arrangements of the church may also have been focused by the coronation of King John and his queen at Canterbury in 1201.[74] Though Hubert was now seldom at Canterbury, these years of reconciliation provide exactly the right political context for the provision of a throne by the monks as a sign of the end of the threat to their electoral and metropolitan rights, indeed as a positive celebration of them. For this reason there is no inherent reason why the references in the cathedral treasurer's accounts to payments *pro sede archiepiscopi* in the years 1201–4 should not refer to the manufacture of this throne, designs for which could have been provided by English William.[75]

Similar rather thick-set detailing in Purbeck was used for Hubert Walter's tomb, raised on the south side of the shrine ambulatory after his death in July 1205 (figs 36–7), doubtless authorized by his executor Elias of Dereham, and presumably designed by English William, the overseer of the surrounding architecture.[76] The composition is that of an ornate sarcophagus raised on an arcade with trefoil-headed arches and somewhat overscaled moulded bases, which resemble the one surviving rose-pink marble base which purports to come from the main shrine, of which the tomb may have been an offshoot. It is self-evident that the design owes something to the *ferramenta* of the stained glass – and ultimately Mosan metalwork – in the sophisticatedly overlapping geometrical forms of its lid; and the same type of source, namely the foliage borders of some of the windows (fig. 66), may also account for the small foliate brackets that link the chest to the stubby free-standing shafts of the arcade, a device already appearing to different ends and on a much larger scale on some piers at Lincoln (fig. 67).[77]

Hubert's tomb is strikingly modern. Prospective too are the very bold and fine heads carved in quatrefoils inscribed in diamonds on the lid (fig. 37), for these are an early manifestation of devices used on thirteenth-century micro-architectural seals (fig. 89) or, indeed, on the west front of Salisbury Cathedral.[78] The use of heads in sunk quatrefoils first occurs on the seal of St Augustine's Abbey around 1198–9.[79] On the other hand their basic debt to antique sarcophagi and to a small group of tombs dating to around 1190 at Lisieux and Rochester suggests the same deliberate searching-out of old motifs as the chair.[80] The jewellery discovered in the tomb, including gems cut in Italy or Asia Minor (fig. 35), also points to a breadth of taste scarcely compatible with the *laicus* and *illiteratus* castigated by one of St Augustine's chroniclers.[81]

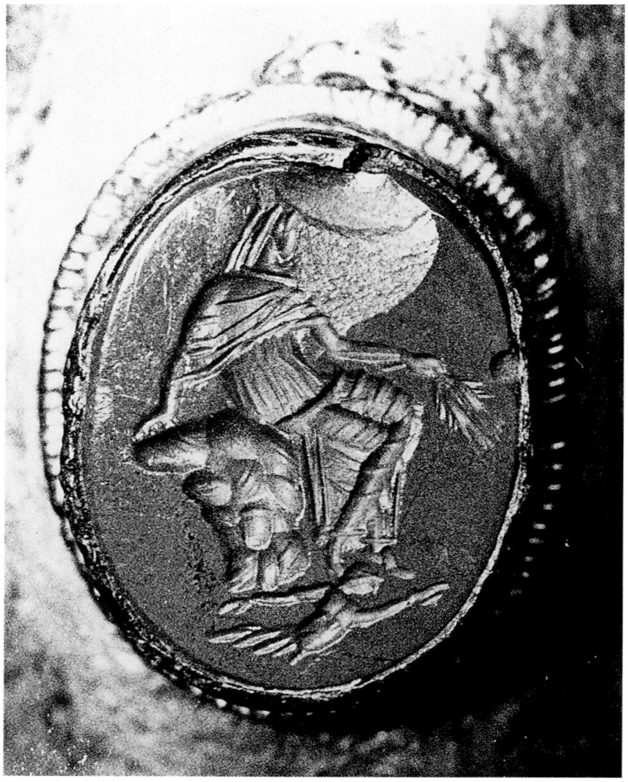

35 Tyche of Antioch, intaglio gem from head of Hubert Walter's crosier (Dean and Chapter of Canterbury).

Hubert Walter was a magnificent patron, justifiably so given his position as the most powerful man in England after the king. Gervase of Canterbury came to the double-edged view that Hubert was so bountiful and open-handed in entertaining guests, including the poor, and also of such incomparable magnificence (*gloriae incomparabilis*) that some men thought him covetous (*cupidus*) and arrogant.[82] The critique of *vanitas* followed hot on the heels of any lavish display. Gerald of Wales took a similar view, praising Hubert's 'incomparable

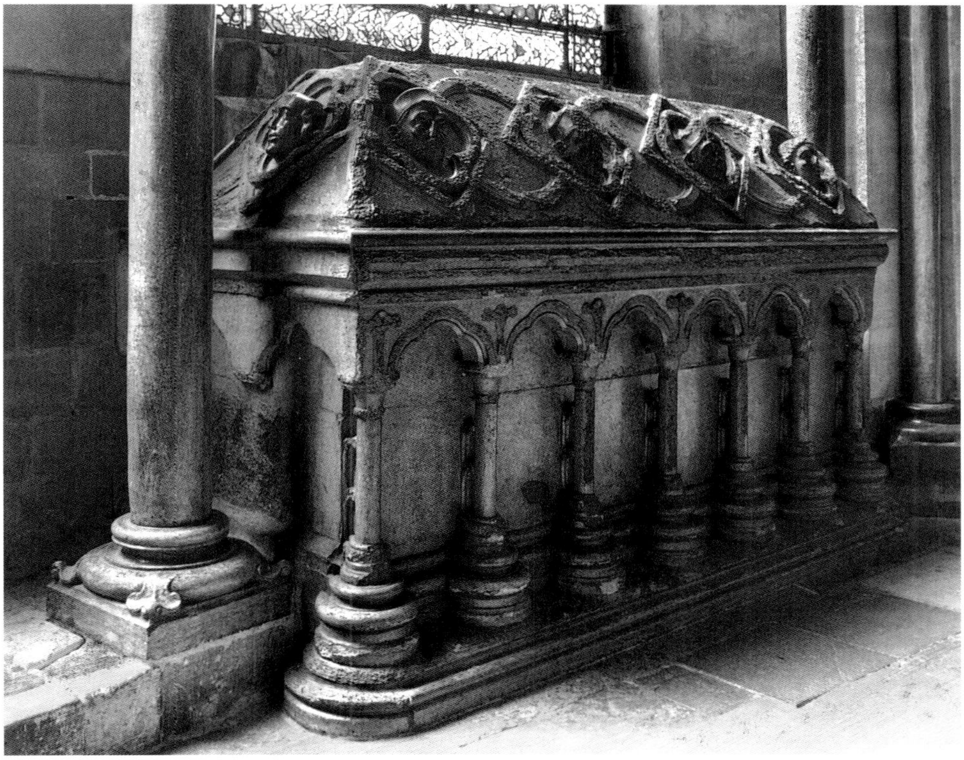

36 Canterbury Cathedral, tomb of Archbishop Hubert Walter, d. 1205 (Christopher Wilson).

37 Canterbury Cathedral, tomb of Archbishop Hubert Walter, detail of lid (Christopher Wilson).

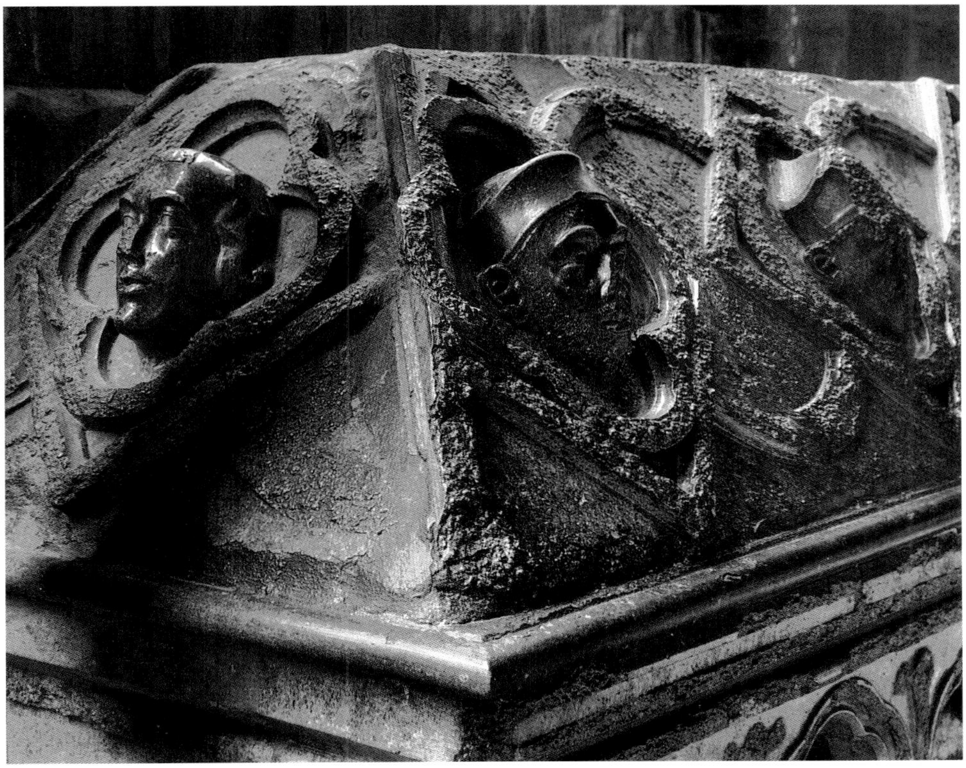

bounty' but connecting it directly to his desire to amass riches.[83] Other commentators pragmatically accepted that a man of his station was justified in living in great, indeed royal, estate, keeping a grand table and sustaining what was in effect an episcopal court.[84] Gervase therefore did not hesitate to describe Hubert as a great builder, wonderful in the raising of large and excellent buildings.[85] By this Gervase presumably meant not the aborted and provocative projects at Hackington and Lambeth, but rather the works undertaken at Canterbury itself (*in curia Cantuariensi*), of which the new archiepiscopal hall was the most extraordinary.[86] One later monastic chronicler regarded it as worthy of comparison with Solomon.[87]

The new Gothic Great Hall at Canterbury (now largely demolished) was probably begun by Hubert though its surviving window tracery indicates that much of the progress was made on it by his successor Stephen Langton, who according to Matthew Paris 'perfected' it, doubtless in time for the epic feast that accompanied the translation of St Thomas in 1220.[88] There is no serious reason to doubt that this immense building, 168 by 64 feet with two interior arcades and bold modern windows, was intentionally planned and begun by Hubert as a sign of his largesse at Canterbury after the collapse of the Lambeth project – for Lambeth was close to the Great Royal Hall at the Palace of Westminster, one of the few secular buildings exceeding the hall at Canterbury in scale. As such, it was in the first instance a political restatement of the metropolitan authority of Canterbury. Øystein had begun a palace at Trondheim for similar reasons. It may equally have followed on from the growth of Hubert's entourage of clerks in archiepiscopal service, and from a recognition that Canterbury's old curial buildings were ill suited to such events as the coronation festivities of 1201. Indeed, provision both for royal entertainment and for the comparatively modest administrative needs of thirteenth-century Benedictine houses was cited as one factor in the erection of the so-called *palatium regium* under John of Hertford at St Albans in the 1230s: Henry III stayed at the house at least nine times.[89] It should also be recalled that Innocent III was essentially a builder of curial, not ecclesiastical, structures.[90]

The idea that the zenith of archiepiscopal and papal power should be celebrated by magnificent halls and chambers also had a serious and coherent ethical grounding: the great table in an equally splendid hall was a recognized symbol of the magnificence and virtue of a great leader, which Hubert Walter undoubtedly was. Nor was this view of magnificence separable from the sacral quality of episcopal leadership. Becket's hagiographers had already provided much the most striking contemporary account of truly educated (and educative) liberality. Hubert Walter was a greater patron than Becket and, unlike Langton and St Edmund of Abingdon, could not be described as his natural follower, even though he had the image of Thomas's martyrdom depicted on the reverse of his seal (fig. 38).[91] The two men were very different temperamentally. Yet both had been tied, for better or worse, to the administration of public power, in a way that tested Becket's hagiographers.[92] Becket had, after all,

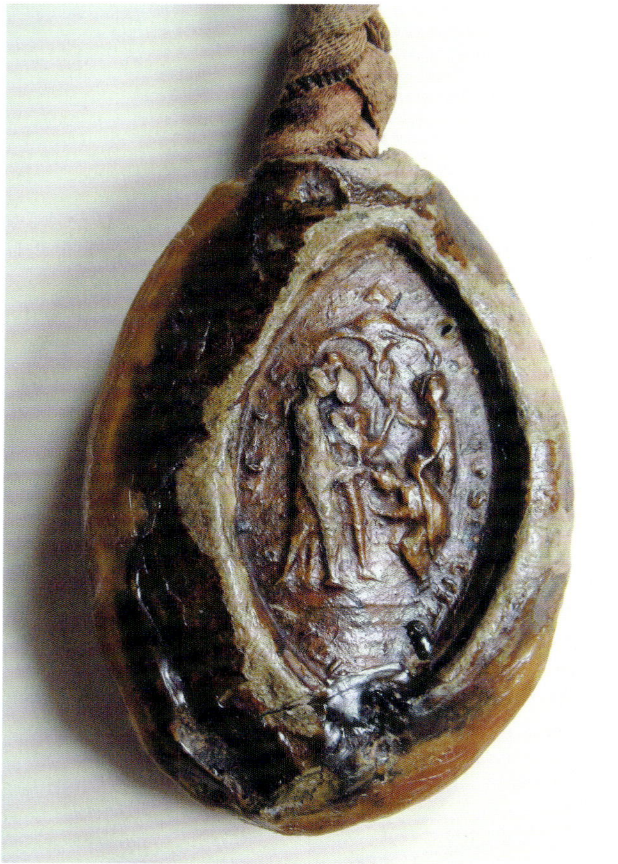

38 Seal of Hubert Walter showing martyrdom of St Thomas, Canterbury Cathedral Library, Ch. Ant. L 130, *c.* 1193 (Dean and Chapter of Canterbury).

loved the trappings of power, and had been a magnificent chancellor. But what is presented in his hagiography as a naturally aristocratic virtue, or magnanimity, redeemed this taste for secular things.[93] Even while he was in disguise in exile, Becket's aristocratic authority and bearing were evident.[94] Becket took the image of Mercury, conferring wisdom, grace and health, for the design of his private seal.[95] For Herbert of Bosham,

Becket was 'extraordinarily lavish, generous to all (*omnibus dapsilis*), excelling all in sumptuousness and grandeur [. . .] as great in heart as he was in appearance'.[96] The terms (e.g. *dapsilis*) plainly adumbrate those used of Hubert Walter by Gervase; for Becket as chancellor, the ideal model of the great-souled man or *generosus*, nothing around him was to lack magnificence: *Nihil circa eum nisi magnum, nihil nisi magnificentia*.[97] Hubert fitted this model imperfectly, but sufficiently, in his liberality to all, spoilt as it was by an undercurrent of acquisitiveness.

The ideal of the great-souled churchman as formulated in Becket's Lives had become inseparable from his role as the leader, in effect, of a court whose ethical character was defined by the ideals of *disciplina morum* which themselves had been codified and practised in cathedral schools and episcopal households.[98] Thus it mattered to the authors of the Lives of Becket, most notably Herbert of Bosham, that Becket's bearing was not only inherently aristocratic or magnanimous, but pedagogic: Becket was a natural educator in *mores*. What is so telling about their absolutely deliberate formulation is the stress it lays, in keeping with earlier Victorine *disciplina morum*, on Becket's banqueting customs and table manners, the proper preserve of the archiepiscopal hall (fig. 39). Herbert of Bosham deliberately construed Becket's dining arrangements as a schoolroom.[99] The matter of table manners and *mores* in general was a sensitive one for the masters of the period: thus Gerald of Wales reproved the monks of Canterbury for ungentlemanly behaviour at table, whistling and gesticulating when they should remain silent.[100] As noted in the previous chapter, Herbert of Bosham devoted considerable space to Becket's conduct at Mass.[101] Herbert's notion of sanctity was always ultimately theological. His account of the exacting customs of the spiritual table is followed by those of the corporeal table, over which Thomas presided with 'courtly breeding', his splendour tempered in Aristotelian or Ciceronian fashion by subtle moderation (*temperantia*), just as his abstinence was concealed by civilized dissimulation.[102] But in its outward aspect his table was more like Caesar's table than a bishop's (*Mensa haec videtur potius mensa Caesaris quam pontificis*).[103] Accordingly it observed not only decorum but precedence. The lower tables were arranged deliberately: Becket's *eruditi* were seated at his right hand, the monks and other religious at his left; knights were placed at a third table, where they would not be disturbed by the readings delivered by the cross-bearer, or by learned conversation – and to compensate, their table was slightly more splendidly laid.[104] Becket's 'courtliness', in other words, had gained legitimacy.[105]

Becket was not high-born, and Herbert of Bosham's aims were not those of the social commentator, but of the theologian and moral mythographer. His image of Becket as the educative courtier is itself reliant upon accounts of moral behaviour formulated by writers such as John of Salisbury, who wrote in his *Policraticus* (Book 8) of the nature of civil, philosophical and popular banqueting in the wordly courtly context – Becket's table combining the civil and the philosophical.[106] It would be incorrect to suppose that all such ideas were essentially clerical in origin, though many of them were unquestionably of clerical formulation. Myths mattered. The careful placement of lay and ecclesiastical guests at Stephen Langton's banquet, documented in one poetic source for the translation of St Thomas in 1220 in the Great Hall at Canterbury, the first major event held there, suggests that such ideals were carefully attended to, indeed adhered to, by Becket's greatest admirers.[107] But the myth was important in other respects. It established a common ethical framework for temporal and spiritual lordship – and so for ideal leadership – of which Becket was an extraordinary example as the embodiment of the *Vox populi*. In doing so it demonstrated the practicality of the pragmatic account of the relationship of the Church to public power as framed, among others, by Gervase of Chichester: if the great bishop was himself an educator in *mores*, so much the greater was his pastoral command and influence. William of Wykeham's motto 'Manners makyth man' is only one of the many echoes of this in the late Middle Ages. Becket's life as lived showed precisely how the clergy could have a role in ethical and spiritual mentorship at court, for the highest clergy were themselves courtiers whose example could be worthy of imitation.[108] The ethical life was inseparable from the spiritual. Smalley was justified in observing that 'It is better to avoid the terms "Church" and "State": secular and ecclesiastical government overlapped', and the mythology of Becket indicated one way in which their ethics too could coincide.[109]

This theme is explored in more detail in Part II, which considers the development of English sainthood. For the present it is enough to note that it also helps us better to understand some of the values of contemporary architecture. The ambitions that provoked the construction of the new Great Hall at Canterbury under Hubert and Stephen Langton acknowledged no serious frontier between 'Church' and 'State': the models were probably secular, but the most compelling and charismatic recent account of the type of life to be lived in such buildings was clerical – not least because it was an archbishop, St Thomas, and not a king, whose biography gave occasion for its rehearsal. This had happened well before 1200; and

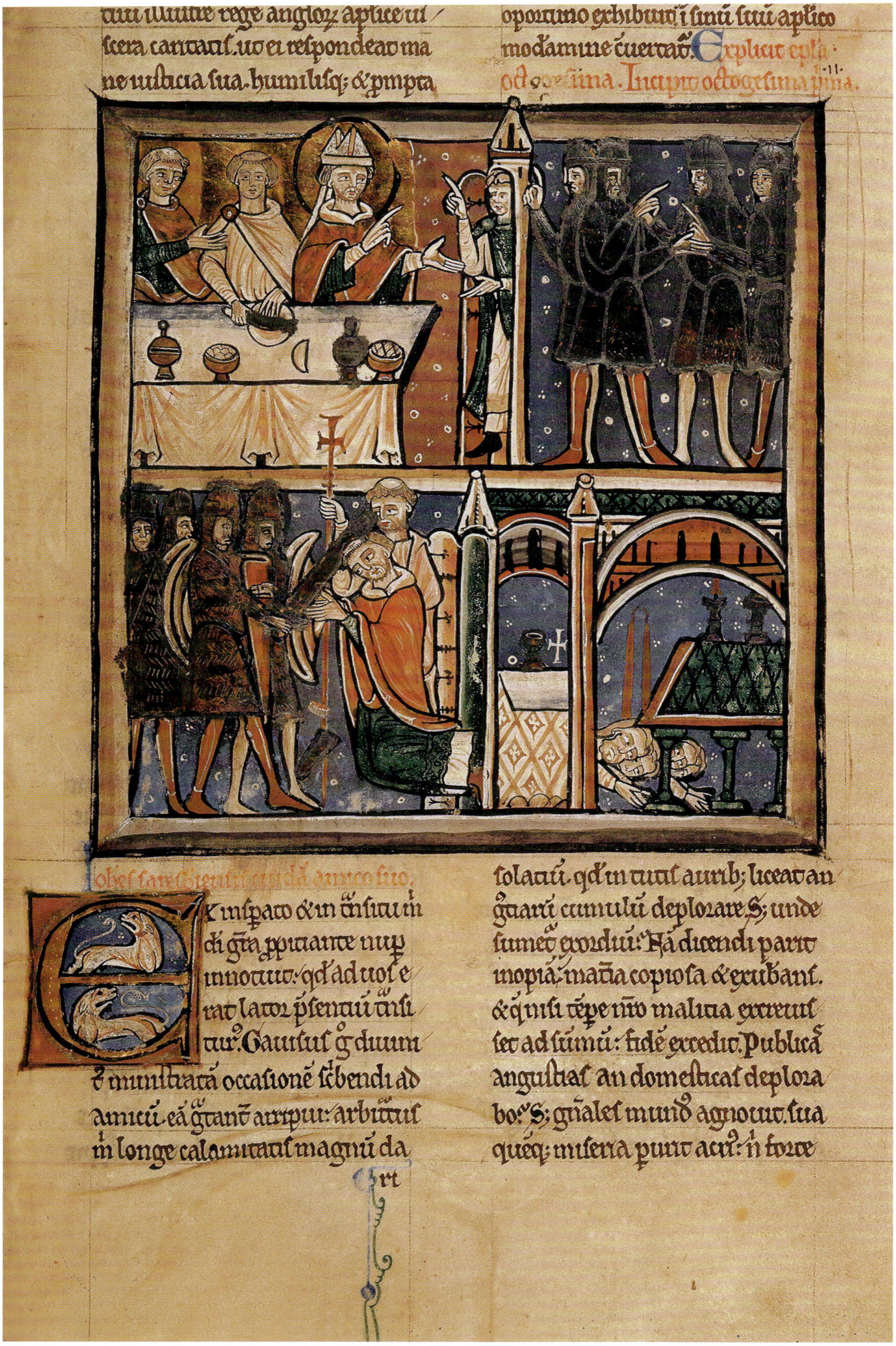

39 St Thomas at table, the four knights and the martyrdom. Life of St Thomas by John of Salisbury, BL MS Cotton Claudius B. II, fol. 341, *c.* 1180–90 (by permission of the British Library).

it is to this period, not the mid-thirteenth century, that one should look for an account of the intersection of the aesthetics of curial (royal, seigneurial and episcopal) and church building.[110] The boundaries between sacred and secular should not be too rigorously policed. Reformist literature in the vernacular was one vehicle by which such ideas and practices spread from the inner sanctum of the episcopal household, as a sphere of practical wisdom, to the lay world, a key process in so much of the thought of the period. When, a generation later, Robert Grosseteste, a reformer, turned his hand to the compilation of regulations for lay household and estate management, he recognized (for precisely the reasons sketched here) that ethical and pastoral mentorship went hand in hand. His *Statuta* for his own household, and his related French rules of around 1240 for the king's sister the Countess of Lincoln (whose cook Robert once borrowed), include elementary ethical advice to the effect that the lord of the household should appear openly (*uvertement*) in hall and not eat in a chamber, that the hall should be as quiet as possible, and that moderation in eating and drinking should prevail.[111] And when, in 1243, Henry III cited the splendid windows of the Great Hall at Canterbury, which he had seen in 1220, as an exemplar for his own new hall at Dublin (in which he was shortly to be painted as if seated with his queen and all his baronage), he too recognized the importance of his most important archbishopric.[112] St Thomas and his successors subscribed, for ethically serious reasons, to the aristocratic aesthetics of properly tempered *magnificentia*, and in ways that were also to be central to the image of the great church. Perhaps not surprisingly, this generally responsible and dignified formulation was to encounter an equally serious contrary position.

The Apostles of Simplicity

The alternative point of view was expressed vigorously. The robust, durable and versatile traditions of the ancient world, which sustained the positive style of commentary on great and magnificent patronage of the type discussed above in relation to Canterbury, also provided a negative critique of worldliness linked explicitly to pride and excess in life and art. This critique was represented by the satirical writings of Lucilius, Persius and especially Horace and Juvenal, and by Seneca and Cicero, in other words the broadly stoic tradition that echoes in the writings of the master-rhetorician St Bernard and in numerous medieval *florilegia* or miscellanies.[113] St Jerome particularly had transfused it into the bloodstream of Christian thought, for Jerome cited Juvenal's attack on the mighty portals, the *latas porticus*, of the Romans in his own critique of worldly ways.[114] In view of this substantial patristic legacy, later medieval commentators were impelled to steer a perilous course between the Scylla of splendour and the Charybdis of denial – and we too must tilt our rudders accordingly.

The issue is especially vivid because this debate was recaptured and amplified in twelfth-century French thought to such a degree that it has been supposed that there was a relation between what might as well be called the 'ascetic doctrine' and architectural practice. Thus the 'Gothic' style becomes for some a strategic response to the earlier formulation of ascetic ideals that exerted 'moral pressures' on patrons and architects.[115] The classic statement of this is one particular reading of Suger's various treatises on his abbacy of Saint-Denis which sees them as justificatory responses to the Cistercian, and particularly Bernardine, critique of excess in the cloister.[116] The critique of superfluity at least had the merit of polemical precision, for hatred sharpens perception. But there are issues attendant upon seeing Gothic as itself a reformist idiom. 'Gothic' – like 'reform' – was a pluralist phenomenon, and it must be said that the arguments set out by ascetic commentators were themselves unsparing of Gothic architectural practices, the creation of lofty, stone-vaulted churches for one. At least one substantial critic, Peter the Chanter (fig. 27), a canon of Notre-Dame – itself a masterpiece of the new style planned in the 1150s (fig. 40) – seems to have been reacting to an earlier 'Cluniac' tendency among such episcopal patrons of Gothic as Maurice de Sully, Bishop of Paris. The ascetic doctrine, enunciated most frequently at the height of the 'building boom' of the twelfth century, was at least in part reactive, rather than constitutive: Gervase of Chichester's brief comments certainly suggest as much, and I discuss another example of this at St Albans presently. Beyond the monastic and specifically Cistercian domain, however, it is difficult to see Gothic buildings in northern France or southern England as some categorically segregated and decontaminated arena of 'reformed' architectural activity. Christopher Wilson has pointed to the comparatively rapid implication of the northern English Cistercians in the architecture of secular great churches in that region, to an extent greater than that imaginable at the time in France.[117] The grip of ideals tended to loosen. In respect of France, Margot Fassler notes that late Victorine liturgical sequences seemed to spread in tandem with Gothic.[118] Yet she states:

> It has been difficult for students of the twelfth century to move from reform and the spirit of reform to artists

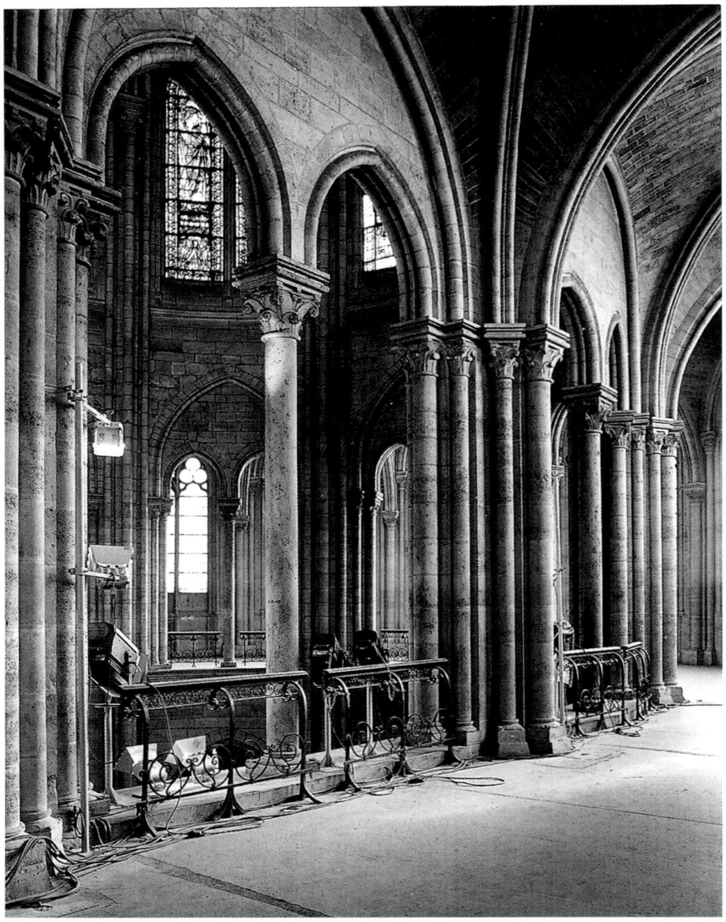

40 Paris, Notre-Dame, tribune at east end (Conway Library, Courtauld Institute of Art).

and works of art. [. . .] if it is true that the Gregorian reform movement helped to inspire an artistic renaissance in twelfth-century France, how did the idea that the church was to be reborn, renewed, and not even to look as it did before, become translated into early manifestations of the art often called 'Gothic'?[119]

For her the answer lay in one particular area of reformist activity by Parisian regular clergy at Saint-Victor which concerned their thought and action on liturgical symbolism, church organization, clerical education and the form of the common life of clergy.[120] These coincided in many respects with the preoccupations of reformist clergy in England in the period covered by this book. Indeed this sphere of thought can be shown to have been directly influential upon English patrons of great church architecture towards the end of the twelfth century – though in stating as much one must try to separate its allegorical from its ethical implications. This educative and symbolist motivation implied no necessary commitment to an aesthetic as such: Øystein Erlendsson or Hubert Walter were certainly reformers, but hardly ascetics in their patronage. The twelfth-century church of Saint-Victor in Paris was if anything magnificently furnished, like Saint-Denis, or indeed Canterbury.[121] And this type of reform failed, in Anna Esmeijer's words, to provide a 'vademecum for commissioners and executants of visual exegetic programmes'.[122]

Gervase of Chichester is the only English writer considered so far to have expressed thoughts much in line with the ascetic doctrine, the character of which was almost always in the first instance monastic. He wrote his late homilies at exactly the time when the terminology of 'superfluity' or 'sumptuousness' was first appearing in Cistercian legislation specifically in connection with building, as in their General Chapter statutes of 1188 and 1192.[123] The salient features of St Bernard's sonorous, entertaining and urbane critique of excess in building (*immensitas*, *supervacuitas*, *sumptuositas*, *curiositas*) in the great *Apologia ad Guillelmum* of around 1125 need not be rehearsed at length here.[124] This work was based, as one might expect, on Cassian, Jerome and Ambrose. Though monastic in origin and initial intent, it was to be taken over by the canons regular.[125] Because the argument could be conducted on the basis of long-standing and eloquent Christian ethical traditions, it had the character of universality: and it was possible and practical to proceed from ideas about monasticism to those of pastoral interest to the wider Church. St Bernard's treatise on the duties of bishops therefore criticizes *amplis aedificiis*, rich vestments and mounted entourages as seigneurial temptations incompatible with the pastoral mission and the Gregorian drive to 'monasticize' the episcopate.[126] It is technically true that subsequent regulations for the Cistercian Order were not 'legislative' in any strict sense, and that the issue of the size, shape and form of Cistercian buildings was never legislated about with any precision.[127] Yet Bernard's point of view indubitably stemmed from what might loosely be called a legislative aesthetic, which posited a total view of human nature and conduct, i.e. the Christian *habitus*. By the same token, although not a single English secular churchman ever 'legislated' at provincial or diocesan level about the size or appearance of great churches, it would be unwise to assume that there was no discourse in the secular Church about these issues, especially given the intellectual training of increasing numbers of its most articulate members.

It is arguably within the history of European architecture, the most social of the arts, that the tradition of legislative aesthetics has been most evident and persistent. In regard to England in the period under consideration, the questions that follow from this observation are, if it existed, what form did this discourse take, to what extent did it become the basis for a widespread doctrine, and did it have practical consequences?

Texts by the French and English writers Hugues de Fouilly, Peter the Chanter and Alexander Nequam seem to answer the first question. All three writers conduct essentially the same sort of argument in terms and ways that suggest the existence of an actual doctrine. Hugues de Fouilly (or Folieto) (d. ?1172–4), a French Augustinian canon, was probably, though not certainly, the author of *De claustro animae* (*c.* 1150), a gloomy and prolix meditation on the condition of the monastic soul written from the viewpoint of the moral theology of St Jerome, the Cistercians and the Augustinians.[128] Hugues's targets were both broad and specific enough: thus in Book 1, bishops are seen to build palaces as high as churches, adorned without by columns and decorated within with rich paintings of secular subjects.[129] Monasteries should not bear battlements, and the buildings of canons should be modest, for while stones can usefully shore up a building, what is the point of them in vaults?[130] The cloister is not to be a sphere of appetite or the bestial activities of warfare or hunting; and nor is it the place of pride, for vaults are prideful. If buildings are to be well finished with polished columns, that finish is to signify *aequalitas*, the equality in their hearts of the brethren, rather than the outward luxury of polished sumptuousness.[131]

The text of the much more widely influential *Verbum abbreviatum* (*c.* 1190–97) by Peter the Chanter (d. 1197) is especially important given Peter's office as Chanter of Notre-Dame in Paris (fig. 40) and his major role as a teacher in the twelfth-century schools of Paris. The *Verbum* is a complex work known in different versions, the shortest of which enjoyed the widest circulation, including England. This version includes the widely cited chapter *Contra superfluitatem aedificiorum*.[132] Like Bernard in the *Apologia* and his work on bishops, Peter understands building as one aspect of the more general *habitus* of the religious life, his discussion being part of a lengthy exhortation against excess in food, vestments and so on: as in raiment, so in building (*sic et in superfluitate, curiositate et sumptuositate aedificiorum*). Peter quotes Seneca extensively.[133] Thus the simplicity of the ancients in building (by which he himself means the Old Testament) is preferable to the luxury of the moderns, a sentiment that clearly alludes to the Senecan stoic understanding of ancient virtue, a *locus communis* in the schools of declamation of Imperial Rome.[134] Pointless building takes the form of towers which resemble Babel, for what is the use to a bishop of lofty palaces, towers and ramparts: *Quid sibi vult ista altitudo domorum vestrarum? Quid Turres? Quid propugnacula in eis*? All this is madness (*quanta dementia*) for great palaces merely demonstrate a lust for building (*libido aedificandi*) that leads to a sort of pathology (*morbus aedificandi*).[135] Peter explicitly cites St Bernard, but his attack on lofty towers echoes St Jerome's commentary on the Pauline Epistles, in which bishops stationed in towers exhibit supercilious pride.[136] Jerome saw this as a fault common both to the palace and the church, and it is clear that Peter accepted this in attacking the immense and lofty chevets of some Romanesque or Gothic cathedrals which, as the head of the church (*caput*) signifying Christ, ought really to be more humble than the body of the church.[137] There can be no doubt that this alludes to the great churches, the *maiores ecclesiae*.[138] Here Peter is attacking the 'Cluniac' tendencies of the Bishop of Paris, Maurice de Sully, who presided over the reconstruction of Notre-Dame, and who, according to other sources, was content, unlike Peter, to accept funds gained from usury to fund it.[139] 'Gothic' was not excused.

Much in Peter, as in stoic doctrine generally, proceeds from a certain view of utility, for Peter also disliked wasteful and distracting litigation over ecclesiastical jurisdictions in Paris which absorbed the clergy's time – a point also made by Gervase of Chichester on Malachi.[140] His moral theology thus has a generally pragmatic character, since in the *Verbum abbreviatum* he takes the view that there are useful and useless arts (agriculture as opposed to architecture for example).[141] It is merely ironic that he died at Longpont, one of the most architecturally ambitious of the Cistercian churches of northern France.[142] Peter's pragmatism modified his puritanical instincts, and in this regard his casuistical outlook was to be important for attitudes towards the arts more generally.

The encyclopaedic *De naturis rerum* by the English writer Alexander de Sancto Albano, better known as Alexander Nequam (d. 1217), was written before about 1205 and has many points of similarity in its ethical reasoning with the high-minded French clerical tradition outlined so far.[143] Brought up in St Albans, he had been educated in the Paris schools at the time of Peter the Chanter;[144] he claimed to have been a 'small pillar of the Petit Pont', which renders it likely that he was lecturing on Aristotle and was acquainted with his ethical views on temperance.[145] Nequam's writing in *De naturis rerum* is also informed by a tiresomely pessimistic Augustinian morality of the type which asserts that human health, though ostensibly a blessing, only provides an incitement to sin.[146] This general tone establishes the context for remarks on all things, including human vanity, of which building to excess is only an aspect. His chapter *De aedificiis*[147] is framed by chapters on agricultural implements (useful) and the Liberal Arts (subtle and dubious), the whole text ending with a comprehensive denunciation of excesses of all types which returns again to building.[148] *De aedificiis* states that the superfluous magnificence of buildings is a product of pride and viciously pleasurable expenditure (*voluptuariae expensae*); lofty towers are built that threaten the stars, excelling the peaks of Parnassus; nature complains she is vanquished by art (*natura se ab arte superari conqueritur*). All is vanity and affectation, Nequam's language echoing St Bernard's.[149] Like Bernard and Peter the Chanter, he invokes insanity: this is a pathology of building, for man, suffering from the fickleness of his nature, has an urge to build endlessly (*Homo, morbo inconstantiae laborans*). Carving and painting show only that wealth leads to folly. Numerous, exhausting and unlawful inventions (*illicitae adinventiones*) prevail, not the least of which are capitals which sustain vaults like spider webs (*celaturae aranearum*).

It is difficult to avoid the impression that this last and imaginatively effective moralization refers specifically to Gothic rib vaults, the spider web being chosen not merely on grounds of visual aptness but also because of its subtlety, *subtilitas* (fig. 41). Gerald of Wales, in attacking dialectical sophistication or logic-chopping (of which Peter the Chanter also disapproved), employed the spider web as an example of subtlety, in contradistinction to *utilitas*: thus a spider web is clever, but merely catches flies.[150] Arachne's stubborn pride cannot have been far from mind. So much for the moral probity of Gothic! As Peter of Blois noted, this hatred of subtlety was Senecan in origin: both Alexander and Peter read Seneca.[151] To judge from his account of the spider web in *De naturis rerum*, Alexander also saw the stone vault as a symbol of vanity's entrapment of the unwary.[152] Alexander was not the first to make such associations: the earlier account of Durham Cathedral by Reginald of Durham, for example, contrasts ancient simplicity (a theme in Peter the Chanter) with modern subtlety, by means of which the ingenuity of 'mere dexterity' had raised arches of 'sublime pride'.[153]

Context is vitally important for an understanding of what Alexander has to say on building, because although his comments imply knowledge of the latest accomplishments of Gothic building, it would be wrong to deduce from them that his was a critique aimed at building in general. The Augustinian view of human nature and the stress on *mediocritas* as an ethical ideal in *De naturis rerum* are likely above all to reflect the circumstances under which it was written, namely not long after Alexander's entry to the Augustinian house at Cirencester between 1197 and 1202.[154] It was for such canons that the *linea canonice mediocritatis* had been put forward in the sermons of Peter the Chanter, and Alexander's work is comprehensible within the style of commentary on architecture as an aspect of the canonical or monastic *habitus* exemplified in Hugues de Fouilly.[155] In being appropriate to a religious order, such sentiments remind one once again that men's views are adaptable. Indeed, after his return from Paris in the 1190s and before his entry to Cirencester, Alexander represented a very different outlook. In Oxford he is known to have preached a sermon appealing for funds for the restoration of St Frideswide's, after a fire in 1190: 'Why do you not reflect, you laymen, that it was said literally Lord I have loved the beauty of thy dwelling'.[156] This is not the idealistic stoical view of the moralists, but the commonplace tolerant view of the secular church.

The Sad Case of Abbot John

One may reasonably conclude that Alexander's sentiments were most likely to have been attended to by those in the religious or monastic orders: in answering the question about the widespread nature of this sort of sentiment, one needs to bear in mind the function and audience of such texts. Alexander's works were sufficiently well known in England to be cited by Roger Bacon and John of Brompton.[157] An illustrated *florilegium* of Nequam's works (CUL MS Gg. 6. 42) includes a leaf with some of the earliest representations of St Francis and other mendicants, drawn much in the early style of Matthew Paris.[158] There is no positive evidence that Matthew himself (fig. 185) knew *De naturis rerum*, but the early manuscript tradition of the work at St Albans shows that he certainly could have had access to it.[159] Matthew was also quite capable of writing in similar vein. The evidence for this is found in his compilation on the deeds of the abbots of St Albans, the *Gesta abbatum*, made after 1236 but before about 1250,[160] and in his own account of the abbacy of John of Cella (1195–1214).[161]

Matthew's famously censorious pen, though strongly chauvinistic about his own house, is ambivalent about Abbot John, a former schoolman at Paris in the tradition of the rather elevated intellectual community of St Albans which, in the time of Abbot Simon (1166–83), was already assimilating the works of the Victorines.[162] According to Matthew, John's most exceptional feat was to have memorized the entire Psalter so that he could recite it line by line, forwards or backwards.[163] The idea is classical: there is comment on committing the works

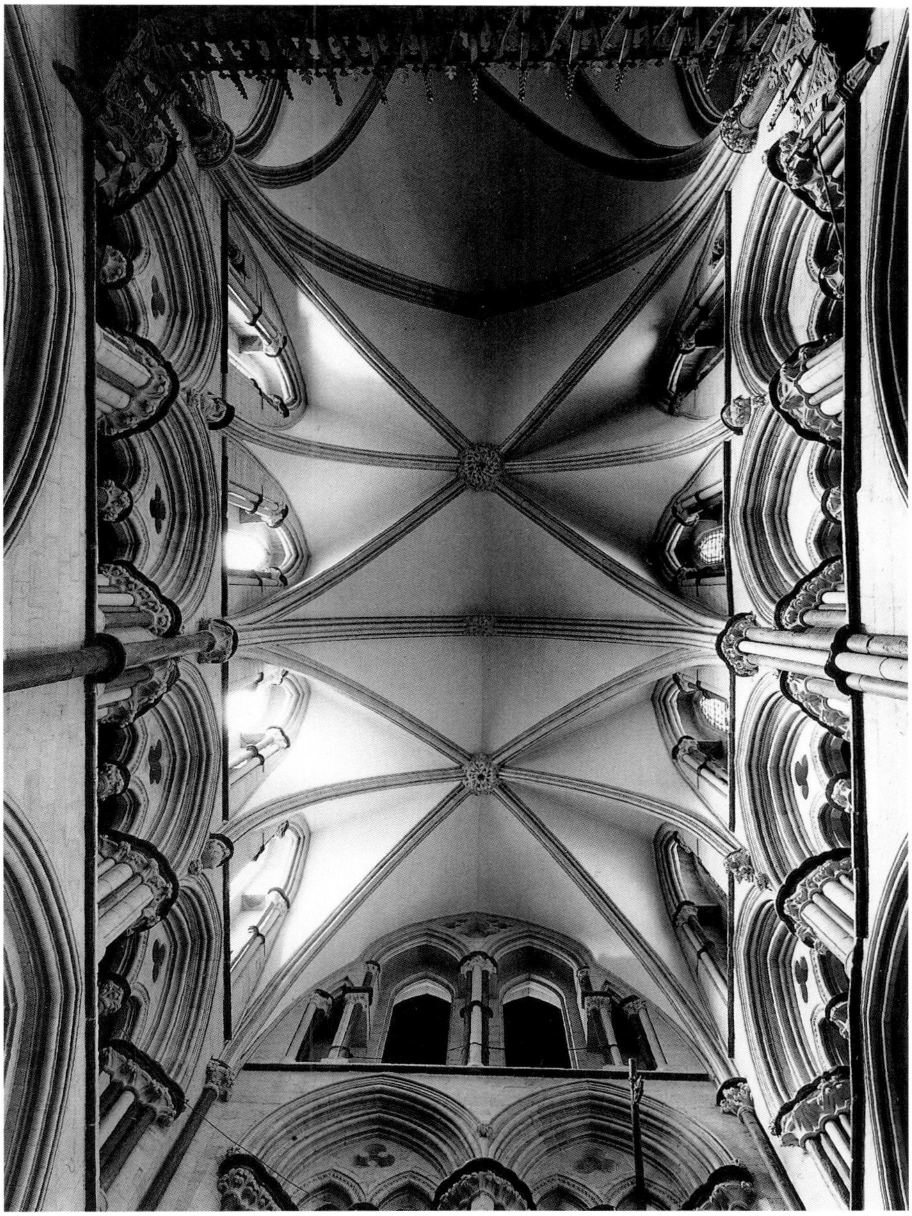

41 *Celaturae aranearum*, Lincoln Cathedral, vault of eastern transept (Conway Library, Courtauld Institute of Art).

of Virgil or Cicero to memory in the writings of Augustine.[164] Matthew is typically witty: he puns on the name Cella, cell, cellar or storeroom of the memory, with moral intent to point up a prodigious, but useless, skill.[165] John was also learned, indeed a veritable Ovid in versifying (*in metrico Ovidius*). But, like many scholars, he was unworldy and ignorant of everyday affairs (*rei familiaris ignarus*), a follower of Mary, not Martha.[166] This failing, whether brought about by the monastic profession or by the absorption of the new subtle learning of the schools, rendered John a poor judge, not well able to cope with the worldly trials and tribulations that fill the pages of the *Gesta*. It made him improvident, and certainly an improbable patron of building. Yet in 1197–8 John elected to extend the nave of the monastic church and to build an elaborate Gothic nave extension and west facade (*murus frontis ecclesiae*) (figs 42–3).[167] It is unclear why he should have done this at a time when it was

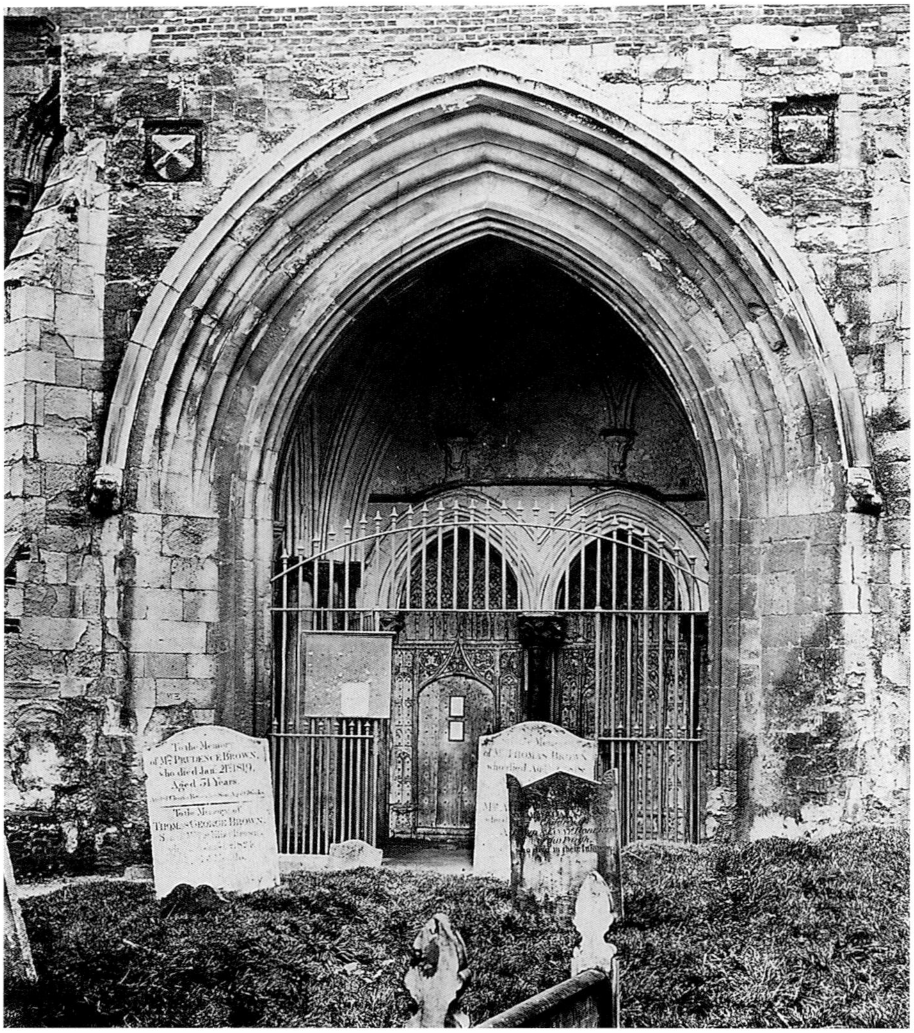

42 St Albans Abbey, thirteenth-century west portal, mid-19th-century photograph (reproduced by permission of English Heritage. NMR).

becoming customary to reconstruct the east and not the west ends of churches in the new style.[168] However, what mattered for Matthew was that he failed to take account of the exhortation in Luke 14: 28–30, where the man who builds without sufficient resources comes to grief and is mocked.

It had all begun well. In an echo of the heroic Benedictine panegyrics of praise of great patrons acquiring great marbles from distant places, John began to drag together (*attrahere*) timber and large stones, including pillars and capitals, and assembled a team of select masons (*convocatis caementariis electis*), in such a way as to suggest that the aim was to emulate and reproduce the best buildings of the time. Matthew used much the same terms in describing Richard Poore's summoning of noble artificers from remote parts (*a remotis*) for the construction of Salisbury Cathedral in 1220.[169] But John had failed to judge the character of the master under whom he placed this team, Hugh of Goldclif, a deceitful man and a liar, but a pre-eminent craftsman (*vir quidem fallax et falsidicus sed artifex praeelectus*). Hugh gave John treacherous advice to add unnecessary, futile and excessively rich (*somptuosis*) ornaments which quickly exhausted the sums the abbot had set aside for the work. Before the facade was half built, John grew weary of the work which duly languished incomplete and began to collapse under its own weight together with its bases, columns and capitals. The fallen remains of sculpted figures and foliage drew derisive laughter (*cachinnatio*) from the onlookers in fulfilment of the warning in Luke

43 St Albans Abbey, nave looking east (John Crook).

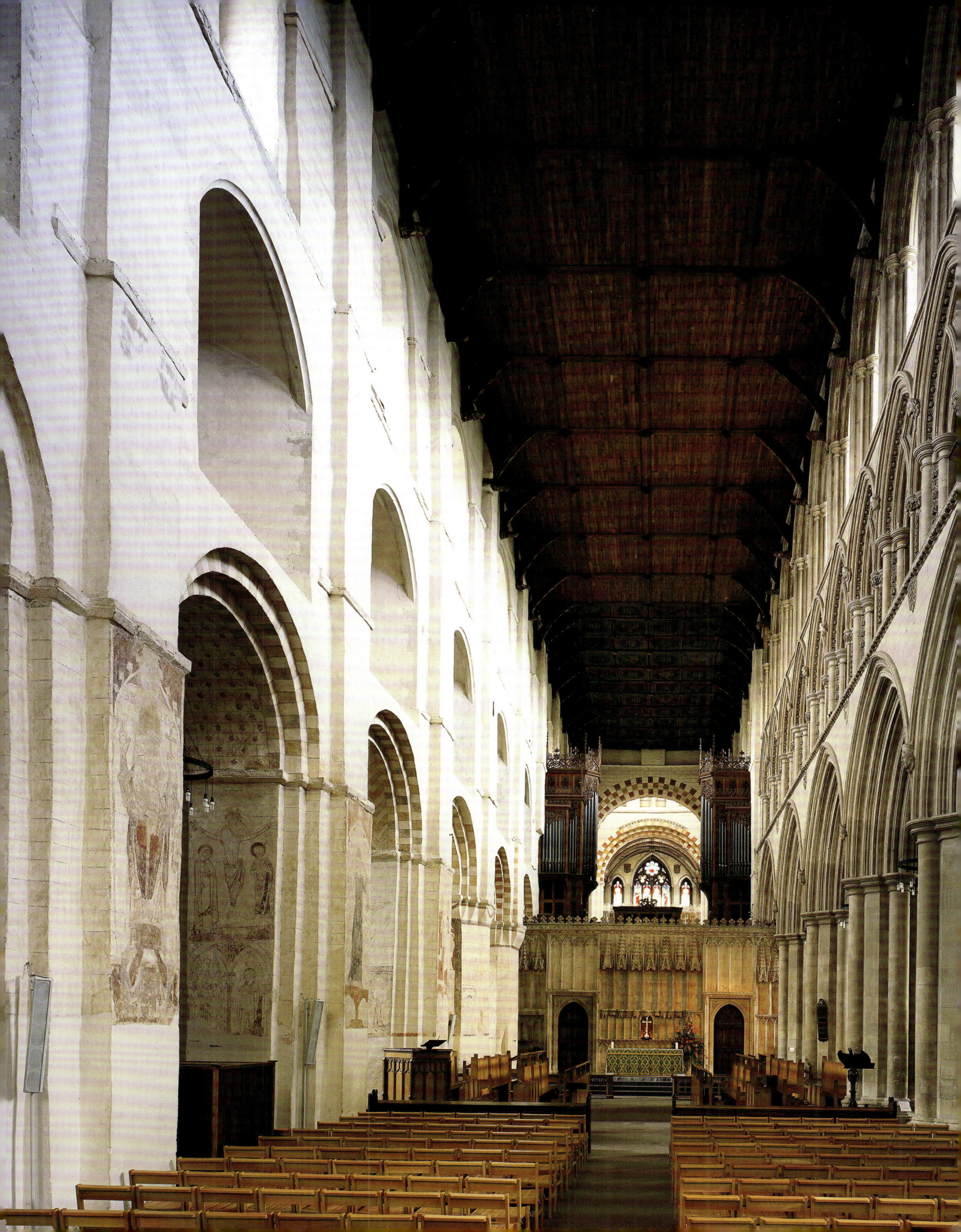

14:28–30.[170] Even though some of the abbey's relics were paraded throughout the land to raise money for the project, the work was never to recover, causing the abbot inconsolable grief.

The moral of the tale for readers of the *Gesta abbatum* is clear: the treacherous advice of a bad though professional man, when given to an improvident patron, leads to excess and dangerous innovation, which in turn leads to lethargy or depression. This is the consequence of the pathological *libido aedificandi* mentioned in the ascetic critiques of *superfluitas*: far from bringing fame, virtue or health, love of innovation is a trap, the vain imitation of nature is worthy of ridicule, and misplaced ambition leads the patron to sink into a moral torpor, as it were dramatized by the image of the building collapsing under its own weight. The abbot was a dreamer, his architect a cowboy.

Matthew's text is haunted by several spectres. One was the possibility, implicit in the moral and institutional framework of Benedictine monasticism which ceded ultimate responsibility for the conduct of a monastery to its abbot, that the head of house might fail as well as succeed. Matthew makes a point of listing Abbot John's various negligencies.[171] The other was debt, incurred by building or by litigation, and which at St Albans and elsewhere was to lead to constitutional reform; to an extent the *Gesta abbatum* is itself a local reformist document which makes moral use of striking *exempla*.[172] It conveys too a deep fear of treachery. This could come from within: Matthew's account is followed in the *Gesta abbatum* by that of the deceitful monk William Pigun, who betrayed the monastery to Robert FitzWalter and who was to expire justly but horribly, while sitting drunk on the abbey's lavatory.[173] More importantly, it could all too easily come from without, from lay professionals such as Hugh of Goldclif, who is simultaneously praised for his expertise and his deceit. This helped to ameliorate the case against Abbot John; yet, as Xenia Muratova argued, it also discloses a new fear on the part of the monastic orders not only of dangerous or vicious innovation, but also of the professional secular world beyond the walls of the monastery, which lacked the praiseworthy virtues of the traditional monastic *Opus Dei*.[174] Abbot John's facade was an eclectic and up-to-date design, and there are still signs from the remaining traces of it (fig. 42) that the scheme was eventually finished in more modest style than originally intended. Hugh of Goldclif was acquainted with the latest works at Lincoln and in the West Country (his name may indicate a connection with the Benedictine priory at Goldcliff on the Welsh side of the Bristol Channel).[175] In turning to Lincoln, a secular church, the monastery was emulating the richest possible exemplar of the new style, and this bold orientation might have prompted internal resistance, provoking wariness of the type of unlawful invention, ambition and prideful sumptuousness excoriated by Nequam.

Matthew was a natural moralist, and his account of Abbot John's improvidence indicates familiarity with the ascetic doctrine, for which the rather tough line taken on human nature throughout the *Gesta abbatum* provided the ideal context for rehearsal. The point of view is also strongly monastic, and it is not inconceivable that even Gervase of Canterbury's generally more positive attitude to building reveals a hint of suspicion about the pride of the new professions. Perhaps having cast an eye at Book 8 of Ovid's *Metamorphoses* and the ruinous skills (*damnosas artes*) of Dedalus,[176] Gervase himself seems implicitly to distance himself from the high-flown art of William of Sens, a capable but persuasive professional spokesman for his new, and perhaps prideful art, in his account of William's Icarus-like fall from the scaffolding. This is one possible reading of Gervase's elliptical but probably conventional remark that William was the sole victim of the 'vengeance of God, or spite of the devil': nor was the example of Dedalus far from the mind of Peter the Chanter in his critique of building.[177]

It is important to ask whether Matthew was reflecting received opinion based on institutional memory of events at St Albans before 1200, or whether his moralizing line was more proper to the period of the composition of the *Gesta abbatum* itself, towards the middle of the thirteenth century. The latter is possible. The events retold in the *Gesta abbatum* predated the writing of *De naturis rerum*. The section of the *Gesta abbatum* written around the middle of the century also contains a rueful reflection on the decline of modern Benedictine monasticism into subtlety and preciousness.[178] By around 1250 it was also becoming evident that the plans to aggrandize the west end of the church had become connected to increased lay use of the nave, another point of tension. Matthew was also to express gloomy thoughts about the morality of mendicant patronage. His celebrated change of heart about the Franciscans and Dominicans, whom he at first admired but came, in the 1230s and 1240s, to regard as malign agents of the king and the pope, culminated in a sharp critique in 1243 of their slide into prideful decadence: scarcely more than twenty years after their arrival 'their buildings rise to regal height. These are they who, in sumptuous edifices which grow daily, and within their lofty walls, spend untold treasures', so transgressing the vows of poverty.[179] Matthew's text raises interesting questions about the identification of height with pride but also regality, already encountered in his description of Abbot John of Hertford's admirable two-storeyed *palatium regium* at St Albans.[180] He was given to double standards, being very willing in his history and hagiography to praise the great building works of King Offa at St Albans.

Matthew's writing demonstrates above all that the ascetic doctrine was known in England at least within its natural homeland, monasticism. Its leading and most rhetorically capable commentators had, in the loosest sense, formulated a legislative aesthetic, even though the signs are that it was summoned only in commentary. What this discussion is moving towards next is the signal failure of the legislative aesthetic to influence the clerical reception, and indeed the actual conception, of the most important churches to be built at the dawn of the thirteenth century.

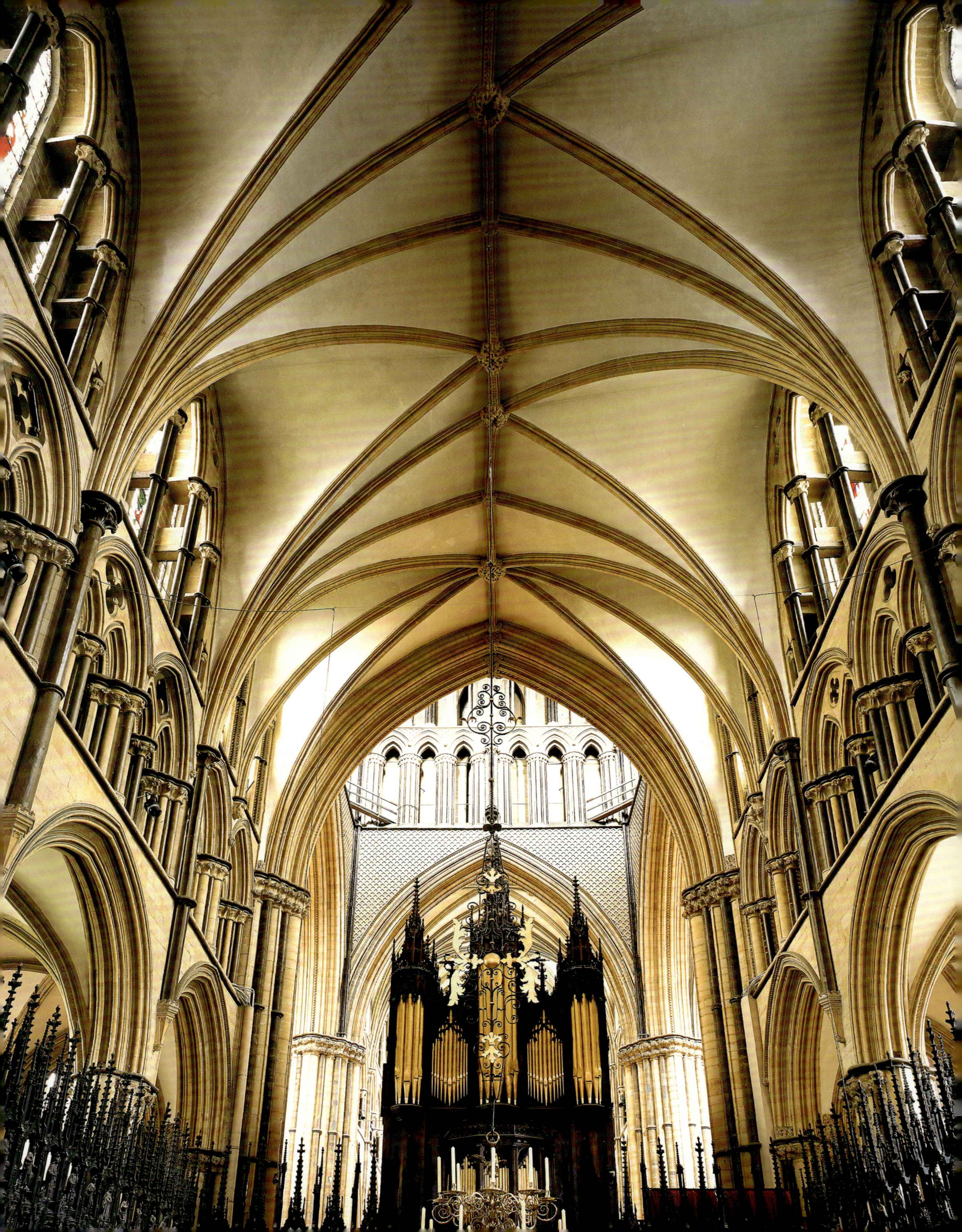

Chapter 3

MARY'S GREAT CHURCHES: LINCOLN AND SALISBURY

Domine dilexi decorem domus tuae.

Psalm 25: 8

Arma virumque cano: *St Hugh of Lincoln and the 1190s*

In order better to understand the character and direction of the various Gothic movements in England in the thirteenth century – and arguably throughout the later Middle Ages – one should trace the apparent lack of success of exactly those ascetic doctrines sketched in the previous chapter, and the corresponding success of what I have earlier called the 'allegorical mode' as followed at Canterbury. At Canterbury this mode actively sustained the conception of a great building; later, its principal sphere was that of reception and interpretation. Throughout this study, the reader is offered numerous opportunities to consider the ways in which Gothic architecture and representation actually moved ahead of signification and interpretation. In itself, the allegorical mode entailed no necessary or obvious aesthetic consequences, though, as explored below, the manner of its rehearsal in the late twelfth century in England was not without an aesthetic dimension. The richness of English great church building, its opulent physical and imaginative character, was the product of a wealthy and powerful diocesan Church. But it was the product too of a more or less explicit (but also flexible) doctrine that great churches should be complex and magnificent. Given the ambitions and capacities of the cathedral chapters and the *magistri*, such a doctrine was pragmatic. Of course, the consequences of this state of affairs did not determine fully the appearance of architecture down to the last detail. Neither the allegorical nor the ethical aspects of these buildings can be deduced from their architecture alone: they are matters for historical and contextual discretion. And since by far the greatest and most influential building site in England in the 1190s was that of the cathedral of the Virgin Mary at Lincoln, the vast diocese of which embraced St Albans, one may profitably follow the evolution of these matters from the viewpoint of those great secular churches from whose mighty towers clamoured praise of the Mother of God: Lincoln; and, later, Salisbury.

It was to Lincoln that the abbots of St Albans had turned for ideas for their new west front and for details of its vaulted nave extension.[1] The objective decided upon at Lincoln in the late 1180s or early 1190s was to build an entirely new Gothic east end, comprising a chevet with chapels, eastern and western transepts and a choir, in effect a separate church for the canons to the east of the Romanesque nave, and a decisive assertion of the chapter's corporate ambition (figs 44–5). According to the one (not entirely reliable) source for the date of inception of the work, the foundations were laid in 1192 following damage caused by an earthquake in 1185.[2] The chevet and eastern transepts were far enough advanced for the presiding bishop, Hugh, to be buried on the site after his death in 1200, and the choir must have followed rapidly thereafter, to judge from the dendrochronological evidence of its roofing timbers.[3] The famously odd wedge-shaped chevet was demolished in 1256 to make way for a new square-ended and slightly longer retrochoir, the Angel Choir (fig. 214), but it had been planned in such a way as to have an easternmost polygonal chapel that could have housed a shrine or some specialized liturgy.[4] The planning and finish, including the lavish use of dark marble shafting, owed much to the example of the new east end at Canterbury, which was largely com-

44 Lincoln Cathedral, St Hugh's Choir, view to west (John Crook).

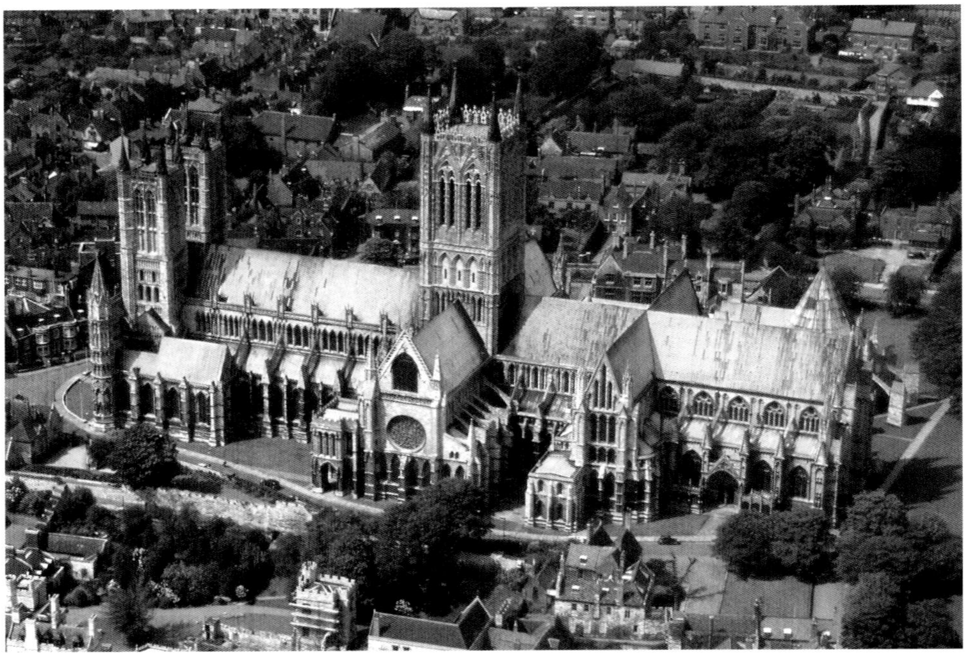

45 Lincoln Cathedral, aerial view from south-east (Simmons Aerofilms Ltd).

plete by 1184; Lincoln's strong and distinctive aesthetic character also entailed the rejection of many of Canterbury's most important (and most French) features, and a serious and committed rethinking of many smaller design elements.[5] Lincoln is a magnificent and imaginatively protean building marked throughout by a trenchant vigour, and occasionally coarseness, of detail; like Canterbury, the impress of which is still very apparent upon it, it must have been costly to build; and its impact was to be both wide and deep.

The new building (fig. 44) was started under the Carthusian monk-bishop Hugh of Avalon (1186–1200), who was to be canonized in 1220.[6] Hugh was a peppery and intransigent reformist champion of the rights of the Church in the face of secular authority, whether invested in the king or the archbishop.[7] His chaplain, Adam, later Abbot of Eynsham (a house associated with the Anglo-Saxon hagiographer Aelfric), composed the official Life of Hugh, the *Magna vita*, around 1212–13.[8] The *Magna vita* says virtually nothing about the rebuilding of the cathedral church, referring merely to the visit to Hugh's deathbed by Geoffrey de Noiers, the church's *constructor*, in order that plans might be made for Hugh's burial there, and alluding to Hugh's immense zeal for the beauty of the house of God.[9] This tact may reflect the monastic origin and intent of the text, addressed to the Prior of Witham, for the *Magna vita* promotes a monastic view of Hugh and his works. Hugh's relation to art is thus presented as essentially that of the moralist, not the patron, as exemplified by its report of the bishop's stern, salutary words to King John delivered before the vivid depictions of heaven and hell over a portal at Fontevrault, the only significant instance of the 'reception' of such images in England in the late twelfth century, and one which conforms to the Gregorian 'Bible of the illiterate' commonplace.[10] The *Magna vita* states that, despite his monastic profession and ascetic habits, Hugh took care to understand the customs and privileges of the cathedral and that he was in other respects a magnificent and liberal churchman, especially in entertainment.[11] In contrast, the Lives of Hugh written by the secular clerks and masters Gerald of Wales and Henry of Avranches take a much more positive view of the architectural works conducted under him than the *Magna vita*: for them, the patronage of a saint naturally glorified the cathedral chapter. These Lives were intended for Stephen Langton and Hugh of Wells, Bishop of Lincoln from 1209, and they represent an important contribution to the reformulation of the idea of the bishop-saint in the Langtonian era.[12]

Gerald's first Life of Hugh, written at Lincoln around 1196–9, was conceived only as a part of his Life of Remigius (d. 1092).[13] His approach to the sanctity of bishops was programmatic, for he treated the lives of great English bishops in pairs: St Thomas and Henry of Blois, Bartholomew of Exeter and Roger of Worcester,

Baldwin of Canterbury and Hugh of Lincoln.[14] Remigius and Hugh were two lamps to illuminate the Church; and if the rose, St Thomas, belonged to Canterbury, the lily, Hugh, was Lincoln's: both were to flourish in the 'garden of delights'.[15] Remigius was the first potential saint at Lincoln to be built up in the wake of the Becket cult: thus St Thomas bid the sick to go to Remigius for health just as St Denis had passed pilgrims on to Thomas; Gerald recalls that miracles by Remigius had been especially frequent during the rebuilding of the church.[16] This is one reason for supposing that the new chevet was intended to house his relics. According to anecdote, Gerald deemed ample space for the clergy to be of symbolic importance.[17] Gerald indeed praises the new east end (*capicium*) of the church, erected with the most sumptuous art (*opere sumptuossisimo*) and adorned with Parian (white) stone and black marble columns. In another image, Hugh is held to have promoted the most able men to his chapter as trustworthy pillars for his church, and to have begun an episcopal palace.[18]

These images were amplified and formalized rhetorically in the second version of Gerald's Life, the *Vita Sancti Hugonis*, finished some time between 1210 and 1214, when Remigius's prospects for canonization were fading from view; the work was probably intended for citation in canonization proceedings for Hugh, which eventually took place in 1219–20.[19] It is likely to be significant that this Life was dedicated to Stephen Langton, not least because this version greatly amplifies remarks on the architecture of the new church.[20] Thus Hugh rebuilt the church with wonderful vaults of stone (*miro lapideo tabulatu constructa*) and (in the common *topos* of outdoing), whereas Remigius built the old church according to the style of the time, Hugh's was incomparably finer.[21] It was brought into conformity with the more subtle (*subtilius*) craftsmanship of modern (*moderne*) invention. Hugh used small columns (*columpnellas*) of Parian stone and marble arranged alternately and harmoniously as if by painted contrasts, and incomparably. The church was made not from lifeless material (*insensibili materia*) but from living stones (*ex vivis lapidibus*), an image connected directly by Gerald to Hugh's summoning of virtuous men to form a properly regulated chapter, from whom he constructed sound and reliable pillars of the church (*firmas et fidelissimus ecclesiae sue columpnas erexit*).

This last pastoral image is reminiscent of the exploration by his hagiographers of the school-like virtues of St Thomas's erudite hall and *familia*; and it is one small point in common with the *Magna vita* which also praises Hugh's ability to appoint skilful men from the archbishop's household, and also from the schools abroad, who could support the unworldly monk in the administration of his diocese.[22] Gerald was a sharp, well-read and sensitive aesthetic commentator, who is said as a boy to have preferred building sand churches and monasteries to sand castles.[23] He was not a member of the Lincoln chapter but, as a Paris-educated clerk working at Lincoln, is nevertheless likely to have understood its general disposition. So, while his language of architectural ekphrasis is absolutely conventional, for example in its classicizing allusions to Parian stone, it also reveals a clerical approval of modernity, for the art of the new church is connected to the virtue of its chapter.[24] His uncritical association of *subtilitas* and *modernitas* is especially striking, since in other contexts Gerald could be critical of *subtilitas* when displayed in other domains, as for example in dialectical sophistication.[25] He knew and used Peter the Chanter's *Verbum abbreviatum* with its utility-based views of architecture and dialectic; yet this utilitarian outlook on building seems not to have guided his unqualified terms of praise of Lincoln, nor the contents of his own reformist text *Gemma ecclesiastica*.[26]

Gerald's *Vita Sancti Hugonis* is important here because it rehearses ideas even more fully developed in the so-called Metrical Life of St Hugh.[27] The Metrical Life is commonly attributed to the prolific itinerant versifier and grammar master, Henry of Avranches, who (if the attributions are correct) was the single most active Latin hagiographer at work in England around 1220 and whose work was methodically collected by Matthew Paris, himself an adroit writer about the English saints.[28] The Metrical Life was composed during the episcopate of Hugh of Wells (1209–35) and refers directly to him as the second Hugh. Henry was adept at turning out timely and locally researched Latin verse celebrations of the English saints for the institutions which possessed their relics, and it seems probable that this Life was intended to be used for public recitation or private contemplation at around the time of Hugh's canonization; it reveals knowledge of information produced for the commission of enquiry into Hugh's sanctity.[29] The Metrical Life also contains the most astonishing account of a Gothic church to be written after Gervase's commentary on Canterbury. In asserting as much, one must be careful to ascertain what this part of the Life does not achieve, for it is not (nor could it be) a methodical commentary on the salient features of the Gothic style: the mindset is much more literary and allegorical than that of the empiricist chronicler Gervase, and almost all its more conventional figures (and there are many) could apply to buildings in other styles, though some, such as his comments on vaults, seem incomprehensible without reference to Gothic rib vaults. Yet its conventions are interesting and revealing in their own right, for there is no reason to suppose that precise technical language is necessarily more truthful (or historical) as an account of such architecture than the allegorical mode. In writing about Lincoln, Canterbury and Salisbury, Henry behaved not as some insensitive mercenary, but as an attentive and artful commentator on local sources and ideas, and readers ignore what he has to say, including his *topoi*, at their peril.[30]

For the Metrical Life, Henry chose the dactylic hexameter, a traditional epic metre. It opens in heroic mode by citing the start of Virgil's *Aeneid*: *Arma virumque cano*, 'I sing of arms and the man', for St Hugh is to be a knight of Christ who overcomes evil and wears spiritual armour as a strong pillar (*robusta columna*) of the clergy.[31] As a youth he virtuously rejects worldly logic (*logica mundana*) and the falsehoods of Ovid and immoralities of Juvenal, in favour of theology.[32] The poet himself, however, adopts a resolutely classical tone, as for instance in his long *descriptio pulchritudinis* (or formalized account of beauty) of a young woman who tempts Hugh to sin.[33] The Life relates Hugh's growth in virtue and sanctity, of which his work as a patron is a part: and so the account of the new building grows directly out of, indeed exemplifies, Hugh's spiritual propriety, his rejection of simony and his charity and just rule.[34]

The poem devotes quite exceptional space, 132 of its 1308 lines, to an encomium of the new work at Lincoln.[35] Hugh is provident in piety, the pontifical bridge-builder (a pun on *pontifex*) to heaven, who in his humility himself laboriously picks up stones in a hod and sweats for the building as the good shepherd.[36] The hod itself proves miraculous.[37] The old church, mother Sion, is downcast, ailing and ugly (*turpis*). Hugh raises it up in cruciform shape, united in one form by arduous labour with soaring walls and a vault reaching towards the stars (*Evolat ad nubes paries, ad sidera tectum*). The poet invokes Ovid's *Metamorphoses*: the costliness of the materials is well matched by the zeal of the craftsmanship.[38] *Evolat* coaxes out the next simile, for the vault seems not only to converse with the winged birds, but actually looks like spread wings. The nature simile is then pursued: though gathered of separate stones, the building coalesces into an entity, a thing not of art, but of nature (*non esse videtur ab arte/Quin a natura*). Hence it has purpose, and can express its own ambition: so, not content with having one colour, it uses black stonework (*lapidum nigrorum*) as well as white. This dense marble flashes and glints, and its hardness can only be conquered by the ingenuity of polishing with sand and strong vinegar. The onlooker's mind is held in suspense with fascination as to the nature of this material, wondering whether it is jasper or a noble marble (*nobile marmor*). The shafts of marble (*columnellae*) encircle the pillars in a ring dance (*ut videantur ibi quandam celebrare choream*). Their starry brilliance is more polished than a fingernail's. It is a triumph of nature's pictorial gifts. Indeed there are a thousand shafts, strong, precious and gleaming, which render the building durable and bright, and of appropriate order, beauty and function. The church has a splendid procession of windows on either side which confront the viewer with riddles (*aenigmata*) and which show the saints. Two other large round windows (in the main transepts) are like, but surpass, the sun and the moon, two lamps to illuminate the church. In addition to the church there is a chapter house which outdoes Roman building, and which the wealth of Croesus could scarcely conceive. Its entrance way is like a square portico (*quasi quadra portico*) and within is a circular space rivalling Solomon's Temple. The poet hopes that the second Hugh (Bishop Hugh of Wells) will complete the work of the first.

This descriptive part of the poem is essentially a catalogue of absolutely conventional figures, combined in its similes with a fresh empiricism. Its tone is strongly classicizing, indeed eulogistic in the best and most shameless of antique traditions. Much would be recognizable to Gervase of Canterbury: thus there are commonplaces of outdoing (the new building surpasses the old), and also inexpressibility (the building is adorned with a thousand marble shafts). Emphasis is given to richness of materials, and to ambition. The motif of starry or altitudinous vaults comes perhaps from the Roman curriculum authors such as Statius, noted above in connection with Gervase. The same sources doubtless explain Nequam's lofty towers which threaten the stars.[39] The citation of Ovid is routine.[40] The ring-dance motif seems either classical or Christian, and one which effectively conveys the dynamic character of pier design at Lincoln, as in the retrochoir at Chichester.[41] The natural and purposeful character of the building as a single entity echoes classical figures in which will is ascribed to inert matter, as in the marbles that 'vie' for attention in Statius's poetry.[42] As Heslop notes, this is 'part of an extended conceit about the interplay of Art and Nature'.[43] Indeed the poem is in some ways even more nature-centred than the building, whose gristly detail has not yet developed the *viriditas* of major shrine-churches in the thirteenth century. Again, hesitation at the nature of the marbles invokes either a Neoplatonic suspension of mind, or simply the ancient *topos* of the inexpressible. The reference to the polished surface of fingernails can be matched in Paulus Silentarius's poetic observations on the marbles of Hagia Sophia.[44] The marble contributes to the durability of the building as well as to its order, fitting beauty and function (*ordo venustas [. . .] decor aptus [. . .] usus gratus*). In a particularly risky figure, the chapter house exceeds Rome and indeed the wealth of Croesus in emulating Solomon's Temple. It is worth recalling that the image of the ancient worlds (especially pagan Rome) was associated with avarice in the minds of writers such as John of Salisbury or Matthew Paris; and even the resolutely non-Christian interests of the English clerk Master Gregorius, who wrote the encomiastic *Narracio de mirabilibus urbis Romae* within about a generation, did not obscure this ancient, and to their minds contemporary, Roman trait.[45] The allusion to a *porticus* is perhaps provoked by the *porticus* of Solomon's Temple, but the combination of a square portico and a round chamber also suggests the Pantheon.

There is nothing of the ascetic doctrine in this poem, nor in Gerald's *Vita* which clearly influenced it. Quite the contrary: where the ascetic doctrine is critical of sumptuously polished surfaces, the Parian stone and effulgent marble of Lincoln are positively vaunted; where Nequam excoriates lofty towers reaching to the stars, Henry lauds the star-striking vaults; where Nequam criticizes illicit innovations, Gerald praises the subtle nature of modern invention; where Nequam espies in Gothic vaults the sticky subtle entrapment of a spider web, Henry sees in them the freedom of birds; and where Nequam attacks colour and sculpture, Henry follows his allegory with praise for the painted and gilded images over the entrance to the choir at Lincoln.[46] No *morbus aedificandi* at Lincoln: Sion is given health by building, and the life of a good if austere shepherd promoted.

That part of the poem conceived in the allegorical mode which follows this encomium is no less important, because it shows how the art-nature nexus could be developed in specific ways.[47] The poet continues immediately with sponsorial imagery. Thus the church is like a honeycomb, waxen on the outside but honeyed (*intus est favus*) on the inside, perhaps like the honeyed lips of the bride in Canticles 4: 11.[48] The church is divided into the spheres of the earth, clouds and stars. Its white stone signifies those who are wise (*sapientes*), and also modesty; and its cutting, doctrine. Its marble signifies the 'toiling' bride, i.e. the Church as handmaid. The clergy of the chapter illuminate the world with heavenly light: thus the windows on either side represent the canons and their vicars. In an astonishing allegory of clerical surveillance, the poet sees the two round windows in the transept as representing the dean and the bishop, on the north and south respectively, the two eyes of the cathedral which look out from it. Thus, according to the text, do unfeeling stones enclose the mysteries of animate ones: *Sic insensibiles lapides mysteria claudunt/Vivorum lapidum.*

Again, the ideas sustaining this vision of a 'moralized' architecture are conventional, but they are not for that reason uninteresting. As described in chapter 1, Gerald had already explored the idea of the members of the Lincoln chapter as pillars of the Church, living stones, the *lapides vivi* of I Peter 2: 4–6, which had also preoccupied Carolingian and Anglo-Saxon explanations of such texts as Matthew 16: 18, I Corinthians 3: 10–11 and 10: 4.[49] At Canterbury in the mid-1170s, as suggested in the previous chapter, such ideas were put into effect in architectural commemoration of Becket. Such thinking was demonstrably current too in the 1190s. The image of the living church understood as a single organism or macrocosm, made up of people or standing for them in general terms, finds a particularly suggestive visual and textual correspondence in an illustrated manuscript with north-eastern English connections executed probably at Durham Cathedral priory in the late 1180s, which contains a full-colour illustration accompanying Gilbert of Limerick's treatise *De statu ecclesiae* (CUL MS Ff. 1. 27, fol. 238; fig. 46).[50] Gilbert, Bishop of Limerick, was the first papal legate in Ireland.[51] *De statu ecclesiae* or *De usu ecclesiastico* was very likely written as a programme of reform, based in part upon Frankish authorities, for the Irish synod of 1111.[52] Its prologue concerns the proper canonical recitation of the hours and the due fulfilment of the duties of the ecclesiastical order. Its focus, however, is a diagram of the general order of the Church, expressed in what the text calls an *imago generalis ecclesiae*. The text sets out to explain the hierarchy of the Church by working up from the smallest units to the largest by means of what Gilbert calls a series of pyramids. Starting at the lower left, the basic pyramidal units are the parish, whose officers number seven from the priest down, and the monastery or nunnery, headed by an abbot or abbess. These units are divided into seven ranks, but also into three other (and by the twelfth century familiar) categories, those who pray (*oratores*), plough (*aratores*) or fight (*bellatores*); and these categories include the laity, male and female.[53] Working upwards and outwards by the Russian doll method, the next major unit governing the parishes and the monasteries is the diocese, which is in turn embraced by the archdiocese and finally the primatial church ruled by a primate, *primatus*. This Church is in turn headed by the pope, whose type is Noah, and over whom presides Christ.[54] Each stage of the ecclesiastical hierarchy finds a corresponding rank in the secular hierarchy, from the emperor downwards to the knights, who rank alongside

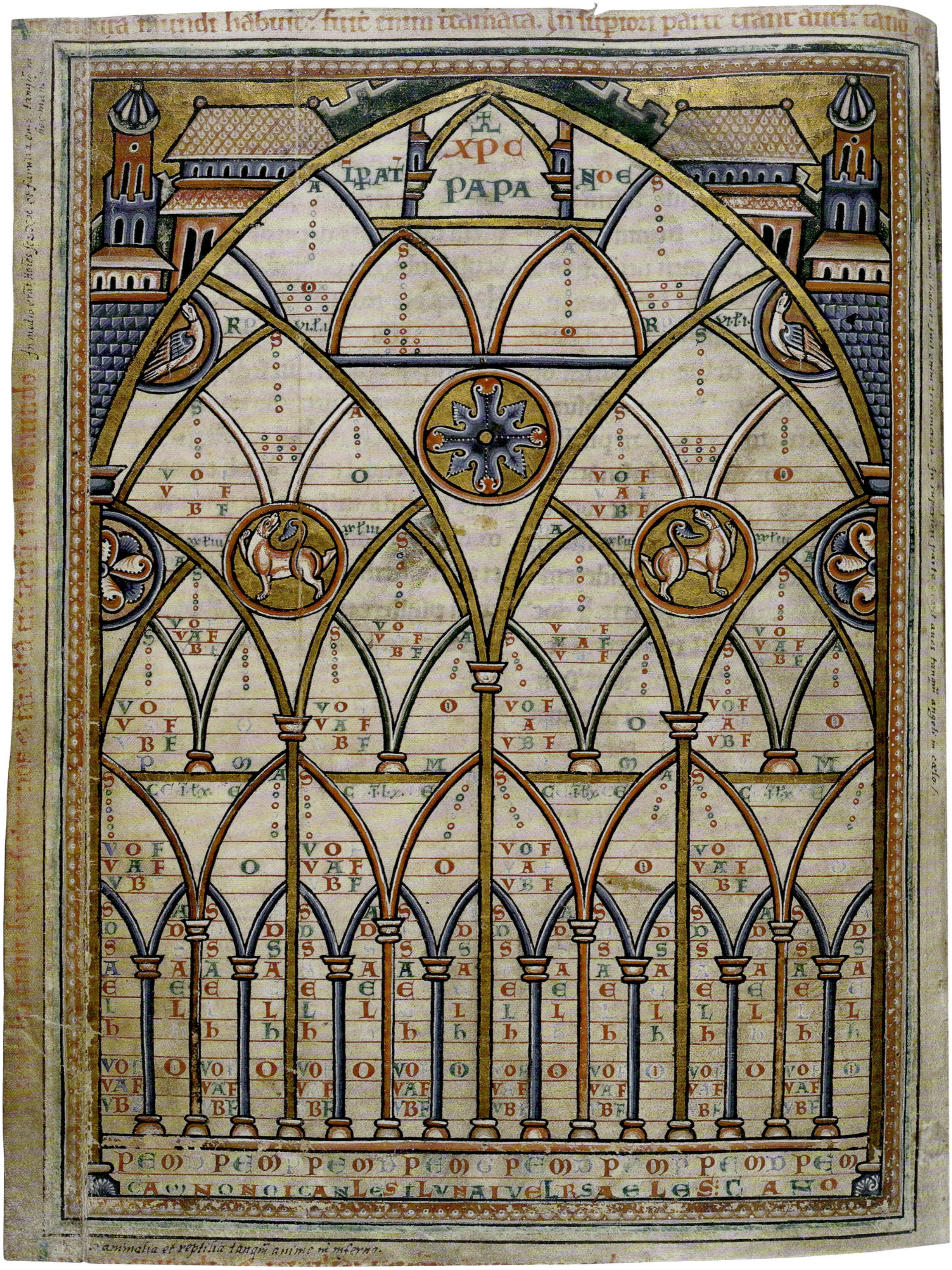

46 Gilbert of Limerick, *De statu ecclesie* showing the hierarchy of the Church from Christ and the pope downwards. CUL MS Ff. 1. 27, fol. 238, *c.* 1188 (by permission of the Syndics of Cambridge University Library).

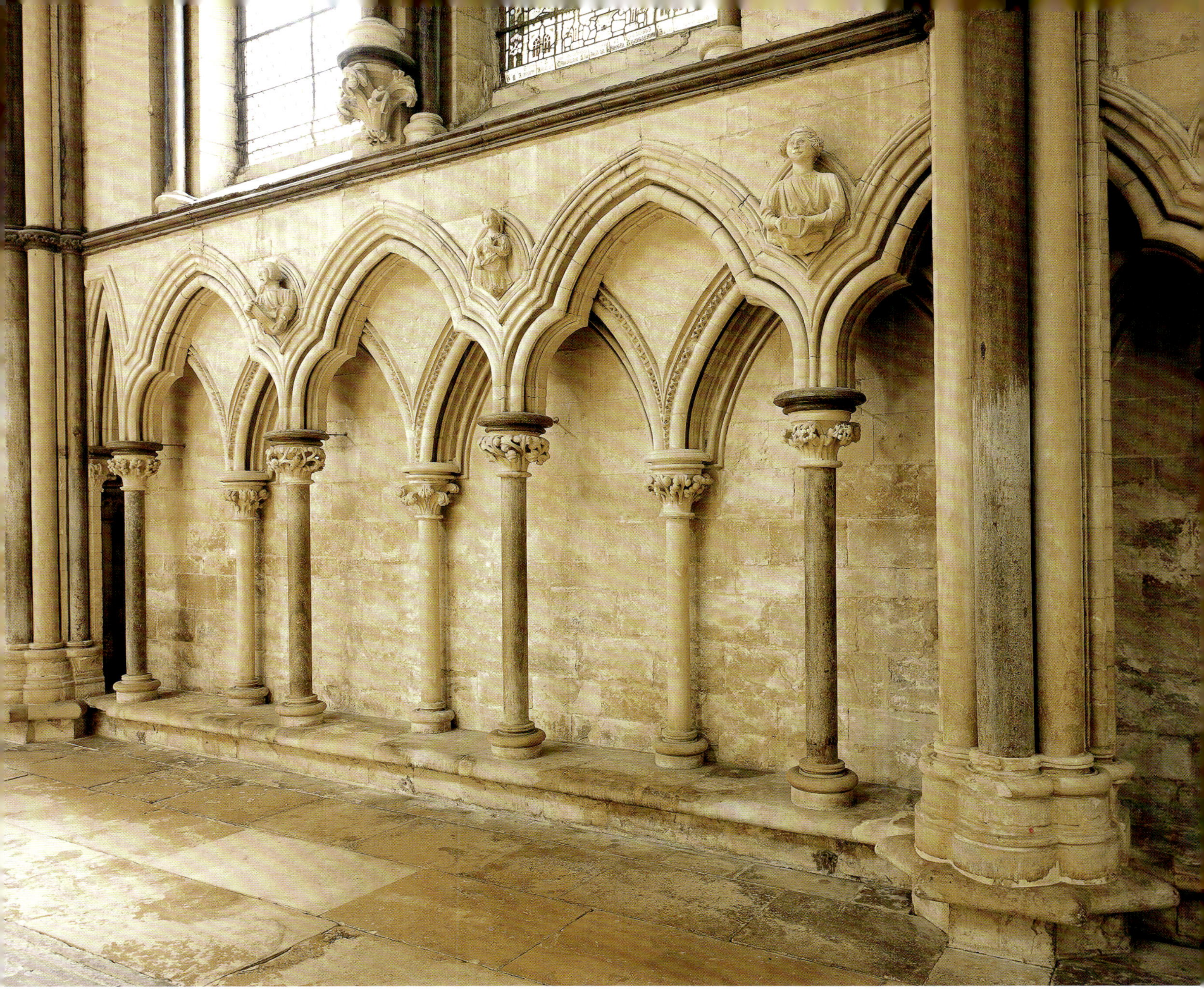

47 Lincoln Cathedral, arcading in south choir aisle, 1190s (John Crook).

the priests. All the spiritual and temporal ranks are identified by capital letters.

Gilbert's text is clear enough, and finds its most accurate counterpart in terms of layout and lettering in a fairly simple diagram in another Durham manuscript of the period (Durham Cathedral Library MS B. II. 35, fol. 36v).[55] The greater elaboration of the full-colour diagram in MS Ff. 1. 27 goes with a rather less coherent design and system of lettering. Yet its interest is formidable, not least because the proposal that the image dates to the 1180s, and not to the period around 1200 or later, significantly enhances its priority. In it, a continuous plinth supports a series of layered Gothic arches with bases and capitals that mount up in symmetrical subdivisions, part answering to part, within a major arch for the *ecclesia generalis*, the pyramidal conceit being almost entirely gothicized into pointed arches except for the solid late Romanesque towers and roofs at the top which serve only to highlight the new lightweight membrification of the image as a whole. Ideal human and spiritual arrangements are here struck from a compass point in smooth and comparatively lucid form, the Church being made up of people whose relationships it itself structures. Part of the interest stems from the likelihood that, stylistically, this is not only the earliest undeniably 'Gothic' illumination in English – and possibly European – art, but also one to which concrete ideas are attached. The designer saw pointed arches as being congruent with the pyramids that form the basic module of the text. This is worth stressing, if only because before 1190 there is no other architectural image or commentary on actual building that shows what sorts of concept might have been linked to the pointed form, albeit in this case by transference from the notion of a pyramid. Gilbert states that in the *imago*, the broad base or foundation of the Church embracing ordinary carnal and married folk, gives way above to a pointed (*acuta*) upper part by means of which the narrow way (*arcta via*) of the life of religious and ordained people is demonstrated.[56]

The force of this is obviously increased by the close relationship between the intersecting arched forms in MS Ff. 1. 27 and contemporary ideas in 'real' architecture in northern and eastern England. Though sometimes likened to a Gothic window, the distribution of the arches is strikingly similar to the 'syncopated' layered wall arcading found towards 1200 in the aisles of St Hugh's choir and eastern transepts at Lincoln (fig. 47), and later in the Lincoln-inspired triforiums of Beverley Minster and elsewhere at Worcester Cathedral.[57] Syncopated arcading appears to have developed before Lincoln in the eastern triforium of the retrochoir at Chichester, designed after about 1187, but it occurs with waterleaf detailing at the Augustinian Priory at Guisborough in the same period or slightly earlier, again in the north.[58] Such early occurrences make a nonsense of the anyway inherently improbable notion that such layered effects were related to thirteenth-century optical theory.[59] The roots of such illusionistic conceits, in this case layered shaft-arch forms which apparently break open of the wall surfaces to stress ambivalent, if not absolutely boundless, peripheral space, lie surely not in optical theory, so much as in a revitalization of the Romanesque taste for interlocked arch forms (as in the Lady Chapel at Bristol or the chapter house at Much Wenlock) brought about by renewed attention to the ultimately classical language of outdoing and inexpressibility (innumerability, boundlessness) encountered in the Latin encomiastic tradition.

The image in MS Ff. 1. 27, datable to north-eastern England in the late 1180s but based on an older text, is clearly part of a current of cunning and assertive formal invention apparent also in 'real' architecture. It does not offer unambiguous grounds for thinking that this figurative mode had aesthetic consequences for actual building, and nor can it be allied specifically with projects planned or realized at either Durham or Lincoln. Given its date, however, it manifests at least one idea of what a portfolio of symbolic and aesthetic concepts for a building such as Lincoln's east end might have included, in the absence of architectural drawings or chapter minutes. In this regard it is very rare, if not unique, and no one is entitled to disregard it, or wholly to segregate this type of concept from 'real' architecture. In saying this one should not lose sight of its actual purpose either: first and foremost it was edificatory, and rhetorical principally in the sense that it created the type of memory structure based on architecture common in the Middle Ages, which had the advantage of permitting formal *amplificatio*.[60] Even the simple arched forms of Gospel canon tables foreshadow the basic method. Its vision of the Church as a rational, highly articulated organism was essentially that of a hierarchy of command, and was not in itself an elaborate theological allegory or meditation, bar the analogy to Noah and the Ark as a type for the Church (the border inscription envisages the Ark of Noah as a tricameral figure for the World divided into angelic, terrestrial and infernal domains). It actually manifests a fine example of what Erwin Panofsky called the 'principle of progressive divisability' which he identified as part of the agenda of *manifestatio* or 'making plain' in scholasticism and Gothic architecture – though its early date suggests an entire aspect to the problem of which Panofsky was apparently unaware.[61] Clearly before 1200, and the true era of scholasticism, such highly articulated patterns could be invested with a more developed significance of the type found also in the Metrical Life.

Here the term 'edification' in its double sense (from *aedificare*) seems particularly apt. The analogy between Scripture and building is found in Philo and in Pope Gregory the Great's *Moralia in Job*.[62] Gregory's approach informs an extended passage in Book 6 of Hugh of Saint-Victor's *Didascalicon* (1120s), according to which divine Scripture is like an edifice, for it too has a structure with a foundation (history) and a superstructure (allegory), the whole of divinity being a spiritual structure raised on high.[63] Hugh's observation that the foundation and principle of sacred learning, history, is like a honeycomb from which the honey, allegory, is extracted, may have been a stimulus for the remark in the Metrical Life that the church of Lincoln was like a honeycomb, yielding a sweet inner meaning.[64] Was the 'honeycomb' image, like the pyramidal progressive subdivision, also a means of singling out the complex articulation of Gothic architecture as something to be analysed and comprehended, as well as admired? Mary Carruthers and Margot Fassler have emphasized the Victorine character of such deliberately sought correspondences between the textual and the visual, in their accounts of Hugh's writings on Noah's Ark as a moral and mystical allegory of the Church, and as 'a model of spiritual building', forming an *arca sapientiae*.[65] Hugh's Ark was an image for speculation, and the same vivid approach to allegory, now in respect of the dedication of churches, is developed further in Hugh's great work *De sacramentis*.[66] Walter Cahn has also drawn attention to the importance of architectural imagery in Richard of Saint-Victor's commentary on Ezekiel.[67] It is therefore striking that Christopher Norton, who has argued for the production of MS Ff. 1. 27 at Durham, should stress the way in which its commissioners 'were aware of the rich and imaginative developments in religious imagery and exegesis' of the period, not least in Victorine circles.[68]

The Victorine symbolic order of the Church and its liturgies forms for Fassler a 'reformer's vision' with a stress on regulation, a well-ordered clergy, and clarity as the basis for teaching and preaching, *verbo et exemplo* – much the same reformist vision as that in Gilbert's *De statu ecclesiae*.[69] The *imago ecclesiae* represents a model or pattern for the form, or re-forming, of the Church, an example of the twelfth-century canonical emphasis of the life of the clergy as a pattern or model for the laity. There is nothing overtly ascetic in this particular reformist and – literally – edificatory position, and it is not surprising that a very similar heuristic approach is to be found in the work of Hugues de Fouilly, a fair representative of the ascetic doctrine discussed above; for this use of structural or mechanical metaphors for the communal life, of Christian life in general, is very much in line with Hugues's regulatory and reformist concerns.[70] In similar vein to Hugh of Saint-Victor, Hugues may well have illustrated his own speculative treatises or regarded them as suitable for illustration.[71] No illustrated version survives of his *De claustro animae*, but Hugues's images are as visually telling as those in the Metrical Life. Hugues likens church windows to the Doctors of the Church (*Obliquae fenestrae sunt doctores Ecclesiae*) in a way that anticipates the Metrical Life's identification of the cathedral's windows with the saints and clergy, the inhabitants of the Celestial City (*cives Urbis supernae*);[72] Hugues also envisages the walls of the mystical temple as being the faithful of the Church, an idea cognate with the pattern in Gilbert of Limerick's *imago*.[73] Both men conceived of images as having the value of dense epitomes conveying complex ideas memorably, the better that they should be mentally and spiritually assimilated.[74] This tradition persisted throughout the twelfth century, since it is found with variations in the *De gemma animae* of Honorius of Autun and in Peter of Roissy's later treatise on the liturgy, the *Manuale de mysteriis ecclesiae*, in which the Doctors of the Church are represented by columns, the prelates and preachers by its towers. The *Rationale* of Durandus was to be its best-known outcome, but other writers of the thirteenth century in England were to deploy architectural allegory to more directly pastoral ends (see p. 182 below).[75]

Such texts and images had a broadly reformist objective, and it is intrinsically probable that their allegorical techniques were familiar to the members of the Lincoln chapter in the late twelfth and early thirteenth centuries. The Metrical Life itself discloses ways of thinking about architecture that had developed well before 1200: as T. A. Heslop has commented, the poem 'is not out of line with some of the intellectual concerns of the cathedral's community in the 1190s'.[76] In terms of sheer intellectual presence, Lincoln was almost certainly the major cathedral of the period in England. Gerald of Wales, who had received education in Paris, was unable to return to Oxford in the 1190s in time of war, but moved instead to Lincoln, a fair indication of its status, and he said as much.[77] The pillars of Hugh's chapter include a significant number of highly educated men of cosmopolitan outlook, about 42 per cent of its chapter being masters in this period.[78] Among these were the former lecturer in Paris, William de Montibus, the Chancellor of Lincoln (1191–1213) and author of the celebrated *Peniteas cito*, the first confessional treatise written in verse; and also Robert Blund, a regent master at Paris and John of Cornwall, a pupil of Peter the Lombard.[79] The chapter included Walter Map, Archdeacon of Oxford, and author of the satirical and generally anti-monastic *De nugis curialium*, and Simon of Southwell, a canonist and graduate of Bologna and Paris and a master at Oxford. Simon was a member of St Hugh's *familia* at Lincoln between 1189 and 1193, and may also have been a member of Bishop Hugh de Puiset's household at Durham around the time MS Ff. 1. 27 was executed there.[80]

In essence the attitude of these men to symbol and allegory was that of the Victorines and the men in the circle of the Chanter in Paris. This attitude was represented in later twelfth-century England by Herbert of Bosham, and in the thirteenth by Henry of Avranches, Stephen Langton and St Edmund of Abingdon, who carried the Victorine vision out into the lay world by pastoral endeavour. The Victorines, at once cloistered and scholarly, had by their nature effected a vitally important bridge between the monastic and secular Church.[81] Their *lectio* was being transformed in this period into the moral theology of the school lectures. The works of Gerald and Henry were composed by masters acquainted with the schools who, as in Gerald's case, were also familiar with the work of at least one ascetic writer, Peter the Chanter. Their view of a building such as Lincoln was authentic – or at least not inauthentic. Yet, and this is my main point, what interested Englishmen in the 1190s was predominantly allegory, and not the harsher morality of the critics of superfluity. So compelling is Henry of Avranches's account of magnificent building in the allegorical mode that, in other circumstances, it might almost have seemed like a riposte to ascetically minded criticism. But there is no evidence that this position was ever struck by anyone at Lincoln. Gerald of Wales demonstrably knew Peter the Chanter's *Verbum abbreviatum*, but in citing it extensively he passed over its chapter on superfluity in building, and did not allow it to restrain his praise of Lincoln Cathedral's magnificence and novelty in his Life of St Hugh, intended, significantly enough, for Langton's eyes.[82] The Metrical Life was probably composed long after ascetic rebukes to the style or form of the new work would have been reasonable. Such texts were written for a chapter of high intellectual standing, with a substantial proportion of internationally educated masters, created and presided over by an austere Carthusian saint – and yet which authorized the construction of what was at the time one of the most opulent new English great churches, and in a style now more obviously resistant to French models. Their thinking is likely to have been broadly reformist: yet the writings from this circle suggest that while some by-products of reform – especially the notion of an allegorized architecture – were deemed beneficial and constructive in the edificatory sense, their ethical stance was disregarded. While it is by no means easy (or absolutely necessary) to argue that Lincoln as conceived in the 1190s was a practical example of the allegorical mode instantiated in architecture, it is certainly arguable that the sheer magnificence of this building owed something to the failure of legislative-aesthetic imperatives to gain the upper hand in the architecture of the English secular great church. This failure created enormous opportunities for stylistic diversification and enrichment which were to be explored thoroughly in the thirteenth century. Allegory was not a means of salvaging a positive ethical content for these buildings, for no such salvage operation was necessary. Ascetic instincts born of stoicism were unrealistic for the ordinary Church. They gave way before the conventional sentiment of Psalm 25: 8, *Domine dilexi decorem domus tuae*: 'Lord, I have loved the habitation of your house'.[83]

* * *

O rerum novitas!: *Salisbury and the Langtonians*

In the literature on what Peter Brieger called the 'Episcopal Style', the figure of Stephen Langton and his circle while he was Archbishop of Canterbury (1207–28) has come, not unreasonably, to occupy a prominent place in speculation on the nature and significance of Gothic architecture at the time of the Fourth Lateran Council of 1215. Brieger regarded the major styles of great church building of the early thirteenth century as being especially adapted to the 'peculiar needs and conceptions of the English secular clergy' of the sort discussed above in connection with Lincoln.[84] These men were believed by Brieger to be bound by common ideals and policies concerning church reform that could 'be made visible in the arts in an unblemished and lasting form'.[85] Brieger was perhaps too hasty in identifying common ethical and aesthetic ideals in the rather diverse buildings in question, and in pursuing his particular idea of 'making visible'. Yet, that Langton and his highly educated and talented *familia* were capable of bringing to the culture of the English Church the school habits of speculation in moral theology and its translation into practical outcomes – which might or might not have included architectural patronage – is beyond serious dispute. Langton's twentieth-century biographer F. M. Powicke indeed regarded the removal of the cathedral of the Virgin Mary at Salisbury from Old to New Sarum in 1219–20 under Bishop Richard Poore, Langton's protégé and closest associate, as 'a deliberate act of emancipation' to be seen in the context of relations between the Church and public power in the post-Becket era.[86]

The period following the end of the Interdict in 1213 and the Fourth Lateran Council in 1215 offered renewed hope to churchmen with a strong instinct for policy formation and concerted action of a symbolic type. Bishops, the 'Langtonians' especially, now made renewed efforts to free cathedral chapters from local or traditional constraints, to promote reform, and to advance the reputation of specifically English saints as an expression of the liberty, sanctity and triumph of the English Church – a theme considered in Part II. The Interdict (1208–13) had come about because of a fundamental conflict between the Church and public power. Langton had been Innocent III's candidate for promotion to the see of Canterbury, but this was challenged by King John: in turn, Innocent III placed the English church under an interdict and excommunicated the king. Langton, though frequently in exile in this period, participated closely in the negotiations pertaining to Magna Carta in 1215, but his rise to real power did not occur until after

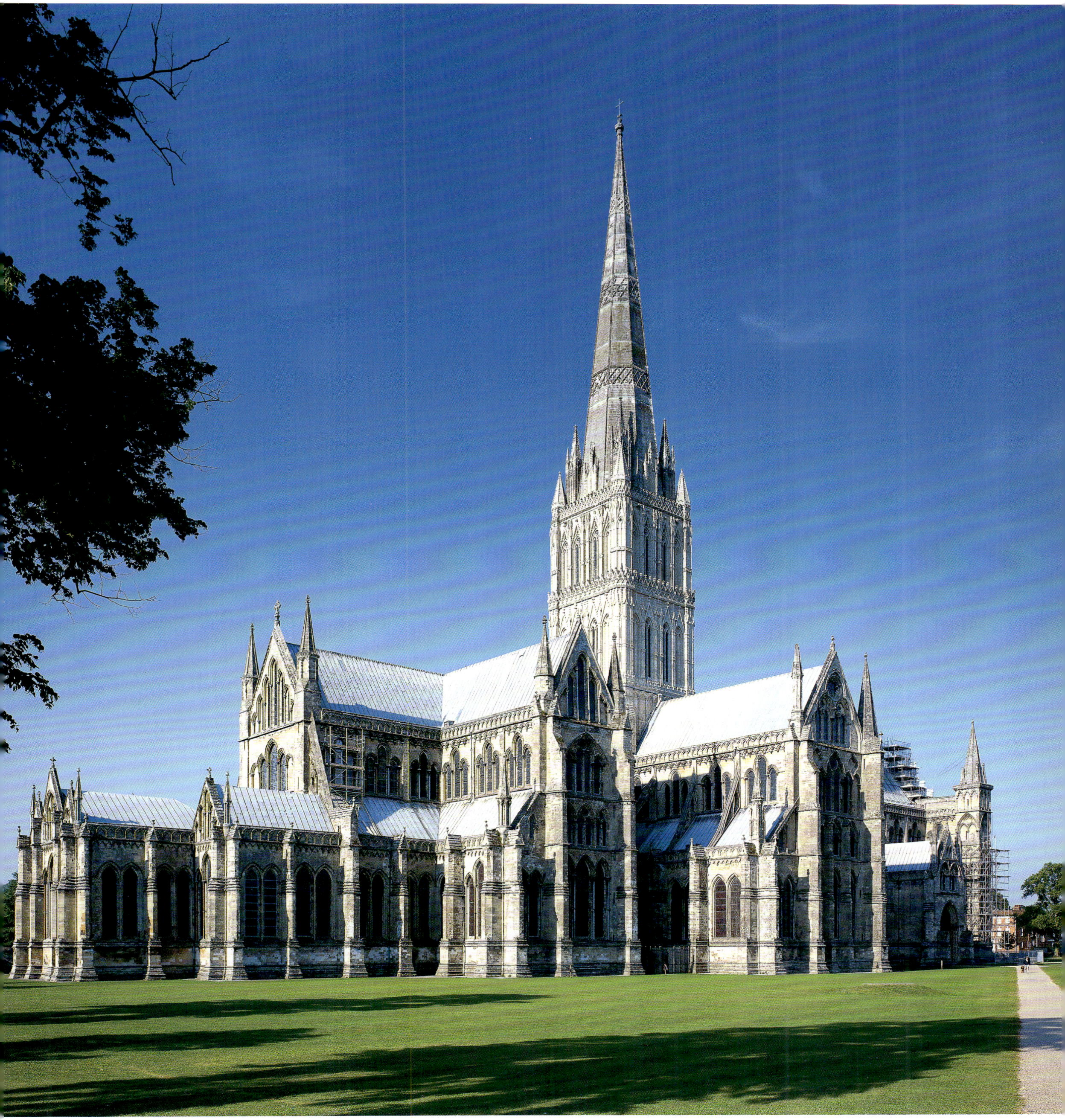

48 Salisbury Cathedral from north-east (John Crook).

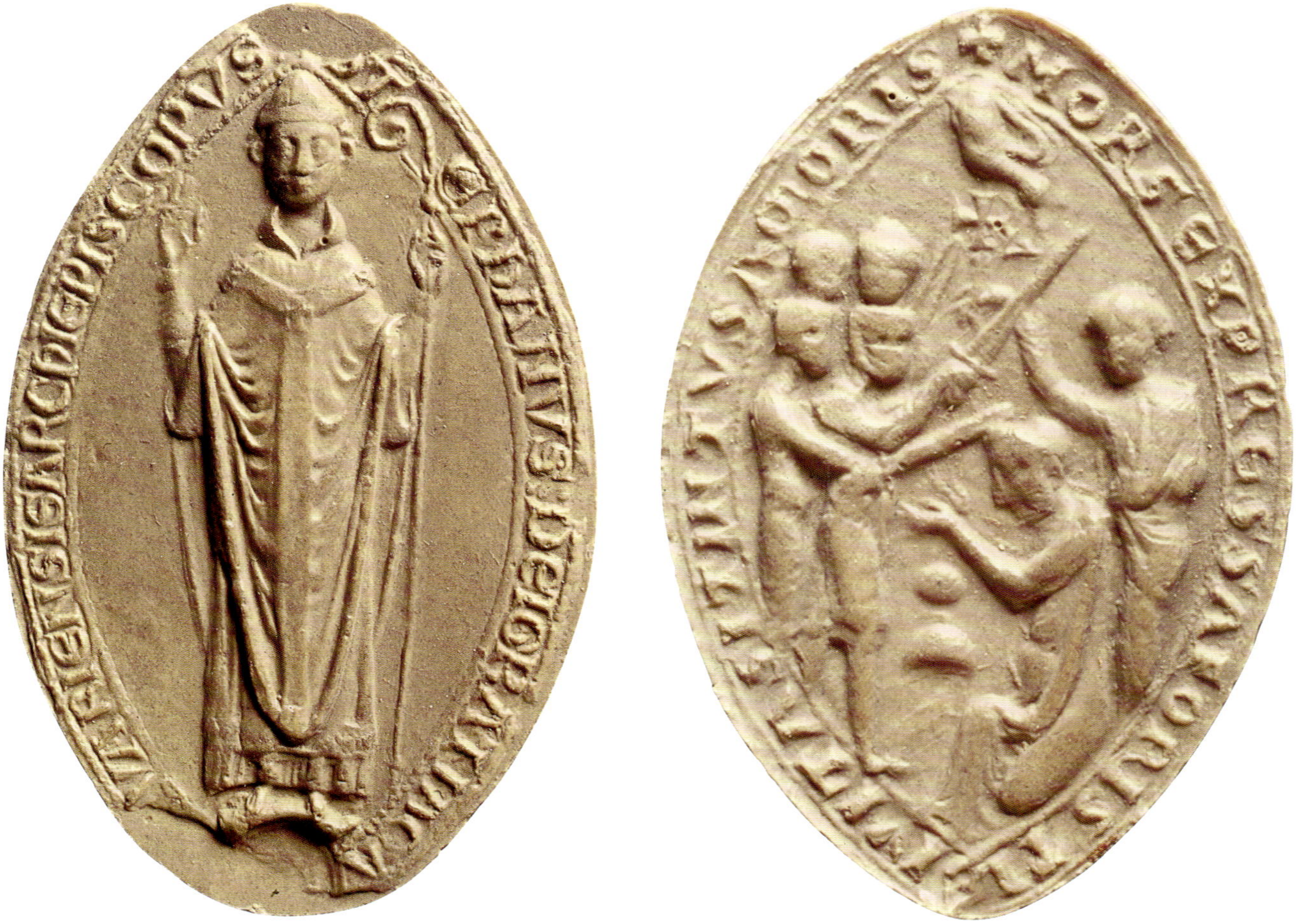

49 Seal of Archbishop Stephen Langton, showing counterseal with martyrdom of St Thomas (right), *c.* 1207 (Society of Antiquaries of London).

the accession of the young Henry III in 1216 and the removal of papal legatine control of the church in 1221.[87] Powicke regarded this phase of Langtonian ascendancy as 'a period of ceremonial stocktaking in the Church in England' which included a series of carefully staged events throughout the year 1220, often with an eye to the royal presence: the canonization of Hugh of Lincoln, the second coronation of Henry III and the foundation of a new Lady Chapel at Westminster Abbey, the start of works on the cathedral at Salisbury, and Langton's most signal achievement, the brilliantly orchestrated translation of St Thomas in July of that year, which has justifiably been regarded as a politically symbolic *adventus* both of Thomas and of the Church at large.[88] This period of public reconcilation was closely and deliberately tied to acts of building, because the ideological and physical reconstruction of the English Church had gained at least notionally in importance in the wake of the Lateran Council (which Langton had attended) and the Interdict, which had initiated a pause in serious building activity.[89]

More hypothetically, the Interdict also created an opportunity for reflection and, according to some, for the formulation of at least one new cathedral with a distinctive aesthetic character driven by a specifically reformist agenda, namely Salisbury (fig. 48). Salisbury, the first important post-Interdict great church, is held by some to exemplify the specific religious and ethical allegiances of Langtonianism; and the Langtonians, it is argued, had such allegiances because they were strongly influenced by the culture of the schoolmen.[90] In Langton's personal case the links with the Paris schools were formative since, as Innocent III (a Paris schoolman himself) well knew, Langton had been a Paris master by the 1180s, and, like Peter the Chanter (fig. 27), had been a prebendal canon of Notre-Dame.[91] Langton (fig. 49) was a phenomenally diligent and prolific theologian and preacher, whose sphere of activity was basically that of

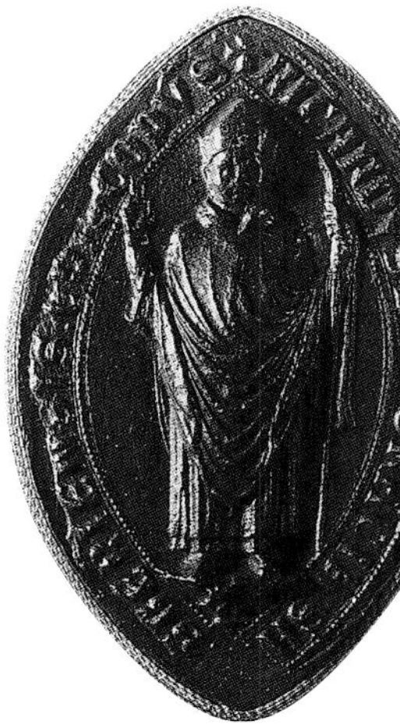

50 Seal of Bishop Richard Poore, *c.* 1217 (Society of Antiquaries of London).

the moral theology of the schools; it was in this context that his theology was rehearsed to moral ends, the reform and the cultivation of the young masters who were later to lead the Church. He is most often associated with the division of the Bible into chapters, so producing a standard reference system for the aid of teaching which was subsequently sharpened further by the Dominicans. He was the most brilliant English practitioner in the Victorine tradition, taking Hugh's *Didascalicon* as the basis for his programme of reading.[92]

In England, Langton found a close ally in his Paris student Richard Poore (d. 1237), who was Dean and then Bishop of Salisbury (1217–28) (fig. 50) and later Bishop of Durham. Poore, whose exposure to the circle of Robert of Courçon and Parisian moral theology has long been supposed, was also an important reformer and legislator, and was to assist Langton at the translation of St Thomas in 1220.[93] He it was who finally codified the Use of Sarum, the most comprehensively influential liturgical and regulative statement of its type, and who moved the cathedral from Old to New Sarum, creating in effect not only a new great church on a virgin site, but a planned cathedral city covering 260 acres.[94] The historical record of this process was furnished principally by the precentor and later Dean of Salisbury, William de Wanda, in his *Historia translationis*.[95] De Wanda's account makes it clear that the scheme to remove the canons' church entirely from Old Sarum had been conceived at the latest by the mid-1190s, indeed under Richard Poore's brother, Herbert, also Bishop of Salisbury (1194–1217), but was then hindered by circumstances.[96] The idea that the move might even have been prompted by Hubert Walter, himself Bishop of Salisbury (1189–93), is fully in keeping with other aspects of his policy, though positive action by him at Salisbury was ruled out by his frequent absences abroad; even so, plots for the canons' houses on the new site may have been determined early on.[97] In 1217 the pope was petitioned for permission to remove to the new site.[98] The ensuing licence was gained in 1218 and the final decision to move taken by the chapter the following year.[99] In April 1220 foundation stones, including a series of brass consecration crosses, were laid in the names of the pope, the archbishop and the bishop as well as the Earl and Countess of Salisbury.[100] In 1225, the year of the reissue of Magna Carta, three altars at the east end of the church were consecrated to the Trinity and All Saints, St Peter and the Apostles and St Stephen and the Martyrs; and income from the new chapels was directed to the fabric now being administered by Elias of Dereham.[101] But further need for revenue was evidently felt, and for this reason Richard Poore pressed ahead with plans for the canonization of St Osmund, a former Bishop of Salisbury, in 1228, following the translation of his relics from Old Sarum in 1226: but nothing came of it.[102] The choir and transepts were complete by 1246 and the cathedral was consecrated in 1258.[103]

The move to New Sarum guaranteed for the canons a freer and larger cathedral church of real distinction (figs 48–51). Unlike Lincoln, Salisbury Cathedral was never to benefit from an encomium of its architecture. But the move itself was celebrated in a contemporary poem, *De translatione veteris Ecclesiae Sarisbiriensis et constructione nove*, also often attributed to Henry of Avranches, and almost exactly contemporary with his Metrical Life of St Hugh. Henry was by now closely allied with the Langtonian party, having also been a protégé of Langton's opponent Peter des Roches, Bishop of Winchester. The poem was included by Matthew Paris in his compilation of verses attributed to Henry (now in CUL MS Dd. 11. 78), and it was cited by him twice in connection with Salisbury in his *Chronica majora*.[104] In 208 lines the poem celebrates the decision to move the church from Old Sarum to a new and more promising location. It may have been used to raise funds for the new church, and it is short enough for public recitation.[105] Since it mentions Richard Poore, it was doubtless intended for him or his chapter around 1220.

The poem's imagery warrants some discussion.[106] Its central, and so one might say broadly Langtonian, theme is the emancipation of the Church. In this respect at least there is no doubt about its political character. It opens immediately with an image of sterility drawn from II Samuel 1: 21, King David's lamentation for Saul and Jonathan: the hill at Old Sarum was like Mount Gilboa,

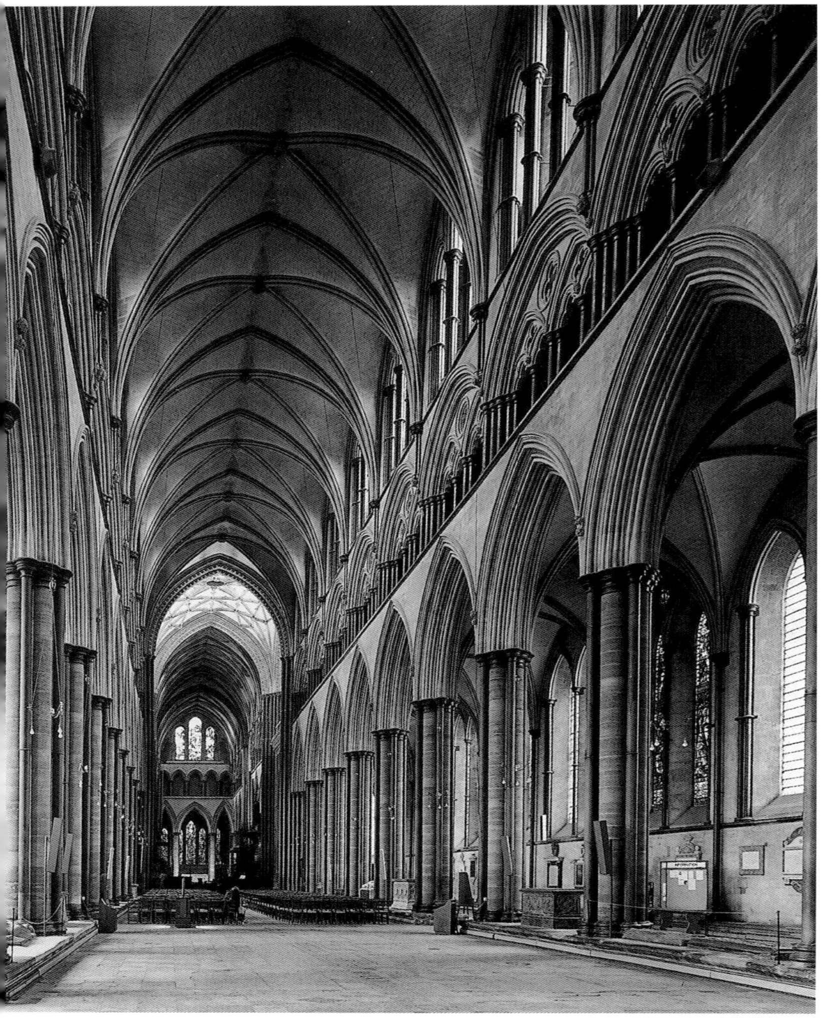

51 Salisbury Cathedral, nave looking east (Conway Library, Courtauld Institute of Art).

the *mons maledictus*, without rain or dew or living things, except wormwood, for a tree is known by its fruit (Matthew 7: 20). It was a place of wind and arid chalk, without birdsong and the solace of nature. The castle, the city within it, and the cathedral were jostled together: God and Caesar were confused, and Caesar preyed upon the rights of God, plundering the clergy. The Ark of the Covenant was imprisoned in the Temple of Baal, Jerusalem was captive in Babylon. But Sion and Jerusalem were to be transformed (*mutata*) and filled with joy. Bishop Richard yearned to free the clergy from the yoke of tyranny and the oppressive character of the old site, which blinded the eyes with dazzling chalk, deafened the ears with the rush of wind, and parched the throat for want of water, so assaulting the senses. The best part of man is freedom, and the valley of new Sarum was much preferable. So Richard moved both the city and the church, which were resurrected on the new site: Oh wonder of renewal! – *O rerum novitas!* The valley was well watered, rich in fruit trees and full of natural life, indeed the hind was not afraid of the bear, nor the stag of the lion. Everywhere birdsong is to be heard, the nightingale and the lark. The fields are full of white lilies, violets and red roses. Here the busy workmen begin a new chapel (*cella nova*) of remarkable beauty which, although on humble ground, is of high standing. The church is begun beside a spring issuing waters clearer than crystal and sweeter than ambrosia, which one day will gladden the city with crops. Royal woods provide the timber, and beautiful flowers comfort the sick, for the virtue of herbs drives away harm. This is a paradise, and Adam would have preferred it to Eden; one can appreciate it all the more because it is directly related to experience. Happy the man who sees this work finished! Let the king give the materials, the bishop his aid and the masons their skill, for in this work will be seen the charity of the king, the love of the bishop and the faith of the craftsmen.

In comparison with the Metrical Life the shift of tone in this poem is striking, especially so if the attribution of both these works to Henry of Avranches is accepted. There are no learned retrospective classical allusions; instead the emphasis is on the *sensorium*, experience, and spiritual figures who are thoroughly prospective. Jerusalem – the cathedral and its city – is restored to a prelapsarian condition expressed through the imagery of fertility, not sterility. Marian themes are important. According to the text *De prima fundacione*, Poore intended to build a *camera* or abode for the chaste Virgin at Salisbury, and it was Mary herself who in a dream indicated to him the land, the Myrfield, where he was to establish his church in springtime, far from persecution by public power.[107] The poet deploys biblical ideas of the valley as a place of hope and salvation as found in the valley of Eshcol (Numbers 32: 9), the valley of vision in Isaiah 22: 1, and the well-watered valley in Isaiah 41: 18. Isaiah 11: 6–7 perhaps prompted the theme of wild animals living together peaceably. Water, verdure, bird life and the 'virgin' site reveal an undercurrent of sacramental, Marian and apocalyptic themes. So the songbirds presumably represent the New Song, the *canticum novum* of the Marian Psalm 97 sung at Matins on Saturday mornings, and the lilies and roses Mary's chastity, after Canticles 2: 1. The birds are also a type for the cathedral canons, who, formerly deafened by wind

52 Salisbury Cathedral, eastern crossing showing traces of vault paintings in right transept; those on the main vessel vaults are nineteenth-century restorations (© Crown copyright. NMR).

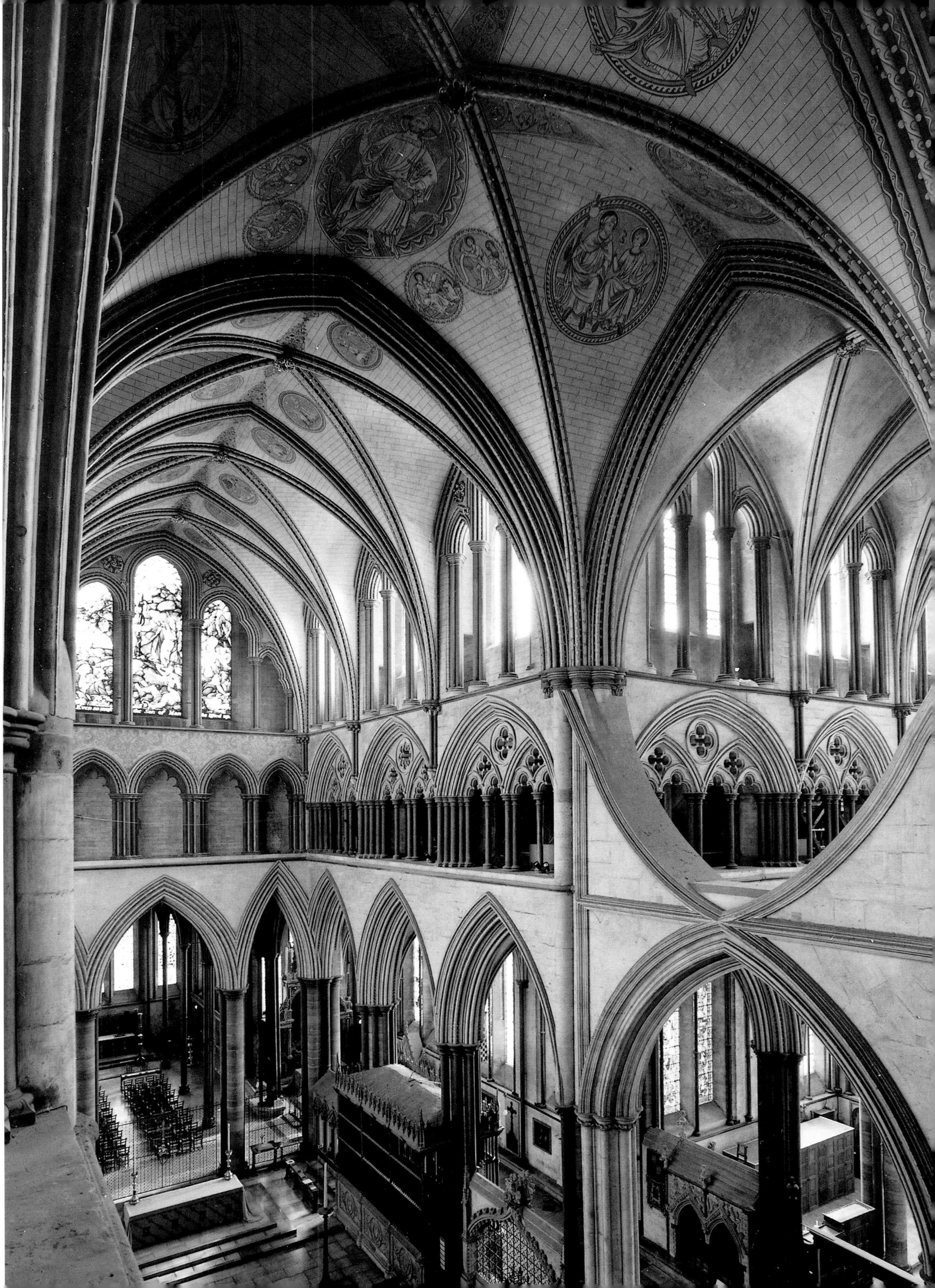

at Old Sarum, can now hear one another sing; and, perhaps as in the Metrical Life, birds themselves evoke liberty. Nature accordingly stands for the Living Church, a theme consolidated by reference to the valley's verdure which offers physical and spiritual nourishment, food and healing; and this new Jerusalem is watered by a spring clearer than crystal, foreshadowing the crystal waters of the Heavenly Jerusalem, Revelation 22: 1.

De translatione thus deftly promotes the political and liturgical interests of the cathedral chapter. Its terms had demonstrably been current at Salisbury before 1220. Some are anticipated around 1200 in the *Epistolae* of Peter of Blois (d. *c.* 1212), a canon of Old Sarum and a former employee of two archbishops of Canterbury, Richard and Baldwin.[108] In a letter to the chapter congratulating the decision to move, Peter observes that Old Sarum was a windy, sterile, arid, deserted and narrow place like Gilboa from which the canons rightly descended, like the sons of the prophets going down to the Jordan (II Kings 6: 1–2); the church was now delivered like the Ark from the Temple of Dagon. 'Let us descend joyfully to the plains where the valley abounds in corn, and where the fields are fertile'.[109] Reference to the canons being unable to hear one another sing is also found in the papal licence granted in 1218 which echoes the complaints of the chapter made in their petition.[110] The poet was clearly in touch with local sources, and it is worth recalling that Henry of Avranches displayed just this thoroughness in compiling the Metrical Life of St Hugh and his poem on the translation of St Thomas, which echoes the correspondence of Honorius III on that subject.[111]

The poem, although essentially no more than a piece of promotional writing, says at least something about the disposition of things at Salisbury around 1220, but it cannot remotely be described as offering a brief for the cathedral church itself, beyond tracing certain interests on the part of its commissioning circle. Indeed in some regards (if not all) it consorts ill with what was actually realized there. Salisbury is rightly celebrated as an instance of thoroughly regulated architectural planning, not only of the layout of the close, but also of the architectural forms for the great church itself, all of which was facilitated by the circumstances of a virgin site.[112] The cathedral is a consistent and deliberative building, much more carefully set out and detailed than, say, Lincoln.[113] The architecture is neat, repetitive and somewhat impersonal (fig. 52). It eschews wall arcading, by now a focus in great churches for the display of sculpted ornament; it has plain quadripartite rib vaulting and a lucidly rectangular east end rather than a polygonal chevet; it also uses variously coloured Purbeck marble throughout, with virtually all the most conspicuous detailing in marble being moulded not carved. Where foliated or figurated carving does occur, it is of high quality yet restricted application, as for instance on the corbels sustaining the short vault shafts.[114] Major foliated marble capitals are found only on the two main piers nearest the high altar, signalling its position.[115] The principal liturgical sectors of the church are thus demarcated by a subtle permutation of forms, and the whole is governed by a calm self-generating logic. In short, the 'cool, dry' tone and 'mechanical excellence' that Kidson rightly attributes to the church convey exactly the sense in which its values are those not of nature, but of culture.[116] There is no easy correspondence here with the Christian nature-imagery of *De translatione*, so easily and yet so misleadingly translatable in the mind into the visual language of Gothic 'naturalism'. Other sanctuaries – notably the great shrine-spaces at Ely (fig. 62) – show that the relationship between the organic and inorganic was a matter of lively and practical contemporary interest. At Salisbury the organic is calmed, neutered and then shed, and the rough made plain: the smooth regular manufacture of all the component parts instead celebrates the inorganic, the crystalline, the lapidary. If this is the New Jerusalem, it is the glossy Heavenly City of precious stones, like unto clear glass.

The relationship of Salisbury's serene, well-tempered architecture to the major projects at Canterbury, Wells and Lincoln, even Old Sarum, whether complete or under way, is in this regard rather telling.[117] Its stance was clearly both derivative and critical. Acknowledgement of Canterbury's Trinity Chapel and the work of English William is especially evident in the ultra-slim shafting and moulded capitals of the spectacular chapel of the same dedication at the cathedral's east end (fig. 54).[118] Lincoln is alluded to in other aspects, notably the form and distribution of the windows of the main elevations and the double-transept plan; and so the explicit rejection of Lincoln's aesthetic of vigorous, trenchant yet erratic carved detail is again likely to be significant.[119] The new canons' church at Wells, a precocious building under way from the late 1170s, had also set an important example, one of regional relevance to Salisbury, not least because it had adopted an early version of the Sarum customs and had some planning features in common.[120] Like Lincoln, Wells has a strong and highly individual aesthetic character, marked in its western parts under construction in 1220 by a bold and spirited use of carved plantiform motifs, and limited use of coloured marble. Salisbury reverses these priorities: internal sculpture is strictly controlled and the use of marble boosted. Wells also makes great play with bold figurative capital and corbel sculptures which, as at Lincoln (fig. 53), include bust-length figures sustaining the vault shafts in the transepts. But such showy, classicizing – and perhaps in their opinion trite and old-fashioned – self-dramatization of architecture was by and large not to the high-minded taste of the Salisbury chapter, for at Salisbury corbel heads are used extensively but remain very small in relation to the overall scale of the elevations, and are placed high up.

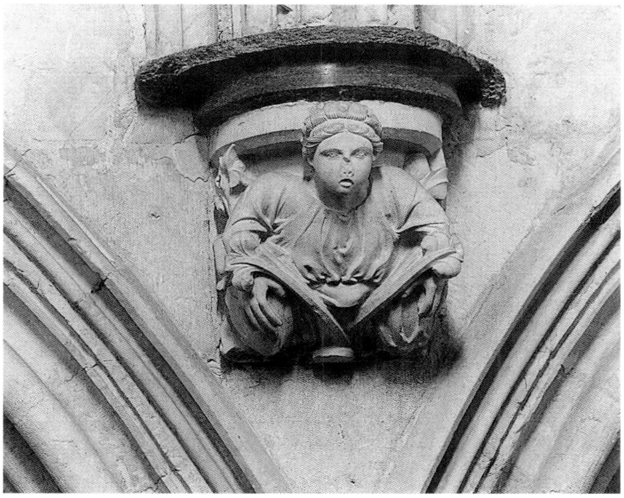

53 Lincoln Cathedral, high vault corbel in eastern transept (Conway Library, Courtauld Institute of Art).

Salisbury's particular refinement could be said to mark a conscious departure from the breadth and opulent *gravitas* of the Canterbury-Lincoln manner, almost a deliberate de-Romanization. Formalist commentaries have accounted for this process in terms of High Gothic tendencies to reduce surface ornamentation and to integrate forms in a new and exacting way, for example through the use of so-called 'dying' mouldings, which call into question the familiar contrast between Salisbury as a paradigm of 'Englishness' and contemporary French Gothic buildings such as Amiens.[121] By this reading, Salisbury is essentially a modern building, indeed 'the very model of Gothic modernity'.[122] In this respect if no other, *De translatione*, with its avoidance of classical imagery and its forward-looking spiritual tone, points to a consonance of sorts with the building. But the sense in which it does so is strictly speaking analogistic: the freshness and independence of Salisbury are analogous to the 'Langtonian' programme of emancipation, blessed renewal, *novitas*: the former things are swept away, *quae prima abierunt* (Revelation 21: 4).[123] Salisbury as it were

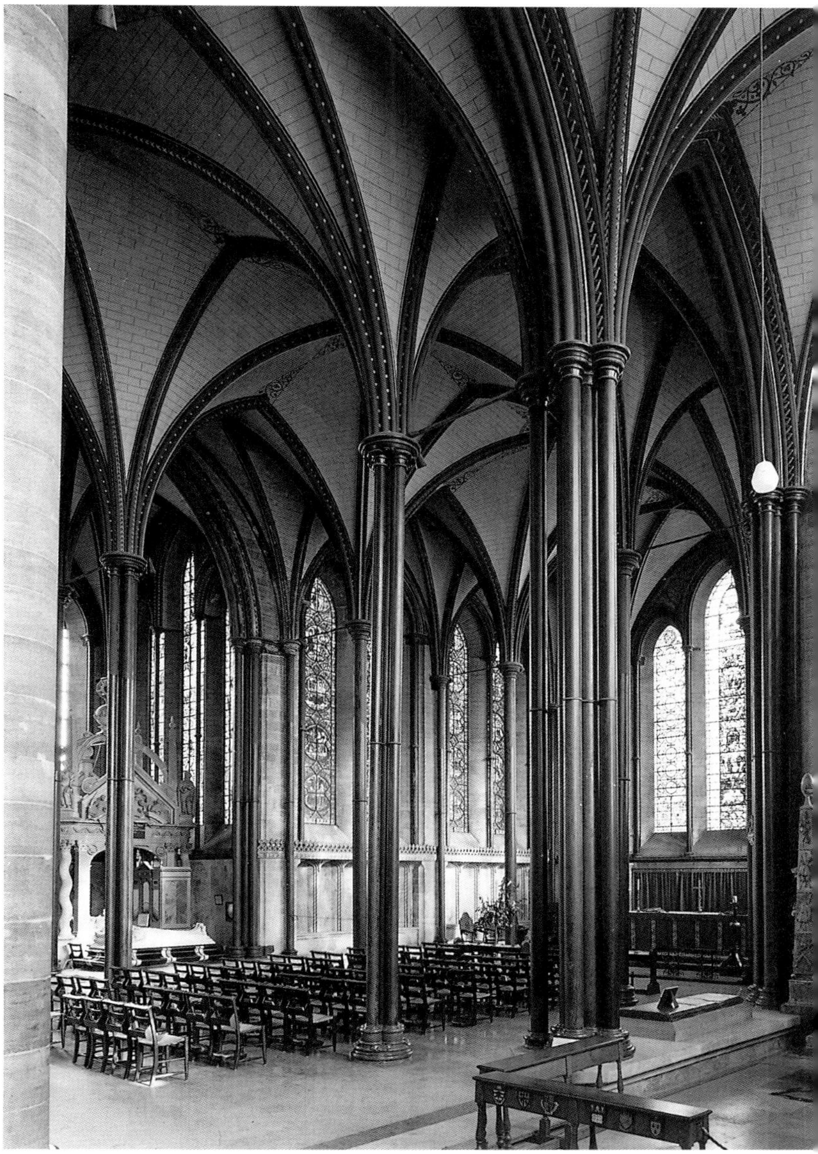

54 Salisbury Cathedral, Trinity Chapel (© Crown copyright. NMR).

manifests not only the politics, but the aesthetics of Langtonian emancipation from the old order, construed spiritually, politically, aesthetically: to pursue the figure, it speaks the language of the *moderni*, not the *antiqui*.

Just how far such analogies can and should be taken is a matter of opinion. Virginia Jansen, in her interventions on the aesthetic of a series of buildings in southern England erected between around 1215 and 1240, including Salisbury, the archbishop's palace chapel at Lambeth and the choir of the Temple Church in London (fig. 55), went so far as to see in these buildings a tech-

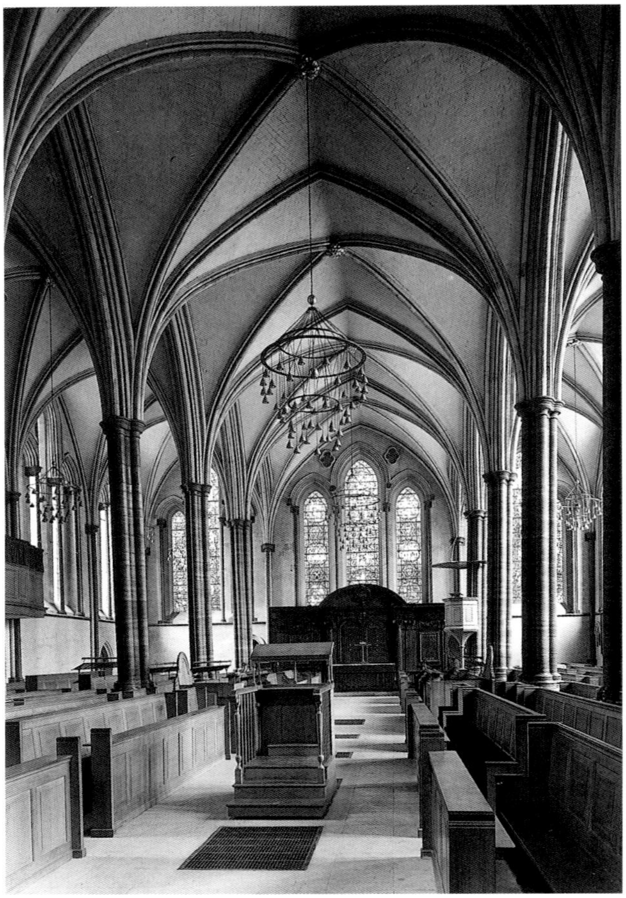

55 London, Temple Church, looking east (A.F. Kersting).

nically disciplined 'mode' of restraint and regularity, which reflects the type of patronage that might be expected of the Langtonians as highly trained reformist administrators: 'The southern Gothic architectural manner seems in keeping with what one might imagine such bureaucrats' minds to be – clear cut, systematic, and tidy.'[124] This theory, while cavilling at Brieger's generalization about an 'Episcopal Style', nevertheless derives from Brieger an interest in what he called the 'needs and conceptions of the English secular clergy', and attributes to that group what Jansen in turn calls a 'kind of world outlook' or 'mental structure' objectified in the architecture.[125] This 'world outlook' may also have been shaped by contact with the Paris schools or with the Cistercians: thus, while in Paris, Richard Poore 'would surely have been exposed to Peter the Chanter's remarks about the extravagance of church building. Peter was probably Langton's teacher and Langton was Richard Poore's'.[126] A version of this theory, which links this mode of thought to the functionalist consideration of architecture and liturgical codification in the Use of Sarum, is also advanced by Peter Draper, who sees in Salisbury 'a conscious selection of features designed to ensure that the church maintained due decorum as a model cathedral of the reform movement', a 'due decorum' which is exhibited in the Use and in the self-conscious dialectical positioning of Salisbury in relation to its major points of reference at Canterbury, Wells and Lincoln.[127] Salisbury thus manifests a 'fine balance between cathedral grandeur and ordered simplicity' attributable again to the influence of Richard Poore.[128]

The echoes here are not so much of Brieger as of Panofsky's cultural holism. Panofsky's *Gothic Architecture and Scholasticism* (1951) postulates 'intrinsic analogies' between the 'mental habit' of French twelfth- and thirteenth-century scholastic thought and the dialectical *modus operandi* and final outcome of French Gothic architecture of this period.[129] At Salisbury the terms of debate have changed only slightly: the building is informed by the 'mental structures' of ascetically minded reform, scholasticism as it were colonizing English architectural practice at one remove via reform, through the pastoral spread of moral theology and a codified and decorous liturgy. The impact of the schools is not upon the allegorical understanding or formal *modus operandi* of such buildings, but upon their ethical content as vested in a sense of decorum. Salisbury, in Wölfflinian terms, accordingly manifests a classical equilibrium.[130]

In considering this illuminating but analogistic *aperçu*, two general points must be made. First, Salisbury cannot be regarded as the very embodiment of everything that Peter the Chanter or Alexander Nequam would have approved of in building. Two features of the building are, superficially, in line with the ascetic doctrine as it had been formulated in the twelfth century: its lack of any military detailing (*propugnacula*) and its lack of substantial towers of the type the ascetics identified with episcopal pride. This absence of military detailing might be viewed in the context of emancipation from the embattled context of Old Sarum; it might reflect the more general ecclesiastical wariness of military culture, which Becket himself had echoed just before his martyrdom, when he ordered that the church's doors should not be closed to the knights because it was not fitting that the church should be turned into a fortress.[131] But this current of thought was very widespread, and was not necessarily inherently reformist: English ecclesiastical architecture had started to part company with military building aesthetically in the previous century, and crenellation was not yet definitely used on major English Gothic churches before about 1240; towers of prodigious scale are not on the whole a feature of early thirteenth-

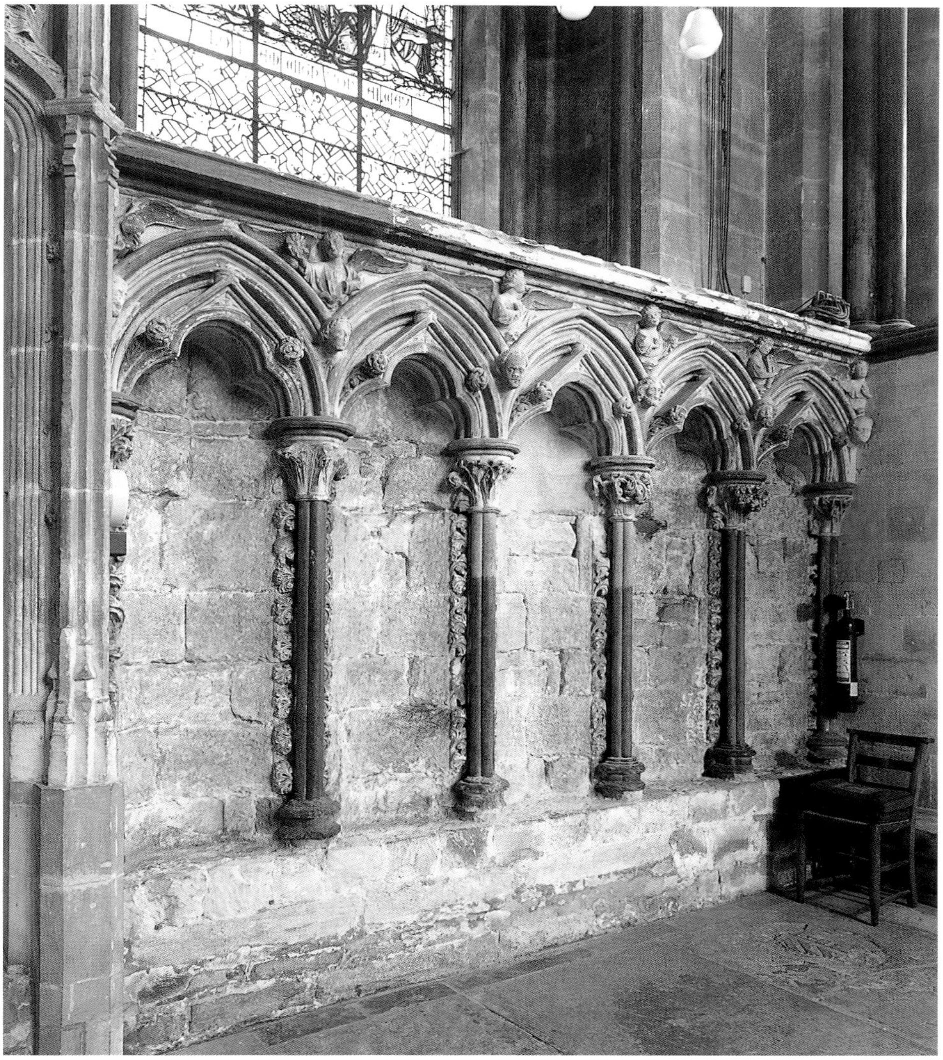

56 Salisbury Cathedral, section of pulpitum screen (reset) (Conway Library, Courtauld Institute of Art).

century church building, though Salisbury had a very substantial free-standing stone belfry.[132] Salisbury is no more or less feudal in appearance than any other great church of the age. And the anti-militaristic position was anyway being subverted by a palpable shift within pastoral writing of the twelfth and especially thirteenth centuries towards a more positive regard for the spiritual signification of military metaphors, especially in England (see also p. 184 below).[133] The cathedral may even have been crenellated in the fourteenth century.[134] Again, because it was a public church of note, Salisbury's commissioners felt compelled to use Purbeck marble throughout its interior, risking the charge – if such a charge be taken seriously – that they were indulging in the sumptuousness that attended upon the use of polished marble adornments. Though tempered by the 'discipline of the lathe' rather than foliate carving, this aesthetic was by now inextricably identified with magnificent building, as were the complex mouldings of the main arcade and triforium arches.[135] Salisbury's mid-thirteenth-century scheme of vault paintings in the eastern arm and transepts is orderly and conventional (fig. 52), eschewing the drolleries found in comparable monastic schemes such as the painted nave ceiling of the same period at Peterborough Abbey.[136] Yet its west facade and fine, cheerfully sculpted and illuminated pulpitum are opulent enough, and were presumably sanctioned by the chapter (fig. 56).[137] Salisbury shows that the practicalities of designing and furnishing a great secular church tended to entail a certain eclecticism; and eclecticism is seldom compatible with hard-line aesthetic ideologies.

A second consideration is the lack of direct and clear evidence for what the Langtonians actually thought about architecture, and for the contention that what they thought differed seriously from the other reformist members of the episcopal class. The premise that they manifested a sort of ascetic 'group thinking' is open to serious question. There seems to have been no tradition of architectural critique at Salisbury. In her study of the twelfth-century manuscripts of Salisbury, Teresa Webber has shown that the canons had long since shed their interest in the more monastic aspects of discipline.[138] Peter of Blois, one of its canons, was familiar with the *Verbum abbreviatum*; yet, in his letter to the chapter celebrating their decision to move to the new site, he invoked Ezekiel's vision of the Temple (Ezekiel 40–48) and Solomon's example, biblical types of great spiritual building which in Ezekiel's case had prompted important Victorine commentary.[139] The vision of Langton's 'reverent sobriety' and study with Peter the Chanter owes much to Powicke's view of him in 1928, which even Powicke himself later abrogated.[140] In recognizing the importance of Peter and his circle, one does him little service in assuming that his ideas were always there to be poached, let alone applied, in a mechanical fashion. It is by no means clear that the circumstantial links between Poore, Langton and Peter the Chanter extended to all their intellectual and moral sympathies. Langton's christology and his biblical commentaries were influenced by Peter the Lombard and the Victorines, and his sacramental theology and Bible study by the Chanter, whose work he cites.[141] His intellectual background was eclectic. Langton himself was preoccupied with liturgical reform, the conduct of clergy and penitential theology; and like Peter the Chanter he inveighed against usury and the 'lucrative' professional arts.[142] Langton had views quite different from those of Peter on key issues such as the debate about the moment of consecration of the Host at Mass.[143] And there seems to be no evidence from his *Questiones* that Langton cared morally about architecture; his principal concern – much in line with the norms of moral theology – seems to have been that buildings should not be raised on ill-gotten gains, from usury or prostitution.[144] Concerns about superfluity in building appear not to have entered the pastoral literature burgeoning in England in this period. Poore might in theory have encountered the homilies of Gervase of Chichester when he himself was Bishop of Chichester; but of this there is no proof. The notion that Langton or Poore might have subscribed to, or even noted, the utilitarian or ascetic position of the twelfth-century moralists simply on the grounds that they had been Paris masters is therefore no more than an interesting but uncorroborated assumption, which evidence from other chapters tends to contradict or at least qualify. Finally, actions speak louder than words: as primate, Langton was in receipt of saints' Lives that eulogized splendid architecture; as a patron, he had presided over the completion of the country's largest and most splendid episcopal great hall, and (with Poore) its most magnificent shrine, in the very year that Salisbury was begun.

This raises the issue of patronage and individual agency. Richard Poore was as much the patron of Salisbury as St Hugh was of Lincoln.[145] When Matthew Paris praised him for summoning noble artificers from distant parts (*a remotis*) for the construction of Salisbury Cathedral in 1220, he was using conventional language that paid traditional regard to the idea of the great churchman as the efficient cause of a work.[146] Poore made the land, part of his own domain, available and undoubtedly acted as a driving force.[147] Yet Poore, unlike Hugh of Northwold at Ely or Jocelin of Wells at their churches, appears not to have been buried at Salisbury, as might have been expected of a founder.[148] Nor did he take the style with him to Durham in 1228, in the way that he undoubtedly took his diocesan statutes.[149] Indeed the Bishop of Salisbury, though a member of the chapter, was tending to lose power to it and to the dean at this time, following the new consuetudinary of around 1210 and the *Nova constitutio* of around 1215.[150] The cathedral itself was demonstrably not funded by Poore in the way, for example, that the retrochoir of Ely was funded by Hugh of Northwold. In 1218–19 the chapter had pledged a quarter of its annual prebendal income to the fabric for seven years, and presumably commissioned Henry of Avranches to write the fund-raising poem, *De translatione*, as part of this effort.[151] The new dean, de Wanda, is likely to have been a significant figure in the new project, but of his mental preparation little is known. In pointing to the chapter of Salisbury and its presumed values, one is forced back onto the character of a collective to which a 'world outlook' can be attributed only with some risk: one needs a 'Langtonian' chapter as well. There is something to be said for tracing in Salisbury's bland idiom the mindset of a chapter committee.[152] Yet, if the canons of Salisbury were motivated by an aesthetic allegiance as a matter of policy, they did not enforce it at all their prebendal churches: so the prebendal church at Potterne on an episcopal manor was rebuilt after 1220 in a style reminiscent of the cathedral; since it was Elias of Dereham's church, however, it is unclear what should be ascribed to the chapter or to his direct intervention.[153] Again, the distant parish church of Grantham was a prebendal church of Salisbury, but its idiom was informed not by Salisbury but by its diocesan church, Lincoln, a pointer to the pragmatic dominance of regional idioms.[154]

Similarly, the Use of Sarum as reformulated by Richard Poore can be seen as the product of a certain highly organized mindset and as an instance of a clerical desire to create well-codified universal exemplars. In this connection it should be remembered that the new Use developed older Sarum regulations which had given Salisbury authority as the main source of orderly written constitutions for secular clergy long before 1200.[155] The metropolitan Church, Canterbury, of course had a monastic use. Salisbury was immensely proud of its liturgical authority, seeing itself as a sun in the firmament in relation to liturgy.[156] There can be no doubt that understanding Salisbury's liturgical customs yields a fuller comprehension of the nature of the building. Yet the aesthetic implications of such customs – their sense of decorum – are less clear when extended beyond the bounds of the human ritual *habitus* to that of architecture.[157] Indeed, the history of the rapid adoption of the new constitutional and liturgical practices of Salisbury by many English churches in the Province of Canterbury by the early fourteenth century – not later, as is often thought – may militate against the idea that it was associated with a specific sense of decorum.[158] Nigel Morgan states that 'the Use of Sarum had been in part or wholly introduced in all dioceses in the province of Canterbury, Hereford excepted, by 1325'.[159] In effect the Use was quickly adopted for churches which, despite very basic functional similarities of planning, were built or rebuilt according to very different, usually regional, tastes. Salisbury's art and its customs could be detached. This warns against seeing Salisbury too readily as the product of some sort of unscripted legislative aesthetic.

The other issue of agency concerns the architect, and the vexed question of the role of Elias of Dereham. Elias held the common fund of Salisbury Cathedral from 1224 as well as its fabric fund from 1225, and in one early source is identified as the *rector* of the cathedral's fabric.[160] Elias was in the first instance a clerk designated (though on what grounds is unclear) as *magister*, who enjoyed a distinguished career as a church administrator. He was steward to numerous prelates, including Hubert Walter, Jocelin of Bath, Stephen Langton and possibly Gilbert Glanvill of Rochester; he was also executor for Hubert, Stephen, Richard Grant, Peter des Roches, Richard Poore, Hugh of Lincoln and William Marshall, Earl of Pembroke.[161] Elias tended to crop up at times and locations where major building works were under way. He was made a canon of Salisbury (Potterne and Lavington) around 1220–22, and was also a canon of Wells (Litton).[162] He had been exiled for his support of Louis of France in 1216 and returned to England around 1219 to Langton's household; and it was presumably with Langton's support that he was moved to assist Richard Poore at Salisbury.[163] Elias was a beneficiary of Langton's rising fortunes, and his work on St Thomas's shrine at Canterbury also came about through Langton's influence. Matthew Paris's account of the manufacture of the shrine of St Thomas for the translation in 1220 praises Elias, together with the St Albans artist Walter of Colchester, as *artifex incomparabilis*.[164] This description of him as an *artifex* must be taken seriously, for there were other connections between the two men which show that Matthew's knowledge was more than casual. It was almost certainly from Elias himself as fund manager at Salisbury that Matthew gained access to *De translatione*, which he copied into MS Dd. 11. 78 (p. 65 above); Elias also possibly availed Matthew of the text of Magna Carta which Elias had handled at the time of its distribution, and which Matthew thoroughly garbled.[165] Matthew noted his death in 1245 in the *Chronica majora*.[166]

Whether or not he was actually the architect of Salisbury Cathedral – a recently rehabilitated view – Elias indubitably acted for several patrons as a favoured guru of good building.[167] He assisted Ela, Countess of Salisbury, in the establishment and building of the charterhouse at Hinton, and on these grounds alone can probably be identified as a 'churchwright'.[168] In 1233 Henry III mandated that windows in a chamber at Winchester Castle should be built to the specification of Elias.[169] At Salisbury, according to a deed of 1232, Elias had built a canon's house at considerable expense intended for his own use, namely the Leadenhall (demolished in the early twentieth century) on the west walk of the close (fig. 57). Canons had been expected to build their own houses as part of the project of 1220.[170] Elias's was dedicated to the Virgin Mary and was intended by him to be an *exemplum* or pattern for the other canons' houses on the site.[171] It may have formed but a part of larger plans drawn up by Elias for the disposition of the new cathedral town and its waterways.[172]

All the buildings linked idiomatically to Salisbury Cathedral and its close are in the south of England, and some, including the Palace Chapel at Lambeth and the Great Hall at Winchester Castle (fig. 58), either have features in common with the known work of Elias of Dereham, or are documented as having been produced under his advice. It takes only a slight shift of angle for one to see these features not as products of the patronage of Poore or Langton, but of the guiding hand of Elias

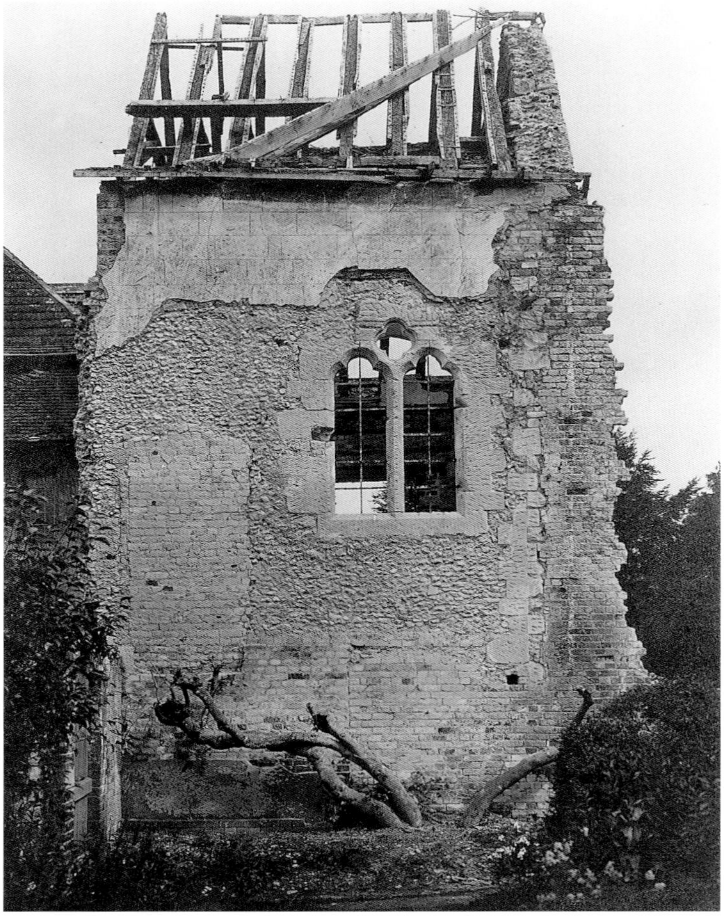

57 Salisbury Cathedral close, the Leadenhall of Elias of Dereham (reproduced by permission of English Heritage. NMR).

himself.[173] Elias's career is exactly of the sort to explain the coalescence of style of a small group of buildings now labelled 'Langtonian'. Yet Elias, though a key common agent in these buildings and also a member of the *familia* of Langton, was not necessarily exclusively 'Langtonian' in outlook.[174] Like Henry of Avranches, he was mobile in his allegiances, for like Henry he was connected both with Langton and, after his death in 1228, Langton's antagonist Peter des Roches, Bishop of Winchester. He assisted des Roches with his new religious houses of Selborne and Titchfield; he provided designs for the royal palace at Winchester under des Roches's supervision; he was the bishop's regular guest in the 1230s, and finally his executor in 1238.[175] In the same period he was also employed by the 'Langtonian' Archbishop of Canterbury, Edmund of Abingdon, in planning a new house for secular canons at Maidstone.[176] This is not the career path of the ideologue, but of the pragmatist or well-placed opportunist, for des Roches was at the height of power at court in 1232–4 and may have brought Elias to the attention of Henry III. Nicholas Vincent indeed has noted his 'apparent ability to span the gulf between bitterly opposed political factions'.[177] Elias was in exactly the kind of position not only to generate designs but to transmit them beyond the bounds, ideological and practical, of the various coteries for which he worked.

And such designs were rapidly adopted for buildings whose association with the Church and clerical interests was at best indirect. Their entrance into the secular domain takes me back to my earlier statement that church Gothic in this period was not some categorically segregated and decontaminated arena of 'reformed' architectural activity. Domestic buildings for episcopal or seigneurial use are a case in point: Gothic 'crossed' building types. The great halls at Canterbury and Winchester, which are certainly closely tied to Elias's idiom, have been cited as instances of the southern English 'Langtonian' style.[178] Canterbury's hall was also selected specifically by Henry III as the example for his new hall at Dublin in 1243: royal and seigneurial halls

58 Winchester Castle, the Great Hall (Conway Library, Courtauld Institute of Art).

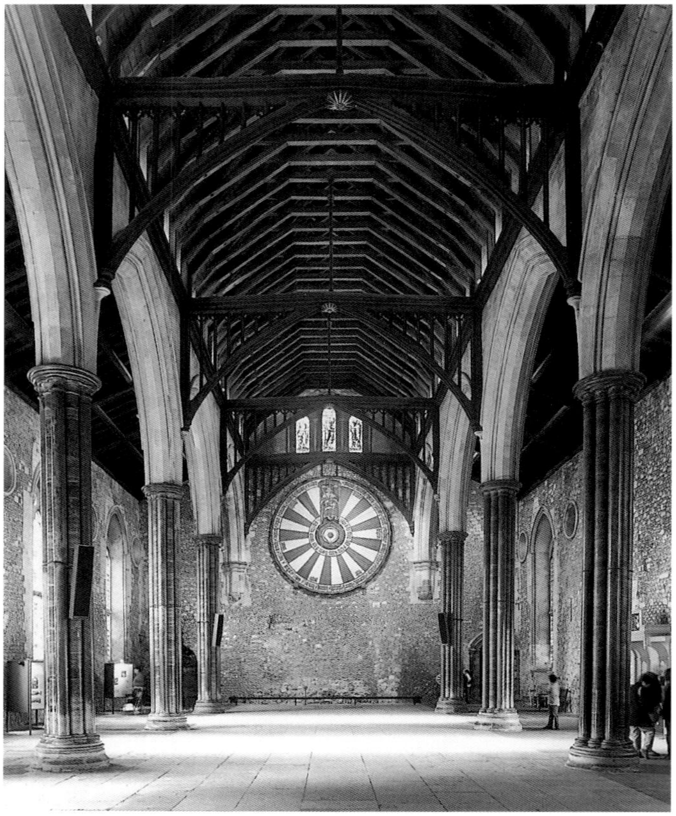

demonstrably had much in common. It was precisely to the neat, elegant and well-executed architectural repertory of his domestic buildings, his chambers and halls, that Henry III's mandates attached the old-fashioned, conventional and morally untroubled vocabulary of *decens*, *pulcher* and *sumptuosas*.[179] The same terminology was used in the 1232 deed relating to Elias's Leadenhall, the 'mansion house sumptuously built' (*domus mansionis [. . .] sumptuose constructa*) which also made careful provision for its use by his successors in order that a hundred poor persons might be fed annually on the anniversary of his death, and which was so expensive to build that his successors there were left to pay for it.[180] This provides at least one instance of architecture at Salisbury referred to by contemporaries both as an *exemplum* and as sumptuous. As discussed above, in the context of the ethical formulation of Becket's conduct, great halls were allied in theory and practice to magnificent conduct and to its natural corollary, charitable largesse, the key political virtue of great men.[181] Temporal and spiritual lordship shared an ethical framework.[182] This aristocratic notion of exemplary public and magnanimous virtue was to influence the iconography not only of royal palace chambers but of the cathedral chapters in the thirteenth century, as at Salisbury Cathedral itself, the chapter house-portal of which depicts the virtues and vices (or sins, see p. 188) including *Largitas* overcoming *Avaritia* (fig. 156).[183] In the true spirit of aristocratic magnanimity, riches should be expended for pastoral, or political, ends as well as in the name of charity. As the motto in Henry III's great chamber put it, *Ke ne dune ke ne tine ne prent ke desire*: Spend, and God shall send.[184]

There could, however, be no doubt that the great diocesan churches were intended to outstrip any lordly building, no matter how grand. Salisbury is no more an ascetic building than Lincoln, their very real differences notwithstanding. Indeed its character might quite as well be said to benefit from the 'reciprocal illumination' offered less by the ultimately stoic ascetic critique, than by Aristotle's discussion of temperance, in which magnanimity appears as the mean between pettiness and vulgarity, in Books 2 and 3 of the *Ethics*, the *Ethica vetus* or 'Old Ethics'. As architecture, Salisbury could be said to have a certain Aristotelian coolness. Again, this is a figure, an analogy, and should be seen as such: it would be rash to argue that Salisbury was in any straightforward causal sense the outcome of the new learning. Yet something stopped Salisbury being either mean or vulgar. If one is to play the analogy game, one might as well consider the widest possible range of historically feasible analogies. It is justifiable to raise Aristotle's ethical writings because these texts were to be found in the curriculum of the schools, were not prohibited like some of Aristotle's other works, and were certainly known to such Oxford-educated scholars as Robert Grosseteste, whose slightly later (1240s) translation of the entire Ethics remained a standard version.[185] Henry of Avranches's sentiment in *De translatione* that 'experience makes pleasures sweet' would not have been inappropriate for a cathedral chapter familiar with Aristotle's thought on pleasure and the senses.[186] According to the Pontigny Life of St Edmund of Abingdon, treasurer of Salisbury from 1222, even the ascetic saint-bishop recognized that largesse (magnificence without gain) was a means to obtaining pastoral influence: he freely entertained at his table courtiers and men of the world, so that he could draw them to the love of God. We have already encountered something like this pragmatic view in Gervase of Chichester's thoughts on the Church and public power (p. 31 above). If this really was Edmund's view, rather than one attributed to him by his later hagiographers, it too reveals an outlook not uncongenial to Aristotelian ethics.[187]

Such tempered magnificence, then, was no more reformist in origin or intent than it was solely ecclesiastical in character: as the great halls and their associated ideals of conduct indicate, its character was also lordly. One index of this is provided by Westminster Abbey, for Westminster's debt to this southern English current of building, and to details of Salisbury itself, is evident and recognized. Henry of Reyns elected to place in the abbey four-shaft marble piers with plain moulded capitals (like those at Salisbury) directly by the shrine of St Edward, one of the richest in the kingdom (fig. 59).[188] In most other respects, Westminster took the Salisbury aesthetic a few notches up the scale of richness to assert parity with the greatest national and international shrine-churches. It was the paradigm of a certain calculated, but entirely sumptuous, aristocratic heterogeneity: in the words of Innocent IV's bull of 1245 granting indulgences in aid of its construction, *opere plurimum sumptuoso*.[189] The long-standing notion that architecture should embody the political virtue of magnificent patronage, *megaloprepeia*, was perfectly fulfilled. The two buildings occupy different places on the scale of decorum appropriate for such buildings; but that they occupy the same scale is undeniable, and to deny the fact is to render the relationship between them incomprehensible.

Caesar, quite as much as God, was the ultimate beneficiary of ideas whose character was formed at the juncture, never harshly drawn at the time, between the aristocratic and the ascetic; and these ideas are explored further in relation to the character of thirteenth-century sainthood in the next part of this book. But in express-

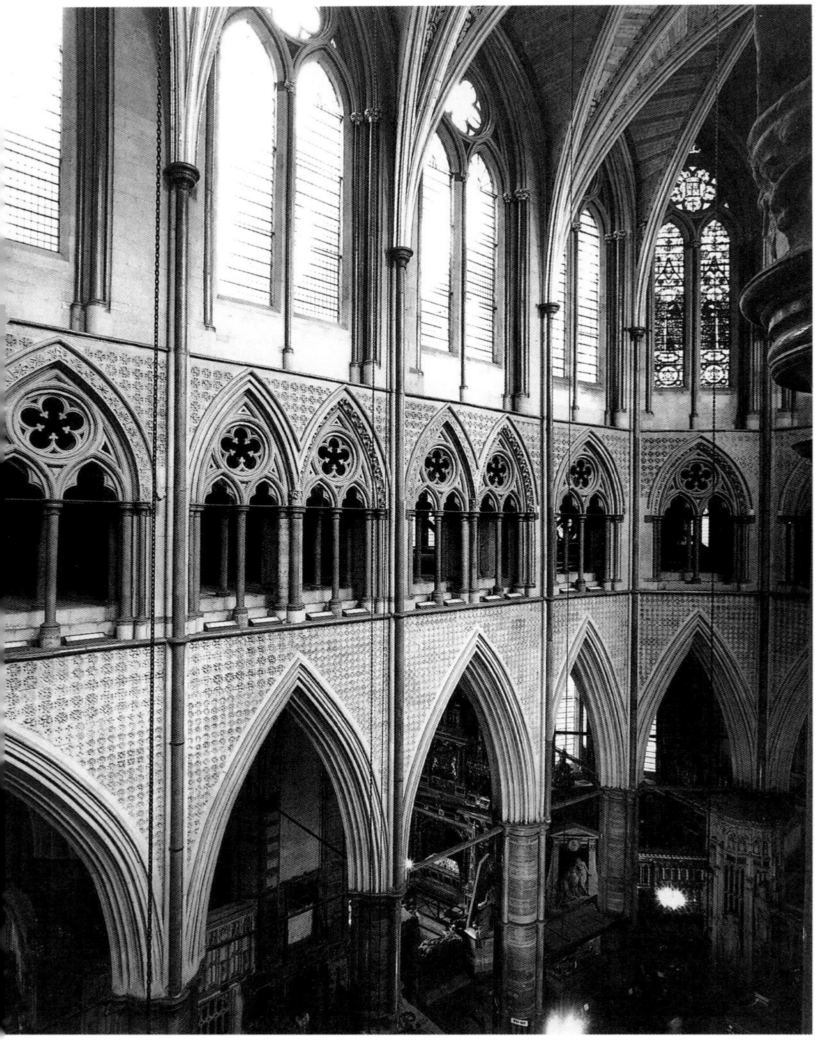

59 Westminster Abbey, main elevation of presbytery and apse (Conway Library, Courtauld Institute of Art).

ing some scepticism about the 'reformist' character of Salisbury and related buildings, one should not lose sight of the more fundamental insight that this theory, however undemonstrable, affords. 'Langtonianism' as an aesthetic current, if such it was, was dead by about 1250. Yet great church and great palace building in this period was gaining in self-consciousness. At Westminster Abbey from 1245, Henry of Reyns made calculated allusions to various northern French buildings that were selected as models for their ideological character (Reims Cathedral, the Sainte-Chapelle in Paris), showing that the notion that buildings could be given a conscious form for political, ethical or religious reasons had now entered the bloodstream of royal patronage.[190] It was precisely diocesan buildings like Salisbury that Westminster was intended to outstrip, as an assertion of Henry III's elevated conception of monarchy. Westminster differs from Salisbury because much more evidence survives about the discourses that framed it. Henry's many mandates relating to his art patronage indicate the discrimination of a thoughtful and restless patron strategically aware of issues of location, taste, materials and subject-matter in relation to the tropological, spiritual, even psychological, character of government and devotion.[191] His art is in a sense the first well-documented 'moralized' art in England.

Yet courts in England operated in practice, not in theory. Theory was the preserve of churchmen. Earlier I asked what the practical consequences of the ascetic doctrine might have been for actual building. The answer is that the ascetic doctrines of the twelfth-century clerks and monks had little, if any, significant direct impact on English Gothic architecture. Reformist arguments about the relationship of the Church to public power failed, at Canterbury, Lincoln and arguably at Salisbury, to shake the fundamental assumption that great church building should embody an aesthetic of magnificence not unworthy of public power. What supported this assumption was an historical fact: the diocesan Church could – and therefore inevitably did – build magnificently, and with the latest technologies. It embraced modernity because its thinking was practical, and attuned to an era of renovation: the most interesting writings on architecture coincided with the great age of saint creation in England. The older order of praise – and blame – was passing away with the emergence of a consensus that accepted that magnificent church building was pastorally appropriate to the secular Church. The rise of monarchy as a serious agent in commissioning great church building can only have consolidated this process. Slowly, the ascetic viewpoint was retreating to the domain of the monastic and mendicant orders. Similar patterns almost certainly applied in France. The gulf there between the position in, say, 1180 and 1280 may be measured by the warm praise accorded in 1272 to the 'wonderful height and size' of the new choir of Beauvais Cathedral, the mighty vaults of which were to collapse in 1284 without any surviving high-minded comment at all about the hubris of architects and their over-mighty buildings.[192] The pragmatic acceptance, indeed harnessing, of progress is a pattern encountered at various points in this book. The schoolmen of the age of reform had learned to think in new ways about art and patronage. They had the most sophisticated ethical and symbolical language with which to reason about it, whatever their exact stance. They raised the stakes intellectually. Their capacity to invest buildings with significance, allegorical or political, went undimmed. Possibly too – and here scholarly research needs developing – they may have thought of new and better ways of producing great church architecture: the idiom of Salisbury and of Elias may in the end have been a product less of a specific and highly theorized ethos, than of a method of exemplary building-site management. Such a method was developing within that 'charmed circle' of the new administrative hierarchy to which Elias, for all the mystery surrounding him, undoubtedly belonged.[193]

The notion that architecture, art and social conduct could be shaped at least in theory by a fundamentally utilitarian ethos entailed that the domain of legislative aesthetics was to be greatly increased in the thirteenth century as its central ideas came to influence and infiltrate the major pastoral mission of the secular Church. The lesson of masters and morals was one component in the formation of the new ethically and psychologically sophisticated arts known as Gothic. And in these arts the saints, too, found their voice: if the ethical ideals traced in this part of my book enjoyed a haphazard fate in regard to church building, in the sphere of the regulation of human conduct and the sanctification of its myths and ideals, the position was very different.

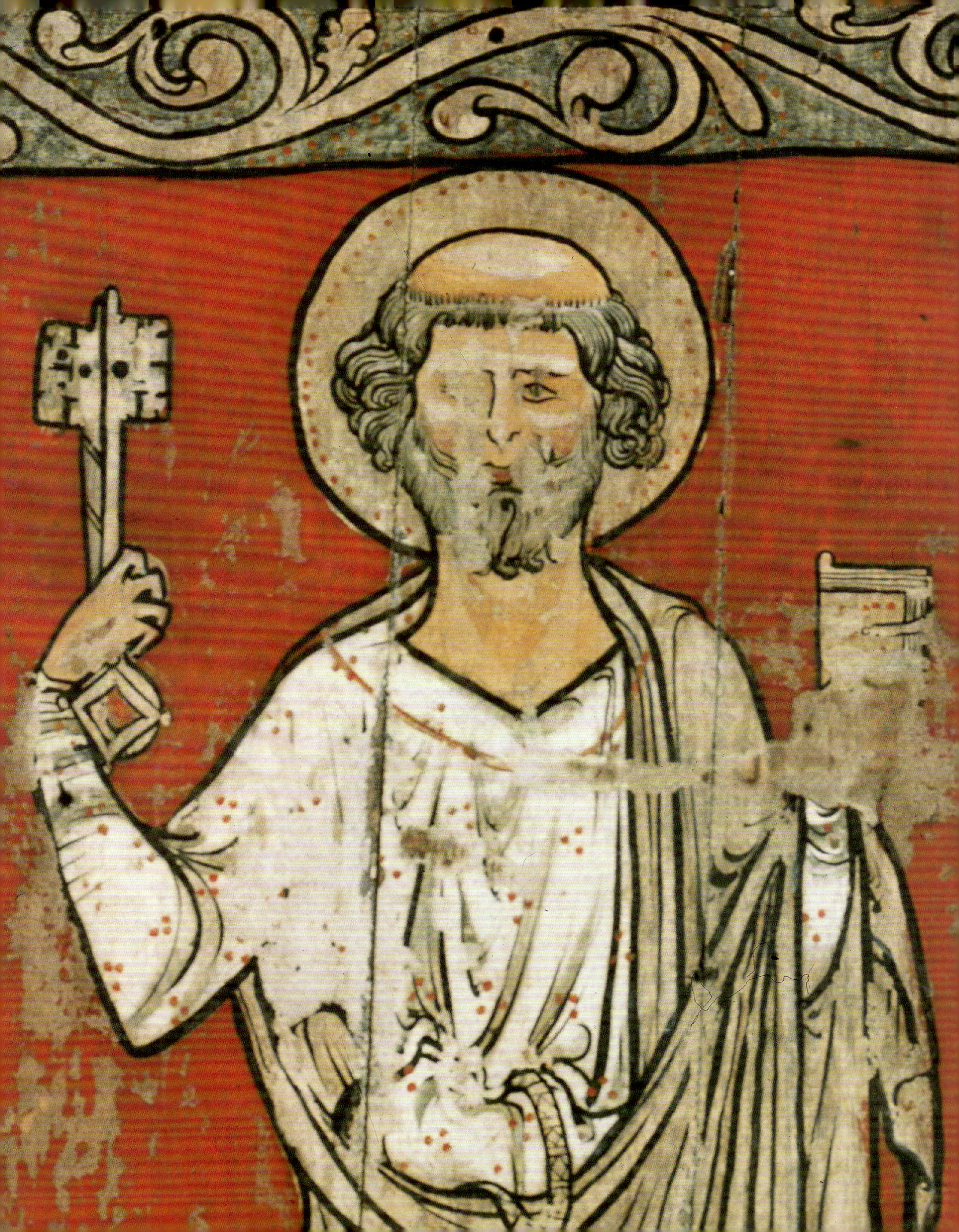

Part II

SANCTIFICATION

FACING PAGE St Peter. Tabernacle wing from Fåberg parish church, Norway (detail of fig. 143).

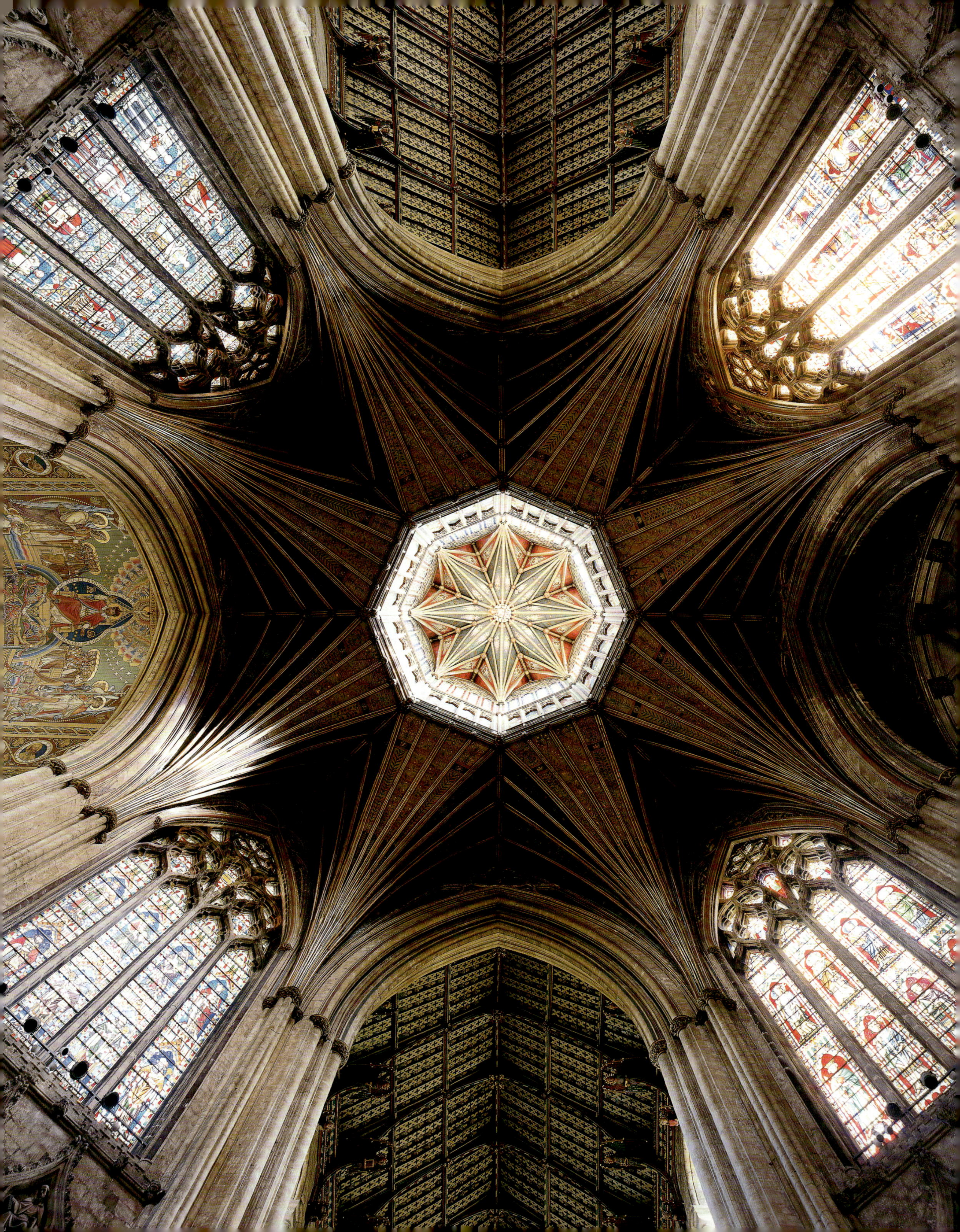

Chapter 4

VIRIDITAS: ELY AND ST ETHELDREDA

Thus unconscious stones enclose the mysteries of animate ones.
Henry of Avranches, *The Metrical Life of St Hugh*

Patterns of Sanctity

In 1250 the talented and pugnacious Benedictine historian Matthew Paris drew breath from his manifold tasks in order to summarize in his *Chronica majora* the remarkable events of the previous half-century, a time of apocalyptic prodigies and novelties of all types: eclipses, earthquakes, inundations and falling stars – all manner of 'signs in the sun'. The time indeed seemed to have returned which St Benedict, full of the spirit of the saints, had mentioned at the start of his Rule. For – to paraphrase Matthew – not only had mighty St Thomas been translated, and the gentle, learned and ascetic Archbishop of Canterbury, Edmund of Abingdon (d. 1240), been found incorrupt at Pontigny and canonized,[1] but even newer saints shone in England and displayed healing miracles, as at the tombs of Roger (Niger), Bishop of London, John of Foxtone, Robert, the brother of St Edmund of Abingdon, and the hermit Robert of Knaresborough.[2] St Elizabeth of Hungary and St Hildegard the prophetess had also proven their worth, as had Øystein Erlendsson in Norway, the rebuilder of Trondheim Cathedral.[3] At Lincoln, Robert Grosseteste and at Chichester, Richard Wyche (both d. 1253) brought forth their episcopal miracles, as if the time of the Apostles was being revived.[4] For Matthew, who actively celebrated the new saints in his Latin and vernacular hagiography, their virtues were those of his nation: they were both in, and of, England.[5] In fact, for all his love of human inventories, Matthew had underestimated the situation. The tally of canonizations and translations of English episcopal saints since the martyrdom of St Thomas, and indeed through much of his adult life (he was born around 1200) was proving phenomenal. Thomas was canonized in 1173, Wulfstan of Worcester in 1203, Hugh of Lincoln in 1220, Lawrence O'Toole (an Archbishop of Dublin) in 1225, William of York in 1227, Edmund of Abingdon in 1247 and Richard Wyche in 1262; and along with these elevations to sanctity there went a host of translations, in effect promotions, of other saints: the hermit St Neot, the Cistercian St Waltheof, St Birinus of Dorchester, St Wilfrid of Ripon and so on. Some cults – such as that of Robert Grosseteste, the formidable Bishop of Lincoln – 'failed'; other saints' bodies were moved or demoted in a period of unprecedented activity nation wide.[6] But the pattern was undoubtedly that of stirring times.

The remarkable rise in the frequency and range of canonization by Roman process in this period should be set against the fundamental continuities – continuities of type, as it were – that characterized the English landscape of sanctity. The courageous, and fundamentally valid, typological distinction drawn by André Vauchez between the aristocratic sainthood of north-western Europe and the more bourgeois or plebeian (rather than 'popular') forms of the Mediterranean world was never truer than for England, for this remained a country of 'holy sufferers', men and women who were born into, or who gained, high rank and whose styles of life and death entailed – or was held to have entailed – the trauma of inner or outer martyrdom.[7] As bishops joined and energized the ranks of this hierarchy, so it grew in scope and variety, but its essential characteristics remained strikingly stable. One reason for this was that the hierarchy was of great antiquity, sustained by substantial institutional sanction. The imprint of the cults of royal saints had been made long before the Conquest among the West Saxons and East Anglians: it was deep, ubiquitous and persistent.[8] The main lines of this style of sanctity were clear: kings or princes who attained physical mar-

60 Ely Cathedral, the octagon (John Crook).

tyrdom (notably Edmund of East Anglia and Edward the Martyr); and women who renounced their high-born station to embrace chastity and the monastic life (Edburga of Winchester, Etheldreda of Ely, Edith of Wilton) as well as those who fell somewhere in between, such as Guthlac, of royal stock, but eremitic inclination.[9]

Quite clearly too, England did not produce other forms of sanctity increasingly prominent in Europe, though the reasons for this extend well beyond the limits of this study. The position of women in this regard is especially interesting. The full extent of the vitality and depth of English female religious culture is beginning to be revealed and appreciated despite being hampered by a shortage of sources.[10] In England, female saints were extremely important, but also highly traditional. Such essentially monastic figures as St Etheldreda were cast from a mould of pre-Conquest royal origin. St Frideswide of Oxford (translated in 1180) belonged to the pattern of aristocratic renunciation, and her new cult owed much circumstantially to Becket's cult at Canterbury.[11] Yet while the existence of holy women was well established in England in the twelfth century, nothing could compare with the extremely diverse European circumstances that nurtured Hildegard of Bingen, Elizabeth of Marburg or such extraordinarily modern figures as Marie of Oignies or Juliana of Cornillon who led what one authority has described as the first 'women's movement' in Western history.[12] The English pattern of female observance was much more closely tied to monastic enclosure and reclusivity than the religious movements of the urban patriciates of the Low Countries and the Rhineland, Liège and Cologne, which produced the Beguines, unenclosed lay females aspiring to the religious life. Texts such as the *Ancrene Wisse* composed for female recluses show every sign of having been conceived for those from the gentle classes.[13] There was less diversity in England, even in the cities. Though Robert Grosseteste and Matthew Paris smiled benevolently upon the new Beguines as a model of female virtue and holy mendicancy, in England royal, monastic and especially diocesan control tended to marginalize and suppress the more extreme – and hence sometimes more revealing – manifestations of female religious independence and mystical and eucharistic piety seen in northern Europe; the prospects for female beatification and canonization were correspondingly dismal. England's religious scene was dominated to a vastly greater extent by the dense network of the rural and city parishes and enclosed monastic orders that created a different religious culture – quieter, less radical, more governed, than the exciting city cultures and eucharistic innovations across the North Sea. Papally sponsored reform in England placed greater limitations on the creation of the circumstances that were tending in northern Europe to produce new and radical forms of spirituality, especially among women; Canon 13 of the Fourth Lateran Council, for example, prevented the establishment of new enclosed orders.[14] This may also in part explain why the images of Francis and Dominic made much less impact on the parochial scene than in Italy. England produced very few saints of obviously humble origin and no education, such as the hermit St Godric of Finchale (d. 1170), whose miracles found a largely lower-class, female and local devotion: the hermits had once been the frontiersmen of sanctity.[15] The cult of relics in medieval England as a social, religious and political phenomenon, involving according to one estimate the relics of at least 644 saints in religious houses alone, was complex, and remains comparatively neglected: the English were the parishioners of saints of widely differing character and origin.[16] My concern here is necessarily limited to some outstanding examples of English sainthood and sanctity which made a manifest impact on the visual, pastoral and ethical culture of early Gothic England.

Vauchez's general distinction between different types of saint seems to hold up. It follows from the traditional character of English sanctity that one of its enduring features was its conservative and political nature; for these saints were above all upper-class patrons associated not with cities, but major ecclesiastical corporations. As such they were inextricably bound up with local institutional customs, rights and claims: they were the immortal members and protectors of the monastic and secular chapters, and before and after the Conquest they provided an enduring focus of loyalty and identity. In this their royal, monastic or episcopal character was important. Late twentieth-century authorities have indeed stressed the political origins of such cults as those of Edmund or Etheldreda, not least in the formation of mighty monastic establishments.[17] As Matthew Paris well knew, the greatest 'national' saints, Thomas, Alban, Edmund, Cuthbert and Edward presided over some of the oldest and wealthiest Benedictine houses.[18] At the Conquest, the main cathedral shrines were predominantly those of the bishops.[19] Hagiography was an important means of institutional self-promotion, and defence. It is not difficult to see how the interests of these establishments came to be closely bound up with the way in which their saints were presented, for example in the matter of monastic exemption from episcopal authority, which is a leitmotif of the hagiography of St Edward at thirteenth-century Westminster; hard-headed claims could be poeticized.[20] Also, the notion of a collective national sanctity, celebrating the extraordinary saintly wealth of England, enjoyed wide currency even under the Anglo-Saxons, not least at a time when the unification of England could be emblematized by such wealth.[21] English sanctity tended to map the fault lines of regional and local, not national, structures, and the stronger these structures the less evanescent the cults. In so far as public assent to certain single great saints can be measured – and official *festa ferianda* or religious holidays free of work probably offer as good a criterion of this as any – St Thomas of Canterbury was by the thirteenth century much the most universally celebrated saint of English origin. Other English saints' holidays enjoyed more limited diocesan or institutional observance, and St Edward remained the saint of a tiny political elite, not even being noted among the *festa ferianda* for the diocese of London.[22] Much about St Edward – not least the form of his thirteenth-century shrine – suggests that his cult was built up in deliberate imitation of such truly popular and miraculous cults as Thomas's. The later medieval phenomenon of canonized 'opposition', first identified somewhat categorically by J. C. Russell in 1929, seems to have extended into the study of medieval England the anthropological notion that 'ritual groupings reflect political oppositions' – proof, to cite Clifford Geertz, that anthropologists have at times been 'firmly dedicated to proving the indubitable'.[23] The notion of canonized opposition tended itself to focus upon royal, aristocratic or clerical figures subjected to physical martyrdom in a fashion not wholly discontinuous with the broad pre-Conquest tradition of the suffering leader. Like the early cults, these too served to focus guilt. But, just as the Church had to reach an accommodation with public power, so too that power could recognize the value of 'sacred union' in the causes of truly great if awkward saints, and indeed some lesser ones – for the cults of St Thomas, the epitome of the *Vox populi*, St Hugh, an outspoken royal critic, and even Gilbert of Sempringham, enjoyed royal support.[24]

The state did not define sanctity; but specific people, classes of people, movements and institutions did. The same applied to the process of canonization itself. The Normans appear not so much to have rejected, as severely scrutinized, the old cults of the English, and in the course of the twelfth century their formidable, pragmatic and rational powers of interrogation of sanctity were put on a firm and universal basis by the papacy.[25] The fact of formal papal reservation of the process of canonization was increasingly recognized: St Edward was the first old English saint to be canonized by Rome, Thomas following him in 1173.[26] In 1198 Innocent III, who did so much to consolidate this process, quashed the episcopal canonization of Wulfstan of Worcester and forced his supporters into a proper canonical procedure.[27] English decretal collections from the thirteenth century regularly include clauses relating to papal rights in the process:[28] indeed in this regard the English were signally obedient. The veneration of old relics without papal authorization was implicitly ruled out by canon 62 of the Fourth Lateran Council.[29] Relics old and new also had to be properly enclosed, which may positively have encouraged the translation of saints, whether old or would-be, to a more fitting place: *in loco decentiori*.[30]

But the consequences of papal reservation affected more than shrines. Arguably it was directing the nature and identity of sanctity itself. For one thing, the juridical methods used in the process of defining the sanctoral were by their nature becoming more costly, and so in the thirteenth and fourteenth centuries the process itself was tending to depress the success rate of new candidatures for canonization. The great age of new saints lauded by Matthew was grinding to a halt under the burden of bureaucracy: now, only the great cathedral chapters had the wherewithal to contemplate the idea; for the monasteries it was increasingly out of the question.[31] So some classes of new saint were now more or less threatened, and the tendency towards the standardization of calendars, most notably as a result of the rapid spread of the Use of Sarum to secular cathedrals by 1325, had further implications for local observance.[32] More fundamentally, papal reservation and its interrogative methods were starting to affect the thing observed: methods of assessment developed their own constitutive power; procedural reform was by its nature prescriptive.[33] The formal process required new standards in the presentation of evidence, a new acumen on the part of the advocates, a change in the standing and integrity of witnesses, and solid documentation of what Innocent III in 1199 called 'the virtue of morals and truth of signs'.[34] Innocent tightened the entire process. The cult of relics was disciplined. Canon 62 of the Fourth Lateran Council also ordained that ancient relics should not be venerated outside reliquaries, while new ones required papal approval.[35] This tightening-up characterized much of the regulative and penitential character of the thirteenth-century Church as a whole, and was first apparent in the rather tough but successful processes for St Gilbert of Sempringham (1202) and St Wulfstan (1203).[36] With it came a significant shift in values: for the new subtlety with which saints and sinners were examined focused less and less on the superhuman wonderworking of the visionary and thaumaturge: miracles were a necessary, but not a sufficient, condition of the new sanctity, and their extensive documentation was anyway costly and disproportionate to the process itself. Innocent IV ordered that the 1244 process for the canonization of Edmund of Abingdon (can. 1247) should be repeated without such extensive recourse to the listing of miracles, for it was better to have a few well-attested ones.[37] The massive labours of William and Benedict in logging miracles performed by St Thomas at Canterbury in the twelfth century bore no relation to the new, sleek, administratively efficient culture of official saint creation in the thirteenth century, which served to challenge the rights of communities to declare sanctity.[38] Edward I doubted the reports of his own father's miracles.[39]

For now – and the difficulties with the nature of Thomas's sanctity in life bore witness to this – what was of greater interest was the inner character of the saint, the nature not of the lightening-rod of divine power, but of the vessel of virtue.[40] How had the saints lived? How and to what extent had they grown in virtue and devotion? In contrast to the old epic sainthood of royal martyrs and its dated and ultimately monastic virtue of chastity, the new sainthood had in some ways a more complex, as it were more romantic, interior articulation. Of it, the cults of the bishops were absolutely symptomatic, for these were the cults of men who, though they performed miracles and attracted limited popular cults, were defined much more essentially by tough intellectual disciplines, by ascetic bodily practices (inner or 'white' martyrdom), by the rigour but also the humane character of their devotions, and by their deportment, their understanding, practice and dissemination of certain styles of behaviour, in short their *mores* in the public and private domains. This type of sanctity embodied a different form of consciousness from that of the old cults, even though it was itself in some ways a continuation and reinterpretation of the old English tradition of aristocratic sainthood (hence the dynastic element in the reported sanctity of Edmund of Abingdon's relations, including his mother and brother) and imported old and familiar ideas, albeit in a new way.[41] For the bishop-saints were, in conduct if not always in origin, a new type of aristocracy, an aristocracy of the learned ascetics who were emerging from the schools at Paris and Oxford. As such they were emblems and exemplifications of a certain style of reform – again, a refinement of the earlier pre-Conquest identification of monastic and wider Church reform in England with monastic bishop-saints such as Swithun or Ethelwold. Their conscious character as scholars and educators was a manifestation of the time-honoured educational theory of *paideia*, according to which students sought out model individuals for imitation. But they were more than emblems of a movement, for they represented too the ideals of a class: it was the schoolmen who, in shaping and promoting this style of sanctity, canonized the finest representatives of a comparatively new order of intellectual leader, an order to the membership of which they themselves aspired. Innocent III was a former schoolman: so too were Langton, St Edmund and St Richard, and the schoolmen also made up a high proportion of the failed episcopal cults of the period. The age of the monk-bishop was drawing to a close, for the monastic virtues had been absorbed and surpassed by the new styles of episcopal sanctity. In its place came new ideals, expressed less by the notion of sacred lineage, than by the sacred friendship of the master and disciple. In most respects, these men were all friends and disciples, above all, of St Thomas.

This development is important for the present discussion for the simple reason that this new style of sanctity, shaped as it was by and for agents of papally sponsored reform, was articulate and influential. Its representatives were few in number, but they were highly placed and committed to new styles and content of pastoral reform which they themselves helped to shape, and in which certain sectors of the clergy and laity took an increasingly lively interest because they offered ideals of conduct. But new cults do not develop in a vacuum, and the situation of sainthood in thirteenth-century England was complex and multi-layered. The cult of bishop-saints is explored below. In turning first to some practical examples of the way the presence of relics (at Ely) or the representation of saints, particularly collective sainthood (at Wells), affected the appearance of thirteenth-century great churches, one must also bear in mind that these newer forms of sanctity existed alongside, and did not displace, much older forms. Much of the interest of the period in fact arises from the coexistence of separate strands of sanctity, some representing older patterns, others newer, and which could also interact.

The Daughters of Anna

As well as interrogating the old English cults, the Normans altered the landscape of sanctity by a policy, inaugurated in 1075, of removing sees to substantial urban centres and converting monastic churches into diocesan churches. Sees which were moved before or after the Conquest (Norwich, Salisbury, Chichester, Lincoln, Coventry, Wells and Exeter) tended either not to have major relic cults, or to have them develop only in the thirteenth century; and so the greatest shrines –

as Matthew Paris, following Reginald of Durham, stated – were located at the important and ancient monastic churches. In such churches, very considerable steps were taken both before and after the Conquest to organize formally the arrangement and display of major body relics, as for example at Canterbury and at Winchester, where in the 1150s Henry of Blois created a significant collective arrangement of shrines of Saxon kings and bishops in the apse of the Romanesque church, the prelude to the creation in the early thirteenth century of a new form of Gothic presbytery and retrochoir.[42] For the East Anglians as well as the West Saxons, the importance of specifically royal sainthood survived the Conquest. This did not always lead in the thirteenth century to the refashioning of the eastern arm of great churches on the model of Canterbury: neither Bury nor Peterborough, both associated with Anglo-Saxon royalty, were to see major interventions in the new style at the east end of their churches. At the Benedictine house of Ely, however, it did; in 1109 Ely was converted into a diocesan church, a cathedral priory, and received quite exceptionally opulent provision for its major patron, St Etheldreda, a royal saint the character of whose cult was defined very early and around whose body architectural miracles were accomplished.[43]

The thirteenth century in Europe was a lively period in the promotion of the cults of royal holy women – St Elizabeth of Hungary (d. 1231), her saintly niece Margaret of Hungary (d. 1270) and St Hedwig of Bavaria (d. 1243), a member of a royal family that in the Middle Ages produced about thirty saints or *beati*.[44] By Anglo-Saxon standards such saintly dynasties were comparatively new, and the family of Etheldreda of Ely provides a classic, but also more ancient, illustration of what Vauchez describes as the 'belief in the hereditary transmission of a charisma within certain families'.[45] The holy women of Ely in fact comprised a formidable clan of nuns, descended from the East Anglian King Anna (d. 654), including no less than seven saints: his daughters Etheldreda, Sexburga and Withburga, a further daughter Ethelburga (of Faremoûtier-en-Brie), Sexburga's daughters Ermenilda and Erkengota, and Ermenilda's daughter Werburga. In 673 Etheldreda (d. 679) founded the first abbey at Ely, a double monastery and in effect a royal *eigenkloster* or private monastery. Sexburga succeeded her as abbess having established a minster at Sheppey, and was followed in turn by her daughter Ermenilda, while Withburga was associated with a community at East Dereham in Norfolk. Of these, Etheldreda, Sexburga, Withburga and Ermenilda were to have shrines at Ely; Werburga also had connections with Ely but was subsequently enshrined at Chester and as a result was not part of Ely's liturgical commemoration.[46] Etheldreda was married twice, to Tonbert and, after his death, to Ecgfrith, King of Northumbria – whom she left – while Sexburga was the widow of Erconbert, King of Kent, and Ermenilda of Wulfhere of Mercia. Widowhood and, more radically, the renunciation of marriage in favour of chastity are central themes in the cult of Etheldreda.[47] She was also a pioneer in the establishment of the religious life of women in England and an attractive figure to reformers, notably St Ethelwold of Winchester, who re-established Ely as a single monastery (i.e. for men only) in 970 and who translated its key saints to the church's east end.[48]

Ely's shrine – or rather cluster of shrines – was dynastic, almost choric, in nature: where Canterbury gathered together the relics of great archbishops, Ely, like the more modest nunnery at Barking, which by the 1020s contained serial shrines of holy women including Ethelburga and Hildelitha, presented both a collective and a royal vision of sainthood.[49] As Susan Ridyard has shown, this genealogical feature was central to Ely's understanding and perpetuation of its tenurial rights and privileges: the pursuit of the patrimony of St Etheldreda by the monks of Ely could legitimately be seen as a devotional act.[50] Ely's undoubted claim to antiquity was sustained, and given apostolic substance, by allusions in its principal historical compilation drawn up in the twelfth century, the *Liber Eliensis*, to an earlier foundation on the site by St Augustine, and by its claim – in fact surprisingly substantial – to possess the relics of the protomartyr St Alban, something which of course greatly annoyed St Albans.[51] Ridyard has also shown that the Conquest did little to interrupt the traditions of devotion to Etheldreda, who continued to be promoted in the twelfth century and beyond.[52]

Etheldreda's miracles as recorded in the *Liber Eliensis* were frequently those of a protector saint regardful of her home.[53] This pattern sheds some light on the significance of an allusion to the power of Ely's female patrons made after the catastrophic fall of the central tower of the church in 1322, after which its great octagon was raised (fig. 60): it is said that the large and beautiful structure at the east end of the church, i.e. the new presbytery and retrochoir with its shrines, was protected from damage during the collapse by God and the merits of his beloved Etheldreda.[54] The passage perhaps says more about the traditional protective role of the saints at Ely than about the function (if single function it had) of the east end as a shrine space – a model of understanding of such spaces shaped ultimately by Grabar's concept of the *martyrium*.[55] But it cannot be denied that this is where Ely's remarkable shrine-complex was to be found. By

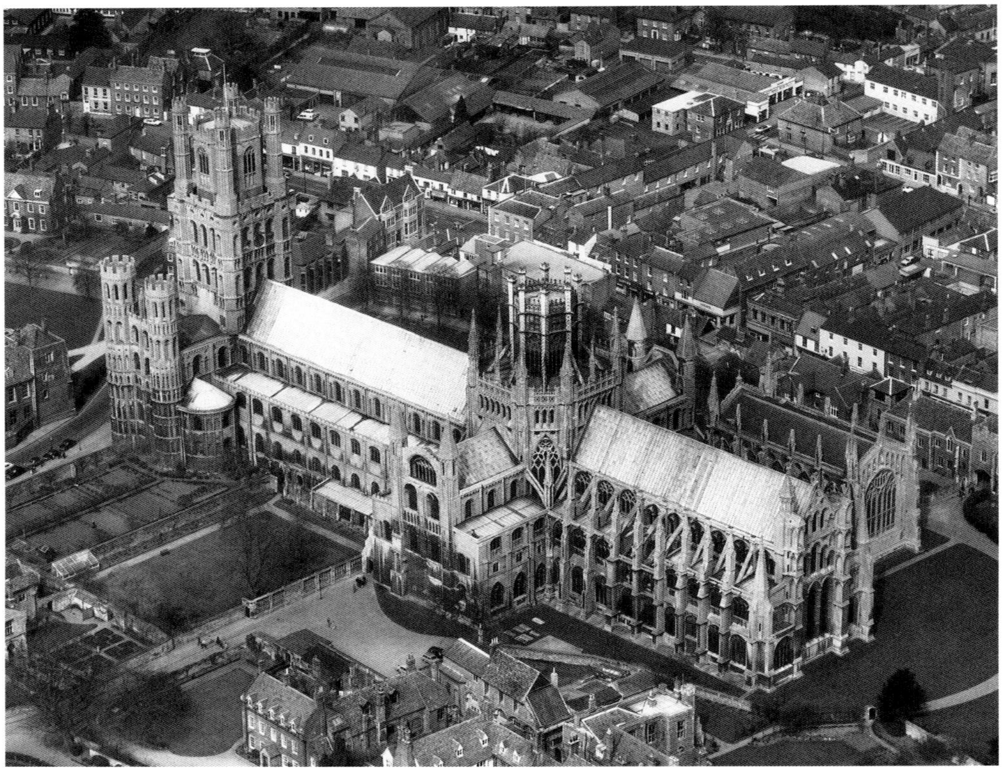

61 Ely Cathedral, aerial view from south-east (Simmons Aerofilms Ltd).

the early twelfth century an inventory in the *Liber Eliensis* shows that the main shrine of Etheldreda was elevated immediately behind the high altar with a Majesty on its western face and sixteen images on each side, a magnificent piece of goldsmith's work. To its north was the shrine of the ever-blooming virgin Withburga; to its east and at its feet lay Sexburga, whose merits never cease to flourish, and to the south of Etheldreda, the bride of Christ, lay the virtuous Ermenilda.[56]

The new Gothic six-bay retrochoir, to which some discussion must now be devoted, was started by about 1234 and completed by 1252; the three westernmost bays were refashioned only after the fall of the crossing tower in 1322 (figs 61–2).[57] It preserved the early topography of feretories with only minor differences.[58] The main shrine of Etheldreda was located at the centre between bays four and five from the east end, with those of her kinswomen at the east end itself; the building's patron, Bishop Hugh of Northwold, was to be buried somewhere in between.[59] It represented a very considerable enlargement of the old four-bay apsidal east arm of the old church, and can be seen as part of the chain reaction to events at Benedictine Canterbury, which had culminated with Becket's translation in 1220. St Hugh's canonization in the same year may also have been a factor, since the papal legate, Pandulph, had secured the election of John, former Abbot of Fountains, to the see of Ely, and John had been appointed to the commission of enquiry into Hugh's sanctity in 1219–20.[60] Other monastic churches in the region were part of this new post-Canterbury Benedictine artistic *risorgimento*. At Peterborough, the sacrist and later abbot, Robert of Lindsey (1214–22), had the church whitewashed and furnished with over thirty stained-glass windows; one of his successors there as abbot, Walter of Bury St Edmunds (1233–45), provided an enlarged choir, a decorated nave ceiling and new shrines for its three female virgin saints, Mercian princesses who had been translated in 963: Cyneburga, Cyneswitha and Tibba, their anchoress kinswoman.[61] This particular promotion looks very like a reaction specifically to Ely's cults. At St Albans in the same period, Matthew Paris records in the *Gesta abbatum* the extensive work on the old church by Abbot William of Trumpington (1214–35), including new windows and altarpieces, enhanced provision for the cult of the Virgin Mary, and a translation of St Amphibalus, Alban's co-saint.[62] Bury's local authority as a royal shrine-church might also have been a factor, since there is one instance in the period of a failed supplication to St Edmund by a Suffolk resident which was diverted successfully to Etheldreda, indicating some degree of rivalry.[63]

But at none of these churches was anything like that at Ely attempted. The names of the heads of houses, ostensibly the patrons – Lindsey, Bury, Trumpington – speak of a strong East Anglian consciousness. Indeed the election as Bishop of Ely in 1229 of another East Anglian man, the former Abbot of Bury, Hugh of Northwold (d. 1254), is likely to have been of decisive importance, not least because of his efficiency and personal wealth. Matthew Paris's eulogy of Hugh in 1254 indeed states that he was buried in his own church in a magnificent presbytery (*presbiterio nobilissimo*), which he had founded and built of marble at his own expense.[64] Hugh was now the sole representative of the Benedictine Order on the bench of bishops, being part of a late crop of monastic appointments including those created by the papal legation at Chichester and Worcester.[65] But Matthew's praise for him suggests that, notwithstanding his profession as a monk, he was a traditionally magnificent prelate: in the same way that he showed devotion at the spiritual table, the altar, where fountains of tears sprung from his eyes, so at the table for bodily refreshment he showed himself hospitable, cheerful and composed (*dapsilis fuit, jocundus et serenus*).[66] As mentioned above, such terms were also applied to Becket and Hubert Walter: of such temperate magnificence, great building was a natural part.

Gems and Buds

Hugh's primary devotion is certain to have been to St Edmund, partly in virtue of Hugh's former office at Bury, and partly because the martyr-king was still an important symbol of liberty from the tyrannical oppression of public power, the sting of which Hugh had felt during his disputed abbatial election.[67] But it is to Canterbury (the generic model), and more especially to Lincoln, rather than Romanesque Bury, that one should look for the specific artistic stimulus for Hugh's new work. The building rejected the Canterbury-derived double transepts and chevet at Lincoln, but shows numerous signs of scrutiny of its main elevations and aisles: so its piers follow those in the nave at Lincoln (fig. 64), and the syncopated wall arcading used in the west Galilee porch follows Lincoln's choir aisles (fig. 47). Ely's approach to the use of materials and surface enrichment is a deliberate amplification of tendencies that seem only latent at Lincoln. Purbeck marble is used extensively. Motifs developed in Lincoln's choir and nave are artfully transposed: the use of small clumps of foliage, which run

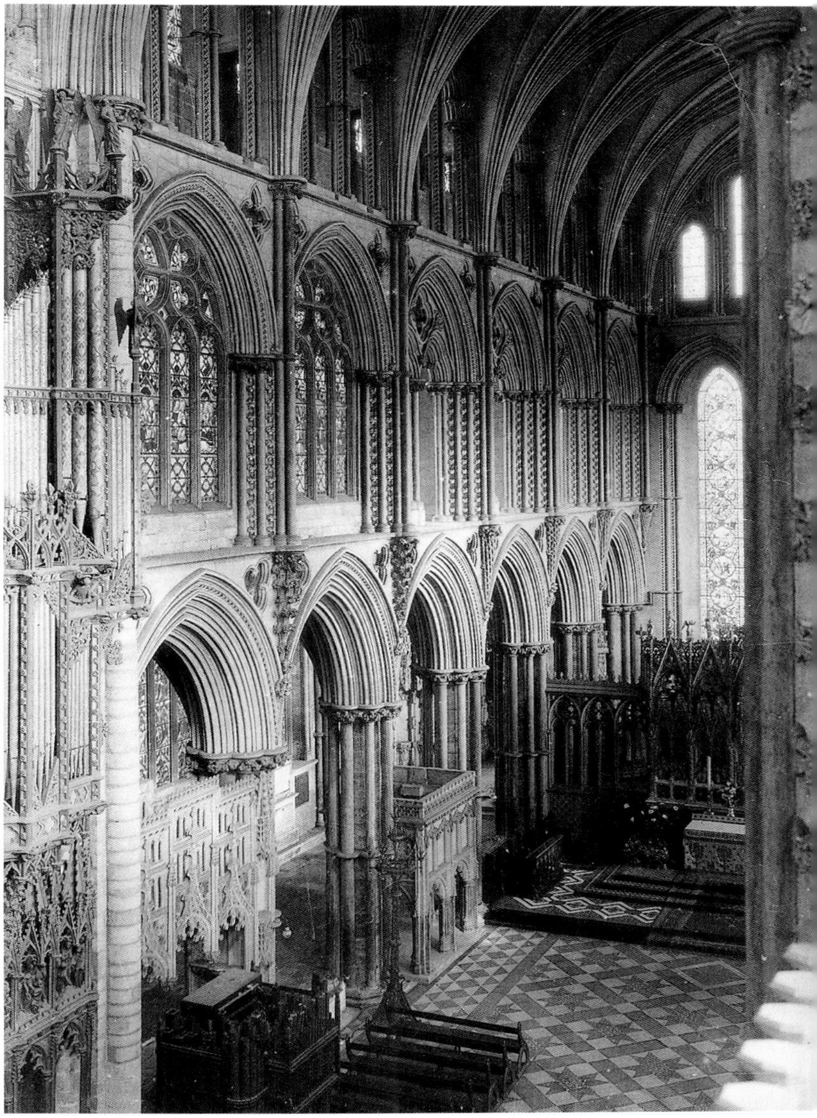

62 Ely Cathedral, retrochoir looking east (Conway Library, Courtauld Institute of Art).

vertically between the slim marble shafts of the Ely triforium (fig. 63), derives from the two crocketted piers at the west junction of the choir and the eastern transepts at Lincoln (fig. 67); the same trick is developed on the central main arch of the near-contemporary west front at Peterborough and also on the facade at Wells (fig. 84). Lincoln's main elevations do not employ such small crocketted shafts. Like Lincoln's nave, the wall surfaces of the Ely elevations are punctured with small foiled openings, sharpened into points and multiplied in number across the wall faces; this sharpening of forms is anticipated in the cross-section of some piers at Lincoln

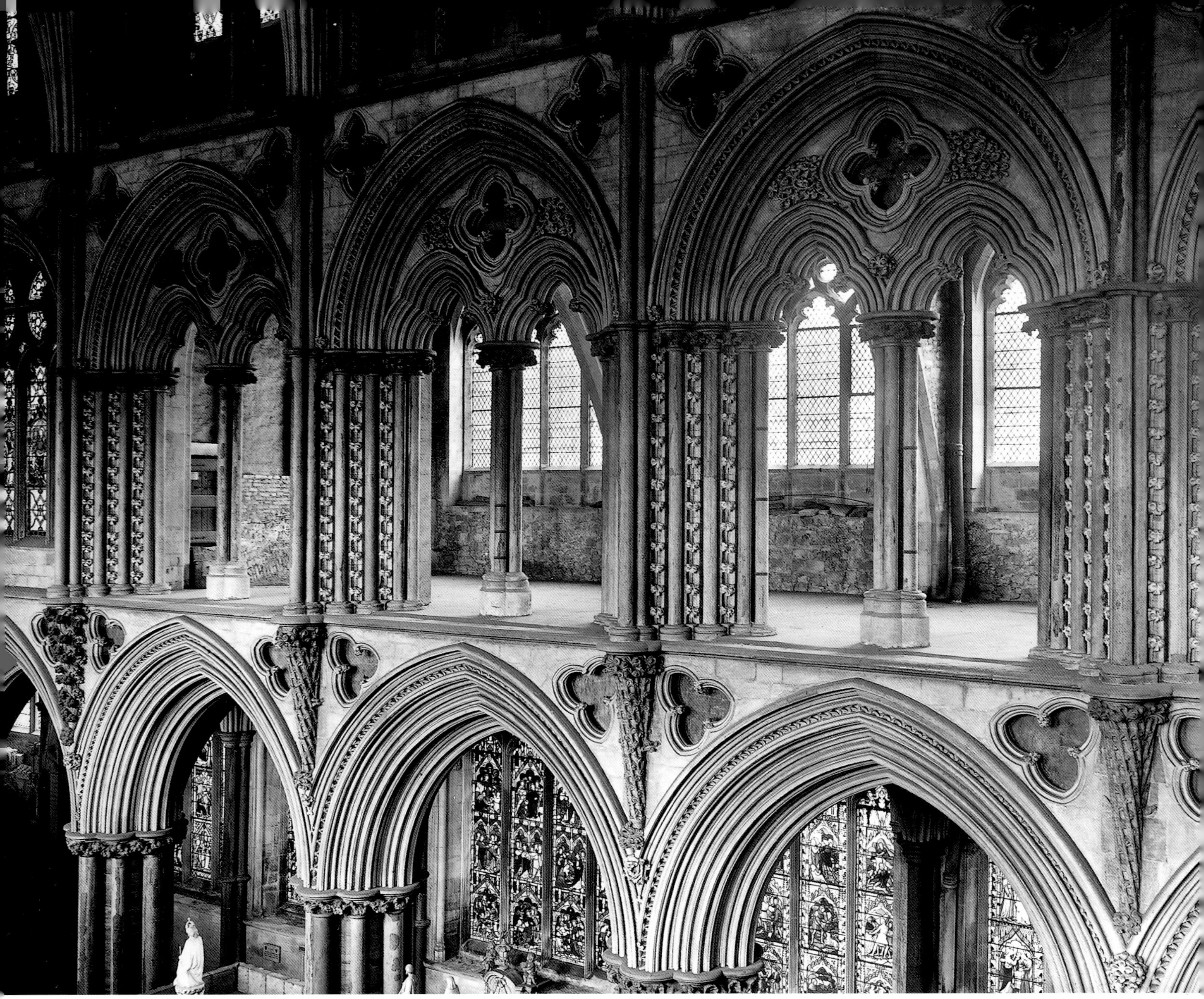

63 Ely Cathedral, retrochoir triforium, north side (©Crown copyright. NMR).

such as those in the morning chapel. Particularly distinctive of this permutative and selective approach to Lincoln are the huge cone-shaped corbels that sustain the high vault shafts, and that fill the height of the main arcade spandrels, a citation less of the comparatively small corbels in the corresponding positions at Lincoln than of the relatively over-scaled corbels in its chapter house, which burst out assertively into lively stiff-leaf foliage, far more vigorous than much later 'naturalistic' foliage proper (fig. 65). The cumulative effect of these enrichments is the most vigorously organic-looking presbytery of the period, a massive development of ideas that were only starting to bud at Lincoln and, of course, a complete contrast to the effects sought at Salisbury.

It is certainly not coincidental that the main legacy of Ely's greenery is to be found at Lincoln's Angel Choir, begun in 1256 (fig. 216), for the two churches seem to have engaged in a sort of reciprocal formal dialogue; since Lincoln had clearly inaugurated this taste in eastern England before 1200, however, one is entitled to look a little harder at why, and to what ends, such organic language had emerged there, before considering what went

64 Lincoln Cathedral, nave looking north-west (reproduced by permission of English Heritage. NMR).

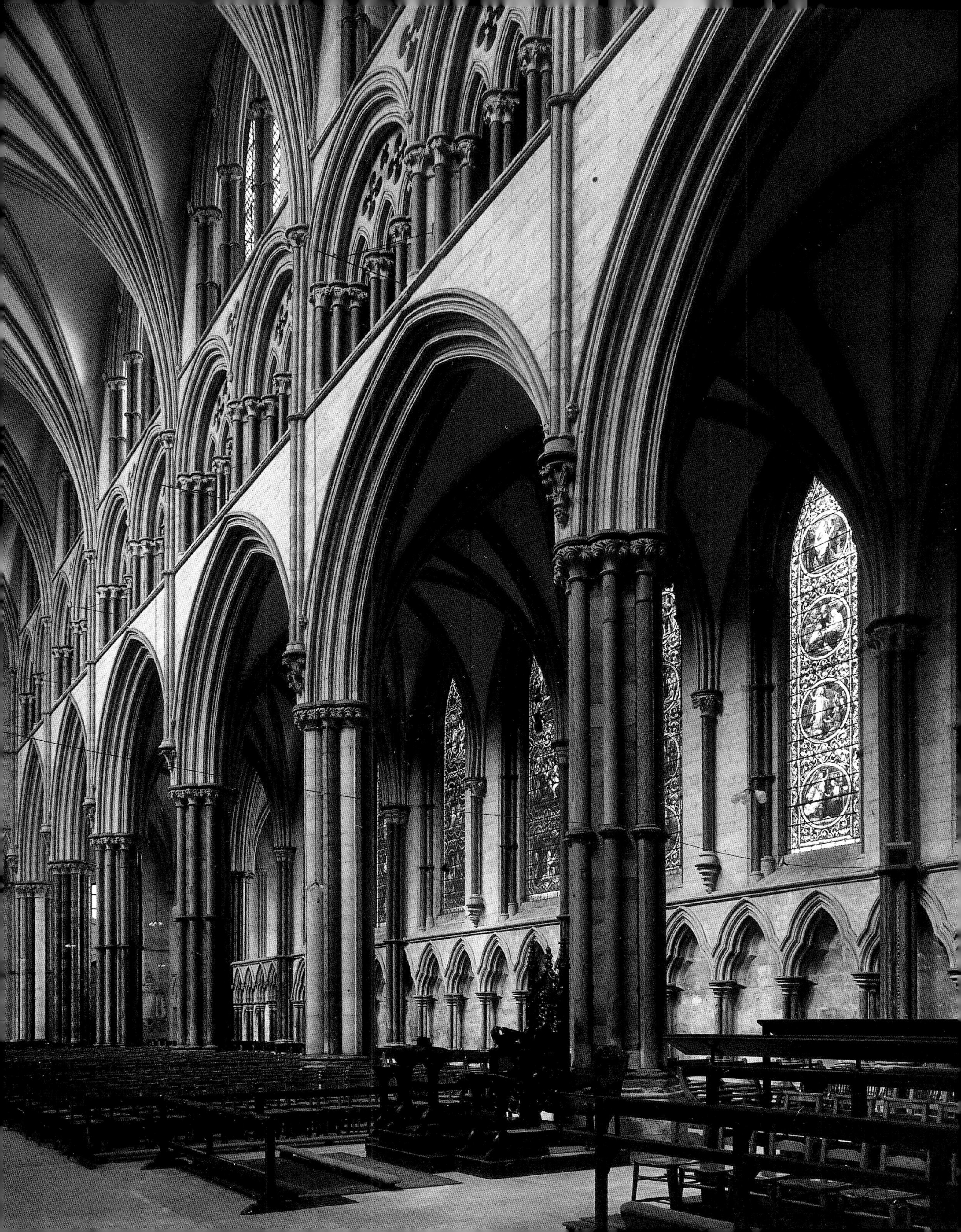

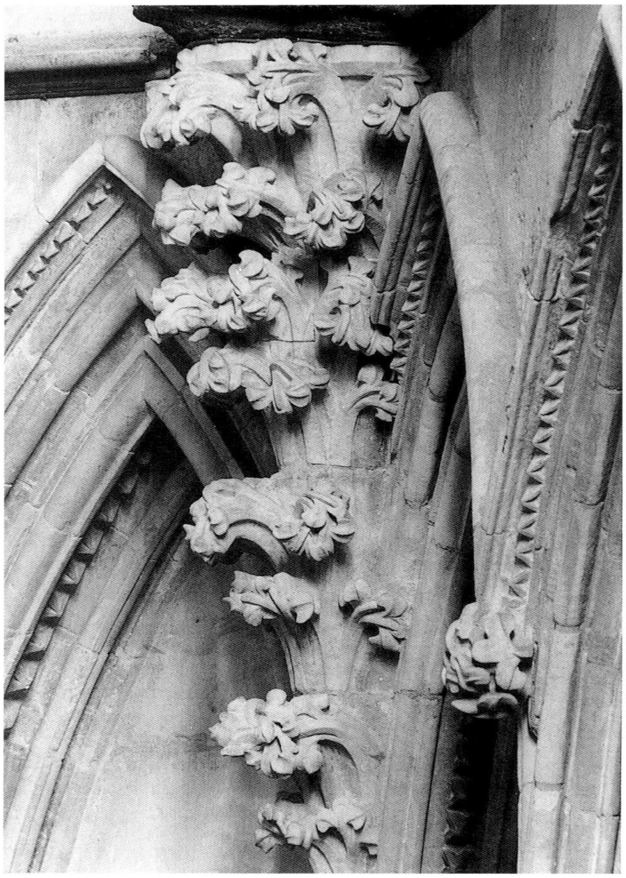

65 Lincoln Cathedral chapter house, corbel (Conway Library, Courtauld Institute of Art).

on to happen at Ely. Lincoln's importance in generating unusual but influential detailing is no better demonstrated than by the two crocket piers at the junction of the choir aisles and western transepts, presumably designed around 1200 (figs 67–8). These are perhaps the oddest manifestation of an important period of experimental pier design in English Gothic architecture.[68] Indeed the sculptural and figurative possibilities of Gothic piers were enjoying a period of unprecedented fertility generally, for example in the extraordinary Angels' or Judgement-Pillar at Strasbourg Cathedral.[69] In general form, the Lincoln piers derive from some of the piers in the presbytery at Canterbury, though large-scale design at Canterbury provided no obvious precedent for the large and rather coarse rounded bud-like crockets that sprout from the entire height of the freestone core of the piers between the four detached Purbeck marble shafts. That Canterbury might however have provided some stimulus to this obviously experimental pier type is indicated by the pairs of small foliated brackets that attach the sarcophagus of the tomb of Hubert Walter to its surrounding stumpy colonettes, designed around 1205 and arguably close to the circle of English William (fig. 36). The use of vertical rows of gemstones on the columns and pilasters of twelfth-century Mosan metalwork shrines such as that of St Anno at Siegburg of around 1183 might also be relevant, given that the formal language of bust-length figures set in spandrels in the choir aisles at Lincoln seems itself generally indebted to *ars sacra*; indeed small shafts adorned with creeping trefoil leaves are a feature of Mosan metalwork at this time.[70] Even more relevant at Canterbury are the rows of symmetrical buds that fill the slim vertical borders of its late twelfth-century stained-glass windows, as in the east clearstory of the south-east transept (fig. 66).[71] Canterbury's Corona also made a positive show of organic imagery in its fine Tree of Jesse window, an image that

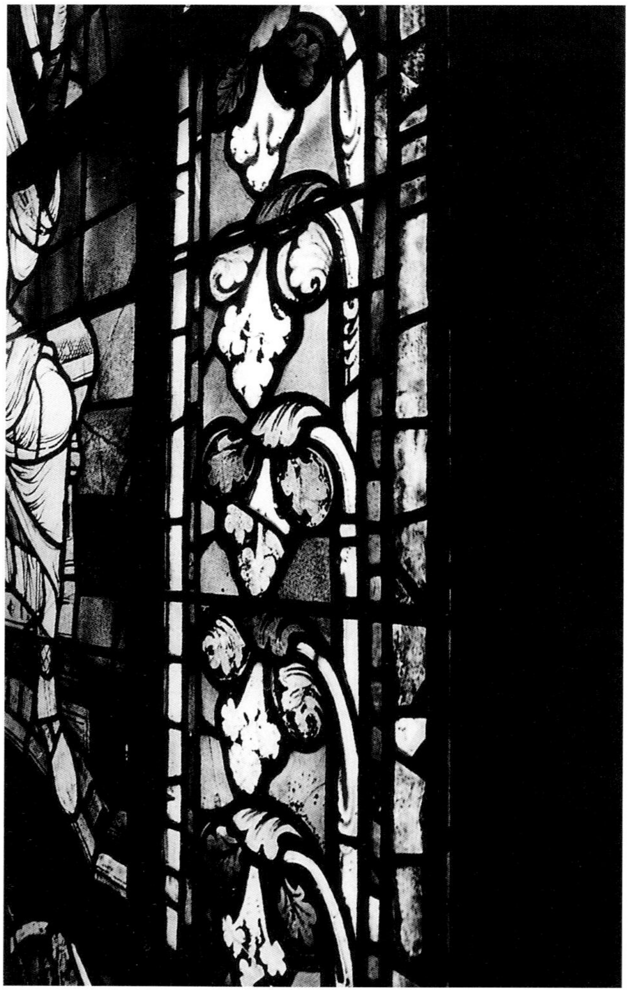

66 Canterbury Cathedral, border of window S: XIV, south-east transept (Sebastian Strobl).

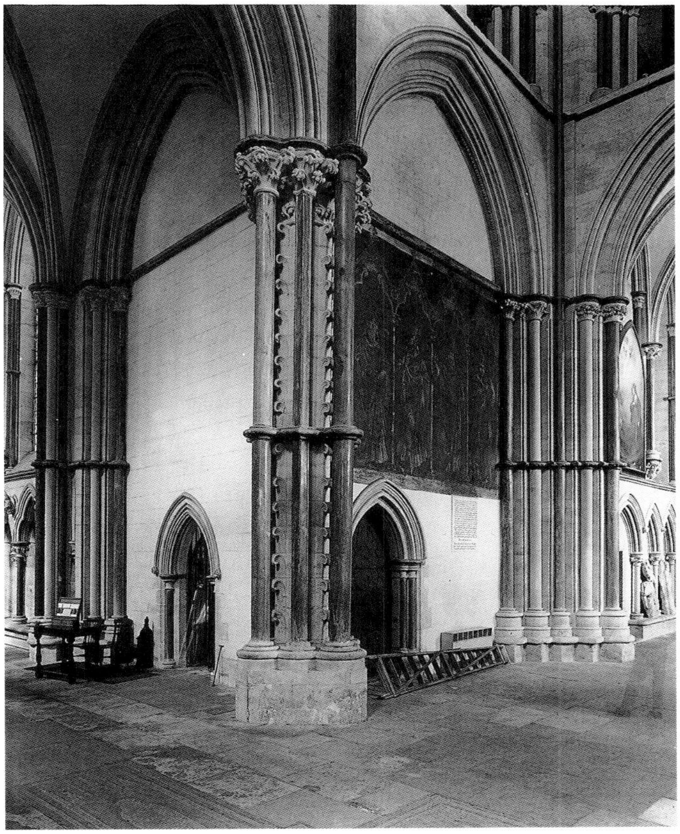

67 Lincoln Cathedral, crocket pier, north-east transept (Conway Library, Courtauld Institute of Art).

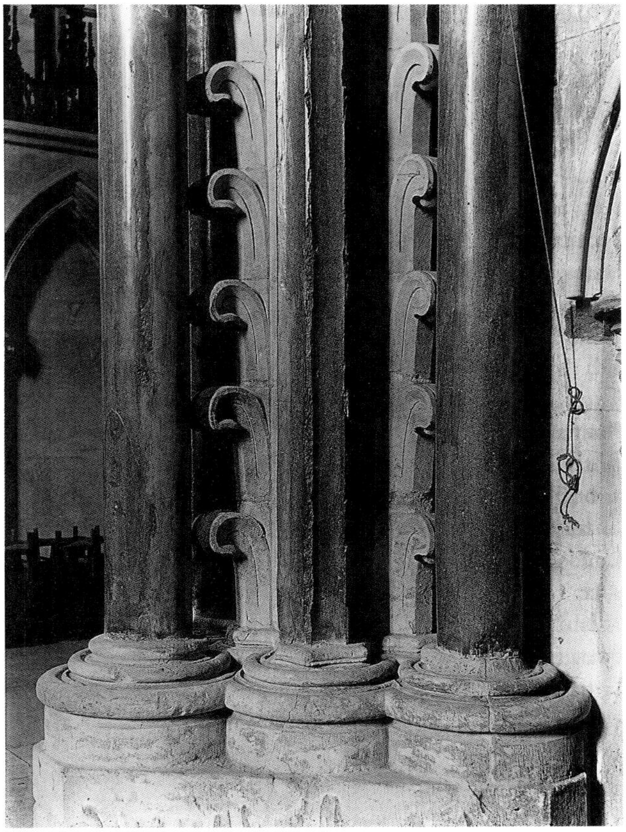

68 Lincoln Cathedral, crocket pier, detail (reproduced by permission of English Heritage. NMR).

frequently acted as a visual cue to Psalm 1, where the righteous man is like a tree that bringeth forth his fruit in season, or the flourishing of the righteous in the house of the Lord in Psalm 91: 13–14. One can understand from the popularity of such metaphors how it is that the Metrical Life of St Hugh attributed to contemporary Lincoln a kind of organic will, as a thing of nature (p. 56 above).[72]

But the crocket piers do not stem literally from Psalm 1 or from the more direct reference to Jesse in Isaiah 11, and nor is it clear why they were placed where they were in the church. They signal no important liturgical division.[73] The example of Salisbury's sole major foliated capitals, by the site of the high altar, might have suggested a higher-status position than this, but at Lincoln the obvious problem is the loss of the original east end, demolished in 1256; the latter may have included more strategically placed instances of the same type of exceptionally ornate free-standing pier. It may have been the failure of this lost east end to influence any subsequent major English great church that explains why the crocket piers were never again taken up in this way, with one important exception: early thirteenth-century Trondheim. Two examples of the same design survive as responds at the junction with the eastern octagon conceived by Archbishop Øystein in the 1180s (fig. 69), but these were originally part of a series of such columns that formed a screen or arcade across the mouth of the eastern octagon holding the shrine of St Olaf.[74] One (by no means conclusive) way of explaining this is to suppose that a similar usage had occurred in the lost east end at Lincoln; and that in turn would mean that the form was thought of at both churches as the accompaniment of their principal shrine and liturgical spaces. Ely took this form up in a slightly different way, in its triforium; though distinct, however, the cults of Olaf and Etheldreda had some points in common in terms of their royal standing, also their association with healing wells and with octagonal spaces.[75]

This speculation prompts a harder look at the kind of discursive associations that might have arisen between cult and church at Lincoln and Ely. Canter-

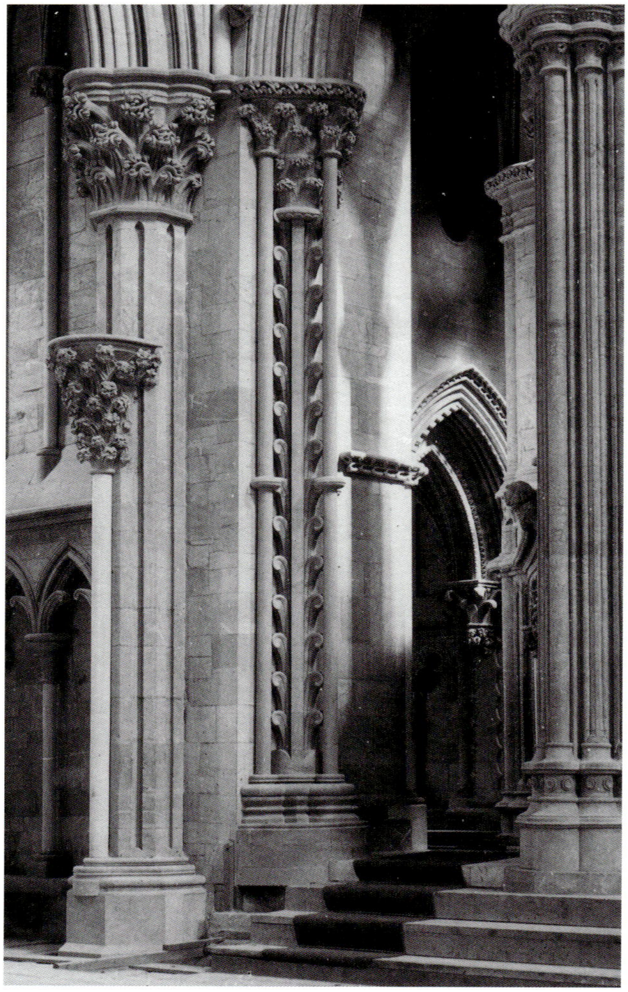

69 Trondheim Cathedral, crocket pier at entrance to octagon (The Restoration Workshop of Nidaros Cathedral).

bury's Corona glazing had introduced not only the organic linking metaphor of the Tree of Jesse but also a typological scheme in its easternmost Redemption window, which culminated in the consecration of Aaron and his sons as a type for Pentecost, and hence the foundation of the Church and the sacrament of ordination. Lincoln's glazing is also likely to have been at least in part typological.[76] This is relevant because much the most feasible point of reference for the crocket pier form is Levitical: Aaron's rod, placed by Moses in the tabernacle which brought forth buds and almonds (Numbers 17: 8), the priests of Israel being types for the Christian priesthood.[77] So, following Isaiah 27: 6 and 35: 1, Israel (the Church), shall blossom and bud. Christological readings of this text, as in Cistercian commentaries or the *Bibles moralisées*, were commonplace.[78] The earlier typological chapter-house paintings at Worcester had connected Aaron's rod, the Virgin Mary and Christ, the divine fruit of the Cross (*fructo deico crucis*).[79] And it is intrinsically likely that this priestly metaphor informed the English tradition of *Lignum vitae* Crucifixions, of which a spectacular Gothic instance is to be found in the fine Psalter made around 1220 for Robert of Lindsey at Peterborough, where the Cross is daintily adorned with pink and white buds as if made of exquisite enamel, or lilies and roses (fig. 70).[80] This is an obvious visual counterpart to the buds appearing on shafts at Lincoln, Ely, Wells and Peterborough itself within a generation.

At Lincoln, organic metaphors for spiritual growth had been applied by hagiographers both to St Remigius, for whom the east end was presumably intended, and to St Hugh: the former is a *planta Christi*, the latter a lily, a rose and the bearer of divine fruit.[81] But it cannot be said that such by now fairly routine analogies had a fundamental role in shaping the physical fabric of a cathedral dedicated to a particular saint. At Ely the position is

70 Crucifixion (detail). Psalter of Robert of Lindsey, Society of Antiquaries MS 59, fol. 35v, *c.* 1220 (Society of Antiquaries of London).

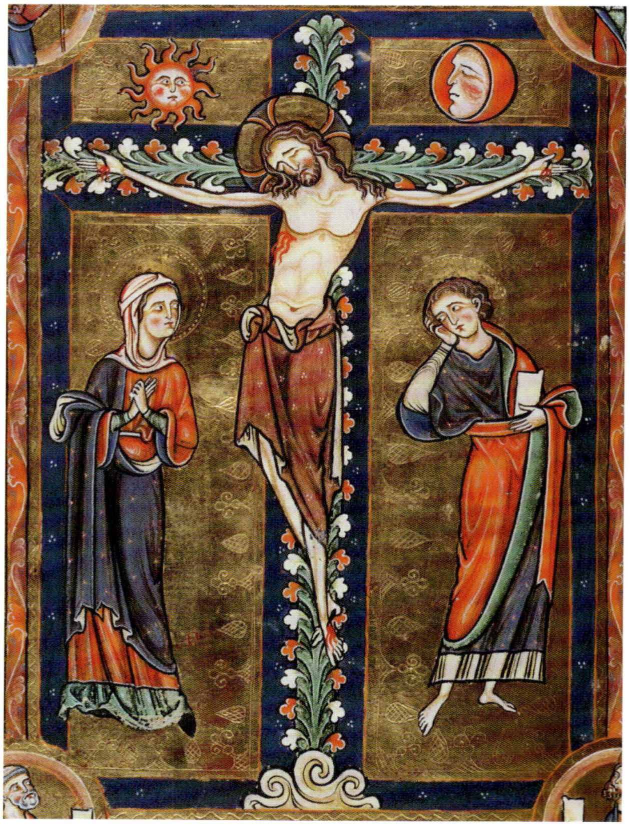

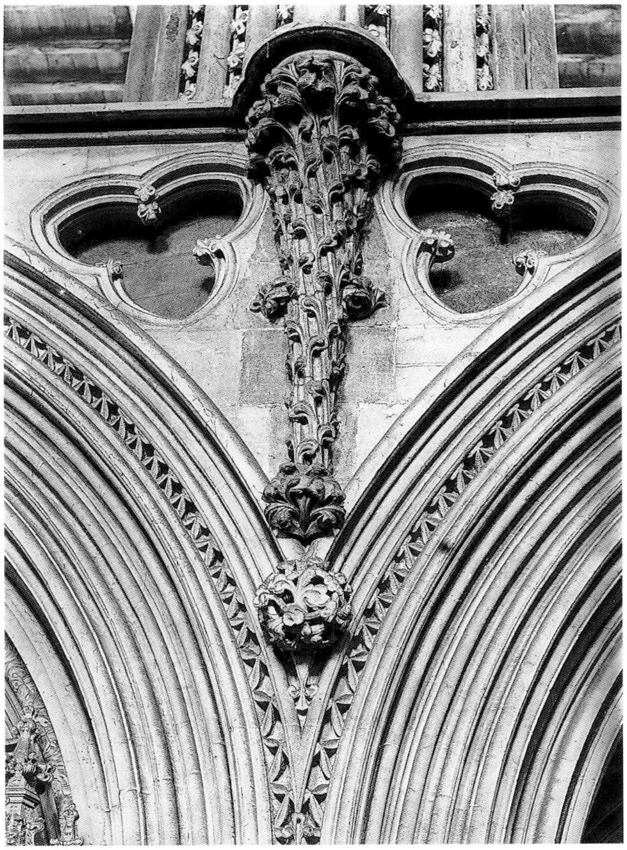

71 Ely Cathedral, vault shaft corbel 'closed' (Conway Library, Courtauld Institute of Art).

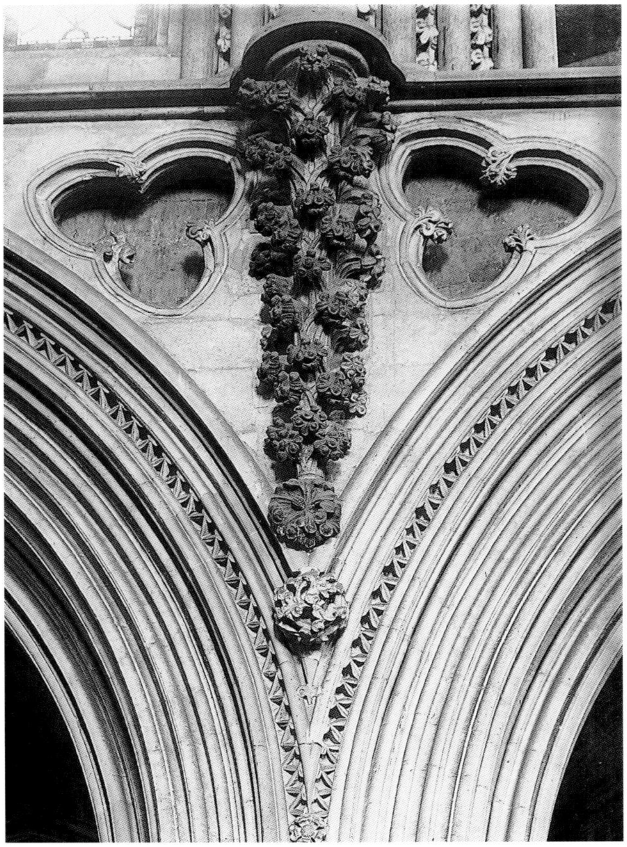

72 Ely Cathedral, vault shaft corbel 'open' (Conway Library, Courtauld Institute of Art).

somewhat different, because it is precisely the hagiography of St Etheldreda that provides a coherent and specific context for the artistic rehearsal of ideas of growth, flourishing and incorruptible virtue which could very well have led Ely patrons to look at Lincoln from a specific viewpoint. That this is so has tended to be obscured by functionalist accounts of Ely's presbytery and retrochoir, which regard its 'decorative qualities' as of subsidiary importance or related to issues of liturgical status.[82] On the contrary: it is precisely the features under discussion that reinforce the functionalist argument for the importance of the presence of the saints here. It is unlikely to be coincidental that the most characteristic miracle of St Etheldreda concerned a miraculously budding staff. A passage replete with nature imagery in the *Liber Eliensis* recounts how Etheldreda, while in the wilds on her way to Ely, took a nap in the heat of the day, and set down her dry wooden staff; on waking she and her witnesses found that the staff had miraculously budded, the arid bark sprouting (*iam viridi amictum cortice fronduisse ac folia prodisse*) and bringing forth an ash tree of legendary size: here it was that a church was founded for the Virgin Mary.[83] As at Lincoln, Aaron's rod and Marian devotion seem to coalesce. That the temple into which Etheldreda was about to enter could itself flower in the presence of this saint is therefore not surprising, and there is no reason not to entertain seriously John Maddison's observation that her holy capacity to bring forth blooms is physically represented, indeed dramatized, at Ely by the progressive budding forth of the huge cones supporting the vault shafts in the space between the procession path to the east and the site of the high altar and shrine-complex (figs 71–2).[84] To the east, the cone surfaces have thin dry stems with small trefoil-leaf sprouts gingerly wound round the surface, but from the fourth pair of piers from the east next to the feretory the fronds burst out, and the corbels remain in this florid state as far as the site of the high altar. The radiance of the shrine and altars brings forth a striking dynamic reciprocity in the 'living stones' of the building itself, which are animated as if in response to the thaumaturgical character of the site and of Etheldreda, as herself *beata stirps*.

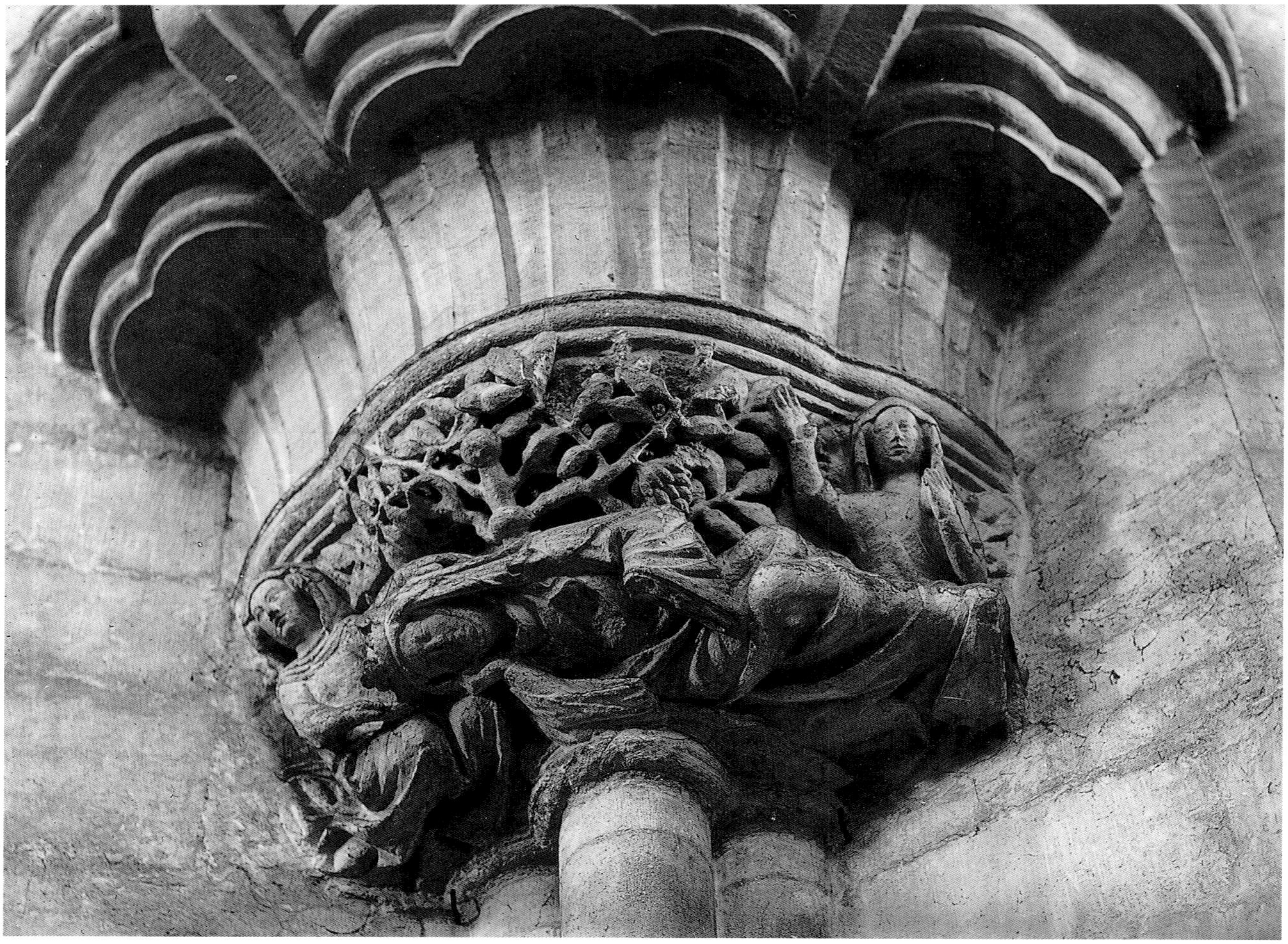

73 Ely Cathedral, corbel with miracle of St Etheldreda's budding staff (Conway Library, Courtauld Institute of Art).

In the sense that symbols can be vehicles for a conception, these are symbols of Etheldreda's style of sanctity.[85]

Such characteristic, if very old-fashioned, miracles had the key tactical advantage of being not only extremely eye-catching, but also of possessing great metaphorical richness, even virtuosity, and one is entitled to regard them imaginatively. At Ely, *viriditas* is the counterpart to the essentially monastic notion of perpetually flourishing virginity and chastity, and hence incorruptibility in both life and death, the mark of Etheldreda and her kinswomen, and indeed of Anglo-Saxon female royal sainthood.[86] The *Liber Eliensis* consistently stresses this theme of chastity; and even in the later Middle Ages episcopal statutes instructed monks at Ely not to engage in illicit conversations with women amidst the shrines of the holy virgins.[87] Virginity ensured the intercessory power of these and other female saints throughout the Middle Ages.[88] The absolute model for this notion of freedom from bodily and spiritual corruption was of course the Virgin Mary. The miracle of the flourishing staff picks up and extends a metaphor established in Etheldreda's earliest hagiography by Bede who, in a hymn of praise to the saint, traced her sacred lineage from Mary, the root of which Etheldreda and her holy kin are holy shoots; and so the Virgin's worthiness bore virgin blossoms (*virgineos flores [. . .] genuit*) including Etheldreda, who flowered in lofty deeds.[89] The stimuli for this organic model of virgin sanctity and virtue were presumably Isaiah 11: 1 and Psalm 1: 3, as indicated by the fourteenth-century sculpted representation of the miracle of the sprouting staff on the north-eastern corbel of the octagon at Ely, to the left of the entrance to the presbytery, which shows a recumbent Etheldreda with the staff rising and blooming behind and above her in a fashion generally reminiscent of the form of Jesse and his stem, a biblical image providing an important metaphor of sacred lineage (fig. 73).[90] So Etheldreda, corporeally East Anglian, is *beata stirps* in virtue of her holy kindred and also of high spiritual descent. Staff or rod imagery was naturally conspicuous because of its association with authority.[91] The Virgin Mary's flourishing sceptre was already a feature of Lincoln's institutional iconography, since she was that church's patron.[92] Episcopal and abbatial crosiers were a natural focus for the imagery of Aaron.[93] Contemporary crosiers brought forth buds as naturally as they yielded the imagery of Mary, as on the Limoges example enclosing the Annunciation at Rochester of around 1220–30 (fig. 74).[94] Staffs as symbols of lineage, virginal virtue and authority – hence also, occasionally, of holy resistance to public power – figure periodically in the history of the older cults of England: William of Malmesbury recalls that the ashen preaching staff of the nobly born St Aldhelm had miraculously flourished;[95] St Wulfstan's staff came to represent ecclesiastical intransigence;[96] and Etheldreda was capable of using hers to punish her enemies.[97]

Besides the prominent flourishing corbels, there are at Ely other instances of the way that this metaphor of perpetual flourishing underwent a transformation into stone. In the *Liber Eliensis*, Etheldreda and her sister Sexburga residing near the high altar are presented not only as the two olive trees of Zechariah 4: 3 and Revelation 11: 9, but also, in the (now familiar) figure of the two columns (*due columpne*) of God.[98] So, at Lincoln, metaphors of the tree and the column are elided and made manifest. In similar vein, the saints are not only columns but cornerstones, for they lock the vault over the site of the main shrine in the form of carved stone bosses (fig. 75). Etheldreda's devotion to Mary is therefore epitomized by the carved bosses showing St Etheldreda with a foliated crosier, and the Coronation of the Virgin to its east.[99] Her capacity to transform stone as if it were a living thing is also demonstrated by a translation miracle. On the occasion of the first opening of her tomb, sixteen years after her death, her body was found to be not only intact but miraculously cleansed of a disfiguring tumour; indeed the very sarcophagus that held her had itself miraculously fused together, as if it too had regenerated and become whole, in what the *Liber Eliensis* called a 'testimony of the saint's virginal intactness' (*virginalis integritatis testimonium*); it also possessed healing powers.[100] A similar miracle of restoring the intactness of stone is attributed to Aldhelm.[101] In a further conventional allusion to the virtue of white Parian marble, already praised by Gerald of Wales at Lincoln, but this time as a sign not only of luxury but also of lily-white virginity, the new sarcophagus was a beautifully made white Roman example discovered by Sexburga at Grantchester, and brought to Ely by ship in the tradition of the importation of expensive marbles from Rome (*locellum de marmore albo pulcherrime tectum*).[102] The *vas marmoreum* of Etheldreda, *tota integra, tota incorrupta*, is recorded within the shrine, 'made by the hands of angels', after the Conquest.[103]

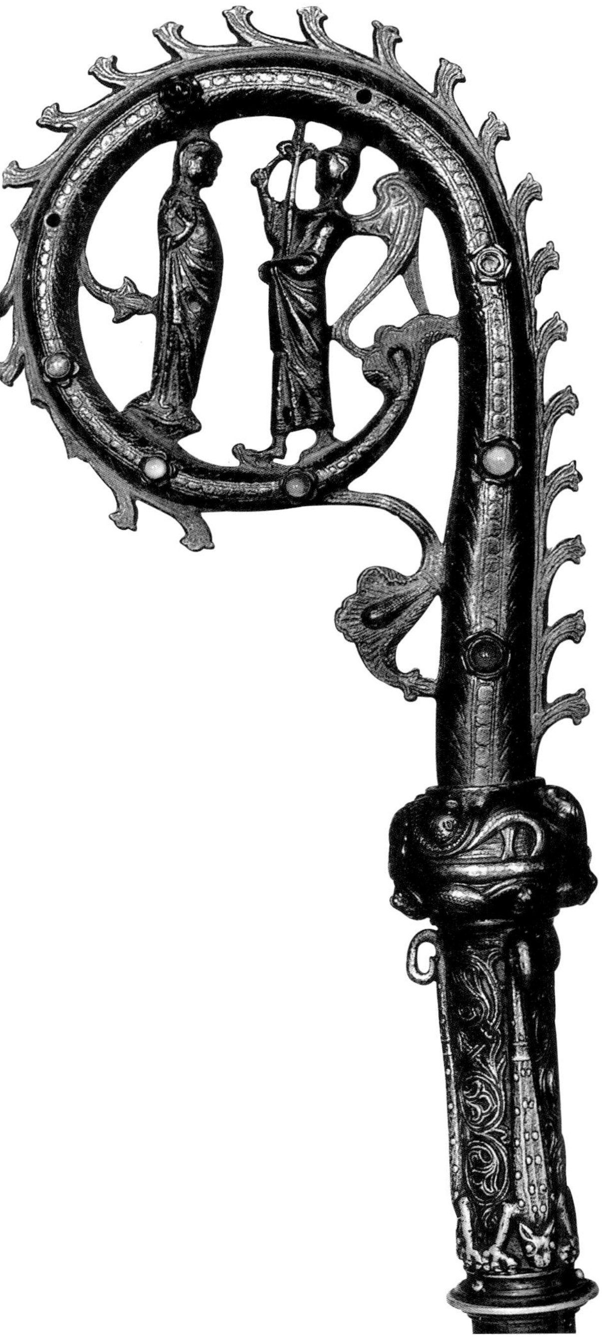

74 Rochester Cathedral crosier with Annunciation, Limoges enamel, *c.* 1220–30 (Dean and Chapter of Rochester Cathedral).

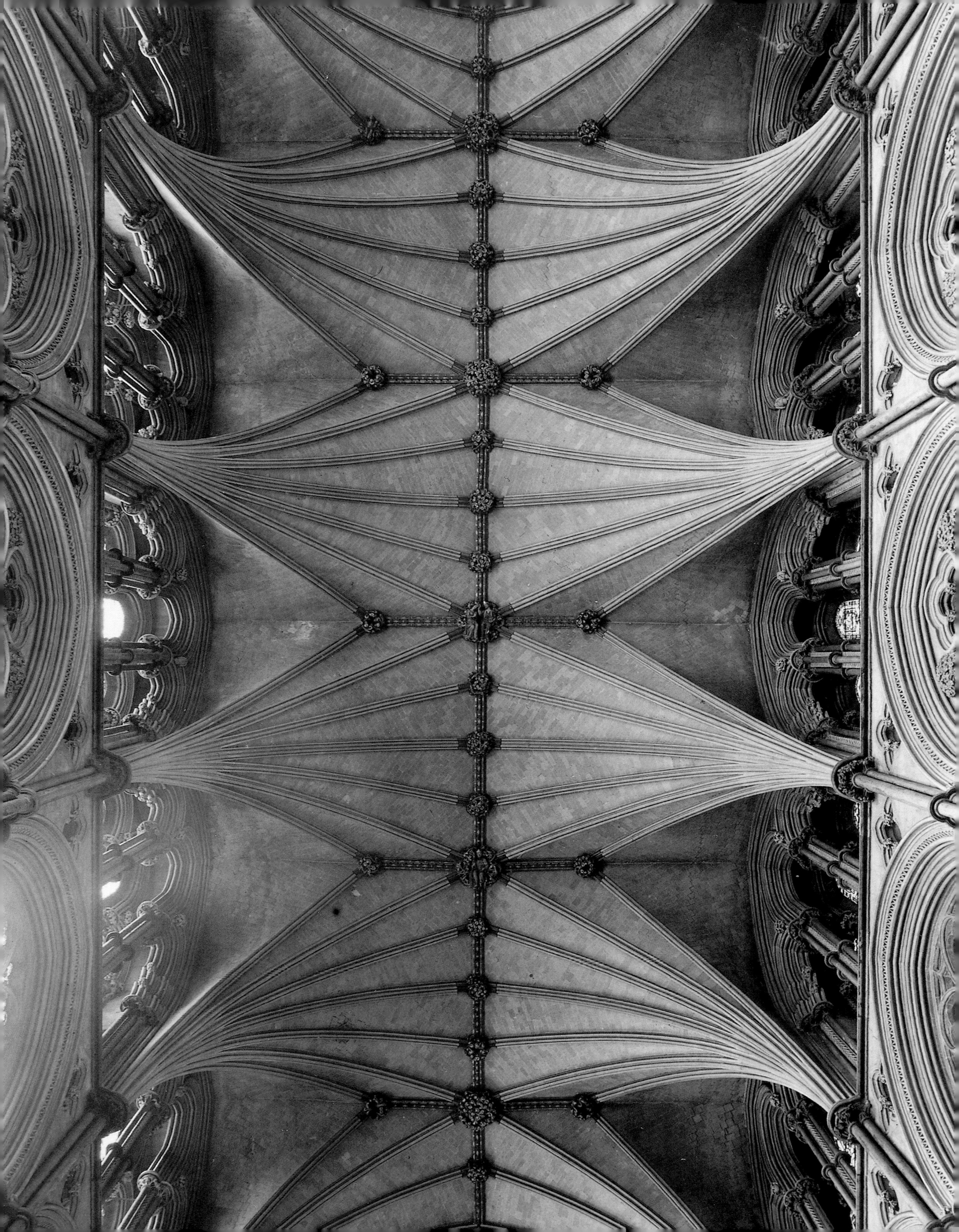

At Ely decay is indeed as foreign as sin. This exploration of analogies between plant, body and stone, the organic and inorganic, may help one to understand the edenic aspect of some English Gothic sanctuaries, their conscious and purposeful recovery in marble and stone of a prelapsarian state of perfectibility. That this owed something to the imaginative relationship between English hagiography, patrons and architects is clear; though the extremely costly form that it took also owed much to the sheer wealth of the English dioceses. It should not be forgotten that such major French High Gothic churches as Reims (1211) and Amiens (1220) were making considerable play with nature imagery. Instances of a conscious and sophisticated reflection on the relationship between the media of stone and wood carving are not unknown in France: at the Gothic parish church of Vermenton, near Auxerre, the porch of around 1170 has very curious piers with attached shafts carved as if they were palm trunks (perhaps following Psalm 91:13?) or roughly hewn wooden poles, growing directly into the capital (fig. 76).[104] This is a form of wit, a conscious acting out of the relationship between the durable and the impermanent and also, perhaps, of the axe-chisel dichotomy employed a few years later by Gervase of Canterbury in his appreciation of the capitals at Canterbury (p. 31 above). That wood and stone enjoyed a positive, and hence potentially enjoyable, hierarchy is indicated by a passage in the Metrical Life of St Hugh concerning Hugh's building-up of the monastery at Witham not in rottable wood, but durable stone (*Non putrescibili ligno, sed perpete saxo*).[105] The contrast here is between something unseemly or rustic, and something essentially virtuous. Ely's sanctuary is virtuous in exactly the same sense: in its naturalistic verve it embodies the paradox that the immutable temple, like the saints, must have none of the corruptibility of the earth, yet must also be a living thing. Peter Dronke's illuminating discussion of the concept of *viriditas* in medieval colour imagery identifies a key focus of this creative ambivalence in the semantic range of the Latin noun *gemma*, i.e. a bud on a plant, or a precious gem: a poetic ambiguity that greatly enriched medieval poetics of the precious stones and edenic garden imagery of the Heavenly Jerusalem.[106] The purchase of the noun *gemma* points directly to the transpositions noted above at Lincoln in the case of its crocket piers studded with *gemmae*, signalling at once something organic (Aaron's rod) and yet precious in derivation and connotation (stained glass or metalwork, the stones of the Heavenly Jerusalem). In this light even the delicate buds of the Peterborough Psalter Crucifixion cited earlier are part of the *Crux gemmata* tradition. Thus, tropologically, the precious stones stand, according to the Latin song *Cives celestis patrie*, for human beings of flesh and blood, their variety being the variety of the virtues adumbrated in the account of Aaron's breastplate in Exodus 28:6–30.[107] Yet because the bejewelled Heavenly Jerusalem is also like a garden, with the pure river of the water of life and the Tree of Life, the

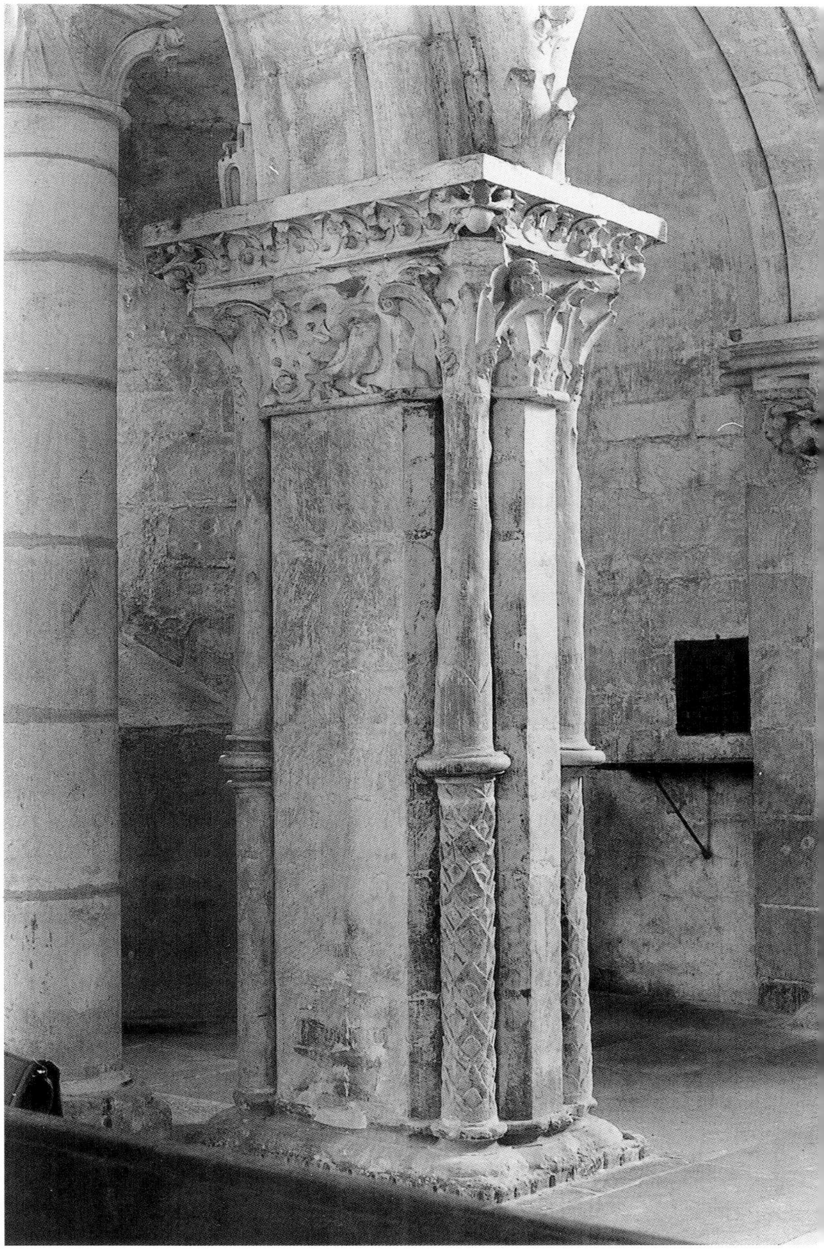

76 Vermenton (near Auxerre, Yonne), parish church, pier, *c.* 1170 (Conway Library, Courtauld Institute of Art).

75 Ely Cathedral, retrochoir vault (east at top), showing principal bosses of St Etheldreda, Coronation of the Virgin (reproduced by permission of English Heritage. NMR).

Lignum vitae with its twelve fruits and leaves which were for the healing of the nations (*ad sanitatem gentium*) (Revelation 22: 2) is both fertile and free of decay. The poem *De translatione*, written for Salisbury around 1220, discussed in the previous chapter, contains restorative imagery broadly in this tradition.

These patterns of thought were far from being solely modern. Ely was a comparatively old cult centre, and devotion to Etheldreda had attained a high degree of articulation well before the Conquest. St Ethelwold's refoundation of the monastery in 970 deserves particular consideration here.[108] Ethelwold translated Etheldreda's remains to an elevated shrine of some description by the high altar, and this was followed by the translations of Withburga, Sexburga and Ermenilda.[109] His first abbot, Brihtnoth, also raised images of the four key saints Etheldreda, Sexburga, Ermenilda and Withburga on either side of the high altar, silver-gilt and jewelled.[110] Ely's tenth-century high altar thus foreshadowed the sanctuary arrangements at Canterbury under Lanfranc, as described by Gervase, where the high altar sanctuary was presided over by precious images of Christ, Sts Dunstan and Alphege, in the manner of prestigious early Christian Roman altars.[111] Whether or not the Ely figures were arrayed under tabernacles, its array of virgin saints was a particularly weighty and effulgent assertion of the visual culture of Ely's second founder, St Ethelwold himself. In Ethelwold's celebrated illuminated Benedictional, also of the 970s or so (BL Add. MS 49598), there is a highly developed choric imagery of male and female saints, confessors, virgins (including Etheldreda) and apostles who stand under tabernacles with grandiose foliated capitals and bases, and apparently sustain them caryatid-like as columns of the Church (fig. 99).[112] It includes a full-page illumination of Etheldreda herself showing her within one of the elaborate acanthus frames so typical of this manuscript, and holding a flowering sprig, perhaps a lily, as 'perpetual virgin' (fig. 77). She turns towards Christ in Majesty, who is enclosed in the initial O for the text of her feast on the opposite page (fol. 91).[113] The benediction celebrates her as the chaste bride of Christ in perpetuity who displayed her purity through her incorruptible body.[114]

Viriditas is arguably a master notion in the conception of the celebrated organic frames or *circi* of the pictures mentioned by the scribe Godeman in the dedicatory poem at the start of the Benedictional of St Ethelwold;[115] and that it was also deemed central to the taste of Hugh of Northwold and his circle is further indicated by the fine marble tomb of Hugh himself, made around or before 1254, which originally lay next to the ornate shrine of the *beata stirps*, Etheldreda, at the heart of the retrochoir.[116] The Purbeck marble effigy of Hugh, garbed in mass vestments, is now set on a low chest and framed by an elaborate canopy, the shafts of which are smothered in energetically creeping and winding inhabited foliage, enclosing birds (fig. 78). The composition of the tomb is a remarkably vivid paradigm of the monk-bishop's devotional preoccupations. The effigy is framed to either side by protector saints standing under richly crocketted foiled arches, forming an early example of the image-towers flanking episcopal effigies which were just becoming fashionable. These small images are segregated by gender, males to his right (St Edmund, a bishop or mitred abbot and a monk), females to his left (St Etheldreda and probably two of her holy kin, one crowned, with an owl at her feet, the other a nun). This ambivalently part-plantiform, part-architectural habitation of the saints perhaps represents the celestial palace (*celesta aula*) into which Etheldreda would surely enter according to Ethelwold's benediction for her.[117] Etheldreda's virtues and destiny are also Hugh's. In illustration of this theme of virtue are pointed allusions to chastity. Two of the female saints have the head of a goat or ram, a symbol of lust vanquished,[118] on the outer frames of their canopies; while Etheldreda, in reference perhaps to the idea that her staff was also a weapon in the struggle against vice, uses her fine flourishing crook to skewer a demon at her feet.[119] The cue to the ensemble is clearly Psalm 90, of which it is an epitome.[120] Thus the whole woven cradle is the *refugium* of Psalm 90: 2, where no evil shall befall him, and into which Hugh's soul is borne, duly censed, by the angels at the crenellated top of the structure, who have been given charge over him and who bear him up in their hands, lest his foot is dashed against a stone (Psalm 90: 11–12). At his feet are the lion and dragon of Psalm 90: 13, and beneath them is the martyrdom of St Edmund with arrows, perhaps in reference to the *sagitta volante in die* of Psalm 90: 6. Since the lion and dragon were also attributes of the Virgin Mary and Christ in this period, as on the west front of Wells Cathedral, it is likely that the boss of the Coronation of the Virgin in the vault overhead was Hugh of Northwold's devotional consummation, as much as Etheldreda's.

The economy, and in some ways modernity, of this monument (such tombs were an emerging and far from fully resolved genre) should not obscure its congruence with the traditional themes encountered here, for the tomb, like the presbytery retrochoir, reveals the extent to which Hugh of Northwold was not only the devotee but also, and perhaps more importantly, the heir of Etheldreda, and perhaps also Ethelwold, in his re-establishment of the building in the centre of which he

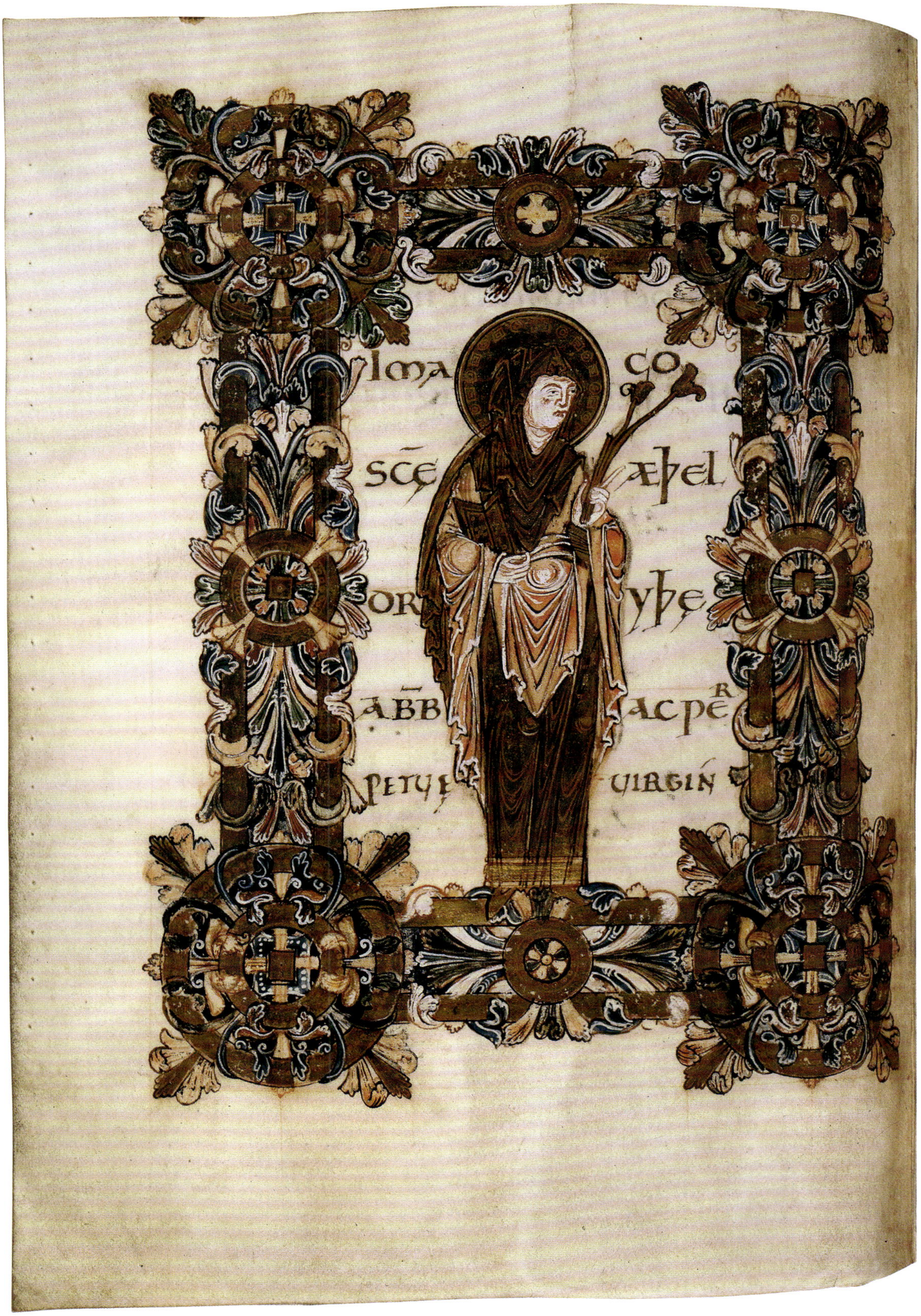

77 St Etheldreda. Benedictional of St Ethelwold, BL Add. MS 49598, fol. 90v, late 10th century (by permission of the British Library).

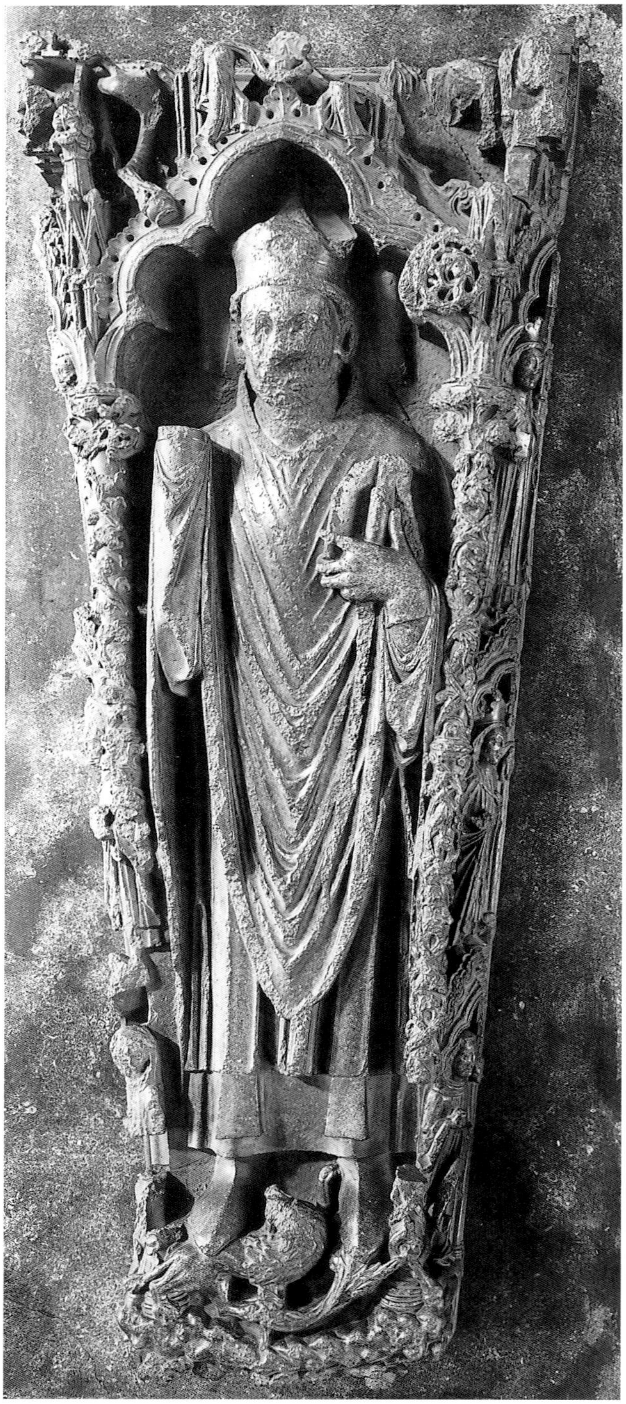

78 Ely Cathedral, tomb effigy of Bishop Hugh of Northwold, d. 1254 (© Crown copyright. NMR).

was buried as *fundator*. In keeping with the current reformist revival of the idea of the bishop as exorcist – to which I shall return – Hugh is shown as the suppressor of evil in the company of the virtuous. Yet the tomb's *agon*, its demonstration of the struggle between good and evil, and its complimentary sense of the force of good as an ineluctable force of nature, correspondingly matched by the vigour of vice, also possesses something archaic, even primitive; something recognizable too in the old Fenland cults, as in Henry of Avranches's characterization of St Guthlac of Crowland battling epically in the wilds as *domitor monstrorum*.[121] The shafts of Hugh's tomb resemble in their luxuriant clotted and inhabited detail not the smooth, sleek colonettes of later episcopal effigies, including that at Ely of Bishop William of Kilkenny around 1256,[122] but the broad assertive carved Romanesque ornament of the jambs of the twelfth-century Prior's Doorway at Ely. It might be going too far to see in them too an analogy to the *circi* of the Benedictional of St Ethelwold; and yet the scaffold-like bars and gripping tendrils that characterize Winchester book ornament of the pre-Conquest period afford sufficiently interesting comparisons to the shafts and trefoil foliage of some early Gothic tomb detailing for the idea not to be wholly absurd. Older art was undoubtedly appreciated, perhaps because at times something new was seen in it. One of the most articulate commentators of the period, Gerald of Wales, wrote at length of his astonishment at the 'well-knitted' ornament he witnessed in an illuminated Insular Gospel book while in Ireland in the 1180s, perhaps another instance of his positive approach to *subtilitas* (p. 55 above) which finds other visual analogies in the period.[123] Francis Wormald wrote authoritatively about the persistence of Anglo-Saxon line-drawing techniques in English post-Conquest and Gothic art, which according to him were undergoing a powerful and widespread 'revival' in early thirteenth-century history and hagiography, as in the great Guthlac Roll.[124]

Yet the temptation to link the artistic celebration of an Anglo-Saxon saint to a wholesale conscious renaissance of Anglo-Saxon art is resistable, for such a supposition would be generally inconsistent with the visual evidence. It is better to think here of something more like a tradition. Hugh of Northwold's Ely was a brilliantly effective and absolutely site-specific harmonization of Gothic art with local traditions and discourses. These discourses obviously entailed a more general sense, apparent from the time of Bede, of the sanctity of the English people, which the Conquest had scarcely undermined. This sensibility was not an innovation: and to suppose that what Hugh of Northwold did at Ely was bound up with a more widespread, even proto-nationalistic, urge to promote well-established old English saints such as Etheldreda may be to overemphasize the extent of their demotion after the Conquest.[125]

In action, Hugh was part of a continuum at Ely; and it was his style of patronage, as much as Etheldreda's style of sanctity, that shaped thirteenth-century Ely. Yet, that this promotion of old saints was undoubtedly a consideration in thirteenth-century England can be demonstrated by other cults of the time which, unlike Ely, saw the production of significant new promotional hagiography and the unexpected emergence of ancient holy figures from much greater obscurity, typically with the support of patrons who, unlike Hugh, were not English. The best instance of this is the support shown in the 1220s for the apostle of the West Saxons, St Birinus, by the French alien Bishop of Winchester, Peter des Roches.[126] For one thing, this style of promotion was connected, as it had been before the Conquest, to the issue of Church reform. But promotion was not always a matter of single relic-cults. Other ecclesiastical patrons of the 1220s and 1230s were thinking just as deeply about the local heritage of their churches; and not all of them had the advantage of a focused and mature local cult. For them, sainthood was a matter of collective representation.

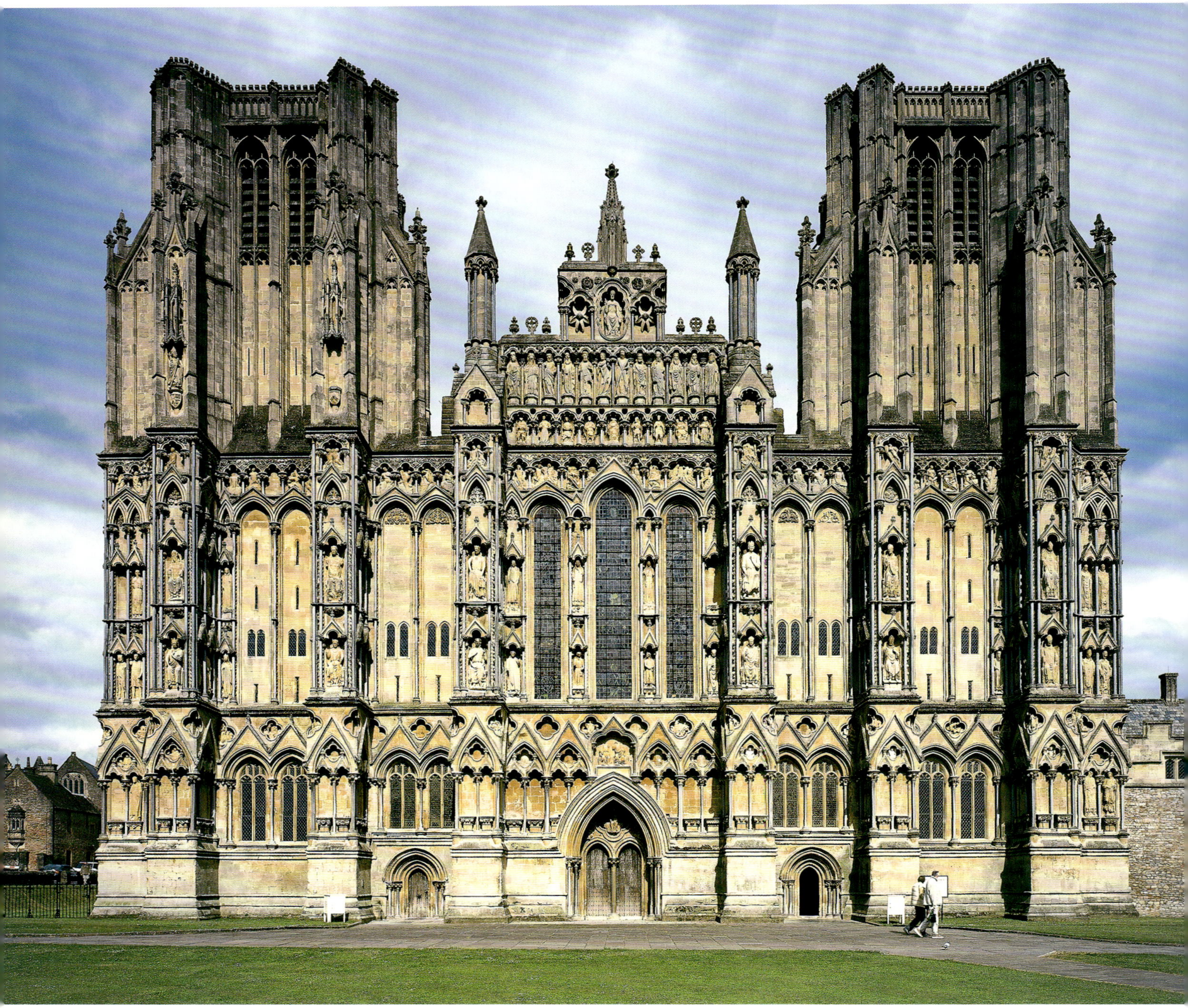

79 Wells Cathedral, west facade (John Crook).

Chapter 5

THE CLEFTS OF THE ROCK: WELLS

O my dove, that art in the clefts of the rock.
Canticles 2: 14

One such patron, a significant bishop who also elected to be buried at the very centre of his church, was Jocelin of Wells. Jocelin, Bishop of Bath (1206–42), and a man with curial experience, presided over a church whose plight was very different from that of stable Ely. Wells had no important relic-cult. Its importance as an Anglo-Saxon diocesan church had been radically affected by the Conquest which, under Bishop John of Tours (1088–1122), had led to its demotion by the removal of the see to the monastic house at Bath, now a cathedral priory. The subsequent creation at Wells of a new cathedral-like church, and with it a major artwork that celebrated sainthood, namely its great sculpted west facade (fig. 79), coincided with the successful struggle finally to regain diocesan status for Wells. Here, if anywhere, one may be entitled to pinpoint the propagandistic and compensatory value of Gothic art for an uncertain institution.

Historiola

The development of patronage at Wells was a response partly to the Norman policy of moving old dioceses to well-developed towns or cities, and partly to the intensification of conflict between diocesan and monastic power. The consequences of this conflict at late twelfth-century Canterbury, including the crises of Hackington and Lambeth, are noted above. The aims of the diocesans were to challenge the customary rights and privileges of the monasteries, either with respect to their electoral rights, or their immunity from episcopal visitation.[1] The Normans had resolved this issue in part by the creation of new cathedral priories, as at Ely and Bath; some monastic houses, such as St Albans, Bury and Westminster, were able altogether to gain exemption from diocesan control. Their abbots were now entitled to wear mitres. But elsewhere no overall solution was found to what were in effect jurisdictional disputes founded on long-standing historical claims to precedence and autonomy. In the twelfth and early thirteenth centuries Wells found itself drawn hither and thither by the gravitational pull of Bath and the exceptionally wealthy monastery of Glastonbury, and it was within this triangle of proud and stubborn West Country institutions that its new cathedral church was eventually to be born. It is not altogether surprising that, given this state of affairs, Wells may have been prompted to reflect on the oldest traditions of the region: and that in turn involved thoughts about kingship and sanctity.

The story of Wells's rebirth as a diocesan church deserves brief discussion here as it is germane to my argument and gives some flavour of the times.[2] Around 909 Wells had become the cathedral church of Somerset, and it remained as such under the patronage of significant Anglo-Saxon bishops who came to rest either side of its high altar, notably Dudoc (d. 1060) and Giso (d. 1088). After John of Tours had removed the see to Bath, the church at Wells saw none of the rebuilding that was typical of great churches under the Normans; in effect it was now a small college of canons located just south of the present great church. For some reason, perhaps because it represented 'good practice' and served to right the wrongs of John of Tours, the college was given a cathedral constitution, based on that of Old Sarum, by Robert of Lewes, Bishop of Bath (1136–66): it is unclear, though possible, that the college nurtured resentment at its demotion.[3] The best single evidence that it did is provided by the start of what was effectively a cathedral-style church at Wells, the present church, under Reginald FitzJocelin de Bohun, Bishop of Bath (1174–91), work being under way not later than about 1180.[4] The possession of a cathedral-like building – indeed a new and fashionable one – was a rational basis for a claim to diocesan status. Reginald was succeeded by his relative Savaric (1192–1205), who sought to extend his diocesan control over Glastonbury in a kind of corporate take-over bid: Glastonbury's power and riches made it seem like a threat to, as well as a natural candidate for, diocesan status, even though its church had been largely destroyed by fire in 1184. This bid, which of course had implications for the cathedral priory at Bath, had been supported by Jocelin, the future bishop.[5] Yet after his elevation to the see in 1206, Jocelin relinquished the claim to Glastonbury and seems almost immediately to have initiated plans, including the erection of a residential palace, to return the see to Wells.[6] That he was a local man was undoubtedly important, for personal motivation – as with Hugh of Northwold at Ely – is an important factor in understanding the origins of Gothic patronage.

From 1214 Jocelin was styled by legatine authority Bishop of Bath and Glastonbury, but the claim to Glastonbury was set aside in 1219, and in 1220 he petitioned Pope Honorius III to be granted the title 'Bath and Wells': the legate Pandulph ordered a search of the registers at Wells to discover if this title had apostolic privilege, as the bishop seems to have claimed; but the search seems never to have been conducted.[7] Wells provides a useful early example – later to be repeated on the national stage under Edward I – of the way that papally sponsored interrogations of local archives could help to shape the production of history.[8] As it was, by 1220 the great church including its west front was well under way. Towards the time that it was being completed, Jocelin, in 1241, issued statutes for the church.[9] In 1244 Pope Innocent IV decreed that the chapter of Wells and the convent of Bath should have equal electoral rights, ceding to both cathedral status, and so resolving the issue put to Honorius in 1220. In 1245 the same pope ordered Jocelin's successor, Roger, to put the legend 'Bath and Wells' on his seal. In 1248 the topping-out of the church was under way: Wells had arrived, and indeed had surpassed physically its rival at Bath.[10]

Though Wells laid claim to St Athelhelm, the uncle of St Dunstan, it lacked a major relic-cult. But in this it was not quite alone, since Glastonbury and Bath also lacked indubitably major shrines: Glastonbury professed to own the relics of St Dunstan and St Patrick, and Bath, St Alphege; but Glastonbury's claim to Dunstan was challenged by Canterbury.[11] Since this issue affected the matter of seniority and privilege of a great house – as became apparent when Savaric launched his bid in the 1190s – Glastonbury had employed William of Malmesbury to compile an account of its antiquity, which included some use of architecture as a witness.[12] In 1191, following the fire of 1184, the monks at Glastonbury made an even more important discovery when they turned up the remains of King Arthur and Guinevere, identified by a clearly inscribed lead cross.[13] William of Malmesbury had not linked King Arthur to Glastonbury but to Avalon; it remained for Gerald of Wales to suggest that Avalon and Glastonbury were in fact the same.[14] In the light of Glastonbury's increasingly well-organized (and in this case spectacular) self-promotion, it is intrinsically likely that during the late twelfth century Wells made a corresponding effort to shape its own history and cultivate its traditions. The principal sign of this is the brief history known as the *Historiola*, compiled at some point after 1174.[15] The declared aim of the *Historiola* was to set down how, why and when Wells became a diocesan church and was later demoted; and though it makes no overt claim to the return of the diocese – a claim surely made much more forcibly by the new church building by 1180 – its implicit purpose seems certain, since it is hard to see why a collegiate church should suddenly have become preoccupied with the historical basis of its former diocesan status, unless it was in some sense still aspiring to that standing. As medieval fabulations of the past go, the *Historiola* is actually a limited document. It relates how the see of Somerset was moved to Wells by (the legendary) Bishop Daniel, who had obtained the town from the great West Saxon King Ine – a founder of Glastonbury – after Ine's marriage there to his beloved Adelburga; after Daniel the bishops succeeded one another down to Giso and Dudoc. Giso, who solicited the support of St Edward and his queen, Edith, had been consecrated in Rome and returned to Wells with the mark of apostolic authority.[16] Great kings are implicated in a kind of local apostolic succession. As the *Historiola* observes, from early times the bishops of Wells were indeed called the Bishops of Wells in the court of Rome, in the registers and in other papal documents,[17] a title that ceased under Robert of Lewes; for this claim to apostolic privilege is exactly what was to be investigated in the registers of Wells at the behest of the papal legate in 1220.[18] Though the *Historiola* makes no mention of any bishop subsequent to Reginald's accession in 1174, its fundamental if oblique assertions seem preparatory to the legatine enquiry about the title 'Bath and Wells'.[19]

The *Historiola* does not provide evidence for the passive acquiescence of the canons of Wells in their demoted status. To the *Historiola* and the fact of the rising

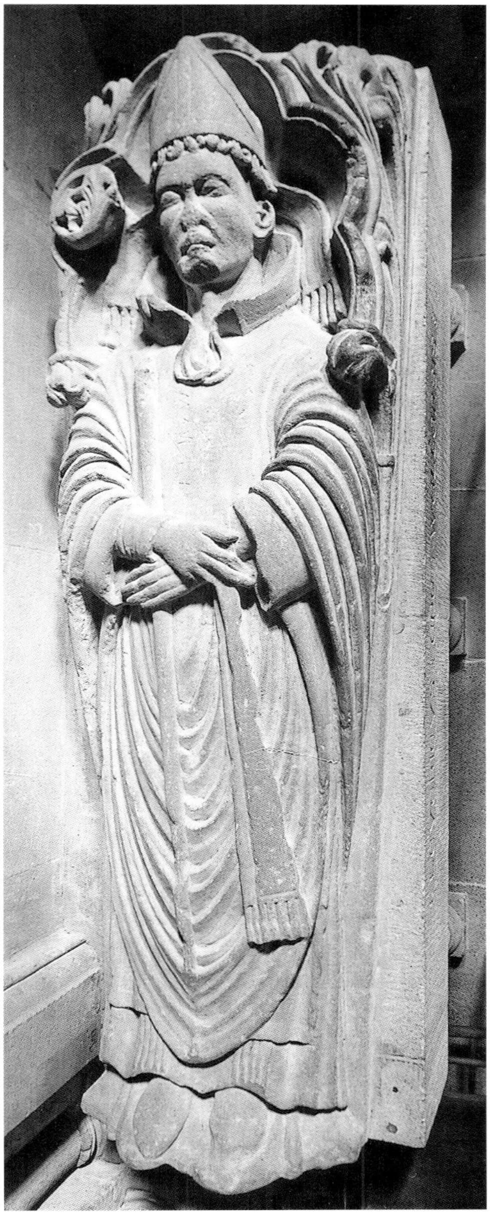

80 Wells Cathedral, effigy of Bishop Levericus (Conway Library, Courtauld Institute of Art).

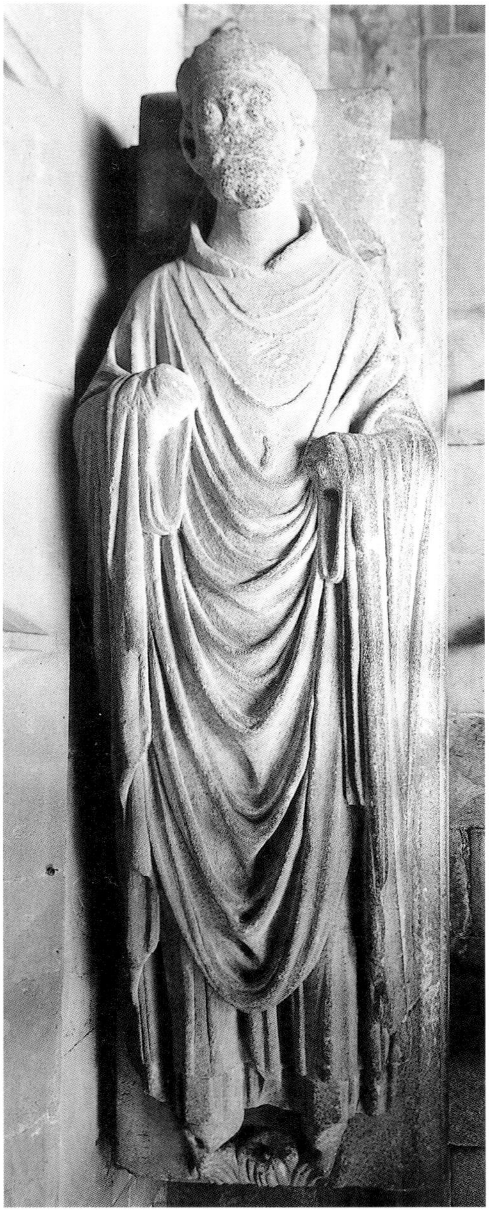

81 Wells Cathedral, effigy of Bishop Giso (Conway Library, Courtauld Institute of Art).

new church must be added a further consideration which lends weight to the idea that the chapter was in fact concerned about its diocesan origins, which is that at some point early in the construction of the new church it commissioned a set of at least seven sculpted tomb-effigies of some of the Anglo-Saxon bishops listed in the *Historiola*, in effect a retrospective commemoration by means of a comparatively new genre.[20] Episcopal and abbatial effigial tombs, typically in low relief, were appearing at Old Sarum, Exeter and Peterborough; and the transfer of the old tombs from Old Sarum to the new cathedral after 1220 reveals the pietas such memorial elicited, not least because Old Sarum provided one possible model for the form of the canons' church at Wells.[21] The remaining effigies at Wells are powerfully wrought representations with some unexpected features, such as folded hands and closed eyes, which may indicate Continental influence (fig. 80); two of them, including that of Bishop Giso (fig. 81), are more conventional in appearance and are also closer in taste to Jocelin's early thirteenth-century seal (fig. 93), so they were either executed by more than one team, or at different dates.[22] Their purpose, however, was to mark the translation of the remains of the bishops to the new church at some point presumably in or after the 1190s.[23] Great care was taken to identify the bishops by means of inscribed lead plaques placed in the wooden coffins, and by external inscriptions,[24] and the forensic value of such texts became apparent in the later Middle Ages when at least one of the inscriptions was cited in evidence in the *Historia major*.[25] William of Malmesbury had already been aware of the evidential power of art and architecture in backing up his account of Glastonbury. Indeed both St Dunstan's and Arthur's remains at Glastonbury were purported in 1184 and 1191 respectively to have been identified by clear inscriptions, a possible incentive to the measures taken at Wells.[26] In effect, the chapter aimed to create a concerted and thoroughly attested display of episcopal tombs surrounding the choir and presbytery, a device perhaps suggested to them by the mode of display of clearly labelled relics at Ely and Winchester, the latter being connected to Glastonbury through Henry of Blois.[27] In their midst, Jocelin elected to be buried.[28] In doing so, he stressed his own, thoroughly local, continuity with his forebears, and also the primacy of Wells, not Bath, as the diocesan centre.[29] The relationship between the *Historiola* and the effigies is harmonious, although it was not so close or self-conscious as that between the history the monk Rigord constructed at Saint-Denis in the 1190s, in which a guide to the abbey's tombs is interwoven with its own institutional history:[30] the *Historiola*, unlike later Wells histories, does not allude to the tombs in evidence, perhaps because its compilation preceded them. Nor is it clear that any significant cults attached to the early bishops of Wells, for there was no hagiographic tradition.[31] What is clear, however, is that serial representations of sculpted figures at Wells, as elsewhere at this time, could be implicated in an institution's assertion of its own ancient identity. Wells, which (for obvious reasons) had seen no episcopal burials in the twelfth century, now demonstrably had more episcopal tombs than its rival, Bath.

The West Front

There are no definitive documents about the creation of England's greatest medieval show of saints (figs 79, 82), but a consensus of sorts exists as to the probable period of its conception and birth. If recent arguments about the chronology of the church's construction from the 1170s are correct, the middle of the nave was being built in the first decade of the thirteenth century; the practical exigencies of setting the foundations of the church in advance of actual construction (which for the west front included the provision of very large footings indeed) would have entailed that plans for the front, as built, were arrived at by around 1200–10.[32] That in turn implied a front of considerable width, one possible corollary of a decision to sculpt it lavishly. The aim was to produce a rectangular screen facade with a single central raised feature, the overall surface of which absorbed the two large towers that flanked the aisles, a type of design already established in Romanesque England, and of which Wells is in a sense a late statement.[33] The front, then, was conceived in the immediate wake of the *Historiola* and the episcopal effigies, and it was almost certainly rising by about 1220. If Matthew Paris's allusion to the fall of a *tholus* (probably a pinnacle) onto the church during an 'earthquake' in 1248 refers to the front and not some other part, it would have been topped out towards 1250, and it is intrinsically likely that the furnishing of sculptures, and their painting, was taken as only far as it could be by that time.[34] Later Wells sources imply that it was Jocelin's work.[35] But there is some doubt as to when it was actually finished. Large – and admittedly invisible – areas of its south tower were never provided with statues. In the 1240s the church appears to have experienced some financial stringency, and from the middle of that decade a significant alternative attraction for capable teams of masons and sculptors had appeared in the form of Henry III's rebuilding of Westminster Abbey, which may have drained away the highly organized talent upon which the production of such sculptures was premised. The topmost gable-like feature with ranks of niches appears not to have been filled with its orders of angels and Apostles until the fifteenth century – exactly the period when at least one medieval witness to the facade, floundering about its meaning, saw it crudely as a sort of play-off between the Old and New Law.[36] Even in its completion, Wells was becoming an elusive monument – historically the fate of much sculpture in the public domain – and attributing some sort of overall meaning to it now is a hazardous matter.[37]

Facades, like towers, were often problematic; the monks at St Albans had already faced the failure of one project to complete the west entrances to their church (p. 47 above), and the Gothic screen-like extensions to the Romanesque front at Lincoln, with their lacklustre expanses of niches and corbels, never gained statues. The comparable projects at Salisbury and Lichfield were carried through architecturally, but not fully furnished with sculpture.[38] Yet for all its imperfections, the Wells

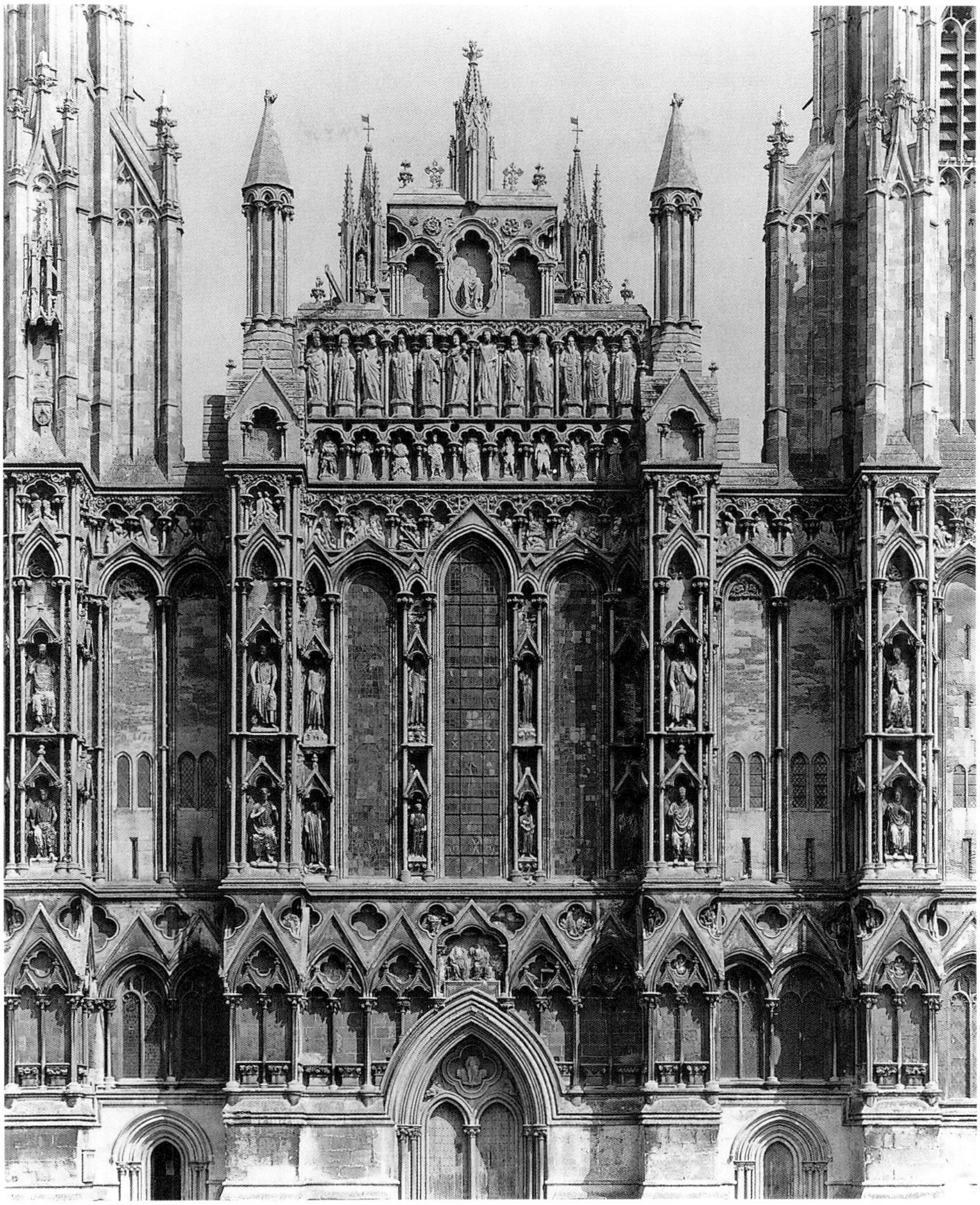

82 Wells Cathedral, west facade, central portion (Conway Library, Courtauld Institute of Art).

front is a strange success, and nothing in the history of English art prepares us for it. Jean Bony rightly called it a 'cliff-face', and the whole composition, though artful, has something of a phenomenon of nature about it.[39] Not only the scale, but also the character, of its hundreds of figures – calm, magnificent, defiant and detached (figs 83–4) – makes the psychological impact of any assured and triumphalist artistic assertion of authority. There is indeed no harm in seeing it as the Church Triumphant. By employing uniformly very few motifs – principally aedicules with projecting canopies supported on blue lias shafts, and quatrefoil sinkings – the facade provided for a scaffold which ripples across its width with a crisp rhythm of brittle components. Yet its underlying structure of giant projecting buttresses, around which the scaffold is turned and folded, is everywhere apparent. It is because of this apparent thickness that the use of forms sunk deep into plain masonry to enclose, even secrete and occlude, statuary as if it were in some way part of its geological history is so effective. The bulk of these

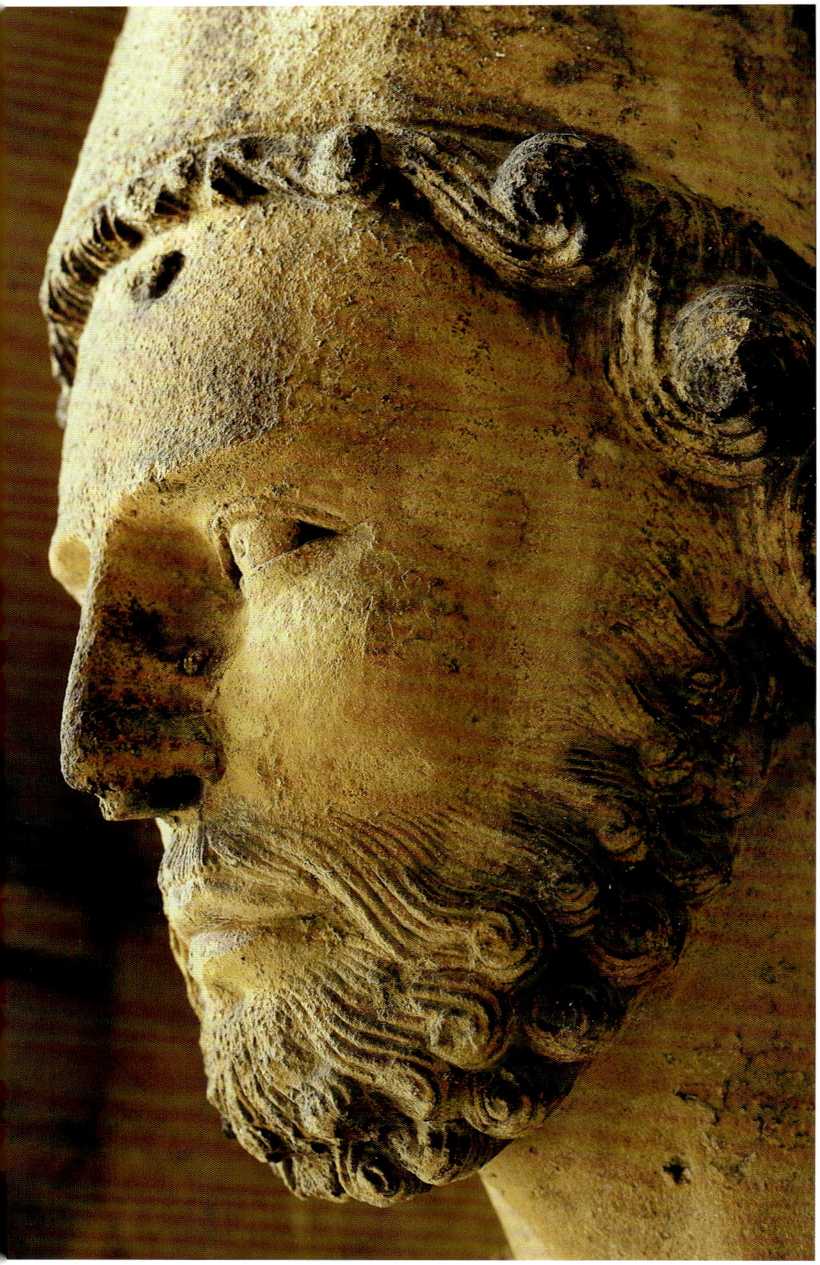

83 Wells Cathedral, west facade, head of king (Jerry Sampson).

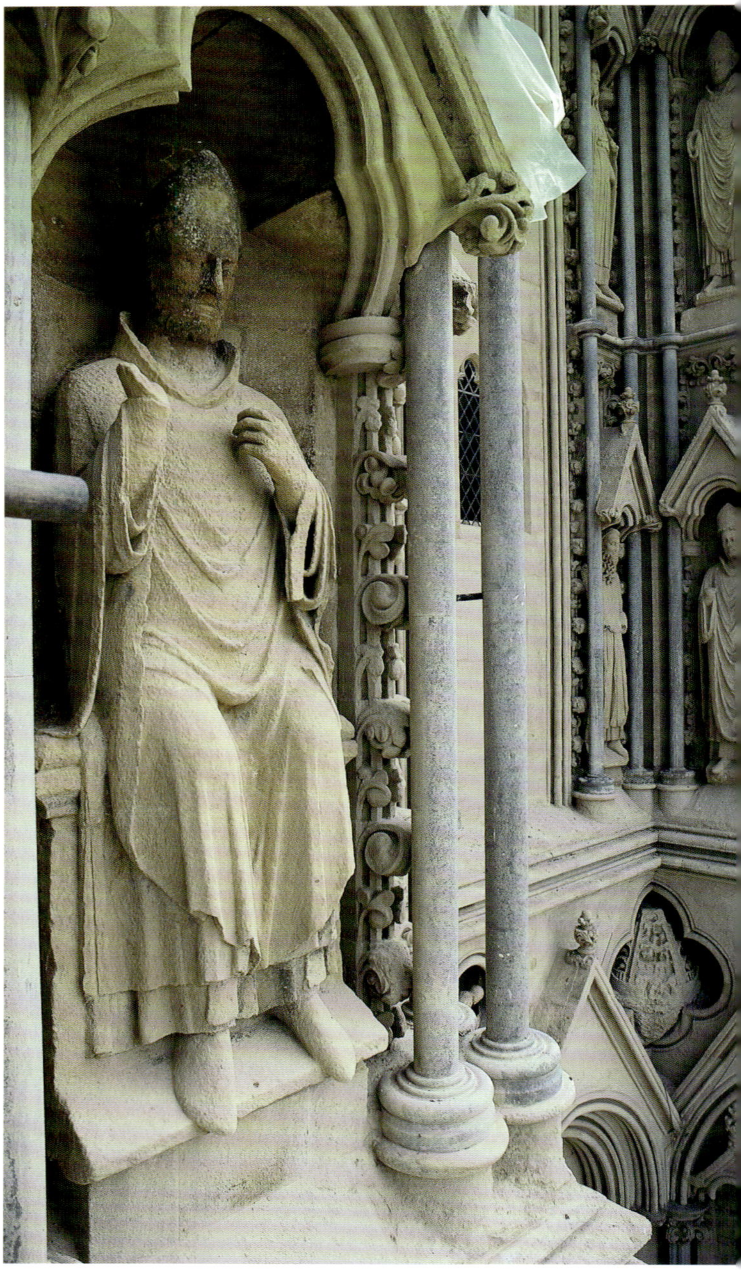

84 Wells Cathedral, west facade, seated bishop (Jerry Sampson).

projections is such that they can bear having their corners cut out by the quatrefoils, as if they had been champed at by some Leviathan. This only strengthens their metaphorical power in showing how the sheltered saints buttress and inhabit the Church. The doors, no smaller than those of most English great churches of the time, are also part of this aesthetic of sunk or hollowed-out forms.[40] The cathedral's north nave porch is extremely finely finished and its portal more ample, and though probably used as the major entrance for the canons, may itself have been the major public entrance.[41] The distinction between the two styles of entrance, respectively narrow and broad, may in turn be symbolic: as noted above, Gilbert of Limerick's reformist *De statu ecclesiae* contrasted the narrow way of the life of monks and priests (*arcta via religiosis et ordinatis*) with the broadness of the church of the secular married folk, the *carnales et conjugatos*.[42]

Strikingly few of the larger ideas can have come from France, and the constant brandishing of the yardstick of French Gothic portals of the period has been one of the less helpful tendencies in the understanding of Wells.[43] Chronology (which the French connection has helped to confuse) is not the least of the problems. If the facade was planned in its essentials by about 1210, the documented presence during the Interdict in 1212 of Bishop Jocelin, his brother Hugh and Elias of Dereham in western France – one of the sectors mentioned in connection with influence on Wells – is of debatable consequence.[44] At Wells, the main statuary is invariably set within niches rather than against columns (fig. 84), a practice that remained normal in England even at so French-influenced a centre as Westminster: this might have been authorized by the setting of figures in aedicules on the major buttresses of French churches, but not by their portals. A certain amount of 'tweaking' of smaller-scale devices, such as the projecting trefoil gabled canopies, may be French-derived, since in England before about 1200 gables tended to be large-scale forms (at Bury, Glastonbury).[45] The dado buttresses on the west front at Amiens, begun after 1220, are adorned with low-relief figurated quatrefoils which fold around the major features of the facade.[46] But for virtually all the Wells practices a wider range of stimuli was possible, which it shared with its French sisters. Serried ranks of big thick gables placed over animated seated figures had started to appear by the 1200s on Mosan metalwork shrines, such as that of the Virgin Mary at Aachen.[47] The great biblical genealogy in the clearstory glass at Canterbury already provided a precocious display of trefoil canopies over its assertive and impressive seated images (fig. 85).[48] This serves to place the otherwise voussoir-like seated presences at Wells in a native context. In fact, where a practice really matters at Wells, it tends to be of English derivation. So, the setting of small lithe figurative compositions from the Bible deep within the quatrefoil sinkings arrayed above door height is exactly similar to the composition on fol. 4v of the Lothian Bible, perhaps from St Albans, of around 1220 (fig. 86), which represents, in thoroughly Augustinian fashion, the Trinity presiding over Creation together with the Fall of the Rebel Angels.[49] At the head of the page is a large quatrefoil enclosing the Trinity, a treatment emphasized by the way in which the Father and Son grip its frame with their fingers disappearing delicately behind it. There is nothing especially French about this arrangement. To put the Trinity in a quatrefoil was a practice of the Anglo-Saxons, as on fol. 126v of the Tiberius Psalter (fig. 87).[50] Lavish rows of vertical crockets frame the major tiers of figures (fig. 84), in the spirit of Lincoln and Ely, and

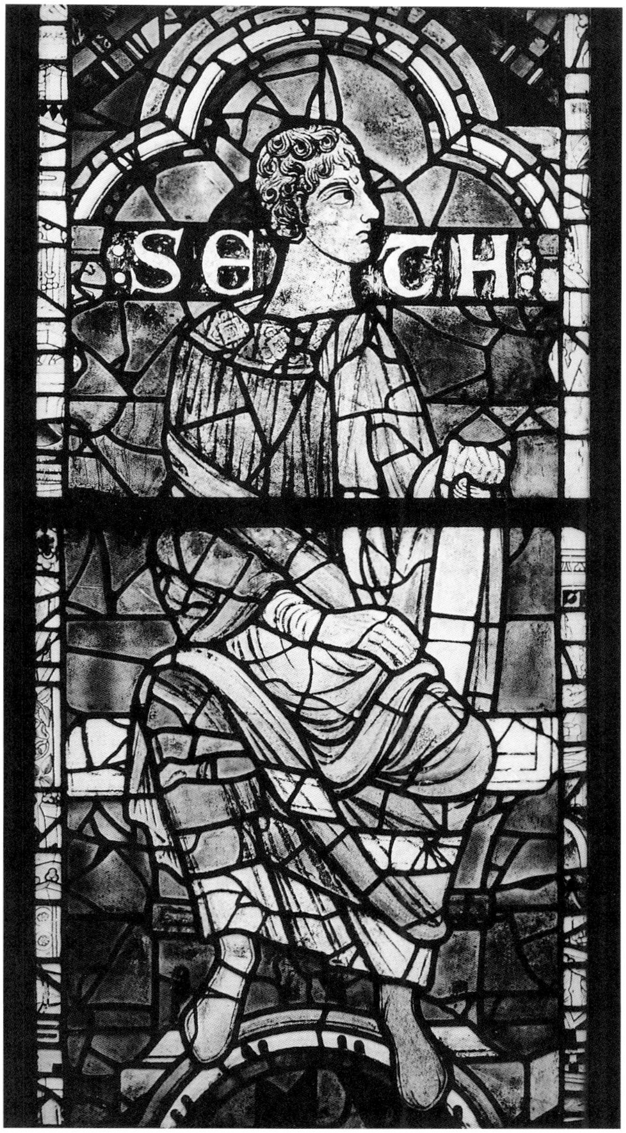

85 Canterbury Cathedral, Semei, from window W: I (Sebastian Strobl).

bring to this show of saints the same metaphorical associations of *viriditas*: the righteous planted in the house of the Lord who flourish in the courts of God (Psalm 91: 13–14). One wonders if this conceit found fresh local authorization at Wells in virtue of its famous springs, since towards the end of the thirteenth century the borough seal of the city adopted on its obverse a fish-filled spring beneath a flourishing tree in allusion to the sources to the south-east of the cathedral church.[51]

Small-scale artworks so often resemble Wells practice that one may reasonably suppose either that this was the kind of scale at which the artists were accustomed to

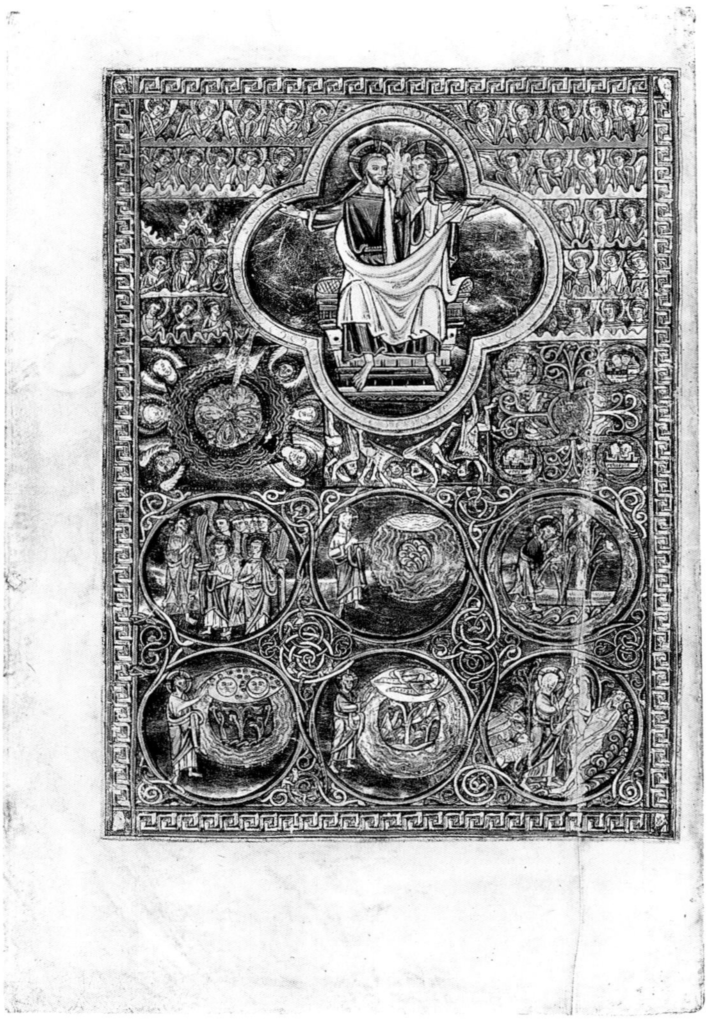

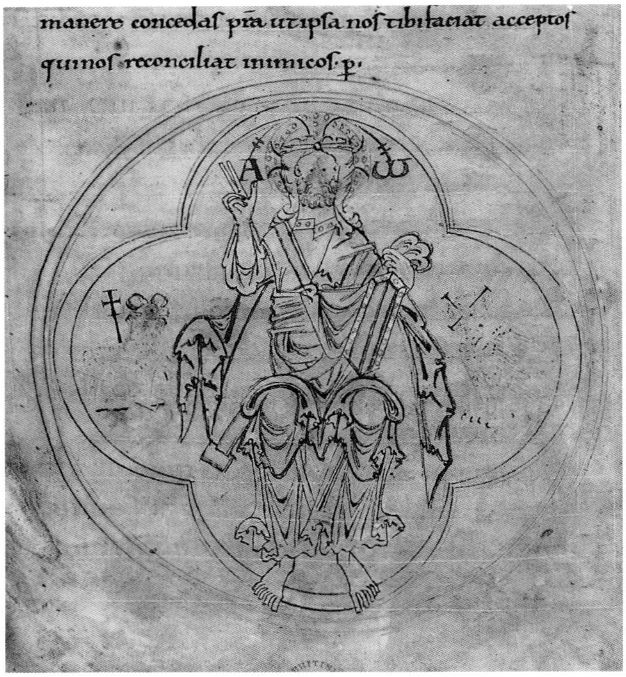

87 Trinity. Tiberius Psalter, BL MS Cotton Tiberius C. VI, fol. 126v, mid-eleventh century (by permission of the British Library).

86 (LEFT) Fall of the Rebel Angels and Creation. Lothian Bible, New York, Pierpont Morgan Library MS 791, fol. 4v, early thirteenth century (The Pierpont Morgan Library, New York).

working (which seems inherently unlikely), or that these artworks in some way point to a much larger repertory of lost monumental, or semi-monumental artefacts, which informed Wells. To set sculpted heads, busts or seated figures in round or foiled openings on tombs, as at Exeter or Canterbury, or facades, as at Lincoln or Peterborough, suggests metalwork-derived practice, as do the reliefs from the fragmentary late twelfth-century screen from Canterbury.[52] Wells in fact is less obviously metalwork-derived, since it eschews many of the techniques of jewellers or goldsmiths. It never uses diaperwork, gewgaws or purely ornamental heads, for example. It does, however, serve as a reminder that the greatest repository of unbuilt great church facade design of the times is to be found on seals. By about 1230 the use of foiled, circular, lozenge or vesica-shaped openings on major institutional seals was fashionable. A good example is the major new seal and counterseal made for Canterbury Cathedral by 1232, which show a pair of church facades conceived in the same sort of brittle, shallow and reiterative decorative language as the west front at Salisbury, and, like the smaller detailing of Salisbury's portals, including tiny heads, busts and figures as a habitation of the saints.[53] The same formal language is spoken by the representation of heads looking out from the walls of Jerusalem, in the Entry to Jerusalem quatrefoil at Wells. Another instance is the seal of Norwich Cathedral of 1258 which includes a tiny image of Herbert de Losinga as *fundator* dominating the frontispiece on the obverse, with on the reverse Christ in a cusped vesica, like the summit of the Wells facade (figs 89, 95).[54] Such feats of miniaturization went hand in hand with the use of multiple-die matrices as a hedge against forgery, as in the case of the Canterbury seal or the *tour de force* of complexity made for Southwick Priory around 1260, though in such cases virtuosity lay precisely in the creation of a multi-layered structure of penetrated, and penetrable, surfaces.[55] The same sort of aesthetic is at work at Wells.

The obviously devotional character of such miniature habitations brings to mind one final reflection on the formal characteristics of Wells, which is the extent to which it may have manifested the same processes of thought as contemporary, though now largely destroyed, church furnishings. Nothing is known, for example, of the design of the (presumably) stone pulpitum at Wells which is likely to have divided the canon's church from the nave in this period, and which might have acted as a pilot for the front; but the surviving fragments from the late twelfth-century screen at Canterbury, and more especially the projecting gabled trefoil arches on the extant pulpitum screen from Salisbury (fig. 56), are fundamentally similar, and the English tendency to transpose motifs and ideas from one context to another should warn against too rigid a distinction between

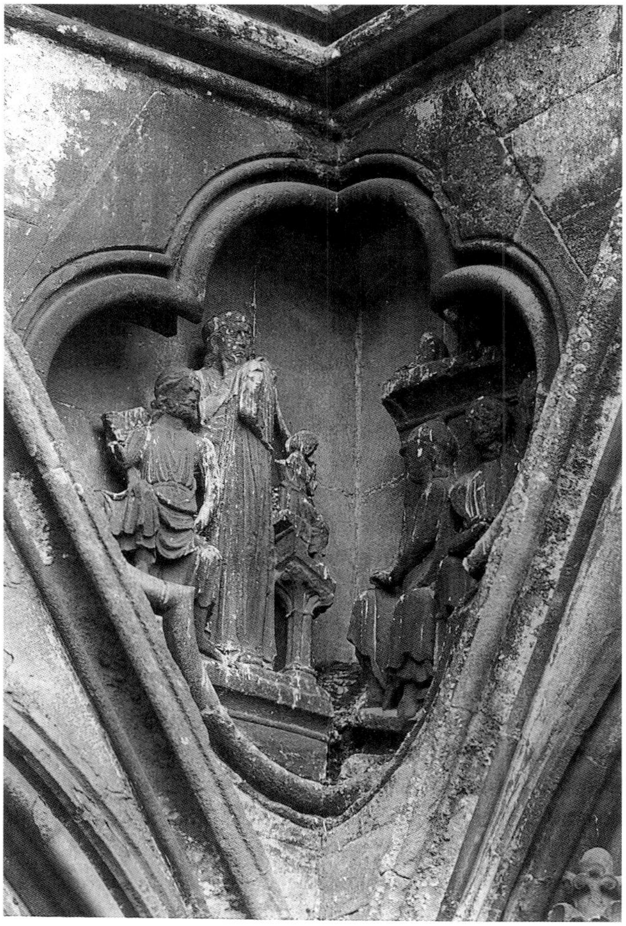

88 Wells Cathedral, west facade quatrefoil showing Christ in the Temple (Conway Library, Courtauld Institute of Art).

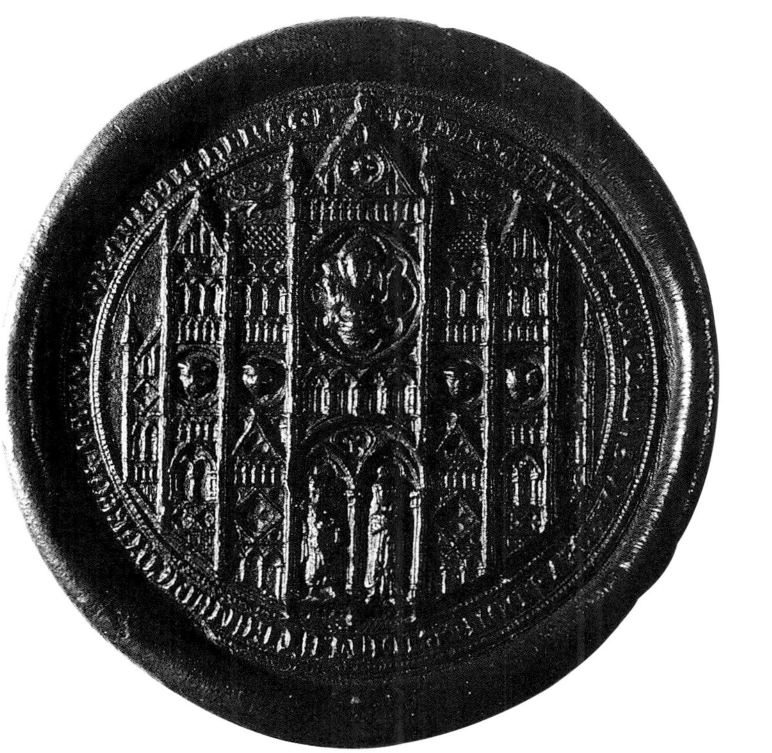

89 Norwich Cathedral Priory, second seal (counterseal) (Society of Antiquaries of London).

'genres' such as great facades and screens.[56] Internal screens such as that of a generation or so later at Naumburg Cathedral employ precisely the same repertory of gables, paired arches and quatrefoils as the Wells facade, and it is partly to such liturgical divisions that one should look for a history of small-scale Bible representation as well.[57] Para-liturgical conceits, such as the young Christ placed in Augustinian fashion as the Word of God on a lectern in the quatrefoil showing the Disputation in the Temple (fig. 88), belong precisely in this sort of context.[58]

To ponder liturgical furnishings is to confront too their performative dimension, for if internal screens or raised divisions were being used in this period for chanting and for the location of organs, so too was the facade at Wells deployed for musical performance. The front has within its thickness a gallery, closed off from the interior of the nave, which runs across the central facade at the level of the angel quatrefoils. It is opened to the west, through the facade and out onto the close, by four triangular groups of three circular openings, which correspond neatly to the outer lobes of the backs of four of the angel niches (figs 90–91). The passageway has rather unusual acoustical properties. As Hugh Shortt spotted in

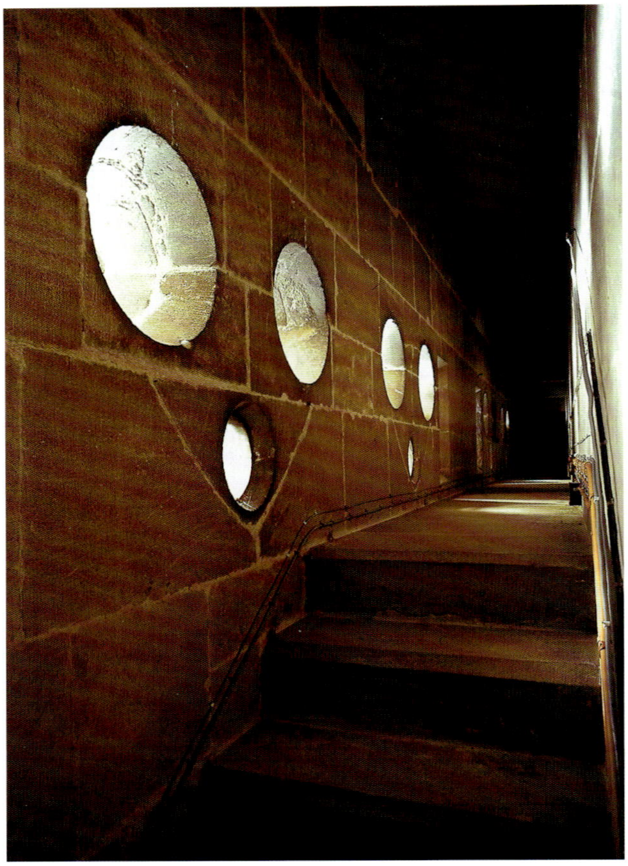

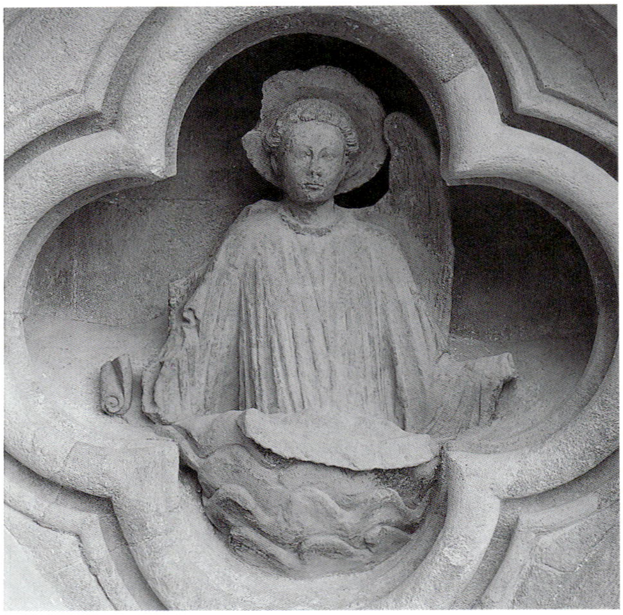

91 Wells Cathedral, west facade, angel (Conway Library, Courtauld Institute of Art).

90 (LEFT) Wells Cathedral, 'singers' gallery within west facade (Jerry Sampson).

1970, through these triple apertures, two at the level of boys and one above for men, choristers sung the *Gloria laus et honor* at Palm Sunday *alternatim* with those outside the church below, a Sarum-derived practice which almost certainly explains why a similar singers' gallery with openings is to be found at both Salisbury and Lichfield, two churches with sculpted west fronts.[59] At Wells there is a further set of eight holes running across above the gable over the niches which now hold the orders of angels; these are suitable for trumpet blasts (Matthew 24: 31, Revelation 8: 2), and may indicate that the plan to have angels in these niches was original. It is not hard to understand the impact of the uncanny effect that human sound projected mysteriously past the angels which inhabited the facade would have had, not least given the long-standing medieval fascination with artefacts, or noises, apparently not made by human means.[60] The facade thus worked on specific occasions as an *organum*, the generic expression for concerted chanting or, more literally, organ playing.[61] The passage at Wells is too small literally to have accommodated an organ of any consequence or profundity. But the analogy with organs is not entirely idle, since the ecclesiastical use of such instruments in England had been encouraged during the pre-Conquest Church reforms of St Dunstan and St Ethelwold, and one possible location for early organs as siren-like sources of clamour, rather than for liturgy, may have been the type of atrium or *westwerk* that existed at Winchester and, possibly, Wells itself.[62] Wulfstan's Life of St Swithun indeed includes the most celebrated (if hyperbolic) description of an early English organ, blown by seventy men and heard throughout the city (*auditur ubique per urbem*).[63] Organs, like bells, were dedicated to saints, and bells too attracted this almost Virgilian mythology of heroic scale and stentorian broadcasting power.[64] Hence the development of separate bell-towers, as at Salisbury. In turning to the substantive content of the west front, then, one must bear in mind its practical and imaginative relationship to automatous *mirabilia* of various types. The heads and bodies which peek out at the viewer from early Gothic facades, and seals, may be understood not just as signs, but as voices, reminiscent perhaps of the 'voices' heard so often in Revelation.

What exactly is being 'voiced' by the stupendous collection of images on the facade is, however, a matter of

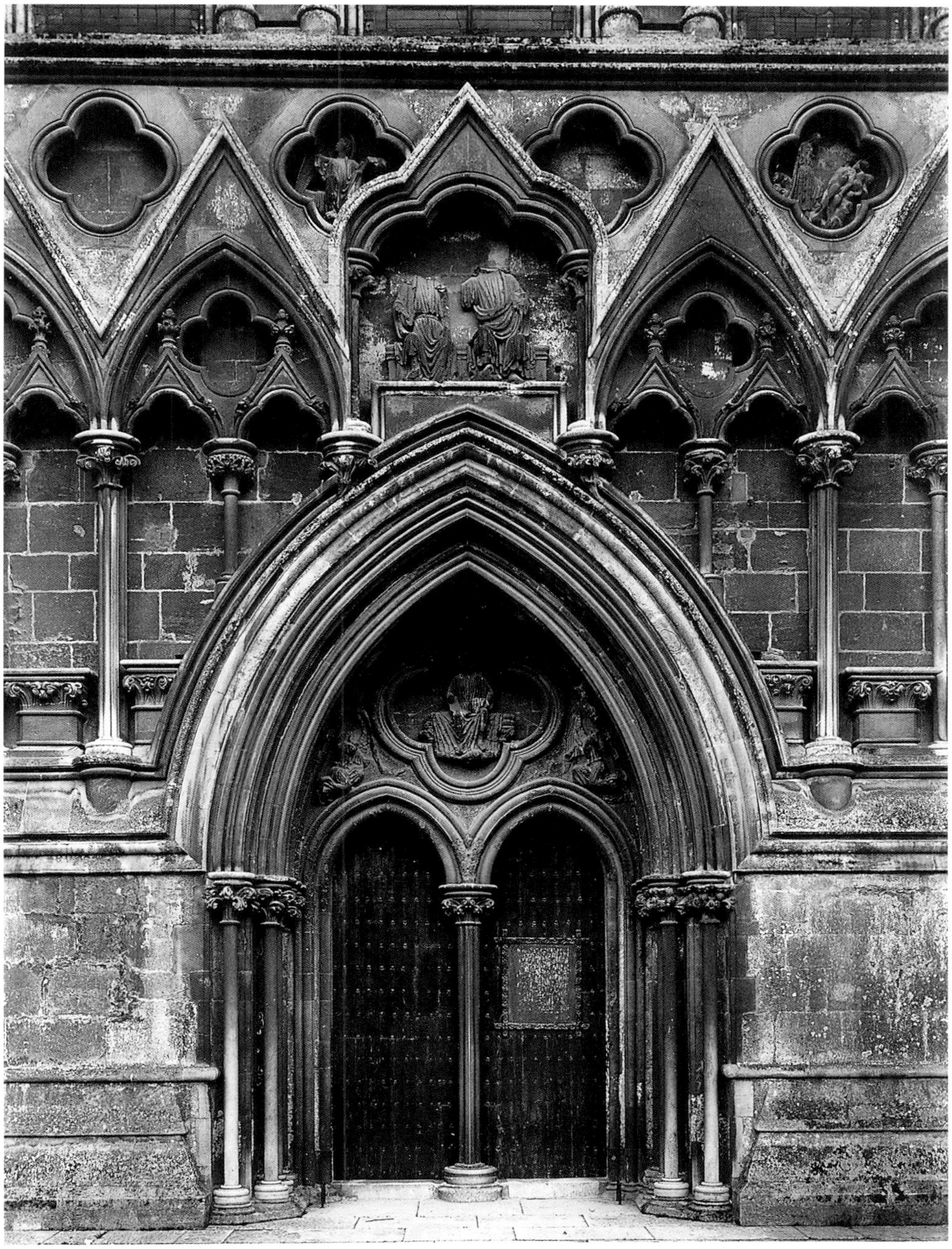

92 Wells Cathedral, west facade, Virgin and Child (below), Coronation of Virgin (above) (reproduced by permission of English Heritage. NMR).

debate, since the facade has certain ambivalences which stem in part from its lack of large-scale focuses, and partly from its state of incompleteness.[65] The quatrefoil over the central portal contains the Virgin and Child, and the niche over it the Coronation of the Virgin (fig. 92), an important sign of the development of the cult of Mary – who prevails here over the patron of the cathedral, St Andrew – and for whom daily Masses had been instituted at Wells under Savaric and Jocelin by 1207.[66] Jocelin's seal as Bishop of Bath shows Mary breastfeeding Christ, the *Virgo lactans* (fig. 93 right), which indicates personal as well as institutional devotion: indeed Jocelin was spoken of as having grown up in the bosom of the Church from infancy, *a prima lacte*.[67] The facade

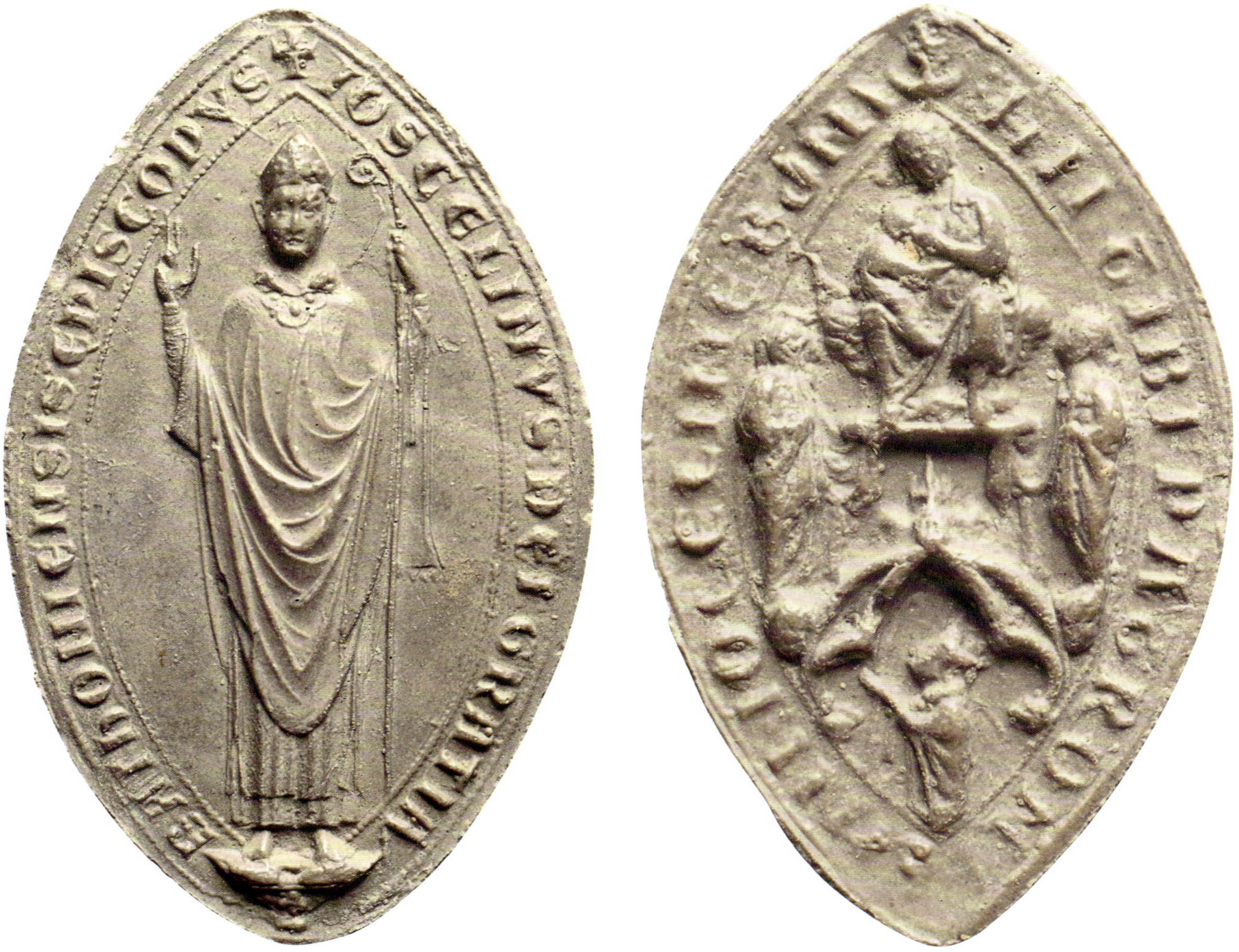

93 Seal of Jocelin, Bishop of Wells, showing counterseal with *Virgo lactans* and Jocelin below, *c.* 1206 (Society of Antiquaries of London).

at Salisbury is likely to have been Marian in focus.[68] If it is correct to identify the two full-size figures in the niches either side of the central window just above the Coronation as Sheba and Solomon (fig. 82), then the central emphasis at Wells can be described as sponsorial, but Brieger is justified in playing down the Marian connotations of the facade as a whole, since no other narrative elements are devoted to her.[69] The marriage of Christ and the Church is, however, the axis or crux for the row of quatrefoils which runs across the facade above the angel-nooks, illustrating Genesis outwards to the south, and the Gospels including the Passion to the north.[70] Romanesque Lincoln had already followed this use of Bible narrative, but there the stress was homiletic; here it much more closely resembles the combination of Genesis and Gospel illustrations, i.e. the Fall and Redemption, in English Psalter prefatory picture-cycles of the twelfth and thirteenth centuries. Since the northern tower is sculpted all around, the Gospel cycle is appreciably fuller than that of Genesis, again in keeping with the proportions typical of the prefatory cycles. That a cast of mind like that of illuminators was at work is suggested too by numerous small points. The form of Noah's Ark afloat, a tall pyramidal object rising from a curved hull which is being locked by God, resembles that of the Noah pictures in the Caedmon and Aelfric manuscripts (Oxford, Bodleian Library MS Junius 11 and BL MS Cotton Claudius B. IV) and also certain thirteenth-century manuscripts (e.g. Cambridge, St John's College MS K. 26).[71] Adam uses a spade while delving, again long-standing pre-Conquest imagery, as deployed on the frieze at Lincoln and by such illuminators as W. de Brailes working in the 1230s and 1240s.[72]

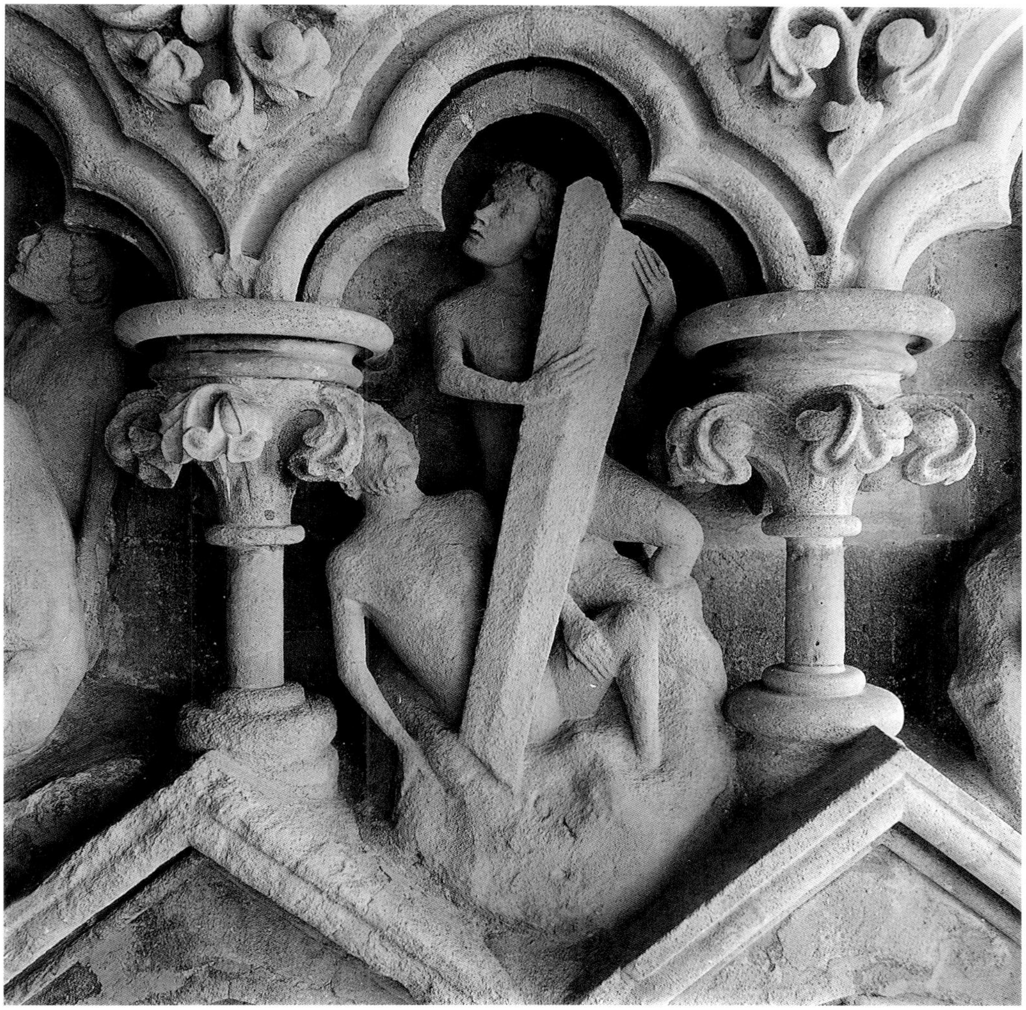

94 Wells Cathedral, west facade, Resurrection (Conway Library, Courtauld Institute of Art).

These various elements are pretty conventional. The lowest tier of the front rising as far as the string courses beneath the main windows is basically redemptive in emphasis and, to judge from the full-scale figures that remain on the north tower at this level, was preoccupied with the birth of the Church.[73] The second (main) tier is filled with the myriad figures that exemplify the historical Church; and the resurrection tier, which also embraces the whole facade, together with the great gable, exemplifies the Church to come: so the fundamental organization is chronological. Though not nearly so systematic, it brings to mind the careful horizontal segregation of subjects, as a revelation of the divine plan in time, on the Klosterneuburg ambo of 1181.[74] Yet there are areas of real uncertainty. The facade is topped by a band depicting the Resurrection (fig. 94), but it includes no judgement or separation of the blessed and damned, as would be expected from Matthew 24–5. Since this iconography was already commonplace, its omission might seem purposeful. Is this the first resurrection of the saints in Revelation 20: 4–6, rather than the general resurrection in Revelation 20: 11–15, since the images of resurrection grow directly out of the tiers of saints below and accompany them across and right around the north and south towers?[75] Yet the fragmentary figure of Christ that occupied the topmost polyfoiled niche of the gable (fig. 95) seems to have displayed the wounds of the suffering Son of Man of the Last Judgement; and it is not difficult to envisage the two niches to either side as suitable locations for angels bearing the Instruments of the Passion, as on fol. 30 of the great early thirteenth-century Psalter in Munich.[76] The text of Matthew 25: 21 – 'Enter thou into the joy of the Lord' – is cited in a contemporary carved inscription on a scroll held by

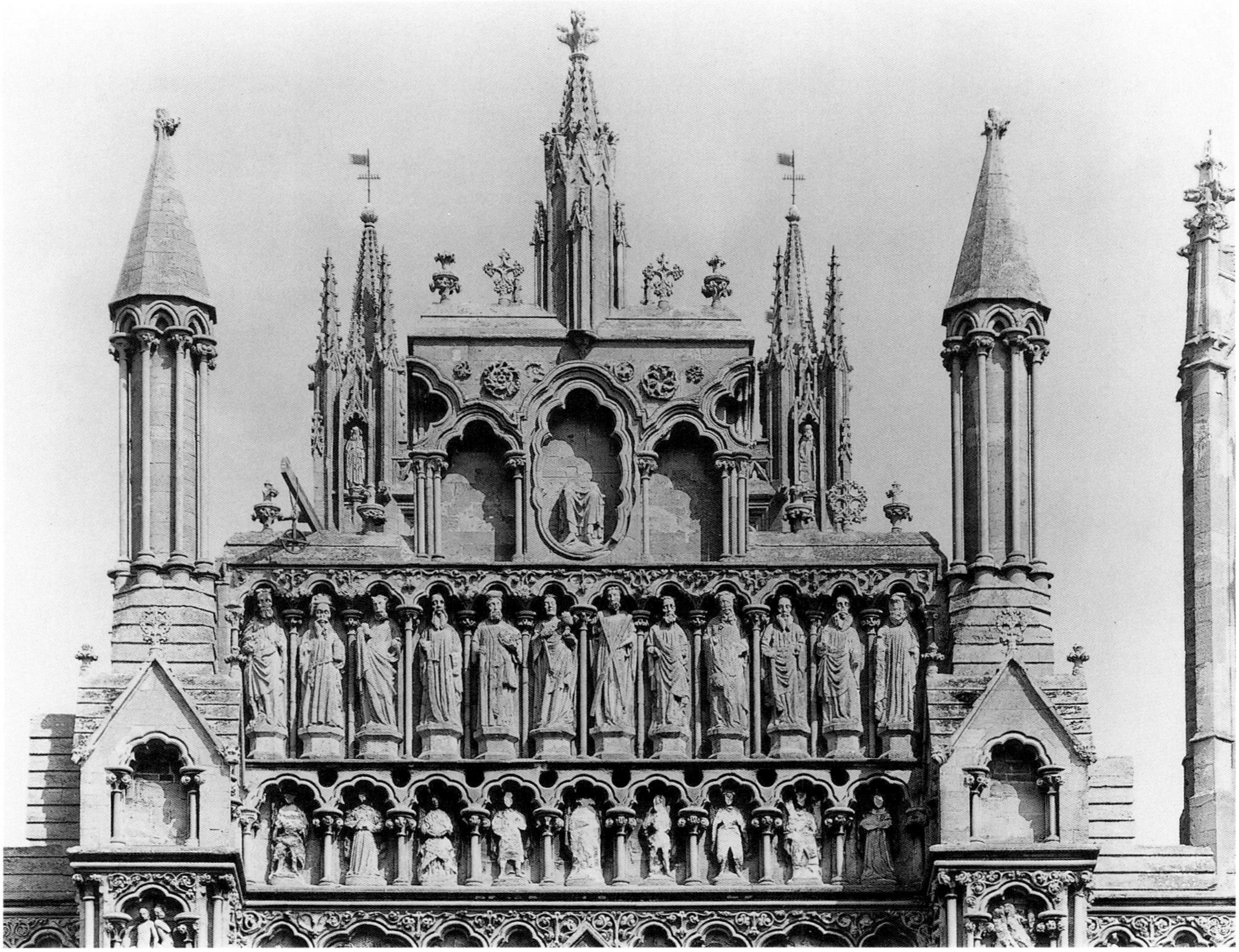

95 Wells Cathedral, west facade, gable, with remains of figure of Christ *in situ* (Conway Library, Courtauld Institute of Art).

a sculpted canon in the north porch, showing that Matthew 25 and its account of the Son of Man coming in his glory to judge were already linked to a portal at Wells. Had the later medieval sculptors turned the topmost west front Christ gently into one suitable for a conventional Last Judgement? Were they merely mistaken? Or are these ambivalences simply signs that the genre of Last Judgement portal in England was itself still settling down?

Viewed politically, the display of saints to which I now turn is likely, from the canons' point of view, to have been the final nail in the coffin of Bath Abbey's ambitions to primacy in the see, which were finally compromised in 1244. Since over 90 per cent of the popes, kings, queens, knights, bishops, priests, monks and sundry holy men and women cannot be certainly identified, the exact stance on sainthood taken by the scheme is elusive, and will remain so.[77] Evidence for the Wells liturgical tradition is fragmentary.[78] So one can be confident of only a few basic points. The first is that the facade seems to have distributed the figures according to certain very general categories. The south tower area is dominated by churchmen (fig. 84), with virtually no women or secular representatives, bar one king on the upper tier of the front face of the south-central buttress, and none of these can be identified with certainty as martyrs, who tend to have their tormentors placed under their feet in triumph. Royalty, martyrs, knights and women govern the north tower area much more exclusively, which suggests some sort of generic division into martyrs (north) and confessors (south). The lowest tier beneath the first string course seems to have been devoted to deacons, subdeacons, holy women and presumably other representatives of the first Church and the Old Law.[79] The

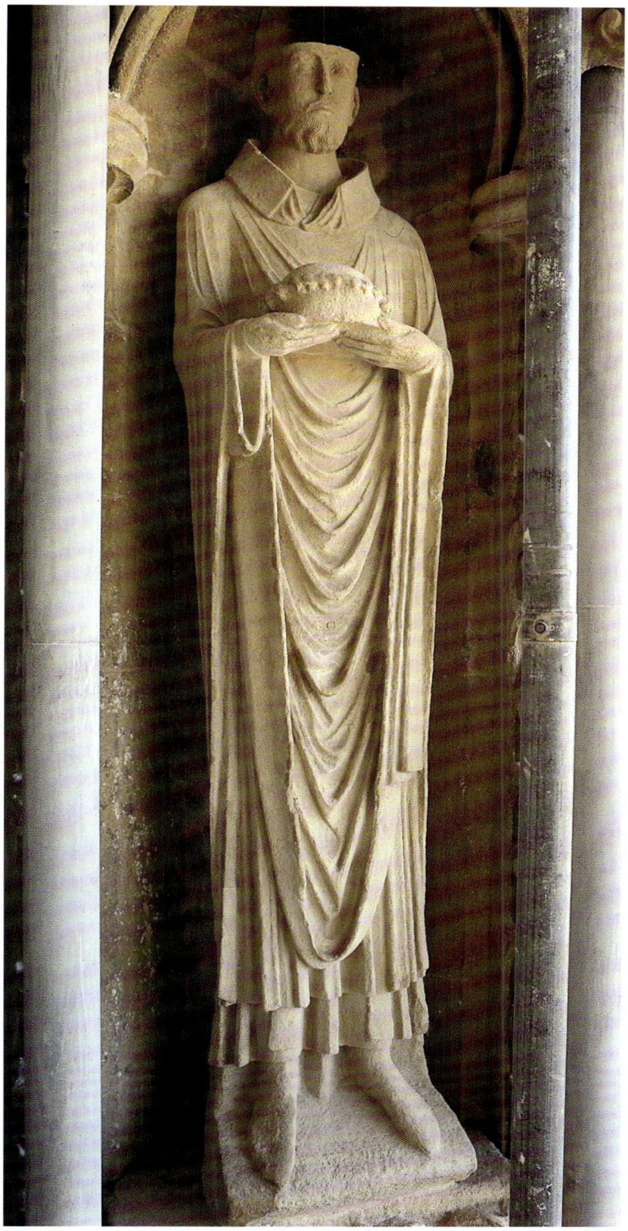

96 Wells Cathedral, west facade, St Thomas (Jerry Sampson).

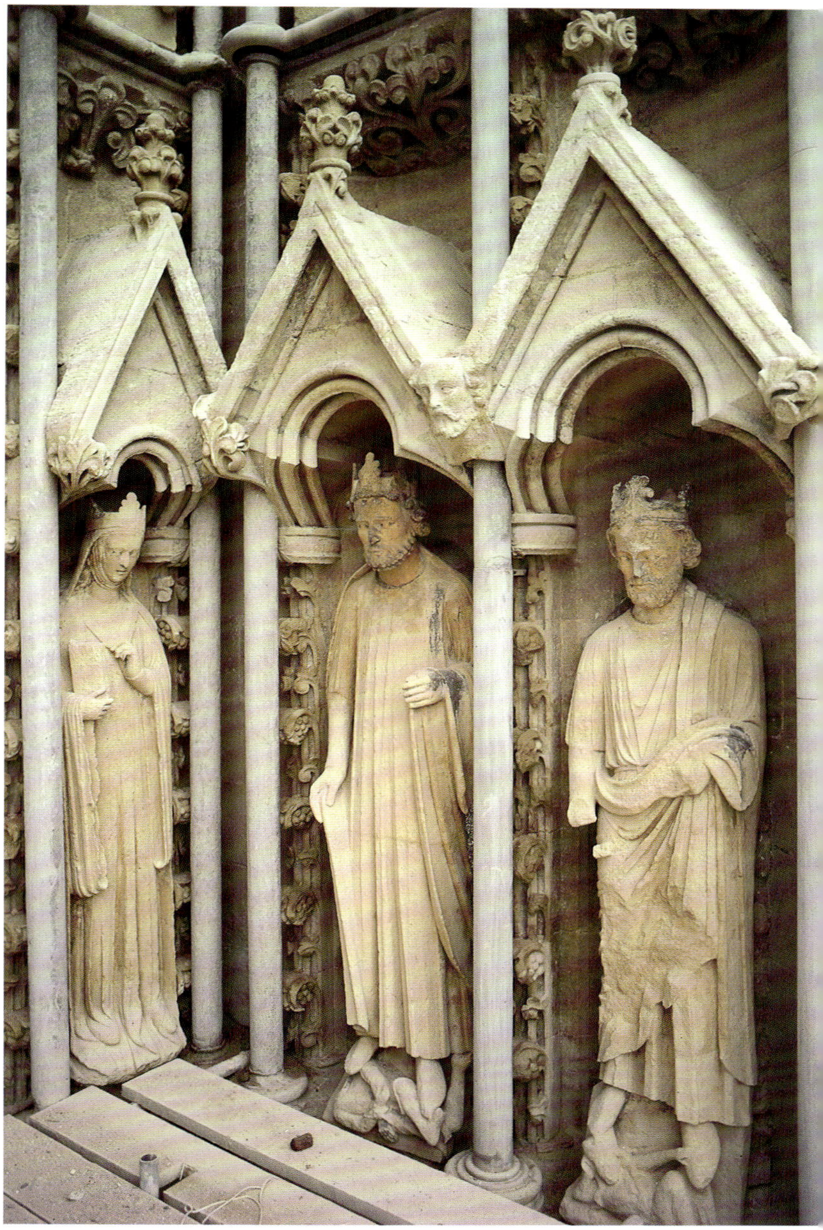

97 Wells Cathedral, west facade, royal martyrs (Jerry Sampson).

clump of martyrs on the north tower (fig. 97) is dominated by kings in the old tradition of the (often youthful) suffering leader, and, in virtue of the figures they trample upon, appears to include Ethelbert of Hereford, Oswald, Edward and Kenelm, and possibly also Edwin, Wistan, Ethelred, Oswin and Edmund.[80] St Thomas is also to be found here (figs 12, 96). But not all the saints belong to insular tradition: St Olaf may be present, and St Eustace certainly is, so the approach is definitely more universal.[81]

This array of choruses of sainthood – to pick up the musical image – was obviously based on organized thought of some sort. Its traditional basis can be established from the striking generic resemblance between the choruses of confessors and virgins in the Benedictional of St Ethelwold and the choruses on the lowest tier of the Wells facade (figs 98–9). Although the detailing of the enclosures at Wells has shrivelled and sharpened, and its figures are appreciably more etiolated, the basic components of standing saints, paired arches

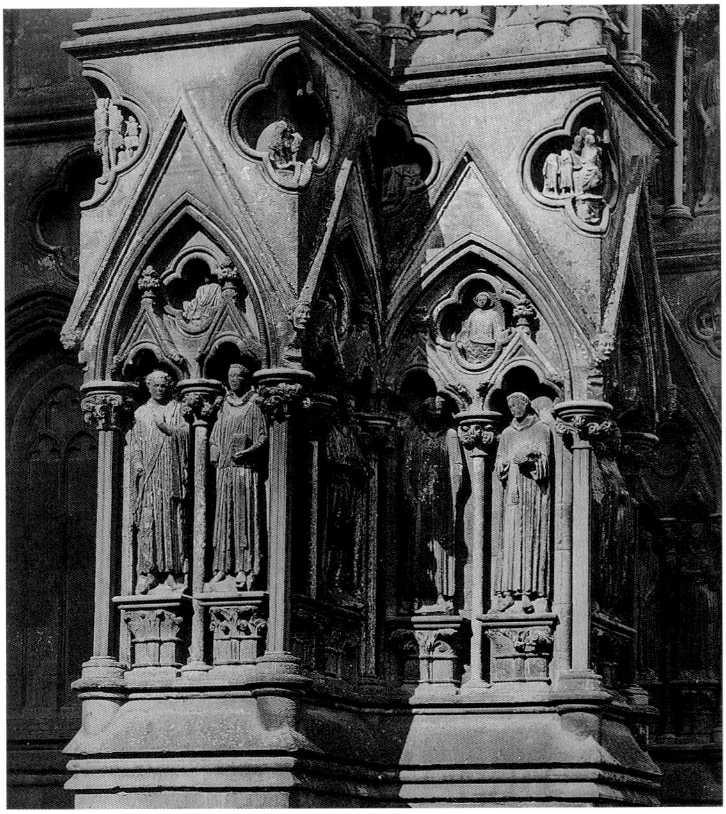

98 Wells Cathedral, west facade, deacons (Conway Library, Courtauld Institute of Art).

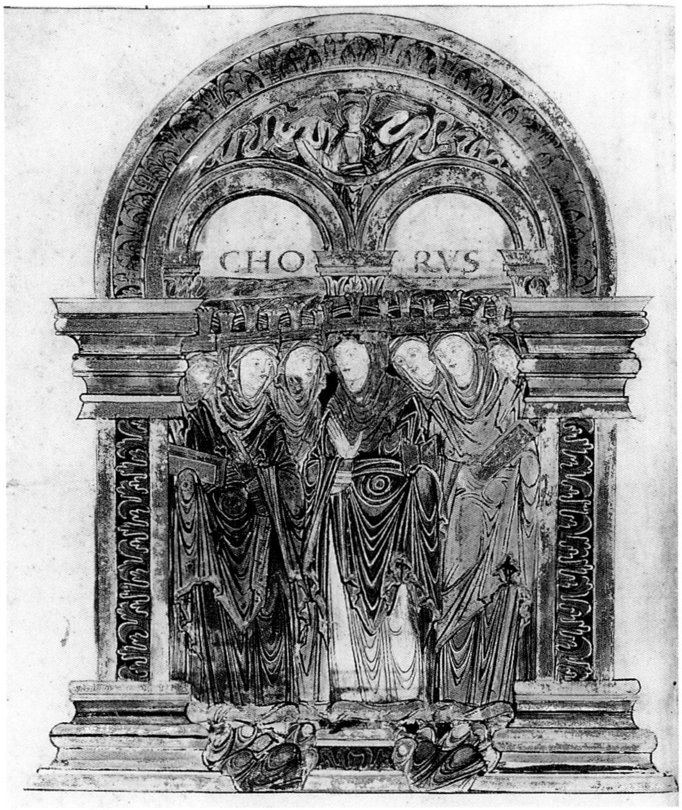

99 Chorus of Virgins. Benedictional of St Ethelwold, BL Add. MS 49598, fol. 1v, late tenth century (by permission of the British Library).

within a major arch, with an angel holding a scroll in the tympanum, are identical.[82] This says nothing specific about the ideas lying behind Wells, beyond their fundamental harmony with the Anglo-Saxon tradition of choric representation.[83] It might, however, prompt one to consider other Anglo-Saxon methods of categorizing the saints, such as the *Secgan* tradition of tracts on the resting-places of insular saints which, as one might expect, includes a high proportion of royalty.[84] The *Secgan*, together with the Old English Martyrology and the Kentish Royal Legend, promoted a sense of the collective strength of English national sanctity during the period of West Saxon domination, and also provided the basis for post-Conquest updatings of such lists of the type produced by Hugh Candidus.[85] It was perhaps on the basis of some such source that Henry III was able to list the names of the sainted kings of England for Matthew Paris in 1257: Edward the Martyr, Edward the Confessor, Albert, Kenelm, Oswald, Oswin, Neithan, Wistan, Fromund, Edwulf and Edmund.[86] Wells, unlike Congresbury and Glastonbury, does not occur in the *Secgan*, and it is a matter of conjecture whether the connection of insular sainthood to more universal types constituted for Wells a broader celebration of 'sacred union'. But the direct implication of Wells's own history and interests is almost certainly proved by the two very prominent seated kings on the topmost front faces of the main central buttresses, who support large charters against their legs (fig. 100). These must be grants of land or privilege of some sort, and that in turn would point to King Ine and St Edward, to follow the *Historiola*, which explicitly cites the testimony of ancient documents, *cyrographis regiae auctoritatis et donationis*.[87] Though the carved documents are not cyrographs, they belong to a new pictorial tradition of the literal depiction of documents granting lands or privileges to ecclesiastical corporations or their patrons, the saints. One instance is found in the series of pictures relating to the Fenland saint Guthlac in the celebrated Guthlac Roll (BL Harley Roll Y 6), in which the benefactors of Crowland, headed by King Ethelbald, hold up their deeds of gift to the abbey and shrine; the texts on the scrolls record the names of the donors and estates.[88] A rotulus of some description is among the items held by the kings paired

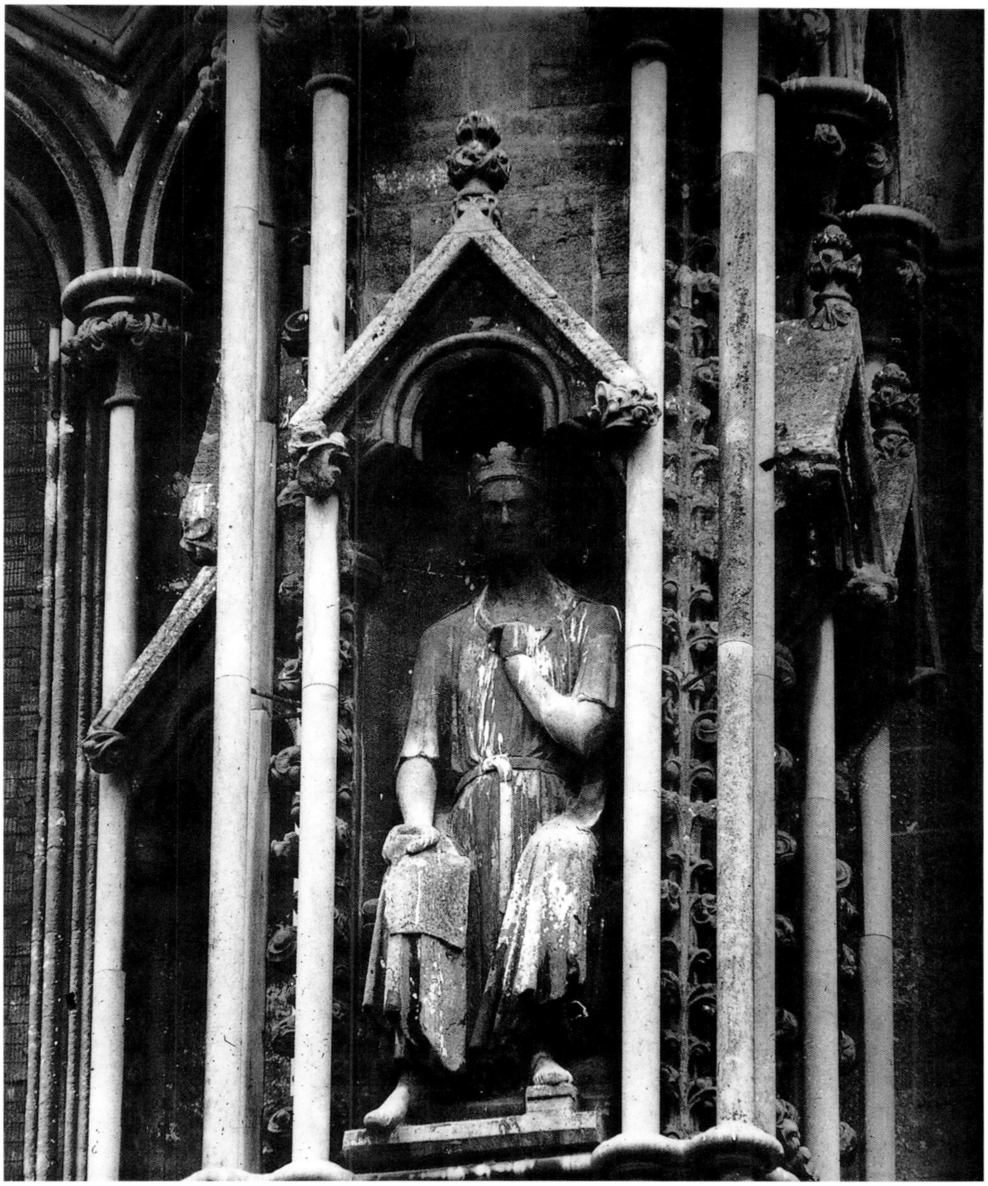

100 Wells Cathedral, west facade, seated king with charter (Conway Library, Courtauld Institute of Art).

with archbishops and bishops on the painted ceiling of Peterborough Abbey, probably begun under Abbot Walter of Bury St Edmunds (1233–45).[89] These are exactly the sorts of local benefactor and founder-figure that could have been assembled from a reading of Hugh Candidus's account of the early history of Medeshamstede.[90] Large-scale displays of the sources of authority and privilege mattered to ecclesiastical institutions after the Interdict, and Peterborough, like Wells or Crowland, was inevitably jealous of its rights.[91]

In so contextualizing the saints at Wells, one runs the risk of seeing them simply as a utilitarian assertion of commonplace rights; yet if this great 'cliff-face' has an instrumental character, it is at least as likely to have resided in its general spiritual signification and, critically, its aesthetic. It is justifiable to see the front in terms of the absolutely conventional symbolism of Jerusalem in its manifold historical and spiritual senses: historically and liturgically it is the Jerusalem of Palm Sunday; spiritually it is the New Jerusalem, the saints of Revelation

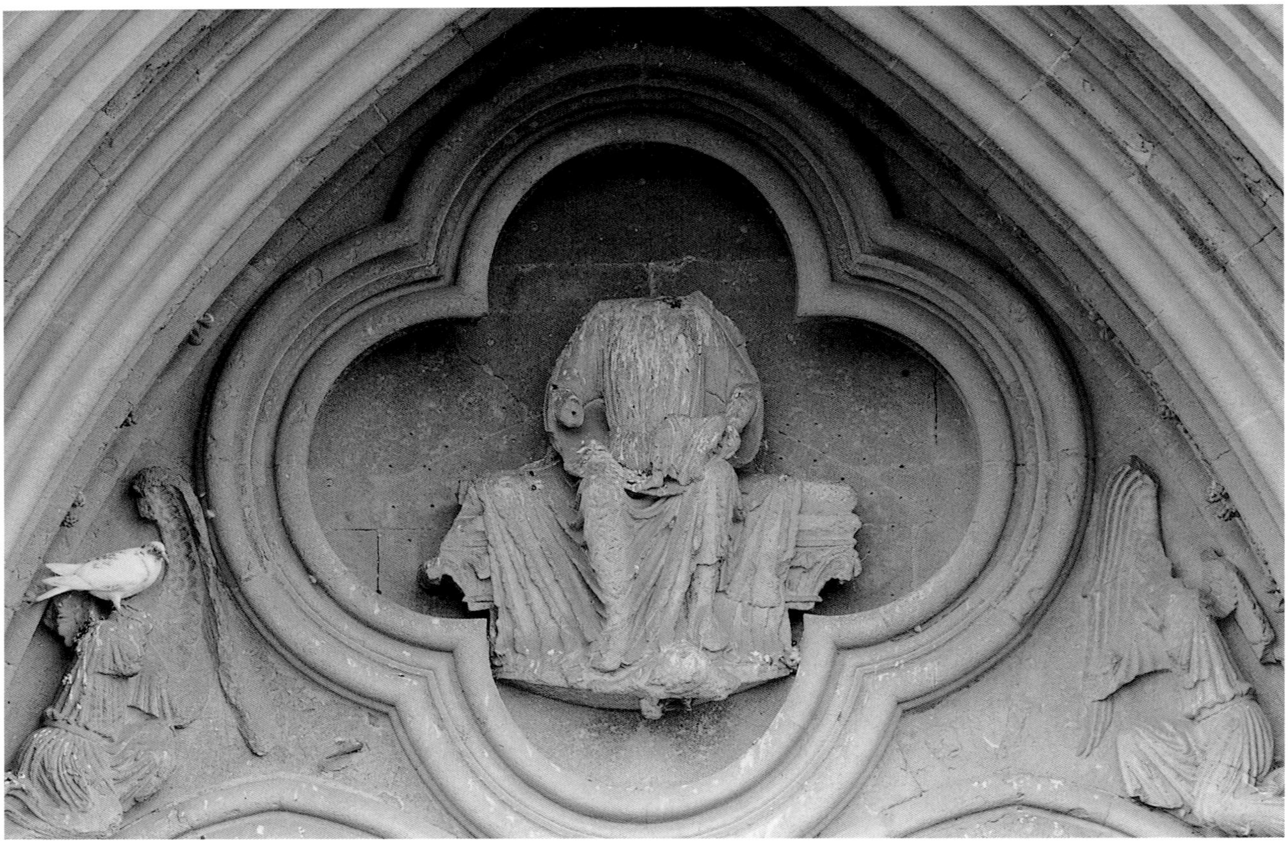

101 *Columba mea in foraminibus petrae*: Wells Cathedral, west facade, Virgin and Child (Conway Library, Courtauld Institute of Art).

20: 4–6 preparing the way, as the priests of God, for the descent of the New Jerusalem prepared as a bride (*sponsa*) adorned for her husband (Revelation 21: 2); and this latter idea accords well with the presence at the centre of the ensemble of Mary-Ecclesia, Solomon and Sheba.[92] No commentary on the Church as bride of Christ by a secular clerk or master can match for spiritual exhilaration the extraordinary, and widely read, sermons on Canticles by St Bernard, one of which (no. 62) catches the mystical sense of Wells's realization of the Living Church with such accuracy that it serves only to demonstrate the astonishing (if proleptic) sympathy of Cistercian poetics with what would now be called Gothic imagery. The sermon in question is on Canticles 2: 14: my dove in the clefts of the rock, in the nooks of the wall (*columba mea in foraminibus petrae in caverna maceriae*).[93] The dove is the bride, i.e. the Church (fig. 101). Thus the wall, *maceria*, is not a mass of mere stones but the communion of saints; the nooks or clefts in the wall have been left behind by the fallen angels, and these imperfections are to be filled spiritually by the *vivi lapides* of I Peter 2: 4–5; indeed the guardianship of the angels is like the wall in the Lord's vineyard. The Church's desire for union with God is consoled by the memory of the Passion of Christ in the past, and the contemplation of her welcome among the saints. Through the clefts in the wall flowed Christ's ransoming blood. The Church joyously explores the crannies, the many and varied resting-places and mansions (*mansiones multae*) which are in her Father's house (John 14: 2), in which God lodges his children according to their just deserts.[94] The clefts are a sign of the Church's desire for completeness, but they are made too by thought and desire, for the holy heavens, living and rational, will look on mortals lovingly and hear their prayers: everyone may hollow out a place in this heavenly wall. Now one can see the patriarchs; now the prophets; now one can mingle with the assembly of the apostles, now join the chorus of martyrs. With the quickness of devotion we can run up and down the dwelling-places and ranks of the blessed orders of the angels, as far as the cherubim and seraphim. God takes delight in these nooks, from which ring out the voices of thanksgiving, the voices of wonder and praise.[95] The hollows in the rock are the means of self-incorporation into God, for while one divine happiness consists in the contemplation of the heavenly city with its multitude of heavenly citizens, the other is concerned with the divinity of God himself, the rock, into which by contemplation worshippers penetrate: the task is difficult, but the rewards sweet.

The sermon uses several familiar ideas: the communion of saints as the living stones of the Church; the act of contemplation, of spiritual penetration and ascent; the Church as the penetrable body of the wounded Christ and so on.[96] The language of the nooks vacated by the rebel angels which are to be filled by the just is reminiscent of the formal and theological scheme in the Lothian Bible Genesis page mentioned above.[97] But its elucidation of the terms *foramen* and *caverna* (*foramina* being a contemporary term for the holes in shrines by which access was gained to the relics of the saints) offers a particularly suggestive commentary on the spiritual potential of the Wells aesthetic (shared, as already noted, by some contemporary seal designs) of the punctured and inhabited wall. It is into these *foramina* that one delves to disclose to oneself their secrets, for they are a means to union with God. Wells's sonic quatrefoils are literally those holes from which ring out the sounds of thanksgiving, wonder and praise. Contemplation, visualization and interpretation become one, for Bernard's extraordinarily vivid powers of ideation are founded upon an exhilarating scanning process, the dove hovering and swooping across the wall surface to see the company of heaven lodged within it, in a sort of flight of the mind.

The depth and specificity of this Cistercian discourse on the wall and nook should not delude one into supposing that it demonstrably represents anything like a positive source for the Wells accomplishment. It may or may not be significant that Cistercian ideas have been invoked more generally in accounts of the earliest designs of Wells Cathedral; too little is known about the readership of Bernard's sermons in the West Country or about its Cistercian culture in general.[98] Wells Cathedral, having history but no cult, had no obvious hagiographical context within which such ideas might have been rehearsed. Yet by the early thirteenth century the aesthetic, and perhaps conceptual, gulf between the Cistercian churches and the secular churches, in northern England at least, had virtually disappeared.[99] And although they belonged in the first instance to older traditions of monastic *lectio* and mystical speculation, Bernard's sermons were extremely widely known; what they provide for modern readers at the very least is an horizon of expectation, a set of limits within which one might establish some general account of Wells in terms of the greatest intellectual and imaginative capacities of the time. As discussed, Bernard's material, Canticles, furnished the speculative mind of the period with allegories of fundamental importance, and it is intrinsically likely that such texts as Canticles 2: 14 were to be found in the broad mental hinterland of those who formulated the west front at Wells.

In considering the cult of saints as something represented, and not invested in an actual cult of relics, one is reminded that at Wells such collective representations were now also implicated in something which was not only historical, even atavistic, but much more modern: an affective piety which recognized and exploited the capacity of artistic conceits to realize a particular sensibility and a particular mode of engagement, and which the new models of episcopal sanctity emerging in the thirteenth century were helping to propagate. It is to these that I turn next.

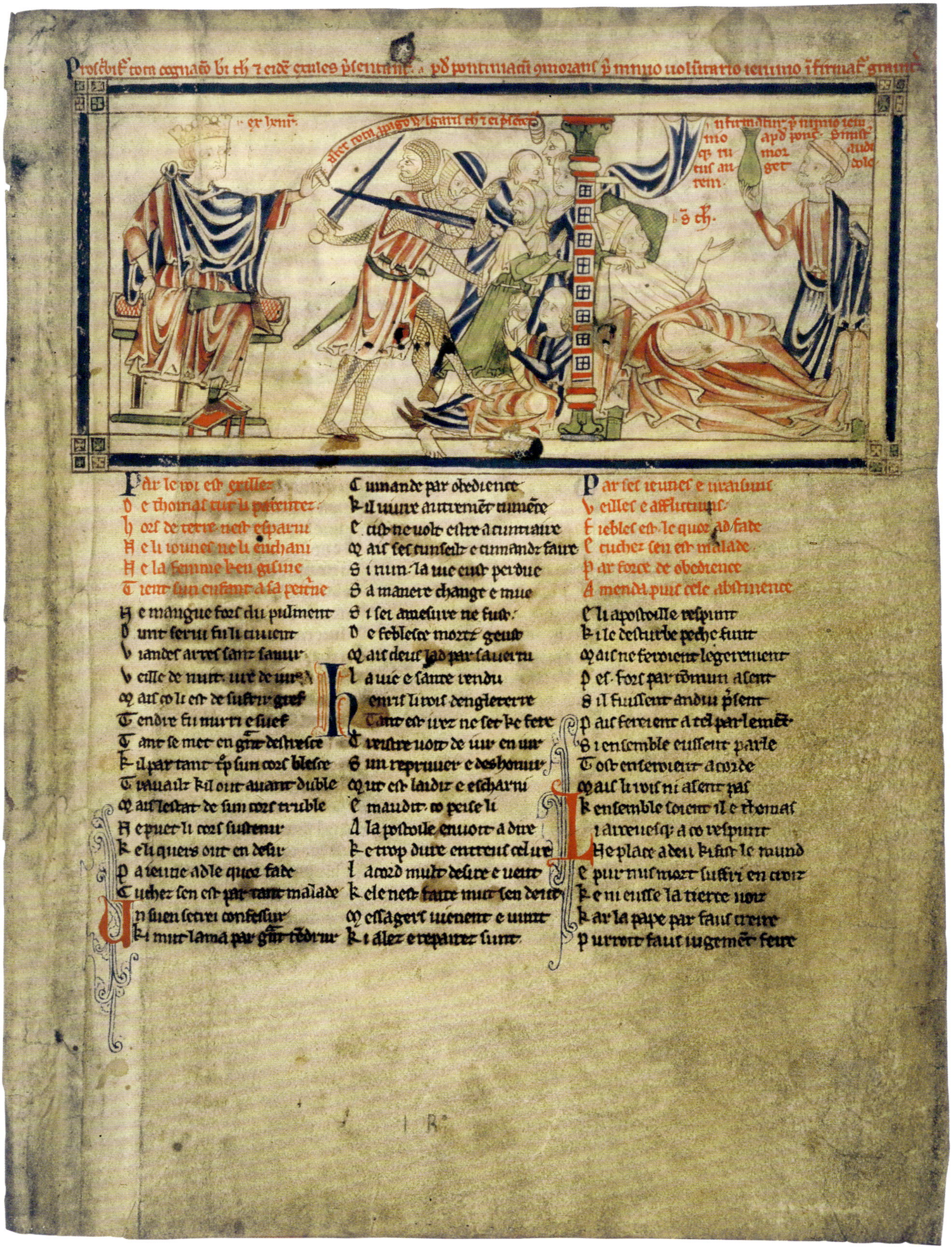

Par le roi est exillez
De Thomas tut li parentez.
Hom de terre nen est esparni
Ne li iounes ne li enchani
Ne la femme ke en gisine
Tient sun enfant a sa peitrine
Ne mangue fors du pulment
Dunt servi fu li convent
Viandes autres sanz savur
Veille de nuit, ure de iur
Mais co li est de suffrir gref
Tendre fu nurri e suef
Tant se met en grant destresce
Kil par tant ad sun cors blesce
Travail kil out avant duble
Mais le estat de sun cors truble
Ne puet li cors sustenir
Ke li quers out en desir
Pasience adle quor fade
Cuchez sen est par tant malade
Un suen secrei confessur
Ki mult lama par grant tendrur

Cumande par obedience
Kil vivre autrement cumence
E cil ne volt estre a cuntraire
Mais ses cunseilz e cumandz faire
Si nun la vie eust perdue
Sa manere change e mue
Si sei amesure ne fust
De feblesce morz geust
Mais deus iad par sa vertu
La vie e sante rendu
Henris li reis dengleterre
Tant est irez ne set ke fere
Destrure voit de iur en iur
Sun repruver e deshonur
Kar est laidiz e escharni
E maudit, co peise li
A la postoile enuoit a dire
Ke trop dure entent celui
La acord mult desire e veut
Ke ele nest faite mult sen deut
Messagers vienent e vunt
Ki alez e repairez sunt.

Par ses ieunes e travailz
Veilles e afflictiuns
Febles est le quor ad fade
Cuchez sen est malade.
Par force de obedience
Amenda puis cele abstinence
E li apostoille respunt
Kile destuibe peche funt
Mais ne feroient legerement
Pes fors par comun asent
Sil fuissent andui present
Pais feroient a tel parlement
Si ensemble eussent parle
Tost en serroient a corde
Mais li reis ni asent pas
Kensemble soient il e thomas
Li arceuesq; a co respunt
Ne place a deu kifist le mund
Ke pur nus mort suffri en croiz
Ke ieo nen eusse la tierce voiz
Kar la pape par faus creire
Purroit faus iugement feire

102 Henry II (as a type for King Herod) sends into exile Becket's relations; St Thomas ill at Pontigny from excessive fasting. Leaf (fol. 1) from fragmentary Anglo-Norman verse Life of St Thomas, *c.* 1230 (by permission of the British Library and the Estate of the later Sir Paul Getty, K.B.E., Wormsley Library).

Chapter 6

BECKET'S CROWN

His court was of courtesy
The school, and of accomplishments.
Matthew Paris, *La Estoire de Seint Aedward le Rei*

The Inner Consecration of Life

The young and formidable Isabel, Countess of Arundel, showed no fear before the fickle King Henry III: Matthew Paris loved her for her defiant defence of English liberty, and his *Chronica majora* presents her as a model of feminine fortitude in a dramatic set-piece confrontation with King Henry, laughing derisively at her in his chamber, in 1252.[1] The issue was a baronial one, her rights in regard to wardship. Yet her examples, her mirrors, were the English male saints, the bishops in particular, Thomas (fig. 102), Edmund, Richard – the last two of whom she may have known personally, and of whose cults she was a patroness.[2] Like her, the great bishops – Anselm, Thomas, Hugh, Stephen – stood up to arbitrary public power, the *vis* and *voluntas* of the Crown. Their moral prowess could be understood as in some sense 'baronial'. In virtue of what is sometimes called the 'political character' of his scepticism towards royal and papal authority, Matthew was implicated in Isabel's world-view. He shared it; but he also helped to shape it.[3]

By the 1240s Matthew was circulating manuscript copies of his Lives of the English saints to female aristocratic and royal patrons. One such was an illustrated book of Anglo-Norman verses about St Thomas and St Edward the Confessor, which he lent to Isabel and then to Sanchia, Countess of Cornwall.[4] A later source also attributes to him illustrated Lives of St Thomas and St Edmund, Archbishops of Canterbury.[5] In the *Chronica majora*, Matthew noted that the Life of St Edmund, compiled after Edmund's canonization late in 1247, was available to readers at St Albans in 1253.[6] It still survives in Latin and French versions, though unillustrated.[7] Matthew's Anglo-Norman verse translation is dedicated to Isabel, the *Riche cuntesse d'Arundele*, and includes in the verses his own name, 'Maheu', a rare confessional touch which helps to secure the attribution.[8] Isabel was patroness of one of St Albans's dependent cells, Wymondham, and presumably also knew Matthew's Life of St Alban.[9] Matthew's general aim was clear: Isabel should follow in Edmund's footsteps, *De saint Edmund suez la trace*.[10] Isabel's fortitude was matched by her thoroughness, since in the 1270s she received a copy of a Life of St Edmund's friend and colleague St Richard of Chichester (d. 1253, can. 1262), composed by the Dominican Ralph Bocking between 1262 and the translation of the saint in 1276; this Life, dedicated to her, had been commissioned by Robert Kilwardby, also a Dominican.[11] So, while churchmen took the initiative in commanding such Lives, the aristocracy had an important role in receiving and, presumably, learning from them. Isabel was useful; but she seems also to have been learned. Like these sainted schoolmen, noble laywomen were to be scholarly, literally versed in the asperity of the holy dons: the construction of the ascetic bishop was not unrelated to the conduct of the virtuous widow, and Richard's Life was to be a mirror to her own.[12] Ralph noted that Isabel indeed possessed an entire set of such Lives, read along with the 'mirror of scripture', and which presumably included Matthew's works: she had become an erudite widow indeed.[13]

Matthew's pastoral emphasis on the traces of the saints reminds one once again that the language of the pattern, model, imprint or footstep had long been developed allegorically by reformist churchmen, in the first instance for other churchmen. Some of its consequences for the notion of edification – building physically and spiritually – in the sphere of architecture are noted above (p. 61).

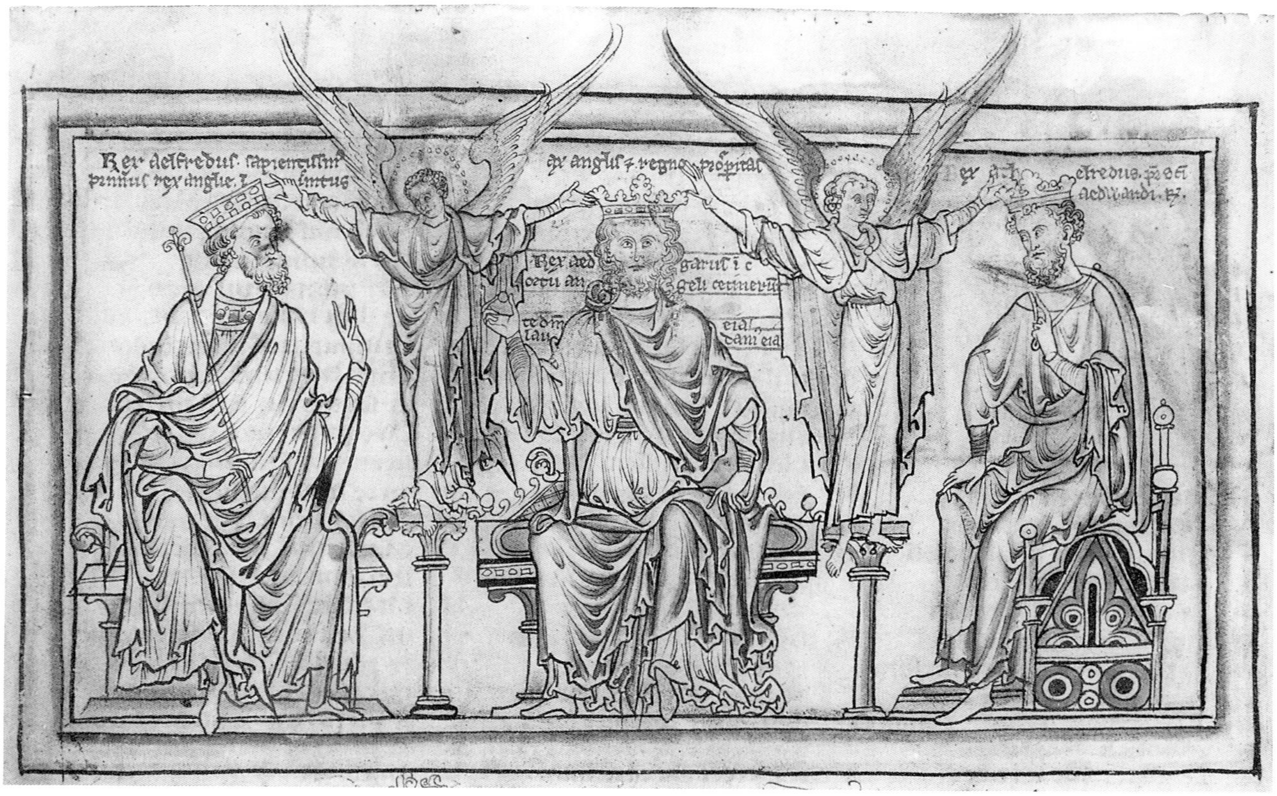

103 Holy kings of England crowned in heaven, Alfred, Edgar and Ethelred. *La Estoire de Seint Aedward le Rei*, CUL MS Ee. 3. 59, fol. 3v, *c.* 1255 (by permission of the Syndics of Cambridge University Library).

The model or impress of sanctity, especially learned sanctity, was part of this reformist endeavour, now carried out beyond the schools and cloisters into the world of laymen and of women. Papally and episcopally sponsored reform from the late twelfth century encouraged an unprecedented spread of edificatory literature about the saints in the vernacular (e.g. the *South English Legendary*).[14] Strong as the impetus from the centre may have been, demand was also huge. With Matthew's work the process of translation, typically for female readers, was well under way, but it was also prompted by cathedral canons such as those at Chichester, who in the 1270s commissioned a translation into French of Bocking's Life of St Richard, doubtless because of the extent of aristocratic interest in his shrine.[15] The Lives of the saints were a vehicle of evangelization particularly among the aristocracy and gentry classes as well as royalty. Matthew's Anglo-Norman Life of St Edward the Confessor, composed after 1236 (fig. 103), was dedicated to Queen Eleanor of Provence with the explicit aim of recommending to her Henry's favourite saint; in the late 1280s her daughter-in-law Eleanor of Castile also possessed a book of the Lives of Thomas and Edward, perhaps based on, or identical with, that being lent out by Matthew in the 1240s.[16] It was pastorally appropriate to educate foreign princesses in the history of English sanctity, preferably in a vernacular language; St Edward's Lives tend to crop up shortly after royal marriages or the births of sons called Edward (the future Edward I was born in 1239, Edward II in 1284). There is good reason to think that they were regarded as mirrors for princely conduct. Matthew's autograph illustrated Life of St Alban in Dublin was to be copied by clerks and artists at the behest of his patronesses. His pen-and-wash illustrations were a powerful vehicle; restrained, yet direct and compelling, their tonal simplicity seems like a counterpart to the new models of temperate, aristocratic sanctity they depict. The style was also ideal for the kind of rapid copying of books lent out for the purpose of circulation. The fragmentary French verse Life of St Thomas based on the *Quadrilogus* contains gauche but powerful illustrations of royal vice and clerical virtue in similar vein (fig. 102); made around 1230, these leaves were not the work of Matthew, but their remarkable survival illustrates the popularity of the form.[17] Thomas and Edward especially were the new exemplars of the Church and public power respectively. Their patrons and patronesses were to love their Lives and their example; indeed Henry III came to love the Confessor, who in turn loved St John; and St Edmund and St Richard loved each other. Holy lineage was giving way to divine friendship. And with this new notion of the holy bond came a new piety, for the Lives that now circulated at first among the privileged also propagated a new affective style of belief and practice: lachrymose, eucharistic and empathetic, but also harsh, self-mortifying and cerebral.

In its practical manifestation the new sanctity, though in important respects aristocratic in tenor, was male and clerical, and for the most part resolutely episcopal. It was a symbol of the power of the reformist diocesan Church in England, premised, like its new cathedrals, on large and wealthy dioceses.[18] It was not entirely new: bishops had dominated cathedral cults since before the Conquest.[19] Nor was it restricted to England. Scandinavia, for different reasons – comparatively recent conversion to Christianity and the lack of older saints – saw the rise of the cult of bishops led in part by the example of St Thomas; and the physical impact of this made by the survival of painted wooden sculptures of bishop-saints in Norway and Sweden (fig. 104) is reminiscent of a significant lost dimension to the visual culture of the corresponding English cults, which certainly existed.[20] From the late twelfth century in England and Ireland, additions to the sanctoral were almost entirely bishops, eight being canonized between Thomas of Canterbury in 1173 and Thomas of Hereford in 1320, and three of them under Langton alone.[21] A portion of them were either monks or entered monastic orders at some point – St Wulfstan (1203), St Hugh (1220), William of York (1227), Lawrence O'Toole (1225) – while the others – Edmund (1247), Richard (1262) and Thomas of Hereford (1320) – were masters at Paris or Oxford; and the *magistri* tended increasingly to produce those bishops who were either designated saints or who had limited cults (Roger Niger of London, Robert Grosseteste of Lincoln).[22] Failing the monarchy, it was onto such ascetic and learned men of the diocesan Church that the desire for ideal rulership was projected. Not all of them were able administrators, but a fair measure, the masters especially, were certainly competent, though limiting their skills to diocesan, not public, governance and reform. By nature and ideology they stood apart from the worldly values of the royal curia.

The bishops' virtue and learnedness was an aspect of their *nobilitas*, for erudition added lustre to noble origins and office, quite as much as it offered a fast track to preferment. Their social origins were generally also substantial.[23] Hugh, William of York and Thomas of Hereford were of noble descent, Hugh's *Magna vita* showing a 'quiet but firm insistence on and interest in aristocratic origins as a source of saintliness, holy courage and authority'.[24] Becket was a scion of the London merchant class.[25] St Edmund was of middling (*mediocris*) yet prosperous stock – hence perhaps Edmund's family name, Rich; and St Richard's origin was described euphemistically as *non ignobilis*.[26] Langton's family was modest, but none was as base in origin as the most brilliant of them, Robert Grosseteste, the son of a peasant.[27] Indeed, the English episcopate was by no means restricted to those of noble birth, certainly less so than in Germany;[28] and while it would be anachronistic to see the saintly bishops as the product of a meritocracy, the construction of new sainthood in this period entailed an acceptance that nobility of blood was insufficient: what mattered was that growth of virtue, that 'inner consecration of life',[29] that nobility of the spirit, with which the process of papal canonization now concerned itself.

A cluster of ideas was associated with this concept. In respect of *nobilitas* it mattered, first, that as a spiritual lord the bishop should be a *generosus* in the widest sense of the term.[30] The point that a saint-bishop was magnanimous and exhibited magnificence (largesse distributed with no regard to material loss or gain) is made repeatedly in the hagiographies, and the ethic is also present in the more austere monastic writings.[31] The reader has already encountered it in St Thomas's courtly conduct in hall, in St Hugh's liberality and in Langton's spectacular feasting for the translation of St Thomas in 1220 (p. 41 above). St Edmund's hospitality, contempt for gain and habitual indebtedness were famed, as was St Richard's

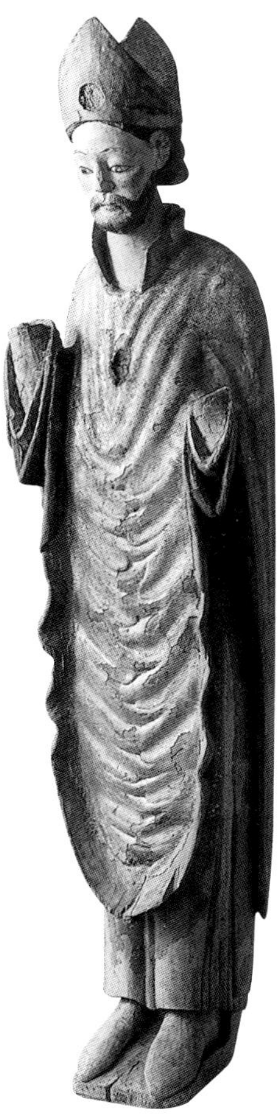

104 Painted wooden sculpture of a bishop from Ekerö, Sweden. Stockholm, Statens Historiska Museum, no. 24725:2 (Statens Historiska Museum).

hospitalitas;[32] St Thomas of Hereford expended and abounded greatly both in life and death, a reminder that the thaumaturgical powers of a great shrine were themselves a form of spiritual largesse.[33] Such ideas are likely to have influenced the art of commemoration. One of the earliest canopied tombs of the thirteenth century, that of the thoroughly curial (and reformist) Archbishop Walter Gray (d. 1255) at York Minster (fig. 105), not only marks the giant transepts that he built for the church as patron, but explicitly echoes the form of the elevated shrines that stood at Durham and especially Canterbury (fig. 21). The latter was the probable model (St William, though canonized in 1227, remained in a tomb) in view of York's deliberate attempt under Gray to surpass the southern province.[34] Given this impressive lineage, it is not surprising that it was the bishops who had a leading role in the development of tombs of this type. Great building was, as already noted, the most durable sign of this ethic of magnificence and, like grand tombs, another important sign of the nexus of clerical and royal patronage in the thirteenth century. The parallel between episcopal generosity and royal alms-giving and support for the mendicant orders is obvious, for it is unlikely to be coincidental that the various iconographies of largesse were being very fully developed in the halls and chambers of Henry III, at the time that this new model of sanctity was being given final and definitive form.[35]

It mattered, secondly, that the bishop as *generosus* and as saint-courtier should also exhibit temperance and good manners. A key motif in the hagiographies of the new saints is equilibrium, the balance between the inner and outer spheres of a virtuous man.[36] This marked a return to the patristic ideals of Pope Gregory the Great's *Liber regulae pastoris*, with its schedule of virtues of sobriety, courtesy, hospitality, moderation and benevolence.[37] It also reflected an ancient ethic of leadership, for the avoidance of extremes and a stress on balance, *mediocritas*, were part of a long-established philosophy of aristocratic and royal *mores* common to much of Western Christendom.[38] It manifests itself in a constant regard for external signs, civilized and pleasant bodily deportment, facial expression, even physical beauty. Its character was thus aesthetic. Princely saints such as the hermit Guthlac were adorned by distinction of appearance, chastity of body and good looks.[39] William of Malmesbury connected St Wulfstan's physical radiance to his virtue.[40] Peter the Chanter very clearly had a theory of graceful movement as an attribute of suitability for political office.[41] St Hugh had been recommended for his *morum elegantia*.[42] Becket's biographers noted how Becket's natural nobility made itself apparent physically, even in disguise: his was the gestalt of the great-souled man, well-mannered, magnificent and patient in suffering.[43] And so too with Edmund, who was affable to all, always joyous and cheerful.[44] St Richard possessed a body of angelic beauty.[45] Even St Richard's name, according to the etymology of his hagiographer, encoded the words 'laughing', 'dear' and 'sweet', *ri*dens, *car*us et *d*u*lcis*, for his outward bodily carriage, being the 'simulacrum' of his interior disposition, revealed the stamp of his mind.[46] He cultivated sobriety and prudence, and avoided excess in dress, eschewing

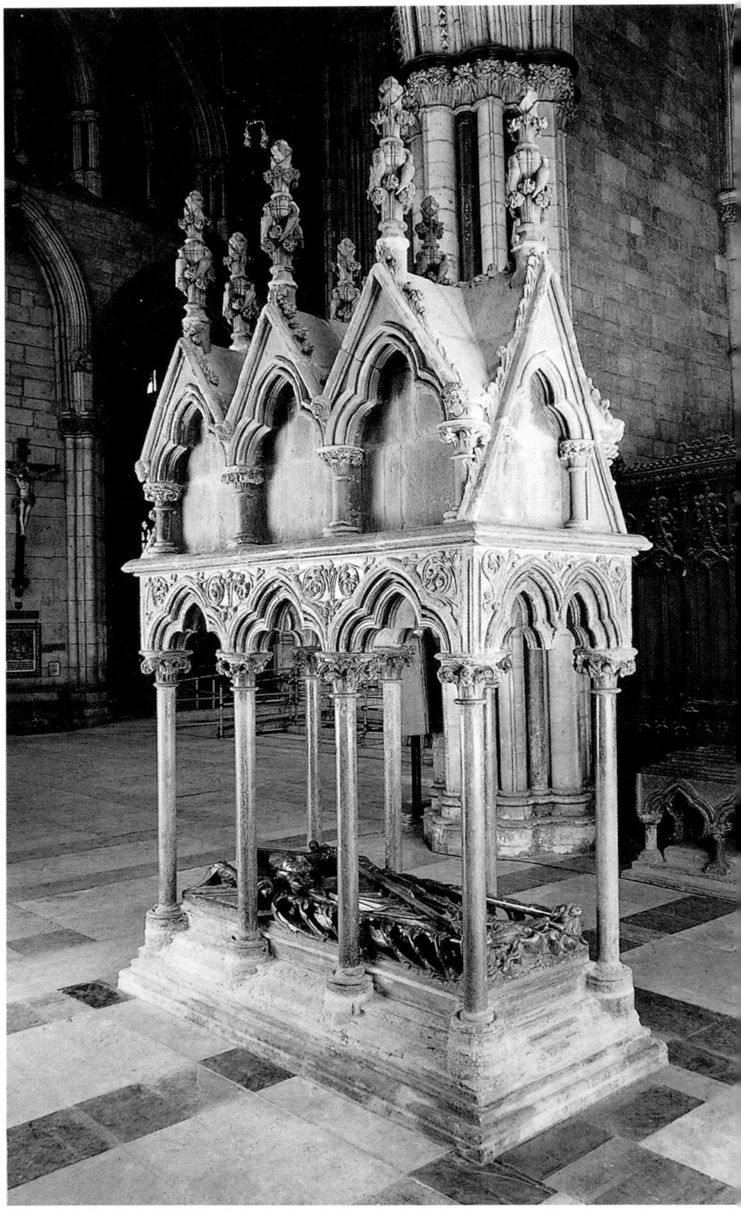

105 York Minster, tomb of Archbishop Walter Gray, d. 1255 (© Crown copyright. NMR).

novelty, vanity and superfluity, and knowing nothing of hunting and hawking – St Bernard would have approved.[47] All these criteria of decorum – as understood by St Ambrose, Peter the Chanter or Thomas Aquinas – are recognizably classical.[48]

A third and more specialized attribute of this type of nobility was asceticism.[49] The increasing stress on the ideal of episcopal asperity – in effect 'white' martyrdom – in the thirteenth century reflected efforts to revive monastic standards of conduct in the secular church which, in the English context, had been anticipated during the reforms under Dunstan and Ethelwold.[50] This remonasticizing of the episcopate was gaining ground at exactly the time when the actual monastic presence among the English bishops was declining: between 1215 and 1272 only eight of the seventy-eight bishops who held office were monks.[51] In so overtaking the monks, the masters had in effect appropriated their values. They did so by attending afresh to the models for clerical conduct offered by the Bible (e.g. I Timothy: 3), by patristic writing, by St Bernard's treatise on the conduct and duties of bishops and, above all, Sulpitius Severus's Life of St Martin.[52] Martin's example is cited directly or indirectly with great frequency. Yet severe asperity as a quality of inner life posed problems for the ordinary mortal. It involved, or at least could involve, a kind of disequilibrium, a flouting of reasonable *mediocritas*. The Aristotelian-minded Grosseteste (*De confessione II*) classified such behaviour as pious excess, and potentially as the vice of *curiositas*, the immoderate (*immoderatum*) exercise of good works.[53] Even for the saintly its practices thus entailed a form of concealment, discretion, a hidden piety, which in turn permitted eventual exposure. St Thomas's case was particularly problematic in view of its conspicuousness and exemplary standing. As Jennifer O'Reilly has shown, Becket's biographers employed considerable ingenuity in reconciling the key facts of Becket's life and his claim to sanctity, his 'red' martyrdom and his miracles, with the notion that sanctity should also be based upon the development of virtue in life, for St Thomas, because of his public conduct before and after becoming Archbishop of Canterbury, was not an obvious model of the confessor or 'white' martyr.[54] The recuperation of St Thomas's inner growth of sanctity, in the face of the nature of the man, involved ingenious disclosure, of which the discovery of his inner garb of verminous sackcloth was the most potent instance.[55] Herbert of Bosham confidently claimed that Thomas was not to be wondered at for his signs (*in signis*) but to be imitated for his works (*in operibus*),[56] the changes in his inner self and in his public attitude to the Church – for whatever his external nature, 'within, all was different'.[57] Dietary austerity, ritual flogging and the wearing of hair shirts were necessarily confessional activities based on the imitation of the early martyrs and St Martin; the process of exile too linked Thomas to local exemplars, notably St Anselm.[58] Exile as pilgrimage, *peregrinatio*, becomes a self-conscious theme in the Life of St Edmund, and the association of both Thomas, Stephen Langton and Edmund with Pontigny a compliment to the spiritual authority of the Cistercians.[59] The emphasis on Thomas's concealment of his asperities by 'civilized dissimulation' (for example taking food in hall but picking at it) is thus an aspect both of episcopal *mores* and of a more complex representation of sainthood itself, which was immediately picked up, and in effect codified, by Thomas's followers such as St Edmund, who hid his fasting with a serene face (*serena facie*) and holy dissimulation.[60] Edmund was also paired effortlessly with Martin,[61] and Edmund's disciple St Richard, also a model of asceticism, is shown with St Martin among the painted representation of All Saints, dating to the late thirteenth century, on the vault of the Ante-Reliquary Chapel at Norwich Cathedral.[62]

Not all thirteenth-century bishops or masters were ascetics, and asceticism itself could entail a certain anti-intellectualism, a contempt for worldly subtlety and for the activity of teaching.[63] But learning in the schools especially was undoubtedly a means to social and professional advancement for the most able.[64] The stress on the virtue of learnedness, and with it the notion that Christianity could be defined as a scholarly religion, was one of the most enduring consequences of Gregorian reform.[65] It generally entailed the type of prudential learning (in the sense of learning in arts and theology) for which the saint-bishops, products of the schools of Oxford and Paris, were famed.[66] The image of learning itself could also come to constitute part of the public iconography of the episcopal tomb in the period. A striking instance of the new importance of the *cursus vitae* of the bishop, including his birth, education and teaching, is provided by the shrine-like biographical narratives sculpted on the courtly-looking tomb canopy of Bishop Giles Bridport at Salisbury (d. 1262) (figs 106–7), himself not a saint – though such tombs were part of the dossier of sanctity – but a *magister* and *pastor bonus* imitating the examples of St Martin or St Nicholas, or the learned saints of his own generation.[67] But the notion of episcopal erudition suggested something more subtle, yet also more practical. Because its natural sphere was the school or the episcopal *familia*, it also entailed the more 'charismatic pedagogy' of the episcopal household, the education of young men in *mores* by word and by example which can be pinpointed in the case of Becket

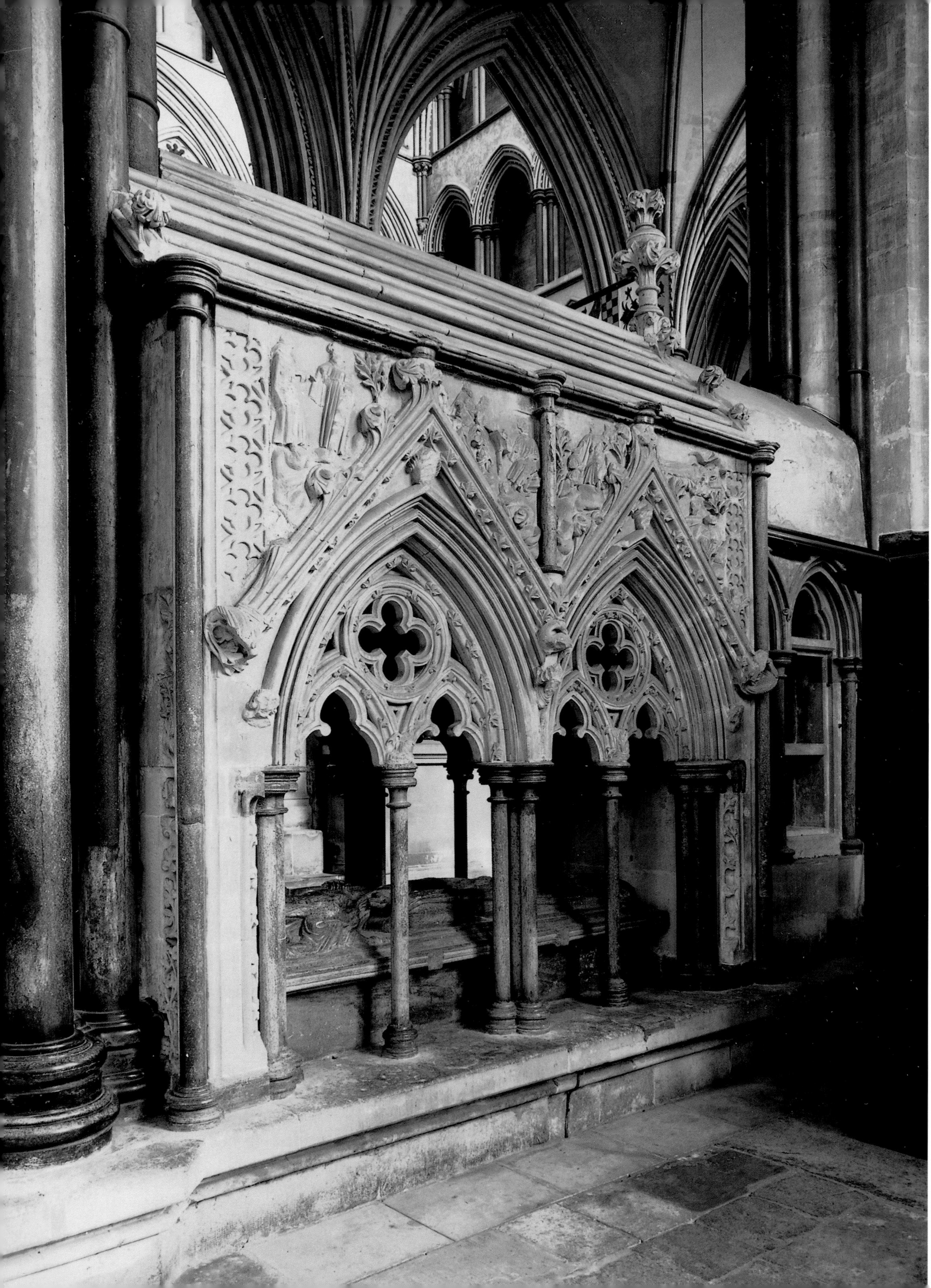

(whose signet ring depicted Mercury, for wisdom, grace and health), or Robert Grosseteste (who produced widely read household regulations), or St Richard, who wanted his pupils to be graced by manners.[68] Pedagogy was a vital dimension of the pastoral mission: the interconnectedness of all the elements – few of them absolutely original in themselves – that made up the thirteenth-century vision of saintly nobility is striking, not least because, as the library of Isabel of Arundel shows, they were arguably of wider importance for social and religious practice. As R. W. Southern has said, such processes were 'the outward and visible sign that the schools, which had begun by creating a universal system of doctrine and institutions, had now turned to the task of bringing the results of their work to the people'.[69]

Holy Bishops, Holy Kings, Holy Friends

Matthew Paris and his highly placed patrons regarded the finest representatives of the episcopal class as a check on the claims of public power, if not as representatives of a wholehearted 'opposition' to kingship.[70] Their greatest model, St Thomas, was an embodiment of the *Vox populi*; and the recognition that sainthood – whether episcopal or royal – had a social and political character was, as I have shown, integral to the nature and understanding of English sanctity throughout its history. But it was especially in the era of Becket's followers, notably Stephen Langton and St Edmund of Abingdon, that this recognition was given formal shape in the new wave of hagiographical writing, liturgical formulation and preaching. Matthew himself assembled a biography of Langton, the character of which is essentially hagiographical, even though Langton himself enjoyed no cult. Matthew, one of culture's magpies, collected Langton's sermons in the same way that he gathered together the poetry of Henry of Avranches.[71] The surviving fragment of his Life of Langton is apostolic, exorcistic and anti-papal in tone: Langton is portrayed travelling to Rome, excoriating French usurers, outwitting demons – for demoniac possession was currently an important topic – facing down the wrathful Pope Innocent III and generally measuring up well to the fathers

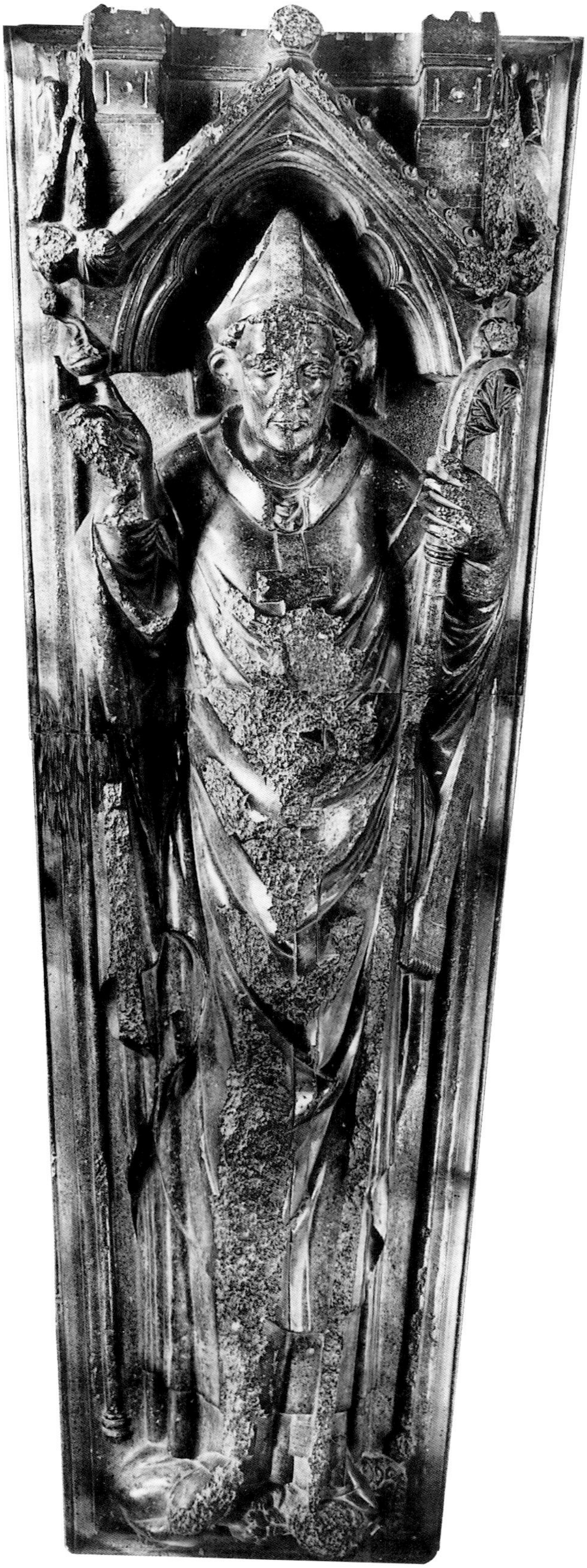

106 (FACING PAGE) Salisbury Cathedral, tomb of Bishop Giles Bridport, d. 1262 (© Crown copyright. NMR).

107 Salisbury Cathedral, tomb effigy of Bishop Giles Bridport, (© Crown copyright. NMR).

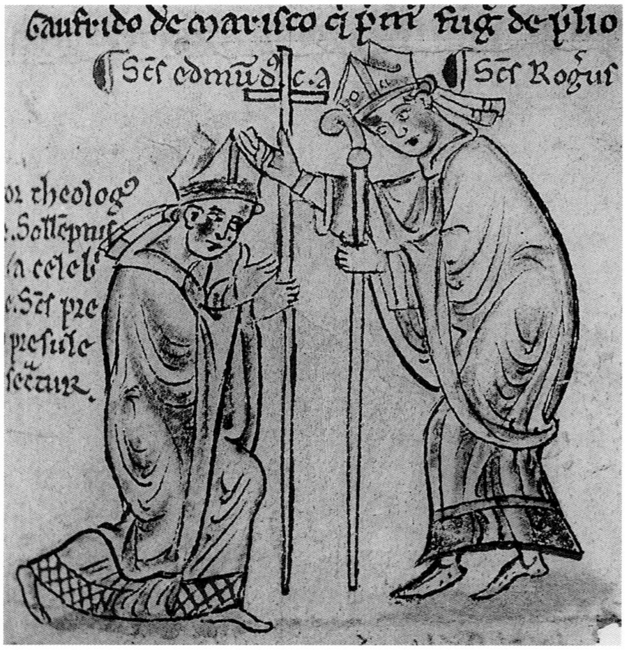

108 Roger Niger, Bishop of London, consecrates Edmund of Abingdon as Archbishop of Canterbury. *Historia anglorum* of Matthew Paris, BL Royal MS 14. C. VII, fol. 122, 1250s (Conway Library, Courtauld Institute of Art).

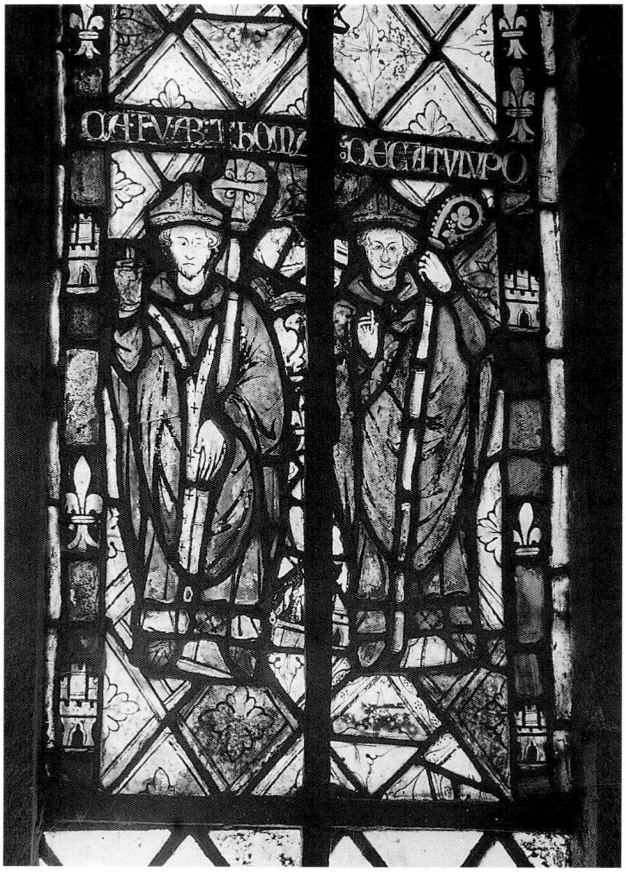

109 St Thomas Becket and St Thomas Cantelupe, stained glass at Credenhill (near Hereford) (reproduced by permission of English Heritage. NMR).

of the Church, especially as a preacher – in short as the very model of a reformist, outspoken and patriotic English bishop.[72]

This perception of Langton's life may owe something to Matthew's views on Rome of the 1240s and 1250s, but it does not totally misrepresent the general character of Langton's policy towards the papacy, the Church and the saints. Langton's policy was doubtless more papally inspired than Matthew would allow: he wanted to preserve the integrity of episcopal appointments, and inaugurated the first important provincial council in 1222, implementing canons of the Fourth Lateran Council.[73] His attitude to the sanctoral was typical of the expansionist era of Innocent III. He had a sharp eye for the symbolic and political weight of concerted ritual, especially in 1220, a remarkable year during which his influence reached an apogee, and a series of events of national standing took place: the canonization of St Hugh, the second coronation of Henry III at Westminster, the start of work on the new cathedral at Salisbury and, above all, the translation of St Thomas in July 1220.[74] The last event was the most cogent and orchestrated assertion of Langtonian symbolism: Becket was carefully moved in the presence of the king to his dazzling new shrine; a great feast was summoned in the new archiepiscopal hall; a new liturgy for Thomas's translation was assembled; and a programme of suitably allegorical preaching on the apotheosis was inaugurated in England and Rome.[75] Langton's sermons on the translation deploy the symbolism of Canticles and Revelation in a potent allegory of divine harmony gathered around St Thomas, in effect as an allegory of the whole community of the realm (*communitas regni*), the king and his baronage, harmoniously united in a celestial and sponsorial banquet.[76] For a 'political Augustinian' this was remarkably optimistic.[77] Langton understood that the *adventus* of a saint could make a powerful political statement, in this case, as Richard Eales has argued, of the 'renewal of peace and right order in the English Church and Kingdom'.[78]

But it would be wrong to assume that these events merely conscripted the cult of St Thomas to the domain of political utility, for Thomas's shadow fell long and hauntingly across the landscape of the English Church for generations. His spiritual and imaginative influence on the bishops was persistent. The idea of Becket, the 'Becket model', was an organizing principle which affected not merely political action, but spiritual and psychological identification.[79] Langton's six years of exile during the Interdict resonated immediately with Becket's six years of exile before his martyrdom, a point made in Langton's sermons; so too did their shared association with Pontigny.[80] Retreat to the Cistercians had been a feature of such leading schoolmen as Peter the Chanter, who retired to Longpont.[81] But action was matched by content. Sacred puns reveal a sense of essential identification: thus Henry of Avranches's poem for Langton, *Ad Stephanum*, states that 'not an atom should separate you from Thomas': *ut te non a Thoma separet ulla athomos*.[82] Matthew Paris's treatment of the dazzling array of saintly bishops in the mid-thirteenth century consistently stresses the theme of union and succession; so in his Life of Edmund he noted that Edmund was consecrated by Roger Niger, Bishop of London, one saint, theologian, virgin and ascetic consecrating another (fig. 108).[83] Yet his alertness to the theme of saintly friendship and holy union was scarcely peculiar. Gerald of Wales had already linked saintly bishops in pairs in his Lives of Remigius and Hugh of Lincoln,[84] and the 'Becket model' is almost ideally illustrated in the late thirteenth-century glass at Credenhill near Hereford (fig. 109), in which St Thomas is coupled with his namesake Thomas Cantilupe (d. 1282, can. 1320), Bishop of Hereford, presumably with the aim of promoting the latter.[85]

Edmund of Abingdon's example as the first canonized Oxford don is perhaps the most characteristic of all, in so far as it reveals with particular directness the complex relationship between these pedagogic, affective and ultimately pastoral preoccupations. Born around the time of St Thomas's canonization, by training he was a schoolman, versed in the moral theology of the schools in Paris, and associated with Oxford from around 1214. One of the few near-contemporary images of him is to be found in the chancel glass of St Michael's, Oxford (fig. 111), in the company of St Nicholas, the Virgin Mary and St Michael.[86] His promotion to treasurer (in charge not of money but of liturgical vessels and furnishings) at Salisbury in 1222 was owed to Richard Poore, and his outlook and alliances were broadly 'Langtonian'. Elected Archbishop of Canterbury in 1233, his relationship with the monks was not easy; indeed he fell out with them over the same causes that had split the convent and the primate under Baldwin and Hubert Walter.[87] His exile and death near Pontigny followed in 1240, and it was here that he was buried at his request (fig. 110), and eventually translated to a new shrine. Because he died and was enshrined abroad, the physical impact of his cult in England was limited; his days spent at Canterbury were few.[88]

The appearance of Matthew Paris's illustrated Life of Edmund is a matter of conjecture. Yet the saint's cult carried ideological weight. What the Benedictines lost the French Cistercians gained, for it was they who promoted the cause of his canonization with the support of the English members of the order, John of Toledo and Stephen of Lexington, Abbot of Clairvaux from 1243 and an associate of Edmund.[89] The process was completed with his canonization early in 1247, and by 1255 the convent at Pontigny gained permission to relax its regulations about lay access to shrines, including especially access by noblewomen, who are likely to have included Isabel of Arundel.[90] The importance of the cult of Edmund for the French monarchy exceeded that for the English king. The translation of the saint at Pontigny in 1247 was attended by Louis IX and his mother Blanche of Castile, who, according to Matthew Paris, kept a vigil at the shrine with fasting and prayer. Matthew also relates that Henry III's brother Edmund, Earl of Cornwall (whose wife Sanchia had been among the readership of Matthew Paris's Lives), regarded Edmund's 'exile' and death abroad as a rebuke to the English, and volunteered to pay for one-quarter of the cost of the precious feretory holding his relics, finished in 1249.[91] Henry III, though rumoured to have been involved in an attempt to stall the process of canonization, himself came to the shrine in 1254 and made oblations there.[92]

In emphasizing that St Edmund's cult was in part the product of a deliberate (and effective) formulation of an aristocratic style of sanctity, I should also point out that the conduct and style of his life were not a remotely realistic model for general imitation: the notion of the *pedisequus* (which had Cistercian forebears) had clear and obvious limitations in the pastoral domain.[93] Though Herbert of Bosham had advised that St Thomas was not to be wondered at for his signs but to be imitated for his works, severely ascetic conduct was something proper to a small and specialized class, a stimulus or starting-point, rather than an attainable end. Herbert was probably directing his remark to the *eruditi*. As Caroline Walker Bynum has noted, there was a practical distinc-

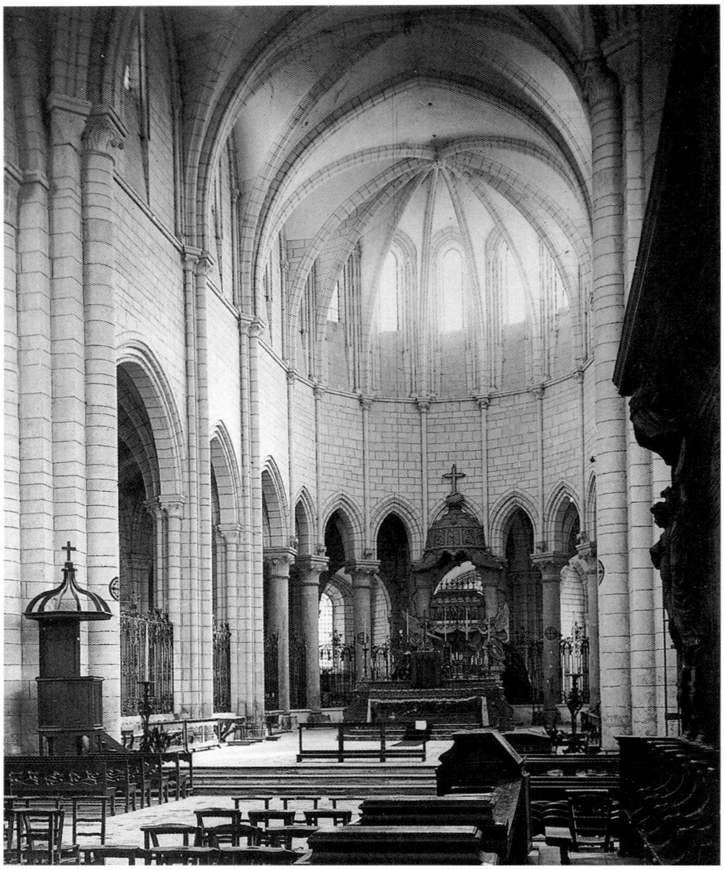

110 Pontigny Abbey, shrine of St Edmund (Conway Library, Courtauld Institute of Art).

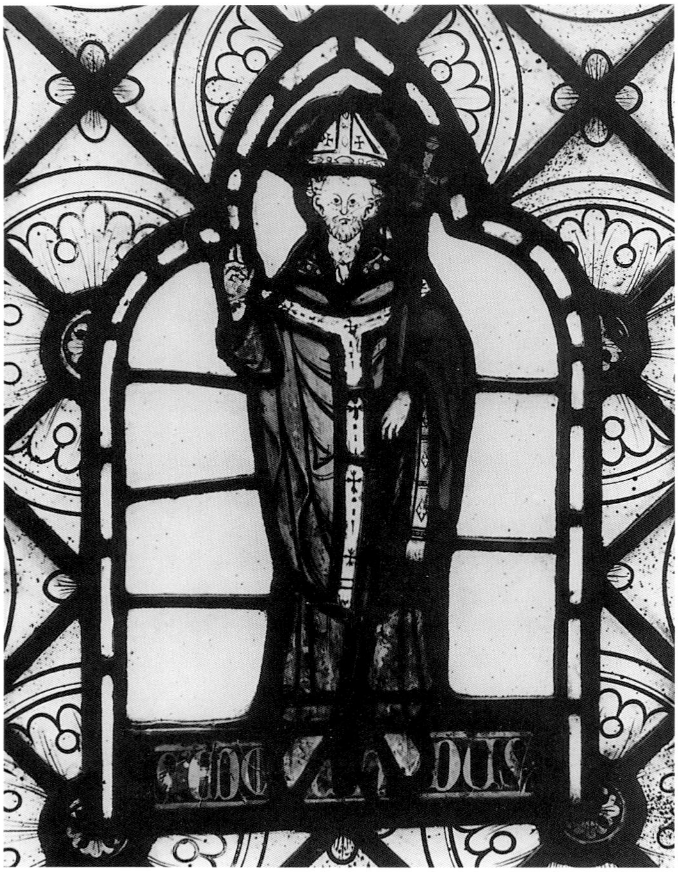

111 St Edmund of Abingdon, stained glass at St Michael, Oxford (reproduced by permission of English Heritage. NMR).

tion between admiring or wondering at such extremes, and actually imitating them, between absorbing them into consciousness, and actual practice: this had been summed up by the phrase *non imitandum sed admirandum*.[94] But this raises a further issue: the extent to which this style of sanctity was conceived in the first instance precisely as a model not for the ordinary faithful, but for the clerical class itself, as an aspect of the reflexive dimension of self-reform of the Church.

Matthew Paris's Life, though planned for a laywoman, is striking for exploring the theme of *imitatio* and the imprint or signature, whose formulation owed much to the increasing interest in the humanity of Christ of the previous two or so centuries.[95] Early in the Life, Christ, having appeared as an infant to St Edmund in a miracle echoing in form that of the Burning Bush, exhorts the saint to sign himself frequently in the name of Jesus of Nazareth.[96] The vision is a sort of epiphany or transfiguration, and following it Edmund turns to his life of wonderful asceticism. He is held to have signed himself in this way from head to foot, daily; Matthew Paris also records that he possessed a sapphire engraved with a figure of the crucifix, which passed into the possession of St Albans after his death.[97] Later, in a somewhat anti-intellectual vision, Edmund's dead mother appeared to him in a dream at a time when he was preparing lectures on arithmetic, and she asked about the geometrical forms to which he was paying such close attention. Edmund replied that the forms were for his lecture, whereupon she grasped his right hand and painted three circles in it, and in the circles she wrote the names of the Holy Trinity. Edmund was to direct his attention to theology, not the Liberal Arts.[98] The tale is partly a reminiscence of the moralizing stance towards the inutility and subtlety of the Liberal Arts met earlier in Alexander Nequam. But the sign of the Trinity is of course also the perfect image of God and a prognostication of Edmund's promotion to Canterbury. He was to know the Trinity like he knew the palm of his hand. The use of a diagrammatic representation of the Trinity resembles the increasing use of diagrammatic epitomes of doctrinal instruction in contemporary pastoral manuals (p. 189 below). Also, this mark of the Trinity as a set of circles finds an exact counterpart in the image of the Trinity, again as a set of three heads within circles, on the reverse of an *ad causas* seal dating around 1290 of Canterbury Cathedral itself (fig. 112), the other side showing St Thomas's martyrdom.[99] Was the allusion to the three circlets on St Edmund's palm based upon earlier Canterbury seals showing the Trinity, or did the *ad causas* seal echo an image in the Life of one of Canterbury's greatest saints? The form was certainly not new. In the twelfth century one of Canterbury's archdeacons and an opponent of Becket, Roger of Pont l'Evêque, had possessed a gem engraved with a triple-faced mask of Greek comedy and the legend *Caput nostrum trinitas est*.[100]

Since Hubert Walter's time it had also been conventional for the seals of the Archbishops of Canterbury to show the passion of St Thomas (figs 38, 49).[101] Matthew relates the horror expressed at the action of Robert Grosseteste in trampling upon a sealed letter sent to him by the convent at Canterbury, because its seal bore St Thomas's image.[102] In his Life of Edmund Matthew states that, in time of tribulation, the saint was directed in a vision to contemplate the example of the image and legend on his seal showing the passion of St Thomas and the legend *Edmundum doceat mors mea non timeat*: 'let my death teach Edmund to be fearless' (fig. 113 right); this was immediately followed by Edmund's decision to follow in Thomas's footsteps, *sequi vestigia pedentim*.[103] Thomas the model should literally 'inform' his followers with the stamp of his authority and example. At Canterbury, Eadmer and St Anselm were familiar with the seal metaphor in their spiritual writings.[104] The apocalyptic and sponsorial cues for this understanding of the waxen seal, commentaries on Canticles 2: 14 and 8: 6 (*pone me ut signaculum super cor tuum ut signaculum super brachium tuum*, 'set me as a seal upon thine heart, as a seal upon thine arm') were conventional enough.[105] Hugh of Saint-Victor, author of *De institutione novitiorum*, a foundation text for the Christian *habitus*, used the image of the seal in a pedagogic sense, in a fashion anticipated by Aristotle: the teacher is a seal, the pupil the wax.[106] St Edmund's writings reveal the profound influence of Victorine patterns of thought, and Matthew's report of his attitude to the image of St Thomas on his seal is absolutely in sympathy with Hugh of Saint-Victor's citation of the wax sculpture of the great man as a sort of exemplar:

> we who seek to be reformed through the example of good men, as through some marvellously sculpted seal, perceive in them the traces of actions, some of which are sublime and eminent. [. . .] When (saintly men) act in such a way as to arouse the admiration of human minds, then they appear as exquisite sculptures.[107]

Wax was viewed as a pastoral metaphor for the ductile or malleable character of the soul to be improved or 'informed'.[108] But that sculpture itself might be seen as the image of conduct was to have important implications, a topic pursued in Part IV (pp. 257–9).

By the time that Matthew was writing his Life of Edmund, the image of the model or imprint as a means of instruction had become associated with the newer styles of affective and somatic spirituality in a manner that was almost habitual. Their most powerful and vivid example was the stigmatization of St Francis in 1224; but St Francis was part of a wave of stigmatic, or at least parastigmatic, episodes in the period.[109] The stigmata were associated with those who bore the marks of involuntary crucifixion, notably St William of Norwich, and

112 Holy Trinity. Seal *ad causas* of Canterbury Cathedral. Canterbury Cathedral Library, Ch. Ant. F 33, late 13th century (Dean and Chapter of Canterbury).

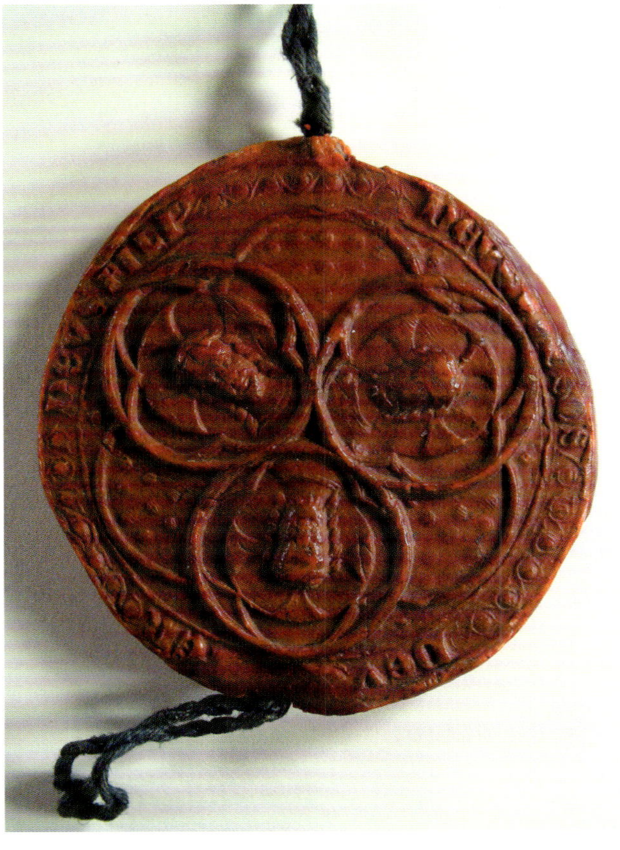

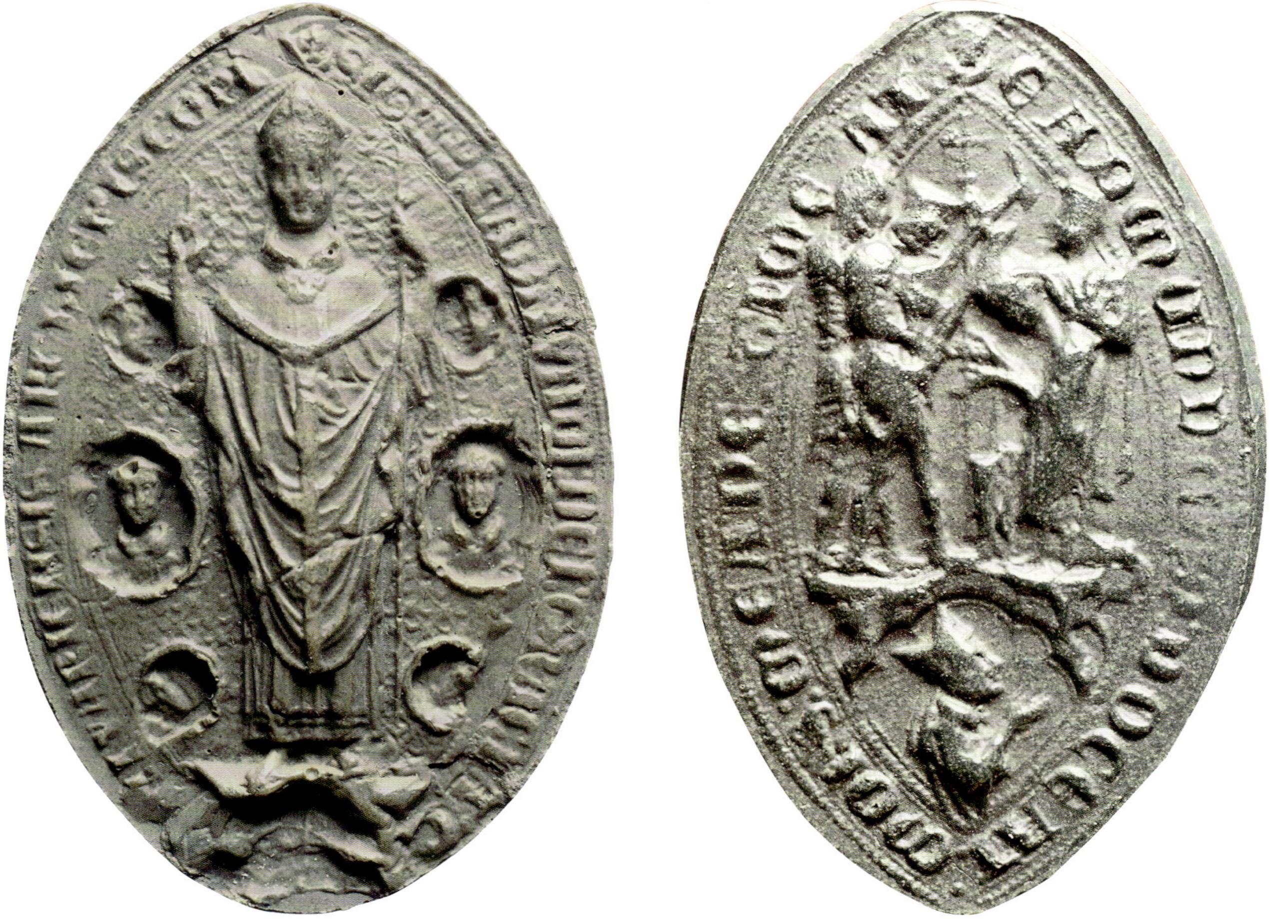

113 Seal of Edmund of Abingdon as Archbishop of Canterbury, showing counterseal with martyrdom of St Thomas (right), *c.* 1233 (Society of Antiquaries of London).

usually as part of anti-Jewish activity. In the early thirteenth century there were some true stigmatics: Marie of Oignies (d. 1213), Dodo of Hascha (d. 1231) and the dauphin, Robert of Auvergne (d. 1234). Others were either mad or heretical, as in the case of illicit self-crucifixion brought before the Council of Oxford in 1222: a young man, the first English 'stigmatic', was accused of having allowed himself to be crucified, so bearing the five wounds of Christ, and of being associated with adoring women, one of whom called herself Mary; the perpetrators were sentenced to death.[110]

Edmund of course was not a stigmatic; the type of imagery in Matthew's Life has instead a parastigmatic content, stressing the spiritual or figurative importance of the imprint, seal or signature, rather than literal harm to the flesh and its attendant dissolving of the boundaries between internal and external conduct, allegory and reality. The character of Edmund's asceticism is internal: he is the saint whose flight from pleasure is like the daily bearing in his body of the dying of the cross; his martyrdom is the white, and not the red, of St Thomas, the living victim.[111] Edmund's asceticism is also aristocratic: as already noted, like St Thomas his model, Edmund hid his fasting with serene face and holy dissimulation; and Robert Grosseteste classified pious excess as the vice of *curiositas*, the immoderate exercise of good works.[112] St Edmund in his own pastoral text *Speculum ecclesiae* (see p. 193 below) is also familiar with this basically classical language of temperance in advocating *mesure* as against *demesuré dolor*.[113] The bishop-saint's words define for others the natural or decorous limits of pious behaviour, but his own actions test them by example. Edmund's piety is severe; but it is not without sweetness, tears and affection – and in this regard at least its practical or pragmatic character is much more notable.

Matthew's Life of Edmund is a *locus classicus* of this type of moderate affective religion. At its heart lies a particular empathy with both Mary and Christ. The relationship with Mary is bound up with Edmund's relationship with his mother, who, like the *Virgo lactans*, feeds Edmund with the milk of doctrine and virtue; later, as the very example of pious widowhood, she sends to her son (then a student in Paris), a hair shirt to be used for the sake of Christ. It is characteristic of such piety that it never fails to invoke the symbol and the allusion. The 'Mary-mother-saint' complex is partly a by-product of the Becket apocrypha, since it is in the later accounts of Becket's miracles and his secret asperity that one discovers that it was the Virgin Mary who bestowed upon St Thomas his rough, hairy undergarments, and who indeed later repaired them maternally for the unkempt prelate at Pontigny.[114] This is but a short distance from the lively patterns of association between Mary, spinning Eve and St Thomas which preoccupied the illuminator W. de Brailes in his Psalters and Books of Hours (fig. 114).[115] Asceticism is almost an inherited trait – an echo of the older English tradition of blessed lineage. At the symbolically important age of twelve – the age of Christ's first theophany and rejection of his worldly parents, famously celebrated in an allegorical treatise by Aelred of Rievaulx – Edmund dedicates his virginity to the Virgin Mary while praying at a statue of her in church, and then seals the bond by placing a ring on her finger, invoking the virtue of St John the Evangelist, a sponsorial gesture which Mary recognizes by refusing to relinquish the ring.[116] Once again, St Edmund's relationship to Mary at the age of twelve is a consolidation and enrichment of a tale in the Becket apocrypha relating how at a tender age St Thomas, a great devotee of the Virgin, tearfully approached her image and dedicated his virginity to her, taking her as his bride; in return she gave him a tiny pyx, an adumbration of his identification with the Passion of Christ.[117]

114 Virgin Mary vests St Thomas in a hair shirt. Hours of W. de Brailes, BL Add. MS 49999, fol. 49, *c.* 1240 (Conway Library, Courtauld Institute of Art).

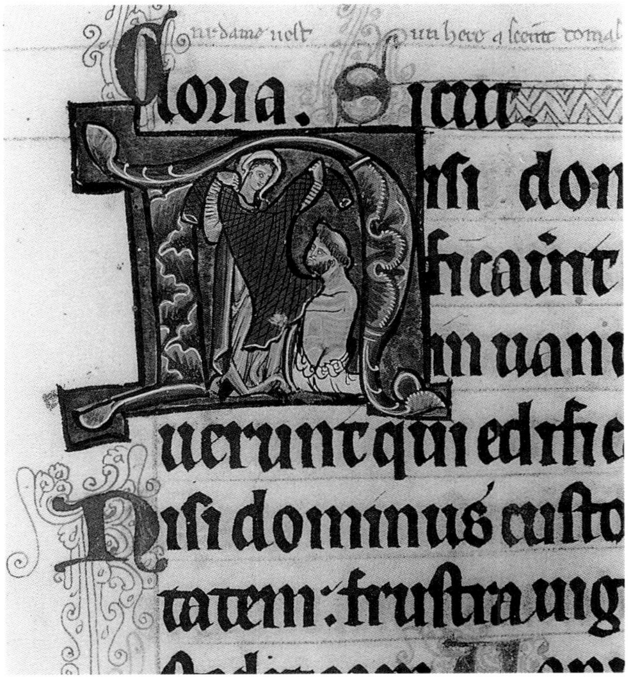

Note how important images are to this style of devotion. Edmund's hagiography is unusually interesting in this regard. In his *Chronica majora* Matthew, recording early signs and wonders of St Edmund in 1244, noted the survival in England of painted pictures (*tabulae pictae*) which the saint used to carry; in his Life of Edmund he relates that these images, which included a silver panel on which was carved (or painted) a figure of the Virgin and Child, the Crucifixion and the martyrdom of St Thomas, were sent by him to his sisters as nuns at Catesby.[118] The Pontigny Life of St Edmund sheds further light on how he used such images, not solely as a means of connection to his devotions, but to the apparently combined practices of *lectio* and devotion. Edmund sat at his reading desk with his books placed on the top part, and a most beautiful ivory statuette (*imago eburnea*) of the Virgin Mary, whose throne related the story of Christian redemption: what holy scripture expressed in letters, a sculpture could clearly do in its form (*apertius in figura*), throwing open meaning to the senses and permitting the sweet refreshment of the spirit in the combination of prayer and reading.[119] The mildly justificatory tone of this passage is distinctly Cistercian in that it recognizes – as does the text *Pictor in carmine* of around 1200 generally attributed to an English Cistercian – that legitimate images (of the saints, biblical typology, etc.) may act as a stimulus to those who are literate and of spiritual, not carnal, inclination.[120] As Suzanne Lewis has noted, this combination of reading and prayer provides a coherent context for the miscellany of pastoral illustrations added to the Lambeth Apocalypse of the 1260s (Lambeth Palace Library MS 209); these include a frontispiece showing a Benedictine monk painting a statuette of the Virgin Mary (the *Opus Dei*), a portrait of the patroness of the book Lady de Quincy kneeling in prayer with an open book before a large image of the Virgin Mary (fig. 115), various martyr saints, the Crucifixion (fig. 181), two archbishop saints and an allegory of penance (fols 48–53).[121] Lewis also notes that the archbishop-saints, presumably Thomas and Edmund (the first

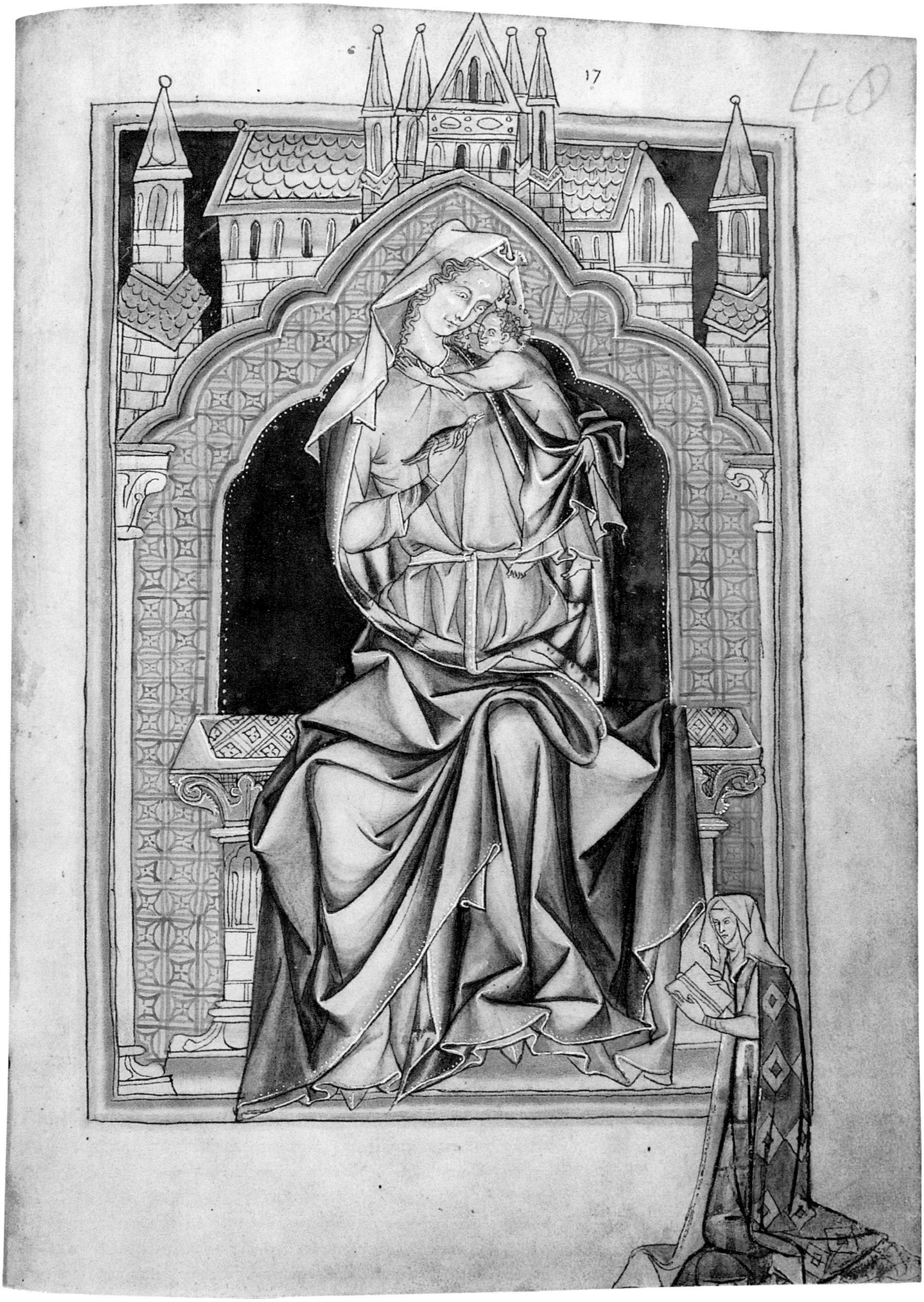

115 Lady de Quincy prays before the Virgin Mary. Lambeth Apocalypse suffixed illustration, Lambeth Palace Library MS 209, fol. 48, 1260s (Lambeth Palace Library).

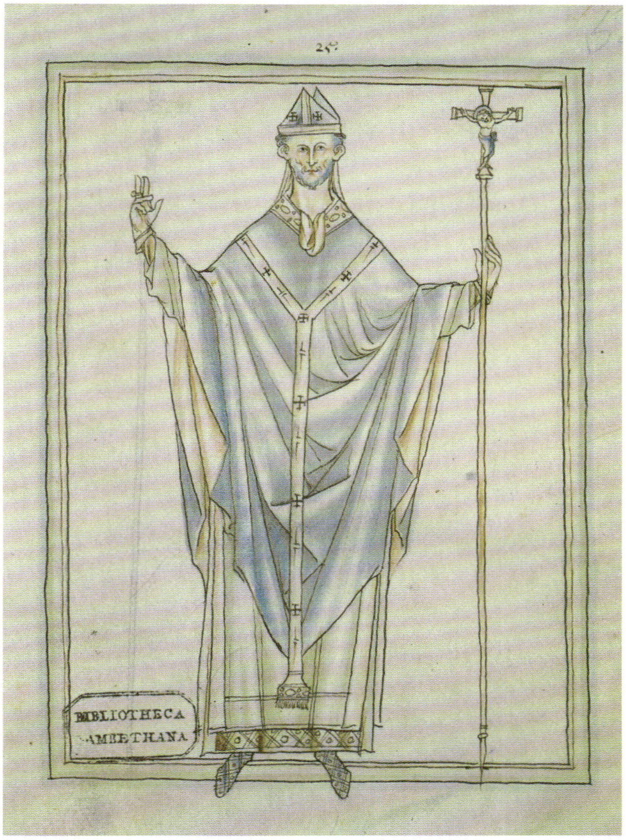

116 St Thomas the 'patron' or model. Lambeth Apocalypse suffixed illustration, Lambeth Palace Library MS 209, fol. 52, 1260s (Lambeth Palace Library).

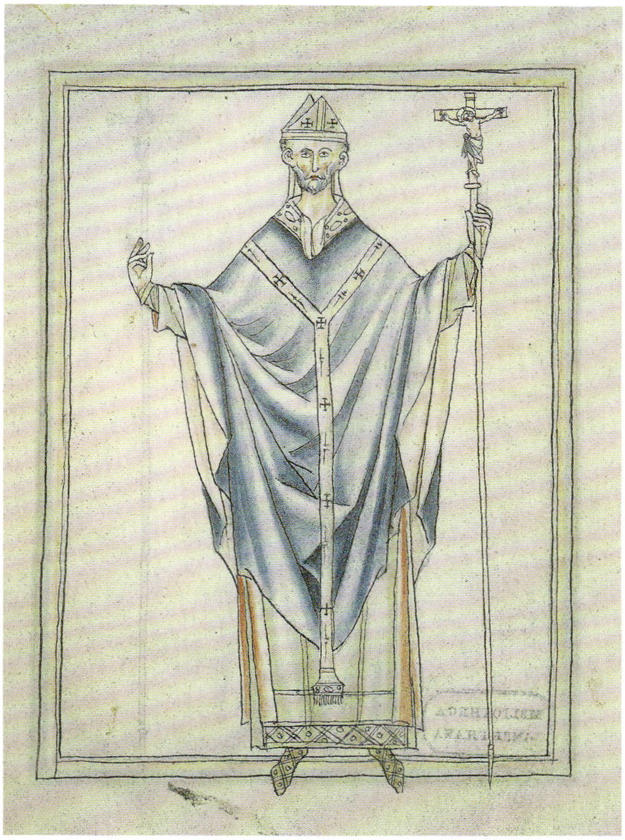

117 St Edmund the 'copy'. Lambeth Apocalypse suffixed illustration, Lambeth Palace Library MS 209, fol. 52v, 1260s (Lambeth Palace Library).

archbishop opposite the Crucifixion is likely to be St Thomas in view of his *passio*, and the second, St Edmund, falling after the sequence of martyrs and opposite the allegory of penance in virtue of his pastoral importance), are painted on recto and verso of the same folio (52), one design providing the 'ghost' for the other to follow on the back of the vellum (figs 116–17). This is a fine example of the medieval understanding of the word 'patron' to include the idea of a design or model for an artist, as much as for ideal conduct. This idea immediately brings to mind the 'model' or 'imprint' theme followed throughout this discussion.[122]

Though such schemes of pastoral reading and prayer were not wholly affective in intent they were significantly so, and in ways that would have been recognizable to earlier monastic and specifically Cistercian poetics. The Life of St Edmund emphasizes the infantile aspects of Christ and the saints, and the imagery of breasts and wounds as sources of spiritual nourishment.[123] The tone is therefore strongly eucharistic. In Matthew Paris's Life, Edmund, having been given the *viaticum* on his deathbed, seizes the crucifix from the hand of the administering priest and presses the blood red wounds of Christ to his mouth and eyes, constantly kissing them, and sucking the wound at Christ's side, saying 'With joy shall you draw water out of the wells of the Saviour' – an allusion to the sacraments of the eucharist and penance. Matthew relates that this devotion caused no little astonishment, not least on account of its novelty.[124] Given the occurrence of this sort of maternal and ingestive imagery in the writings of Aelred of Rievaulx, St Bernard, Rupert of Deutz and – perhaps most significantly – St Anselm and the *Ancrene Wisse*, this last observation by Matthew is odd, unless it points to the real possibility that the episcopal saints were only now carrying such basically monastic devotional and doctrinal ideas out into the wider world through their very conduct.[125]

Not the least of these affective themes, one which ties Edmund to other saints in terms of male notions of love, is of course friendship. Edmund's hagiography emerged directly from his *familia*, from his chaplain Eustace of Faversham, from the Dominican Robert Bacon, and above all from his talented young chancellor, Richard Wyche, who became St Richard of Chichester. These were the sources that Matthew Paris himself used. One collection of depositions made about Edmund – doubtless in conscious reference to St Thomas – was called the *Quadrilogus*; indeed Eustace's draft Life copied out pages of John of Salisbury's Life of Becket wholesale.[126] For the present argument the most important of these relations was between Edmund and Richard. The Lives of Edmund and Richard both revive the *candidus et rubicundus* figure noted earlier in St Thomas's hagiography.[127] In a note on Richard's death in the *Chronica majora*, Matthew Paris claimed that Richard's relationship to Edmund was one of special intimacy; Richard knew Edmund's secrets and sought to walk in his footsteps; and it was to Matthew in turn that Richard disclosed these secrets.[128] Richard Wyche, like Edmund, was a holy don: born in the late 1190s, he had been a regent master at Oxford by the 1220s and was its chancellor by 1235, becoming Edmund's clerk in 1237.[129] His association with Edmund was almost certainly formed at Oxford.[130] Richard was elected Bishop of Chichester in 1244 against Henry III's wishes, and the ensuing resistance he showed to the king's will marked him out as a staunch champion of the Church. He was a reformer, and his diocesan statutes were promulgated in 1252, the year before his death; he was canonized in 1262 and thereafter had a limited cult following.[131]

Above all he was the disciple of Edmund. Theology was never far away: Richard's Life composed for Isabel of Arundel likens the two saints protecting the church of Canterbury to the two cherubim either side of the Ark (Exodus 25: 18), one being the archbishop, the other his pupil.[132] Nor were older patterns of virginal miracle-making wholly foreign: like Etheldreda, St Richard could make grafts bloom miraculously – his hagiographer explicitly mentions the example of Aaron's rod – and could repair cracked stones.[133] But what matters more here is their relationship, for, as presented in the hagiographies, this has an especially confessional tone. Richard was Edmund's constant companion, his adherent, in life, exile and death.[134] Their Lives use similar types of anecdote. On Edmund's death Richard sought solace learning theology with the Dominicans.[135] In 1253 Richard's entrails were buried by the altar of the chapel of St Edmund at Dover, which he had dedicated; his body was placed by the altar of St Edmund on the north side of the nave at Chichester.[136] The words put into his mouth by Ralph Bocking, that Edmund had long taken Richard into his heart – *quem iam diu nobis invisceravimus* – were scarcely idle, and burial practices expressed them succinctly.[137] Such heartfelt love (the image of love stemming from the viscera is common in such texts) pinpoints exactly the place of such holy alliances within the affective piety of the period, and its capacity to find in bodily imagery powerful metaphors of the spiritual. The model for the ideal of romantic spiritual friendship referred to here was monastic, and was most richly developed in the writings on the topic by Aelred of Rievaulx (derived explicitly from Cicero's *De amicitia* which Aelred had discovered as a schoolboy), and above all by St Anselm.[138]

Matthew Paris's Life of Edmund is shot through with somatic, parastigmatic and affective imagery, whose principal objects are Mary and Christ, and St Thomas. Ralph's Life of Richard, portraying the bishop on his deathbed gently kissing and stroking the wounds on the Crucifix, was in the same mould: for the time was coming when he, like Edmund before him, would not merely touch Becket's feet, but kiss him on the lips, in fulfilment of Canticles 1: 1.[139] So familiar and stable is this pattern of imagery connecting St Thomas to his holy precursors and successors – whom one may fairly call friends – that it is easy to dismiss its reiteration of themes merely as a conventional reflex, as sterile pattern-making. But this would be to miss the point: the regular imprint or pattern, the steady drip-drip of familiar images, was not a sign of exhaustion, but (from a widely held Aristotelian position at least) the positive assertion of the techniques, habits, repetitions needed for a structured, disciplined religious ethos or *habitus*; by such means, *verbo et exemplo*, were spiritual consolation and edification to be found and propagated.[140] The saint's Life was one powerful vehicle for such ideas because it could be rendered into the vernacular. So too could the most direct forms of pastoral instruction for religious and layfolk, for an intimate relationship existed between what was said about the bishop-saints as regulators of *mores* and affective piety, and what they themselves wrote as pastors. St Edmund's widely influential *Speculum ecclesiae* was a case in point, and I return to this text in Part III, where I consider in more depth the consequences of this style of religious life and human relationship for the Church at large.

To begin to understand this broader dimension, I conclude this chapter by examining the political domain of the English saints. As Matthew Paris noted in his summary of the year 1250, during the reign of Henry III (1216–72) there was a striking efflorescence of English sainthood. Langton's promotion of St Thomas indubitably provoked a chain reaction of events, the consequences of which were felt throughout the second quarter of the century and beyond. Canterbury's example informed the architectural reformulation of such major churches as Ely, and also a new wave of promotions of the English saints. St Thomas's translation and the canonization of St Hugh were followed by the translations of St Augustine at Canterbury and Wilfrid of Ripon, the canonization of William of York and the attempted canonization of St Osmund at Salisbury.[141] Not all the patrons concerned were 'Langtonian': Langton's powerful adversary Peter des Roches, Bishop of Winchester, refounded a hospital at Southwark which acted as a centre of the cult of Becket, and promoted the cult of St Birinus, the apostle of the West Saxons, whose relics were 'invented' at Dorchester in 1224.[142] In doing so he commissioned a Life of Birinus from Henry of Avranches who, with characteristic diplomacy, connected Peter, a French alien, to his reforming Anglo-Saxon forebears St Swithun and St Ethelwold as well as to St Martin.[143] This conscious promotion of English sainthood by alien churchmen takes on a particular significance in relation to sainthood and alien royal dynasties. Des Roches was Henry III's tutor, and may have been aware of the conscious efforts that Henry's father King John had made to align himself with the protective aura of the saintly English episcopate. John had been buried in 1216 at Worcester, near the shrines of Sts Oswald and Wulfstan, both Anglo-Saxon monk bishops.[144] Wulfstan was canonized by the new, tougher papal procedure in 1203, and his translation in 1218 was followed by the total reconstruction of the east end of the church: Henry III attended the translation with des Roches.[145] John's marble tomb effigy (fig. 118) is accompanied to either side by small figures of Oswald and Wulfstan wearing Anglo-Saxon mitres, an attentiveness to outmoded detailing anticipated by the retrospective effigies at Wells; carved bosses on the vault behind the high altar also show two bishops.[146] Wulfstan's cult had enjoyed a revival at the end of the twelfth century in the wake of events at Canterbury,[147] and there is some evidence that his famous action of ramming his episcopal staff into the tomb of St Edward in defiance of the Norman Archbishop Lanfranc – so bolstering the authority of English kingship in Church affairs while also connecting Wulfstan and Edward – was conscripted by John or his apologists in his dispute with the papal legate during the Interdict.[148]

The tactic failed, as such tactics are wont to do: but John provides the first example of positive English royal recognition of the value of holy union of saint and king. Henry III's devotion to St Edward the Confessor provides the second. The rise of St Edward's fortunes at the court of the young Henry has never been fully explained, but the cult had certainly come into royal favour at the latest by the mid-1230s, just as Henry gained his majority. The king's tutelage under Peter des Roches may have been one factor in this somewhat unexpected ascent. Des Roches had already promoted the cults of Birinus and Swithun, and his will of 1238 made provision for the foundation of a Cistercian house at Netley, alias Edwardstowe.[149] Des Roches also installed a new Abbot of Westminster, Richard of Barking, in 1222, the year in which the bishop had served alongside Langton and Poore in obtaining for Westminster its exemption from episcopal authority.[150] Richard of Barking was himself a supporter of the cult of St Edward and commissioned a set of tapestries of his life for the choir of the abbey.[151] It would be entirely in keeping with the patterns sketched out in this chapter for the clerical or monastic stimulus of a coterie of this type to have played a major part in influencing the formation of a royal cult. Indeed St Edward's role at Westminster was twofold. His twelfth- and thirteenth-century hagiography makes it clear, first, that St Edward's Life was the pretext for the rehearsal of Westminster Abbey's rights and privileges with regard to exemption from diocesan control, the housing of royal burial and the coronation of the English kings. Its importance was thus institutional; so, when in the late 1230s Matthew Paris composed an illustrated Anglo-Norman verse Life of the saint, using the model of Aelred of Rievaulx's Latin Life, and dedicating it to Eleanor of Provence, he was acting as a Benedictine apologist for a major monastic shrine in royal hands.[152] Everything about this Life seems to anticipate the major new provision for the shrine (fig. 119) and abbey church that Henry III was planning in the early 1240s.

But St Edward's second role, for the court at Westminster, was even more important because it exemplified the pastoral importance of St Edward for royal spiritual and ethical mentorship. Matthew conceived his poem, and its opening epithalamium for Queen Eleanor, with the same objectives in mind as his Life of St Edmund for Isabel of Arundel, *attavis regibus*, descendant of kings;[153] and since his Lives of Edward and Thomas were bound in a single volume for Isabel's readership too, St Edward's example is likely to have been considered alongside that of St Thomas. It would therefore be quite wrong to see these Lives as expressing some sort of oppositionist antagonism, and more profitable to consider in what ways their viewpoints on ideal leadership might have been complementary, even dialectical.[154] It is worth recalling that despite the stress on holy virtuous marriage in St Edward's hagiography, Henry III and

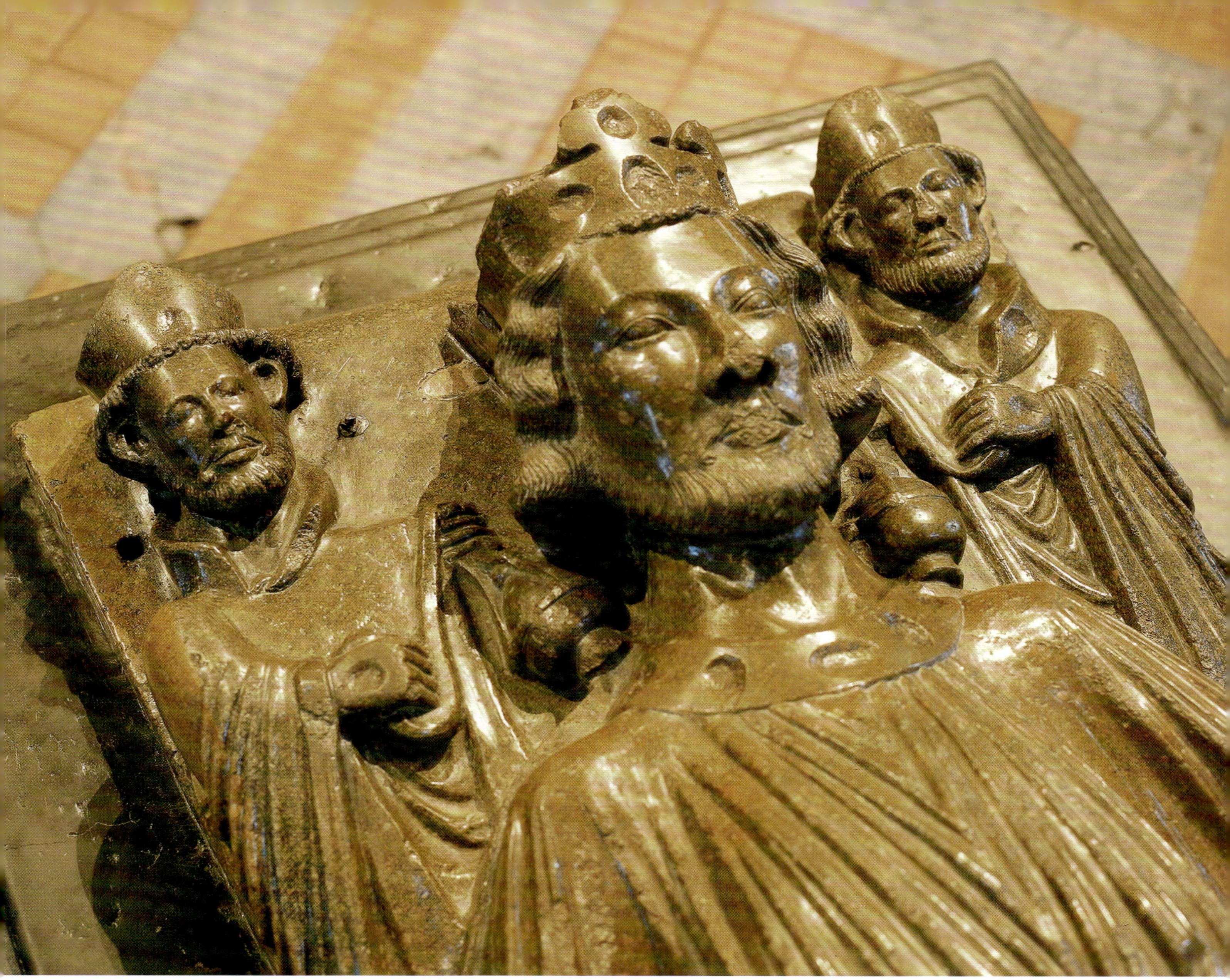

118 Worcester Cathedral, tomb effigy of King John with Oswald and Wulfstan, 1230s (John Crook).

Eleanor were married not at Westminster, but before the shrine of St Thomas at Canterbury in 1236.[155] The extant copy of Matthew's Life of Edward, *La Estoire de Seint Aedward le Rei* (CUL MS Ee. 3. 59), is on the face of it a document which reasserts the ancient traditions of English royal sanctity considered earlier in this chapter. So, Edward is presented as a model of peaceable kingship, the text of the poem opening with a contrast between those pre-Conquest kings who increased their political strength by being mighty and bold (*forz, e hardiz*), and those such as Edward who were wise, peaceable and moderate (*ki erent plus senez/ Peisibles e atemprez*) and whose power came from good counsel and intelligence (*par bon cunseil e lur sens*) (fig. 103).[156] This immediate rejection of a chivalric or warrior ethos amounts to a revival of the pre-Conquest stress on innocence and chastity among the Anglo-Saxon English saintly princes and kings, to whom Edward is now joined as a pacific king who rules by virtue, simplicity and wit.[157] The *Estoire* also uses old-fashioned nature allegories of a type found in traditional English sanctity (p. 93 above), whereby ideas of good and holy lineage are expressed in terms of the root, stock or branch,[158] most notably in a prognostication by St Edward (whose saintly powers were principally visionary) of the downfall and eventual recovery of the kingdom in terms of

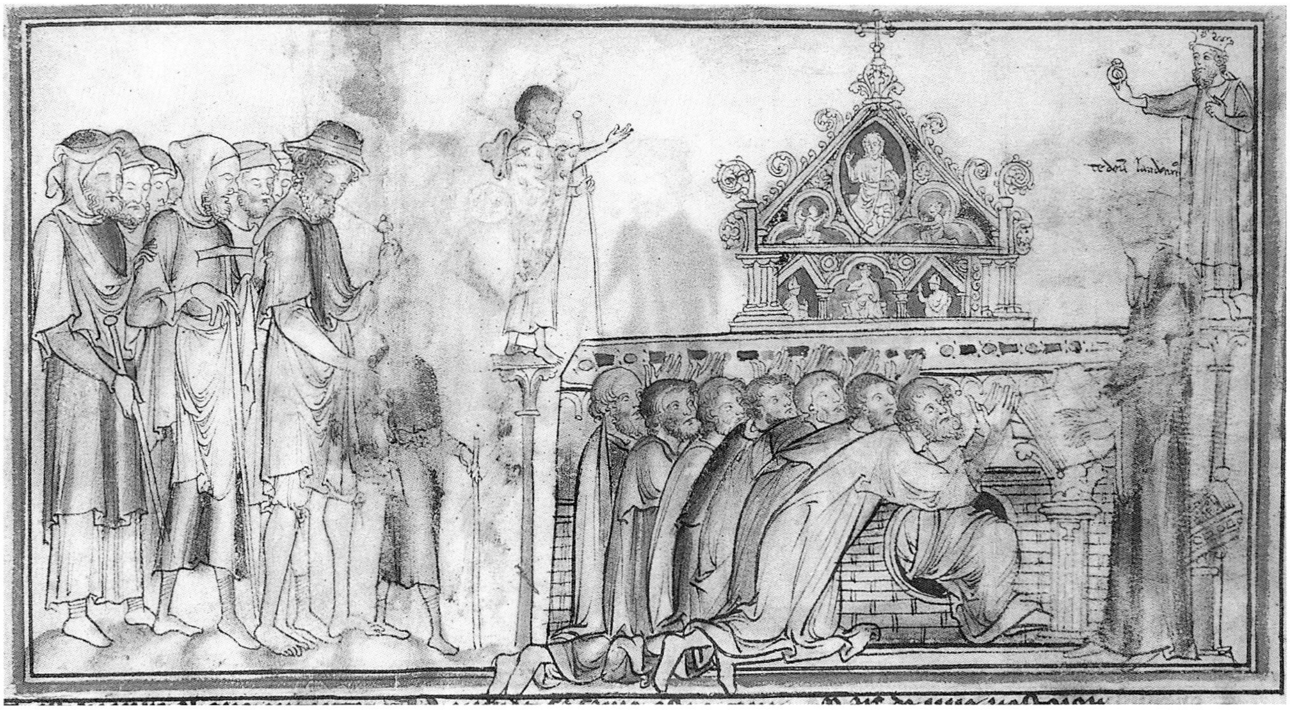

119 Healing of the sick at St Edward's tomb, with the Miracle of the Ring. *La Estoire de Seint Aedward le Rei*, CUL MS Ee. 3. 59, fol. 30, *c.* 1255 (by permission of the Syndics of Cambridge University Library).

an extended root and branch metaphor.[159] Here, however, the principle is not merely lineal, but restorative: Edward's reign – to use an image of Matthew Paris – represented the 'golden centuries' of good laws, holiness and harmonious rule, the calm summer of the English people before the Conquest;[160] and it is up to his successors (principally Henry II and Henry III) to put matters right. Edward's harmonious relations with his baronage are therefore a sort of prescriptive mythology, a necessary nostalgic fiction, for the Plantagenets. Fittingly, one of the earliest rehearsals of this concept of St Edward as the touchstone of political nostalgia is to be found in Herbert of Bosham's account of the translation of Edward in the presence of St Thomas and Henry II, Edward symbolizing their brief unity.[161]

The skill of the *Estoire* lies in part in this ability to reconcile traditional sanctity with the new rulership ethos of the thirteenth century that I have attempted to describe in this chapter. It is tempting to think of an annexation of traditional models of English royal sanctity to a Langtonian morality of kingship. St Edward was a natural protector of the Church. His asceticism was important. Edward's miraculous powers – his visionary powers especially – derived from sexual chastity and the subduing of the flesh.[162] Edward's model in this was St John the Evangelist, with whom he formed a holy union. So Edward made a chaste marriage with his queen, Edith, living with her 'as if in a monastic order' under the protection of the Virgin Mary, St John and St Peter (fig. 120).[163] Yet the theme is also a variant of the monastic emphasis on chastity encountered above with Anglo-Saxon innocent male martyrs and saint-queens, in the sense that Edward's and Edith's chastity involves a renunciation of sex, not marriage, unlike Etheldreda's. This was of relevance to courtly wife and widow: it had been Ralph Bocking in his Life of St Richard who, in praising Isabel's voluntary chastity, deplored the female lust which drove the contemporary aristocratic marriage market.[164] Nor, more importantly, does it involve the renunciation of power, the throne itself, one possible corollary of the stress on virginity in the old sainthood: kings who fled into monasteries tended not to be canonized.[165]

Precisely because marriage is not renounced in the Life, its pastoral authority as a document about virtuous marriage is sustained, opening as it does with a tribute to the marriage of Henry and Eleanor of Provence. Its view of royal chastity thus retains a certain courtly equilibrium, for Edward is not a crowned monk, merely like one, and his conduct is not that of the wholehearted

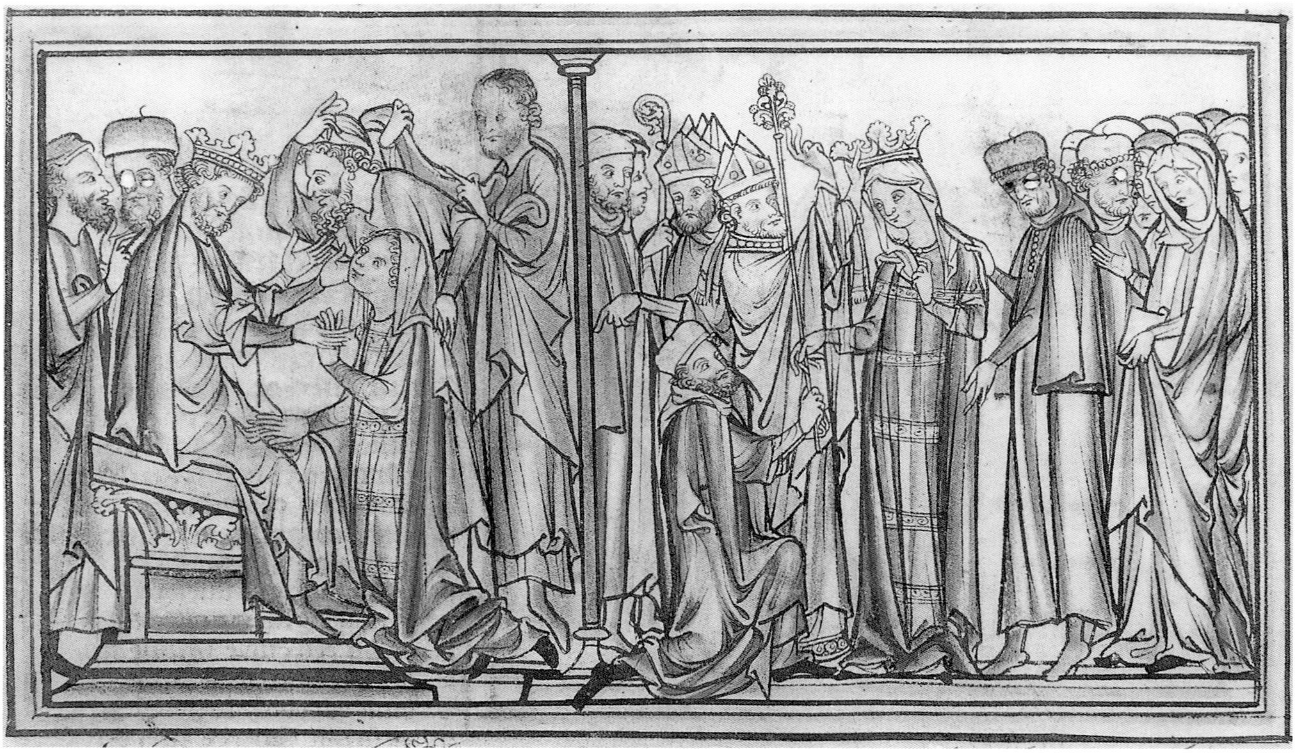

120 Marriage and coronation of Queen Edith. *La Estoire de Seint Aedward le Rei*, CUL MS Ee. 3. 59, fol. 11v, *c.* 1255 (by permission of the Syndics of Cambridge University Library).

clerical or monastic ascetic. So, in keeping with the aristocratic model of episcopal temperance derived from the 'Becket model', Edward's and Edith's chastity is a matter of dissimulation: their desire to preserve the flower of chastity, the white lily and the red rose, is the great secret (*le grant secrei*) of St Edward.[166] Where Becket had dissimulated about food, Edward dissimulated about sex.

That such para-clerical behaviour involved discretion is a sign of the sophisticatedly courtly apparatus of sanctity apparent in the Life of Edward. The king's principal virtues aside from chastity are magnificence and temperance (*mesure*), aristocratic qualities that again harmonize well with the ethics of ideal episcopal conduct (pp. 125–9 above): Edward forgives thefts from his treasury, remits taxes, has a groaning table in his hall, and sheds his treasure greatly (*largement*) for the poor before his death.[167] This theme was coming to dominate the public iconography as well as the fact of public charity at the court of Henry III.[168] In comparison with his monastic sources, Matthew Paris also enlarges on the 'charismatic pedagogy' of Edward's court. In celebrating Edward's restorative role, the king is likened to Solomon: rulers and magnates positively seek out his presence, and all nations see embodied in him the ideal of virtuous rule. This ideal is essentially pedagogic, for they come

> Ses leis oir e establies,
> Ses sens e curtaises;
> Checuns ki veit le rei Aedward
> Plus est curtois quant il s'en part;
> Checuns i prent, checuns aprent
> Mesure, sen, e afaitement [. . .]
> Sa court fu de afaitement
> Escole, e de enseignement.
>
> To hear his laws and his judgements
> His sense and courtesy;
> Each one who sees King Edward
> Is more courteous when he leaves him;
> Each one receives there, each one learns
> Moderation, sense, and good manners [. . .]
> His court was of courtesy
> The school, and of accomplishments.[169]

Not surprisingly, a reciprocal diplomacy marks St Edmund the peacemaker.[170] As Jocelyn Wogan-Browne concludes, these Lives 'engage in the politics of

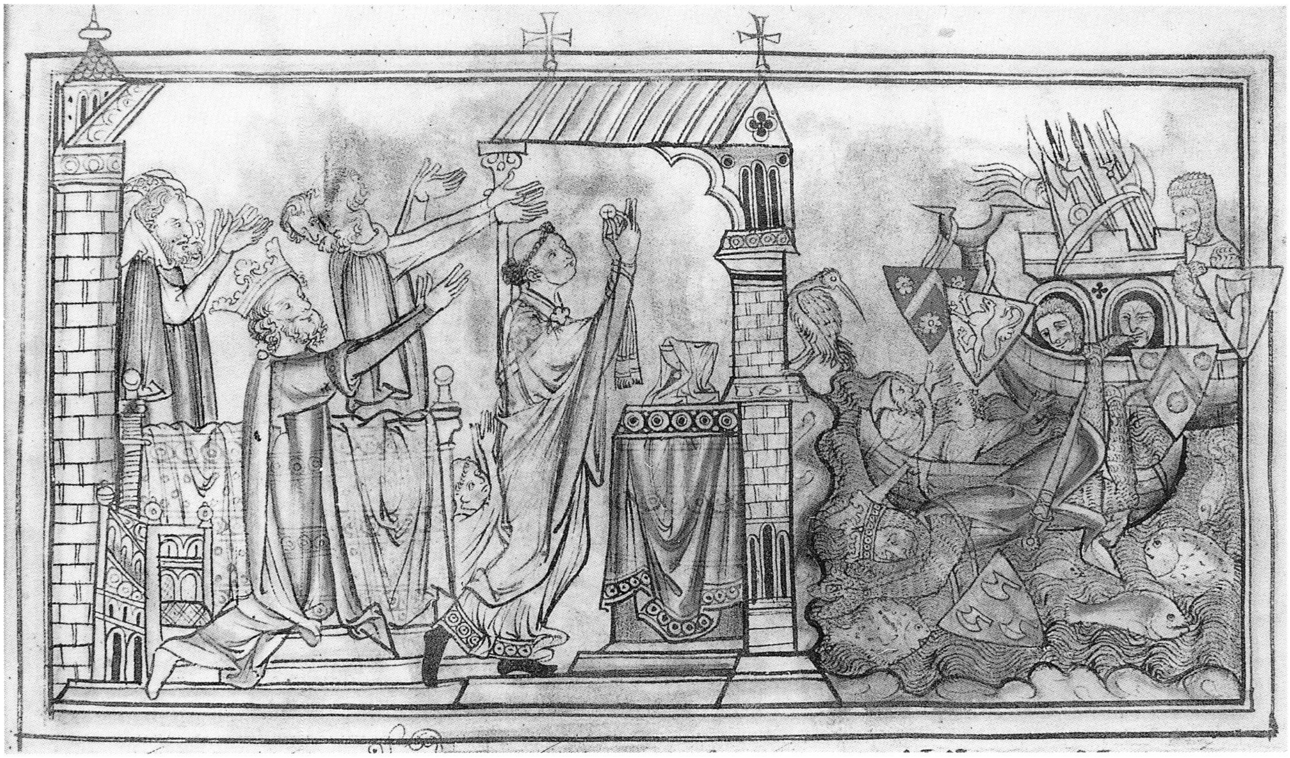

121 Vision of the King of Denmark drowning seen by St Edward at Mass. *La Estoire de Seint Aedward le Rei*, CUL MS Ee. 3. 59, fol. 12, *c.* 1255 (by permission of the Syndics of Cambridge University Library).

thirteenth-century curiality' and in 'the construction of courtliness'.[171]

A further aspect of this charismatic formulation of royal sainthood from the late twelfth century is its emphasis on affect, in the sense of 'emotion understood as disposition'. In Edward's case the saint's affective nature is governed by *mesure*. An important instance of this is his bodily expressivity, particularly his willingness to smile (fig. 121) – but never (for reasons considered below, pp. 247–56) to laugh out loud. The *Estoire* is also absolutely typical of its time in its lachrymose eucharistic piety – for Edward was also greatly disposed to gentle weeping at Mass, not least on the occasion of witnessing the Christ Child in the Host (fig. 126).[172] Host miracles of the latter sort were comparatively common. One is related in the *Magna vita* of St Hugh, another in the Life of St Edmund of Abingdon. They formed part of the burgeoning 'Christ-oriented infantilism' which Giles Constable has identified in contemporary imitation of the Body of Christ.[173] Again it is likely that Matthew felt authorized to develop this angle by Aelred of Rievaulx's Life. More importantly, the *Estoire* contains precisely the same eucharistic and empathetic devotional preoccupations that were coming to feature too in the Life of St Edmund. It is within the Life of Edmund by Matthew, and not the earlier *Estoire*, that one reads of the reception by Henry III in 1247 of the relic of the Holy Blood, whose nature reflected common Anglo-French interdynastic rivalries.[174] The reception of Christ's blood doubtless explains too the related interest in the relic of the Ascension at Westminster, the holy footprint indicating that Henry was to be the *pedisequus* not just of St Edward, but of Christ.[175]

Also in keeping with this affectivity – as one might expect of Aelred's interest in friendship – is a stress on conubial imagery. The *Estoire* offers guidance as to an ideal marriage between a king and a queen, but its notion of sainthood as a form of chaste, divine union is extended into a chain of friendship between the royal patrons, St Edward, and his saintly companions St John and St Peter. It was to John, Edward's model of chastity and visionary power, that the king offered a ring as a sign of his spiritual marriage to the evangelist (fig. 122, also fig. 119), who in turn returned it to the saint because of his love for King Edward – *Pur l'amur Aedward lu roi*.[176] This conubial theme was important to ascetic hagiography which also promoted the idea of the Church as the saint's bride, following Canticles: as noted above, St

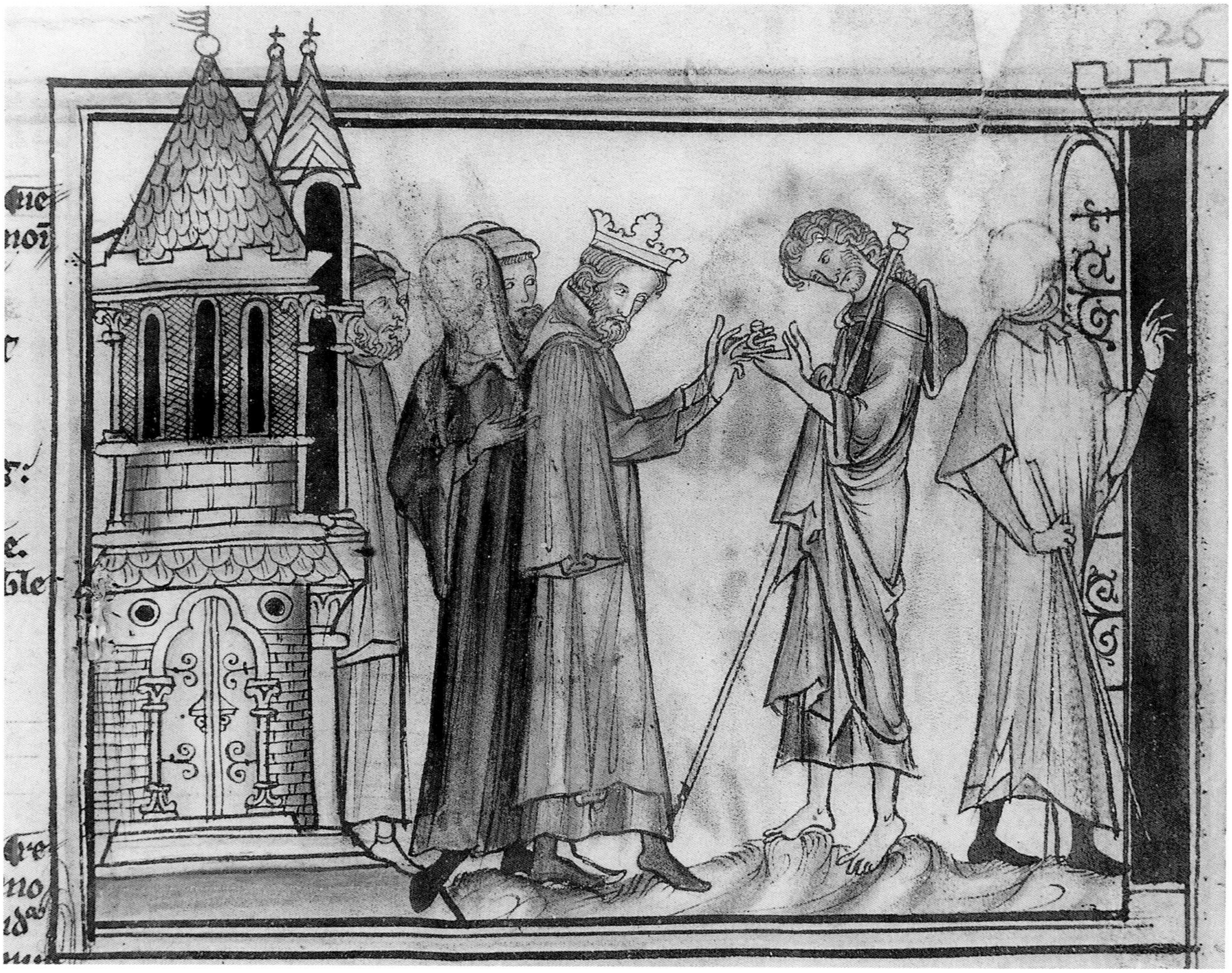

122 Miracle of the Ring. *La Estoire de Seint Aedward le Rei*, CUL MS Ee. 3. 59, fol. 26, *c.* 1255 (by permission of the Syndics of Cambridge University Library).

Edmund of Abingdon had placed a ring on the finger of a statue of the Virgin Mary in a similar sponsorial gesture, while invoking St John's virginal example; St Richard's virgin flesh was unstained, and he 'betrothed his soul to the heavenly bridegroom'.[177]

The legend of St Edward and St John was the defining moment of Edward's public iconography. It occurred commonly in the royal palaces and at Westminster Abbey, not least in the images that surrounded the shrine of the saint.[178] Westminster's shrine and tomb complex can legitimately be seen as the most sublime physical expression of the impact of the notion of holy union in thirteenth-century England. St Edward lies at the very heart of the building in a shrine of Roman Cosmati mosaic (fig. 123); Henry rests immediately to his north in a tremendous shrine-like tomb of the same manufacture, their abode being the same.[179] The inscription recorded on the shrine, giving the date of completion of this remarkable complex of memorials, 1279, and the reasons for its coming into being, is eloquent: 'O man, if you wish to know the cause, the king was Henry, the friend of the present saint' (*Homo, causam noscere si vis, rex fuit Henricus, sancti presentis amicus*).[180] The term *amicus* has a particular richness, for it implies not only artistic patronage, but patronage in the fullest political and spiritual sense. Though saints ranked above kings, Henry and Edward are shown here as mutual sponsors, patrons, protecting each other in a commemorative union expressed through the shared aesthetic order of their tombs, whose language of porphyry and other rare inlaid stones is

123 Westminster Abbey, the shrine of St Edward (John Crook).

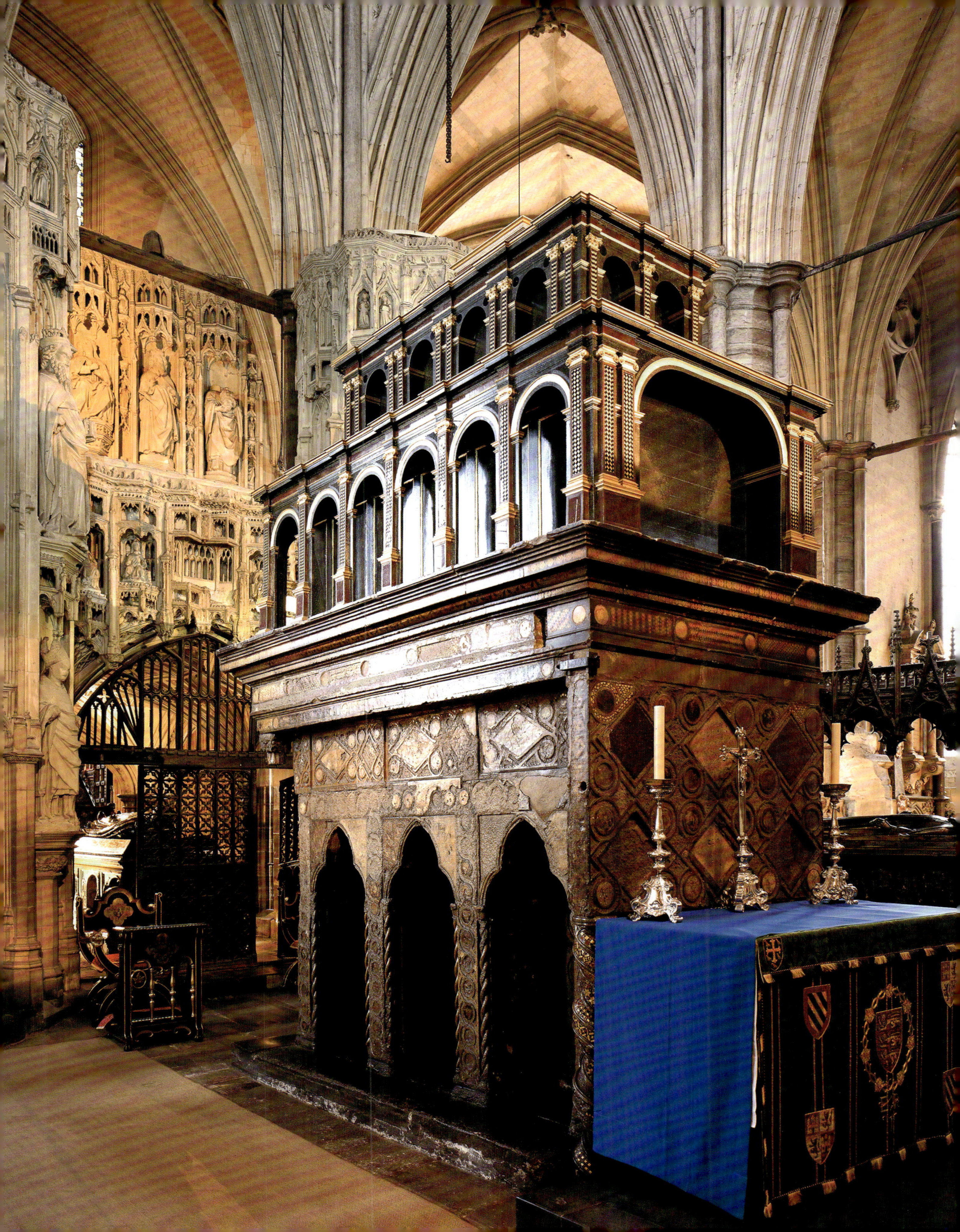

expressive of the charisma of power. Henry slept next to an image of St Edward in his great chamber; here he sleeps with the saint in death.[181] To share a bed or clothes was the highest sign of spiritual love.[182] The bishop-saints Edmund and Richard had also known such a heartfelt love in life and death, indeed 'in death they were not divided' – *in morte non esse separati*.[183] Matthew Paris understood that Edward was Henry's 'own dear one' and that Henry was the *amator Sancti Aedwardi*.[184] Their common habitation at Westminster is the perfect fulfilment, even the dramatization, of the pastoral objectives of contemporary hagiography. It created something strikingly reminiscent of a contemporary definition of love by a Neapolitan genius working in Paris under the influence of Aristotle, namely Aquinas – love as a 'mutual indwelling' (*mutua inhaesio*). For as St John, Edward's patron, said 'He that dwells in charity dwells in God, and God in him' (1 John 4: 16).[185] Cicero had expressed it succinctly in his theory of *amicitia*: that, in ideal friendship, several are united in one.[186] The ideal was an old one; here at Westminster it attained its highest aesthetic embodiment in the English Middle Ages.

This chapter on the saints of England accordingly ends with the investment of sublime friendship between the saints and their patrons in the visual culture of medieval *romanitas*. It is no part of the present argument to suggest that the intimate connections and resonances between episcopal and royal sanctity were necessarily causal, for they seem to shed light on the broader pastoral and ethical character of ideal leadership invested in the communion of saints. Reform was not only an issue for the mass of ordinary faithful, but for the highest reaches of the Church and public power itself. The harmony between the elements traced in this chapter is striking, and was probably unique to the situation of the mid-thirteenth century in England. The cult of St Edward as reformulated in the reign of Henry III, and with the aid of the considerable literary and artistic resources of Matthew Paris and his contemporary hagiographers, was a form of resolution of the various ancient traditions of English sanctity with the 'Langtonian' concept of the *communitas regni*. In the boldest sense this resolution can be seen as part of a post-Becket, post-Magna Carta accommodation of sanctity and public power. Yet the model of Canterbury, and with it the powerfully formulated and persistently influential model of Thomas Becket, is everywhere to be felt in the thirteenth century. The art of Westminster in effect reintroduced to sacral kingship concepts of sanctity whose major and most powerful formulations, in the widest aesthetic sense, were monastic and clerical. Canterbury itself, so richly informed by the heroic, humanistic and charismatic language of Benedictine patronage, as well as by the example of French Gothic architecture, remained an important point of reference for Westminster's own alert and self-conscious rapprochement with France and Rome. The shrine of St Edward and the tomb of Henry, surrounded by gorgeous mosaic pavements and inscriptions referring directly to the 'heroic mode' of great patronage at Canterbury, were the finest, and indeed the last, English instances of the feudalization of the highest ideals of the post-Gregorian Church. This was a high point in the art of English sanctity. From it proceed the next stages of this enquiry: how the ideals of reform, the aesthetics of affective piety, and the representational means at the disposal of artists working at this time, came to coalesce and spread under a new regime of pastoral regulation, whose primary aim was to put the Church itself in order.

Part III

REGULATION

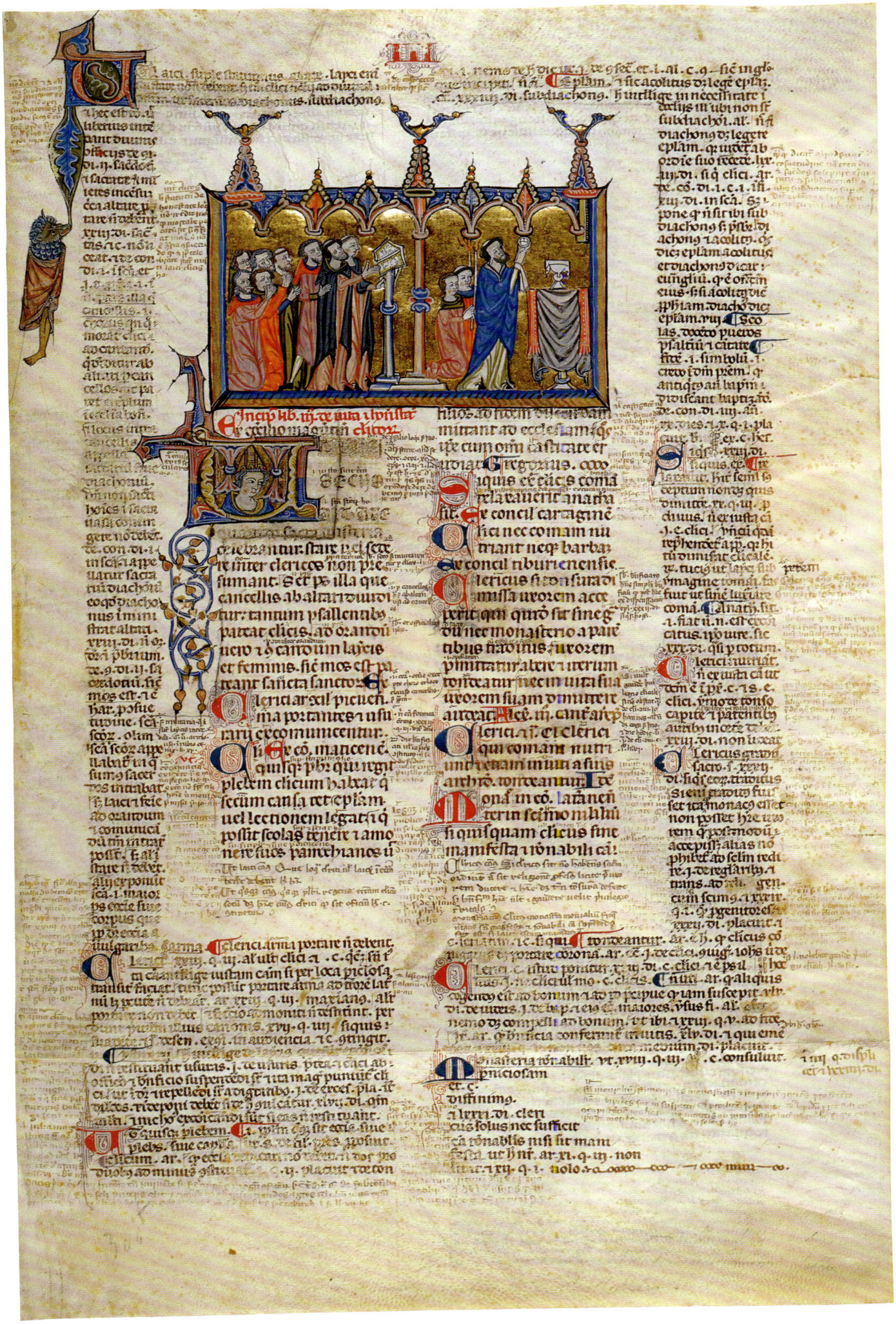

124 Elevation of the Host. Decretals of Gregory IX. Cambridge, Fitzwilliam Museum, Marlay Cutting Fr. 2, *c.* 1340 (by permission of the Syndics of the Fitzwilliam Museum, Cambridge).

Chapter 7

ORNAMENTA

As we are to deal with meaning, let us begin with a paradigm: viz. that sacred symbols function to synthesize a people's ethos – the tone, character, and quality of their life, its moral and aesthetic style and mood – and their world-view – the picture they have of the way things in sheer actuality are, their most comprehensive ideas of order.

Clifford Geertz, 'Religion as a Cultural System'

All matters should be diligently attended to by him to whom an altar is committed: also he should not permit sundry images or lights to be placed on or fixed around altars in a disorderly manner, as happens in country churches, but only the images of the saints in whose honour the altars are dedicated, with a cross in the middle and two candlesticks to either side which burn equally.

Statutes for the collegiate church of Ottery St Mary, 1339

So far this book has addressed such issues as allegory, morality and sanctity; and because my concern is to consider yet more deeply what Clifford Geertz identifies as the ethical content of symbols – their 'moral and aesthetic style' – the reader must now confront the most palpable ways by means of which such symbols were lent a framework of official coherence and legitimacy, namely through the regulative practices of the Church. This is a complex and in some ways intractable matter, but because it concerns the history of images in this period, it is inescapable and must lie at the centre of this enquiry. It will quickly become apparent that regulations can offer only an incomplete view of what was actually happening in the thirteenth-century English Church at large. One has to recognize the numerous loopholes in law-making and enforcement, as well as the new countervailing pressures, including a massive surge of lay interest and investment, which render a solely 'top-down' view of the history of images as at best inadequate, and at worst actively misleading. But that the Church and its agencies were positively intent upon regulation with increasing precision and determination as the century progressed cannot be gainsaid: and the issue is of interest here because law is at least one index of expectations, if not of outcomes.

The regulation of art had wider dimensions. In so far as art is undoubtedly an outcome of human conduct, the Church saw that it too could be drawn into the domain of the theology of human behaviour, which itself had become one of the most ambitious and fertile aspects of the thought of the monasteries and the schools in the generations around the year 1200, and which was being codified as part of the reformist drive. The Church recognized, on the basis of its own increasingly sophisticated and self-conscious theoretical accounts of human morality, that the image, the installation, the altar, as well as the forms of behaviour associated with and implicit in such things, were part of the *habitus* of contemporary religion. One was constitutive of the other. Ideals about 'church furnishings' and what was foreign, or proper, to the Church at the parochial level, implied a view of ethical propriety, and the belief that such propriety was related to art's instrumentality. This was an aesthetic issue in the fullest sense of the word. The desire to create legitimate patterns, models, pathways, is one that is traced throughout this account of the products of early Gothic art and architecture in England. The post-Gregorian project of reform led, from one viewpoint, to 'the first programme of mass education ever carried out in the West', as set out in the canons of the Fourth Lateran

Council of 1215.[1] The episcopal and magisterial class was deeply implicated in these measures. This class, this regime, led the way in shaping the rational, versatile and self-consciously universalizing formulations for liturgy known as the Use of Sarum, which was spreading from Salisbury throughout most of the English dioceses in the Province of Canterbury by the early fourteenth century.[2] As early as 1257 the statutes of Salisbury were describing its position among churches as being like the sun in the firmament.[3] That there was also what R. I. Moore calls a 'dark underside' to the contemporary clerical regime, involving the currency of repression, stigmatization and marginalization of undesirable thought or conduct, or ethnic origin, is undeniable. This has to be set against such seemingly innocent accomplishments as the recognition of the concept of the minimum wage for parish clergy, or the discrediting of trial by ordeal.[4] In the objective of regulating not only justice but the visual culture of the Church down to parochial level, lay an implicit scepticism about the validity of the community as a source of proper practice – and so an anti-communitarian instinct, characteristic (for some) of the emergent bureaucratic state and of newly authoritarian attitudes to popular cults, miracles and canonization.[5]

But the fact of law is established (fig. 124); what matters are what differences its existence made, how it worked in detail, and whether it worked at all. The English outlook on these universal issues within the Catholic Church is both privileged and inadequate. England, at least in the period under discussion, was not a land of widespread heretical belief, as the *Ancrene Wisse*, composed for western-English anchoresses in the early part of the century recognized: 'heresy, thank God, is not prevalent in England'.[6] Indeed it was comparatively thoroughly regulated, both at the parochial and diocesan level. As a result the final consolidation and regulation of the English parochial system in the twelfth and thirteenth centuries is remarkably well documented. Coercion has benefits for historical understanding. In contrast, the physical traces of the images, installations, altars and so on surviving from the thirteenth century have been radically compromised by later medieval provision, to say nothing of hammer-happy Protestant zeal. In considering (and only in passing) the art of the highly organized parochial system as it was recognized in ecumenical and diocesan legislation, the exercise is to an extent counterfactual, much 'text' and comparatively little 'image'.

Yet there are solid grounds for proceeding, and they are best established in two broad stages. The first involves the practical exercise of establishing what the law was in regard to the ethos and details of the art of the secular Church down to parish level; and to do this one must examine the ecumenical, and more local provincial and diocesan, adjudications on the matter, starting with the framework provided by the Lateran Council of 1215. How the law was formulated and implemented is one thing. What it embraced is another. The local was in some ways of much greater interest than the ecumenical, and the network of control was surprisingly open in texture. There were considerable but very fertile gaps in regulation which hugely shifted the emphasis onto what may usefully be called *adiaphora* – things inessential in the eyes of the Church, but fundamental to the history of art. Much that was of most interest in the visual archaeology of the thirteenth- and fourteenth-century English Church was adiaphorous, and so not a matter of useful legislation at all.

The second stage requires one to see in what ways the ordering of external things, *ornamenta* as they are often called in the documents, was related to the ordering of things internal to the Christian person, especially how models of edification through pastoral instruction were turned inwards to discipline, and ornament internally, the self. These can be approached under the heading *pastoralia*. This stage, the subject of the next chapter, entails facing up to the most radical pastoral activity by the Church, the suppression of illicit activities or images on the grounds of 'error'.

Lateran IV: Scope and Limitations

The Council at the Lateran, summoned by Innocent III (1198–1216) in 1213 and convened in November 1215, had an extensive and original agenda; it was larger in attendance than the previous Lateran Council of 1179, with over four hundred bishops as well as representatives of the monastic orders, and it was new in respect of the form of its seventy-one constitutions or canons, which were proposed to the Council by Innocent himself, and approved in a single session on 30 November.[7] Following Roger of Wendover's sceptical text about the event in the *Chronica majora*, Matthew Paris depicts Lateran IV as a sort of contentious parliament of prelates (fig. 125). The Benedictines had reason to be wary of the Council's reformist agenda towards the monastic orders, embodied in its canon 12.[8] They knew that Lateran IV was important because its attention to issues in the contemporary Latin Church was comprehensive. But they could gain too. In his account in the *Gesta abbatum*, Matthew (whose view of the papacy was not unlike Margaret Thatcher's attitude to the European Union), notes that the Abbot of St Albans, who attended the Council, had gained papal agreement to the invocation of the names of the principal saints in churches during the secret of the Mass, and observes that at the Council there had been a 'diligent discussion on the Mass and matters pertaining to the Mass; and some things were abolished which had been done for a long time before'.[9] In closing some doors, it opened others. Lateran IV was regarded in the Middle Ages as an ecumenical council of the Church. Subsequently it has had to bear the burden of numerous competing historical ideologies: those stressing the positive angle of pastoral care, education and doctrinal clarity; and those seeing in its provisions the foundations of what T. N. Tentler called 'a comprehensive and organized system of social control', foundations which helped to establish, in Foucault's words, 'the main rituals we rely on for the production of truth' – and indeed (according to some) created the first truly Catholic Church.[10] Those who hold this last view have seen in its provisions the dark underside of the clerical mentality of the period, not so much closing, as slamming, doors in the faces of specific groups.[11] But in regard to both broad positions, each of which invests great faith in the standing of the Council as a 'watershed', some balance is necessary. Not every aspect of Lateran IV was new, surprising or final. Canons 1 and 21 of the Council are held to be among its most important. It is often asserted that the Council promulgated a dogma of Transubstantiation in its first canon. But, as Gary Macy has indicated, this was far from so: the Council merely promulgated the doctrine of Transubstantiation, without in any sense providing a definitive or final dogmatic account of this extremely complex issue, one best seen in the context of the theological pluralism of the age.[12] Its recommendations about 'the production of truth', the kernel of which, canon 21 (*Omnis utriusque sexus fidelis*), set out the obligation of Christians to confess their sins, perform penance and receive communion at least once a year at Easter, actually sanctioned a customary relaxation of existing requirements.[13] Indeed Richard Poore's statutes for Salisbury produced in the Council's wake were altogether tougher and more traditional on the point of confession and communion, repeating not the Lateran's new formula but that of Langton's earlier statutes which favoured thrice annual communion.[14] This again warns of the necessity to see the Council in due proportion.

Medieval law-making tended to be conservative, and the canons agreed at the Council should also be seen in the context of developments in the so-called interconciliar period (1179–1215), during which Innocent's own outlook had largely been formed: his mental preparation was at least partly Parisian.[15] The canons of the Council

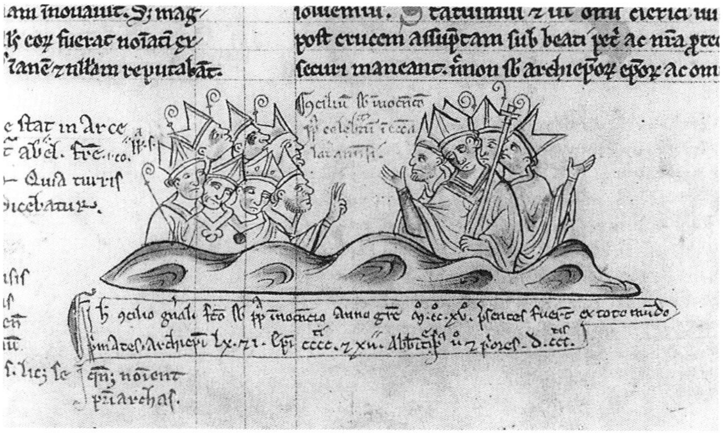

125 The Fourth Lateran Council. Matthew Paris, *Chronica majora*, Cambridge Corpus Christi College MS 16, fol. 43v, *c.* 1250 (by permission of the Master and Fellows of Corpus Christi College, Cambridge).

also reflected the intellectual energies of English participants in the Paris schools and in the Council itself, attended by Stephen Langton and Richard Poore among others: the type of men who demonstrated the existence of a developed 'scholastic consciousness' in England.[16] Its stress on the outcomes of the moral theology of the schools – the role of preaching and other forms of pastoral education, penance, proper understanding of and regard for the sacraments and the role of the parish – were all congenial to an advanced English clerical mindset which had indeed provided much of the material, and which took a lively interest in the development and diffusion of canon law.[17] Old Sarum, already an important post-Conquest centre of liturgical codification, provides an instance of this mindset. Teresa Webber's study of Salisbury Cathedral's twelfth-century manuscripts shows how, even before 1179, the canons had begun to develop an interest in a practical pastoral moral theology which had started to free it of the harsher aspects of monastic discipline; the results may have lacked the sense of system of later *pastoralia*, but they indicate the local ways in which the ground had been prepared for the most ambitious ecumenical and diocesan pronouncements of the next century.[18] The interconciliar period itself had also seen the first major post-Conquest wave of English provincial and diocesan statute-making. This included the provisions concerning the education of parish priests, clerical celibacy and the sacraments made by the Council of Westminster in 1200, held under the auspices of Hubert Walter; this major Council cited the canons of Lateran III, and its deliberations were much in line with the contemporary legislation of the Archbishop of Rouen and the Bishop of Paris.[19] The theologians of Paris were 'in the background of the sacramental provisions' of the Westminster Council before they made their impact at the Lateran fifteen years later.[20] Stephen Langton incorporated a large part of Hubert's statutes in his own diocesan legislation a year before Lateran IV.[21] As the greatest English authority on the textual history of English Church legislation, Christopher Cheney, concluded, Lateran IV 'was not the *fons et origo* of all later legislation'.[22] It was essentially the most important universal component in a developing machinery of Church management. This very basic truth about the Council holds good for some of its most important formulations about doctrine and discipline.

There was also the issue of implementation. Lateran IV was promulgated by two principal mechanisms. The major universal one was the incorporation of its canons into canon law, in the Decretals of Pope Gregory IX of 1234, compiled at the behest of the canonist Raymond of Peñafort.[23] This may explain the lack of numerous surviving manuscripts of the canons in England in comparison with some of the synodal decrees.[24] The second was the provincial and diocesan synods themselves, which were in theory to be held annually according to canon 6 of Lateran IV, and where the canons of the Council were to be read.[25] Since the requirement of annual synods was one of the measures of the Council that signally failed to be implemented (with exceptions that indicate that this was a matter for the inclinations of individual bishops), one cannot be sure to what extent this was observed.[26] But Richard Poore's statutes for Salisbury of 1217–19 cite the Council's opening profession of faith;[27] and the mandates of the Council are stated to have been read at the influential provincial council held by Langton at Oxford in 1222,[28] the final canon of which expected the canons to be promulgated without delay in subsequent episcopal synods.[29] The Oxford Council in fact formed the basis of the local law of the English Church.[30] It is also unlikely to be coincidence that the earliest English legislation to incorporate parts of the Lateran Council was produced by some of the prelates who actually attended it.[31] Once it had been incorporated, however, the Council formed but one part of the complex of regulations actually enforced at the level of archdeaconries and parishes, either by ensuring that parishes or parish priests had copies of diocesan legislation, or by obliging priests to attend to public recitations of such legislation at synodal gatherings, by applying the sanction of fines in view of ignorance of the law, and finally by enforcement by the archdeacons themselves in parochial visitation.[32] This was no more than a system whereby detailed regulation was devolved. By such means were the ecumenical pronouncements of Innocent III supposed to have percolated down to the furthest and most obscure parish; and it was for the visitations to reveal the sorry lack of compliance, or sheer ignorance, that was the reality in many – but certainly not all – parishes throughout much of the century, not least in respect of formal possession of copies of diocesan statutes.[33]

The net result of this was that the canons of Lateran IV were quickly assimilated directly into canon law, and less directly into the broader mass of statutes which archbishops and bishops enacted in England with some frequency, especially in the first half of the thirteenth century, the great era of legislation.[34] Not a single collection of diocesan statutes produced in this period imports Lateran IV wholesale. Marion Gibbs and Jane Lang prudently saw the canons as being instead gradually clothed in the 'localized and particular detail' of the diocesan reformist projects, which greatly softened the rubber stamp of episcopal approval of Innocent's project.[35] Indeed, their still useful account of this process of assimilation is essentially one of failure and tepidity, brought about partly by the seemingly unsystematic nature of episcopal legislation, but above all by the collapse of the plan to impose annual provincial and diocesan synods.[36] The monstrously complex textual history of this most important era of the English Church's self-reform explains in part why Powicke's remark in 1928 that 'the history of the reconstruction of the Church in England after the interdict, in accordance with the Lateran decrees, has yet to be written' has held true until fairly recently.[37] But there is another reason: namely that the predominance of textual enquiry may itself have reflected a lack of positive curiosity about what its results might mean for the visual archaeology of religion in this period. Neither Lang nor Cheney were drawn to this question.[38] Given that a lot seems to have gone on outside the letter of the law, this is perhaps understandable.

Even a comparatively quick glance at the Decretals of Gregory IX (fig. 124) discloses how small a part 'art' played in the central compilation of canon law of the period – the obvious starting-point for the Church itself – 'art' usually being among the topics gathered under the heading *De ornamentis*. Indeed, aside from some prescriptions about the proper care due to altars, and hence to the sacrament of the Mass, and about the propriety of lay behaviour at the elevation of the Host (at which priests are to instruct the congregation to bow reverently) the Decretals actually say nothing.[39] This is salutary, because it puts in proportion any type of art-historical enquiry which regards medieval Church regulation as an absolute point of reference rather than as a starting-point. Slim and relatively non-specific regulations were easy to enforce sedulously, for law tangles with local detail and tradition at its peril.[40] Part of the intelligence of ecumenical legislation was that it offered no more than what would nowadays be called 'guidelines' based on lowest common denominators, adaptable to the local truths of medieval western Europe. But the regulation of art was in no sense the principal purpose of such regulations, and one must be as wary of retroactively conscripting them to the aims of the history of art, as of deducing local practices from central forms.[41] The local arrangements mattered: pondering only the ecumenical and canonical position is like being unable to see the trees for the wood.

Lateran IV also requires careful handling. Only five of its seventy-one canons appear to have any implications for *ornamenta*. The first is canon 1, *Fermiter credimus*, with its profession of faith in one universal Church in which Christ is both priest and sacrifice, whose 'body and blood are truly contained in the sacrament of the altar under the forms of bread and wine, the bread and wine having been changed in substance'.[42] The other four are: canons 19–20, which relate to the custody of the sacraments; canon 21, relating to the sacraments of penance and communion; and canon 62, concerning the veneration of relics.[43] Of these, discussion of canon 21 *Omnis utriusque sexus* belongs to the domain of pastoral education (in the next chapter). The four remaining canons are of more direct interest, and the first one of all of them, *Fermiter credimus*, has had to bear the heaviest burden of interpretation. The issue is obvious: a profession of faith in the Trinity or Transubstantiation is not an art manifesto. As already noted, *Fermiter credimus* clarified the issue in so far as it bolstered the universal authority of the Mass by way of refutation of heresy; yet this concern to regulate sacramental theology was part, and in no sense the conclusion, of a widespread movement within the theology of the schools in the twelfth century which formed a wider penumbra of belief, opinion and practice.[44] Canons 19 and 20 of the Council were its logical extensions. So was the framing of much diocesan legislation in terms of the seven sacraments. Nevertheless, one would be misguided to see this canon in itself as having sole constitutive importance for the type of thing that was going on from the later twelfth century in regard, say, to the increase in the size of church chancels and altars of all types. Like a vitamin, *Fermiter credimus* fortified existing patterns, but created none: it monitored development, not change. General physical provision for the Mass is one thing; much more detailed or coercive prescriptions about conduct and ritual at the Mass another.

The elevation of the Host (fig. 124) is a case in point. Of all gestures and signs, the elevation and the Host together have come to enjoy extraordinary (and perhaps exaggerated) critical attention as indices of medieval attitudes towards incarnation and visuality.[45] The origins of the elevation from one point of view therefore matter greatly. One obvious art-historical heresy that has grown out of a casual – one is tempted to say typically art-historical – reading of Lateran IV has been the belief that it brought about this most familiar and important liturgical gesture at Mass, quite commonly represented in the art of the period.[46] This is an interesting mistake because it exposes assumptions about the relationship between ecumenical statement and locally devolved beliefs and practices. As with the doctrine of Transubstantiation, it also pretends that the issue was not in some way contentious. The remarkable studies of the early history of the elevation by V. L. Kennedy are in this regard inescapable. Kennedy's basic proposition was that the major elevation of the Host after its consecration was reasoned about and performed in Paris before 1215.[47] At this time the Parisian Peter of Roissy noted an admirable custom, evidently known about or extant in Paris by the 1200s, that at the elevation the congregation should raise their joined hands and bow (fig. 126).[48] But Peter's thought reflected even earlier concerns of the Parisian theologians on such matters. There was considerable

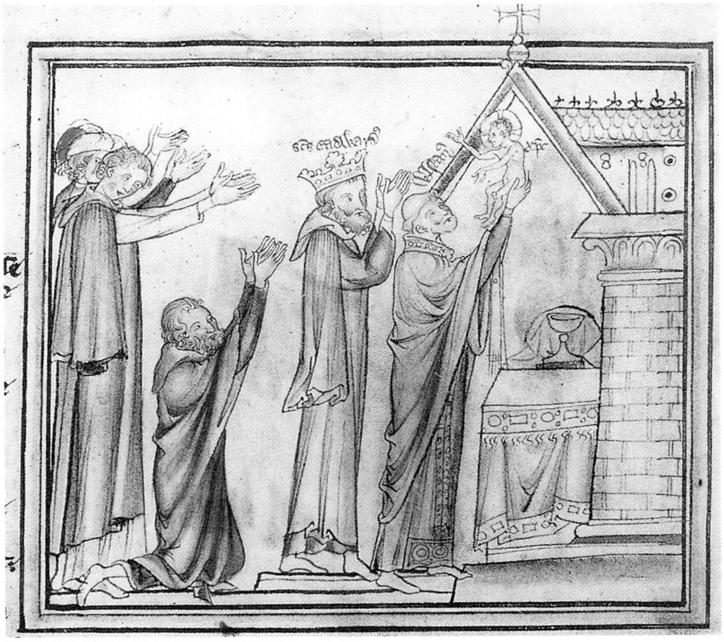

126 St Edward witnesses the Christ Child in the Host. *La Estoire de Seint Aedward le Rei*, CUL MS Ee. 3. 59, fol. 21, *c.* 1255 (by permission of the Syndics of Cambridge University Library).

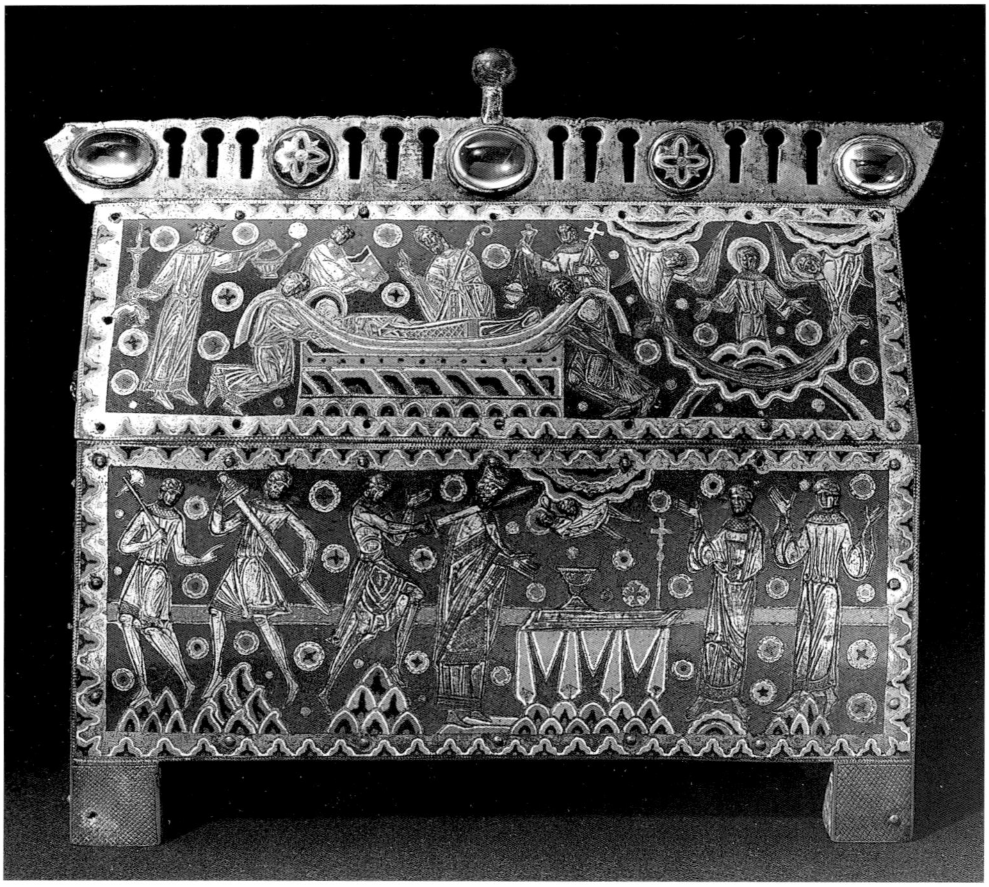

127 Limoges enamel reliquary casket showing the martyrdom of St Thomas (V&A Picture Library).

debate in late twelfth-century Paris about the exact moment of the consecration of the Host, particularly whether it was consecrated before the blessing of the chalice or after. This mattered, because to elevate the Host before its proper and complete consecration would be to practise wafer-worship, i.e. idolatory. Langton and Peter the Chanter produced contrary opinions on the issue, Langton dealing with it in such a way as to suggest that, while the congregation genuflected at the moment of the consecration in England, the major elevation was not performed there before 1206.[49] However it was certainly known in England by 1213–14, since Langton's own provincial statutes state that the congregation should behave reverently at the consecration and should perform a sustained genuflection after the elevation. This debate also concerned itself with the visibility of the Host, the elevation allowing it to be seen by all, *ita quod possit videri ab omnibus*.[50] This also mattered, because the question of forms of devotion to the sacrament implicit in the expectation that it should be visible after its consecration were among the most important of all the issues of late medieval sacramental theology. Miracles attended the moment (figs 121, 126). Devotion at the elevation was certainly practised by about 1220.[51] Yet Lateran IV says nothing on the matter at all: it was the cold, blank tip of an iceberg. Quite clearly what was going on in Paris under Bishop Odo of Sully (1196–1208) or Peter of Nemours (1208–19), or under Langton at Canterbury in 1213 in regard to such issues, was of much greater interest, and warmth.

Indeed of the Lateran canons only numbers 19, 20 and 62 relate unambiguously to *ornamenta*. In the case of canon 19, *Relinqui nolumus incorrectum*, the aim was to reinforce existing norms. Profane items were not to be stored in church; liturgical vessels, vestments and altar cloths were not to be mired in filth; they should instead be kept neat and clean.[52] Hubert Walter's Westminster provisions of 1200 are in a similar spirit.[53] Canon 20 of Lateran IV decreed that the eucharist, i.e. the consecrated Host, should be locked away safely to guard against profanation; and canon 62 forbade the display of ancient relics outside their containers.[54] Of all the canons these last two are the most specific, since they encouraged the use of lockable aumbries or tabernacles for the sacrament, and reliquaries (fig. 127). The ensuing object domain can be readily imagined. Reliquaries were certainly not novel, but the constraint applied here on undisciplined relic-cults formed part of papal policy towards sanctioned sanctity examined above (p. 83). In respect of the reservation of the Host, Parisian regulations were in the vanguard; this was not simply an attempt to reinforce the reservation of the sacrament outside Italy.[55] Langton's statutes of 1213–14 make provision for the reservation of the Host in a clean pyx for no more than seven days after its consecration.[56] Canon 20 is cited directly in the canons of the Council of Oxford in 1222 and periodically thereafter, notably in Archbishop Pecham's Lambeth canons of 1281 which specify a lockable tabernacle.[57] Indeed it is in regard to the regulations about sacramental purity in Lateran IV that one approaches anything like an aesthetic statement. But again it was at the diocesan level that the picture sharpened radically. Among the pure materials deemed suitable for eucharistic reservation in diocesan statutes are included silver, ivory or Limoges enamel pyxes (fig. 128).[58] The reference to Limoges enamel, a comparatively new and very widespread medium known to have enjoyed the patronage of Innocent III in Rome, is especially striking.[59] Decent pure materials at the Mass were part of the same regime as decent pure behaviour, and up-to-date French art forms were one of its expressions.

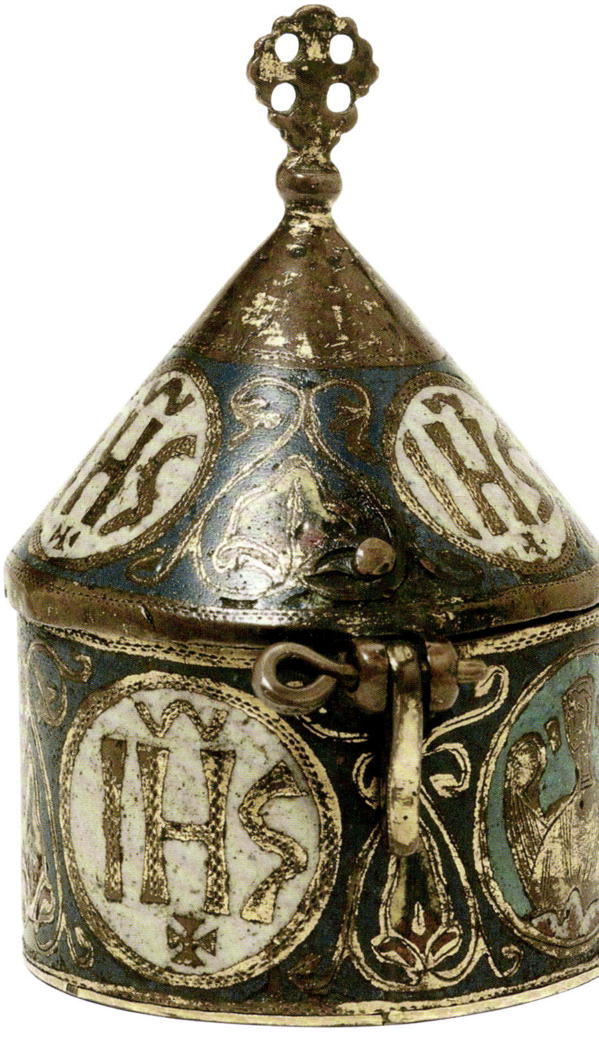

128 Limoges enamel pyx (V&A Picture Library).

Adiaphora

Even at the diocesan level the picture is somewhat mixed. The body of thirteenth-century English church legislation edited by Powicke and Cheney provides the single most important source for this enquiry, yet it is clear that quite as much is said in such documents about (for example) the education and care of children, as about *ornamenta*.[60] The first customs for an English diocese to mention images pertain to Salisbury at some point around the middle of the century, and only then specifically in relation to the parish's liability to provide such things as bell ropes, crosses and images.[61] This was a matter not of art provision, but of conflict resolution (p. 176). Images are mentioned more frequently in the second half of the century, again in the context of disputes over who was to provide them. What is very apparent is the virtual absence of references to what would now be identified as significant art forms known to have been developing at this time: one looks in vain for references to chancel or rood screens, wall paintings, figurated stained glass and painted altar panels. The issue here was partly that at least some of these items were themselves emerging in such a way that legislation was highly likely to spotlight them only retrospectively, and partly that a medieval taxonomy for such forms was only starting to become common. One can more usefully think of items such as altarpieces as being governed by conventions, not regulations.[62] Indeed altarpieces were scarcely even a genre.[63] Yet a taxonomy of sorts did exist, because items such as painted panels, *tabule depicte*, used for the front or over the altar (i.e. frontals and retables), are identified in visitation records for parish churches by 1250 at the latest. Precept lagged well behind practice, and unless diocesan authorities were able to exert pressure on local communities to provide artefacts of this type by means other than statutory legislation, the likelihood is that much about the art of the period fell into the category of *adiaphora* because there was nowhere else to put it.

One can examine this by looking at the most important sacramental object in any church, the altar. Here the 'regulations' were clear, at least in principle, from the top down.[64] Altars had to be dedicated to God in honour (as a rule) of a saint, and treated with reverence. The issue of dedication was long-standing: in keeping with older customs, the year and day of the consecration and the names of the dedicator and the titular were to be written distinctly and clearly (*distincte et aperte* or *evidenter*) around all consecrated altars.[65] Altars were to be kept clean and were not to be usurped for profane purposes, of which the most commonly cited was the use of the stone altar-block for grinding pigments, presumably by wall painters.[66] This abuse seems especially to have exercised Robert Grosseteste at Lincoln, since his statutes of around 1239 are the first to mention it, and there is also reference to it in his letters.[67] The appearance of the altar during Mass was signally important. Here Innocent III, while still Lotario de' Conti, had made an important intervention in his *De missarum misteriis* of before 1198.[68] *De missarum misteriis*, though exegetical in nature, has a much more practical tone than late twelfth-century English writing on the Mass such as Baldwin of Ford's *De sacramentis* of the 1180s.[69] It was being read before 1213 by Parisian theorists, notably Peter of Roissy, who was concerned with the issue of conduct at the elevation.[70] In his treatise, Innocent purported to explain aspects of current practice in Rome itself, and his text is celebrated principally for its observations on the symbolism of the five main liturgical colours used in the Church (white, red, green, black and violet), which were to change with the calendar.[71] In effect this gloss on colour, the tincture of the altar, and the liturgical year, was a form of Christian heraldry, rooted in the exegesis of Exodus.[72] Given Lotario de' Conti's mental preparation in Paris, the question whether or not such heraldry was actually a Roman innovation is worth asking. Whatever the answer, this type of codification, finding in colour and time a memorable symbolic congruence, was to be typical of the thirteenth-century Church. Innocent's text reflects a mounting sensitivity to colour decorum which may be reflected in canon 16 of Lateran IV, which instructed clerics not to indulge in red or green cloths or other superfluous apparel, apparently because these colours also had secular connotations.[73] The citation of this canon in Richard Poore's Salisbury statutes of 1217–19 in a section on Pride is the only certain instance in which Richard sanctioned remarks against superfluity, doubtless simply because of their ecumenical authority.[74] Yet there is no hint of the issue of liturgical colours in English diocesan legislation.

But one aspect of Innocent's writing does find its legislative counterpart: his remarks on lights. Cleanliness of vessels and vestments was an aspect of the desire for effulgence.[75] The symbolism of lights at Mass had been discussed in Rome far earlier.[76] By 1200 the question of the location of artificial lights around or upon altars, and indeed the issue of supplying the altar areas of churches with sufficient natural illumination, was current. In the twelfth century lights tended not to be put directly on the altar itself.[77] Even in the 1180s the Cistercians were 'legislating' for the presence on the altar at Mass of a cross only, and no lights at all upon the table.[78] But Innocent's *De missarum misteriis* states that for Mass on feast days the altar is to have a cross and two candles to either side of it.[79] In his later *Rationale* Durandus extended Innocent's words to apply not to feast days but ferial, i.e. ordinary, usage.[80] This also seems to be the understanding in English diocesan legislation of the period. By the 1220s in England at least one set of statutes had specified the presence on the altar at ordinary Mass of one or two candles.[81] The Winchester statutes of 1224 stress the need for the cross to be on the altar at Mass.[82] The Salisbury statutes of 1238–44 are the first to require the cross and two lights – i.e. Innocent's formula – and make a point of the visibility of the Host at the elevation to excite the devotion of those standing, or better kneeling, in church: *cum propter hoc excitetur devotio fidelium*.[83] There is also reference to two lights in the section *De sacramento altaris* in Grosseteste's pastoral *Templum Dei*, but not in his statutes, another sign that diocesan legislation was only one aspect of a larger penumbra of ideas.[84]

A rational strategy, both cognitive and aesthetic, governs these stipulations about conduct, dedication, colour and light. Its aims are purity and intelligibility. Neatness and cleanliness, colour and effulgence (of lights, of ornaments) are part of the same discourse as the proper advertisement of the facts of an altar's dedication, the proper marking of the calendar by means of colour, and the availability of proper light to see the Host and to read and pronounce the Mass loud and clear – for the phrase *distincte et aperte* is used not only in reference to dedicatory inscriptions but also to the audible vocal pronunciation of Mass and Office by the clergy according to the appropriate Use.[85] Richard Wyche's statutes for Chichester of around 1252 explain that such pronunciation should not be garbled or slurred because of excessively fast reading.[86] Such rhetorical errors had been identified in the course of the disciplining of prayer by Peter the Chanter in the section *De malo oratore* in his *De oratione*.[87] They mattered doctrinally because they might subvert proper performance, due action, and hence the efficacy of the sacraments or prayer.[88] It may be that the size and form of illuminated initials in liturgical manuscripts gave guidance as to the raising of the voice by the priest at appropriate moments in the Mass and Offices. It should also be noted that the same prescription, *distincte et aperte*, occurs in connection with the communicative medium of wall painting in this period, as in a royal mandate for the clear execution of murals in the best colours at Westminster in 1253.[89] The expression *apertement* was used of his own drawings by Matthew Paris.[90] There was some connection of a rhetorical order between clarity of diction and the visual arts.

It was also important that the sensorium should be engaged fully. Thuribles for incense are commonly mentioned in the statutes among the desiderata for all churches.[91] Lights were of universal symbolic importance. Also, they assisted the priest in the clear reading and delivery of the text of the Mass when appropriate; their presence cannot have been unrelated to the visibility of the elevated Host and so to sacramental devotion; and the absence of adequate natural and artificial light in chancels or around altars is an increasingly well-documented concern in the thirteenth century, not least when new ambitious tombs blocked out the sunlight.[92] The statutes repeatedly link the ringing of bells and the elevation or procession of the Host to the excitation of devotion and to genuflection (fig. 129).[93] It was only a matter of time before all five senses were integrated into the structure of prayer.[94] Underlying this is a choreography of affect and effect, and a very practical grasp of the role of synaesthesia in focusing attention, enriching understanding and structuring recall.[95] Issues of intelligibility are related to, and marshalled in the service of, belief and practice. Sights, texts and sounds were to act as signposts on the map of liturgy and devotion; and in doing so they formed a complex of techniques, mapping prescribed routes of action and response for the lay faithful to follow. These techniques of course ran quite counter to monastic suspicion of the senses and stress on an 'interior' liturgy.[96] Though strongly attuned to the visual and so to the 'incarnational' aesthetics of Gothic most apparent to the faculty of sight, such techniques were multi-sensory. (The auditory and musical sphere are discussed in chapter 11 below.)

What they showed above all was that sensory signposts – what John Beleth (d. 1182) called the 'layman's book of painting and ornament', *pictura et ornamenta* – were increasingly necessary because the 'map' of public activity in Church was growing appreciably more complex.[97] Not only were liturgies and liturgical actions becoming more developed and more codified, but the proliferation of mass provision was also giving rise to larger and more numerous altars, and hence to a basic problem of 'labelling', especially in the great churches.[98] Image complexes that served the purpose of clarifying the identity of altars, either through the presence of more or less fixed retable altarpieces showing the titular saint of the altar, or accompanying sculpted images within tabernacles (and sometimes both), might be expected in any church with several altars, not least because the later thirteenth-century synodalia of Durandus (d. 1296) indicate that images could fulfil the role of texts in advertising dedication loud and clear.[99] This in turn implies that such image complexes were prompted directly by the cult of saints, and not by eucharistic devotion as such: as Charles Hope has noted, altarpieces were in the first instance not about events or doctrines, but people, and then usually not Christ, but the saints.[100] Again, however, prescriptions for such images are relatively late. The earliest positive example occurs in the section *De ecclesiarum ornamentis* in the Exeter diocesan statutes drawn up by Bishop Quinel in 1287, which somewhat expands the lists of desiderata for churches in earlier statutes by including the image of the Virgin Mary, the patronal saint and the altar *celatura* or flat canopy.[101] This consorts well with the sheltered images of the Virgin surviving in early fourteenth-century Suffolk wall paintings (fig. 130).[102] But none of the statutes specifies medium.[103] The Exeter statutes are the only ones from thirteenth-century England positively to cite frontals among these desiderata (*sit* [. . .] *frontellum ad quodlibet altare*), but these could have been decent embroideries, rather than painted, carved or even precious panels.[104]

Crucially, and considering particularly that such documents were in part trying to clarify the issue of provision between the parish and the rector – the 'principal chancel image' is singled out solely in this regard in Archbishop Winchelsey's statutes of 1295–1313, and so must have been a pre-existing innovation[105] – not a single diocesan prescription mentions the retable above the altar. Yet panels in the retable position, which by their nature were not circumscribed by the shape of the front of the altar-block but only by its width, not only demonstrably existed in many English churches by this time, but are recognized to have been the major site of innovation in altar imagery in the late Middle Ages throughout the Latin Church.[106] The great age of the frontal as a major focus of images attached to the altar had not

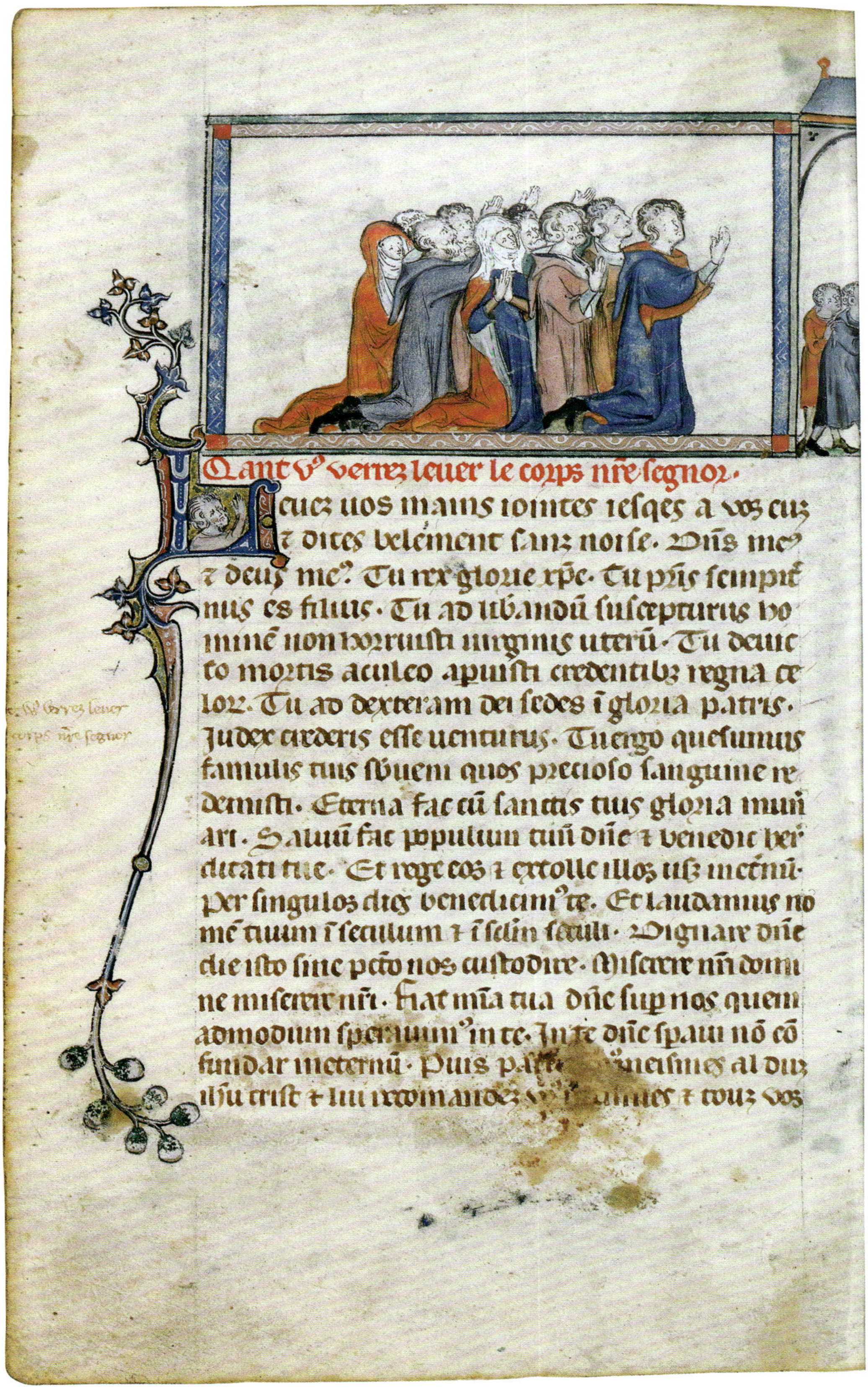

129 (ABOVE AND FACING PAGE) Elevation of the Host, with bell. Anglo-Norman tract on conduct at Mass, BN MS fr. 13342, fols 46v–47, early fourteenth century (Bibliothèque Nationale, Paris).

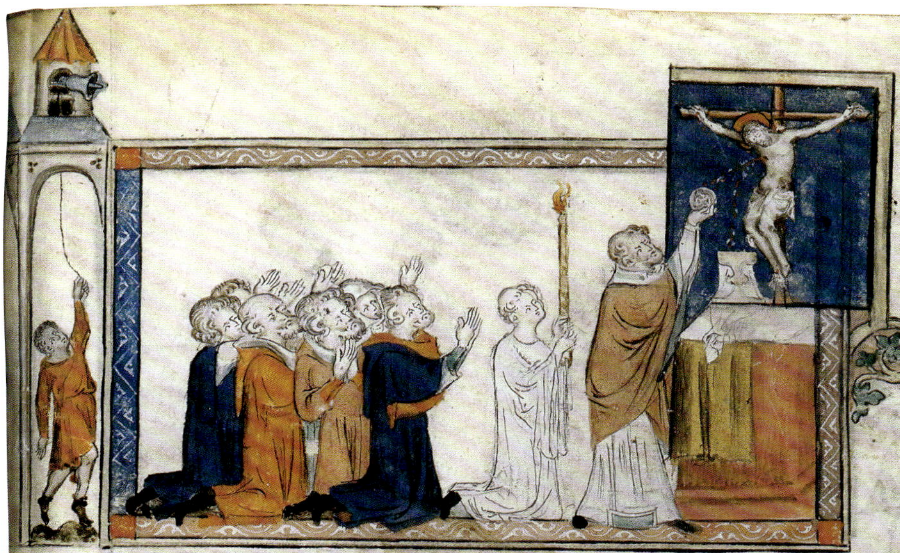

anius et toutes vos especiales besoignes si com
vostre quor vous a prendra.

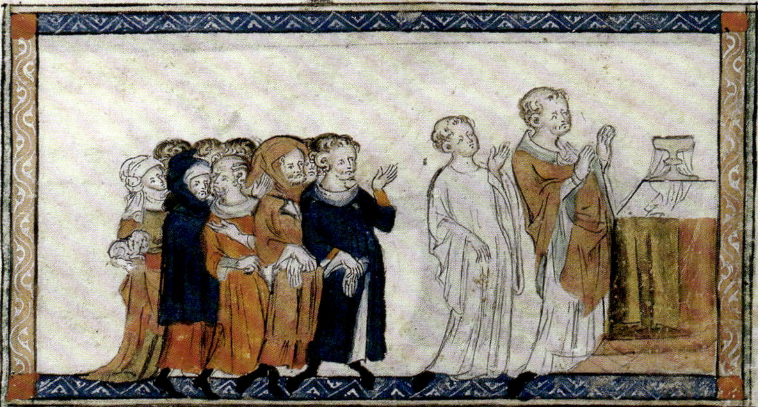

A per omnia secula seculorum devant le pater nostre
Responez devoutement amen. E dites vostre pater
noster. E loez en silence aille ewangele et respo
nez ame. et puis dites vostre pater noster mesmes et a la
fin dites. per dominum [illegible] Ihesum Christum filium tuum qui tecum
vivit et regnat [illegible] spiritus sancti deus. per omnia secula seculorum amen.

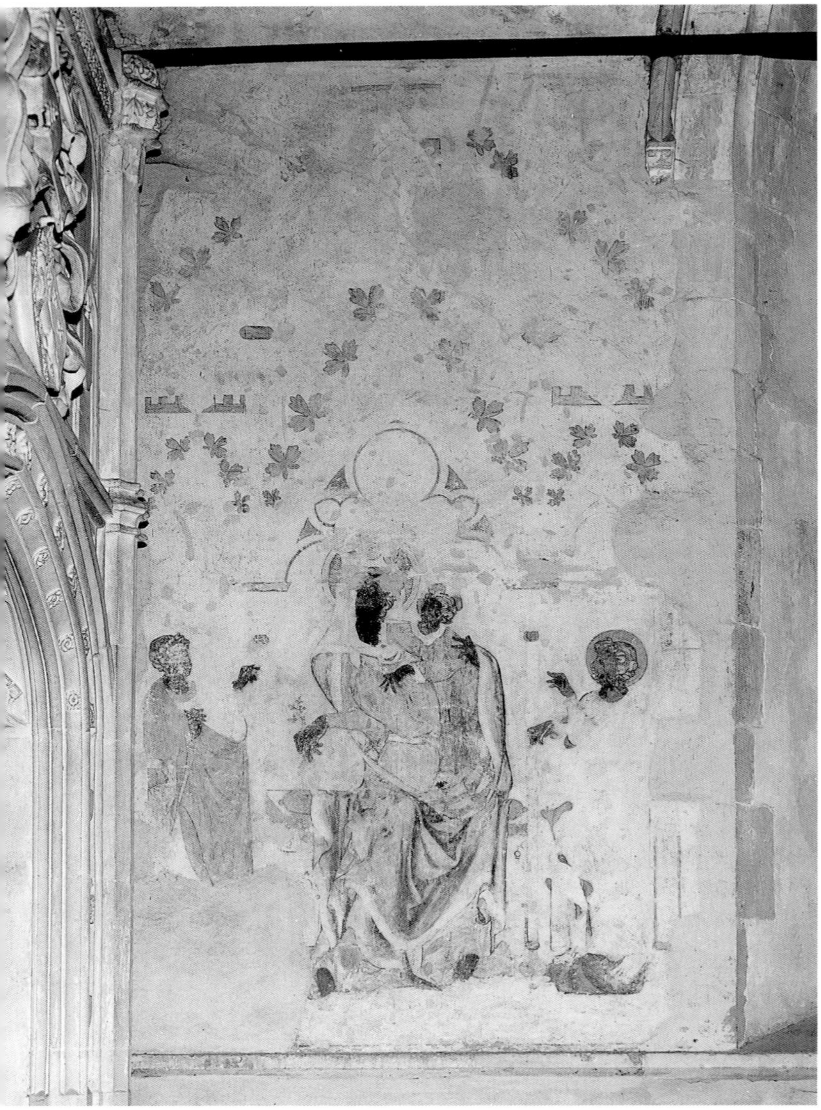

130 Virgin and Child censed by angels, beneath tabernacle. Mural to right of high altar, parish church of Little Wenham, Suffolk, early fourteenth century (© Crown copyright. NMR).

ended, but it was drawing to a close. In England the evidence for this is entirely documentary, though one's image of the process is fleshed out somewhat by survivals in Scandinavia. The Scandinavian material is important because the currency of artistic ideas between England and the territories along the North Sea was long-standing; the case of the architecture of Trondheim around 1200 is a notable example (see p. 33 above). But the pattern was established even earlier. Direct English influence on Scandinavian altar panels is proved by the style and content of the mid- to late twelfth-century metalwork frontal from Broddetorp (Statens Historiska Museet, Stockholm), which corresponds exactly to aspects of an eleventh-century precious frontal recorded in an inventory in the *Liber Eliensis* of which it may have been a reflection (fig. 131).[107] Precious bejewelled frontals were common in English Romanesque great churches, and are part of the paraphernalia mentioned in the Lanfranc constitutions for, among other places, Canterbury Cathedral.[108] Like shrines, they were a useful way of securing or hoarding capital that could be liquidated, gifted or stolen.[109] It is therefore inherently probable that the prosperous English ecclesiastical culture of the twelfth century was familiar with the metalwork retable and frontal combinations with overarching crosses now represented by the surviving altar from Lisbjerg (Nationalmuseet, Copenhagen).[110] Metal retables of low rectangular format such as that showing Christ and the Apostles supposedly from St Castor in Coblenz (Musée de Cluny, Paris) were also being produced in the Mosan region by the mid-twelfth century, anticipating by over a century the form of central Italian painted dossals. Such objects are reminders that it was still fashionable to display reliquaries and other precious objects on altars, or to connect major shrines to the altars themselves.[111] But even these had been foreshadowed in tenth-century England under the patronage of St Ethelwold at Abingdon, who provided for the monastery there a precious retable (*tabula supra altare*) showing the Twelve Apostles.[112] Even the liturgically advanced centre of Notre-Dame in Paris was provided in traditional fashion with a precious metal frontal for its high altar in 1196, and not (so far as is known) a retable, as might have been expected from those arguments which try to link causally the use of retables to the elevation so energetically discussed by Parisian theologians at the time.[113] Such stone retables as survive from the thirteenth century at Saint-Denis (fig. 132) and elsewhere tend to preserve the low, wide proportions of their rectangular twelfth-century metal precursors.[114] They cannot plausibly have acted as elevation backdrops. Northern European retable and frontal combinations emerged not only well before 1215, but well before the middle of the twelfth century at the latest; and neither their existence nor their character is readily explained by doctrinal or liturgical change.

What happened next was a decisive shift towards more plentiful production of such objects in the baser currency of painted wood. This is partly to be explained by an increased demand for *tabulae* on and in front of altars which acted as surrogates for metalwork.[115] Catalan evidence shows that this process had begun in the twelfth century.[116] Not surprisingly, painted panels continued to mimic the effulgent aesthetic of precious ones by using

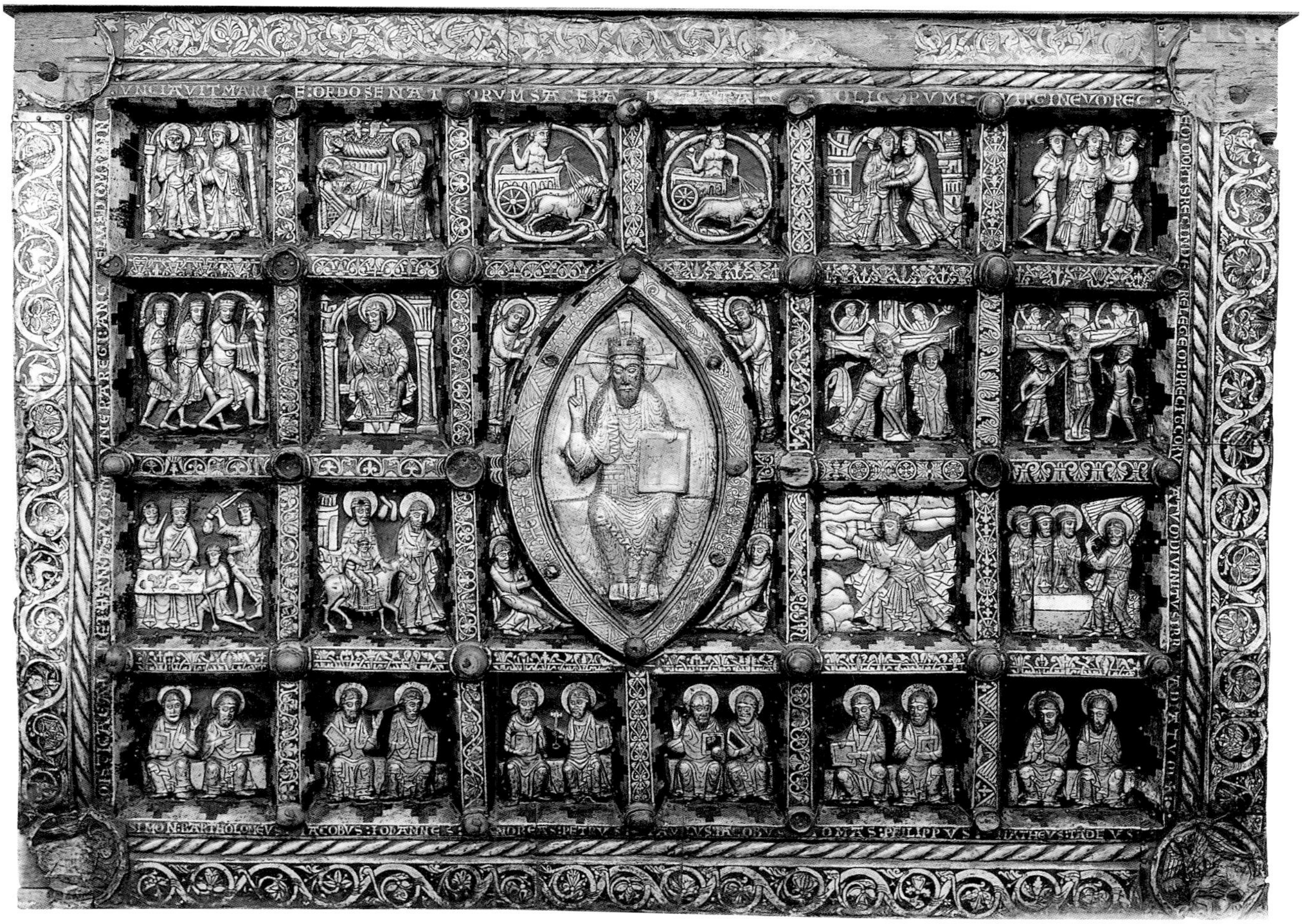

131 Christ, Apostles and Gospel scenes. Metal altar frontal from Broddetorp, Sweden, twelfth century. Stockholm, Statens Historiska Museum, no. 4674 (Statens Historiska Museum).

gold and silver leaf, painted enamels, glass ornaments and translucent enamel-like paint glazes for much of the thirteenth century.[117] But when supply really exploded to meet demand after about 1300, techniques appear to have been somewhat simplified; the currency was prone to debasement as circulation increased. The transition towards the more common use of painted wood panels can be followed with relative ease from the closing decades of the twelfth century in England, and only the earliest examples of it need to be given here. Around 1200 a monk of Rochester, Robert of Hecham, gave to an altar in the cathedral priory two painted panels above and in front of the altar, i.e. a joint retable and frontal donation.[118] Salisbury Cathedral possessed a painted frontal or retable by 1222,[119] and at least one parish church in its diocese, Arborfield, had a retable by 1214 (or at least before 1222).[120] A Marian retable of some description was donated by Robert of Lindesey, Abbot of Peterborough, to the chancel of Oxney church, also before 1222.[121] In other words cathedral priories, secular cathedrals, parish churches and monastic patrons were involved in the rise of this new genre around 1200. Thereafter, as the visitation records of dioceses such as London show quite clearly, painted altar panels, wooden roods and other polychrome images were to become normal in churches of all ranks.[122] But at no point do the visitations suggest that such items were necessary; they merely record what they found, and tend only to comment about the quality or state of repair of such items. This increasingly developed culture of polychrome woodwork is again faithfully registered by the remarkable survivals of painted panels, tabernacles and statuary in Oslo (fig. 143), Bergen (fig. 133) and Stockholm, which give a good impression of what has been lost from thirteenth-century England, not least because the earliest Scandinavian examples reveal English artistic influ-

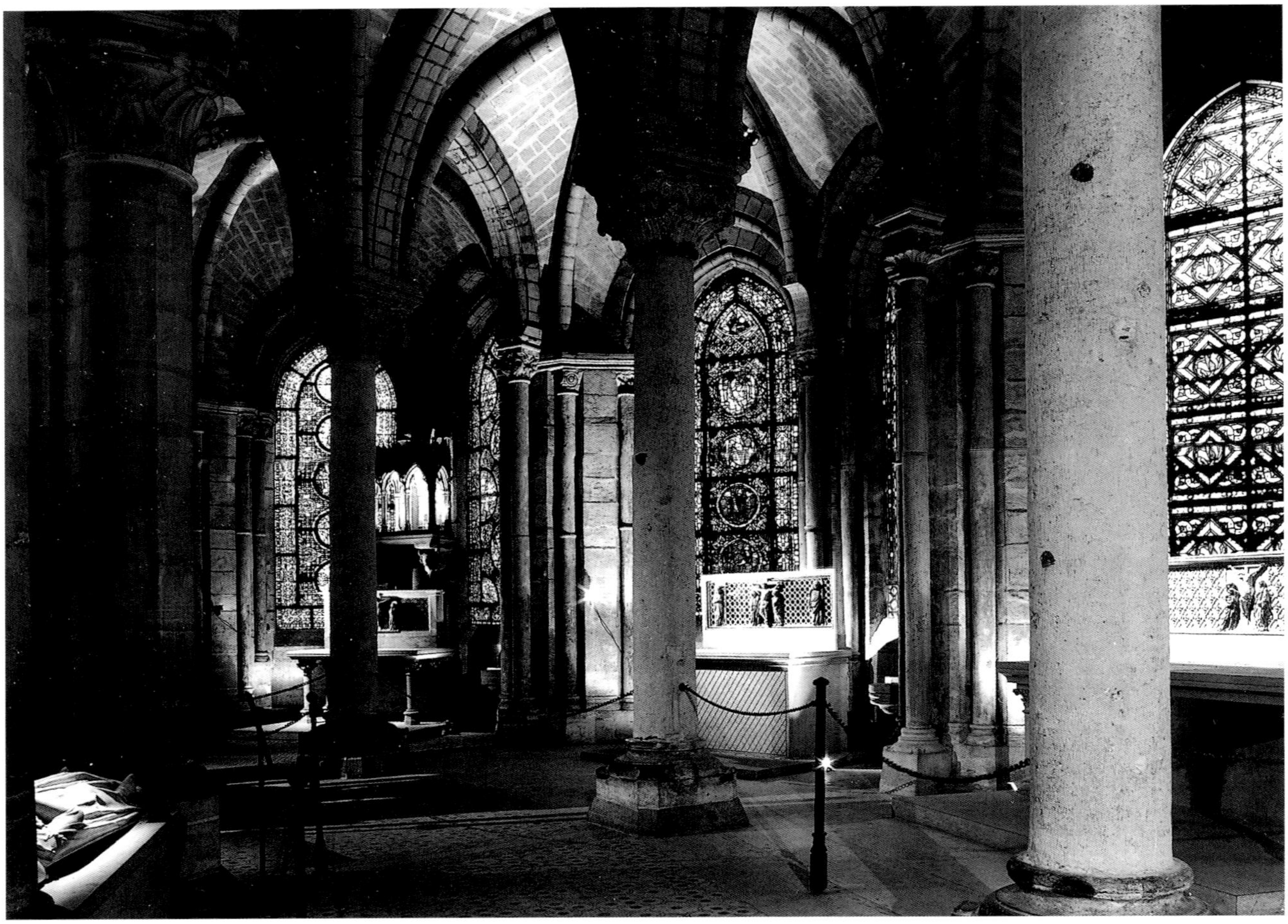

132 Paris, Saint-Denis, eastern ambulatory with rectangular stone retables, thirteenth century (Conway Library, Courtauld Institute of Art).

ence.[123] It was against polychrome retable altarpieces that the Cistercians – still quick to pick up on superfluity – protested at their General Chapter of 1240, which duly legislated that 'all panels with various colours should be removed or painted white'.[124] The only substantial early legislative reference to altarpieces was thus negative. Such things cannot have been legislated into existence: other factors were at work, and among them were specific cults.

The Becket Model

One reason for noting the early chronology of polychrome altarpieces is to stress that such panels were not solely a Mediterranean, and specifically Italian, innovation. Yet the Italian example is not irrelevant to England. The retable altarpiece seems to have emerged coevally in both countries, and at least two related factors common to both milieux can be traced. The first was a shared heritage of high-quality, Byzantine-influenced painting on wall and panel. In the late twelfth century some of the finest practitioners of essentially Byzantine-style painting in western Europe were at work in the scriptoria of the monastic centres of Winchester, Canterbury and St Albans; the technical and imaginative leap to panel or mural (or indeed glass) painting from such illuminated manuscripts as the Winchester Bible, or the last copy of the Utrecht Psalter made towards 1200 at Canterbury (BN MS lat. 8846) is unlikely to have been great, as the superb wall paintings of St Paul in the chapel of St Anselm at Canterbury, probably of the 1160s, and in the Holy Sepulchre Chapel at Winchester, prove.[125] The second common consideration was undoubtedly the cult of saints, not least the universal cult of Mary. The most important byzantinizing images of the mid-twelfth century to survive from England consist of the diptych showing the *koimesis* or Dormition of the Virgin,

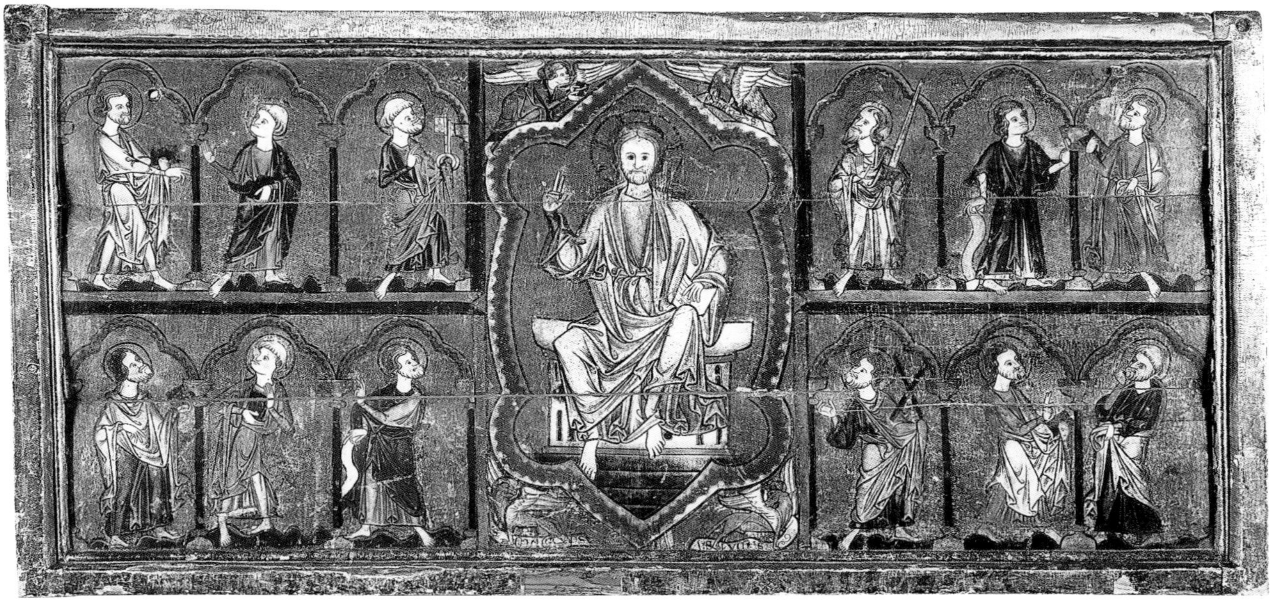

133 Christ and Apostles. Painted altar frontal from Ulvik, Norway, *c.* 1250 (Historisk Museum, Universitetet i Bergen).

and her glorification, in the Winchester Psalter (BL MS Cotton Nero C. IV), which are little more than English copies of Greek or Roman icons.[126] Iconic paintings of this type played a much greater role in English liturgical and devotional activity, especially in relation to saints, than the extant material suggests. This can be demonstrated from a single but striking instance from the court of Henry III. In April 1237 Henry commissioned five portable square or rectangular painted panels (*tabulae quadratae*) specifically to be carried in the king's processions in the manner of 'texts': a Majesty of Christ, the Virgin Mary, a Crucifixion with Mary and John, a Coronation of the Virgin and the Transfiguration.[127] Henry's mandate implies that they were to be used first at Easter, but their form and content as large processional icons carried like the Gospels points to a function probably very similar to the processing of icons of Christ and his Mother in contemporary Roman civic ritual for the Feast of the Assumption.[128] It may be only coincidental that the papal legate, Otto, cardinal deacon of San Nicola was shortly to arrive in England, convening a legatine council in 1237.[129] In fact there is no reason to suppose that Henry's was an especially 'papal' policy towards images, notwithstanding other aspects of his later patronage which might prompt this idea. Ritual processions of this type merely place in context the illustrated account by Matthew Paris of the processing through London to Westminster of the Holy Blood relic which Henry III had gained in 1247.[130] Henry III is also the first thoroughly documented English patron of painted altarpieces for use in his court chapels and elsewhere from the 1230s onwards.[131] The commissioning of processional icons and of altar panels from favoured court painters seems to have been linked, for the two genres were not quite separate. At court – and arguably within contemporary or earlier ecclesiastical institutions too – the technical potential of significant centres or networks of art production was as vital a factor as tradition, personal preference, regulation and innovation in encouraging the production of certain forms of art.[132]

The concentration of early painted retables within a comparatively limited geographical sphere in central Italy, principally the archdiocese of Pisa, is a case in point.[133] There, the explosion in the numbers of painted retable altarpieces from the second quarter of the thirteenth century is commonly linked specifically to the cult of St Francis of Assisi (d. 1226). Images of Francis, in the form of relatively large gilded tempera paintings depicting the saint standing full-length and flanked on either side by small panels relating salient moments from his life, appeared with quite striking speed after his canonization in 1228: the earliest surviving instance is a panel at San Francesco in Pescia dated to 1235 (fig. 134).[134] Formally, these objects, combining the iconic presence and biographical history of a saint, are known as *vita*-retables, and Francis is generally credited with being the first western European saint to have been depicted in this way, though the form is not uncommon

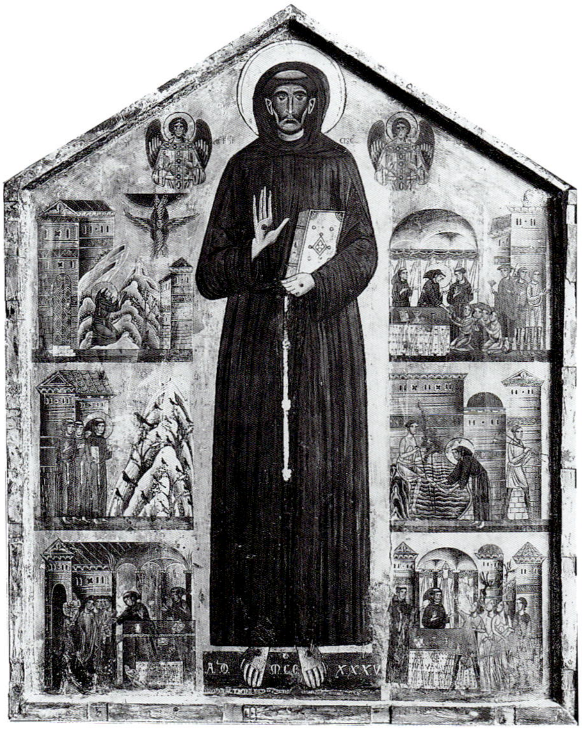

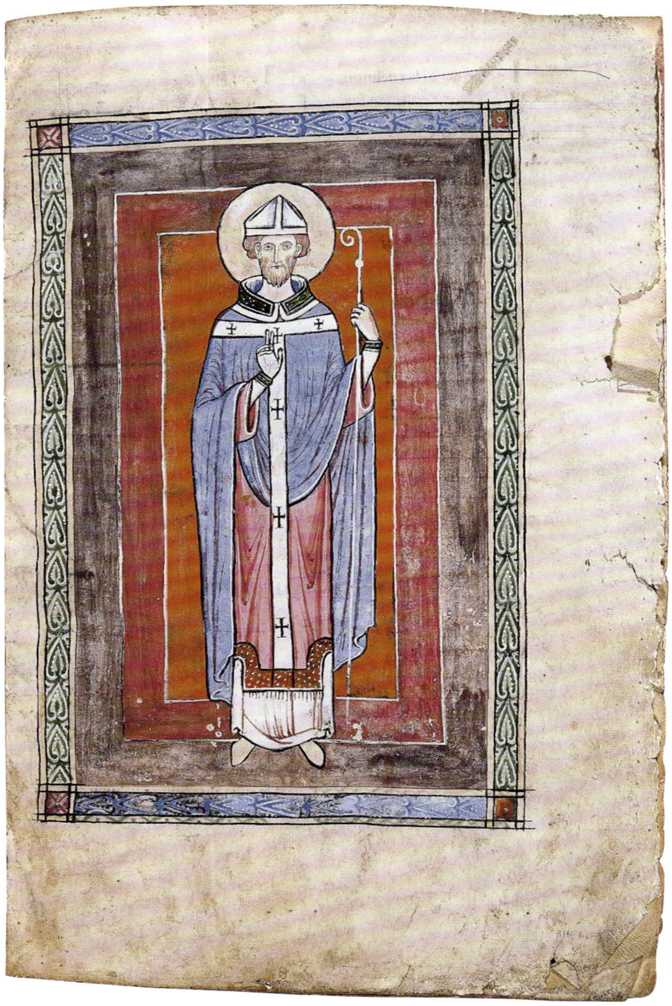

134 St Francis *vita*-retable, 1235. Pescia, San Francesco (Alinari).

135 (RIGHT) St Dunstan. Cambridge, Corpus Christi College MS 161, fol. 1, early thirteenth century (Master and Fellows of Corpus Christi College, Cambridge).

in Greek icons.[135] Later examples include St Dominic. Francis's case was obviously exceptional, or nearly so, in view of the strong element of cult of personality deliberately propagated by his biographers, and of which such painted panels were demonstrations.[136] No one can doubt the universal, profound and almost immediate imaginative impact of the *poverello* on contemporary art and spirituality.

Yet there are reasons for thinking that Francis was not in fact the first saint whose image was propagated by the *vita*-retable. To compare the vain, grand and often worldly personality of St Thomas Becket with St Francis, the very model of thirteenth-century asceticism and virtue, might at first seem incongruous. Spiritually the two men represented quite different constituencies, quite distinct paradigms of sanctity, one aristocratic, the other urban, one characteristic of the northern European ideal of the suffering leader, the other of the Mediterranean culture of the city.[137] The cults brought with them very different emphases on the role and importance of images. While Becket's passion was governed, at least in the eyes of his biographers, by an insistent Christomimesis, Francis in contrast was himself the very image of Christ, an *alter Christus*, a walking manifestation in life of the wounds of the Passion following his stigmatization in 1224. Images, such as the eloquent crucifix at San Damiano which spoke to Francis, play an important role not only in depictions of Francis's life but in those of his followers and devotees.[138] In contrast images of Becket, indeed images of any sort, play a negligible part in the Lives of Thomas, much less so than in the Life of his follower St Edmund of Abingdon.[139] This is one reason why the view of his art patronage is somewhat hazy. But the analogy is not entirely hopeless.[140] The speed with which St Francis's image was institutionalized was matched by St Thomas.[141] Both men had exceptionally strong personalities and inspired spectacular followings; each was regarded as a pillar of the Church; each enjoyed not only rapid canonization but swift entry into the pantheon of universal sainthood; in the name of both, Gothic double churches were constructed; and though images played roles of very different proportion within the two cults, both men were widely and comprehensively depicted in such a way that their cults could affect the development of art.

The truth of this is of course obscured by the fact that while Francis's image was sheltered by the subsequent history of religion in Italy, Thomas's was exposed to the full brunt of censorship during the Henrician Reformation.[142] A sense of how exactly he was represented, and in what contexts, is severely warped and impoverished by a massive level of systematic destruction which erased St Thomas's image from the domain of English visual culture with Stalinist zeal. But a few deductions can still be made about the early period. One of the earliest images of Becket, in the apse mosaics of the cathedral at Monreale in Sicily, executed around 1180 probably as a result of the new dynastic links between Henry II and the Norman kingdom, shows him as a gaunt and somewhat impersonal standing archbishop making a blessing.[143] Standing or seated images of saints were common on icons. The pictorial form of the Monreale mosaic finds an excellent counterpart in the sensitive full-length depiction of an archbishop, perhaps St Dunstan, making a blessing at the start of a volume of Lives of English prelates executed towards 1200 either in Canterbury or in the diocese of Rochester (Cambridge, Corpus Christi College MS 161; fig. 135).[144] This volume does not contain a Life of Becket, but it is a reasonable presumption that St Thomas himself was frequently commemorated in this way.[145] Two early instances demonstrate the presence of his image standing over altars. One is a magnificent mural of around 1200 in an altar niche in the nave of the parish church at Hauxton, near Cambridge (fig. 136).[146] The second is more revolutionary. An altar niche in the north transept of the church at Stow in Lincolnshire retains traces of an excellent but fragmentary mural that depicts the figure of St Thomas standing full-length amidst small panels containing scenes from his Life, including his last supper and martyrdom.[147] The painting was uncovered and drawn in the 1860s (figs 137–8). The style, and the form of St Thomas's cap in the flanking feast scene, are compatible with a date of around 1200. Stow was an episcopal manor of the Bishops of Lincoln, famously associated with St Hugh of Lincoln and his pet swan.[148] Hugh himself, to judge from the *Magna vita*, seems to have accorded St Thomas only formal respect as the princi-

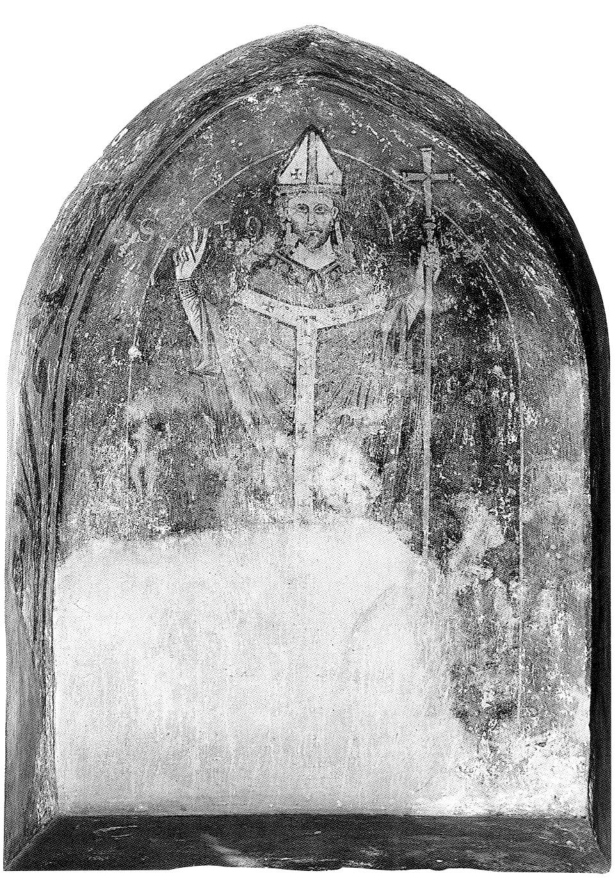

136 St Thomas. Mural in altar niche, Hauxton parish church, near Cambridge, *c.* 1200 (© Crown copyright. NMR).

pal model of resistance to public power: yet it was quite possibly during Hugh's episcopate, 1186–1200, that this picture was done. This is of interest principally because, although it is a wall painting, the Stow mural is in its form unmistakably a *vita*-retable, imitating, as wall paintings often did, the form of panel paintings or sculptures. As in Scandinavian frontals with two tiers of narrative, the legends to either side of the standing figure are separated by a broad band. From this two conclusions can be drawn. The first is that this type of icon-cum-narrative altar-image cannot have been associated principally with specific feasts, as has been suggested for the Franciscan retables, since it also manifested itself in permanent murals presumably as a sign of their dedication.[149] The second is that it was again in the inter-conciliar period, 1179–1215, and directly as the result of a spectacular cult, that painted altar-images of this sort were first developed, arguably half a century earlier than the extant Franciscan examples, and possibly in the light of the adoption of this *vita* form in Greek icons around

1200 or earlier.[150] That this appears to have been so argues for a more complex pre-history of such narrative icons than is usually assumed.

Becket's cult did not 'invent' the *vita*-retable, but it may have been as major a catalyst for the widespread emergence of the English painted retable as was Francis for its counterparts in Italy. Destruction renders the pursuit of this idea into the thirteenth century extremely difficult. If this was indeed the case, one might expect early signs that painted panels of this type were being produced within the Province of Canterbury. Canterbury Cathedral itself is absolutely uninformative on this point, bar a few signs at the east end of the crypt of the Trinity Chapel of lost wooden or stone installations that may have related to St Thomas's cult, and which might have been painted.[151] The record of an early painted retable donation to an unidentified altar at Rochester Cathedral might well fit this pattern, and the specific documented instance of an early painted retable-frontal combination (*tabula Beati Thomae superior et inferior*) for an altar to St Thomas at St Albans, before 1214, certainly does.[152] By the middle of the century an altar niche in the south transept at the Holy Cross in Winchester was provided with a mural altarpiece with events from the Life of St Thomas.[153] These examples are no more than isolated and fractured records, but they are greatly supplemented by the astonishing instances of polychromatic

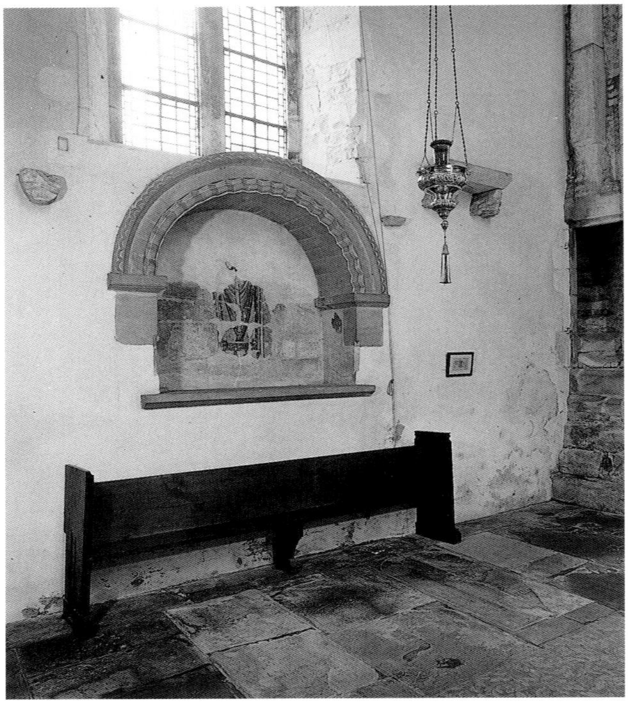

137 St Thomas. Mural in altar niche, Stow parish church, Lincolnshire *c.* 1200 (© Crown copyright. NMR).

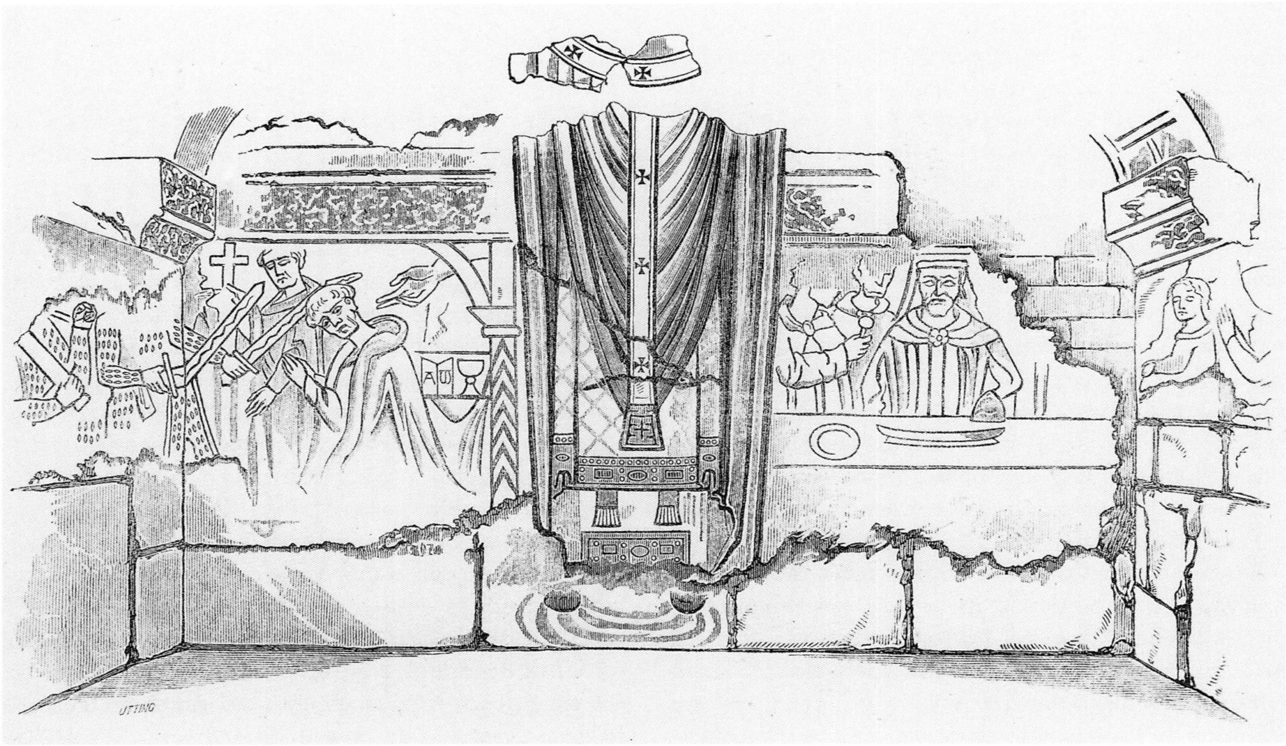

138 (BELOW) Drawing of mural of St Thomas at Stow (after Trollope 1866).

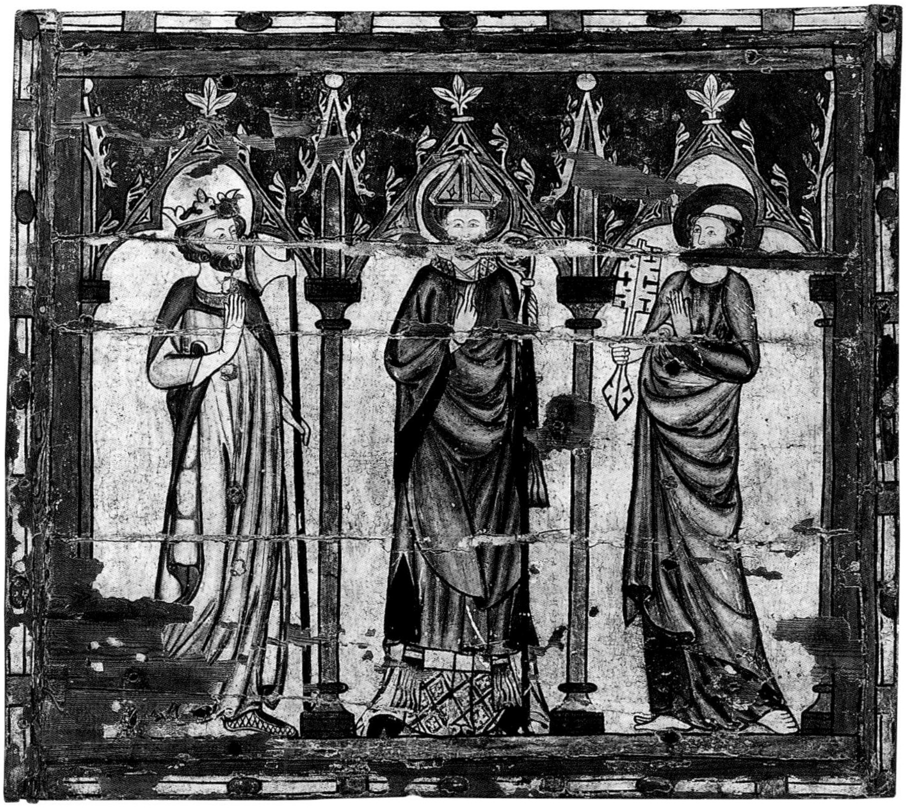

139 St Olaf, Archbishop Øystein and St Peter. Painted altar frontal from Kvaefjord, near Trondheim, 1330s (© University Museum of Cultural Heritage, University of Oslo, Norway).

woodwork made in the celebration of the cults of episcopal saints in Scandinavia (see p. 125 above). Something of the appearance of early Becket-altarpieces may be gauged from the early fourteenth-century *vita*-panel depicting St Martin, a key episcopal model, from Möðruvellir in Iceland, now in Reykjavik.[154] Becket was the object of what Anne Duggan calls a 'pervasive' cult in Iceland, at least thirteen churches being dedicated to him there, with numerous images: and these should be seen in the context of the Old Icelandic Thomas Sagas, an extraordinary record of Becket's international popularity, and themselves based upon the English biographies.[155] An important early fourteenth-century panel showing the three standing figures of St Olaf, Archbishop Øystein and St Peter from Kvaefjord near Trondheim (fig. 139), and so from an area falling under strong influence from Canterbury, Lincoln and the 'Becket model', reflects another range of possibilities.[156] The most important sequence of Becket paintings on wood are now those that decorated the walls of the remarkable church formerly at Björsäter in Sweden (fig. 140), which couple his legend with that of the invention of the Holy Cross.[157] These images all celebrated the ideals of the Scandinavian diocesan Church. But many, especially those in the parishes, were provided by painters working within towns and cities, with the laity acting as patrons.[158] The retables and frontals which were becoming so routine a fixture in parish churches on the perimeters of the North Sea towards 1300 owed much to the stimulus offered by the cult of saints to the increasingly assertive lay classes. Their origins doubtless lay in a sophisticated dialogue between high ecclesiastical patronage in England and the image-world of the Mediterranean; but their development was also a matter for a newly engaged range of patrons.

St Albans: Edification, Consolation and Monastic Reform

One way to examine the relationship of ecclesiastical patronage to the laity in regard to images is to see what could happen when the lay and clerical, or monastic, domains actually overlapped; and a fairly well-docu-

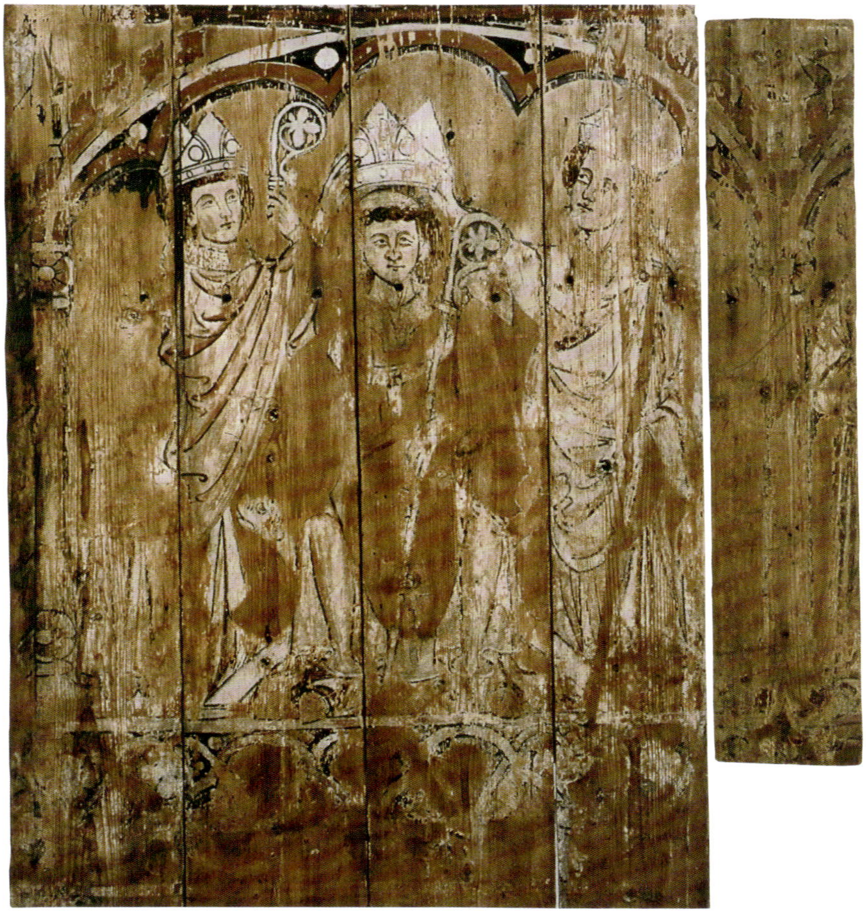

140 Consecration of St Thomas, formerly in Björsäter parish church, Ostergotland, early fourteenth century (Stockholm, Statens Historiska Museum).

mented instance of this is provided by the nave of St Albans Abbey and its wall paintings. The thirteenth-century paintings adorn the Romanesque piers of the north side of this elongated space (fig. 141), and though only one or two of them are of real quality, their context prompts questions as to what, and who, they were for.[159] Answers to this are forthcoming not only because of the extent of the survivals, but also because of the *Gesta abbatum* and its concern for the abbey's works.

Of all the monastic houses in southern England, St Albans, in virtue of its strong tradition of historical writing, and especially Matthew Paris's range of activity as an artist and writer, had an exceptionally well-developed mythology of the quality and standing of its figurative art. It was in part this medieval self-belief – on the whole not borne out by any surviving artwork – which lent substance to the later art-historical claim, since largely discredited, that the monastery indeed had a 'school' of painting to vie with the 'schools' of Westminster, or indeed Florence or Siena.[160] In fact among the older Benedictine houses, St Albans was no more distinguished in this regard than Canterbury, Winchester, Peterborough or particularly Bury; and it was certainly eclipsed by Westminster. Matthew Paris's own training seems to have been tied very closely to the substantial tradition of late Romanesque painting, illuminating and metalworking represented at these houses.[161] The various works, attributed to the abbots by Matthew Paris in the *Gesta abbatum* especially, belong in part to a more general effort, after the completion of the east end of Canterbury, to upgrade the churches and liturgical fittings of the Benedictine houses (p. 86 above). After the failure of the first campaigns on its west front (p. 47 above) the church at St Albans saw only a partial rebuilding, in effect an extension, of its nave, including an aborted plan to provide it with a vault: work on the east end was postponed to the second half of the century.[162]

From the twelfth century onwards St Albans had made positive efforts to attract capable artists with a wide range of competence in different media. It did this by drawing into its ranks professional artists who professed as monks, i.e. *conversi*.[163] One early instance is the metalworker Anketil, a monk-goldsmith, who had worked for the royal Danish mint before executing the shrine of St Alban, with an assistant called Solomon of Ely, around 1129.[164] Exactly this type of connection might account for the English links with Scandinavian *ars sacra*. Matthew Paris relates that it was under the impractical Abbot John of Cella (1195–1214) that an important East Anglian professional craftsman of wide competence, Walter of Colchester, was attracted to St Albans by one of the monks, and later professed, becoming sacrist.[165] He may have been poached either from Colchester or Bury, and it is a measure of the common aspects of Benedictine culture of the period that he also worked at Canterbury.[166] Matthew says enough about Walter to indicate that he was in fact one of a clan, having a brother, Master Simon, and a nephew, the monk Richard, who were painters providing altarpieces for the church, including the high altar frontal, a *tabula picta* before the altar of the Virgin Mary and a retable and frontal for the altar of St Thomas of Canterbury, all before 1214.[167] Matthew also gives Walter of Colchester the fulsome praise that he himself might have encountered in the writing of Pliny on ancient painters in Book 35 of the *Historia naturalis*: thus Walter was *pictor et sculptor incomparabilis* whose like was never to be seen again; *mirabilis artifex*; *pictor praeelectus*; and the *artifex incomparabilis* who worked with that other *artifex*, Elias of Dereham, on the shrine of St Thomas at Canterbury.[168] Matthew also attaches the Ovidian tag *artificio materiam superante* to Walter's work on the shrine.[169] The assimilation of such clans into the house as *conversi* exemplified a certain moral virtue, the values of the professional world as it were internalized and purified in the service of the monastic *Opus Dei* – an issue encountered in Matthew's critique of Hugh of Goldclif, *vir quidem fallax et falsidicus sed artifex praeelectus* (p. 48 above). In contrast, St Dunstan had furnished the ideal of the virtuous all-round monastic craftsman and rounded moral and spiritual personality.[170] Indeed exactly this language of praise was to be extended to Matthew Paris himself after his death in 1259, as *pictor peroptimus*, and *nulli secundus*, second to none in the world, in respect of his art.[171]

In all this there is of course a measure of institutional chauvinism. As an inventory of works accomplished, Matthew's *Gesta abbatum* was a text somewhat in the mode of Suger's *De administratione*, or the similar text by Henry of Blois as Abbot of Glastonbury,[172] except that it tends to take the side of the convent in its various conflicts with the abbots. Indeed in this difference lies its character: the aim of the *Gesta* was political and didactic. Its portraits of individual virtue, including artistic

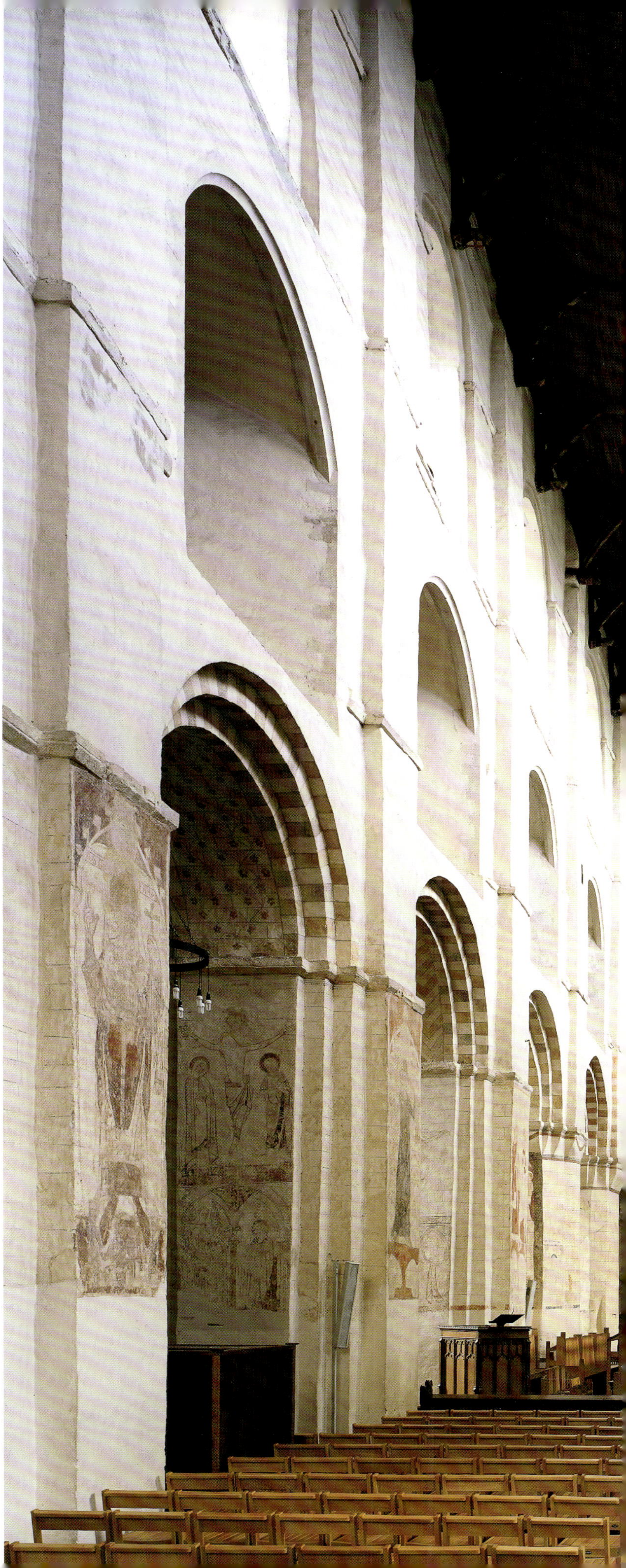

141 St Albans Abbey, nave looking east (John Crook).

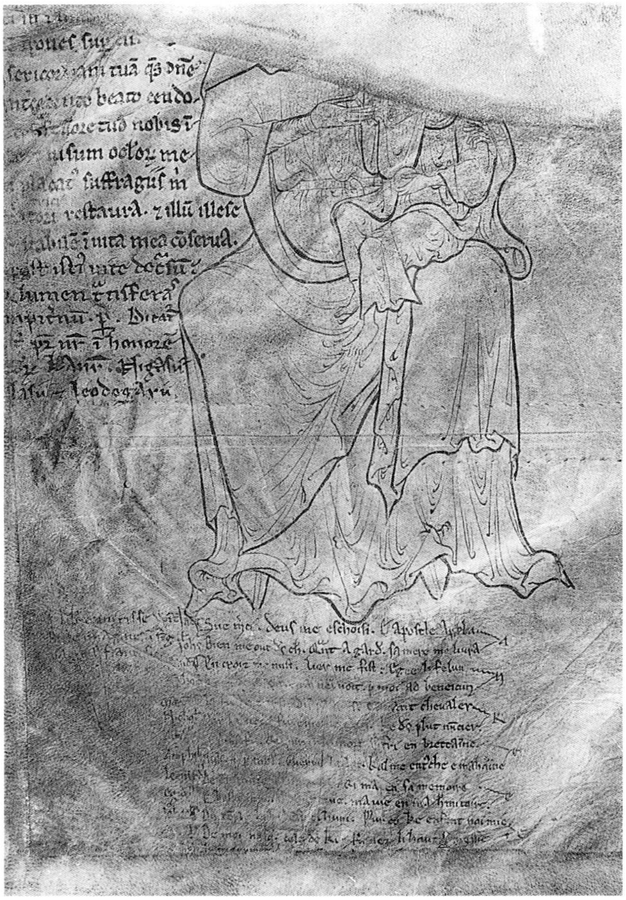

142 Virgin and Child, with (to her right) prayer to St Cendonius for eyesight, and below, suggestion for subjects in Psalter for the Countess of Winchester. Matthew Paris, Trinity College Dublin MS 177, fol. 2, *c.* 1250 (The Board of Trinity College Dublin).

virtue, become signs of the collective virtue of the house, counter-examples to the treachery of the world without and, occasionally, within. This in turn is part of an agenda to demonstrate how St Albans adhered firmly to the observance of the rule of St Benedict, how its monks still possessed a certain ancient toughness, how they contrasted with the rapid decline into laxity and pride of the friars, and so on. In short, the *Gesta abbatum* reclaimed rigour in face of the increased sanctions on the monastic orders imposed by Lateran IV, which Abbot William of Trumpington (1214–35) had attended; and also of the burden of papal control of houses such as St Albans which enjoyed freedom, or 'exemption', from diocesan control.[173] Though not an overtly reformist manifesto so much as a moralized history in the mould of Matthew's generally censorious approach to history writing, the *Gesta* may usefully be regarded in the light of reformist endeavour. This aspect of Matthew's own work – Matthew as the active provider of examples or models as part of a reforming moral and spiritual world-view – has received insufficient emphasis in recent literature, in which Matthew Paris's artistic activity is seen as inventorial and passively responsive to superior artworks at St Albans or elsewhere.[174]

In my chapter on the saints I described how Matthew produced Latin and vernacular saints' Lives for the pastoral edification of highly placed layfolk. Works such as the illustrated manuscript Life or *roman* of St Alban and St Amphibalus (Dublin, Trinity College MS 177) were produced by Matthew for loan, for transfer into bespoke versions by the artists and scribes employed by his patrons.[175] The Alban manuscript is a signally important document of these methods since its second flyleaf (fol. 2) contains a series of notes relating to the provision by Matthew of books for none other than the Countesses of Winchester, Arundel and Cornwall, the last two apparently borrowing from Matthew a French illustrated volume of the Lives of St Thomas and St Edward translated and drawn out by him. It is unlikely to be coincidental that this folio began life as a larger piece of vellum with a fine drawing by Matthew of the Virgin and Child, which was eventually cannibalized by Matthew for various *ad hoc* memos about his provision of books or book designs, and a prayer for intercession to St Cendonius for the preservation of eyesight, an artist's or scribe's preoccupation (fig. 142).[176] This image may itself have been a model for transfer, and it perhaps offers some indication of how Matthew may have influenced distant commissions by means of his lending library.

This in turn leads to Scandinavia. In 1247 Matthew was appointed by Innocent IV to reform a small Norwegian Benedictine house, St Benet Holm on the island of Nidarholm near Trondheim, which had got into financial and practical difficulties. Matthew was not a little proud of his appointment to restore proper observance, which he records as having wider validity *ad reformandum Ordinem Sancti Benedicti*.[177] How his connection with Norway came about is unclear, but some high diplomatic connection is implied by the fact that he carried with him letters from Louis IX to King Håkon of Norway during his visit in 1248–9, and received gifts from Håkon in return.[178] According to a later St Albans source, Matthew's reform caused religion to flourish again at St Benet, and Matthew 'carefully added to its possessions'.[179] In context, this is likely to have meant that Matthew added not land, but liturgical appurtenances and books.

It is in this context that one should note a panel painting in Oslo which, as Andreas Lindblom recognized, answers in all its aspects to the style of Matthew Paris (fig. 143).[180] It is either a product of his hand or the work of someone closely following his models; nothing else from contemporary Scandinavia can explain its character so well. The painted oak panel, measuring some 6 by 2½ ft, is the wing of a tabernacle which once enclosed a statue of the Virgin Mary. Its interior face had attached to it sculptures of the Annunciation, Visitation and Adoration of the Magi; its exterior face, the one visible when the tabernacle was closed, shows St Peter. The English identity of the work can be established by the correspondence between the figure of St Peter and the image of St Peter in the Jesse Tree as depicted in the Great Canterbury Psalter (BN MS lat. 8846, fol. 4);[181] but the idiomatic resemblance to Matthew's work of around 1250, in respect of the supple line ductus, foliage forms and triplets of small red dots on Peter's pale tunic, is exact. The panel is stated to have come from a church in Fåberg (Oppland), well inland from the areas, Bergen and Nidarholm, with which Matthew is known to have had contact, but still on an important pilgrim route from the south.[182] The comparatively large size of the tabernacle to which this wing belonged suggests that it is the type of thing which may have been produced for, or under the influence of, altar ensembles in rather larger churches. To judge from the *Gesta abbatum*, this is very likely to have been the type of object that the workshops at St Albans were producing between 1214 and 1235. In the *Gesta* Matthew notes that in this period Walter of Colchester erected certain most noble structures (*structuras nobilissimas*) around the high altar of St Albans, which consisted of something called an *artificiosa machina* under a beam carved with the Life of St Alban which ran across over the high altar – a conventional fitting also known at Bury, Canterbury and elsewhere.[183] The *machina* was therefore set below a trabeated contrivance of the sort often used to display reliquaries, as at St Augustine's, Canterbury. Perhaps it consisted of some form of tabernaculated screen with relic cupboards and painted doors, in other words a prototypical reredos bearing some relationship to the type of painted reliquary furniture now surviving at Løgum in southern Denmark, or Doberan in Germany.[184] Since such tabernacles were increasingly common in Scandinavia, there is no need to assume that Matthew himself was respon-

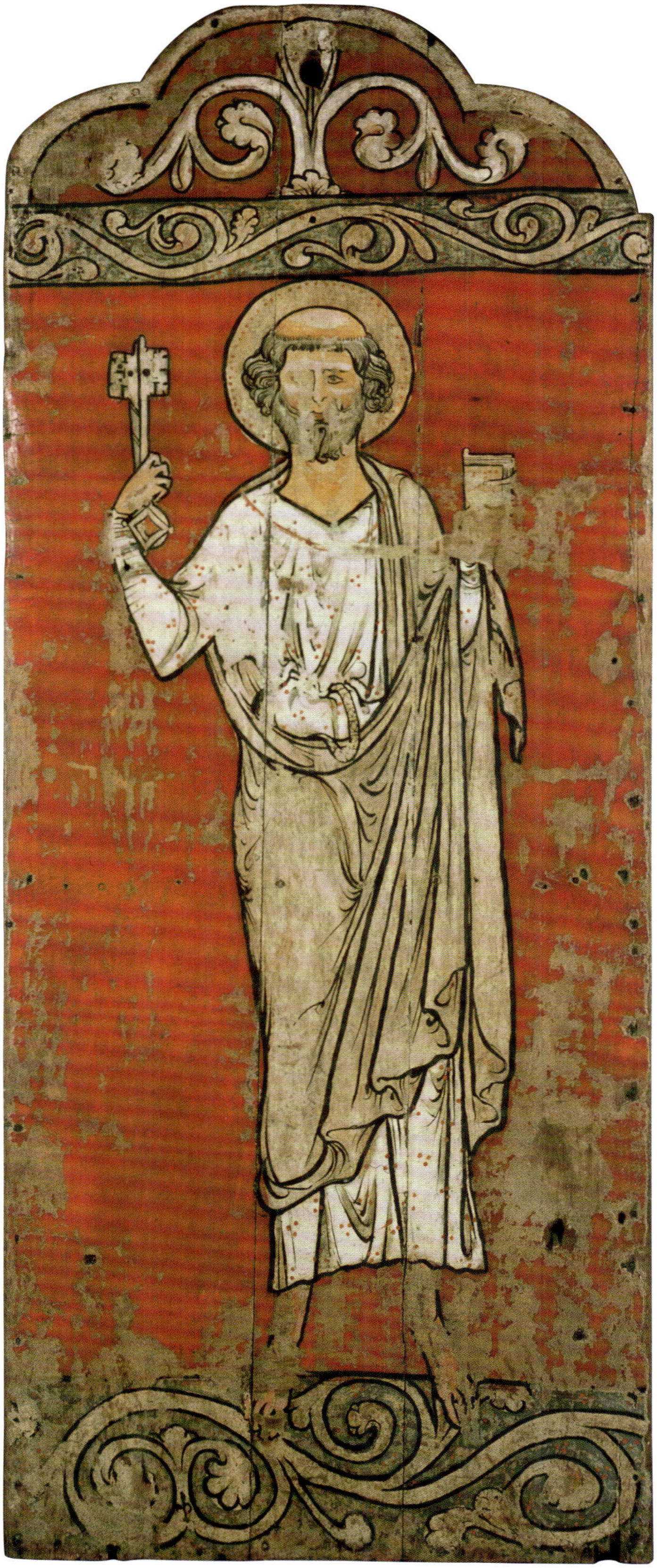

143 St Peter. Tabernacle wing from Fåberg parish church, Norway, *c.* 1250 (© University Museum of Cultural Heritage, University of Oslo, Norway: Eirik Irgens Johnson).

sible for starting a trend of which the Fåberg panel was merely part. What the evidence does suggest is that there may have been some connection between the provision of up-to-date altar furniture and the process of internal reform, which served to bring this small house of St Benet Holm into line. If so, one may begin to understand the ways in which objects such as painted retables and reredoses, strictly speaking *adiaphora*, started to arise and spread not by direct legislation, but by example. The development and spread of art forms of this type in this period are often seen in the context of the mendicant orders: the role of the reforming Benedictines also deserves consideration.

This is certainly a subtext of the inventory in the *Gesta abbatum* listing works at St Albans that exemplified the virtuous attention of its abbots to liturgy and furnishings. Under John of Cella, an accepted form for a major altar devoted to the Virgin Mary was to equip it with a frontal, retable and a cross (probably on a beam or ciborium over the altar).[185] William of Trumpington's scheme of works undertaken before 1235 was more ambitious, and more strategic. After 1221 William had a rood screen erected at the east end of the nave of the church (i.e. *in medio ecclesiae*) together with a new shrine, near the rood altar and behind railings, for the relics of St Amphibalus, the companion of St Alban.[186] The intention, to create a specific shrine-space for the nave, is clear. William was especially intent on promoting the cult of Mary. Lights were provided for her altar, and vestments by the laity – a point of note.[187] William instigated daily musical Masses for the Virgin as well as the established Saturday Mass.[188] These were to be held at a new Lady altar in the south choir aisle or transept of the church, which was also soon the object of benefaction.[189] Care was taken to provide this altar with a revered Mariola, or statue of the Virgin Mary, with its own canopy, as well as the old and richly figurated rood formerly over the high altar, with a Majesty of Christ, the Apostles, Patriarchs, Ecclesia and Synagoga.[190] The church was extensively whitewashed. Finally, and most revealingly, the old rood from the pulpitum in the nave was moved, together with another old Mariola, to the northern part of the church, presumably the north aisle or transept, specifically for the 'edification and worldly consolation of the lay people and anyone else who came there' – and lest the abbot's new works should be in any way damaged.[191]

Provision for the laity, in this case with the old Gregorian maxim in mind about images and edification, thus went hand-in-hand with their segregation.[192] Liturgical reform brought about new altars, lights, images, music and liturgy, and the repeated combination of the image of Mary and the Cross or Christ, but in such a way as either to locate shrines behind stout grilles, or to distance safely the best images and most important monastic liturgical complexes, from the contaminating press of the people. The nave images exactly replicate the type of combination of images documented in the *Gesta*. Six of the Romanesque piers on the north side of the nave are painted, five of them with various combinations of Marian themes (below) and the Crucifixion (above) on the west faces of the piers, all done in the thirteenth century.[193] Further images of such saints as Thomas Becket and Christopher, and donors, were executed on the south sides of the piers facing into the nave in the fourteenth century.[194] Internal and stylistic evidence suggests very strongly that the earliest of the paintings, dating to around 1230, is the westernmost, and that the pictures were added progressively to each pier in turn to the east, ending around 1300.[195] The first shows a Crucifixion supported on a beam, and a Mariola with censing angels much in the style of an image in the Glazier Psalter, and so representative of metropolitan style (fig. 144).[196] This picture could well have been part of the repainting of the church undertaken under Abbot William.[197] The second painting, much retouched, repeats this general formula and seems to have been closest to the idiom of Matthew Paris himself around mid-century; and the last of the sequence, showing the Coronation of the Virgin and the Crucifixion, done around 1300, is the most striking (fig. 145).[198] The final effect, though not that intended, is that of a series of stations, but clearly this is not a single programme of paintings, rather the result of a process of accretion of images of Mary surmounted by the Cross. There are many examples of this type of hierarchy of Mary and Christ in the period, as for example in the Bible of William of Devon (fig. 188): but these are certainly among the earliest and most important.

The function of these Mariolas and roods was probably both to act as votive images and as mural image-complexes – not exactly retables, but reredosses – over altars set against the piers. In form and content these murals and statues anticipate exactly the type of material envisaged for lay imagination in the later so-called layfolk's Mass books (fig. 161).[199] Not all the piers need have had altars attached to their fronts, and it is seldom wise to be categorical about the function of an image simply on the basis of its appearance. Pillar paintings – again creating scope for the metaphorical association of the saints as columns of the Church – are a case in point.[200] The real issue is not so much use (for altars could be used for extra-liturgical devotion and the

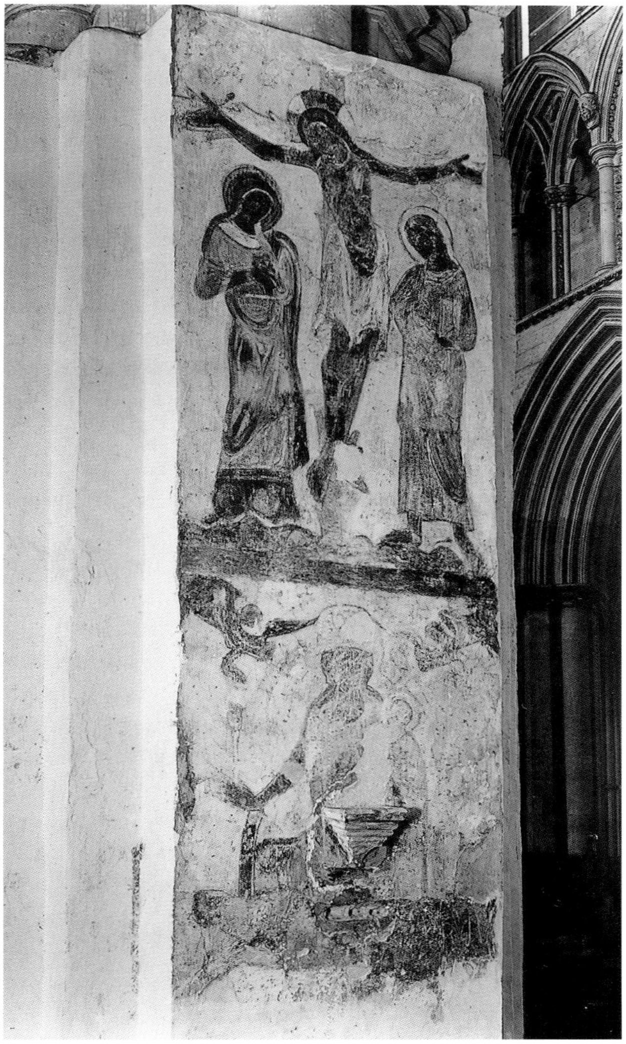

144 Crucifixion and Mariola with censing angels, mural on west face of north nave pier, St Albans Abbey, *c.* 1235 (Conway Library, Courtauld Institute of Art).

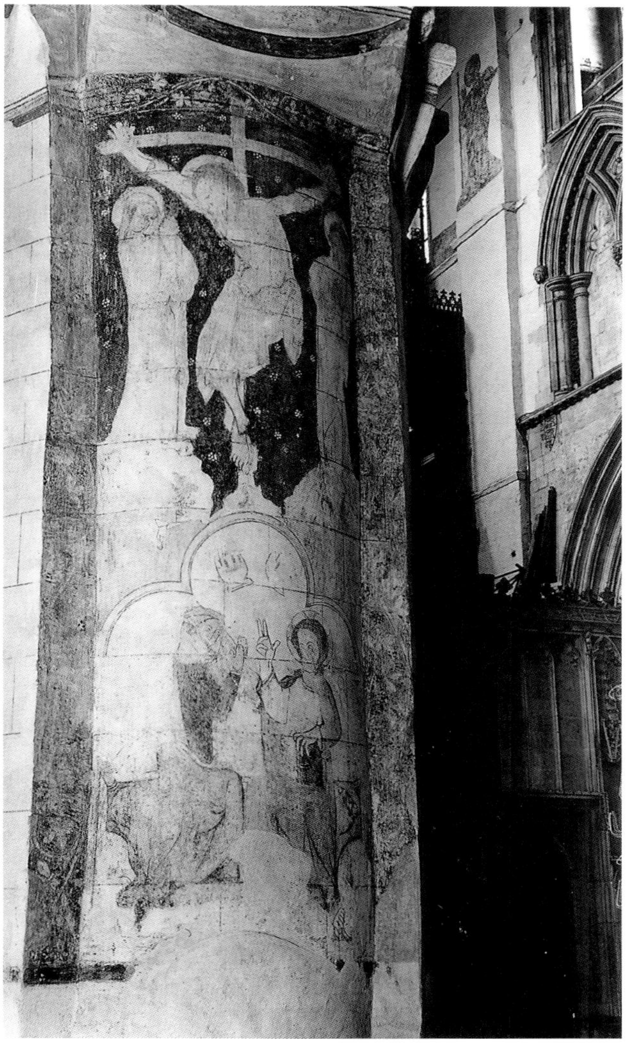

145 Coronation of Virgin and Crucifixion, mural on west face of north pier, St Albans Abbey, *c.* 1300 (Conway Library, Courtauld Institute of Art).

boundaries between 'liturgical' and 'devotional' images were naturally hazy) as audience and clientele. The decorated piers are in a part of the church that the convent in the 1190s had undertaken to extend, vault and close off with a fine but controversial facade. Their paintings seem to have been executed only after plans to rebuild the nave were aborted in the 1220s.[201] Naves in Benedictine churches were, functionally speaking, the most superfluous parts of the church, being principally routes for conventual processions. Though the numbers of monks being ordained to the priesthood had increased very significantly, there is little evidence that monastic masses tended to be said in the nave space at specially segregated altars.[202] Quite the contrary: the evidence points to increasing lay parochial access to and use of naves in monastic and secular, especially cathedral and collegiate, churches in this period.[203] The *Gesta abbatum* is specific on the issue of the press of crowds of laity in the nave at St Albans.[204] It is almost as if the plans to extend the nave for monastic purposes – plans that had already exposed beliefs and prejudices about the convent's relationship to the outside world – had backfired on the monastery by creating a huge potential parish church. That there were indeed problems of containment and discipline is indicated by the provision, from some point in the twelfth century, of a parish chapel for the laity which adjoined the nave at around the location of the westernmost Mariola and Crucifixion mural.[205] St Albans was far from unique in this respect. A parish altar in the north aisle of Dunstable Priory had similarly been allowed to the burgesses of Dunstable in 1219, but in such a way as not to obstruct processions.[206] Ely Cathedral faced similar problems, having what were in effect parishes which formed out of groups of worshippers at its nave altar of the Holy Cross, and for which buildings were to be erected on the north side of the nave.[207]

What is known of the new arrangements of the nave shrine and altar at St Albans points to a similar situation. In keeping with the segregative policy of William of Trumpington, the initial intention was to allow an altar or votive complex for the laity just within the nave space next to the parish chapel, with sanctioned images as it were *ad edificationem et consolationem*, conveniently located for the laity at the west end, yet sufficiently far from the monastic choir to isolate the conventual masses and offices from disturbance. The laity were to be kept for as long as possible to the north and the west, gaining access to the images in the north transept via the north aisle only. Yet segregation was overtaken by events. The murals, like a creeping tide-line, chart the steady advance of the lay presence in the nave towards the choir screens, exactly up to the time when the addition of an enlarged Lady Chapel was begun in the first decade of the fourteenth century.[208] The Lady Chapel and retrochoir were one solution, a kind of pressure-valve, to a problem in the nave, in effect lay self-provision, of which the paintings are a sign. The nave was becoming a parish church. The fact that the nave key was handed over to the parishioners in 1553 was merely the formal recognition of something that had been obvious for a long time, and that at medieval Wymondham, Rochester and Waltham had produced disputes of a far worse order.[209]

Contentions

In setting out an account of thirteenth-century St Albans in terms of a 'tide' of lay activity which had in some way to be contained, one runs a slight risk of presenting the question in terms of certain operating 'forces' – the 'rise of the laity' versus the increasingly entrenched attitudes of large, privileged ecclesiastical corporations, for example. Such collectivist assumptions can help best (and not least as 'plot devices') only when grounded in specific case histories, of which St Albans is one. Yet there is some justification for seeing the cumulative effect of a vast range of human activity and events as being something like the operation of a force. The various documented territorial expedients adopted by monastic and secular establishments in defining the internal organization of their churches – typically by using screens – indicate that something fairly new was being managed from the late twelfth century: and that 'something' was a complex of social and religious factors which operated too within the parish churches.[210] Throughout this period the outlook of many ecclesiastics becomes noticeably more managerial.[211] This is demonstrable from such exceptionally detailed regimes of maintenance of churches and their images as that set out by a great fourteenth-century patron, John Grandisson, Bishop of Exeter (1327–69), for his collegiate foundation at Ottery St Mary. The statutes of 1339 for this church are a fair indication of the highest ideals of the period.[212] Altars in the new church are to be assigned to individual canons for care. The altars and surroundings are to be cleaned at least three times a year for the major feasts, the altars, windows and walls being dusted in such a way as not to damage the images. There is to be a weekly round of inspection. Those in charge of altars are not to permit the placing of sundry images or the affixing of candles around the altar in a disorderly (*incomposite*) manner, as happens in country churches (*ut fit in ecclesiis ruralibus*), but only the images of the saints in whose honour the altars are dedicated, with a cross in the middle and two candles, which burn equally. The objectives are much in line with the diocesan statutes of the previous century, notably those of 1287 for Exeter of Bishop Quinel. Ottery was not Exeter, yet it aspired to its standards of appearance and management: it was to have a 'cathedral' style of ornament. The sideways glance at the festooned altars in rural churches is therefore as revealing as it is picturesque. There may have been some anxiety about images of non-sanctified people, objects of local cults, being put on altars in contravention of the requirement that such altars should be properly dedicated to a saint. It offers a signal example of the high-minded clerical distancing from the popular and the rustic: rurality here (as elsewhere in the period and earlier) is identified with the untidy and the ignorant.[213] Grandisson exemplifies the essentially urbane academic current of thought which had been running through ecumenical and diocesan legislation for a century or more. If one is to identify clerical tidy-mindedness anywhere – the mindset of the pinafore as much as the mitre – it is to be found here, in the domain of detailed regulation of images, rather than in the hazier domain of architectural decorum in general. Panofsky's scholastic *manifestatio*, the 'postulate of clarity for clarity's sake', finds its outlet not on the heroic scale, but in the micro-management of the Christian *habitus*.[214]

Yet here too there are risks. Grandisson's disdain for the rural should not seduce one into too ready a belief in neat distinctions between 'popular' and 'official' piety, as if the social status of piety could be confused with its form, or authenticity.[215] The later history of the medieval altar at all levels throughout western Europe is one of the peaceful coexistence, at various levels of patronage, of formal works of art, and the clutter of pilgrimage and the *ex-voto*.[216] *Manifestatio* demonstrably had its practical limits. Indeed, in seeing the rise of genres such as retables, reredosses and screens as the outcome of long-standing currents of thought, opinion or artistic activity, one runs the risk of teleological error, confusing hesitant prototype and perfected outcome, and assessing the former by means of the latter. Again, creativity lay not in the legislative domain, but in the exploitation of the interstices, the loopholes, in law or official statement. By 1300 – if Durandus is to be taken as a universal example – retable altarpieces or statues could fulfil the obligation to advertise properly the dedication of an altar: but the prescription is only 'image or sculpture, picture or writing'. The forms taken by altar-reredoses in England from the late thirteenth century onwards were manifestly extremely diverse. Public Church art was still a vital focus of innovation, not because it was a sphere of wholly autonomous activity, but because its norms were determined generously. So – to address the arguments of Hans Belting – it would be misleading to single out 'private' art as the special domain of late medieval innovation, as if 'public' art had somehow ground to a halt under the burden of coercive and authoritarian precept.[217] The constant hunt for signs of authoritarianism can result in overlooking key features, including a lack of authority at the 'centre' itself.

Indeed the boundaries between what is now regarded as public and private, liturgical and devotional, and official and unofficial, were in reality much more blurred. In guarding against an (often unconscious) teleological viewpoint of later medieval art 'genres', one must also be wary of the assumption that the realm of the private can be identified as that of personal 'self-realization' – for this concept must contend with the philosophically respectable position that 'self-realization' is quite as much a matter of publicly accessible activity as of private worlds. The relationship between liturgy and devotion illustrates the point. It is commonly, and quite rightly, stated that from the late thirteenth century specific forms of religious image were developed, the character of which was apparently premised upon a particular form of devotional attention – devotional images or *andachtsbilder* – which stood slightly to one side of the conventional categories of public art, and within a seemingly more personal sphere. Such images both test, and reinforce, the categories created by art historians. For this reason one must be cautious. It was indeed the near impossibility of deciding *a priori* exactly what a 'devotional', as opposed to a 'liturgical', image should be functionally and aesthetically that encouraged that freedom from category, that wit, that underlies the metaphysic of late medieval devotional art. As Jeffrey Hamburger has put it succinctly, 'Any work of art can prompt a vision'.[218] Far from distancing public objects from private sensibilities, this connected them. For one thing liturgy, publicly ritualized piety, was the very basis of devotional practice, for it was in this activity that the mutually informative spheres of social and individual awareness – apart from actual devotional texts and practices – had their starting-point.[219] Again, the importance of certain devotional images, for example the Veronica, resided in part in their association with formalized prayers granting papal indulgences.[220] Sarah Beckwith has reminded scholars that the domain of devotional 'subjectivism' was not automatically asocial.[221] This was not so much the start of a 'privatized' religious culture, as of a publicly sanctioned religious 'inwardness'.

It is therefore unhelpful to see altarpieces simply as liturgical paraphernalia, or as public expositions of sacramental doctrine, for this polarizes and circumscribes their importance and imaginative potential: there is no reason why these ostensibly 'public' objects should not have been perfectly suitable objects for 'private' extra-liturgical (Leonard Boyle and others use the expression 'para-liturgical') devotion.[222] Nor can their provision be neatly parcelled out into 'lay' and 'clerical' aspects. The layfolk's Mass books that were appearing around 1300, which deploy images as cues for devotion at certain moments of the Mass, also illustrate this point (see p. 197 below): these texts stand at the intersection of liturgy, devotional regulation (whether public or private) and pastoral instruction. But they cannot really be thought of as instances of what Boyle also calls 'spontaneous' (as opposed to 'popular') piety, i.e. piety that existed outside liturgy or the constraints of obedience to ecclesiastical directive: the manuals were written by clerics and reflected the epistemology and moral theology of the schools.[223] Images could be provided by the laity or the clergy. In some cases – and here perhaps the idea of 'spontaneous' piety rings true – they might have been the product of both, of the sheer weight of consensus, as in the case of the possibility that Becket's very socially inclusive cult – a popular cult of the heroic – lent impetus to the development of the painted altarpiece in England. There can be no doubt that a top-down account of the origin and spread of such forms has to take into account the essentially collusive and reciprocal relationship between the public and private, the official and the 'spontaneous'.

The thirteenth-century English Church itself recognized this; and it was characteristic of its pragmatism that it handled the question by legislating about liability. At parish level the need was increasingly to sharpen the definition of the roles of the parish and the priest in the maintenance of churches and the provision of their equipment. For most practical purposes the territorial frontier between the two was generally held, at least from the early thirteenth century, to lie at the junction between the nave and the chancel, between the lay and clerical domains.[224] In theory the laity (though actually only those of lower station – the laity was not a collective) were forbidden to sit in the chancel among the priests.[225] This division of liability is set out as a precept in the Winchester synodal statutes of 1224, and is fully developed in the customs for the diocese of Salisbury of 1228–56: the parson (*persona*) is to maintain the roof of the chancel as well as some of its equipment; the parishioners are responsible for the equivalent parts of the nave, and also the bell tower, bells and ropes, the crucifix, crosses and images and other items including the service books and lights in both chancel and nave.[226] Bishop Quinel's Exeter statutes of 1287 restate the same liabilities even if they ran against accepted local custom. But it is evident from these increasingly careful regulations about lay patronage that disputes (*contentiones*) were starting to arise, not least in connection with control of the parish alms-boxes, which necessitated legislative explicitness. Parishioners bore the brunt of provision and care of most of the *ornamenta*, including the vestments, altar frontals, liturgical equipment, crosses, images of the Virgin Mary and dedicatee saints, font and bells, while the rector or vicar was to maintain the Psalter, the chancel window-glass and the chancel altar canopy.[227] So perhaps by 1250, and certainly by 1300 in the Province of Canterbury, the idea that the parishioners had only one zone of responsibility was clearly redundant: the chancel was a zone of overlapping responsibilities which cannot be expressed adequately by categorical and polarized modern notions of 'social space'.[228] The prescriptive (and unprecedented) statement in the Exeter statutes that there 'should' be frontals and images in churches also shows that yesterday's luxuries had become present-day necessities.[229] In effect, the parochial burden had increased, and the realm of *adiaphora* was shrinking. This makes comprehensible the remarkable statement about disputes (*altercationes*) which opens the section on *ornamenta* in one of Archbishop Pecham's directives of 1272–92, which itself actually attributes less chancel responsibility to parishioners than Bishop Quinel's.[230] Even the directives of Archbishop Winchelsey of 1295–1313 allude to misunderstanding (*ambiguitas*) on the matter: here, the provision of the principal chancel image (i.e. the dedicatee image) is shunted back onto the parish.[231] The matter is difficult now – and it was pretty hazy even then.

Parishioners on the whole had more duties than rights.[232] The extent of the burdens obviously varied from parish to parish; some parishes had larger communities of priests, others particularly prosperous and assertive layfolk; many others had been appropriated by monastic houses running deficits.[233] The tendency after around 1200 for the chancels of parish churches to be greatly enlarged, generally for liturgical reasons, with better illumination and more expensive stone fittings (piscina, sedilia), created greater liability for the rector or vicar.[234] But at the same time the formulation of lay liability was associated too with growing lay initiative to edify, and also to furnish churches. There are numerous signs of this. Growing lay activity in great churches, such as the nave at St Albans, is one. Another is crime. Since more was given, there was more to steal, leading to disputes over security arrangements and burglary.[235] Yet another is the establishment of boundaries around private initiatives. The foundation of chantries, private non-congregational spaces, required some assurance that the burden of private initiatives by the laity would not eventually fall upon the entire parish.[236] Another still is mass-production of artefacts: the rise in lay provision of painted altarpieces led to their serial production by workshops, and to a simplification of technique. Churches were beginning to attract significant lay endowment, of lights, of altars, as belief in the efficacity of suffrages for those in Purgatory became firmly established by the final decades of the century.[237] One line of defence, probably coming into existence in the third quarter of the century and seemingly first recognized in the Exeter statutes of 1287, was the introduction of the office of churchwarden to represent the parish and to help fulfil its responsibilities, administer endowments, raise funds and look after the ornaments.[238] Responsibility, and with it collusion, was one aspect of growing activity. The politics of provision were gaining in complexity, for lay liability and lay initiative were connected in what Drew, in his study of the churchwarden, astutely called 'the political education of the English parish'.[239] It is exactly this understanding that renders any clear-cut distinction between secular and religious domains within the parish meaningless: patronage was not a 'secular' activity except in the sense that it could be conducted by lay people; 'subjectivity' was far from being a product solely of secular discourse.[240] The drive to educate both clergy and laity, which formed a central part of the policy of the thirteenth-century Church, was fundamental. Instruction in spheres of responsibility was part of this education. As Eamon Duffy notes, 'What was imposed on the laity as their collective responsibility became the focus of their corporate awareness'.[241] To explore what this notion of awareness might have entailed, I now move on to consider the formal means by which the cure of souls and the domain of practical morality were lent form and content, namely though the techniques developed in *pastoralia*.

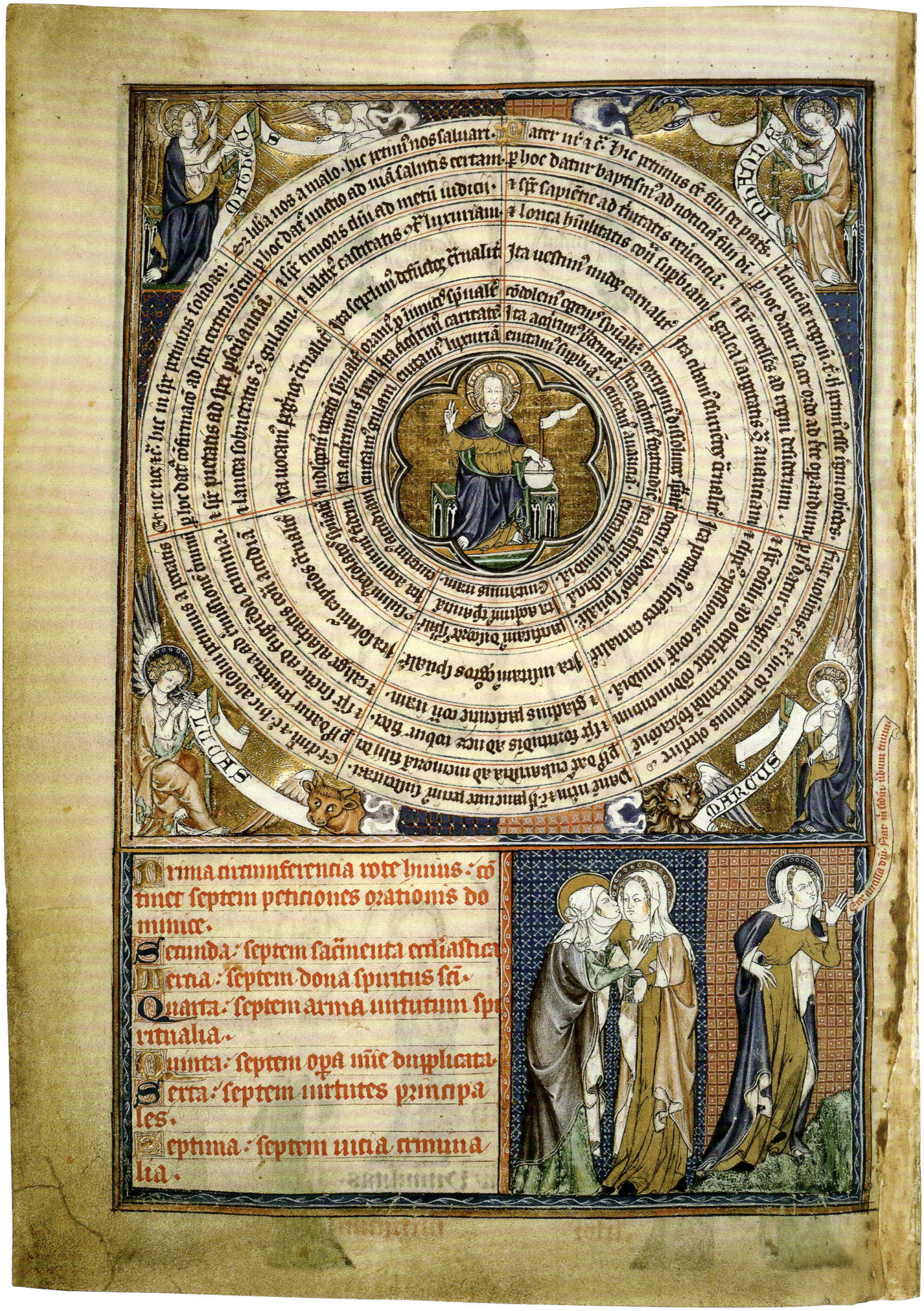

146 Wheel of Sevens divided into seven concentric rings and seven radial segments, with *Pater noster*, seven sacraments, seven gifts of the Holy Spirit, etc. Psalter of Robert de Lisle, BL Arundel MS 83 (II), fol. 129v, early fourteenth century (by permission of the British Library).

Chapter 8

PASTORALIA

Idle and, even more, foul and profane talk must stop; chattering in all its forms must cease. Everything, in short, that may disturb divine worship or offend the eyes of the divine majesty should be absolutely foreign to churches.

Second Council of Lyons, 1274, canon 25

Ther beth so manye bokes and tretees of vyces and vertues [. . .] that this schort lyfe schalle rathere have an ende of anye manne, thanne he may owthere studye hem or rede hem.

Orologium sapientie

School and Confessional

Various points in this book consider the importance of the type of moral theology developed in the twelfth-century schools, in the emergence and spread of which Englishmen played a considerable part. I mentioned it first in regard to the moral dimension of architecture. But its scope is obviously larger. The moral theology of Paris was practical in its reasoning and objectives; it sought to show, not least through example, how Christian revelation could be harmonized with ethical reasoning, in such a way as to produce a total account of human behaviour in its public and private aspects.[1] Because this account was rational and technocratic in character and universal in its claims, it followed that its public expression could, and should, be educational. Earlier I claimed that the very general prescriptions for Mass and the engagement of the sensorium involved the use of certain techniques which could be expressed as prescriptions. Moral theology too was invested in didactic techniques, at the heart of which lay the new science of casuistry, the resolution of cases of conscience, dilemmas, by the application of general rules to specific instances, in order to effect the cure of souls (*cura animarum*). This science reflected the methods of resolving problems, the *sic et non*, of the schoolmen. These techniques had several formal vehicles – the confessional, the sermon, the pastoral manual on the seven deadly sins and so on – which, their extraordinary diversity notwithstanding, I call *pastoralia*. Texts on the virtues and vices alone were extremely common, numbering at least 6,500 and preserved in over 10,000 manuscripts; few of such texts of pastoral theology were glamorous in appearance. As the second epigraph to this chapter shows, the problem was acknowledged even in the Middle Ages. Here only the most limited account of some of the most outstanding is possible.[2]

The 'general rules' of pastoral theology consisted of the repertory of ideas and principles that formed part of the catechism, or examinable schedule of belief. These concerned principally articles of faith: what it was necessary to believe in order to be a Christian. But because such techniques claimed to inform not only faith, but conduct, they were associated with a wider ethical claim: that the Church could influence behaviour more generally. The reader has already approached this issue above, where I describe what the Church tried to say in this period about one aspect of human behaviour, namely the production of art, as one (actually subsidiary) part of the *habitus* of contemporary religion. The step to statements about general conduct (particularly, though not exclusively, conduct in church) was a logical one. *Pastoralia* were a further, ethical aspect of the 'the political education of the English parish' that arose in the definition of communal rights and responsibilities. Their aim was to codify a 'theology of human behaviour' which would develop the skill of living properly – *bene vivendum*, in the words of Thomas of Chobham.[3] The founders of the new pastoral movement and the leading innovators in the theory of the confessional and penance were such men as Peter the Chanter and his English-born pupil Robert of Courçon. The scope of their agenda, both positive and negative, is breathtaking. Peter was not only an important moralist, penitentialist and sacramental theorist, but the author of a text on prayer, *De oratione et speciebus illius*.[4] This text is partly of concern here because, as with the work of some of the Victorine symbolists on 'edificatory' architecture and imaging considered earlier, it was intended to be illustrated. In his study of *De oratione*, Richard C. Trexler has established a case for it being a document of 'behavioural history' which, along with Peter's other works, 'had a seminal role in elaborating the theological foundations of scholasticism at a crucial point in the early life of that intellectual system'.[5] Peter emerges from this as 'an early behavioral scientist', giving doctrinal, rhetorical and expressive shape to the understanding and practice of prayer as a skill, something teachable and invested in words, practices and images (indeed practice 'as' image), all of which demonstrates the correct public disposition towards devotion and *captatio benevolentiae*, the winning of God's favour.[6] This reinforces a point made in the previous chapter about the public and private sphere; for prayer, the dominant form common to both, is something 'publicly performed, yet also privately binding'.[7] Prayer is a skill that lies, first, in the public domain. It carries with it a certain objective view of mental, verbal and physical discipline, the connection of those components, and the necessity for decorum and moderation.[8] This technocratic character helps one to understand the character of the new penitential thinking. Living properly entailed shaping the inner and outer person. It presupposed self-knowledge, in the acquisition of which self-examination was essential. To that extent it was a matter of the interior, moral and spiritual, of a person. But this 'private' dimension of a person was subject to regulation in terms recognizable to public activity, through conventional casuistical and catechetical methods. As discussed in regard to ornaments, it was of the nature of the Church that its regulative mentality extended, or tried to extend, to conduct. The reformation, or remodelling, of the interior person was not something which took place in an individualistic space of personal self-realization. The culture of the confessional, which is so often regarded as being the most important outcome of the canons of Lateran IV, was on the contrary absolutely formulaic and public. It was a coercive para-bureaucratic technology, invested in skills and the formal recognition of duties. The 'rhetorical empowerment' of the priest-confessor is exactly what guaranteed his authority.[9] It was one aspect of the broader reformist drive of the Church examined above in the contexts both of architecture and the figurative arts. In it, the episcopal church quite as much as the new mendicant orders played a fundamental part.

Again, the interconciliar period (between the Lateran Councils of 1179 and 1215) was key to the construction of the new pastoral techniques. It was from the circle of the Chanter and Robert of Courçon that a new type of practical manual of confession was to emerge; the Chanter's *Verbum abbreviatum* formed part of this output.[10] Such men greatly influenced English penitential speculation between about 1200 and the mid-fourteenth century.[11] It should be noted that this moral theology was already being developed in England in the twelfth century, and was to be disseminated by the circle of the prodigious Stephen Langton and his pupils somewhat before 1215.[12] Langton himself promoted the example of Mary Magdalen as a penitent sinner.[13] Robert of Flamborough, a canon-penitentiary of Saint-Victor, wrote his *Liber poenitentialis*, a handbook of what would now be called conflict resolution, for Richard Poore around 1210.[14] Poore's sub-dean at Salisbury was the influential penitential writer and author of the *Summa confessorum*, Thomas of Chobham.[15] The Paris schoolman William de Montibus, Chancellor of Lincoln, was in the vanguard in writing the earliest verse confessional treatise before 1213, the confessor (in a by now commonplace idea originating with Pope Gregory the Great) probing the diseased soul as a doctor might probe an illness of the body.[16]

And so by 1215 the scene was already set. Lateran IV was without doubt the most pastoral of all the medieval ecumenical councils, acknowledging not only the importance of moral theology for clergy and laity alike, but also the role and importance of the parishes within the diocesan system as the principal vehicle for a general transformation of *mores*.[17] Naturally it went hand-in-hand with efforts to improve the standard of conduct and especially the literacy of clergy. Its role was in effect to consolidate the development of a veritable industry of *pastoralia* whose didactic objective was in the first instance to explain the relationship between the seven sacraments – especially the sacraments of penance and the Mass – within a strict catechetical framework that had been emerging gradually in the post-Gregorian Church. Such texts were scarcely known before 1179. In this regard its two leading canons were its first, *Firmiter credimus*, and canon 21, *Omnis utriusque sexus fidelis*, the latter requiring adults individually to confess their sins to their own priest at least once a year, to perform any penance imposed on them, and to receive the sacrament of the Mass at least at Easter.[18] The priest is to probe the nature of sin discerningly and is not to betray the sinner; penance is not based upon a fixed tariff, but upon a more subtle understanding – whose origins were derived ultimately from classical theory of 'plot' – of the 'circumstances' (or 'totagges', trimmings) under which sins were committed, which the *Ancrene Wisse* defines as who, where, when, how, how often and why.[19] In effect, private, or auricular, confession, and the seal of the confessional, were established.

Omnis utriusque sexus fidelis required that this canon should be published in churches, and, to repeat, the canons of the Council were promulgated through diocesan legislation. Stephen Langton's statutes of 1213–14 had already made provision for the instruction of adults in the Lord's Prayer and the Creed.[20] Richard Poore's statutes of 1217–19 were the most systematic of the early post-conciliar English legislation, drawing not only on Lateran IV but also on the work of Courçon and Langton.[21] Poore side-stepped canon 21 by retaining the more demanding schedule of thrice-annual confession set out by Langton,[22] but he reiterated the Council's opening profession of faith and some of the terms of canon 21.[23] Significantly, his statutes include an exposition of the seven sacraments, reflecting their codification by Peter Lombard.[24] In effect, as his final statute implies, diocesan legislation could itself be regarded as a handbook in the exercise of pastoral care.[25]

The importance of this new pattern in legislation, in effect the importation of an expository and didactic structure into the framework of central regulation, cannot be overstated. It set a pattern for much of the diocesan legislation promulgated for the rest of the century.[26] The method of attaching short doctrinal tracts to episcopal statutes can be found, for example, in the decrees of Alexander of Stavensby for Coventry and Lichfield (1224–37), which include a treatise on the seven deadly sins and confession.[27] The statutes of Worcester (1229) required the clergy to instruct the laity in the Creed before confession, and in the seven deadly sins afterwards.[28] An episcopal origin for some teachings on confession is rendered certain by references in Bishop Cantilupe's statutes for Worcester (1240) to the existence of a tract by the bishop – probably resembling the later *Manuel des pechiez* – which was to be copied out and used by all chaplains when they heard confession, and also in the examination of clergy before being instituted to livings.[29] It is hard to envisage a more centralized process. By the late thirteenth century these treatises had grown greatly in extent. The *Summula* of Bishop Quinel of Exeter of around 1287, probably issued with his statutes of that year, runs to several chapters, on the Ten Commandments, the seven deadly sins, confession, penance, the Creed and seven sacraments: copies of it were to be kept by every parish in the diocese and examined by the archdeacon on pain of fines, and priests were to know it, if necessary, by heart.[30] This programme of diocesan instruction culminated in the most influential compilation of all, the section *Ignorantia sacerdotum* in the proceedings of the Lambeth Council of 1281, held under the Franciscan Archbishop of Canterbury, John Pecham.[31] This was to form the basis of the layfolk's catechism.[32] *Ignorantia sacerdotum* was a scheme of instruction for the laity in the articles of the faith, set out under the heading 'information for priests of simple learning', which was to be expounded to the people in the vernacular (*vulgariter*) four times a year. In essence it was a syllabus, framed around the Creed, the Ten Commandments, love of God and of one's neighbour, and the symbolically rich and memorable 'sevens' (fig. 146): the seven works of mercy (including the burial of the dead), the seven deadly sins, the seven virtues and seven sacraments.[33] A memorable syllabus implies examination: by such means were church and confessional converted into a schoolroom, and into the testing ground of the Christian conscience. But to be memorable, a text must also engage the attention: and it was a measure of the wit of the thirteenth-century episcopal leaders that they managed so skilfully to transform ultimately monastic disciplines into something altogether more accessible and comprehensible to the lay mind. Here mental and physical images played their part.

Castle of Love, Temple of the Lord

As already noted, by the thirteenth century, the episcopal class had become associated with the drive to pastoral reform either by example, as in the case of the new episcopal saints whose hagiography enjoyed pastoral success in the circles of highly placed laypeople, or by word, through preaching, legislation and the compilation of pastoral manuals. Two examples of this, both of whom were associated with Oxford, and both of whom had strong sympathies for the Franciscans, namely Robert Grosseteste and St Edmund of Abingdon, are particularly striking. St Edmund's canonization in effect ensured that he would continue to teach *verbo et exemplo*, and this immensely influential figure reappears more than once in this study. I dwell on Robert Grosseteste, Bishop of Lincoln (1235–53), for other reasons. He was the object of a failed and probably local cult, but his humble origins, outspoken manner, prodigious writings, activity as a translator, weighty intellectual reputation and

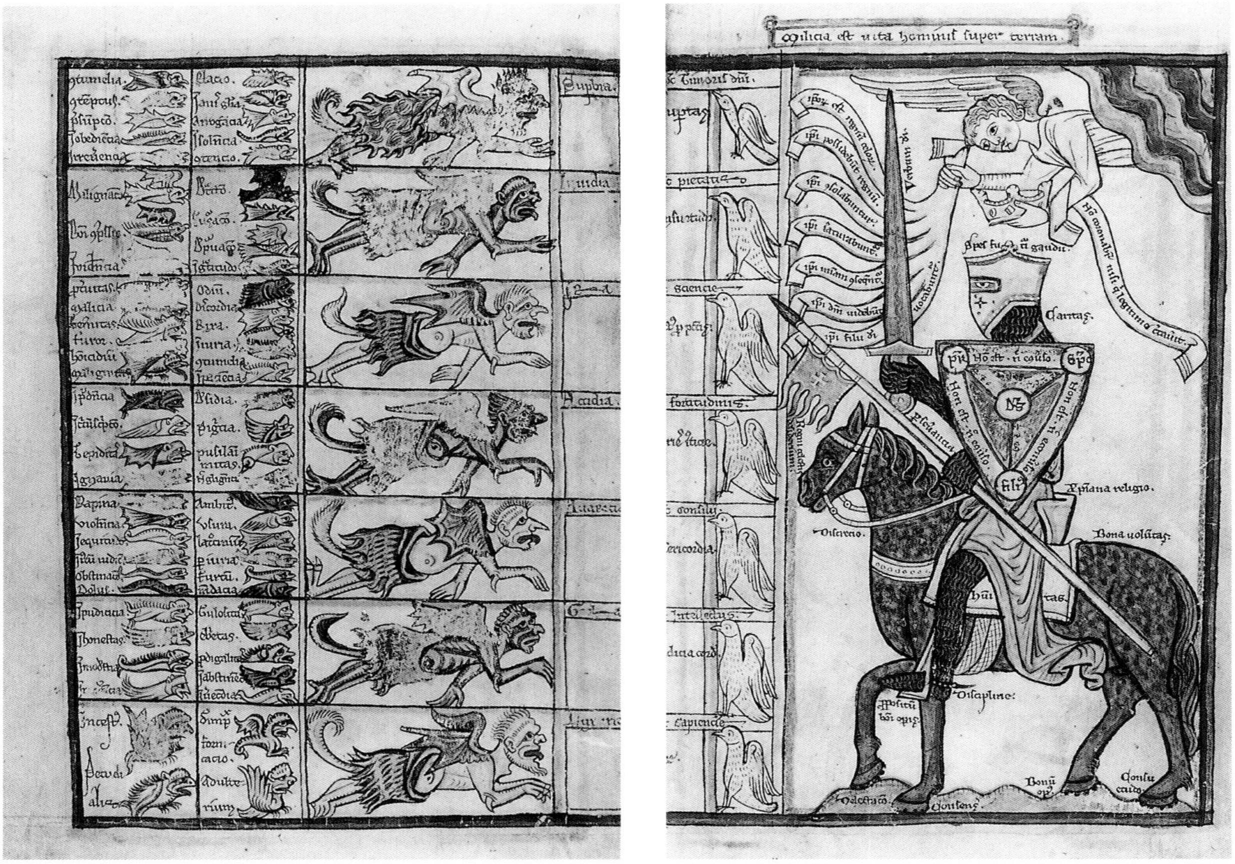

147 Allegory of the armed struggle against sin. Peraldus, *Summa* of Vices, BL Harley MS 3244, fols 27v–28, copy of 1240s (by permission of the British Library).

strongly reformist instincts placed him almost in a class of his own.[34] The extent of his reforms may be judged from his vigorous visitations of the secular clergy in his diocese, which are the best documented of any in the period, not only through his letters but through his diocesan legislation.[35] In keeping with other legislation, Grosseteste lays down a syllabus for priests and layfolk (especially the boys of the parish), including teaching the Ten Commandments, the seven deadly sins and seven sacraments, the Lord's Prayer, Creed, *Ave Maria* and the sign of the Cross.[36]

But Grosseteste's writings on *pastoralia* also take the form of considerably more developed expositions of moral theology in Latin and the vernacular. Of them, two are outstanding, one for its allegorical outlook, the other for its ethical framework: *Château d'Amour*, and *Templum Dei*. *Château d'Amour* is an allegorical poem written in Anglo-Norman French in octosyllabic couplets, and is addressed to an audience of lay readers, or more probably listeners, of high social standing – *Seigneurs*, as they are called in the text, which dates perhaps to the 1230s or 1240s.[37] The intended context was almost certainly household performance – and here one should recall Grosseteste's writing on household conduct in his *Statuta* and related French rules of around 1240 for the king's sister Hawise, Countess of Lincoln.[38] The audience is assumed to need instruction in elementary moral theology. What is interesting is the form this instruction takes, for the fundamental allegory, suggested by Luke 10: 38, *et (Jesus) intravit in quoddam castellum*, is that of a castle of up-to-date design, standing for the Virgin Mary.[39] The castle is thus an incarnational image.[40] It consists of a keep, four towers, baileys and seven barbicans. It is painted in three colours, green, blue and red, for Faith, Hope and Charity. In the midst of the keep is a well from which run four streams, and also an ivory throne with seven steps leading up to it.[41] The castle is a 'moralized' architecture, its floors, towers and barbicans being the Christian virtues that protect Mary from the assault of the sins, its great ivory throne the Solomonic Throne of Wisdom.[42] The text takes over the moral and theological possibilities of architectural allegory itself, as found in *De claustro animae* and the other texts produced within the Victorine milieu considered in Part I.

Here the great Bishop of Lincoln reveals his grasp of the tactics of what would now be called associative psychology. Memorable and effective pastoral writings should catch the imagination of the *Seigneurs* not only by the use of the vernacular, but also by deploying images attractive to the dominant (military) discourse of that particular class, so engaging it imaginatively in order to imprint sound doctrine on it. Grosseteste's debts not only to Victorine, but also to earlier English monastic speculation, are evident, and not the least of them was to the writings of the pseudo-Anselmian *Similitudo militis*.[43] In his analysis of the English illustrated manuscript of the widely known *Summa* of Vices (BL Harley MS 3244), written by the Dominican Peraldus around 1236 (fig. 147), Michael Evans has noted the relative frequency with which English spiritual writers from the twelfth century onwards deployed military metaphors and knightly allegories in the service of (typically monastic or anchoritic) spiritual edification, as in the *Ancrene Wisse*.[44] The illustrated Peraldus reveals a process similar to that of the contemporary *Château d'Amour*. The agenda in Peraldus is however much more austere. Grosseteste's military-religious pastoral allegory is much better attuned to the wider, lay, ethical perspective. Grosseteste was rather given to this sort of martial imagery. It was almost certainly he who first developed the so-called shield of faith or *scutum fidei* (as well as the 'shield of goodwill' and the 'shield of the heart') in his pre-1231 *dicta* (fig. 148).[45] Shield imagery was of course already

148 Shield of Faith. *Dicta* of Robert Grosseteste, Durham Cathedral MS A. III, fol. 14v, before 1231 (Durham Cathedral).

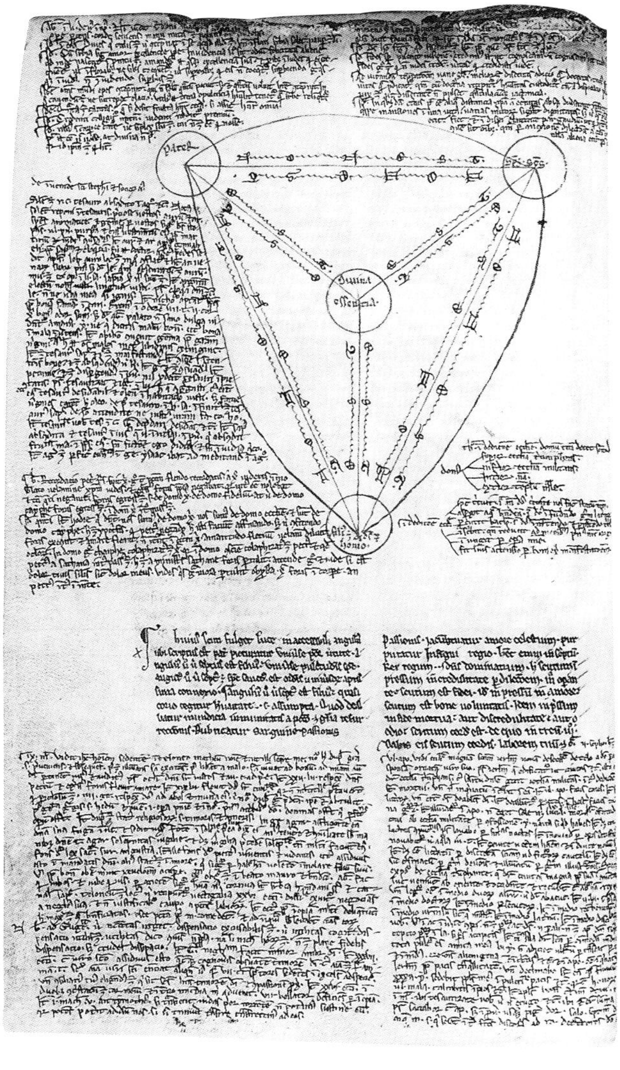

149 Shield of Faith. *Miscellanea* of John of Wallingford, circle of Matthew Paris, BL Cotton Julius D. VII, fol. 3v, *c.* 1250 (Conway Library, Courtauld Institute of Art).

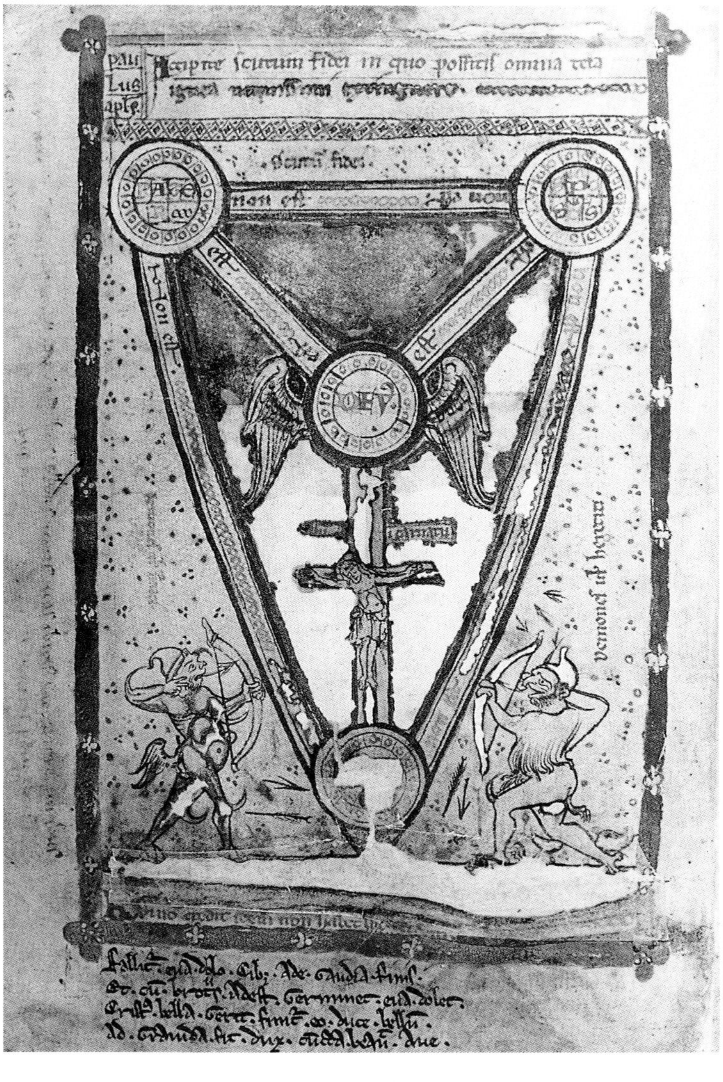

developed in the *Ancrene Wisse*'s celebrated theme of Christ the noble knight-lover, whose shield, reinforcement against evil and temptation, was his body spread on a cross, broad above and narrow beneath, where his feet tapered to overlap with a single nail; like a shield hung up in a church, the cross is raised up on the rood-beam to bring to mind Christ's chivalry.[46] This analogy from warfare was surely intended to move and captivate the upper-class women for whom the text was initially conceived.[47] Grosseteste's particular treatment of it is Trinitarian, and in this form it was quickly noted by the artist of the Peraldus *Summa* (whose knight in emblematic armour bears it); by Matthew Paris and his circle (fig. 149); and by the artist of the pastoral drawings suffixed to the Lambeth Apocalypse made in the 1260s for Eleanor de Quincy, Countess of Winchester, a lady of similar standing to the Countess of Lincoln.[48]

What had been rather specialized monastic and clerical ideas were now drawn into the instruction of the parish and household, so creating, in plan at least, a common symbolic language. The spread of *Château d'Amour* by the Franciscans outside England, as far indeed as Assisi, where it was to find its greatest pictorial exposition, is notable.[49] But even more striking is the possibility that the reversal of values it espoused was one important prelude to a much more widespread, and far from mendicant, phenomenon in England first known in the 1230s and 1240s in the court milieu: the introduction of military motifs of all types into the domain not only of secular, but religious architecture, in such a way that they became one of the defining features of the so-called Decorated Style.[50] Grosseteste's imagery of the virtuous tower and rampart is revolutionary precisely because, its reformist objective notwithstanding, it completely reverses the moral priorities of the older ascetic critique of militarization of the episcopal ethos encountered in the writings of Hugues de Fouilly and Peter the Chanter (p. 45 above). Once again, an English writer takes up the allegorical, but not the ethical, content of this critique. What once stood for supercilious pride and dangerous secularism is now equated with the most positive spiritual ideas conceivable. Grosseteste has in effect imported romantic notions of the Christian-chivalric mindset into a category of exposition – 'edificatory' exposition – whose original character was very different. Given the tone of twelfth-century prohibition, military-looking churches require more explanation than military-looking castles. The Christianization of the military ethos – the invention of chivalry – had long been under way; and it was perhaps inevitable that the reverse process, the militarization of the Christian ethos, would eventually accompany it, starting from the fundamentally monastic premise that the Christian struggle for virtue, far from being contemplative, is itself a kind of *agon*, or conflict.[51] But the entry of these ideas into mainstream pastoral thought was not thoroughly under way until the thirteenth century. *Château d'Amour* represents the new mindset in more than one way. Its imagery of an allegorical castle with multi-coloured towers and a keep enclosing an ivory throne coincides strikingly with the account of the visionary fortified city seen in the dream of Macsen Wledig in the *Mabinogion*, which A. J. Taylor juxtaposed very plausibly with the walls of Caernarvon, the masterpiece of Edward I's campaign of castle-building in Wales, and a cynosure of the new militarism.[52] *Château d'Amour* differs importantly in being religious allegory, not Celtic myth, and is unlikely to have been an alternative source for Caernarvon: but its vision of what a castle might look like is similar. It was 'in touch'. The key point, however, is that this text suggests that the tendency to see the militarization of church architecture as a form of secularization or romanticization over-simplifies the issue. It is tempting to consider the possibility that this new taste in architecture and the figurative arts owed at least something to the sanction not only of the romance ethos, but also of a pragmatic reversal of attitudes towards the moral and religious signification of the military, not least on the part of the period's most alert and responsible prelates. Such a reversal, even reappropriation, had, after all, occurred in the attitude of moral theology towards other social realities of the period.[53] The ideas were not necessarily new; what was new was their injection into the disciplinary and edificatory programme for the laity.

Grosseteste's roughly contemporary *Templum Dei* (or *Templum Domini*) also takes as its starting point the model-building 'edificatory' mode,[54] but it is a compilation of an altogether more schoolmasterly sort. It was written in the 1220s or 1230s with reference to Robert of Flamborough's *Liber poenitentialis*, and so, arguably in the light of Robert's Victorine associations.[55] A copy of it, together with other penitential texts, is included in the illustrated Peraldus just noted.[56] The basis is once more monastic, and it is worth noting that a copy of *Templum Dei* was in the hands of Walter of Bury St Edmunds, Abbot of Peterborough, by 1246.[57] However its purpose, very much in line with the bishop's pastoral injunctions of 1239, is to create a basic catechism or syllabus for parish priests.[58] The Temple in question is not the type of edificatory macrocosm described above in the context of Gilbert of Limerick's *De statu ecclesiae*, but rather the microcosm of the soul, the Temple within, more on the lines of Hugues de Fouilly's *De claustro animae*. As St Paul put it (I Corinthians 3: 16), his brethren

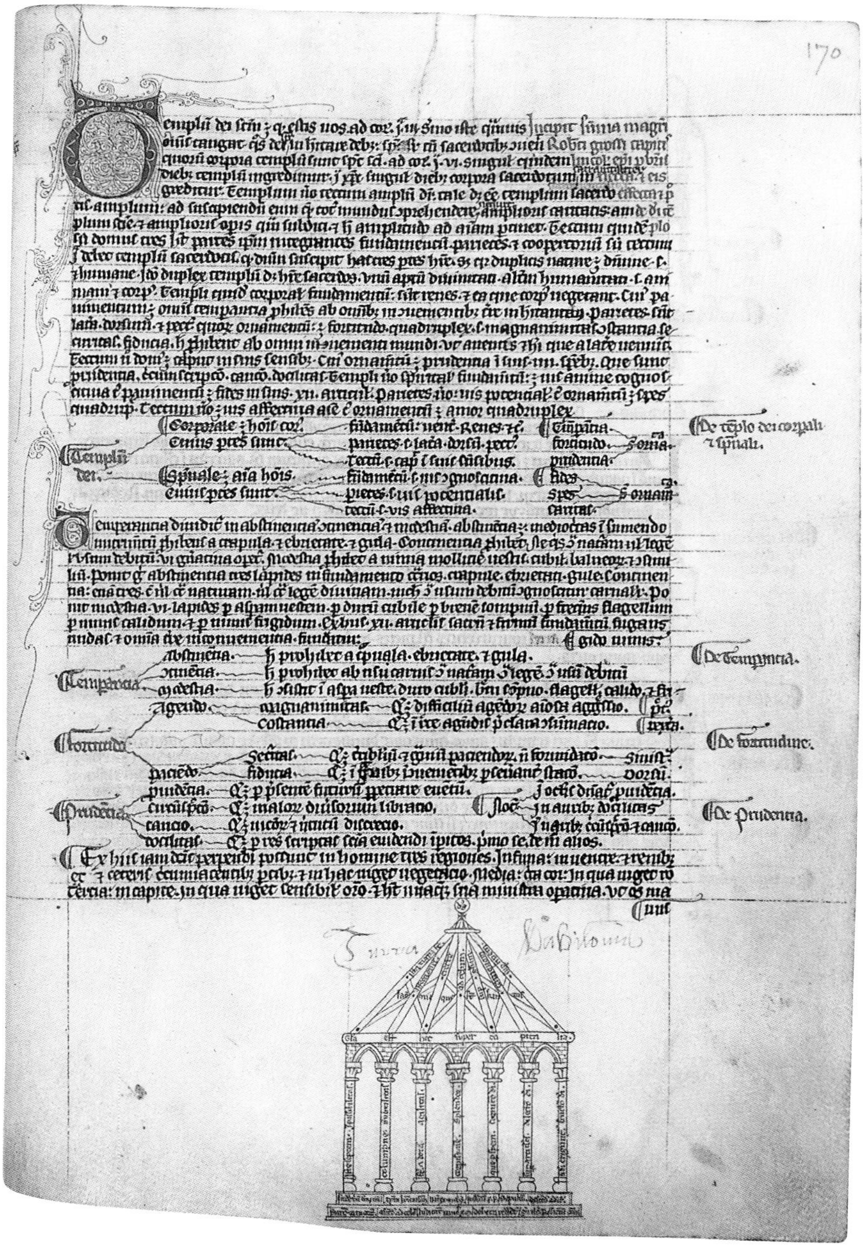

150 *Templum Domini* of Robert Grosseteste. CUL MS Add. 3471, fol. 170, mid-thirteenth century (by permission of the Syndics of Cambridge University Library).

are the Temple of God and the Spirit of God dwells within them, the Temple having a foundation of Faith, walls of Hope and a roof of Charity, the three theological virtues. The aim of life is the building up and preservation of this Temple. A mid-thirteenth-century copy of the text includes a small bas-de-page drawing of the Temple raised up on the basis of the Twelve Articles of Faith with seven pillars of Hope and a wooden roof of Charity (CUL Add. MS 3471, fol. 170; fig. 150). In keeping with this practical tone, *Templum Dei* proposes a dry, mnemonic ready-reference system divided up into *distinctiones*, a handy checklist of the Christian episteme taking the form of what would later be called a 'fist-book' or concise manual of no aesthetic pretension whatsoever, and mercifully shorter than Thomas of Chobham's *Summa confessorum*.[59] In layout it is barely more than a series of tables and lists, the type of thing that could usefully exploit the mnemonic value of 'sevens' in the setting out of a syllabus.[60]

Its interest here lies not only in its structure, but also in its ethical theory. Chapter 11 of *Templum Dei* sets out one possible model for the understanding of virtue in the context of penitenital examination.[61] In thinking about virtue and vice, one might ordinarily expect each to have its own opposite in a sort of binary model. Grosseteste, however, explains that every virtue has not one, but two, corresponding vices: a vice of excess and a vice of insufficiency, of which the virtue is the mean or medium. 'Faith' is thus the desired mean between its excess, *infidelitas* (the capacity to believe absolutely anything) and *perscrutacio* (the capacity to believe absolutely nothing); Hope is likewise the mean between its excess, *presumpcio*, and its deficiency, *desperacio*; and Charity is the mean of *inordinacio* and *odium*. This triadic system yields the pattern for the seven deadly sins, which, with the exception of Envy, are the deficiency of the virtues (thus Pride is the deficiency of Humility, its excess being Hypocrisy, and so on).[62] The model for this is obvious: Aristotle's doctrine of the mean, expounded in Book 2 of the *Ethics*, part of the Old Ethics discussed in the schools.[63] By the 1240s, Grosseteste was of course to furnish the mind of thirteenth-century Europe with the first complete translation of the *Ethics*, but it is clear from the exposition of the mean in *Templum Dei*, and from its Aristotelian division of the soul into vegetative, sensible and rational parts, that he had already been moving in this direction by the 1230s.[64] The same doctrine on human dispositions is to be found in Grosseteste's *De Confessione* (in which, it will be recalled, the bishop classified excessive asceticism oddly but logically with *curiositas*, the immoderate exercise of good works); and also in the text *Deus Est* attributed to him.[65] Echoes of this ethical structure were to be heard in high-art *pastoralia* like the *Somme le Roi* and throughout the parishes in the fist-books; Grosseteste himself advocated a systematic moderation of behaviour in his practical household *Statuta*;[66] and even the excessively pious St Edmund observed the doctrine of the mean in his account of *mesure* in his *Mirour*.[67] There is an important contrast here with the rigorous stoic tradition of patristic ethics, based on Cicero and Seneca and found in Peraldus, a tradition suited principally to the enclosed religious life.[68] The standards of this tradition were less than realistic for the secular Church. Grossteteste seems to have seen some connection between Aristotle's commonsense account of human disposition and the daily needs of the confessional. His Aristotelianism lends to his *pastoralia* an explicit and systematic moderation that, far from being alien or idiosyncratic, was becoming something like an ethical norm in confession.[69]

Picturing the Curriculum

Vernacular instruction in these matters was key, and reminds one that the didactic ethos of the period was committed to a range of teaching techniques which could not be premised solely upon having good Latin, which many priests, among whom there was but a small proportion of *magistri*, were judged from the diocesan viewpoint to lack.[70] To point this out is not to disparage the parish clergy as a whole. This issue of poor clerical latinity was recognized often enough by the diocesan authorities. The episcopal agenda, though contrasting in its ideals with some of the realities of the parish, was unavoidable.[71] In 1222 the Council of Oxford instructed archdeacons to make sure that parish priests could recite and understand at least the unvarying words of the canon of the Mass, a fairly elementary exercise.[72] Robert Grosseteste severely recommended that priests with weak Latin should turn to their neighbouring priests for instruction: his letters portray inadequate pastors as veritable slayers of souls.[73] Ignorance of basic liturgy that poor Latin brought about informs one story about St Thomas Becket. The small and very early Book of Hours illuminated around the middle of the century by the Oxford artist W. de Brailes includes a series of historiated initials to the Hours of the Virgin Mary; these relate the account of her intercessions on behalf of the priest Theophilus (fig. 212) and, from Sext through to Vespers, the story of the ignorant priest in the time of St Thomas who only knew one Mass, that of the Virgin herself (BL Add. MS 49999, fols 44v–58; fig. 151).[74] St Thomas, learning of this limitation to his office, duly suspends him, and harshly rejects his imploring, even in the initial to the consoling gradual Psalm 125. At this point the Virgin Mary herself rewards the devotion of the priest, by divulging to him the secret of how she herself bestowed upon the martyr his hair shirt (fig. 114). The priest wastes no time in reporting this intercession to St Thomas, who kneels before him, begs forgiveness, and reinstates him. The priest, however, has gained no new learning, for he immediately repeats the Mass of the Virgin in thanksgiving.[75]

In this miracle Mary rewarded faith before knowledge; the Church recognized that knowledge was the key to faith, and theology its premise; and it had to be accepted pragmatically that vernacular instruction in doctrine was inevitable, at least for the laity. Richard Poore's statutes of 1217–19 specified that the laity were

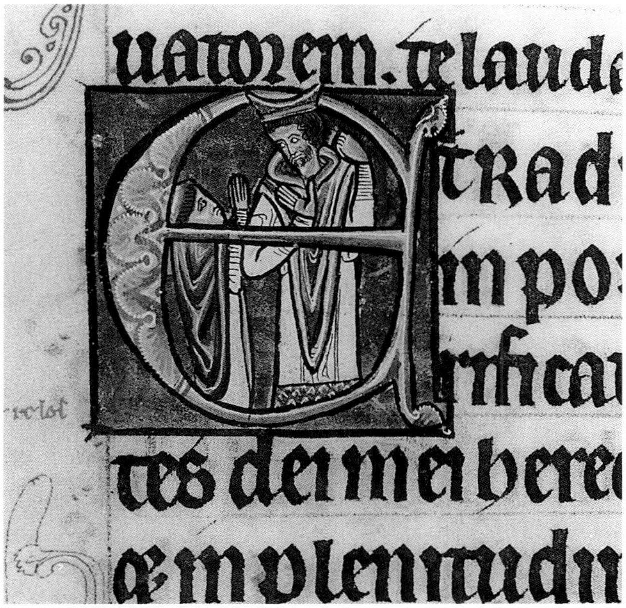

151 St Thomas rejects the petition of the illiterate priest. Hours of W. de Brailes, BL Add. MS 49999, fol. 50v, *c.* 1240 (Conway Library, Courtauld Institute of Art).

to be taught in their own languages, and similar provisions were made in the statutes for Worcester and Winchester.[76] Manuals of instruction were likely eventually to find their way into the home.[77] Preaching in the vernacular was common, and the role of the sermon itself had been reinforced by canon 10 of Lateran IV, *De praedicatoribus instituendis*, and by the establishment of the preaching orders.[78] Episcopal luminaries such as Stephen Langton were prolific writers of sermons.[79] Yet, texts such as the *Château d'Amour* aside, the great age of the vernacular manual, including manuals with illustrations, really only dawned in the second half of the thirteenth century, with what Boyle identified as a second wave of *pastoralia* aimed as much at the laity as the priesthood. This was the first great age of high-art pastoral discourse on the virtues and vices in such texts as the *Manuel des pechiez* and the *Somme le Roi*, and also the period when vernacular translations of favourite saints' lives became widespread, and the illustrated Apocalypse fashionable.[80]

The *Manuel des pechiez*, generally attributed to William of Waddington around 1260, is a vernacular verse handbook on the Creed, Ten Commandments, seven deadly sins, sacrilege, the seven sacraments and confession.[81] Only one illustrated copy survives, in a manuscript miscellany (Princeton University Library Taylor Medieval MS 1), with diagrams of the various 'sevens' and also telling examples – in effect the diocesan schedule of instruction made visually manifest. Some of the *exempla* are striking. The discussion of the sin of anger is illustrated by the tale of the merciful knight who spared the life of an opponent and was rewarded for his virtue with an embrace by the crucified Christ (fig. 152).[82] The text on the seven sacraments includes the unpleasant tale of the man who, not believing in Transubstantiation, is convinced by a vision at Mass of the Christ Child appearing in the elevated Host and then sacrificed and carved

152 The reward for overcoming the vice of anger: Christ embraces the merciful knight from the Cross. *Manuel des pechiez*, Princeton University Library, Taylor Medieval MS 1, fol. 44, late thirteenth century (Princeton University Library).

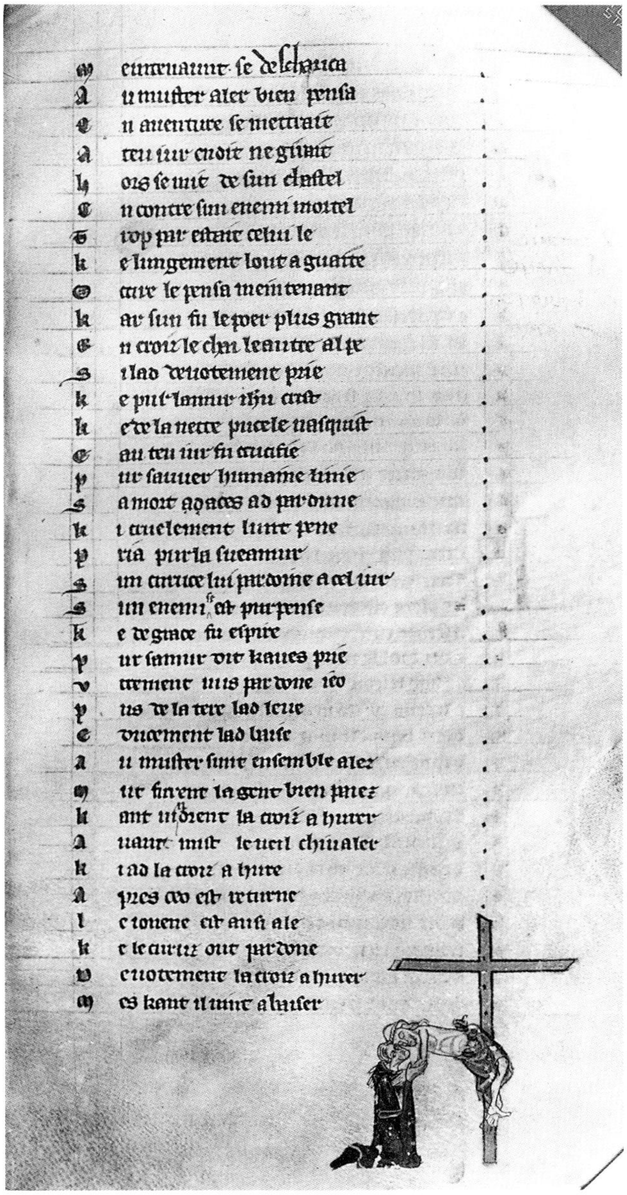

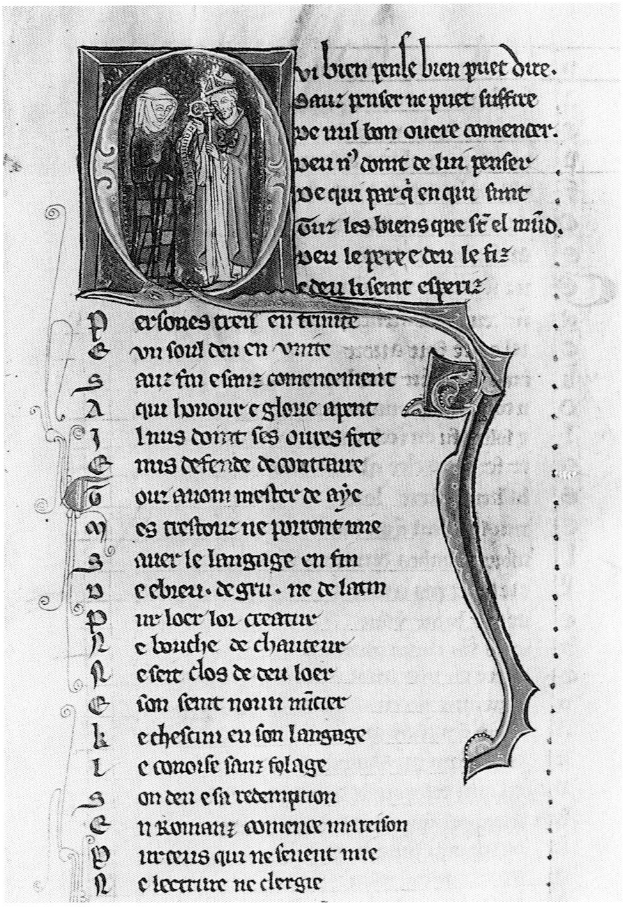

153 Joan Tateshal (d. 1310) face-to-face with 'Saint' Robert Grosseteste. *Manuel des pechiez*, Princeton University Library, Taylor Medieval MS 1, fol. 173, late thirteenth century (Princeton University Library).

up into small pieces. This miscellany also includes *Château d'Amour*. As Adelaide Bennett has indicated, the reason for this is not hard to find. The Princeton manuscript includes two representations of a woman in an heraldic mantle, identifiable as Joan Tateshal, the wife of Baron Robert Tateshal of Tattershall Castle in Lincolnshire.[83] One of them, showing Joan standing on equal terms with a bishop (fig. 153), precedes the text of *Château d'Amour*; the bishop is thus presumably Robert himself. The viewer is reminded of the stature of another aristocratic patroness of *pastoralia*, Isabel, Countess of Arundel, who was acquainted 'face to face' with the saint-bishops she so admired (p. 123 above).[84] In Joan's case the issue was local: her husband was one of the correspondents backing the ultimately unsuccessful canonization of Robert Grosseteste in the 1280s, around which time the manuscript was compiled and illustrated. Local too was the well-known English version of the *Manuel*, the text *Handlyng Synne* ('Handlyng' being a translation of 'manuel' but meaning also 'considering' or 'weighing up' in the reflective sense of the texts on confession) by Robert Mannyng of Brunne (i.e. Bourne, Lincolnshire), begun around 1303.[85]

The rarity of the Princeton manuscript proves how seldom texts of pastoral theology attracted figurative illustration. A gorgeously illuminated work on the virtues and vices (or sins) such as the *Somme le Roi*, compiled in 1279 by the Dominican confessor, Frère Laurent, for King Philippe III of France, was probably conceived to have illustrations (e.g. BL Add. MS 54180); but in this it was the representative of a very small class surrounded by an aesthetic wilderness.[86] Yet in keeping with its much more modest grass-roots cousins, the aim of the French *Somme* was remedial and deliberative: the seven deadly sins find their remedies in seven virtues which spring from the seven petitions of the *Pater noster*, which in turn spring from the seven Gifts of the Holy Spirit: thus Pride is remedied by Humility which springs from Fear of God, and so on.[87] In the illustrations in BL Add. MS 54180, attributed to Master Honoré and datable to the 1290s, each virtue is personified in queenly form, each sin is 'figured' by a personage from the Bible, and the virtue and the sin are then exemplified by 'types'. Thus Humility gracefully faces the Fall of King Ahaziah as the figure of Pride; and Humility and Pride are also typified by the contrite sinner and the conceited hypocrite, who in their behaviour mime their respective internal dispositions (fig. 154). This acting-out of moral disposition is important, for it is an indication of the means by which remedial theology could be invested in a tropology of behaviour, a topic I pursue below. For the present, note that only one major English work of art anticipates this formal exposition of the theology of sin: the orderly sculpted entrance portal of the chapter house at Salisbury, conceived and probably executed not long after around 1260.[88] The entrance consists of two cusped arches within a major arch sculpted with a single order of fourteen female crowned figures, seven to the north and seven to the south, with a central empty niche beneath (figs 155–6). As Rosalie Green demonstrated, the fourteen regal figures which triumph over their supine adversaries are personifications not merely of virtue overcoming vice but, in the case of the seven figures on the north side, specifically of the remedies for the seven sins, accompanied on the south by the three theological and four cardinal virtues.[89] The selection thus has a rather sharper focus on the theology of sin than more conventional displays of the *Psychomachia*. It is also highly likely to have been centred upon an image of the Virgin

Mary in the now vacant main niche. One might expect Marian iconography in this context, not least in view of the dedication of the church, but also because Marian imagery is often found at this place in great churches (as at Westminster Abbey and York Minster).[90] The presence of Mary as *sedes sapientiae*, with, to her right, the figures which Rosamund Tuve regarded as a 'Seven of gift virtues', would make absolute theological sense.[91]

Salisbury's chapter house and the *Somme* differ from a work such as the illustrated *Manuel des pechiez* in Princeton not least in regard to the formality of their methods of visual exposition. Salisbury was the beneficiary of the co-ordinated and articulated expository methods of French Gothic sculpted portals, put to the service of the style of moral theology presumably favoured by the Salisbury Cathedral chapter, of which the chapter house was the corporate expression. Other, rather less synthetic, methods were used in a very few illuminated spiritual miscellanies, of which an early example is the series of pictures suffixed to the Lambeth Apocalypse of the 1260s, which co-ordinates images of saints with images relating to the confessional or penance (e.g. Mary Magdalen with the cherub of the confessional, fols 48v–49; St Edmund of Abingdon with the allegory of penance, fols 52v–53).[92] The Psalter too could attract material of this type. The Oxford illuminator W. de Brailes must at least have conceived of Psalters that contained a range of homiletic material, of which a fragment survives (Cambridge, Fitzwilliam Museum MS 330).[93] Matthew Paris certainly did, since he not only planned a Psalter manuscript with additional hagiographical material for a Countess of Winchester, but there is a surviving Psalter for the use of the St Albans monk John of Dalling which includes this type of thing (BL Royal MS 2. B. VI).[94] Such works provide a context for the illustrations in the early fourteenth-century Psalter of Robert de Lisle (d. 1344) (BL Arundel MS 83 (II)).[95] This now-fragmentary work stands on the dividing line between the kind of diocesan didactic programme envisaged in 1281 by *Ignorantia sacerdotum*, and the mirrors of theology compiled by mendicant writers, in this case the so-called *Speculum theologie* by John of Metz, a Franciscan.[96] Robert de Lisle evidently had Franciscan leanings, as he became a tertiary in 1341.[97] The Psalter pays direct compliment to the cosmology of the Franciscan John Pecham by including his 'sphere', and is distinguished by an entire string of smoothly arranged theological diagrams organized according to the symbolic numbers, including such fundamentals as the Ten Commandments, the Twelve Articles of Faith, a Wheel of Sevens (fig. 146) and that practical epitome of the confessional, the cherub with lettered wings, which are interspersed with Gospel narratives and full-page miniatures, climaxing with John of Metz's *Turris sapiencie* (fig. 157), a superb and entirely crenellated example of the now familiar 'edificatory' agenda for building up virtue, including even modest illustrations to Grosseteste's *Templum Dei*.[98] No satisfactory reason suggests itself as to why the Gospel illustrations, whose tone is exceedingly cool, were combined in the way they were with these versions of scholastic theology; the absence in this work of hagiographical illustrations, by now the natural way to amplify a Psalter aside from Gospel stories, deserves comment in view of

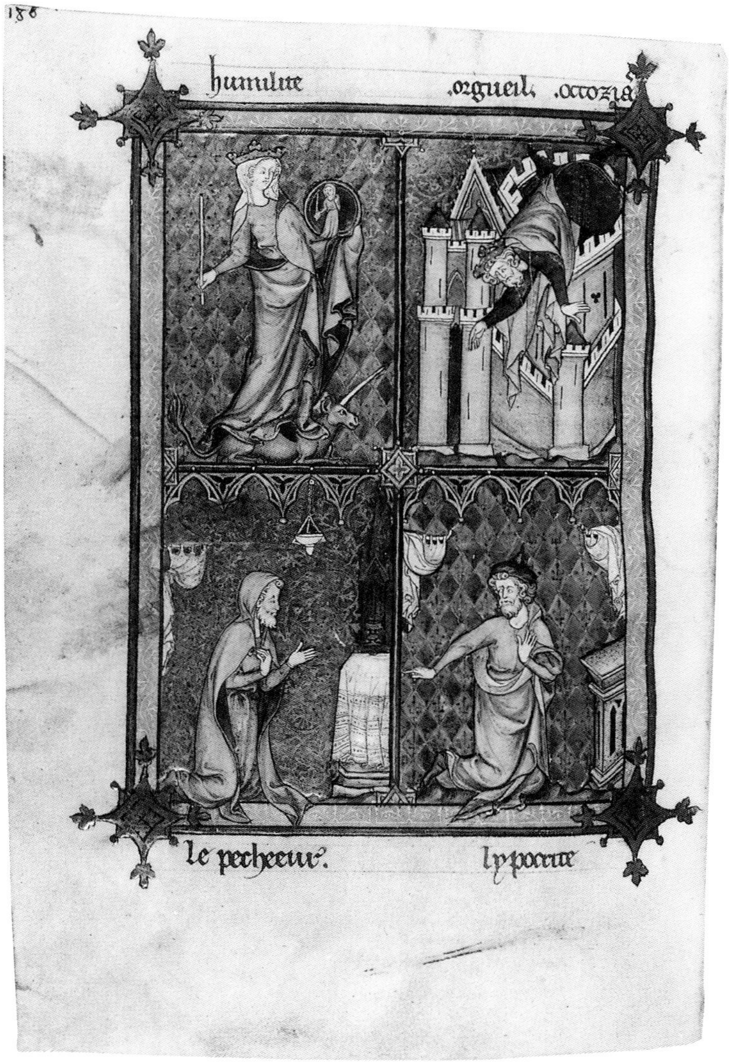

154 Humility personified, top left, with biblical 'figure' of the sin of Pride, King Ahaziah falling; below, humility is typified by the contrite sinner confessing from his heart, hypocrisy (the excess of humility in the Aristotelian moral scheme) looking back in distraction. Parisian *Somme le Roi*, BL Add. MS 54180, fol. 97v, 1290s (by permission of the British Library).

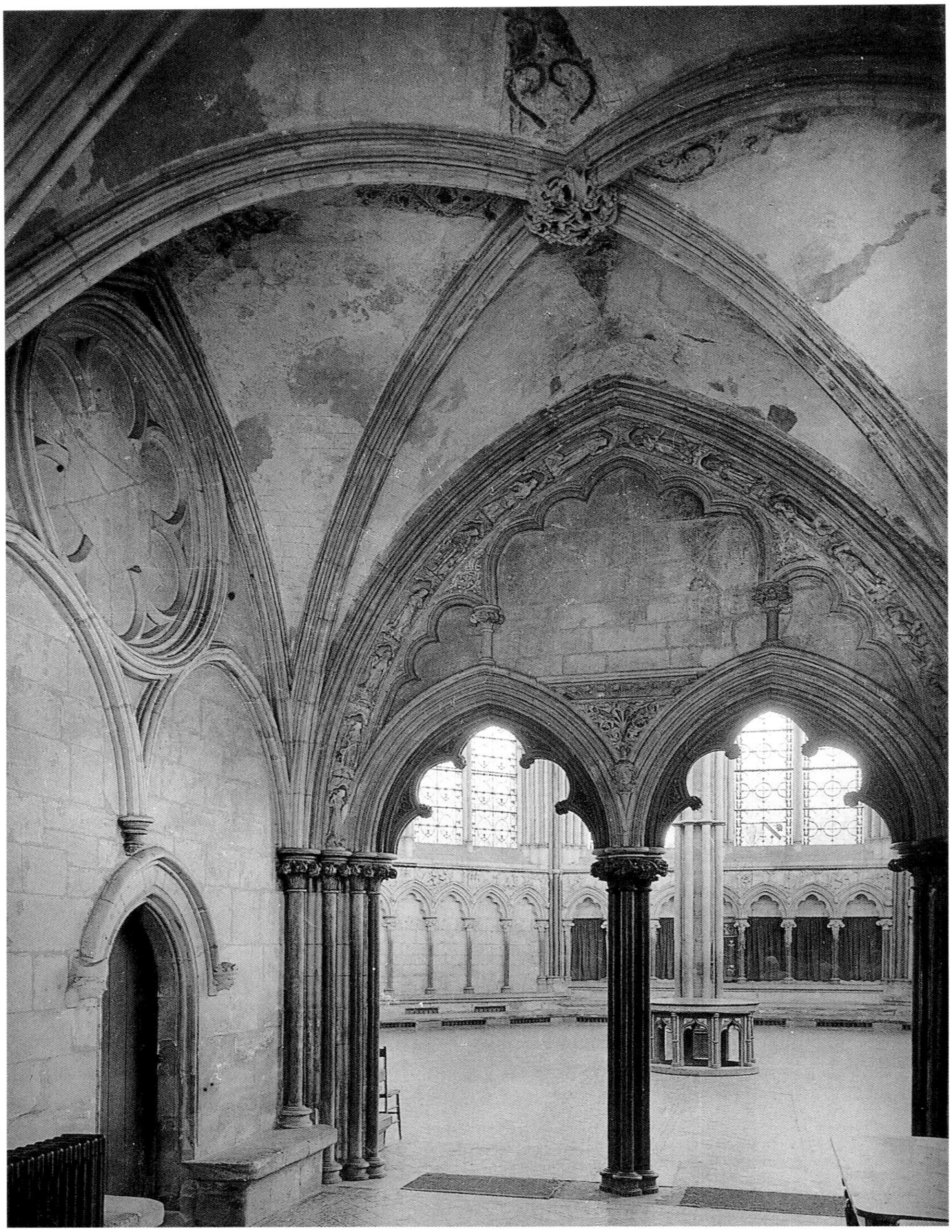

155 Salisbury Cathedral, chapter house entrance (Conway Library, Courtauld Institute of Art).

this slightly detached quality. What matters is the general model of knowledge that this sort of compilation was intended to instil. That the final effect is one of chilly elegance should not obscure the range of techniques at the disposal of those who planned, or at least compiled, such programmes.

The relationship between compilation and planning is of some wider interest. The De Lisle Psalter was not unusual in being the product of more than one campaign of work, in the course of which the elastic character of the miscellany format was realized by the addition or substitution of new images for old within a manufacturing time span of some three decades (*c.* 1310–39). So common is the format of the miscellany in such pastoral sequences that it itself takes on, or seems to take on, the character of an organizing principle. Few

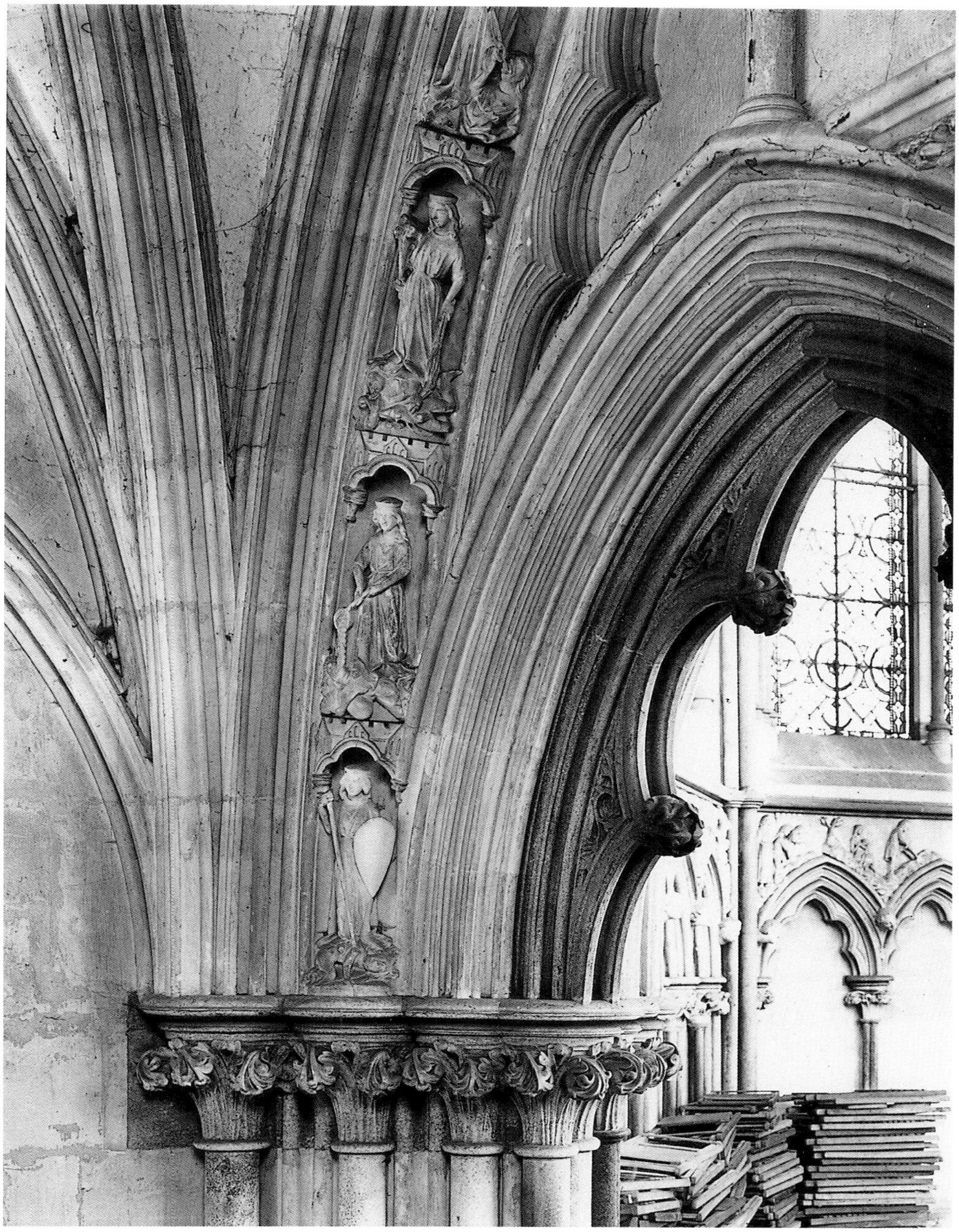

156 Salisbury Cathedral, chapter house entrance, detail of virtues (Conway Library, Courtauld Institute of Art).

such miscellanies are absolutely random, but their overall structural premises often seem more covert than explicit, and sheer happenstance, brought about by the availability or non-availability of texts for copying, may have been a factor in the shaping of compilations of the more utilitarian sort.[99] A text such as *Templum Dei*, disposed in strings of discrete units or schemas of practical instruction which are incomprehensible to those ignorant of the texts, nevertheless seems quite alien to modern literary sensibilities.[100] Similar issues arise in the understanding the sometimes paratactic or disconnected logic, the 'logic which escapes us' in David d'Avray's apt phrase, of the sermon form, which could differ greatly from the forms of thought of scholasticism.[101] Such forms had intrinsic organizing principles, principles which cannot necessarily be established by looking outside the forms

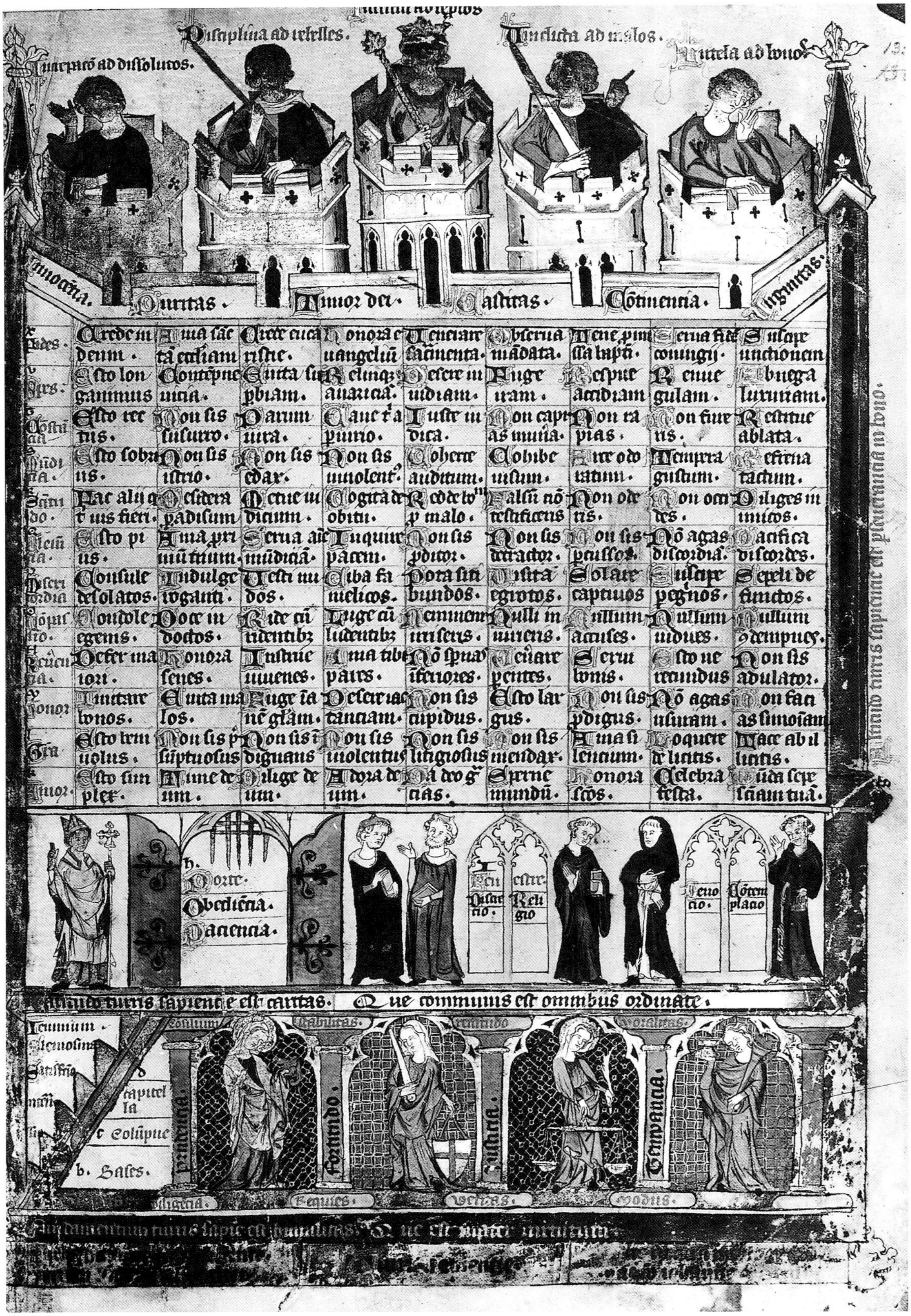

157 Tower of Wisdom. Psalter of Robert de Lisle, BL Arundel MS 83 (II), fol. 135, early fourteenth century (by permission of the British Library).

themselves: some admittedly were liturgical, others may have been spelt out in the *ars praedicandi*; others may just have been aesthetic, in keeping with the Horatian principle that the poet must please in order to instruct.[102] So much also appears to have been true of the medley-like organizational regimes of contemporary parish church wall paintings, which also defy judgement in terms of universal literary or decorative traditions. Here again, the medium was to an extent the message.[103] Church wall paintings (few of which betray any signs of the impact of the new syllabus of belief much before 1300) may on occasion be seen to exhibit the pastoral regime of the miscellany of commonplaces, a regime in some ways ideally suited to the contingencies of wall-space, and much less imaginable in, for example, the Gothic stained-glass window.[104] Gothic murals may also reveal that tropological subtlety, that sense of the impact of an image on day-to-day life, so apparent (indeed apparent for the first time on a large scale in the documentation of medieval art) in the highly strategic specifications for image placement in the Chancery mandates of Henry III for the painted decoration of his palaces.[105] Research into the structuration and tropology of wall paintings of this period has scarcely begun: for the present one may note in them the possibility, perhaps not new to this period but certainly more widespread and developed, of a specifically thematic moral and aesthetic intelligence.

St Edmund's Speculum

How this intelligence came to be related to religious sensibility and daily life – the worthiest practical objective of moral theology – may best be understood by looking at the highly influential pastoral writing of the ascetic and contemplative Archbishop of Canterbury, St Edmund of Abingdon (d. 1240), specifically the text he wrote well before 1234 (probably between 1210 and 1220) most commonly known as the *Speculum ecclesiae*. As already emphasized, St Edmund was a formidable example of ascetic and academic episcopal sainthood, a quasi-monastic role model in life. An early version of the *Speculum* is entitled *Speculum religiosorum*, suggesting that its original purpose was pastoral guidance for enclosed religious, including women. A sign of this last possibility is that the early manuscripts are dominated by an Anglo-Norman French version of the text, the *Mirour de Seinte Eglyse*, and before 1300 it was in this form that the text became arguably the most important spiritual work of its type composed in thirteenth-century England; later it passed into English.[106] The *Speculum* is a classic instance of the transmission of ideas from the monastic to the lay world. It is a treatise on perfect living, which takes the form of a concise manual of moral theology combining the insights of the penitentialists with advice about techniques of contemplation that owe a great deal to the Cistercians and Victorines; H. P. Forshaw showed conclusively that its debt to patristic thought and to St Bernard is explicit, its borrowings from Hugh of Saint-Victor being palpable, but more covert.[107] As a 'speculative' text, the *Speculum* is in fact one of the most coherent signs of those various currents of influence from the Cistercians, Augustinians and the schools noted repeatedly throughout this study, not least in the context of contemporary sanctity.[108] These currents serve to shed light on the intellectual origins of the syllabus in *Ignorantia sacerdotum*, which has one or two points of similarity with it.[109] Its wide currency as a Latin and vernacular text ensured that the *Speculum* did for formal moral theology and monastic meditative techniques what the Book of Hours did for the Breviary, namely to epitomize and broaden access. St Edmund is in a sense the English Bonaventure.

In structure and content the *Speculum* is a guide to intellectual and spiritual ascent. It asks first what it is to live perfectly. The answer (basically Cistercian) lies in part in friendship, humility and honour, but also in the possession of self-knowledge in heart and soul.[110] We are invited to ask ourselves diligently and frequently what we are, what we have been, and what we shall eventually be, for through self-interrogation comes self-knowledge, and self-knowledge is destiny.[111] This is gained specifically by the speculative contemplation of God as revealed in his creation, and in scripture. By scripture is understood the catechetical programme, the Ten Commandments, the Creed, virtues, the other 'sevens' and so on – the scheme of the 'sevens' coming from Hugh of Saint-Victor's *De quinque septenis*. God is then contemplated in his humanity in a series of fourteen meditations before the canonical hours of the Office, specific events or 'mysteries' in Christ's life being the object of reflection at the appointed time. In the last exercises completing this chain of speculation, God is pondered in his divinity in three final stages of contemplation.

It is not difficult to see why this text had appeal, for it offers a focus and a sense of direction both intellectual and contemplative – a sort of journey of the soul – seldom found in other pastoral compilations.[112] No part of it was without impact; but for the purposes of this book the most telling chapters are those which relate to the contemplation of God's humanity in Christ. The reason for this is twofold: their overall scheme was influential, and their mapping-out of the actual character of devotional attention and disposition – its affect – was set out in a more detailed and explicit fashion than in most other texts. The scheme of meditating upon historical events, whether biblical or hagiographic, before or at the Hours is the one aforementioned in the illuminated Hours by W. de Brailes, with its story of St Thomas and the illiterate priest, distributed at intervals in the Hours of the Virgin. It was in no sense St Edmund's invention. Indeed as Forshaw and others have shown, it substantially pre-dated the thirteenth century.[113] The custom of linking episodes of Christ's Life to the Offices is found in Beleth's *Rationale* and in Rupert of Deutz.[114] As in the case of the De Brailes Hours, the events could be set out diachronically, in narrative order; but it was also possible to divide a narrative up synchronically, or thematically. Edmund adopted the latter approach in the *Speculum*, in which the Hours are prefaced by two sets of episodes for meditation, usually including events from the Passion, shuffled out of Gospel order.[115] Before Vespers, for example, the meditation on the Deposition of Christ from the Cross precedes that for the Last Supper. This reordering, isolating episodes from their narrative context deliberately in order to establish other relationships ('Joys of the Virgin Mary' and the Passion, for instance) is highly artificial, and necessarily regulated.[116] For one thing the focus of devotional attention is strictly the text of the Vulgate itself: the *Speculum* is unusual among pastoral manuals in eschewing extended allegories, *exempla*, tables and *schemata* and, unlike Franciscan compilations of the same sort (e.g. the *Meditations* of the pseudo-Bonaventura), apocryphal Gospel narrative material.[117] For another, the objective is to render the objects of devotional attention available in an absolutely affective way. Fragmentation becomes a contemplative aid: events in the 'past', and details within those events, are severed from their temporal continuum in order that they might be relocated in the contemplative subject's imaginative 'present'. The meditation before Matins says that one should diligently consider the time, place and hour of the Gospel event in question.[118] This is obviously a technique for mental and emotional 'focus' on images, symbols, states into which one should enter imaginatively in the here and now. As a style of engagement it is active and affective, and in no sense passive.[119] It makes practical demands on the subject.

It also provided practical options for planners of prayer books. By about 1290 the *Speculum* had made a substantive impact in its programme of meditation before the canonical Hours, as can be gauged by the illuminations of the Hours of the Virgin in the Nuremberg Hours (Nuremberg, Stadtbibliothek Solger 4.4°), a hybrid Anglo-French manuscript (English script, French illuminations) executed wholly or partly in Paris in the 1290s for a highly placed patron with English connections.[120] The manuscript includes images of St Thomas and St Edmund of Abingdon (fig. 158), St Edmund the Martyr and St Osyth, the rare office of St Thomas appropriately following the Hours of the Trinity, and an English and especially Canterbury-influenced calendar and litany.[121] Whoever framed the illuminations of the Hours of the Virgin also had access to a Latin, or perhaps more probably French, version of the *Speculum*, to which access in France was just as likely, given Edmund's revered standing at the French court and his shrine at Pontigny.[122] The Gospel sequences before the Hours (fig. 159) are in the same order as those of St Edmund's scheme.[123] Another point of harmony may be the initial to the fifteen Gradual Psalms (fol. 179v): this shows a woman ascending in prayer to God up a staircase with

158 St Thomas and St Edmund of Abingdon, St Nicholas and St James. Nuremberg Hours, Nuremberg, Stadtbibliothek Solger MS 4.4°, fol. 17v, 1290s (Stadtbibliothek Nuremberg).

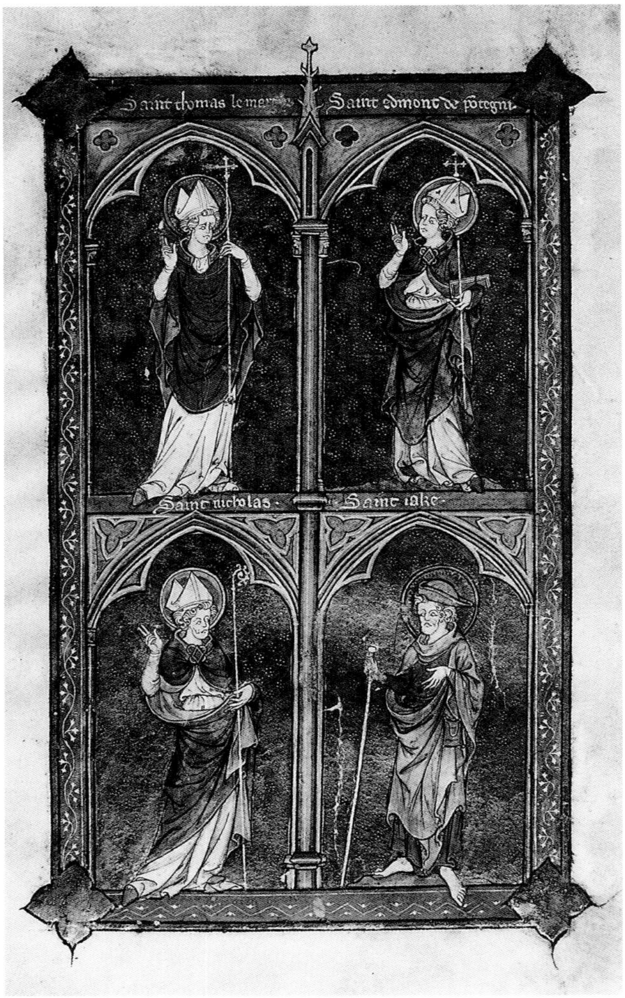

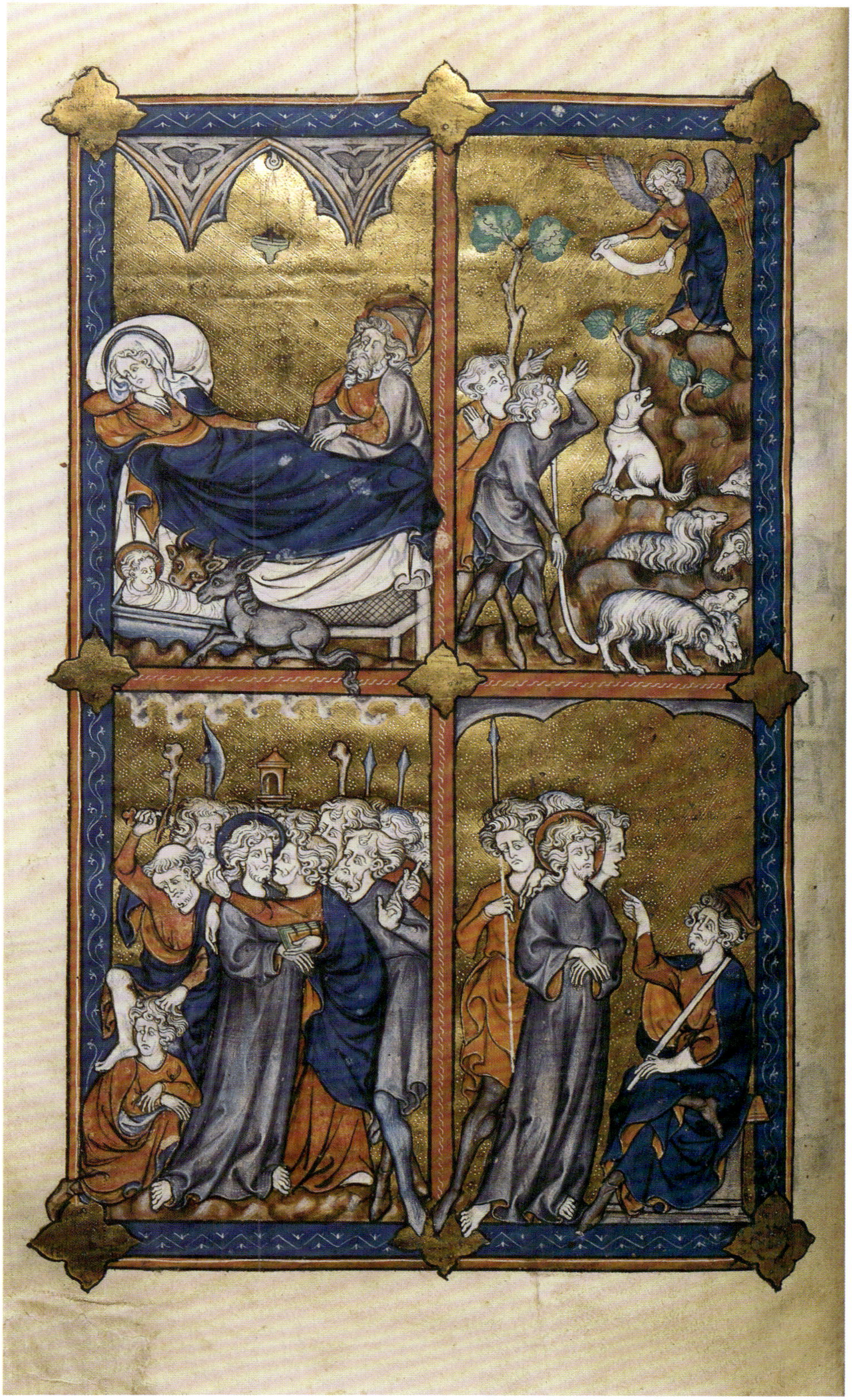

159 Meditation before Lauds, Nuremberg Hours, Nuremberg, Stadtbibliothek Solger MS 4.4°, fol. 39v, 1290s (Stadtbibliothek Nuremberg).

fifteen steps (fig. 160); she stands either for the soul, *anima*, or perhaps for the patroness, on the final contemplative ascent to union with God, according to the Gregorian and Bernardine climactic scheme of mystical prayer with which the *Speculum* culminates.[124] The basis of this overall discipline was the contemplation of history

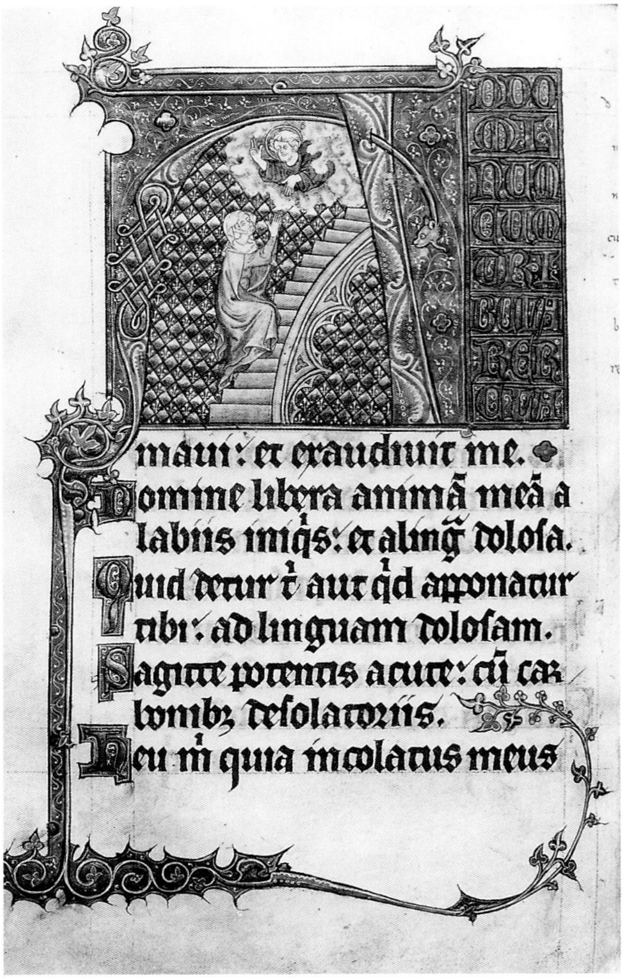

160 The progress of the soul/patroness up the 15 steps of the 15 gradual Psalms, to God. Nuremberg Hours, Nuremberg, Stadtbibliothek Solger MS 4.4°, fol. 179v, 1290s (Stadtbibliothek Nuremberg).

as the foundation for allegorical, and so spiritual, understanding in Victorine thought; the particular genius of the *Speculum* lies exactly in its resolution of Victorine doctrinal formality and *lectio* with Cistercian empathetic spirituality.

This connection also accounts for another technique in the *Speculum* directly related to this imperative of making the Gospel imaginatively present: the 'inflaming' of affection.[125] Edmund will have encountered this technique in the affective prayers of his precursor at Canterbury, St Anselm, notably his second prayer to Christ in which Anselm laments his absence at Christ's Passion: contemplative and imaginative absorption restores that which should so willingly have been present.[126] From Hugh of Saint-Victor this conscious exploration of affect can be traced through the writings of Alexander Nequam, who himself cultivated meditation on the Gospel by the aid of forming vivid mental pictures, articulated in affective language: 'Therefore let us form before the eye of the mind the Mother of sweetness and the Son, sweetness itself, embracing each other'.[127] The use of mental and sensory, especially visual, imagery to excite compunction, *ad excitandum compunctionem*, is recommended by Alexander of Canons Ashby, and is implicit in many English religious lyrics on the Passion.[128] Edmund, like Alexander Nequam, is fond of vivid affective and sensory vocabulary. Thus at Matins, the *Speculum* advises one to think of the diligent care taken of her Son by Mary, and of the great joy of Joseph; of the sweet throng (*dulci turba*) of angels; of the coldness of the season (*quando maximus frigus fuit*); of the hardness of the hour of midnight (*hora durissima*); and of the bitterness (*amaritudine*) of Christ's sufferings: diligence, joyfulness, sweetness, bitterness, coldness, hardness.[129] Such meditations engage the senses rather more comprehensively than some authorities on the affective lyrics of the period have maintained.[130] To judge from the common use of *dulci*, *dulcis*, *dulciter*, *magna dulcedine* and *dulcissima*, 'sweetness' is an especially common attribute of Christ, Mary and the angels, and the reader will have cause to savour this (by no means original) attribute again at a later point in this study.[131] Edmund invites the worshipper at None to ponder Christ's seven last words, a very early instance of this new devotion. These are all cues for imaginative absorption in a 'mysticism of the historical event' in which 'imaging' has a central role in both intellectual and affective persuasion.[132] Self-knowledge, like historical insight, is the outcome of a process rooted in contemplative particularity of awareness which can be disciplined by skill, in order to effect spiritual insight and remedy, and so to rise from 'the pleasing qualities of objects to the real presence of divine grace' in a way in which 'the pleasures of sensation could be justified as a new means for edification'.[133] But in the link between affect and effect – *affectus-effectus* – lies art as well as skill: the recognition that imagination and contemplation could, and should, be an ethical catalyst, galvanizing and shaping (and of course also managing) the emotions. These were lessons that the Middle Ages learned from

Aristotle and Horace; Edmund's version of it was attractive because it was no less fundamentally poetic, creating in Forshaw's words 'a landmark in the history of medieval religious sentiment'.[134] As demonstrated above, it was also of practical importance.

What to Do and Think at Mass

In advising worshippers what to do, what to think about, when, and with what sentiment, the *Speculum* of St Edmund provides a deliberate, coherent and influential paradigm for another type of relationship, whose nature will be of mounting importance in the rest of this study: that between inner and outer human conduct. Edmund's text, in its French, Latin and (later and fuller) English versions, is a text on self-discipline, carrying out into the lay world patterns of internal and external conduct, spiritual deportment, developed earlier in monasticism but given shape and new authority by the ethical, logical, legal and religious culture of the schools. In her extraordinary work on the constitutive importance of such patterns and their dissemination, patterns that often took metaphorical shape in the language of the habit or model, Caroline Walker Bynum has shown how such metaphors 'express intense concern for conforming personal behaviour and community life to prescribed patterns [. . .] the precondition for the flowering of souls towards God. Thus the affectivity or psychological subtlety so emphasized in recent interpretations of the twelfth century is rooted in a new concern with external behaviour.'[135] In saluting this fundamental insight one needs to enquire a little further into how this new concern took practical form in the secular Church in thirteenth-century England. That it was gaining in psychological subtlety may be ascertained from the new language of enquiry into circumstances, and of religious affect, that Gothic *tendresse*, of the new religious lyrics and pastoral manuals; and also by a delicate, but perceptible and optimistic, shift of priorities in the confessional arena, away from a negative emphasis on vice-to-be-exorcised and towards a positive remedial emphasis on virtue-to-be-cultivated.[136] The virtuous reform and discipline of conduct was thus a preventative rather than remedial activity.

The ethical and aesthetic ramifications of this current of thought are explored further below. For the present I need to place some emphasis on the shaping of the actual practice of belief, implicit in St Edmund's *Speculum*, and increasingly explicit elsewhere in the sphere of grass-roots religious conduct: one obvious focus for this is the issue of conduct in church. There was comparatively little legislation about this until the ecumenical pronouncements of the Second Council of Lyons, held in 1274, especially the canon regulating the immunity of churches from secular business.[137] According to canon 25, churches should be entered humbly and devoutly; behaviour inside should be calm, a source of instruction and mental refreshment (this generalized notion of lay behaviour as 'instructive' is striking but consistent with notions of discipline developing since the twelfth century). In fulfilment of the text *ut in nomine Iesu omne genua flectat*, 'at the name of Jesus every knee should bow' (Philippians 2: 10), at Mass each should 'bow the knees of his heart' at the mention of that glorious name, which can be done even by a bow of the head. The liturgy should possess the whole heart and mind. Idle (*vana*), foul and profane talk, gossip (*confabulationes*), must cease. Everything that may disturb divine worship or offend the eyes of God should be absolutely foreign to churches. This increasingly stern regime manifested itself in England in a variety of ways, often misogynistic. The *Speculum* of St Edmund exhorts those in good health to rise regardless of sleepiness, cold or fatigue, go to church and say Matins devoutly, or at least hear it without chatter.[138] The topic of Tutivillus, the devil perched over gossiping or 'jangling' women who records their nattering, recurs in *Handlyng Synne*.[139] From the late thirteenth century corrective parish church wall paintings appear, showing Tutivillus and the women who, as at Melbourne (Derbyshire), jointly hold a mirror, the symbol of their *vana colloquia* and of catoptromancy, divination by mirrors.[140]

The moralities spawned by the Council of Lyons were thus largely prohibitive, and they create some considerable scope for wondering how generally unstructured or inarticulate lay behaviour in church might have been shaped by positive precept. Here comments on conduct at Mass are useful. As mentioned above (p. 153), around 1200 Parisian thinkers such as Peter of Roissy noted that certain activities accompanied the elevation of the Host, such as that the congregation raised their joined hands and bowed.[141] Precept was clearly related to practice: Peter was describing a gesture that was being illustrated precisely in English art by the 1250s, as on folio 21 of the *Estoire* of St Edward in Cambridge, St Edward's vision of the Christ Child in the Host (fig. 126). In England the way action at this moment of the Mass is prescribed varies and develops. As early as 1222–5, synodal statutes specify that at the sight of the Host the people should immediately genuflect and join their hands; the Exeter statutes of 1287 exhort parishioners to bow, to genuflect, to adore the Host with suitable reverence.[142]

Yet, as already suggested in this discussion of St Edmund's writings, precept could extend to more than action at one specific moment, and the evidence for this is to be found first towards the end of the thirteenth century in the category of vernacular manuals edited under the title layfolk's Mass books.[143] An important illustrated Anglo-Norman French example illuminated somewhere in south-eastern England or East Anglia dates to the first decades of the fourteenth century (BN MS fr. 13342). This short manuscript is in small and eminently handy format, and, like many pastoral works, is a compilation. Its two main texts are the Anglo-Norman French version of St Edmund's *Speculum ecclesiae* and a short tract on the Mass in Anglo-Norman French beginning *Ceo qe vous deuez fere e penser a chascon point de la Messe*, 'What you should do and think at each point of the Mass'.[144] The text was illuminated by artists associated with the great Queen Mary Psalter, who also illuminated the only surviving English example of the *Somme le Roi* (Cambridge, St John's College MS S. 30 (256)).[145] In the Paris manuscript the text of the *Mirour de seinte Eglyse* is prefaced by a fine initial of St Edmund preaching, while that on the Mass contains thirteen text miniatures which offer, as the heading indicates, a sort of step-by-step *vade mecum* for lay deportment, physical and mental, during the rite, which is shortened into an epitome. This manuscript is only one example from the Queen Mary Psalter group to show an interest in the depiction of ritual actions at Mass; another is the finely illustrated Sherbrooke Missal, which includes initials depicting ritual actions by the priest at Mass.[146] But in the Paris manuscript the focus is on the laity. Each stage of the Mass acts as a cue to conduct or reflection, 'conduct' being specified by the images acting as a directory, 'reflection' by the text and images together acting as an *ordo*. The distinction is not unlike that found in the increasingly numerous illustrated liturgical manuscripts of the late Middle Ages. Where the manual differs, however, is in its extreme compression, which owes much to the tendency to abbreviate and epitomize liturgical texts for clerical use.[147] Note that none of the congregation represented in the tract holds a book: the ideal was presumably that its substance could easily be memorized, not least because it could be fairly easily represented.

This text differs too in the way in which the stages of the liturgy of the preface and canon of the Mass are marked out as imaginative or discursive prompts. On folio 45 the congregation and deacon kneel behind the priest at the altar for the Confiteor, the image-text spelling out the response and the instruction 'next, say your Confiteor devoutly'. This is followed by the Introit, where the picture-space is partly occupied by an image of the Harrowing of Hell in response to the instruction (doubtless prompted by the prayers for the dead at the start of the Mass), 'Think (*Pensez*) of the desire the holy patriarchs and prophets had for their release by Our Lord'. At the Kyrie eleison (fol. 45v) the instruction 'Think of the humility of his incarnation and birth, the gentleness (*deboneireté*) of His Life and Death, and the sweetness (*douzor*) of His Resurrection and Ascension' is accompanied by appropriate Gospel pictures as imaginative cues (fig. 161). At the *Sanctus* the people stand. At the elevation, in a particularly spectacular picture stretching across a whole opening (fols 46v–47), the entire congregation kneels as the bells are tolled and as the Crucified Redeemer appears over the altar (fig. 129). The bell is rung for the benefit of all, whether in church, 'or in the fields or houses', in the language of the diocesan regulations.[148] The instruction here is 'Lift up your joined hands and say nicely and not raucously *Dominus Meus*' (i.e. the *Te Deum*), ending with the admonition that each should 'speak personally to the sweet Jesus Christ'. The canon of the Mass then becomes the prompt for the catechism, starting with the Our Father, at which the people stand, then the seven deadly sins, Ten Commandments and seven gifts of the Holy Spirit at the *Agnus Dei* (fig. 162), fraction and communion.

Several points will be clear from this summary. The first concerns the striking discursive similarities between the instructions in the tract and the *Mirour* which must explain in part why they are bound up together.[149] Note the repeated use of the word *Pensez*, and the affective vocabulary deployed for the devotions: compare the sentiment *Pensetz la humilité de sa encarnacion e de sa nessance la deboneireté de sa vie e de sa mort la douzor de sa resurrection e de sa assencion* at the Kyrie eleison, with the text before the first meditation before Matins in the *Mirour*, *De sa humanité devez penser .iii. choses: la humilité de sa incarnacion, la duceur de sa conversacion, la charité de sa passion*.[150] The second is the way in which the Mass is used to provide a series of devotional cues in the tract, in the same way as the Hours of the Office are used in the *Mirour*. The third is the integration of catechetical material into devotional activity itself: the syllabus and religious practice have become one. Had St Edmund ever planned such a book, this is what it might have looked like. Did the compilers of MS français 13342 indeed believe that Edmund was the tract's author?

The final point relates to representation itself. Layfolk are being taught how to pray, and when to stand or kneel, through the 'Gregorian' medium of pictures which allows them to learn more than the text might

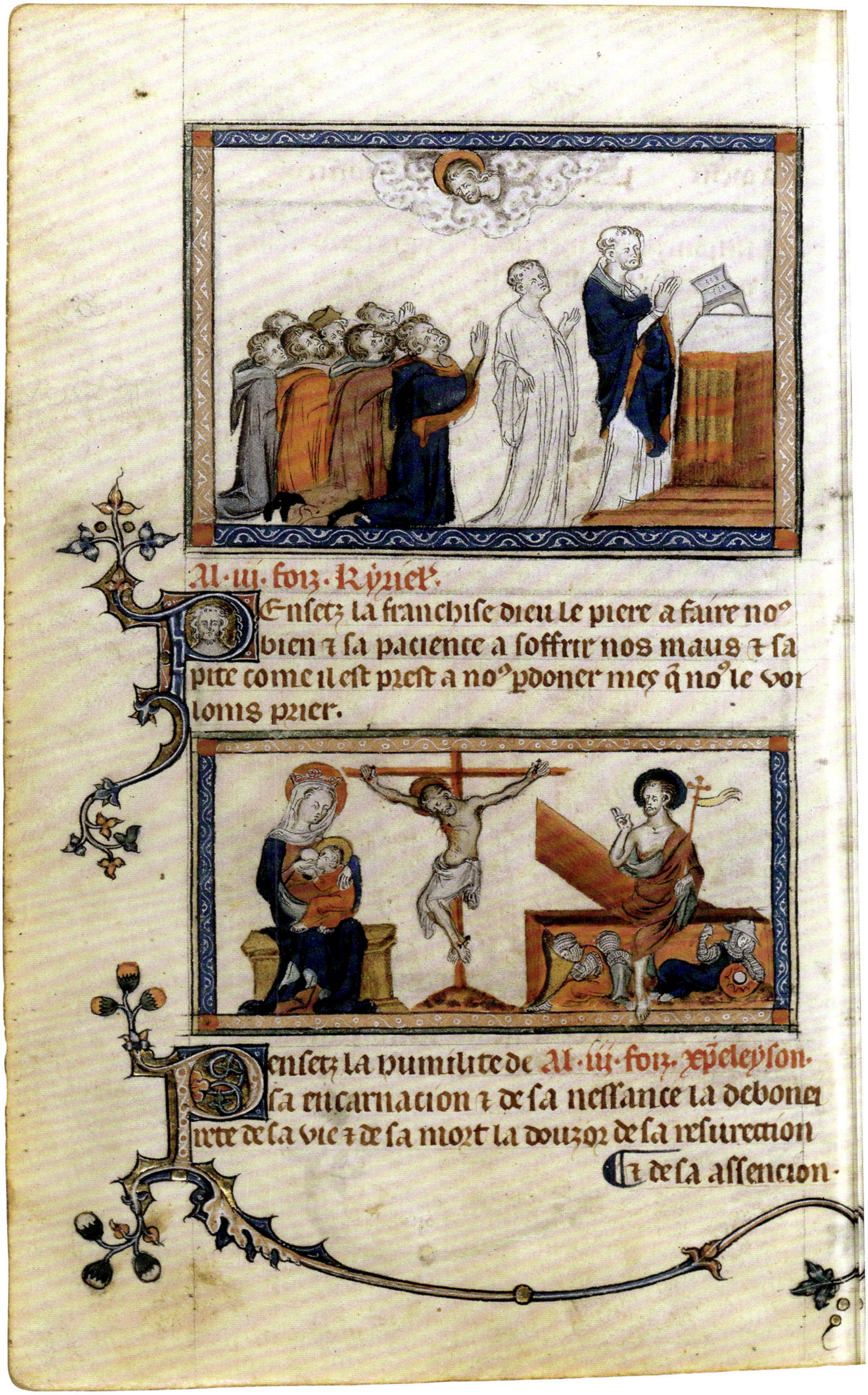

161 Kyrie eleison with instructions. Anglo-Norman tract on conduct at Mass, BN MS fr. 13342, fol. 45v, early fourteenth century (Bibliothèque Nationale, Paris).

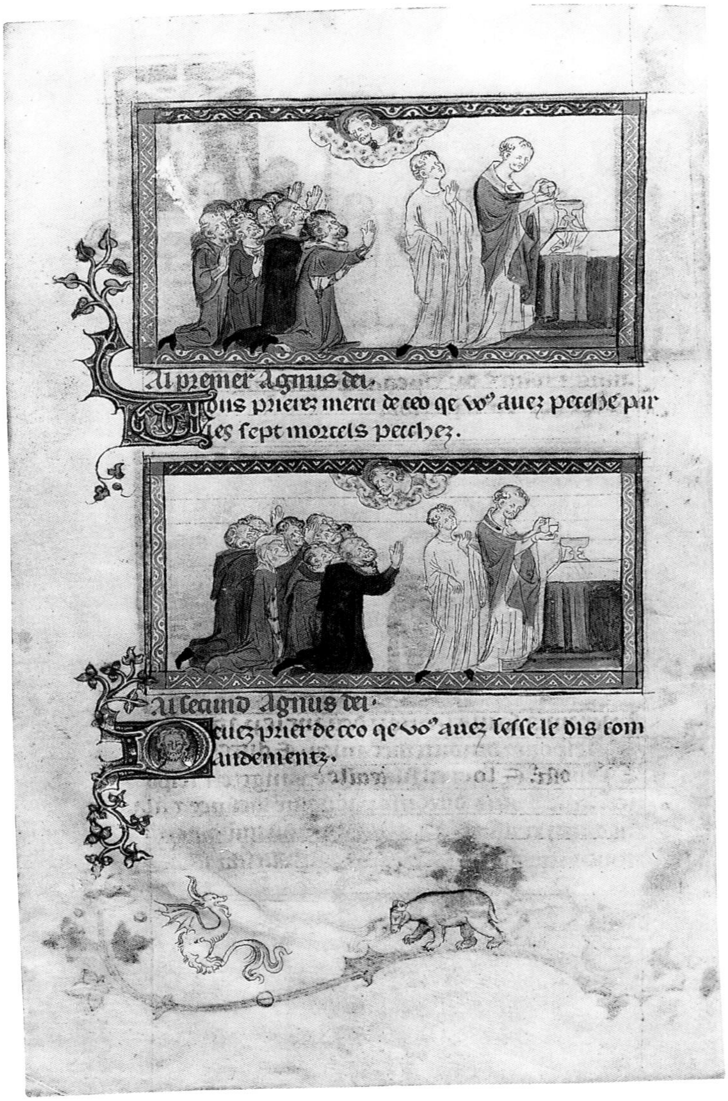

162 *Agnus Dei* with catechetical instructions. Anglo-Norman tract on conduct at Mass, BN MS fr. 13342, fol. 47v, early fourteenth century (Bibliothèque Nationale, Paris).

proffer – which 'show' as well as 'tell'. The notion of an illustrated text on devotional behaviour, whether or not in church and albeit of the most simple and generous type, was not new. It had been established appreciably earlier in exactly the circles most closely associated with formulating the new technologies of penance and prayer, and in Peter the Chanter's illustrated *De oratione* especially.[151] *De oratione* proposed a series of seven prayer modes which corresponded to the Hours, and disciplined the bodily activity of prayer in a decidedly athletic fashion. Peter's text – which also appears not to have enjoyed wide circulation in England – is markedly more sophisticated than anything in *Ceo qe vous deuez fere e penser a chascon point de la Messe*; in this later work the images, as befits a picture book, carry much greater responsibility for directions about comportment at Mass. There can be no question of theorizing about the doctrinal and expressive or rhetorical aspects of prayer comportment: it is simply shown, and in ways that reflect the gradual codification of manual prayer gestures and bodily postures at the clerical, and then lay, level in the course of the thirteenth century, of which Peter's text on prayer is an important instance.[152] At the Confiteor the parishioners mimic the prayer gestures of the priest and deacon, a nice illustration of the role of clerical behaviour as itself an image to be copied. Here again it is best to think of lowest common denominators, 'guidelines', as the by-product of more sophisticated clerical discourse. This formalized behavioural language stresses the public character of devotion, as something 'publicly performed, yet also privately binding', in which the formation of mental images is seen as a corollary of action and devotion, and in which action itself is a form of disciplined representation.[153]

The tract *Ceo qe vous deuez fere e penser* is one of the most attractive – indeed deliberately attractive – outcomes of the new 'concern with external behaviour' that accompanied the diffusion of the thought of the schools and the affective piety of the monasteries out, as it were, into the parishes and fields.[154] It is the final, somewhat watery, product of a long process of filtration. The images themselves cast some doubt on the notion – itself contestable – of a growing divide between clerical and lay spheres of action, whereby segregated clergy perform an enclosed rite, leaving the laity merely within the domains of thinking and feeling, rather than action, sight and hearing; on the contrary, the impression that the orderly, obedient and quiet little groups of figures give in relation to the central action is entirely communitarian.[155] The idea is that of a single ethos. Pictorially this work is scarcely a document of lay alienation from the liturgy, and of lay descent into religious 'subjectivism'. Rather the contrary: the premise is that public liturgy is the central point of departure for all devotional activity.[156] The illustrations hint gently at accepted gender divisions within church, since the women are shown towards the back of the congregation.[157] Yet it is not obvious from these pictures that the bulk of the laity were not to sit in the chancel, as indicated by the legislative guidelines: no screen obtrudes between priest and people.[158] No hint is given of the existence of pews and the squabbles over rights that they were starting to provoke by the 1280s, perhaps because sitting for prayer had been deemed inappropriate by authorities such as

Peter the Chanter.[159] To an extent differences were smoothed over to disciplinary ends. The manuscript is not a mirror of reality, but proposes a basically clerical agenda of orderliness, doctrinal clarity and decency of behaviour. One might even say that the suave harmonious pictorial style of the manuscript, the style of wealthy London and East Anglia, seems to answer to the work's aristocratic delicacy, moderation of sentiment, and discretion about social and religious frictions. There is no reason to doubt that this was a book for an upper-class patron. Yet that its rather smooth – one is tempted to say diocesan – vision of the ethos of public religion was not entirely representative of early fourteenth-century southern England had already been shown by recent events in London itself.

Crux horribilis: *Censorship in London and the* Cura animarum

In a commentary on Psalm 100 written for use in the Oxford schools around 1230, Robert Grosseteste stressed the importance of episcopal exorcism: 'by the word of God, and by judicial power, and in every possible way, sinners are to be driven from the City of God [. . .] just as a farmer aims at destroying the weeds among his growing corn'.[160] Grosseteste's prescription formed part of the same language of suppression of evil as the new episcopal tomb-effigies of the age showing prelates crushing vice, in allusion to Psalm 90: 13. A few years previously the Provincial Council held at Oxford had taken stern action against aberration: a deacon was convicted of apostacy to Judaism and was burnt by the sheriffs' officers; a priest was degraded for homicide, a deacon for sacrilege and theft; a man who allowed himself to be crucified was brought before the council bearing the stigmata, together with a female associate who called herself Mary: both were walled up.[161] Anxieties about 'Albigensian' heresy had surfaced in England during the Interdict and may have provoked the suppression of local cults; before 1200 St Hugh of Lincoln vigorously put down superstitious and magical abominations.[162] The frontiers of belief were being carefully policed. Sorcery and superstitions were to be extirpated by diocesan power: worship at springs is mentioned in the statutes of Worcester of 1240; the statutes of Wells of around 1258 link devotion to improperly sanctioned relics and the worship of stones, trees and springs, as practices injurious to men's souls.[163] Despite the new stress on the cultivation of virtue, in the second half of the century the tone of the diocesan church becomes if anything sterner; a sharper note is sounded, an attitude less forgiving is struck, the focus on abuse becomes clearer. To general guidelines are added specific precepts. A new delicacy is shown towards images as embodiments of the Church and of its doctrines. The Council of Lyons of 1274 recommends 'harsh retributive sentences' to those committing sacrilege, especially those who, in the event of the suspension of a church, commit the detestable abuse and horrible impiety (*horrendae indevotionis*) of treating 'with irreverent boldness crucifixes and images or statues of the blessed Virgin and other saints, [who] throw them to the ground in order to emphasize the suspension of divine worship, and leave them under nettles and thorns'.[164]

This attitude to images, to illicit worship, and to the *cura animarum* was neither sentimental nor irrational; on the contrary, as an episode in the history of London in the first decade of the fourteenth century shows, it was struck by logically and legalistically minded bishops who were perfectly capable of exerting their authority quickly and effectively in one of the most radical possible of all pastoral measures, bar condemnation for heresy: censorship. Ralph Baldock, Bishop of London (1303–13), was one such man. In 1305 this expert canon lawyer was confronted by a problem that was as rare as it is revealing of the pastoral mentality in regard to images.[165] Since it encapsulates many of the issues I have raised in this part of my enquiry, with regard to images and the pastoral *cura animarum*, I have decided to end this chapter with it.

The London Annals for 1305 relate the following:

> In that year, on April 15th, a certain cross of terrible aspect (*Crux horribilis*) was taken to the chapel of Conyhope, and on the following day called Good Friday was adored by many (*adorabatur a multis*); on account of which Geoffrey of Wycombe, the rector of that church, incurred considerable harm at the instigation of the canons of St Paul's (Cathedral). On May 1st of that year, the aforesaid cross was taken away by night to the canons of Holy Trinity (Aldgate).[166]

A year later Baldock gave the verdict on this event in a letter to the Prior of Holy Trinity, Aldgate:

> August 2nd 1306. Commission to return a crucifix incorrectly made. Concerning an erroneous sculpted image of the crucifixion (*yconia crucifixi erronee sculpta*). [. . .] We have heard on trustworthy authority that a while ago one Thidemann of Germany has sold to Geoffrey, Rector of St Mildred's in the Poultry, a certain carved crucifix with a gibbet lacking a cross-beam, which does not represent the true shape of the cross (*cum patibulo sine ligno transversali veram crucis*

> *formam minime pretendente*); this cross the rector raised in his church, and to it the indiscreet populace flocked in crowds as if to a true image of the cross – whereas it was no such thing; as a result, as we foresaw, their souls might very well be imperilled. Because of this cross we caused Thidemann and Geoffrey to be summoned to our presence and, having examined both diligently, we have ordained as follows, in case persistence with this error should lead to even worse things: that Thidemann should take (and he has indeed so taken) his oath on the Gospels that he would never henceforth make, nor allow to be shown for sale, within our city or diocese of London, a crucifix such as this, or crosses with arms contrary to the accustomed fashion, under pain of excommunication for disobedience. Because the said Thidemann claims to be a simple foreigner, who might probably and innocently have ignored the accustomed mysteries of the crucifix and the image attached to it, therefore we have graciously granted to him as follows: that he, having first restored to us the letter of obligation for twenty three pounds sterling which he has from the aforesaid rector, shall obtain restitution of this crucifix, which has been sequestrated and deposited in your keeping (at Aldgate), for the avoidance of peril to men's souls, by the discreet Master Richard of Newport, who was then our vicar and official. Wherefore we enjoin and command you that, having received from this Thidemann the aforesaid obligation (which you will faithfully transmit to us), you will without delay deliver to the said Thidemann his image; provided always that it be borne from your monastery to some place outside our diocese, either at early dawn or late in the evening, when it can be done most secretly and with least scandal; and that you shall set up a watch to assure the execution of this command and to intimate the same to us [. . .] given at our palace at Fulham, August 2nd 1306.[167]

The events of Easter 1305 had taken place in a small and now long-lost chapel which lay just to the west of the parish church of St Mildred, Poultry, in London, the area where butchers, poulterers and purveyors of game worked. 'Conyhope' means little more than 'rabbit field'. The chapel certainly existed by 1303 and, according to later sources, was dedicated to the Virgin Mary and Corpus Christi, in the name of which a fraternity had been formed there before 1349.[168] Several things are striking about the two reports in question, which clearly show different attitudes to the scandal. The account in the London Annals suggests that, though the cross had been purchased by the rector of the parish church of St Mildred's, it had been moved by him to the chapel at Conyhope at Eastertide, for use in the Good Friday public procession of the Cross. The Good Friday veneration of the cross entailed its procession while veiled into the church or chapel, the chanting of the *Improperia* or reproaches, and the unveiling of the cross and its procession into the midst of the people. Presumably it was on this occasion that this particular cross had first been unveiled to gasps of astonishment, but thereafter kept in place in such a way as to remain a 'problem'. Note the strong language of the London Annals: *Crux horribilis* is an unusual term in the annals of English art; infrequent were episodes of outrageous image-worship; mercifully exceptional were attacks, presumably on both person and property, by cathedral canons on local priests. The bishop's letter is also an extraordinary document. The cross in question was made by a German craftsman and sold for the considerable sum of £23 to the rector of St Mildred's. Both were hauled up before the bishop. Its lack of a proper cross-arm rendered it erroneous, and so an illicit object of veneration endangering the *cura animarum*.

The events at Conyhope in 1305 were especially fascinating to art historians preoccupied after the Second World War by the issue of control and freedom within the constraints imposed by the Church.[169] One can scarcely disagree about their importance, for they are a quite exceptional illustration of the role, albeit implicit, that notions of restraint and decorum played in adjudication about images and their effect on souls. Decorum is 'more honoured in the breach', to use Hamlet's proverbial phrase, and changing the central symbols of a faith in the interests of greater impact is a risky business. Of all Christian signs the Cross of Christ was the most delicate and susceptible barometer of sensibilities. A Spanish bishop, Lucas of Tuy, writing some time after 1227, had already complained of the cunning innovations in Christian iconography made by heretics depicting the cross with three, not four, arms, and the crucified Christ being nailed to it with three, not four, nails, one being driven through his overlapping feet. To this devotees were attracted instead of the True Cross of Christ.[170] By 1230 or so this was already a quite common form for the *Christus patiens*, and Lucas was on the losing side: today's vice is tomorrow's custom. Yet there was nothing heretical as such about the Conyhope cross, which presumably had three nails. Instead its lack of a proper cross-arm for the gibbet rendered it erroneous in a rational and commonsense way. *Ipso facto* a cross requires a cross-member. Lucas of Tuy expatiated at greater length about the dangers of such images than did Ralph Baldock, and from the viewpoint of what he deemed to be acceptable (i.e. papal) doctrine on the matter of the shape of the cross and the number of its nails.[171] But Ralph's position is likely to have been similar. A wrongly shaped, in effect three-armed cross shaped like a Y disastrously subverted not only conviction in the historical validity of the Cross as the Christian sign, but the whole Christian semiotic of the cruciform, whether in relation to the sign of the Cross on the body as taught to children, priestly gestures at Mass, Cross-typology, cosmic symbolism of the number four, the breadth, length, depth and height of Ephesians 3: 18, or cruciform bodily modes of prayer.[172]

It is of course true that the English could be more than tolerant of unusually shaped crosses, such as the Coptic *crux ansata* form of the cross-relic associated with St Alban, or the miraculous Holy Rood at Bromholm shaped like a patriarchal cross – that is to say, crosses that were established or authorized cult objects.[173] In regard to Conyhope, Rudolph Berliner was one of the first to make the logical deduction that because the sculptor concerned was German, and because his cross lacked a cross-beam, the cross was therefore of a type known in German as a *Gabelkruzifix* (fork-crucifix); and one may judge something of its appearance from the most celebrated early German instance, the spectacular and supposedly miraculous cross in Sankt Maria im Kapitol in Cologne of around 1304 (fig. 163). It seems likely that Thidemann was himself Rhenish in origin and that he was working in an area of London – not far from the site of the Cologne Guildhall – with strong commercial and family ties between London and Cologne.[174] The form of cross he made had become common in Germany and Italy only in the second half of the previous century; but it was one which had scarcely any currency at all in the Anglo-French 'homelands' of Gothic before 1300, or later. Only one instance, in a late thirteenth-century manuscript associated with La Grasse (BL Add. MS 17006, fol. 130v), is known in contemporary France (fig. 164), and even this seems to have been produced under German influence; one can be fairly confident, not least from the reported reactions to it by all parties, that nothing quite like it had been seen before in England.[175] Perhaps there was some implicit view that German art and customs were barbaric; a few years later two Irish friars visiting St Paul's contrasted its choir's sweet and joyous chanting with the 'howling of the Germans'.[176] But one must be cautious about this, since there is no evidence that nationalistic sensibilities were involved in the case. What the cross did contrive to do was to embody all at once the vices of error and novelty. If it also looked rather like the Cologne example, it was also (and here value judgements seem inescapable) quite

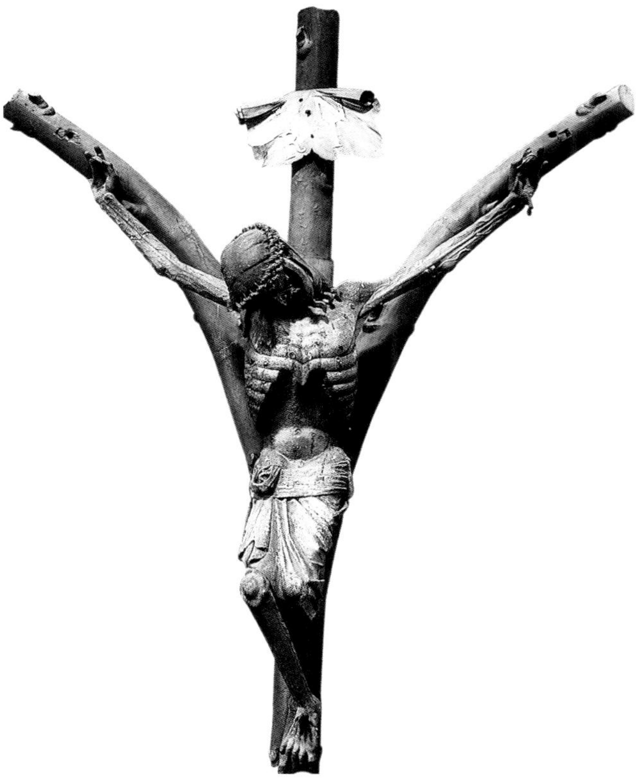

163 Crucifixion, Sankt Maria im Kapitol, Cologne, *c.* 1304 (Bildarchiv Foto Marburg).

out of line with the usual English crucifixion, a *Crux horribilis* indeed.[177]

In asking why the bishop banned this image one might well debate which of these vices – error, foreignness, novelty or sheer ugliness – might have been uppermost in his mind. The two documents suggest different slants on the problem, the Annals pointing to its aesthetic character, the bishop's letter to its symbolic form. The bishop's case reveals the thinking of a lawyer, establishing an unimpeachable case and precisely avoiding value judgement. A sign is either right or wrong; doctrine is doctrine. Yet something in what he had to say does not ring quite true. For one thing, had the problem merely been the shape of the cross, it might have been possible to 'correct' it by retaining the figure of the crucifix and substituting a normal cross. Instead the whole object went; and this suggests that the image in its entirety was in some way offensive to Christ's body, to the sacrament of Mass and to the Church. For another, it is unclear why the cathedral's canons should have sanctioned actual harm to the rector of St Mildred's: if this was justified merely by high-minded aesthetic distaste, concern for symbols or snooty disdain for popular religion, it sug-

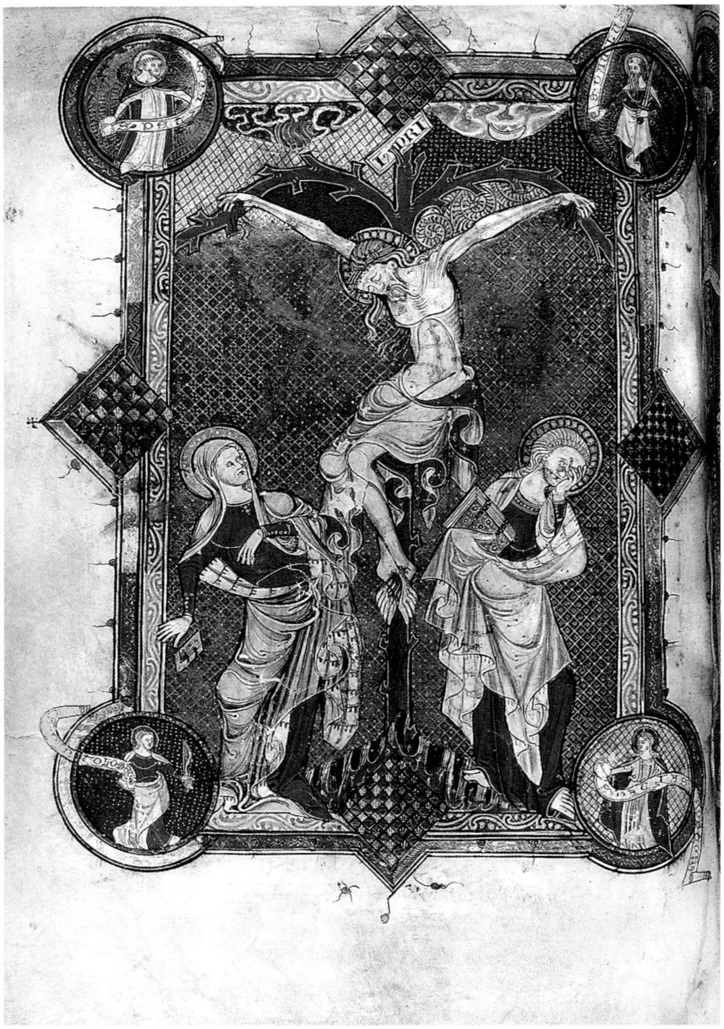

164 Crucifixion. BL Add. MS 17006, fol. 130v, France, late thirteenth century (by permission of the British Library).

gests nothing so much as corporate over-sensitivity. The artist got away scot-free: this was a matter for the Church.

There are really two styles of reply to this question. The first is essentially practical. In 1300, five years before the display of the cross at Conyhope, St Paul's Cathedral had enacted an ordinance that directed that the income from donations to a certain great cross at the north transept of St Paul's itself should be directed to the new works on that great building until they were finished.[178] This cross was still attracting donations in 1331, when Queen Philippa made an offering to it to the accompaniment of minstrels.[179] The drain on the chapter's resources implicit in such a great – indeed huge – building project might well have heightened the chapter's sensitivity to anything which offered competition to the cathedral's own cult images, shrines and revenues. Geoffrey of Wycombe had been rash enough to set up a rival to the cathedral's own money-spinning crucifixion; and the weird form it had taken, and its role as the focus of enthusiastic but unsanctioned local devotions, had played straight into the bishop's hands. From this point of view Ralph Baldock was simply supporting his cathedral chapter at a time when the canons were making increasing efforts to detach themselves in a variety of ways from the unruly urban milieu which surrounded them.[180] In 1310 Edward II himself intervened to instruct the mayor and sheriffs to ensure the safety of the cathedral canons and their possessions.[181]

The second style of reply – by no means incompatible with the first – forces one to confront the power that this image had for an early fourteenth-century London congregation. The Conyhope cross was not merely a faulty symbol, but the sign of a certain form of devotion. In banning the symbol, the ulterior motive was to dispel the attendant behaviour: Geoffrey and Thidemann were together responsible for introducing innovations at Conyhope of which the cross was an exceptionally forceful expression; ugly images shaped ugly practices. Yet an image was easier to suppress than belief or conduct. A clue as to what such conduct might have pertained is provided by the existence at Conyhope later in the century of a Corpus Christi fraternity. When this came into being is unclear, but it is not impossible that the agitations there in 1305 were connected to the sowing of the seeds of the new devotion. The cult of Corpus Christi was a product of the extravagant forms of eucharistic piety that had developed in the thirteenth century in the towns and cities of the Low Countries and the Rhineland, particularly in the dynamic sphere of the rapidly proliferating Beguines and such figures as Juliana of Cornillon.[182] It received its first official sanction by Urban IV in 1264 and was finally universalized by the decretals named the Clementines (after Clement V), promulgated in 1317.[183] In England it had been formally instituted at the latest by 1318.[184] But, as already noted in my treatment of Church legislation, formal institution and actual practice are two different matters. It was not uncommon for feasts to be celebrated locally before they received absolutely official approval. Well before 1300 the feast itself had been adopted in Liège and, critically, in Cologne itself.[185] There is some evidence from Norwich and London that it was also being established around then in the major eastern English cities.[186] To a stickler like Ralph Baldock, the spread of a cult that, though in no sense illegal or heretical, had not received formal universal sanction, might well have been a matter of legitimate diocesan concern, not least given the possibility that in Cologne the *Gabelkreuz* itself had been adopted as a miraculous icon of Corpus Christi devotion.[187] Bishop Baldock could very reasonably have foreseen the possibility that the new devotion was spreading more quickly, with a greater popular intensity – the reference to people flocking in crowds to see the cross is revealing – and with reference to a potentially miraculous but erroneous image than was desirable either for civic discipline or for the economy of the cathedral church. As described in the next chapter, the image of the cross continued to give rise to exactly these questions.

The Conyhope episode thus lay at the intersection of a host of anxieties about unofficial cults, objects of superstitious veneration and lack of pietas in regard to images that the religious climate of England at the opening of the fourteenth century was doing little to dispel. This was a climate in which official or semi-official cults of episcopal *beati* were starting to falter, and in which the always potentially diverse and disorderly urban religious milieu in England was beginning, in official eyes at least, to fall prey to forms of piety and behaviour imported from abroad. In a sense it was a typically, if not exclusively, urban episode.[188] Perhaps the real issue might have been a sort of religious multiculturalism, invested in the existence around the Cologne Guildhall of a German ghetto with its own religious needs; certainly the importance of German (and Italian) commercial interests in London is sometimes neglected.[189] The history of this cross, quietly removed from London and disposed of by night, was part of the same general history of diocesan control of spontaneous outbursts of enthusiasm as that which determined the history of female religious observance and organization in the English towns. At the Council of Oxford, and indeed earlier, heretical or unorthodox belief had been dealt with harshly.[190] The very different forms taken by female religious observance in England from those across the North Sea, and the 'late' arrival of the feast of Corpus Christi in England, are sometimes cited as products of this official caution.[191] In London the issue was cleared up quickly and decisively, if only for the time being. In the years 1309–11 Ralph Baldock had found other targets in his diocese: the heresies of the Templars and the black arts, against which he issued a substantial mandate.[192] By 1323 the crowds had returned to a miracle-working image in St Paul's Cathedral itself, this time of Thomas of Lancaster.[193] Officially it must have been recognized that the power of the *Crux horribilis* at Conyhope to shock and scandalize – its particular visual sorcery – lay in the profound challenge that this type of image and its associated practices mounted to the norms of temperance and symbolic rectitude favoured by the Church. If it indeed looked like the Cologne example, it offered little short of a reproach of the most severe and dolorous sort to the smooth if elegant platitudes of the arts of the cathedral towards 1300. This was not an issue of national, so much as of group or institutional identity: the ethos, even theology, of suffering apparent in the Conyhope cross had no place in the specific milieu of a properly regulated diocesan Church. The sheer power of images to constitute behaviour was being officially recognized. A local affair, almost a clash of ethos and aesthetics, had wider implications for the boundaries and very basis of the signification and expressivity of Gothic art. This is a complex but rewarding problem, and the final part of this study examines it more closely.

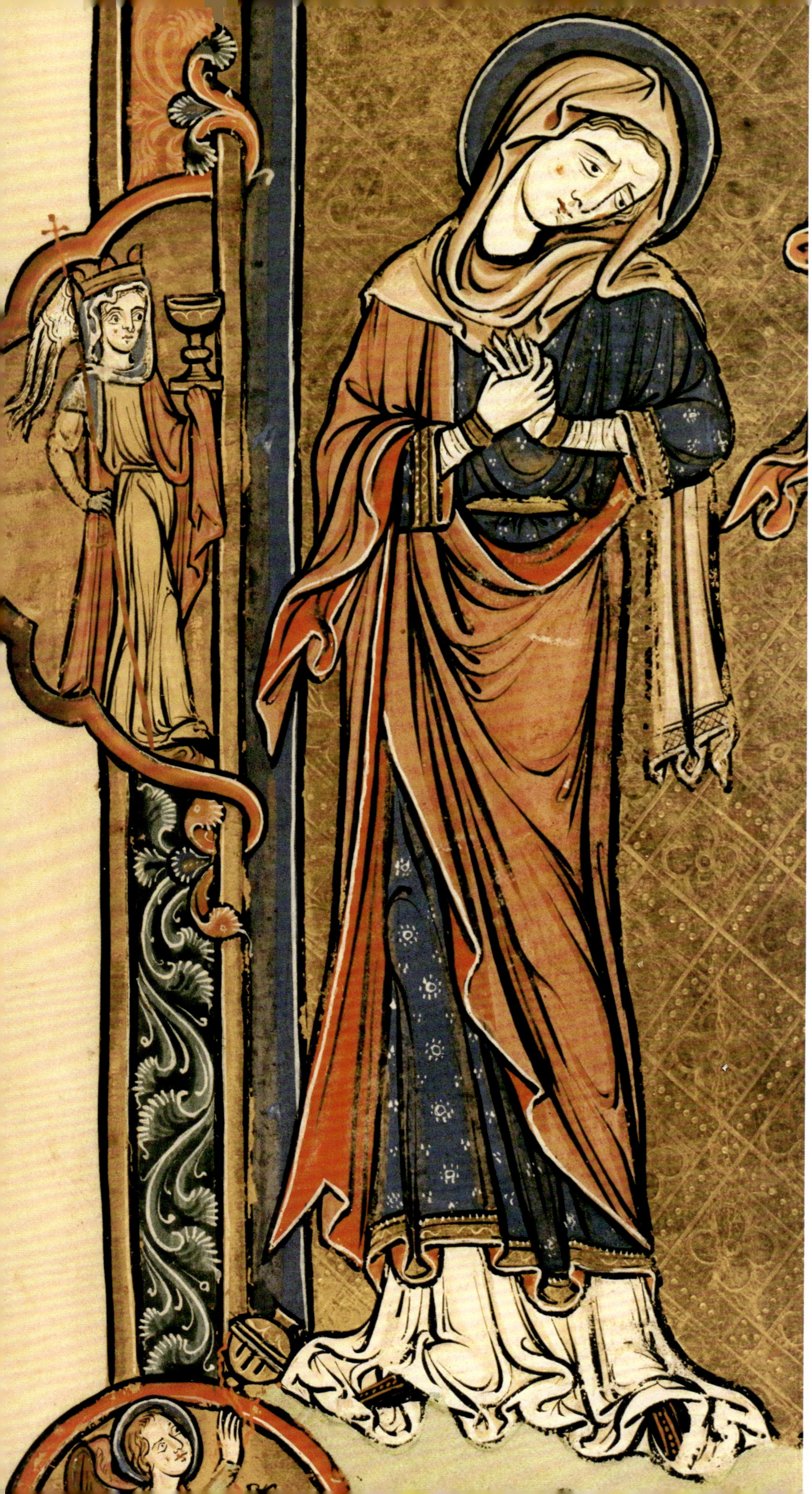

Part IV

EXPRESSION

FACING PAGE Crucifixion. Amesbury Psalter (detail of fig. 165)

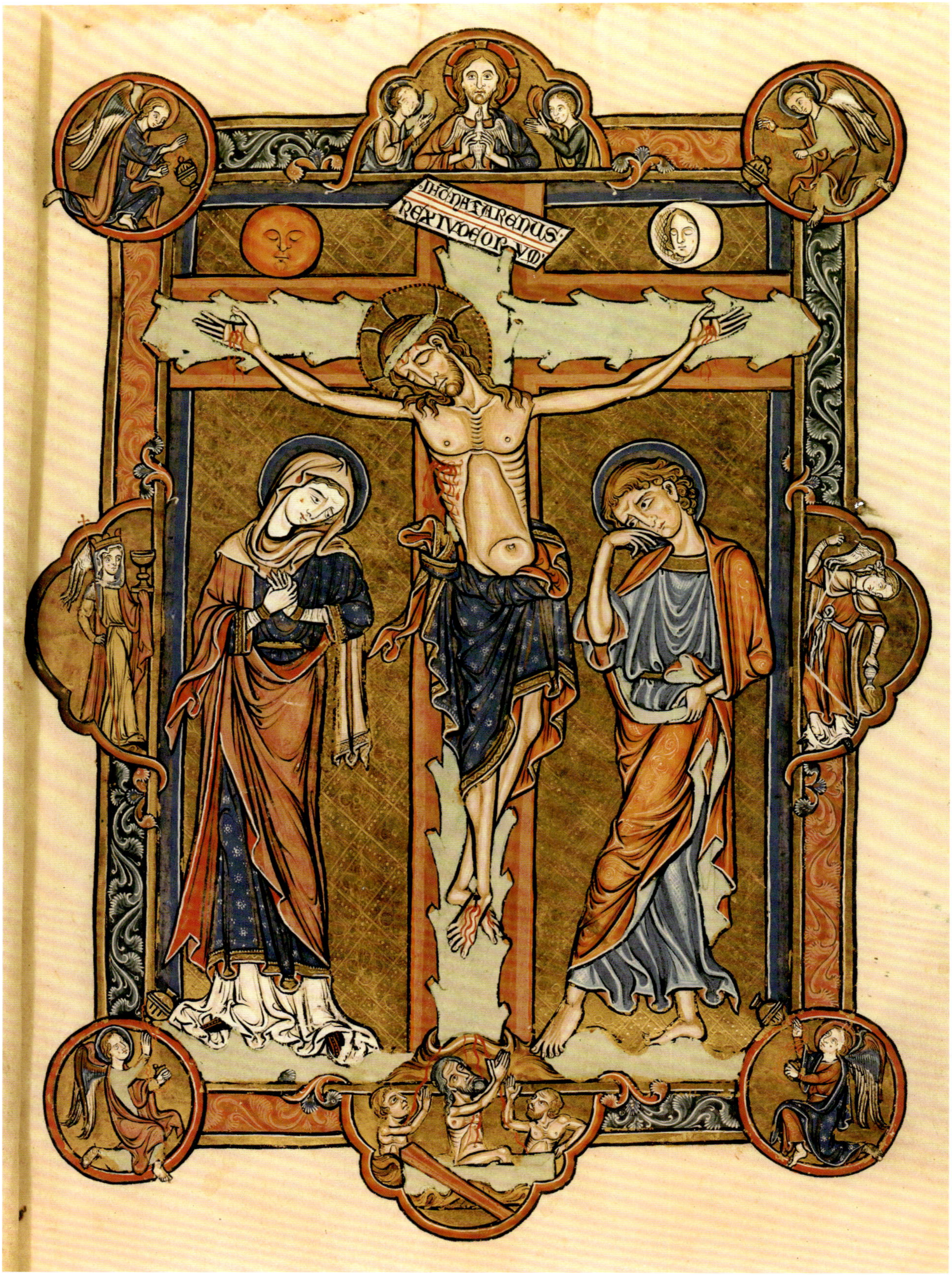

165 Crucifixion. Amesbury Psalter, Oxford, All Souls College MS 6, fol. 5, mid thirteenth century (The Warden and Fellows of All Souls College, Oxford).

Chapter 9

THE TREE OF LIFE

Jesus sweet Jesus my dear my darling my Lord my Saviour my honey-drop my balm sweeter is the memory of you than honey in the mouth.

The Wooing of Our Lord

In His rebukes He is terrible, but in His abominations He is gentle and kind; He is cheerful but always maintains His dignity. At times He has wept, but He has never laughed. In stature He is tall and erect, and His hands and arms are fine to behold. His speech is grave, reserved and temperate.

Publius Lentulus on Christ

Ralph Baldock's suppression of the cross at Conyhope had a rational aspect in regard to religious signs. Because its form was unlike that of a proper cross, it fundamentally subverted the doctrines associated with the idea of a cruciform image. Worse: according to the first of the two sources for the events of 1305, the cross was also a *Crux horribilis*, a cross of terrible or fearsome aspect. The difficulties with it were both symbolic and aesthetic, or socio-aesthetic. From the account of its suppression, its removal from the city of London quietly and by night, one may infer that the bishop saw some connection between the cross, its aberrant form and actual religious practices. Usually, only very attractive, fascinating or powerful things, such as famous relics, were moved by night. So the image was not only in one very exact sense wrong, but also effective and dangerous; it was the expression of a certain style of religious observance, and it must also have been suspected that it was potentially constitutive of that style. What that 'style' consisted of is hard, in practice, to discern. The term *horribilis* conveys at least something about its appearance as a representation of Christ, which one can supplement only imaginatively by reference to the Cologne *Gabelkruzifix* of 1304, historically the nearest analogue. One cannot necessarily extrapolate from the appearance, or presumed appearance, of this image to the style of observance it served and encouraged; but nor can one necessarily detach the two. Balancing these considerations is not easy, for they serve to point to the subtle relation between religious doctrine, experience and affect. In any event, Bishop Baldock's problem serves as a useful bridge between the regulation of the art of the *cura animarum*, discussed in the previous chapter, and the moral, psychological and aesthetic issues of affectivity to be examined in the final part of this book, and which will help to draw together some of its longer strands of argument.

In pointing to the problem of the cross's affect, my argument moves a little closer to the history of the emotions. I have used the words 'affect' or 'affective', from the Latin *affectus*, throughout this study in such a way as to indicate something like 'emotional effect' or 'capacity to move' (emotion coming from *emotus/emoveo*) – common usage in what might be called the history of spirituality.[1] The sense of the term now needs a little sharpening. An affect in medieval usage is not exactly an emotion in the modern (or Platonic) sense of something spontaneous, instinctive or natural in the domain of feeling, distinct from thought or will. On the contrary: integral to affect, or to an affective attitude to the world, is the idea of conscious will, of striving towards something; an affect is a state of mind or attitude, a disposition towards the world and things in it, which may be informed rationally. In its medieval form the notion of an affect owed much to the fundamental connection between emotion and cognition in Aristotelian psychology.[2] In this psychology, the relationship between emotion and cognition, or feeling and thinking, is not merely close but causal: cognition is causally related to emotion, because emotions are prompted or moved by rational thoughts. It follows that because thoughts are open to rational persuasion, emotion itself is also in turn open to argumentation: 'emotional response is intelligent behaviour open to reasoned persuasion'.[3] Since emotions are part of the rational human faculty of judgement, they may also be disciplined morally: virtues are cognitive dispositions which inform thought and feeling. The ethical and educational consequences of this psychology will be clear. It follows that the patterns or habits of inner feelings, quite as much as the external *habitus*, are subject to rational scrutiny and regulation. Many of the pastoral techniques that I have commented on in passing assume this fundamental relation between virtue, reason and feeling. Hence the possibility of setting out appropriate affective responses in pastoral literature giving guidance on contemplation or on liturgical behaviour. The language and techniques of the confessional, pastoral literature and some hagiography are premised upon the possibility of the regulation of human disposition by the cultivation of good habits and a virtuous ethos. Often, and particularly in *paedeia* – the training of the young, of novices or of the simple – they rely on set visual or emotional models which embody the metaphor of repetitive form (the wax seal, or footprint, for instance).[4] Equally clear are the aesthetic and rhetorical consequences. Because an image's affect constitutes its persuasive power in eliciting thoughts and feelings, it may itself be a means of reasoned persuasion. The image not only reflects, but participates in, discourse. So when one speaks of a cross eliciting a problematic affect, one is referring not simply to the play of the emotions, or to the ugly or beautiful as disinterested aesthetic categories, but to something more total, 'aesthetic' in the Aristotelian sense: the ethos of the object, what dispositions and values it represented or proposed, and so might have fostered. A *Crux horribilis* might rationally be said to elicit both thoughts and feelings about fear inappropriate to the ordinary understanding of the crucifixion and its representation (fig. 165) within Christian ethics (compare 'love and pity'): thus one may begin to understand why the appearance of religious artefacts mattered, and why they could be thought appropriate objects of ethical and aesthetic, as well as semiotic, regulation. The rest of this book returns persistently to these issues.

None of this is stated explicitly in the documents, such as they are, relating to Ralph Baldock's act of censorship: for him the pretext for discipline was the character of the cross as a malformed sign. His claim has the semblance of ordinary doctrinal regulation. It is premised upon the idea that there was a more or less stable 'lore' for the representation of the crucifixion in the Latin West, rooted in theology and textual authority. That this lore existed is beyond serious dispute. One of the most rigorous modern exponents of its nature and development was F. P. Pickering. An historian of literature and a philologist, Pickering was not interested in the types of question (moral, social, aesthetic) under discussion here. His objective was to trace the way in which the general lore of the crucifixion as a representation was formed from within textual tradition, rather than from within the history and contexts of religious sentiment, the 'theology of suffering' (*Leidenstheologie*) or late medieval 'realism'.[5] How was it, Pickering asked, that the simple term *crucifixerunt* of the Gospels gave birth to the rich and diverse, yet fundamentally stable, representational tradition that it did? To 'explain' the representation of the crucifixion, in terms of an antecedent history of spirituality which had itself been deduced from the images, was little more than circular reasoning confusing outcome with cause. Instead, Pickering suggested, Christian knowledge was 'a self-sufficient economy' formed within clerical exegetical traditions, which expanded and clarified the bald Gospel *crucifixerunt* by reference to the texts of the Old Testament, and the Psalms in particular.[6] Thus Christ, speaking through David in the Psalms, offers a description of the crucifixion especially in Psalms 21 (the 'Passion Psalm') and 56, which is then confirmed by the Gospel account of the crucifixion as the fulfilment of prophecy.[7] The crucifixion is therefore a biblical-symbolic, not an historical representation, subject not to the methods of historical, but rather textual, enquiry. This exegetical tradition was old, and was simply reformulated in the twelfth and thirteenth centuries in the theologies of Anselm, Bonaventure and others in such a way as to produce a coherent, stable lore or code, harmonizing prophecy into an historical sequence explaining in turn exactly how the cross was a fulfilment: the story of the crucifixion is thus 'aetiological', setting out the events which led to it as a particular result. To this lore, finally established and stabilized in the thirteenth century, images were naturally subject and secondary.

As an explanatory account and as a practical exercise in 'medieval' reading, Pickering's analysis is in some respects irrefutable. It is an important and useful corrective to the idea that a purely contextualist account could explain why crucifixion images look the way they do. Yet, as a way of embracing all the ends to which religious images were directed, something important seems to be missing from it – a point of which Pickering was himself fully aware.[8] The supposition that lore, doctrine and images could stand independent of context, use, function, human experience or faith itself, would be disquieting even if it were practicable. Texts manifestly do not always determine the content of images. Nor is it clear that the understanding and value of a religious image can be determined by its discursive explanation. According to Pickering, the aim of harmonizing prophecy was not 'primarily to encourage a more fervid piety or a deeper compassion. What characterizes the Crucifixion story is [. . .] its capacity to *convince* rather than to move'.[9] One is obliged to ask what notion of conviction Pickering was using here. My brief review of the basically Aristotelian doctrine of cognition and emotion shows why it is unlikely to have found favour in many circles in the Middle Ages. The sense of belief or assent which it implies is – to borrow a concept from Cardinal Newman – purely notional.[10] One might be convinced by something notionally (i.e. intellectually) without being moved; but the human and religious reality of that assent or belief would be limited. I may assent to the idea of Christ's terrible sufferings, but in a purely notional way: the idea perhaps 'leaves me cold'. But if I engage in the meditative exercises of St Edmund of Abingdon, or a reading of the Psalms and crucifixion lore, in such a way as to contemplate and grasp fully and imaginatively the Passion in all the depths of its possible interpretations, then my assent to the idea 'Christ suffered terribly' becomes 'real', directed to an object and not a notion. Real assent in this sense is inevitably accompanied by emotion, vitality, by a certain disposition or affect. Were it not, much in the meditative and lyrical-affective traditions of the period becomes unrecognizable, or even pointless. Pickering's account is thus fundamentally Platonic or dualistic in its suspicion of emotion and its separation from instruction and the word. It is certainly unsympathetic to the main currents of demonstrative rhetorical and poetic theory in this period, which were usually Aristotelian in form, and which saw intelligent behaviour in emotional response. This consideration has to an extent been acknowledged by useful later developments of Pickering's method which have reinserted its findings into the history of spirituality.[11]

To argue the point is not to devalue the importance of the notional or intellectual aspects of doctrine, or for that matter liturgy or devotion. Here two supplementary points are necessary. The first is that the recognition of the depths and complexities of doctrine, or allegory, or ritual – as of any powerful idea – may in itself be emotionally stirring and satisfying, may possess actual aesthetic power, albeit of an austere sort. In chapter 1, for example, I noted the possibility that the architecture of the Trinity Chapel at Canterbury, its rose-pink and white columns, may have had a conscious and purposeful allegorical character in relation to the symbolism of St Thomas's passion and its foundation in biblical exegesis. To accept the truth of this suggestion is to perceive something beyond the observable form of the building: in some sense one's view of the 'presence' of the building is changed and enriched imaginatively. The architecture takes on a greater density of signification, and experience of it takes on a new vitality. And so it is with some of the most important Western traditions regarding religious representation.[12] To comprehend a building or a religious artefact allegorically or emotionally is to see it imaginatively – and it is for this reason among others that I have pursued both media throughout this study, as manifestations of various imaginative regimes. This density of signification is true of the image of the crucifixion quite as much as of the newest genres of 'devotional image' emerging in continental Europe and the Rhineland especially around 1300: the *Gabelkruzifix*, the *imago pietatis*, the *Vesperbild* or *pietà*, Christ and St John, and so on.[13] These *Andachtsbilder* are demanding works not only in terms of their manifold bases in scriptural exegesis and doctrine, but also in their complex, paradoxical and unsentimental affect.

The second point relates to the fact that what all figurative images have in common as images is their 'carnality', the fact that they have an ostensive form. They possess this form not least because of the Gregorian understanding (by now habitual in medieval commentary on art, not least because it found its way into Gratian) that real, as opposed to notional, religious assent requires an overt, palpable, object of contemplation.[14] The theme of the relatively greater eloquence of images rather than texts, and the cognitive primacy of the sense of sight in stimulating the understanding, the emotions and the memory – a theme derived ultimately from Horace – may be traced from patristic writing through Bede and Peter Lombard, to Durandus.[15] A similar assumption underlay the 'naturalistic' Bernardine theory of love, which proceeds hierarchically from carnal human affection to spiritual love.[16] It is essentially this theory of the emotions which underlies the method of affective contemplation of Christ's humanity set out by St Edmund of Abingdon, proceeding directly from attention to the 'presentist' and carnal aspects of Christ's Incarnation and Passion, to contemplation of the divinity of God (p. 194 above). Such methods have a psychological as well as an intellectual purpose; they presuppose an emotional design on the reader or beholder. They also reinforce the conviction – for which we must now provide some grounds – that not every aspect of the ostensive form of a representation such as the crucifixion can readily be explained by doctrine or 'lore' alone: for that form cannot but register changes to the general ethos within which, and for which, images were produced. Equally, if not more importantly, it was demonstrably the sphere of artistic innovation or 'freedom'.[17] Agency and context, doctrine and affect have reciprocal relationships, and this is one reason why the image of the crucifixion has a history. To explore this, it is necessary both to consider the form of the cross itself, and the image of Christ hanging from it. This will be useful, because in the case of the first, textual 'explanations' are readily forthcoming, while in the case of the second, they are less so.

Tree and Flower

Ralph Baldock's censure of the Conyhope cross at first sight suggests antagonism towards absolute modernity; yet the ultimate origins of its problematical shape went back at the latest to the ninth century, and so to a period when the psychological and affective issues I have raised are generally regarded as having been less important than theological ones.[18] Even at this time, a range of formal options existed within the visual 'lore' of the cross, at least beyond England. A ninth-century carved ivory from Metz shows Christ and the thieves crucified together on a striking and perhaps deliberately incongruous range of gibbets, Christ on a regular timber cross, the bad thief bound to a tree with his arms behind his back, and the good thief nailed to a tree with branches diverging to form a Y.[19] It is as if the *Gabelkruzifix* originated as an attribute not of Christ, but of his companions on Golgotha. In the same milieu and period emerged the 'rough-hewn' cross, made from plain trunks retaining the stumps of lopped-off branches, as in the large ninth-century Liuthard ivory crucifixion panel from Metz (Munich, Bayerische Staatsbibliothek).[20] The important point for the present discussion is that some, but not all, of these cross-forms had textual authorization. No text 'explains' the Y-form. But in the case of the organically informed cross generally, the authoritative texts were several: the Trees of Life and Knowledge in Genesis 2: 9; the Tree of Life, the *Lignum vitae* of Revelation 22: 1–2, the leaves of which were for the healing of the nations; the text *Regnavit a ligno Deus* from the Old Latin text of Psalm 95: 10; and the text *Ascendam in palmam* of Canticles 7: 8.[21] As Jennifer O'Reilly has suggested, the lopped-timber or 'rough-hewn' form common in later Anglo-Saxon crucifixions, though at first sight suggesting as it were 'dead wood', in fact signified the living potential of the sign (fig. 166). It first emerges in Anglo-Saxon cross-iconography in the illustration accompanying Psalm 21 in the early eleventh-century Harley Psalter, where the cross, accompanied by instruments of the Passion, is clearly to be understood as a *tropaeum* or victory sign, rather than an object of affect.[22] It is presumably in relation to this relatively new tradition that one should see the remarkable tau-shaped cross with sprouting fronds which forms the T of *Te igitur* at the start of the canon of the Mass in the eleventh-century Sherborne Missal (the Red Book of Darley), which is the only significant precursor of the *Gabelkruzifix* type in English medieval art.[23] The important pre-Conquest crucifixion repertory of ordinary timber crosses, rough-hewn crosses and hewn or sprouting tau-crosses was thus part of a substantial and generous 'lore' whose basis was theological, whose vision of Christ was generally that of the suffering or dead Redeemer, and whose purpose was to explore the mysteries of the Redemption itself.[24]

166 Crucifixion. Gospels of Judith of Flanders, New York, Pierpont Morgan Library MS 709, fol. 1v, 11th century (The Pierpont Morgan Library, New York).

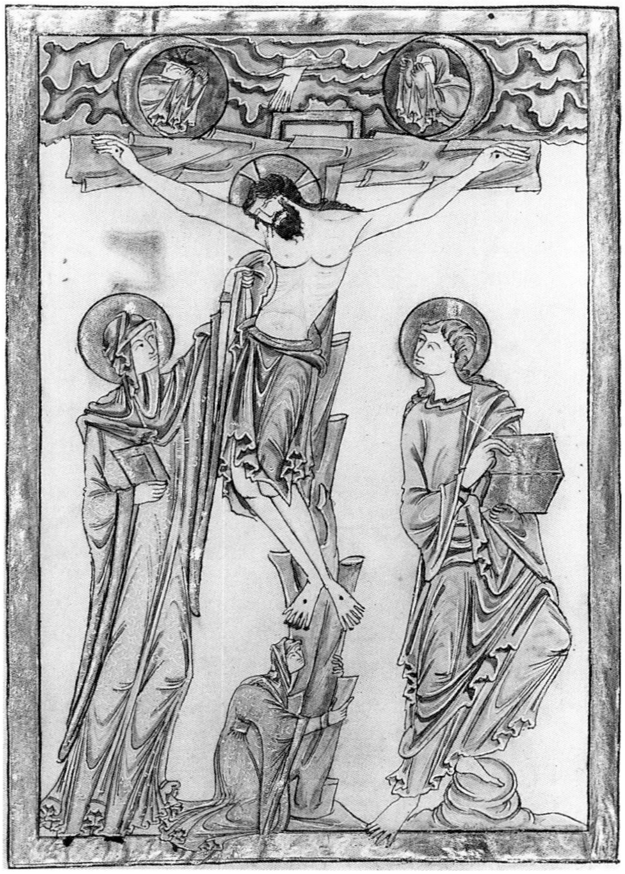

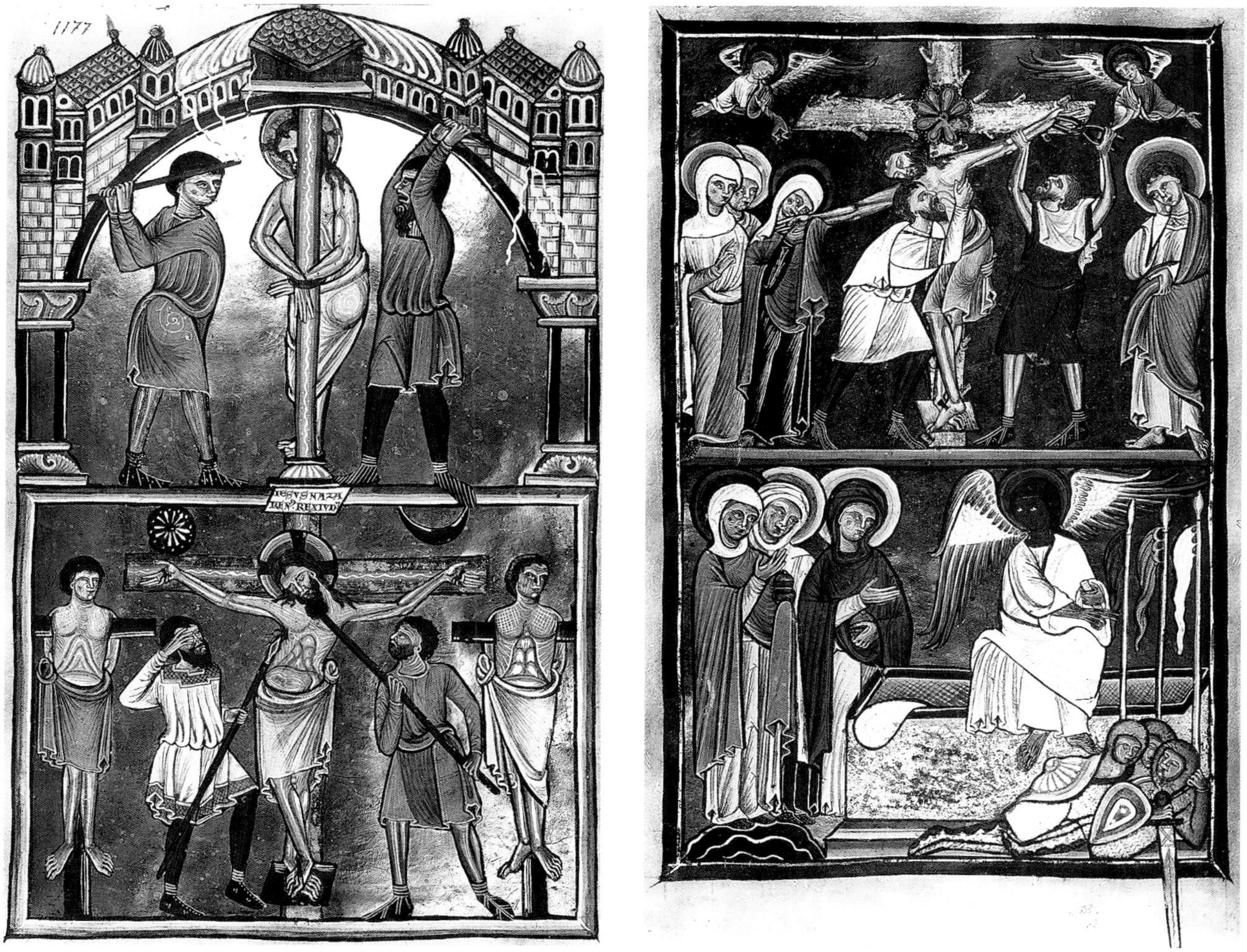

167 Flagellation, Crucifixion, Deposition and Resurrection. Munich Psalter, Munich, Bayerische Staatsbibliothek MS CLM 835, fols 26–26v, *c.* 1200–10 (Bildarchiv Foto Marburg).

Thirteenth-century English Gothic crosses deployed but also narrowed this basic formal range, while continuing to explore these mysteries through the organic cross-type. They were certainly part of the same tradition – a tradition exemplified in the twelfth century by the astonishing walrus ivory cross in the Cloisters Museum in New York.[25] Given the near-total destruction of the several thousand sculpted wooden rood-crosses which one may safely estimate were to be found in England's churches at this time – and of which the Scandinavian survivals are very likely a reliable reflection – the evidence is restricted very largely, but by no means unhelpfully, to paintings and manuscript illuminations. Psalters and Missals are the principal resource. In the extensively illustrated Munich Psalter (Munich, Bayerische Staatsbibliothek MS Clm. 835) of around 1200–10 the sequence of Christ's Passion (fols 26–26v) takes up the two commonest types of cross encountered before the Conquest, the plain timber cross and the rough-hewn cross, in its sequence showing the Crucifixion and Deposition (fig. 167): Christ dies on the plain cross, but is taken down from a rough-hewn cross which should theoretically be exhausted, but which is in fact already regenerating in anticipation of the Resurrection account that follows.[26] The pictures use two types of cross not arbitrarily, but in order to reveal a wonderful process. The same familiar repertory is found in the two very refined Psalters made around 1220 for Peterborough Abbey (Cambridge, Fitzwilliam Museum MS 12; London, Society of Antiquaries MS 59) (figs 168–9).[27] The Fitzwilliam Psalter image is of a consciously plain but exquisitely delineated type; that in the Society of

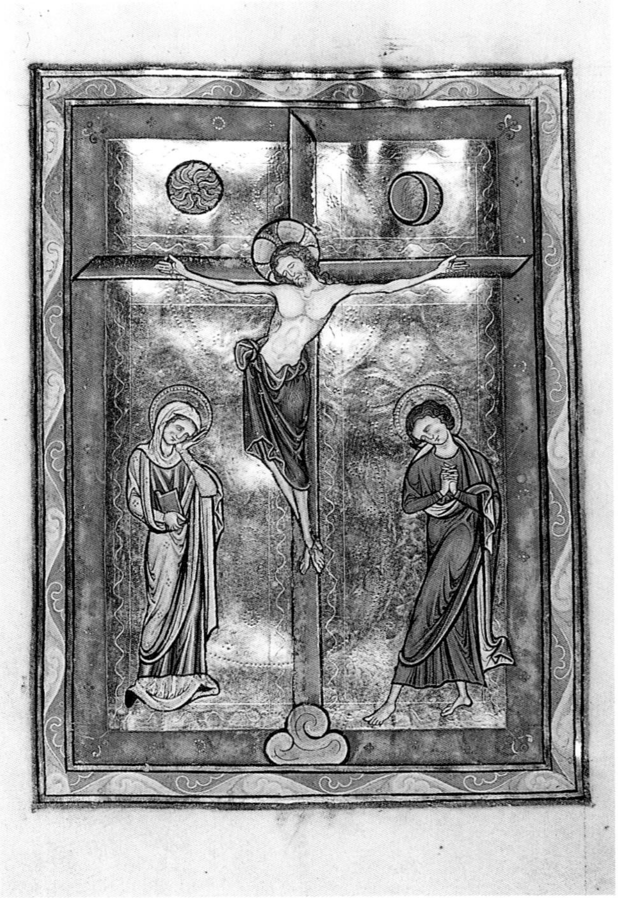

168 Crucifixion. Peterborough Psalter, Cambridge, Fitzwilliam Museum MS 12, fol. 12, *c.* 1220 (The Syndics of the Fitzwilliam Museum, Cambridge).

Antiquaries Psalter, a manuscript originally in the possession of Abbot Robert of Lindsey (d. 1222), has the same poise but is more developed symbolically. In it the cross consists of green symmetrically sprouting stems tipped with neat alternating white and red trefoil buds, regenerating exactly at the moment of Christ's *kenosis* or emptying-out: *sicut aqua effusus sum* in the words of Psalm 21: 15. Christ's drained image is one of extreme frailty, a gentle study in pathetic etiolation; his very fair skin harmonizes with the white buds of the cross, his wounds with the red buds. The commentary here is clearly on Canticles 2: 1 (*ego flos campi et lilium convallium, sicut lilium inter spinas*) and 5: 10 (*dilectus meus candidus et rubicundus*), the red-white, rose and lily sponsorial symbolism encountered in my discussion of St Thomas's passion at Canterbury, and the way his hagiographers introduced imagery from Canticles commonly associated with traditions of affective meditation on the Passion of Christ (p. 8 above). This implicit mutual love of Christ and his Church is accordingly rendered explicit in the Psalter by the traditional typology of the small images in the roundels and half-roundels of the frame: Mary, Ecclesia and St Peter facing John, Synagoga and Moses. The manuscript lacks the Tree of Jesse often found in Psalters in connection with Psalm 1; but a related function linking the two covenants may be suspected in the flowering cross understood as the righteous tree that brings forth its fruit, the leaf of which shall not wither (Psalm 1: 3).

This is also reminiscent of the formally very similar foliage corbels and crocket piers of early thirteenth-century Lincoln (p. 92 above) and the likelihood of their priestly allusion to Numbers 17: 8 and Isaiah 27: 6 and 35: 1, the blossoming of Israel, i.e. the Church. Canterbury and Lincoln are in this regard premised upon the same capacity for metaphysical wit as the English Passion images. The architecture of fleshly rose-red and white marble, and of blossoming piers and corbels, as argued earlier, embodies the same paradox as the flourishing cross: the new covenant is immutable, incorruptible; yet also living, organic. The *gemma* may be a precious stone, or a bud. The cross is the key image of the Living Church. In this ambivalence between the inorganic and organic lies not simply a contrast – the contrast of the rough-hewn or sprouting cross and the *crux gemmata*, the exalted precious trophy – but also an intellectual and spiritual dynamic: the possibility of a shift and growth of spiritual understanding itself within a complex but overlapping scale of values. This dynamic is perhaps most marked in the pre-Conquest period.[28] In English literature it is exploited eloquently in the Dream of the Rood.[29] The cross, like the Church itself, is a mystery which, in O'Reilly's words, presents 'riddling ambiguities and the possibility of a series of apprehensions'.[30] It may not be coincidental that the tradition of riddling *aenigmata* popular in England since Aldhelm included the voice or 'I-persona' of the timber cross spun about with glory, yet afflicted by burning,[31] for here the cross itself speaks eloquently, as it was later to do, with rather different purpose, to St Francis. But there are grounds for supposing that it was not solely a pre-Conquest phenomenon.

As a central sign of the new and explicit taste for living organic forms and metaphors in English thirteenth-century art, the lopped or flourishing cross inevitably developed various branches, a full study of which is badly needed. In sketching it in very quickly one notes, first, that the Anglo-Saxon tradition of rough-hewn timber crosses persisted throughout the century, and is to be found in English *Opus anglicanum* in the fourteenth. It is to be found in works intended for nuns, such as the

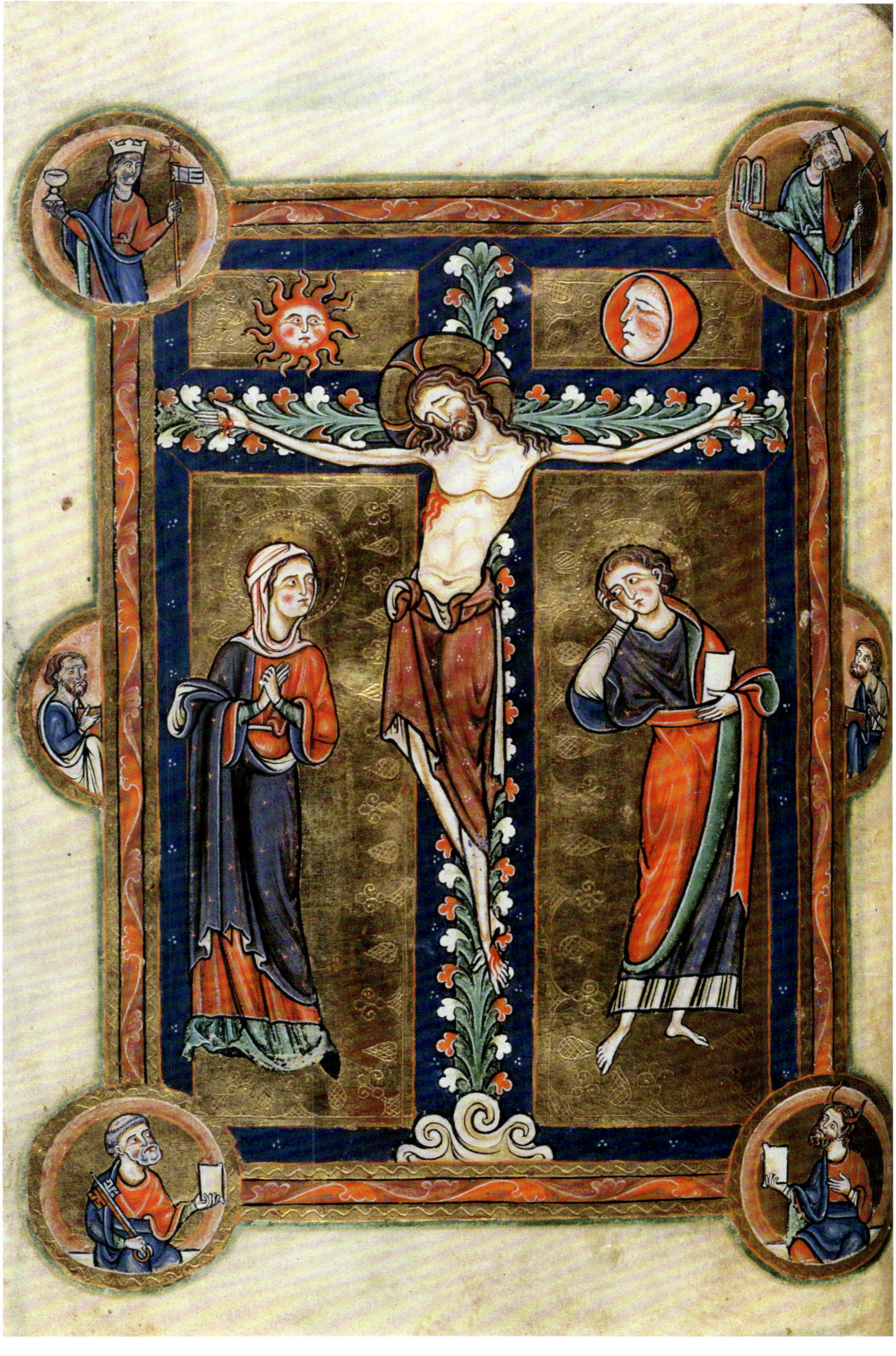

169 Crucifixion. Psalter of Robert of Lindsey, Society of Antiquaries MS 59, fol. 35v, *c.* 1220 (Society of Antiquaries of London).

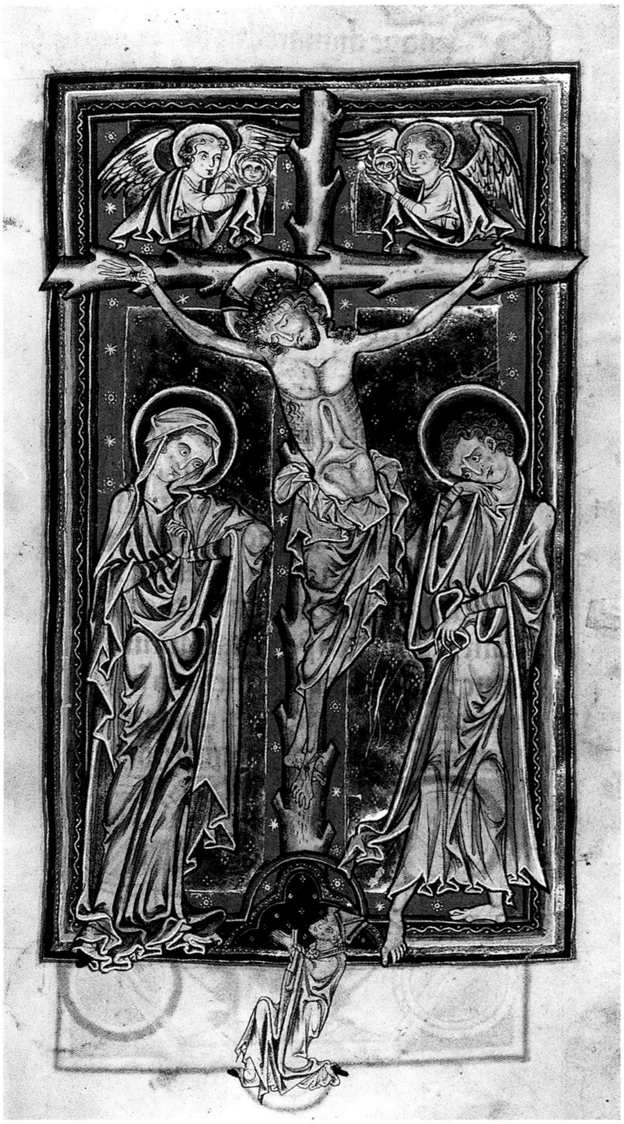

170 Crucifixion. Evesham Psalter, BL Add. MS 44874, fol. 6, mid-thirteenth century (by permission of the British Library).

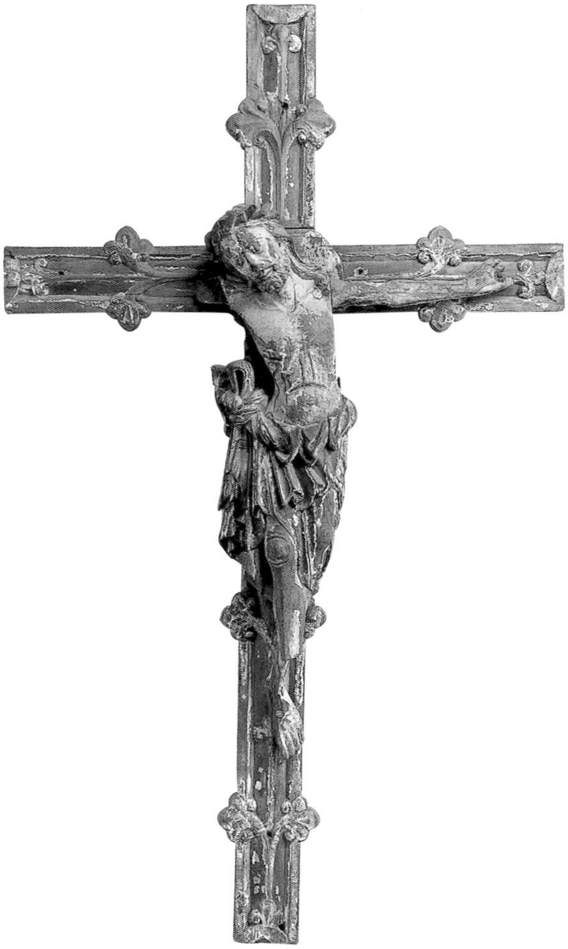

171 Crucifixion. Painted wooden sculpture from Øren parish church, Oppland mid-thirteenth century (© University Museum of Cultural Heritage, University of Oslo, Norway).

Amesbury Psalter (Oxford, All Souls College MS 6, fol. 5), where the pale green cross is combined with the Trinity, Ecclesia, Synagoga and Adam restored by the fruit of the tree (fig. 165); and in works for abbots, such as the contemporary Evesham Psalter (BL Add. MS 44874, fol. 6), where the monastic patron takes Adam's place beneath similarly green timbers (fig. 170).[32] Much more vigorously flourishing crosses were the preserve of the wooden rood-sculptors, where the tradition represented by the Peterborough De Lindsey Psalter is manifest throughout the period: it is tempting to see in the wood carvers an artistic sensibility especially attuned to the potential of the wooden medium itself – a form of craftsman's wit exemplified by the remarkable Scandinavian survivals, as in the case of the beautiful crucifix from Øren in Fåberg (fig. 171).[33] A surviving English example of such florid crosses is the stone crucifixion finial from one of the gables of the tomb of Peter of Aigueblanche, Bishop of Hereford, erected after 1268 (fig. 172).[34] The type was therefore known throughout the broad swathe of lands between the west of England and the Baltic. Other branches of this tradition were more specialized.

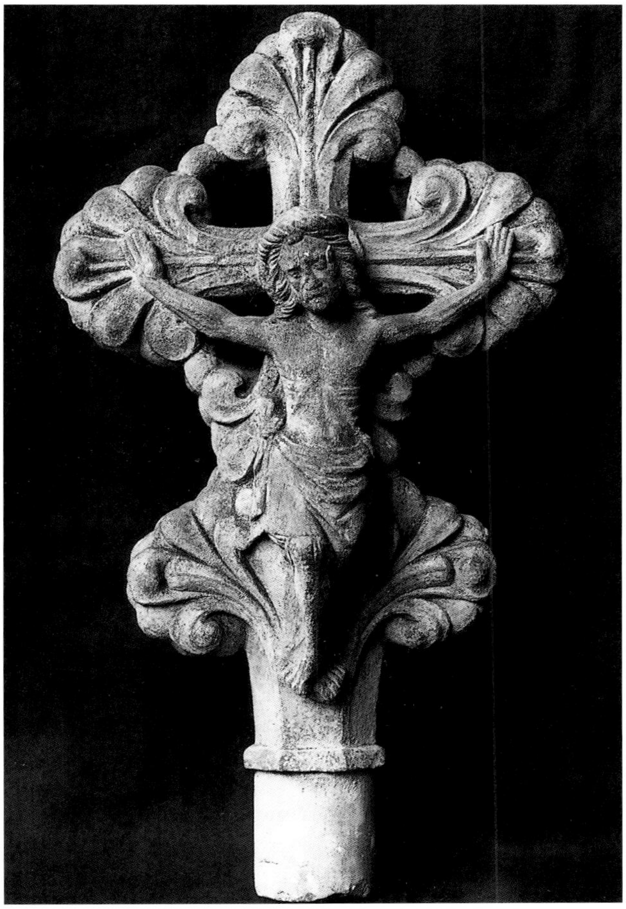

172 Crucifixion. Sculpted finial from tomb canopy of Bishop Peter of Aigueblanche, Hereford Cathedral, after 1268 (reproduced by permission of English Heritage. NMR).

One rare but vigorous offshoot may be found in an illustration for St Bonaventure's mid-century affective and meditative text *Lignum vitae*, where the fruits of the tree in Revelation 22: 1–2 yield a series of contemplations on the mysteries of Christ's humanity and divinity. An English copy of this Franciscan text is found in a theological miscellany dating to around the turn of the third quarter of the thirteenth century, and connected with manuscripts from the area of Bury St Edmunds: a remarkable six-armed cross with numerous tendrils and shoots (BL Royal MS 11. B. III, fol. 289; fig. 173).[35] The illustrations in the Lisbon Apocalypse of the same period include another, somewhat esoteric, crucifixion image based upon Berengaudus' commentary on Revelation 13: 11–14 (Lisbon, Museu Calouste Gulbenkian MS LA 139, fol. 38v; fig. 174). Here, while Antichrist's disciple preaches to the Jews and Gentiles, the prophet Elijah, a magnificent broadly draped figure, preaches to the Jews about Christ. The Jews are gathered attentively at the foot of a sprouting bright green tree trunk sustaining the image of Christ, partly veiled by a mantle over his head and body, which indicates the partial revelation to the Jews of the new covenant, a classic *velatio-revelatio* figure raised up on a Levitical rod in allusion to Psalm 95: 10, *Regnavit a ligno Deus*.[36]

This very particular, as it were priestly, image of Christ on a flourishing cross and spoken of through the prophets leads one to a reflection on the fate of the *Gabelkruzifix* in England. After (and possibly as a result of) Ralph Baldock's suppression of the Conyhope cross, the overt form of such roods seems to have disappeared

173 Crucifixion. *Lignum vitae* of St Bonaventure, from Bury St Edmunds, BL Royal MS 11. B. III, fol. 289, third quarter of thirteenth century (by permission of the British Library).

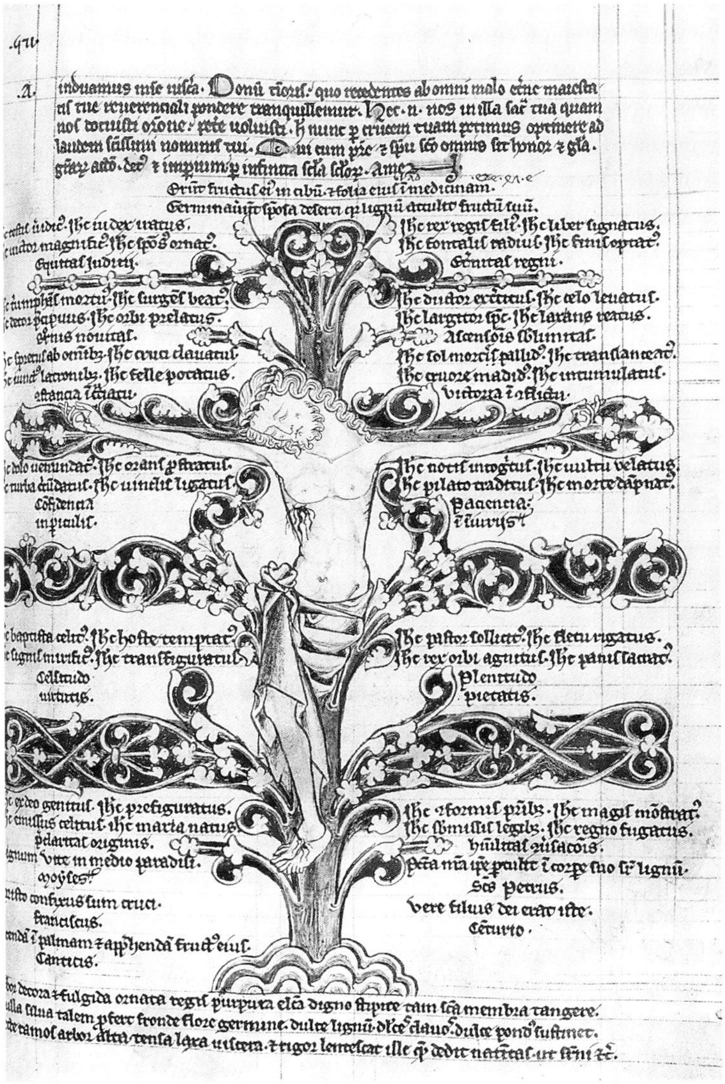

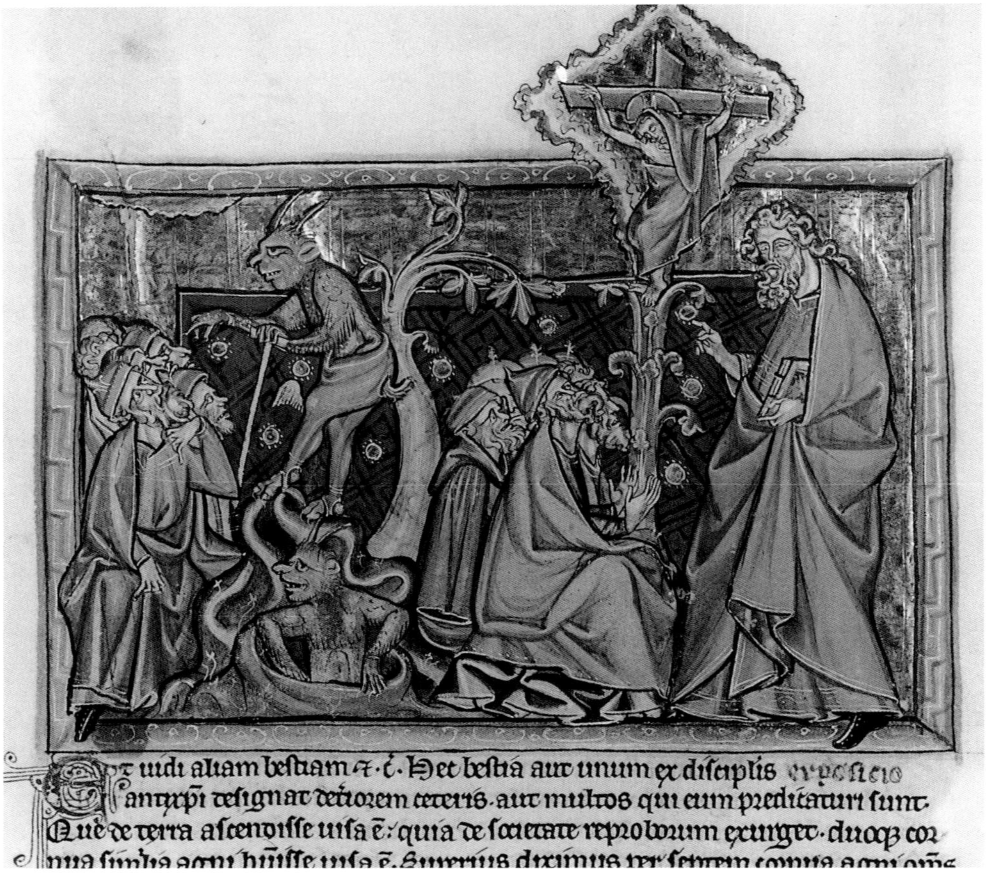

174 Jews brought to the Cross by the teaching of Elijah. Commentary illustration to Apocalypse, Lisbon, Museu Calouste Gulbenkian MS LA 139, fol. 38v, *c.* 1270 (Conway Library, Courtauld Institute of Art).

from England almost entirely, with the exception of one related occurrence on a showy but provincial tomb of the 1340s at Cartmel Priory, an Augustinian foundation in the north-west of England. Yet its underlying shape enjoyed a subsequent, albeit covert, afterlife in another and uniquely English cross-type known only in the late Middle Ages. Crucifixes attached to slim Y-cross forms characterize a number of the so-called 'lily' crucifixes, in which Christ is pinned to a cruciform bunch of lily flowers standing in the midst of the Annunciation, and so within a Marian context (fig. 175). This leads one to suspect that these were an acceptable version of the basically Italian or German Y-cross form, tempered by the loving and sponsorial imagery of Canticles 2: 1 (*ego flos campi et lilium convallium, sicut lilium inter spinas*) or Hosea 14: 6 (*germinabit quasi lilium*), which had long been part of patristic and later Bernardine commentary.[37] In other words, through its metamorphosis into the immaculate white and fragrant lily, a terrifying Rhenish icon of Corpus Christi and of the theology of suffering was quietly assimilated into an older discourse of virginity and martyrdom, and a newer Mariological discourse of the Tree of Life.[38] This shift in ethos is striking, and obliges one to consider further the actual form of Christ himself on the Cross.

Imago Agens

So far, then, it is clear that certain aspects of crucifixion imagery had a distinct discursive basis. But not every aspect of this most central sign was so coherently determined, most importantly the form of the crucifix, Christ's body and the manner of its attachment by nails to the cross. The main lines of artistic development were clear: well before the twelfth century, the representation of Christ as a collapsed or collapsing semi-naked figure with drooping head and closed eyes, suffering or dead (as opposed to covered, crowned, erect and open-eyed) was known in Byzantium and France and was fairly common in Germany and England; the issue of which region or sphere enjoyed absolute priority in regard to this innovation is unimportant for my purposes.[39] This new style of Christ, the *Christus patiens*, was already familiar in Anglo-Saxon art, and was the basic Gothic form. Between the Conquest and the thirteenth century other important continuities can be found, not least in the representation of Mary and John in their various postures of grief to either side of the cross. John's dynamic role as seer or chorus in thirteenth-century Apocalypse illustration of course rendered his psychosomatic reactions quite as much a focus of artistic *inventio* as Mary's.[40] It would be wrong to project back onto the Anglo-Saxon tradition the styles of affectivity appropriate to the century of St Edmund of Abingdon and St Bonaventure; but it is not entirely incorrect to see in the sphere of affectivity itself something of the character and purpose of these nuances.

175 Annunciation with lily crucifix. Aberystwyth, NLW MS 17250, fol. 1, fifteenth century (National Library of Wales).

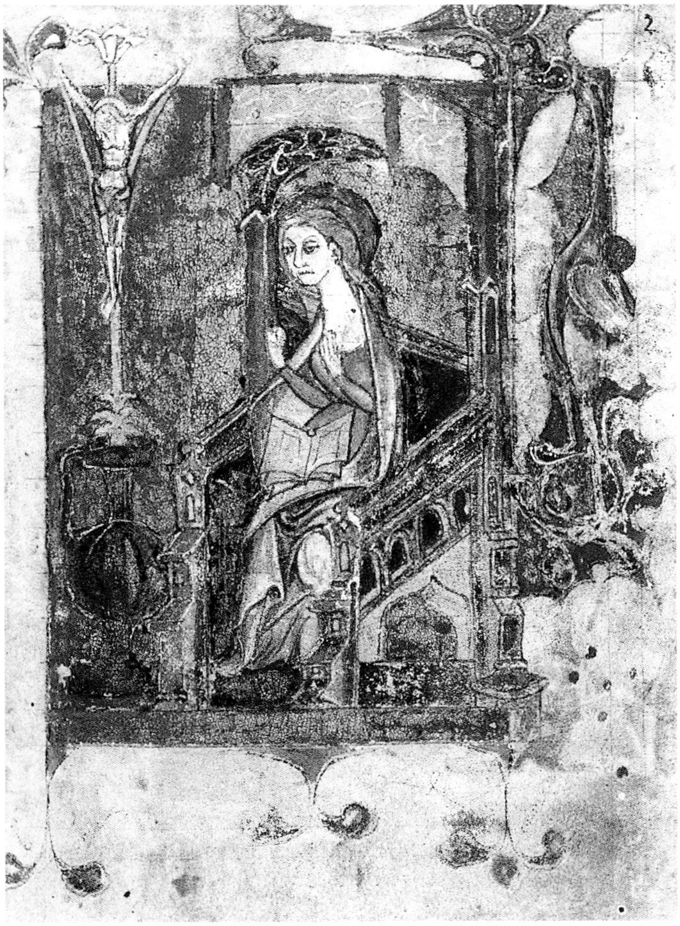

However, within this broad understanding, there were to be important changes. The first, scarcely apparent in England before about 1200, was the abandoning of the well-established four-nail attachment of Christ to the cross (with one nail through each hand and one through each foot, the feet being placed side by side and the figure being calm and erect with outstretched arms) for a three-nail attachment with only one nail through the two overlapping feet.[41] Usually the right foot is placed over the left. The second change, which seems to have depended upon this three-nail formula, was to the form of Christ's body. From around 1250 or so, the nail driven through Christ's feet tended increasingly to be placed relatively high in relation to his body, so in effect bending Christ's legs at the knees, turning his torso somewhat sideways and pushing his stomach inwards to form a concavity. In the earlier three-nail versions the legs tend to be straighter and the stomach protruberant. The new effect creates a profile shaped like an open Z, the lower legs echoing the form of Christ's diagonal right arm, the head hanging forwards, the ribcage projecting and the feet crossed over. The figure now seems not so much to be fixed against the cross, as to hang down and out from it. The three-nail formula is already present in the Munich Psalter (fols 26–26v; fig. 167) and in an initial in BL Arundel MS 104, both of around 1200–10, and seems to be the increasingly accepted type in English manuscripts executed from about 1220 onwards, as in the Robert of Lindsey Psalter (fig. 169).[42] There was clearly room for variance around 1220 or 1230 since the old four-nail type is used in the earliest crucifixion painted to the west end of the nave of St Albans, but abandoned in the crucifixes executed there around and after the mid-century, which culminate in a fine Z-bend example towards 1300 at the east end of the nave (figs 176–7). Matthew Paris used the four-nail version in his various drawings. The Z-bend first occurs in works such as the Oscott Psalter well within the third quarter of the century (fig. 178) and remains the most common formula up to the middle of the fourteenth century (fig. 129 right). Almost exactly the same pattern of change is to be found in thirteenth-century French representations of the crucifixion between the *Bibles moralisées*, the sketchbook of Villard d'Honnecourt and the works of Jean Pucelle and his circle.

This progressive reformulation of the crucifix in the period 1200–1250 resulted in what one may call (echoing Judith Butler) a distinctively new 'corporeal style', the product of an apparently deliberate rejection or undermining of the old formulas.[43] The three-nail

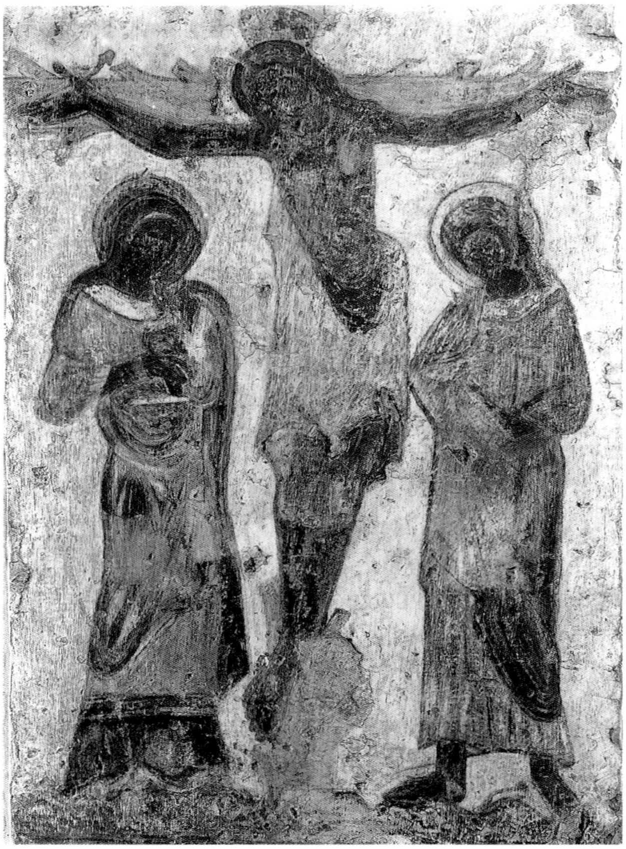

176 Crucifixion. Mural on west face of north nave pier, St Albans Abbey, *c.* 1235 (Conway Library, Courtauld Institute of Art).

formula became the norm; a new consensus had been established. The explanations offered by modern scholars for this are many: Greek and Latin affective writing on the crucifixion, changes to the number of nails shown in representations of the Instruments of the Passion in the Last Judgement, developments within liturgical and Trinitarian symbolism, and so on.[44] But no single account holds sway. This explanatory pluralism arises at least in part from the near-total lack of any contemporary explanation of the three-nail cross: in the period under discussion quite striking changes could occur to central signs without even the slightest contemporary justificatory defence, as opposed to later rationalization.[45] How new traditions come to establish themselves (as opposed to originate) is seldom clear, but the role of important and persistently influential models cannot be discounted. The Abbey of Saint-Denis was one. One of the earliest three-nail crosses, of stupendous scale and artistic and semiotic virtuosity, was commissioned in the 1140s for the main altar at Saint-Denis by Abbot Suger, and so in one of the most authoritative cynosures of the Gothic style in northern France.[46] Suger in his writings on Saint-Denis volunteered no particular comment on the nail-iconography of his great cross (an iconography inferred from later inventorial evidence), describing the cross and its 'suffering image' (*imago patiens*) in a traditional way, as the banner (*vexillum*) of triumph.[47] Its three-nail type may have been part of a new Lotharingian or Mosan sacramental art, since the earliest extant three-nail cross, now in Brussels, is from Tirlemont, dated 1149.[48] As a measure of slightly later twelfth-century Parisian thought, it is notable that the widely read *Historia scholastica* of Petrus Comestor opts for the three-nail formula.[49] Whether or not these statements amounted to a new lore or code for the cross is however manifestly debatable, and it will be clear that

177 Crucifixion. Mural on west face of north nave pier, St Albans Abbey, *c.* 1300 (Conway Library, Courtauld Institute of Art).

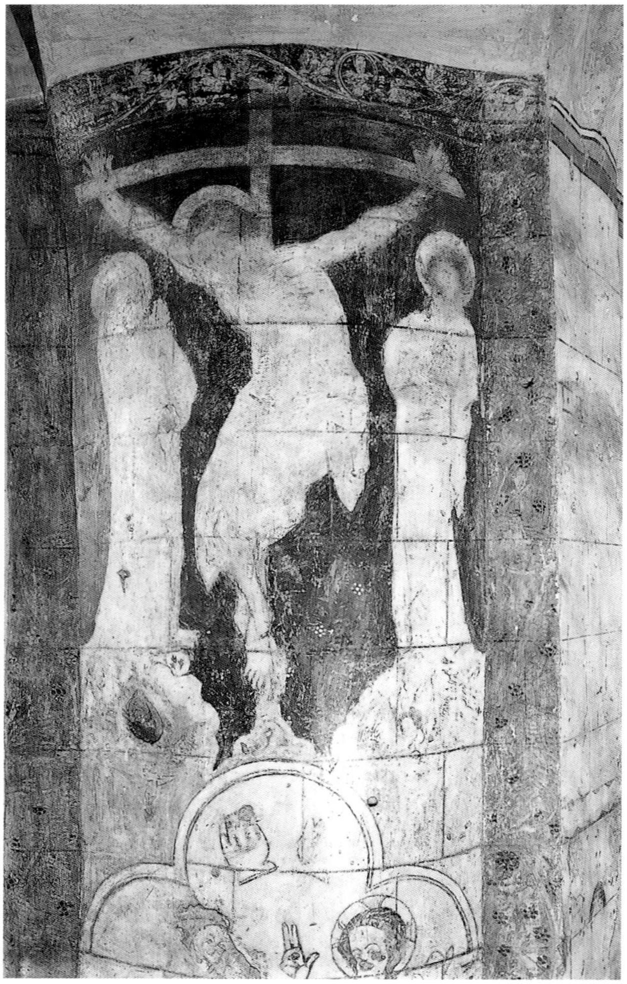

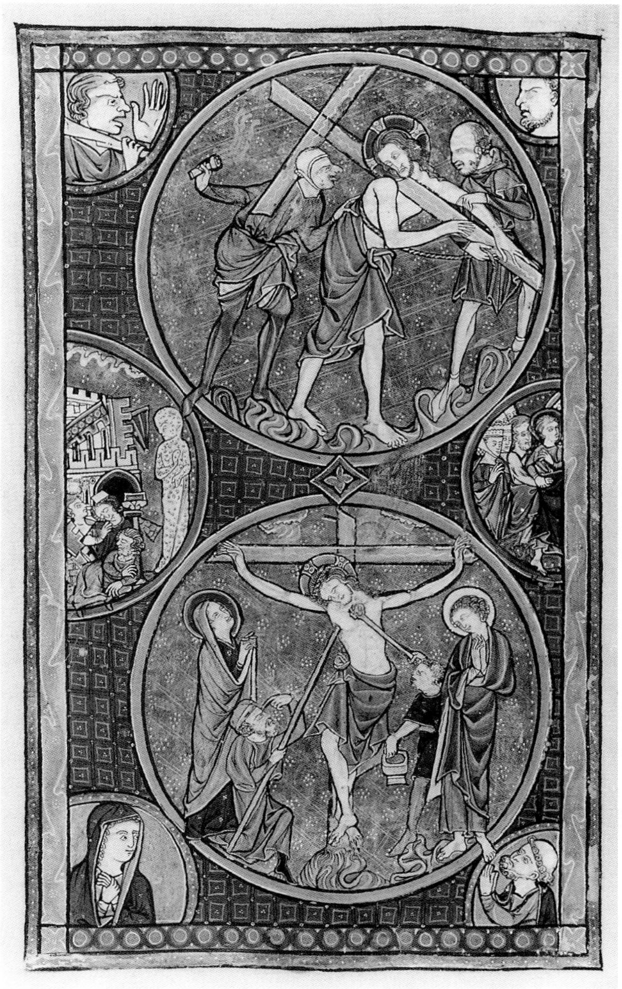

178 Carrying of Cross, Crucifixion. Oscott Psalter, BL Add. MS 50000, fol. 11v, 1260s (Conway Library, Courtauld Institute of Art).

such 'explanations' as there may be do not necessarily embrace the signification of the new forms. The factors initially giving rise to new formulas may be totally different from those that ensure their eventual acceptance and development.

In terms of the very few contemporary statements about the nails and the bodily form of Christ, the picture in the key period of transition around 1200 is in fact mixed. The tradition of affective writing associated with pseudo-Anselm reveals a similar current of thought in twelfth-century England to that in the Mosan region and Paris in regard to acceptance of the three-nail form. The Anselmian meditation 10 and the *Dialogus* on Christ's Passion refer explicitly to only one nail through the feet.[50] Even in the early years of the thirteenth century, the signs are that there was greater willingness to recognize pluralism than to force any issue of doctrinal purity on the point. As Pickering pointed out in regard to the two 'modes' of crucifixion, the 'Anselmian' and the 'Bonaventuran', 'The two rituals were tolerated side by side because either of them allowed the faithful [. . .] to see *one* fulfilment'.[51] Christ could be nailed to the cross lying down, or raised up. The deed may be imagined this way, or that; with four nails, or three. The *Ancrene Wisse* is of signal interest here. The celebrated section of its seventh part, which is devoted to Christ the noble wooer and knight and likens the tapering form of the crucifixion to a shield, observes merely that Christ's feet overlapped on the cross 'as many think', *efter monies wene*: neither disparagement nor defence, but the recognition of diversity of views and, perhaps, of the relative novelty of that particular solution within a characteristically English melding of the affective and the literary.[52] Later in the century Durandus, who notes the basically patristic tradition of four-nail crosses largely adhered to by Italian artists before 1300, also adds that 'others say that Christ was fixed with only three nails'.[53] The pseudo-Bonaventure takes one nail as a norm for the feet.[54] But there is no sense of the need for doctrinal explanation as such in any of these fairly liberally minded texts.

The contrast with the attitude of the strongly papally minded Spanish Bishop Lucas of Tuy, writing before about 1227, will be obvious. Lucas cites the issue of the cross in his determined polemic on the production by heretics of new and erroneous images.[55] His methods are those of the smear. Lucas either did not know about, or chose to ignore, the rapid and widespread adoption of the forms he excoriated by numerous legitimate Church patrons. 'Heretic' is not a term applied as a rule to Abbot Suger, or for that matter Petrus Comestor. Instead, those who make crosses showing Christ with one foot nailed over the other are identified by Lucas with those who deride Christ on the cross as revealed in Psalm 21: 8.[56] These artists are tormenting Christ and the Church anew. Their error is directly linked by him to the making of wrongly shaped tau-crosses with only three arms, which people adore instead of the True Cross – a foreshadowing of the authoritarianism of Ralph Baldock.[57] Lucas understood the danger of 'irrational' signs well, and his attribution of motive to such heretics is insightful, even if born of a ludicrous provincialism. He puts these words into the mouths of his adversaries:

> We say that Christ was crucified with one foot over the other pierced with one nail, and that we wish to change the customs of the Church so that we might

be able to excite the devotion of the people by the greater intensity of the Passion and to prevent boredom by replacing long-standing customs by something new (*ut maiori acerbitate passionis Christi populi excitetur et novitate in consuetudinibus succedente fastidium relevetur*). For these things are neither a matter of the sacraments nor articles of faith, and may be changed daily and at will.

The passage concludes, 'This sort of thing they say as if it were rational.'[58] His defence of the four-nail tradition includes reference to the stigmata of St Francis, to the existence of four nail-relics, and to 'legitimate' images such as the *volto santo* at Lucca, but above all to the preaching of Innocent III which summarized the old patristic line on the true form of the cross with a proper cross-beam and top arm, and four nails.[59] The main point of reference is thus simply tradition, the reformist defence of the customs of the Roman Church, *consuetudines Romanae ecclesiae*. His approach is less compelling than the resourceful allegorizing of Innocent, who likens the timbers and nails to the virtues, and the two separately nailed feet to two prime affects, dread or fear (*metus*) and longing (*appetitus*) disciplined by the nails of fortitude and justice.

Yet Lucas's understanding of his opponents' position is astute, and like many critiques is also revealing of the nature, strength and inherent pluralism of the position he claims to be identifying as contrary to his own. The appearance of the cross is a matter of disagreement; some claim that changes are necessary because they enhance the affect of the cross, its representation of pain, to religious ends; articles of faith and belief in the sacraments leave the matter open to interpretation. But there is no question here of a fundamental – and more truly heretical – challenge to the notion of image-use itself. Lucas's two discourses, of heresy and established custom, far from being radically different, are in fact fundamentally similar; what is at stake is the authority to determine and stabilize discourse. This similarity makes Lucas's polemic all the more interesting in view of his disclosure of the understanding that Christ's body was shown on the cross in a new way for essentially affective reasons. Lucas, perhaps driven by a Platonic suspicion of emotion, might not have liked this possibility, but he did at least acknowledge it and accord it importance. Corroborative evidence that an affective stance towards the crucifixion was by now perfectly legitimate, indeed desirable, is sufficiently widespread for one to think that Lucas was not just engaging in a peculiar rationalization.[60] Indeed in this regard Lucas was out of line not with heretics, but much of the northern European Church, especially given the exactly contemporary 'official' Church's policy of deploying images, or gestures such as the Elevation, to appeal to the senses precisely in order to heighten or excite lay attention to the liturgy – readers will recall the phrase *cum propter hoc excitetur devotio fidelium* in the Salisbury statutes of 1238–44 (p. 156 above). That this strategy of excitation was allied to the aesthetics or practices of bodily animation had already been established in Peter the Chanter's writing on prayer, in which 'sameness is the mother of satiety'.[61] The respectable pedagogic value of 'variation of activity' had already been extended from the sphere of bodily discipline in prayer, into the sphere of religious imagining and theory of affect.

If what Lucas was actually doing was describing and blackening an emergent 'modernist' position within the orthodox constituency, it follows that the new type of cross, placing greater emphasis on the mobility or potential mobility of the hanging corpus of Christ, and on the excruciating effect of legs and feet twisted and dependent upon one fixing-point, may very well have been perceived as looking more agonizing precisely because it had been intended to look that way. It was no longer the static, hieratic icon of earlier centuries, in which suffering is borne stoically, but the dynamic representation of an imaginatively gripping (because mutable) and memorable (because more extreme) process. Yet neither was it 'naturalistic': indeed, in this manipulation lies precisely a recognition, implicit or explicit, of the artificiality of the sign and its need for intensification. In Aristotelian terms, one might say that its pathos was the self-conscious or calculated product of the physiological or dispositional change implicit in an affect: the crucifixion is now an *imago agens*, an image which is both objectively moved and 'moving'; being physically freed up to writhe in agony, to turn hither and thither and finally to slump, the image of Christ in his torment is rhetorically richer and offers greater scope for moment-by-moment imaginative engagement.[62] This is not surprising, as at least since the twelfth century emphasis had been given increasingly to the dynamics of the cross and crucifixion as a temporal process. Exact proof of this is provided by the eventual appearance in the period of wooden images of Christ with movable arms, legs and head to be used as liturgical props at Passiontide, especially after 1300 or so.[63] Movement was also invested in images read sequentially. Thus in the monumental pictures of the Passion on both sides of folio 38 of the so-called picture book of Madame Marie (BN MS n.a. fr. 16251), dating from the last decades of the thirteenth century, the episodes of the sponge and the spear accompany a Christ who progressively hangs lower on the cross in death across two illustrations.[64] Works of art which by their nature were involved in liturgical action and movement could also dramatize the process. It was possible to activate the bodies of Christ and those of Mary and John by means of the movable art object: since the twelfth century some two-sided processional crosses had shown Christ alive on one face, and dead on the other; and on the early fourteenth-century *Opus anglicanum* chasuble (or priest's Mass vestment) from Melk, which shows Christ crucified on either side of the vestment, Mary's and John's postures are slightly varied, each image being engaged and disengaged not by the turning of a page, but by the rotation of the priest's body while performing the ritual actions before the altar.[65]

Not the least aspect of this new style and artifice was that it simultaneously gave rise to new associative possibilities. Representation was in some ways ahead of signification. The *Ancrene Wisse* text just noted suggests very strongly that the three-nail formula developed in twelfth-century France went on to prompt the cross-as-shield figure as well as Trinitarian associations (for in a shield are three things, the wood, leather and paint: the wood of the cross, the leather of Christ's body and the painting of the red blood that coloured it so carefully).[66] It pointed to other links, as illustrated by the typological medallions in Eton College MS 177, an English manuscript of the 1270s;[67] folio 5 shows a three-nail crucifixion surrounded by Old Testament types, including Moses and the Brazen Serpent (fig. 179). The texts around the crucifixion and Brazen Serpent medallions read respectively: 'Christ delivered and redeemed us with shed blood, not worthy of death at all but dying an evil death', and (following the *Glossa ordinaria*) 'Christ the serpent kills the fiery serpents'.[68] The images are dense with allusion. The serpent figure is drawn in the first instance from Christ's own prophecy in John 3: 14 that he would be lifted up like the brazen serpent raised by Moses in the wilderness (Numbers 21: 9, *sicut serpens – ita Filius hominis*), a conventional typology whose implications are usually triumphalist – for the cross, like the brazen serpent, is a standard of victory.[69] In the Eton manuscript, however, the allusion is also to the winding serpent of Genesis 3: 1, to which a pointer is given by the sword-wielding cherub of Eden (Genesis 3: 24) standing by the cross on folio 5. Christ crucified thus triumphs over the Fall. Like the brazen serpent, the serpent in the Genesis illustration on folio 2 of the Eton manuscript also winds up the Tree, so demonstrating its *calliditas*, or subtlety. The *Christus serpens* appears to allude to this serpentine form by means of the rope-like winding arrangement of his legs on the cross.[70] In such visual harmonies one again encounters the incongruous and the riddle-like: the agonized crossed feet and wound-up legs, pointers to the *mors maligna* of the border inscription of the crucifixion scene, have nevertheless been drawn into a typological allegory through visual similarity. It might even be the case that, as Pickering suggested, the Z-bend Christ on the crosses of the late thirteenth century draw beholders back to the writhing worm of Psalm 21: 7, *ego autem sum vermis et non homo*, referring to Christ's abjection and rejection.[71] But my reasons are not Pickering's: the ostensive form, itself to be understood within the history of representation, has suggested the allegorical link, and not vice versa. These new figurative associations, the shield, the serpent and so on, substantiate the idea that there was no tension or conflict between the affective and the discursive: real assent, the power of images, was premised upon both. New images, techniques of representation – the domain of artists – could be the source, not the product, of new understandings of 'lore', and through them medieval art could continually enrich, even rediscover, itself.

Sweetness

As the century progressed, the affective traits of the crucifixion image tended – at first sight – to increase in intensity, just as its internal organization as a sign grew more complex. A superb document of this process forms part of the sequence of devotional and pastoral pictures suffixed to the Lambeth Apocalypse of the 1260s (fig. 181). Stylistically derived from the bulk of Apocalypse illustrations, this is the earliest important English calvary.[72] The mode of the crucifixion is broadly 'Bonaventuran' (i.e. with the hands and feet nailed to an erect cross by means of ladders), and the objective of the image strongly inventorial or synoptic. Here, as if in a series of *nota benes*, are the Virgin Mary, John and a very prominent and dignified kneeling Longinus, whose blind spear is guided towards Christ's side; all of them may be read as members of the litany of saints of which the suffixed programme generally is composed. Here too are catalogued the sinners and acts of sin, the inscription of the *titulus*, the nailing, the spear and sponge and the mocking.[73] It is as if the images of the saints digress into the Passion narrative, while the Passion narrative digresses into the litany of the saints – a fluid process of enumeration and associative connection or cueing typical of the devotional schedule. The image's pictorial mode is also emphatic in a brittle and somewhat cold way. Again, context is everything, for as Wolfgang Kemp has observed, this supercharged style is intrinsic to the

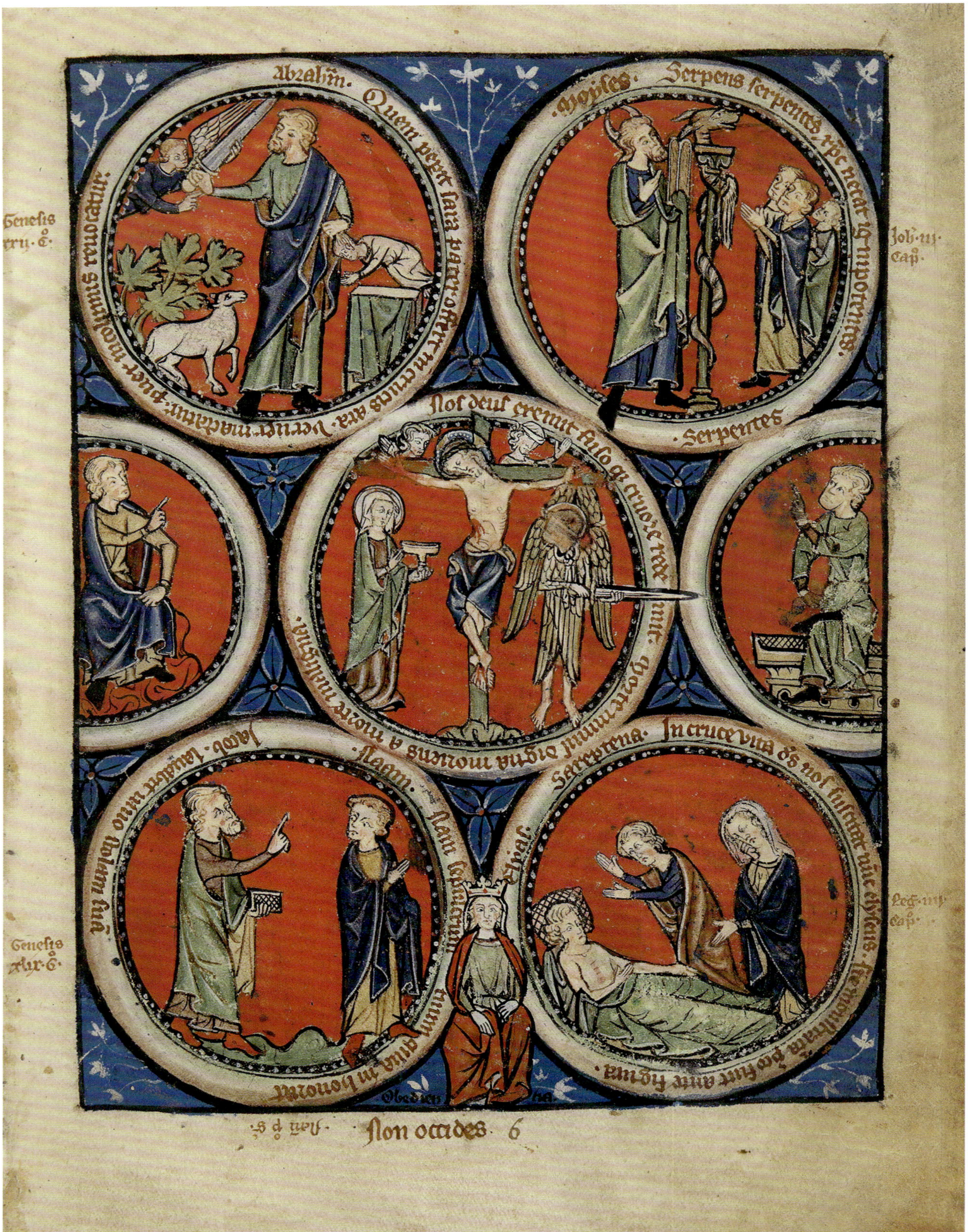

179 Crucifixion with Old Testament types. Eton Apocalypse, Eton College MS 177, fol. 5, 1270s (The Provost & Fellows of Eton College).

methods of the contemporary Apocalypse illuminators, the 'extreme mobility of the figures', the 'visually emphatic nature of the corporeal rhetoric', the new 'exploitation of physiognomy and facial expression', 'pantomime, the play of attitudes, the language of clothes', the 'over strung, hyperactive character' and strong tendency for the story to 'go off on tangents'.[74] The step from this to the devotional crucifixion in the small north-eastern English Huth Psalter of around 1280 (fig. 180) is small:[75] here the sinister flushed and grinning profile heads of abusers and tormentors of Christ offer a physiognomic commentary on Psalm 21: 8 (*omnes videntes me deriserunt me*), in conscious contrast to the stoical comportment of the Saviour and saints standing with him: a further sign of the unprecedented corporeal literalism of the new style of calvary, and of its capacity to reinvigorate traditional crucifixion 'lore' through somatic reference to the Psalms.[76]

180 Crucifixion. Huth Psalter, BL Add. MS 38116, fol. 11v, *c.* 1280 (Conway Library, Courtauld Institute of Art).

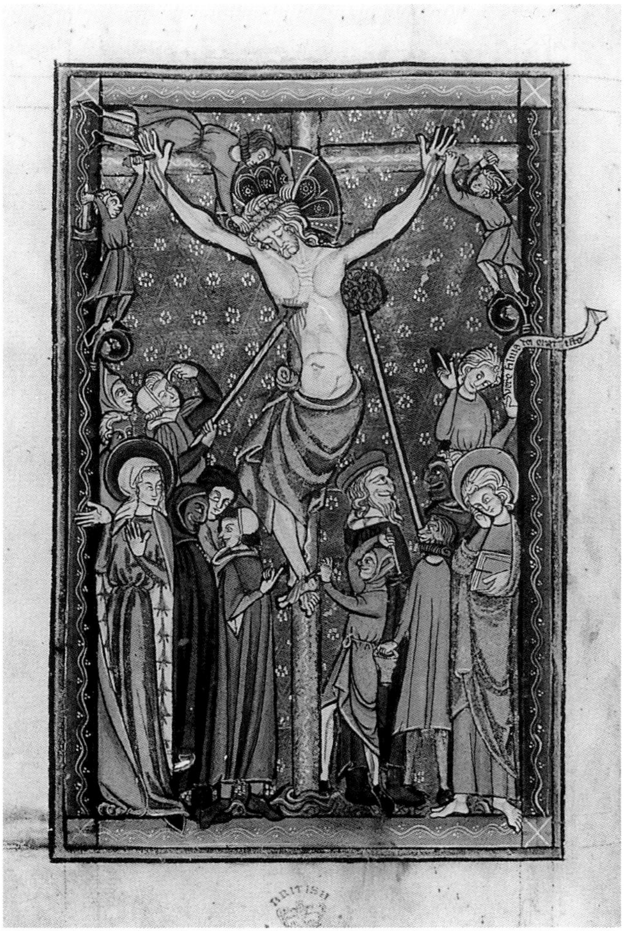

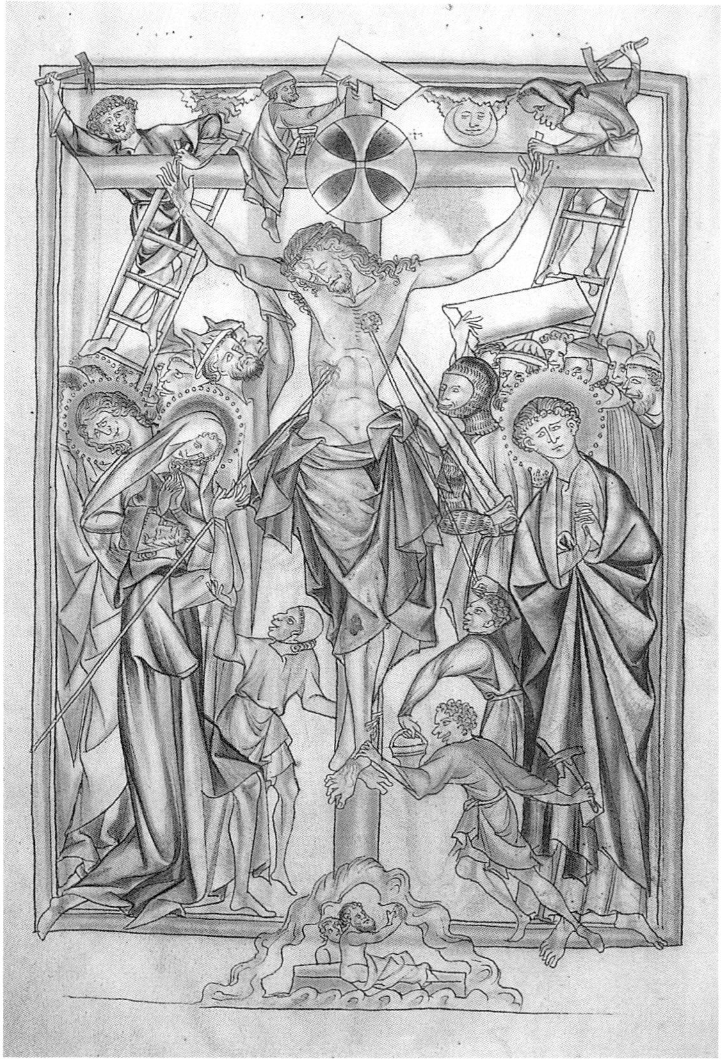

181 Crucifixion. Lambeth Apocalypse suffixed illustration, Lambeth Palace Library MS 209, fol. 51v, 1260s (Lambeth Palace Library).

Works such as the Lambeth Apocalypse and Huth Psalter also raise a major issue concerning the ethos of the Gothic crucifixion in England. These images were produced a generation or two before the Conyhope cross episode in 1305. Yet for all their hyperactivity neither they, nor their fourteenth-century successors, reveal anything of the radical reconfiguration of the body of Christ, the self-evident power to shock, of the *Crucifixus dolorosus*, represented by the wooden image at Sankt Maria im Kapitol in Cologne and – one infers – its sister image once at Conyhope.[77] In them the general character of the crucifix remains quite undisturbed. England has of course lost all its carved or wrought crucifixions from the period, and this loss might be important in so far as the most radical crucifixes of western Europe tended in this period to be executed in sculpture. Nevertheless, if the *Crucifixus dolorosus* had a history in the 'homelands' of the Gothic style before or after 1300 or so, it remains extremely elusive. Very few fourteenth-century crucifixions, such as that in the Holkham Bible picture book (BL Add. MS 47682, fol. 32; fig. 182),[78] present the viewer with the treatment of Christ's absolutely naked body as a leprous integument of weals, as an inventory of holes and wounds to be counted like the bones of Psalm 21: 18, or dwelt upon and penetrated imaginatively, as by the English mystics.[79] In this case the acerbity of the cross belongs to a more extravagant and more focused pattern of visualization than that of the restrained affect of the thirteenth-century images, and one which is also much more characteristic of later medieval religious lyrics on the Passion.[80] Nor is it quite in the tradition of the *Crucifixus dolorosus*. The relatively plentiful English painted wall and manuscript evidence indicates that, as in France and Scandinavia, the period was on the contrary marked by a quite separate and remarkably stable tradition of restraint.

182 Crucifixion. Holkham Bible Picture Book, BL Add. MS 47682, fol. 32, 1330s (Conway Library, Courtauld Institute of Art).

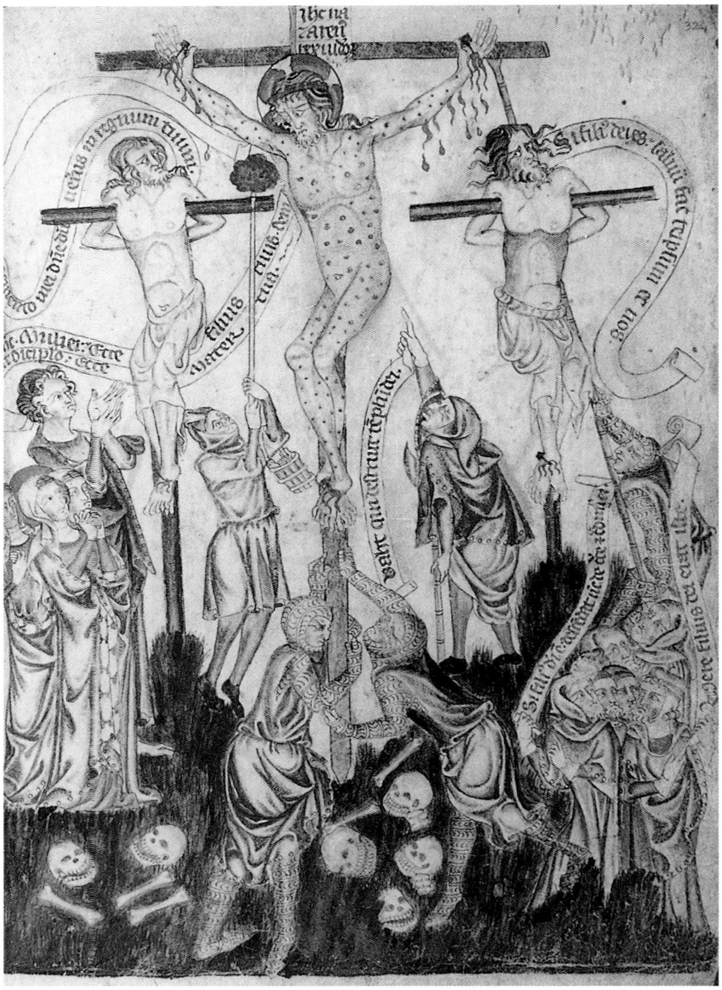

In trying to understand this tradition, it will help to place the central sign of the cross in a wider context. This is not (as the Anglo-German nexus might at first suggest) provided by crudely collectivist notions of national temperament, but rather by the prevailing ethos, or ethical modality, cultivated, perpetuated and inculcated by the publically recognized structures of authority examined at various points in this study, the Church and public power especially. The set of ideas that clustered to form the extremely influential pattern of English sanctity will help me to introduce this point. As will be recalled (p. 81 above), the prevalent character of the older and newer saints' cults was monastic or aristocratic or both: the saints were typically those either born of royal lineage or those, such as the bishops, admitted to the category of the aristocratic by means less of their birth than their virtues. Whether confessors or martyrs, they belonged to the category of 'holy sufferers', red or white martyrs. In the newer cults particularly, there was a persistent and deliberate formulation of this style of aristocratic sanctity in the light of notions of temperance, arguably the dominant personal ethic in the hagiography of the major national saints and role models of leadership – Thomas, Edward, Edmund – composed in and after the late twelfth century. I have already mentioned St Thomas's courtly breeding and temperance, St Edward's *mesure*, St Edmund's affability, St Richard's happy expression and sweet temper. These attributes doubtless represented no more than powerful monastic and aristocratic ideals. Yet in their newer, moderate, Aristotelian form they were now finding their way into the Church's pastoral regulation. As ideals they appear to have been accorded wide assent. It seems that no sphere of English cultural practice, whether male or female, monastic or secular, was untouched by this formulation of the Christian *habitus*. It is therefore worth raising the possibility that it may also help to account for the prevailing ethos of the English crucifixion itself – an image which, as the Lambeth Apocalypse shows, could take its place amidst pastoral illustrations exemplifying and directing conduct, and which was itself demonstrably an object of regulation.

The concepts that are of particular help here are those of sweetness and gentility. These are prominent in the English thirteenth-century religious lyric on the cross, and not surprisingly they stem principally from the monastic style of mystical speculation in the writings of John of Fécamp, St Bernard's sermons on Canticles, the hymn *Dulcis Ihesu Memoria* and Hugh of Saint-Victor's *De arrha animae*. As Rosemary Woolf explained, the latter expounds the love-worthiness of Christ in terms of personal amiability, his supreme fairness and grace.[81] The Anselmian tradition is also of signal importance. Following Canticles 1: 1, meditation 10 in particular makes great use of the notion of Christ's sweetness in his Passion – sweet (*dulcis*) in his lowered head and death, sweet in the extension of his arms, sweet in the opening of his side, sweet in the affixing of his feet with one nail – sweet in his desire to kiss with his lowered head his beloved, whose kisses are sweeter (*meliora*) than wine.[82] This is also the language of affect directed towards the great sweetness (*magna dulcedine*) of Christ, Mary and the angels, contrasted with the bitterness and great anguish (*amaritudine et magno dolore*) of the Passion; as discussed in connection with St Edmund's *Speculum*, this takes its place within the Bernardine and Victorine traditions of affective spirituality, but to pastoral ends.[83]

Edmund's writings take this much older language deep into the thirteenth century, in the context of a text that was aimed originally at socially privileged women and within a century enjoyed wider circulation. Christ's quality of sweetness is a common figure in English vernacular lyrics.[84] Indeed, the most distinguished and moving lyrical examples of this monastic tradition of speculation on the beauty and nobility of Christ are to be found in writings for anchoresses, particularly the closely linked community of texts in the *Ancrene Wisse* and the so-called 'Wooing group' of the first half of the century.[85] Drawing on Latin meditations on Psalm 44: 3 (*speciosus forma prae filiis hominum*, thou art fairer than the children of men), the section of the seventh part of the *Ancrene Wisse* devoted to Christ the wooer and knight, which includes the cross-shield likeness, expatiates on the theme of Christ's beauty and nobility, themes appropriate to women of high rank. His face is the most beautiful of all men's, he speaks sweetly as the wooer of Church, the lady in distress; his shield, his side, is pierced to show her his heart and to draw out hers in return.[86] The gift of her heart is to one who possesses the supreme attributes of fairness, richness, nobility, wisdom, courtesy, generosity, gentleness and sweetness.[87] The same attributes are to be found in the *Þe Wohunge of ure Laverd*, 'The Wooing of Our Lord', a text linked to the *Ancrene Wisse*.[88] *Þe Wohunge* opens with a series of ejaculations to the sweet Jesus, the honey drop, *huniter*, whose memory is sweeter in the mouth than honey, a refrain throughout the text; this is the language of the hymn *Dulcis Ihesu Memoria*.[89] The list of the wooer's qualities is like that of *Ancrene Wisse*: aside from sweetness, one finds fairness (whiteness of flesh especially, after Canticles 5: 10), richness, largesse, wisdom, prowess, nobility, gentility and gentleness (*deboneirschipe*).[90] *Þe Wohunge* speaks unambiguously the language of chivalric and aristocratic virtue which was coming to enjoy wider currency than before: compare the allusion to the gentleness of Christ's life and death, *deboneireté de sa vie e de sa mort*, in the layfolk's Mass book considered in the previous chapter (fig. 161).[91] At no point in the literary or artistic history of the thirteenth-century cross in England is there any suggestion that the crucifixion should prompt the affect of dread, *metus*, a corollary of the notion of a *Crux horribilis* and an attitude much more appropriate to the contemplation of death.[92] Quite the contrary: the dominant themes are those of grief, love and nobility, and the prevailing aesthetic tenor that of beauty and *mesure*, that decorous equilibrium between reason and affect which has also been noted by some authorities in the lyrical and devotional discourse of the period.[93] The cross is not to be the object of histrionics: it is the site of temperance. The wounds of Christ are objects of love, symbols of his supreme love-worthiness, quite as much as his face.[94] The calamity of the crucifixion, Christ's destitution for the sake of his beloved, is understood not in terms of loss of beauty – for Christ retains his loveliness, albeit besmirched – but of the aristocratic concept of shame, being accounted of no social rank, as encountered in the *Ancrene Wisse* and Peter the Chanter's writing on socially suitable prayer postures.[95]

Although beauty and ugliness are relative concepts, this discourse – which was in no sense gender-specific – gives at least some guidance as to how the crucifix was commonly, if not exclusively, shaped and viewed. So it would not be inauthentic to see the Christ of the crucifixion in the Lindsey Psalter (fig. 169), a work intended for monastic viewing, as the embodiment of noble *patientia* or virtuous suffering which, in its technically perfect blending of delicate white and pink flesh tones in Christ's face, breast and limbs, alludes to Canticles 5: 10's *candidus et rubicundus* quite as much as the colours of the budding cross itself. This sweet fairness is again noble and sponsorial, and may be understood in the light of such meditations as *Candet nudatum pectus* of John of Fécamp, and such commonplaces as *Respice in faciem Christi tui* (Psalm 83: 10) and 'Man, folwe Seintt Bernardes trace'.[96] Christ's head is lowered gently, not severely, and his face is not pulled into the rictus of the *Crucifixus dolorosus*, or hung so low as to be obscure, any more than it is in the most beautiful of contemporary English crucifixions, those in the Amesbury and

Evesham Psalters (figs 165, 170), and in the Missal of Henry of Chichester (Manchester, John Rylands Library MS Lat. 24, fol. 152; fig. 183).[97] These images, made for monastic owners or secular clergy, are very delicately nuanced. The ribs of Christ can be counted as well here as in any more severe representation. Yet the cross's role as a love-object is not in doubt, for in her faint before the cross in the Rylands Missal – her absolute affective and compassionate identification with Christ's emptying out of himself – Mary bears a scroll inscribed *anima mea liquefacta est*, from Canticles 5: 6.[98] The emphasis on the fairness in suffering of Christ's face in the lyrical devotional tradition is especially critical given the very marked contemporary shift towards devotion to the Holy Face, traced precisely in the association of the cross and the Veronica on folio 6 of the Evesham Psalter, and in the spread of this devotion within particular religious communities in England.[99] There were therefore important reasons why this most important site of affective exchange should not be excessively agonized or even occluded. As discussed in the next chapter, Matthew Paris was extremely alert to the power of devotional scrutiny of Christ's face, not only as an object of beauty, but as a means of structuring meditation on the historicity and humanity of Christ.

183 Crucifixion. Missal of Henry of Chichester, Manchester, John Rylands Library MS 24, fol. 152, mid-thirteenth century (reproduced by courtesy of the Director and Librarian, the John Rylands University Library of Manchester).

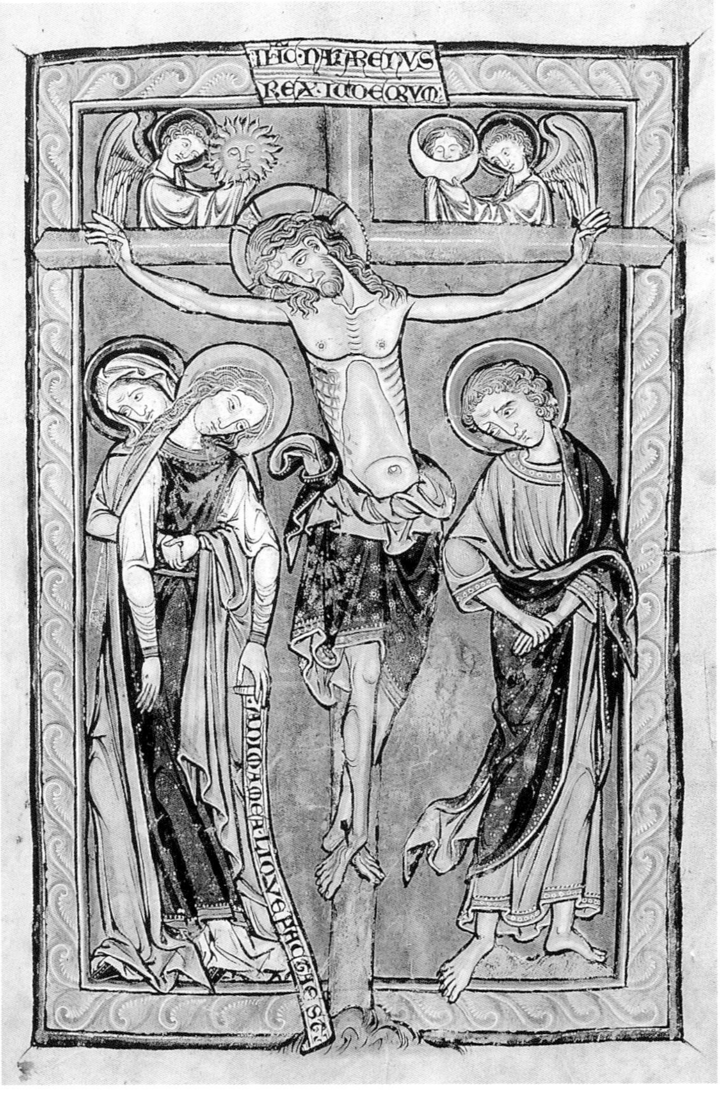

Matthew's treatment of the Holy Face is likely to have been informed by the rich tradition of monastic, and particularly Cistercian, affective writing on the Passion and Canticles whose impact is followed throughout this study. The ethos of restraint, even detachment, upon which I have placed some emphasis here owed much both to monastic and aristocratic aesthetics, as does the emphasis on physical beauty. There is no reason to think it was necessarily limited to such circles, particularly since it seems increasingly to have informed pastoral instruction for those of all ranks in the secular Church, and to have been widespread in the surviving religious lyrics. But its continuing relevance for monastic circles, and female devotion, well into the fourteenth century is illustrated by one curious cross-episode in fourteenth-century Yorkshire, which is also revealing about attitudes to images made for women. According to the chronicle of the Cistercian abbey of Meaux, at some point in the period 1339–49 the abbot, Hugh of Leven,

> had a new crucifix made in the lay-brother's choir. Its craftsman carved (*sculpebat*) nothing particularly beautiful or notable on it except on Fridays, while he fasted on bread and water. The sculptor studied a naked man (*hominem nudum*) standing before him, following whose comely shape (*formosam imaginem*) the cross might be made all the fairer. By means of this cross, God often sought out manifest miracles; and so we then reckoned that if women were allowed access to this cross, the community's devotion might be reinforced, and redound to the great advantage of our monastery. In connection with this, at our request the abbot of the Cistercians granted a licence allowing suitable men and women to go up to this cross, although women would not be allowed to enter through the cloister and dormitory or other offices unless they were a founder, wife or daughter of a founder, or wife of a son of a founder; these were also not to be allowed to remain overnight within the

limits of the abbey, nor to linger before Prime or after Compline. [. . .] Because of this licence, to our misfortune women often came to this cross, but in a state of cool devotion, and quite as much in order to snoop at the church's interior, our wealth being spent on their hospitality.[100]

This narrative is extremely suggestive, not least because it emanates from a monastic order historically opposed in principle to the use of sculpted crosses in churches: only painted wooden crosses had been allowed to the Cistercians.[101] The cross in question was miraculous, and lay access to it was deemed to be a fund-raising expedient, arising doubtless from Abbot Hugh's financial mismanagement of a house already chronically in debt.[102] Very striking is the use of a naked live model by the sculptor, possibly the earliest documented example of this practice in European art. While I have placed considerable emphasis on the growing importance of bodily representation in this account of the crucifix, the issue of mimesis as such has been of secondary importance. It can scarcely help at all with objects like the Cologne cross, whose form indicates that there was no ready correlation between heightened affect and mimesis of a 'naturalistic' sort: quite the contrary, for, though in some sense very real, this dolorous object rejects a smooth correspondence with the world and the platitudes of Gothic towards 1300.[103] On the other hand, the Meaux narrative belongs at first sight to the construction of medieval and post-medieval 'naturalism' and the triumph of the mimetic as a virtue. Yet its purpose is actually quite different. The cross, readers are told, was set up in the lay-brother's choir (i.e. at the head of the nave, distant from the monastic offices) and to it were admitted decent, but also privileged men and especially women, the patronesses of the house. The 'naked man' device is intended to show how the hoped-for devotion of these upper-class women was to be stimulated by the comeliness, *formositas*, of the image. Implicitly, women are to be drawn to the cross by the beauty of the figure as a carnal manifestation of Christ's humanity. This doctrinally acceptable carnality is also rendered licit by the countervailing stress on the ascetic practices of its artist, and more importantly by its instrumental character as a spiritual aid to fostering devotion – an attitude to carnal and spiritual love that can be traced back to St Bernard, and forward via Edmund of Abingdon and others to the writings of Walter Hilton.[104] The Cistercians were hardly immune from eucharistic visions of the cross in which Christ appeared 'not in a picture, not in a sculpture, but in a fleshly body'.[105] Yet the narrative's stress on failure, in effect self-reproach, reveals the hopeless optimism of this project. Here, as at Conyhope, innovation is linked to downfall: in this case, mimesis is nemesis. Devotion remained cool, and the downside of image-making was rendered apparent by the snooping of women around the church, the very embodiment of *curiositas*, the vice of the eyes. Again, another monastic moral: carnal, if beautiful, religious signs are risky and debilitating if they are based on experiment and recruited to pecuniary advantage; women, being naturally carnal, are unlikely to see the point; and the vice of *curiositas* remains an ever-present threat.

Exceptional this case may have been, but it nevertheless reinforces the point about the identification of upper-class female devotion with the beauty of the cross. The basis of such devotion lay at least in part in a long, and much more widespread, tradition of meditation on Christ's sponsorial nature. Such metaphors as Christ the bridegroom and knight-lover were widespread because, although linked to mystical experience, they also offered straightforward moral and doctrinal allegories whose character, as Woolf noted, was persuasive, possessing imaginative potency.[106] As such they influenced the somatic character of the cross. Their lyrical potency could be realized vigorously – and very straightforwardly – in non-somatic ways that bring one back to the tradition of 'edification' in regard to architecture. A very direct response to the Christ-knight metaphor is suggested by the framing of the Crucifixion image in the Fitzwarin Psalter of around 1350–75 (BN MS lat. 765, fol. 22; fig. 184).[107] Here, an exceedingly temperate crucifixion group is lodged within a towering fortress. Many of the Gospel miniatures in the Psalter possess this type of crenellated frame, and no doubt the impulse leading to the adoption of such forms was in part stylistic.[108] Such frank conceits are typical of the Decorated Style.[109] But from what has already been said, their metaphorical power may also be much easier to understand. The seigneurial military-religious allegory had already long been validated by thirteenth-century pastoral writings such as *Château d'Amour* (p. 182 above). The fortress in the Fitzwarin Psalter Crucifixion is both the *refugium* of Psalm 90: 2, 9 and a spectacular expression of the Christ-knight theme. One can begin to sense a fundamental continuity with the allegorization of architecture as traced forwards from Becket's Canterbury.

This dignified, if somewhat stiff and edificatory, realization of the seigneurial metaphors implicit in the sponsorial tradition is a reminder that there was no straightforward progression in this period towards a more dolorous iconography of the cross. It would be quite wrong to project back onto such representations the standards more typical of a later period. Also, to argue

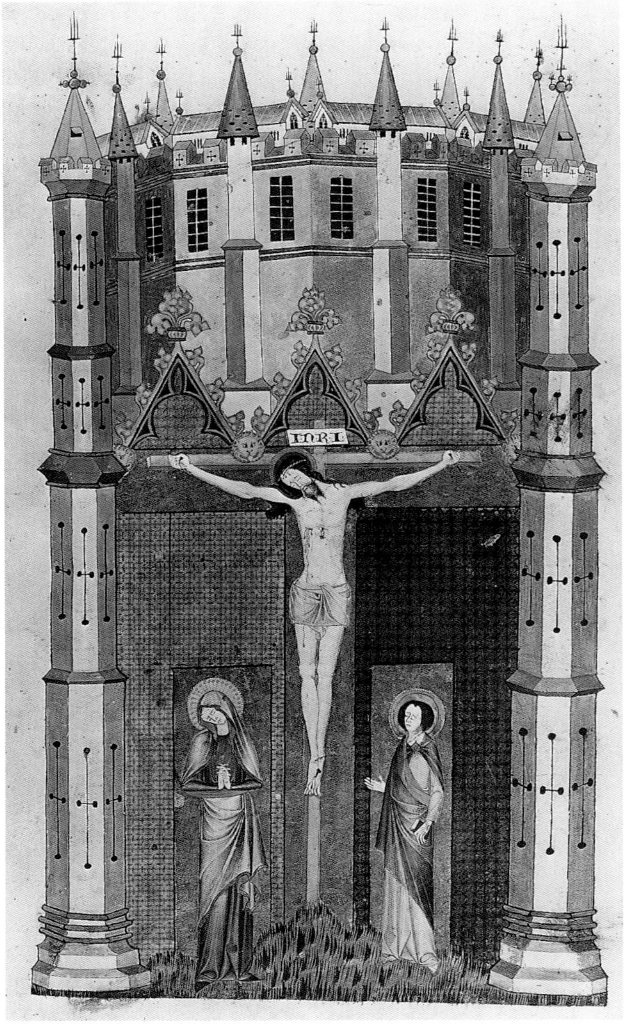

184 Crucifixion. Fitzwarin Psalter, BN MS Lat. 765, fol. 22, *c.* 1350–75 (Bibliothèque Nationale, Paris).

for the existence of a dominant affective ethos in this period is not to deny the very evident fact that the commissioning and consumption of religious art lay ultimately in the hands of several constituencies. The *Crucifixus dolorosus* was obviously fascinating for one spectrum of urban opinion, but objectionable to that of official diocesan authority in London. What held true for the compunctive spirituality of urban and especially female religious communities of the Rhineland did not necessarily hold true for urban south-eastern England or seigneurial and Cistercian Yorkshire: here again, it is more useful to think in terms of institutional or communal, and even regional, not national, identities. It would therefore be misleading to construct an entire history of the crucifixion in these regions of north-western Europe in terms of the 'abject' – the rejection of (ultimately classical) hierarchical notions of beauty by late medieval religious sensibilities in the service of a Christian realist or 'incarnational' aesthetic of the plain or ugly – however illuminating this concept might be in relation to specific religious groupings, and the religious artefacts they used.[110] The idea – a development, via the work of Erich Auerbach, of Hegel's concept of the unbeautiful in Christian or 'Romantic' art – is of very doubtful relevance to the English situation before 1300 or so.[111] On the contrary: the history of the cross as a love-object and a thing of beauty and paradox is sufficiently stable for one to think that principles deriving ultimately from classical rules of style and decorum, far from being deliberately subverted by the new pluralist and realist visual regimes, were for the present also being sustained, at least in some very important quarters. The well-known description of Christ cited in the second epigraph to this chapter, supposedly by Publius Lentulus, procurator of Judea, but probably a fourteenth-century interpolation, is exactly that of the Aristotelian *megalopsychos*, no matter how bizarre Aristotle himself would have regarded the notion of a crucified God. The link between beauty, temperance and truth had yet to be totally severed: and for this assertion one can find at least some evidence in the history of the representation of the Gothic body and the Gothic face, and, best of all, in the two together.

FACING PAGE Vision of the King of Denmark drowning seen by St Edward at Mass. *La Estoire de Seint Aedward le Rei* (detail of fig. 205).

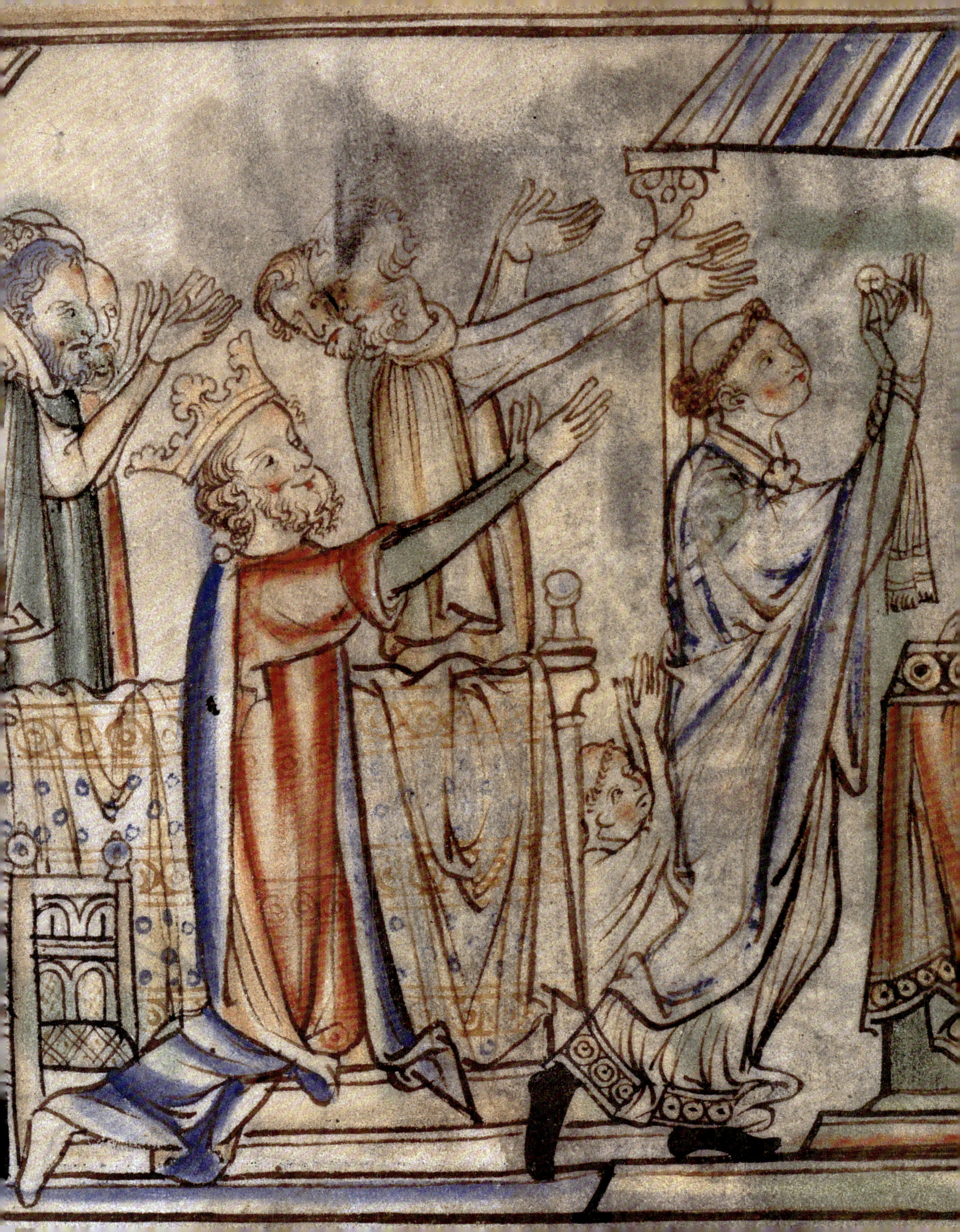

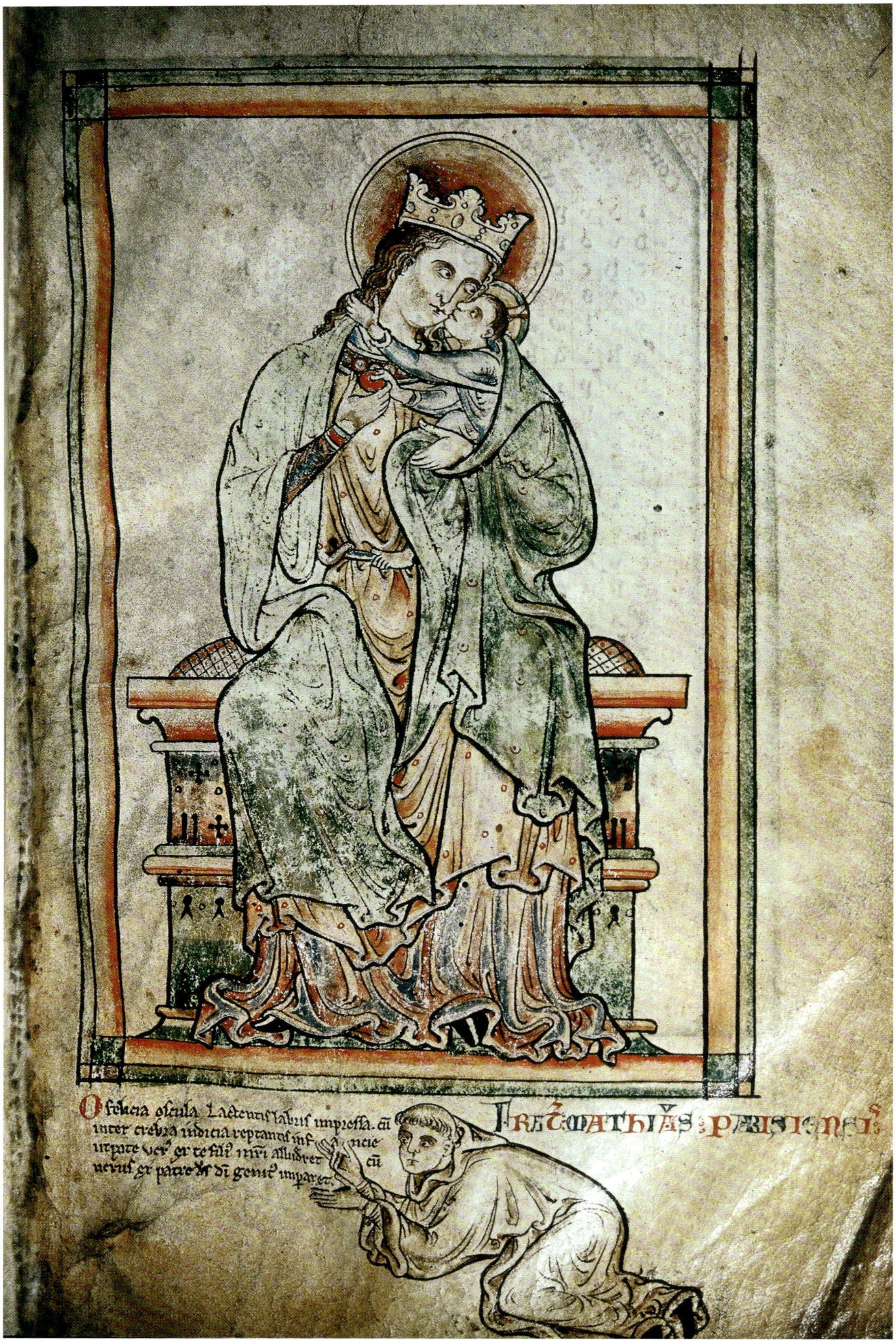

185 Matthew Paris addresses the prayer *O felicia oscula* to the Virgin and Child. Matthew Paris, *Historia anglorum*, BL Royal MS 14. C. VII, fol. 6, *c.* 1250 (by permission of the British Library).

Chapter 10

SUDDEN GLORY

The passion of Laughter is nothyng else but a suddaine Glory arising from suddaine Conception of some Eminency in our selves by Comparison with the Infirmityes of others, or with our owne formerly.

Thomas Hobbes, *The Elements of Law*

There are thousands of masks, thousands of ways of flaring and contracting the nostrils, thousands of twists and turns of the lips which deform the beauty of the face and the harmony of discipline. For the face is a mirror of discipline and it is to be shaped with so much greater vigilance, since the sins which appear there cannot be concealed.

Hugh of Saint-Victor, *De institutione novitiorum*

Jesting about laughter, you draw me into idle debate. But you know that Christ did not laugh.

Umberto Eco, *The Name of the Rose*

Ave Facies Praeclara

The best-known 'self-portrait' of Matthew Paris is a large tinted drawing (in the *Historia anglorum*) which shows him prostrate in prayer before the enthroned Virgin and Child (BL Royal MS 14. C. VII, fol. 6; fig. 185).[1] The form is traditional enough. This is how St Dunstan depicts himself in prayer to Christ in the late tenth-century drawing that opens what is now known as his Classbook (Oxford, Bodleian Library MS Auct. F. 4. 32, fol. 1).[2] The intimate and affective relationship of Mary and Christ in Matthew's drawing is anticipated by the remarkable image of the first two persons of the Trinity, locked eye to eye, on folio 1 of the pre-Conquest Harley Psalter: 'I am in the Father, and the Father in me' (John 14: 10) (BL Harley MS 603).[3] Here, however, Christ kisses his mother on the cheek. It is also tempting, though strictly speaking unnecessary, to see Matthew's group as a version of the Byzantine *Eleousa* Madonna intimately embracing her son. Matthew might also have elected to show a *Virgo lactans*, suckling the child;[4] instead, Christ gently grasps his mother's hair and takes from her an apple, while she bundles him up in a merciful mantle. Interest is focused entirely towards the top of this huge rearing icon. But something of Mary's milk of doctrine and love finds its way in, through the prayer inscribed before Matthew, which he is yielding up to the Virgin: *O felicia oscula lactentis labris impressa*, 'Oh happy kisses, with suckling lips impressed'. The prayer is not of Matthew's composition, since several post-patristic period variants of it exist, often in the context of homilies or other texts on the Assumption of the Virgin Mary.[5] As in Matthew's drawing, such texts often draw on sponsorial imagery, *Osculetur me osculo oris sui* and *mel et lac sub lingua tua* (Canticles 1: 1, 4: 11), to which one might add, 'out of the mouths of babes and sucklings', *ex ore infantium et lactantium* (Psalm 8: 3). Matthew's engagement with these 'tokens of crawling infancy' conforms to a now-widespread style of 'ingestive piety': it had been St Hugh of Lincoln who, through meditation, had 'experienced His sweetness, and sweetly digested it in the depths of his heart'; and, nearer to Matthew's world, Alexander Nequam, who had commended us to 'form before the eye of the mind the Mother of sweetness and the Son, sweetness itself, sweetly embracing each other'.[6]

This mighty picture, similarly formed before Matthew's eyes, has its own logic and coherence, and there is no reason to think it in some way records the appearance of another work of art at St Albans.[7] Such self-sufficiency is surely also true of another even more remarkable image by Matthew, one unprecedented in English art: the tinted drawing of the heads of the Madonna and Child, the suffering or dead Christ and the Majestic Christ (Cambridge, Corpus Christi College MS 26; fig. 186). Like the image in the *Historia anglorum*, this clearly religious picture from the *Chronica majora* indicates the breadth of Matthew Paris's conception of history as an unfolding of the divine plan. These 'close-ups' include Christ and his mother gazing raptly into one another's eyes, as *sponsa* and *sponsus*. From the modern point of view this isolation and focus on parts, not wholes, is perhaps somewhat fetishistic. But its purpose is synthetic, not analytic. The heads are emphatically not to be seen as isolated 'quotations' from other source-images, no matter how impressive (and obvious) the analogies to the Veronica, Man of Sorrows or Christ Crucified might be.[8] Instead they act together as an epitome not only of incarnational theology but of the practices of monastic contemplation of the *imago Christi*. The facial imagery of Canticles 2: 14 and Psalm 83: 10 has again acted as the starting-point for a string of associations. These were not necessarily Greek or Italian in origin.[9] One may understand them better by reference to the type of contemplative speculation on Christ's face developed by such later twelfth-century writers as Thomas the Cistercian. Thomas's commentary on Canticles 3 sets out a similar programme: in it, Christ has four faces, those of his human nativity, worldly calamity or passion, glorified humanity and divine majesty;[10] his followers conform to his humanity, imitate his passion, embrace a new life and aspire to see his divine majesty. These imaginings perform the role of a pilgrimage-like contemplation of Christ's historical transformation, ascending spiritually from the humble and carnal sphere of universal human affection to the beatific vision by means of anagogic interdependence and hierarchy. Matthew has simplified and conflated the details of Thomas's scheme, or something very like it; but the similarity of approach is undeniable.

186 Three Faces of Christ. Matthew Paris, *Chronica majora*, Cambridge, Corpus Christi College MS 26, p. 283 (old fol. vii), *c.* 1250 (Master and Fellows of Corpus Christi College, Cambridge).

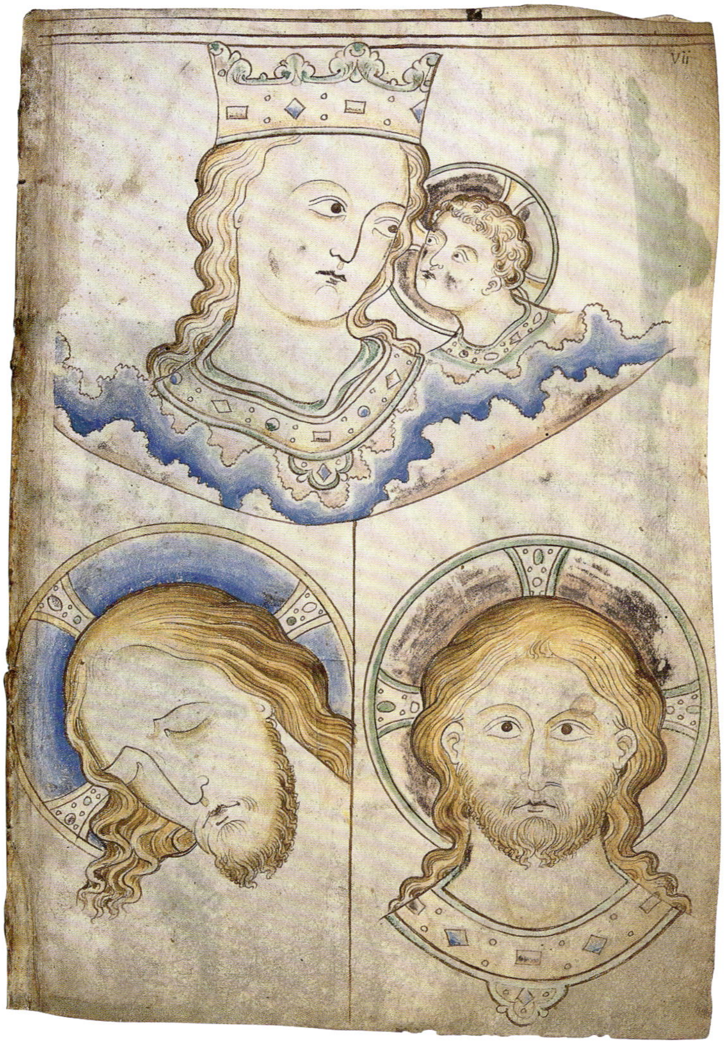

If so, it is intrinsically probable that the activity of viewing such images possessed real imaginative depth, discipline and richness of associative possibility. But in what sense were such drawings attuned to this contemplative style of viewing? They are necessarily large and bold, being physically among the biggest Matthew did on vellum. Yet with that boldness has come no notable increase in descriptive detail or nuance over the drawing in, say, the *Historia anglorum*. One notes that, though the faces seem to chart the history of Christ in his humanity and divinity, their aesthetic character does not change correspondingly. In this sense they are consciously 'timeless'. The features, though neatly drawn, float somewhat blandly across the empty expanses of candid vellum. The eyes are large and impassive, the gaze still and hypnotic. Were the large dot-like eyes to swivel or the mouths to curl, the effect would collapse. To be sure, this is a 'period' feature, reproduced in numerous manuscript and wall paintings with various functions produced around the mid-century, and about to pass out of fashion with the arrival of a new foxy-faced, mobile, Gothic physiognomy.[11] But it is also compatible with a certain form (in this case monastic) of 'rich' viewing. It obviously matters that the viewer's gaze, indeed entire sensibility, should be captivated by the hypnotic look of the images: in this regard, distance between the viewer and thing represented becomes irrelevant. The images help to inform and guide the process of *imitatio*, the meditative and then contemplative ascent to God. Their features are signs which are to be penetrated through or sunk into by way of a contemplative immersion which realizes itself not in, but beyond, the sign.[12] They act as immutable points of entrance, their blandness offering a minimum of sensory interference. The notion of mental life imparted to the viewer by such serene features is clearly that of the Christian-stoic tradition, which emphasized a state of otherworldly constancy, a sublime indifference to the accidents of temporal existence, an idealized emphasis on the harmony of God's creation according to which common rule one is to fashion oneself – a notion as relevant to monastic viewing as it might be to the notions of conformity, the *mos maiorum*, embodied in some Roman portraiture.[13] In Christian tradition, the attribute of *hilaritas* or spiritual joy is a 'deep' attribute of the self, that issues from, but also remains, within. 'Blankness' – the term is imperfect, but will serve for the present – signals inner tranquillity, the positive virtue of inexpressivity; and it also registers the extent to which the faces are in some sense beyond ethical scrutiny. This sense of something being beyond the apparent sign also emphasizes the rapture, the role of loss of self in the activity of viewing such images: loss of the social, psychological and moral elements that in some sense separate the viewer from the concept, the soul from God.

That such impersonal attributes of the face were not the sole domain of certain sorts of medieval image – for the argument being proposed here is not linear or evolutionary – is indicated by Michael Baxandall's discussion of Perugino's use of 'general, unparticularized, interchangeable' physical types which 'provided a base [. . .] on which the pious beholder could impose his personal detail, more particular but less structured than what the painter offered'.[14] Nevertheless it does point to something common in medieval image-making and viewing. The phenomenology of affect may assist in understanding it. Jean-Paul Sartre for example advances the theory that emotions are a manner of apprehending the world which involves a magical transformation of it, such that 'the emotional subject and the object of the emotion are united in an indissoluble synthesis'.[15] The transformation entails a conjuration, which in effect simplifies the world, rendering it manageable. This way of understanding the world is immensely affective, since it entails a powerful sense of will, of striving to comprehend the world in a certain sort of way, and according to a certain disposition: to see the world, or an object or image, 'as' something. This disposition towards the world was clearly very typical of certain kinds of affective religious imagination, and hence stances, towards art. Nor was it necessarily irrational, wilful or intemperate. Matthew Paris's strategies of viewing are highly likely to have been obedient to pre-existing conventional forms, pathways of the type offered by Thomas the Cistercian, which instilled habits of 'reading', and operated within common rules to inhibit self-indulgence or anarchic free association.[16] The point is that this highly affective yet structured mode of viewing may in part help to account for the simplicity of Matthew's images, their poverty in regard to prescriptive detail. It explains why a certain blankness in fact conferred advantages, in simultaneously providing an inlet for contemplative absorption, while also putting forward a traditional ethical and metaphysical view of the inwardness of the self in harmony with a composed exterior, ideally suited to monastic meditation. The *locus classicus* of this mode is provided by surviving images, declared in their own time to be symbols of eloquence, whose mimetic character is plainly limited in the sense we have been outlining. An example is the painted cross from San Damiano which 'spoke' to St Francis of the rebuilding of the Church.[17] As a representation in itself – and in contrast to the sorts of cross examined above – this cannot be described as an *imago agens* so much as a sign of the stoical notion of Christian expressivity. These instances in fact suggest that the notion of a speaking image, a long-standing classical rhetorical ideal, was commonly realized precisely through this style of affective transformation of the world by sheer determination, the representation as it were magically bodying forth that which is required by predisposed viewing. Eloquence was sought in images, and it was found. Again, this was not a peculiarity of medieval art in more or less 'developed' phases, for such productive viewing can also be found in what John Shearman calls the 'Neo-Plinian' style of reading images in the Renaissance.[18] This last point about the historical coexistence of different modes of viewing must surely militate against efforts to generate general (and implicitly linear) theories about medieval 'seeing' which confuse the history of vision, and the history of the theory of vision, particularly in its new 'Aristotelian' guise.[19]

There is clearly nothing primitive in these images: their aesthetic character is the measure of a specific and highly developed form of obedience. They represent the work of a man who, though he was obviously captivated by new ideas (witness Matthew's very early version of

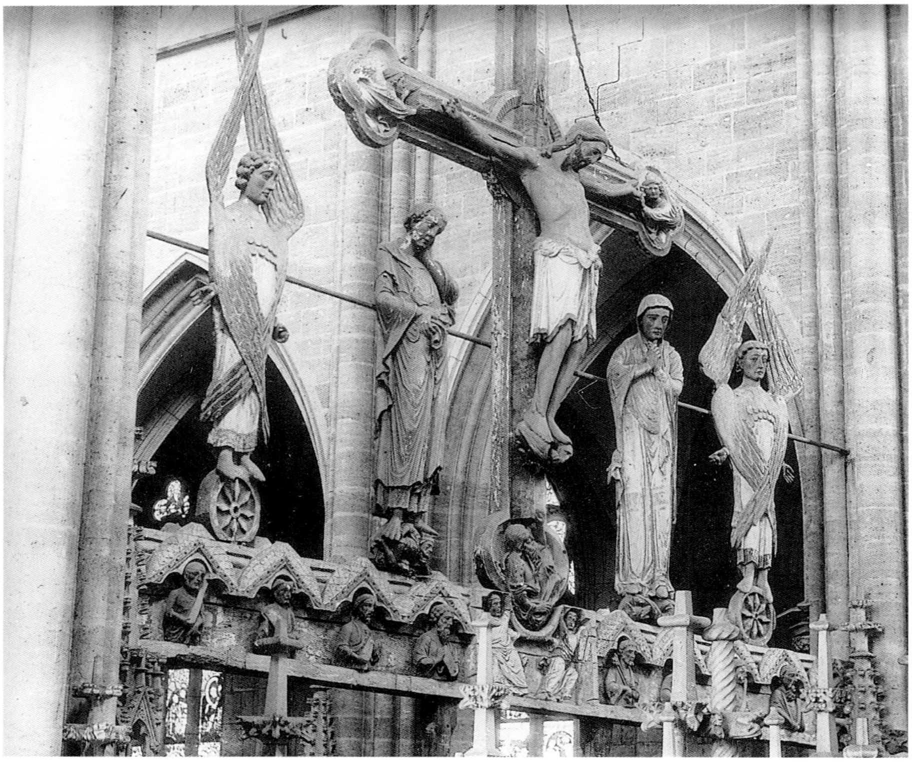

187 Halberstadt Cathedral, rood beam and Cross (Conway Library, Courtauld Institute of Art).

the stigmatization of St Francis in the *Chronica majora*), is nevertheless not usefully understood as either especially conservative, or radical, in outlook.[20] His conception of art and viewing represented one extremely important opinion. But that it was not the only possibility is shown decisively by developments that had already occurred as much as a decade earlier, in the rather more internationalist milieu of Henry III's court at Westminster, and which strongly suggest the coexistence of more than one mode of viewing and representing.

On 10 December 1240 Henry issued a mandate – one of many hundreds giving details of the nature and general purpose of his art patronage – that 'two fair cherubim of joyous and cheerful countenance', *duos scherumbinos cum hyllari vultu et jocoso*, should be made and added to the left and right of the great rood in the Chapel Royal of St Peter ad Vincula in the Tower of London.[21] There was nothing out of the ordinary in the specification that many-winged carved cherubim or seraphim should accompany a sculpted rood-cross. The magnificent early thirteenth-century rood assembly in Halberstadt Cathedral is composed in exactly this way (fig. 187), and the practice is reflected in England in the elegant miniature to the Prologue to Genesis in the Bible of William of Devon (BL Royal MS 1. D. I., fol. 4v; fig. 188).[22] Westminster Abbey possessed such a composition over its high altar in the late Middle Ages.[23] Gervase records exactly this type of rood in his description of Lanfranc's Romanesque choir at Canterbury Cathedral, with a great cross, Mary and John and two cherubim (*duo cherubin*).[24] The basis for this combination is likely to be Psalm 98: 1, *Dominus regnavit [. . .] qui sedet super cherubin, moveatur terra*, the earthquake answering to the crucifixion text *et terra motus est* in Matthew 27: 51. Folio 57 of the great ninth-century Utrecht Psalter (Utrecht, Rijksuniversiteit Bibliotheek MS 32), much studied and copied at Canterbury before 1200, shows a Majesty flanked by cherubim or seraphim at Psalm 98.[25] This Psalm derives its image in turn from the description of the making of the Ark in the Tabernacle in Exodus 25: 17–22, with a mercy seat (*propitiatorium*) with two golden cherubim (*cherubin*) at either end, their faces and wings turned towards the seat: from here, God will meet and will commune with his people concerning the commandments of Israel. A related text of great importance is the account of the throne of God high and lifted up (*excelsum et elevatum*) surmounted by the six-winged seraphim (*seraphin*) crying unto one another 'Holy, holy

holy, is the Lord of Hosts' in Isaiah 6: 1–7.[26] Typologically, then, the Ark is the foreshadowing of the New Covenant revealed either in Christ's Majesty or in Christ raised on the Cross, the cherubim of Exodus 25 answering to the description of the many-winged seraphim in Isaiah 6, which also supplied the *Sanctus* of the Mass.

Henry's mandate was thus in line with substantial and weighty tradition. What is exceptional about it is its absolutely self-conscious recorded prescription that the cherubims' facial features should be delineated with *hilaritas* and *iocunditas*, as it were brightly and cheerily.[27] Here blankness conferred no advantage; something else and fundamentally new was being sought. What the angels looked like may be estimated by means of the brightly smiling seraph from the ceiling of Henry III's Painted Chamber at Westminster, dating probably to the 1260s (fig. 189). *Hilaritas* could no longer reside internally: it was projected onto the surface of facial signs. Doctrinally, this new idea about angels smiling might have been nothing more than a commonsense extrapolation from the liturgical texts of the prefaces to the Mass including *Vere dignum*, where hosts of angels and blessed seraphim join together in celebrating their joy (*exsultatione*) in the *Sanctus* itself. A rood was after all principally an item of liturgical furnishing. The notion that angels may possess emotions, including joy, in the presence of God, was well founded enough.[28] But it was also relatively traditional; and in hunting around for textual justifications, one runs the risk of missing the kernel of the problem, which is not why this ascription was theoretically possible, but why this new and artistically unprecedented cheerfulness actually happened when and where it did. As with the new attitudes of the body of Christ on the Cross, the ostensive form of angels too could change without the sudden or explicit emergence of new beliefs.

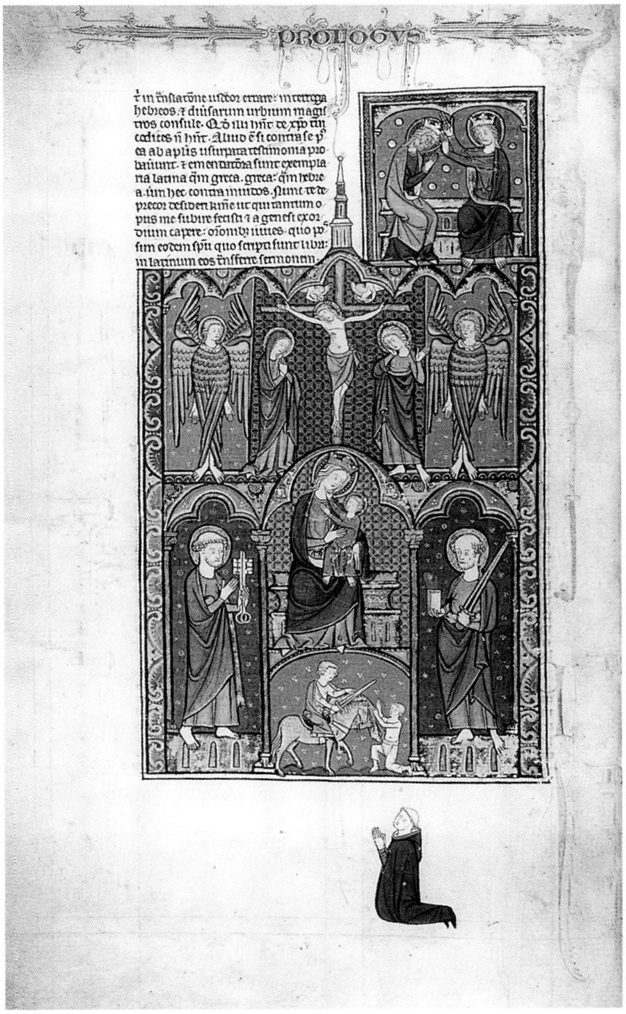

188 Saints and rood. Bible of William of Devon, BL Royal MS 1. D. I, fol. 4v, *c.* 1270 (Conway Library, Courtauld Institute of Art).

The December 1240 mandate for cherubim, though certainly unprecedented in the annals of English art, is not in fact absolutely isolated, and should be seen in relation to a number of other highly suggestive royal documentary references of the years 1240–42. Almost a year earlier, on 20 January 1240, Henry III had ordered that the chimney of the Queen's Chamber at Westminster should be painted with a figure 'which by its sad look and other miserable portrayals (*protractionibus*) of the body may be justly likened to winter'.[29] This shivering hearth-image was plainly meant to be an *imago agens*, a mime relevant not just to its physical, but also seasonal, context. This topicality was a form of courtly wit, worthy of the noun *jocus*. But it was also a style of pictorial jest that could indicate the possibility (in other circumstances) of moral or aesthetic depth, and which could best spring up within an exceptionally lively, capable and topically minded pictorial culture, of the sort nurtured precisely at Henry III's court. Such dramatizations led me to describe Henry III's art as the first well-documented 'moralized' court art (p. 76 above). Readers are perhaps beginning better to understand what the aesthetic implications of this 'moralization' might have been. On the same lines, and on a directly tropological note, a mandate of September 1242 required that images of the Wise and Foolish Virgins should be painted among other paintings in the Queen's Chapel at Windsor.[30] These famous creations of Matthew 25 are known to Gothic art principally in the form of portal sculptures accompanying, but firmly subsidiary to, the Last Judgement, which presumably formed the centrepiece of the queen's murals in her chapel.[31] In 1242 the parable of

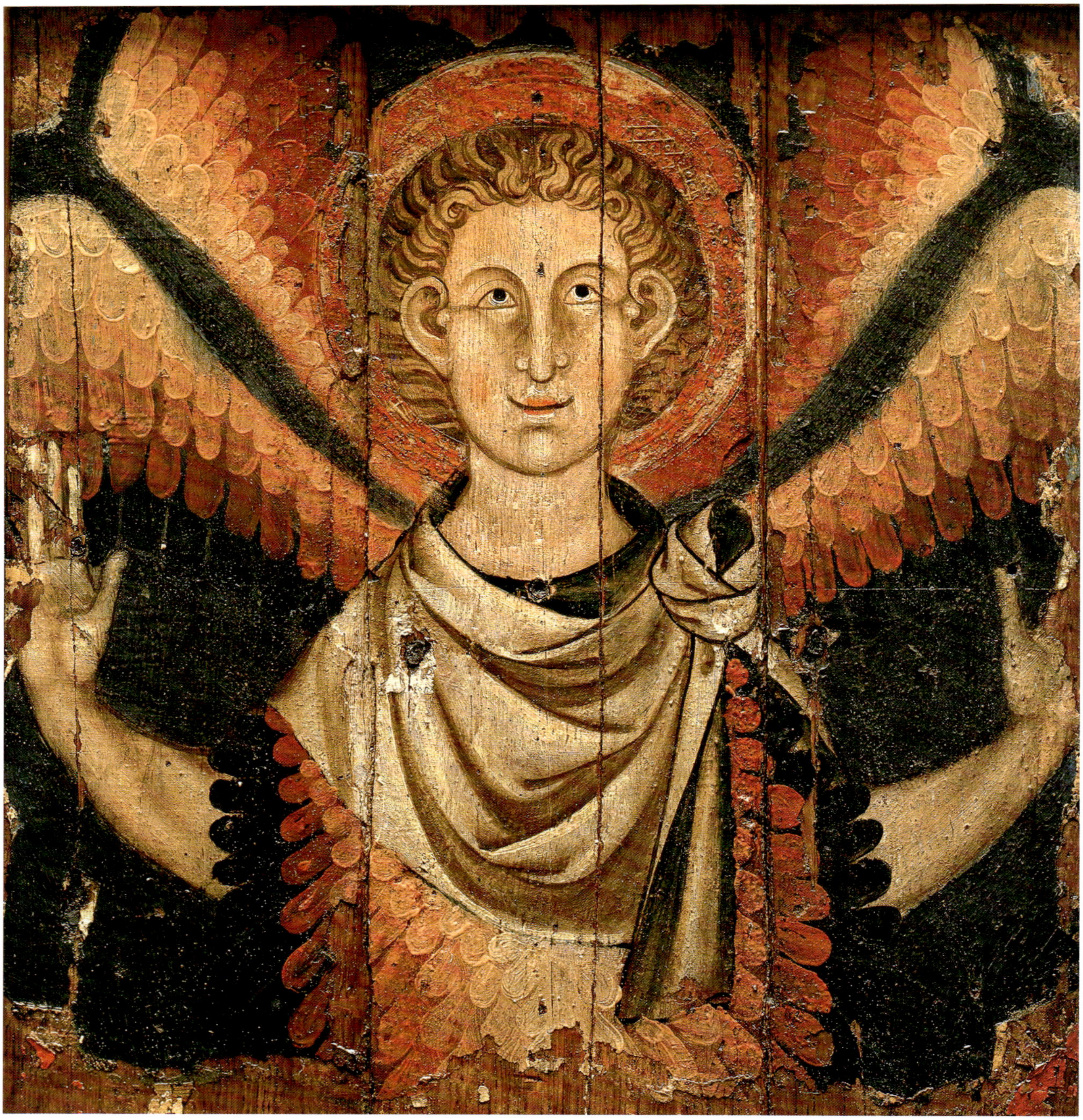

189 Seraph, *c.* 1265, removed *c.* 1819 from ceiling of Painted Chamber, Palace of Westminster, now in British Museum (© Hamilton Kerr Institute).

the Wise and Foolish Virgins scarcely existed as a subject to be depicted in art; and when it finally did gain an impressive degree of autonomy, at mid-century Magdeburg Cathedral (fig. 191), the women offered sculptors unprecedented opportunities for the rendition in stone of that mimetic expressivity which has begun to be traced in these few English royal mandates.[32] There is of course no reason to think that this subject was chosen at Windsor because sculptors in Germany had already started to earmark it as a theme suitable for 'expressive' treatment. The attraction of such subjects lay primarily in their moral content. Rather, it seems that bodily expressivity was now regarded as an aspect of their tropology: *Moralis docet quid agas* as the Latin jingle put it – morality informs action. Behind what seems to have been a new fashion lay a serious ethical purpose.

Explaining this sort of thing is never easy; yet while the available facts will not bear too much by way of a causal account, something at least must be said. The proper place to begin is with specific circumstances and connections: this newly articulated interest in literal expressions was in the first instance the product of creative engagement with one project whose importance as a stimulus and reference-point was to continue for the rest of the century. This was the new work at Reims Cathedral, begun in 1211, and developed to the point where the chapter could take possession of the new choir formally for the first time in 1241.[33] It was almost certainly at Reims between these years that a type of expressivity was first developed on a large scale and in a major Gothic church. Paris's role cannot be forgotten of course, though before about 1240 the surviving signs of this new expressivity in works in Paris or its sphere are few and of less impressive quality (west portal, Saint-Germain l'Auxerrois; Villeneuve-l'Archevêque).[34] The impact of Reims in contrast was wide: it is difficult to overestimate the imaginative importance of this extraordinary building for contemporary projects in the archdioceses of Canterbury, Sens, Reims, Cologne and Magdeburg.[35] As well as being wide, the impact was almost immediate, and had certainly started before 1241: Villard de Honnecourt was spying at Reims on behalf of Cambrai Cathedral or some such organization around 1230.[36] Much of the exterior sculpture of the east end of the church was manufactured between 1211 and 1241, as were the first bays of the nave, in which the liturgical choir was lodged.[37] All this had presumably been descaffolded and revealed to general view by about 1240.

What was encountered by those gaining access to the upper parts of the east end of Reims was (and in some regards still is) shocking: the most brilliantly able explorations of the expressive character of the human face to emerge since the Roman Empire.[38] This style of sculpted work had not yet developed on the sculpted north transept portals used by the canons, or on the tops of the buttresses of the radiating chapels complete by the 1220s.[39] Nor was it a feature of the choir's stained glass.[40] It emerged first at the level of the major buttress-aedicules of the choir, which enclose angels with dramatically extended wings, and at the corresponding levels of the exterior of the choir clearstory and transept towers, which are decorated with numerous masks and figures. The buttress-angels – clearly the mighty guardians of the cathedral church – are an exhilarating

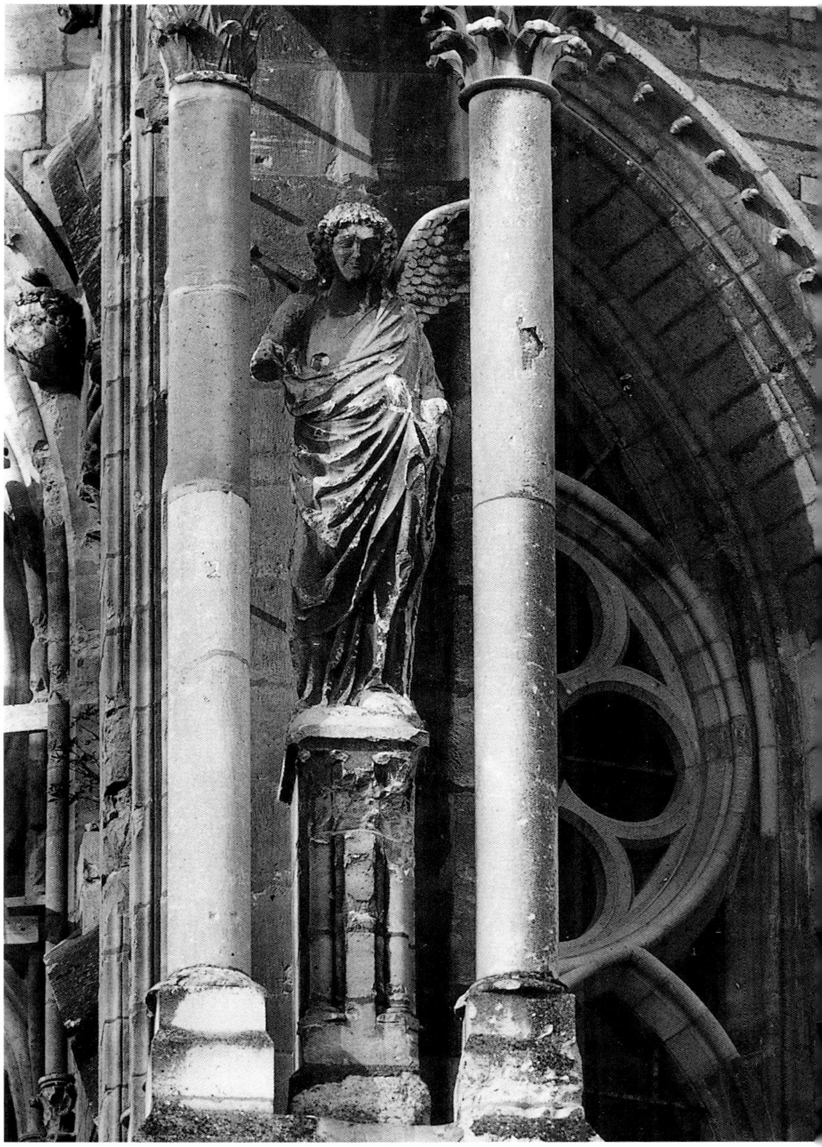

190 Angel in buttress aedicule. Reims Cathedral, east end (Bildarchiv Foto Marburg).

creation in themselves, and it is their facial features that first start to crease gently, almost imperceptibly, into smiles (fig. 190).[41] But the small corbel-heads and figures at the clearstory and rose-window levels of the choir and transepts go much further. Some, such as the toothy guffawing 'prophet', are obviously dazzlingly successful exercises in 'difficulty'.[42] Others are now hard to separate from later traditions of physiognomic study, and certainly seem ancestral to them. A sense of conscious challenge pervades the numerous profane masks of grinning and possibly predatory men and women showing

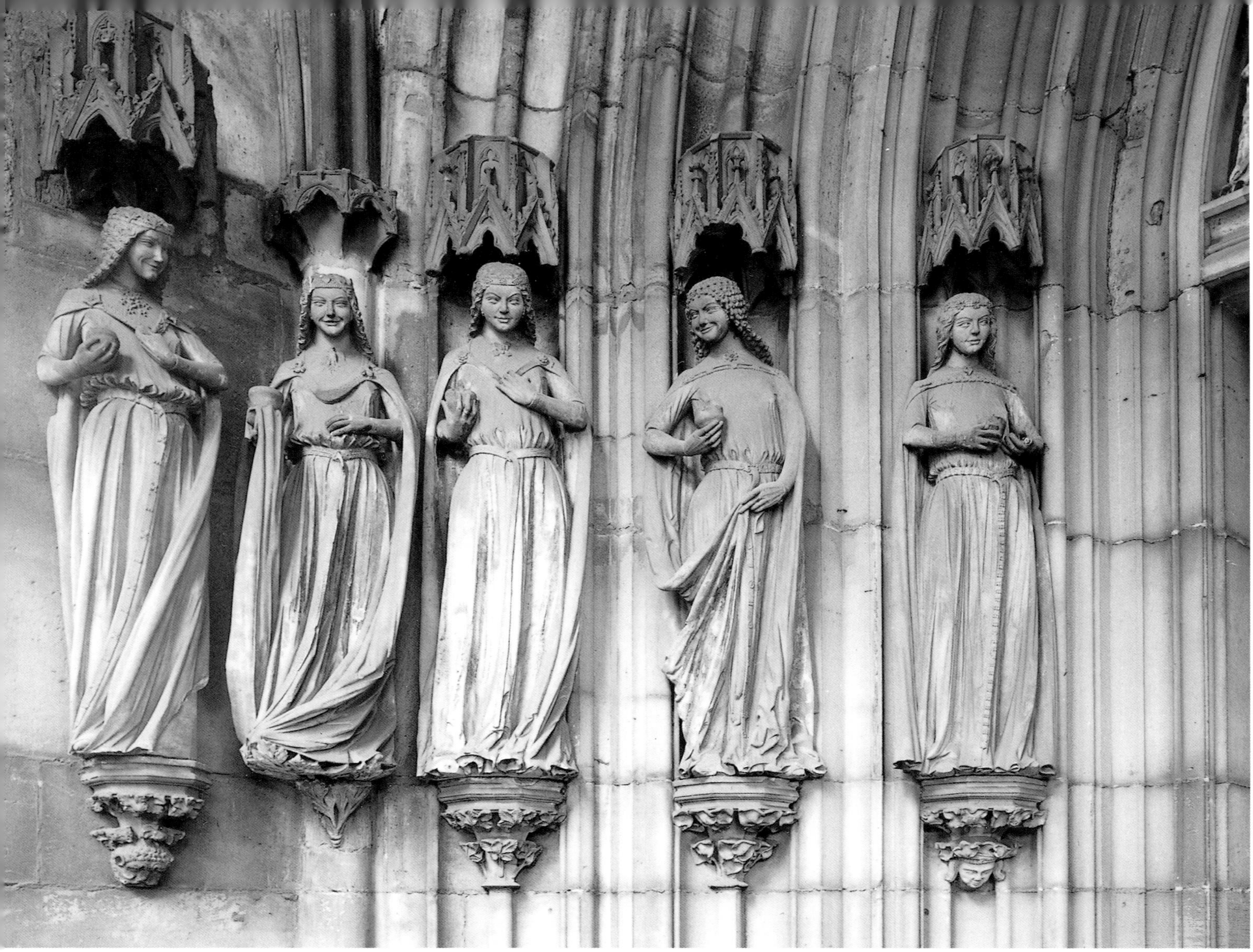

191 (ABOVE AND FACING PAGE) Wise and Foolish Virgins. Magdeburg Cathedral (Conway Library, Courtauld Institute of Art).

their teeth (figs 192–3), sinister frowning and mocking men, men whose jaws fall open in pain or ecstasy, youths with idiotically stuck-out tongues (fig. 194), or with their cheeks sucked in and lips puckered, characters who hoot, shout, sing or chuckle, and handsome strong-boned men who gaze into the distance with expressions of pent-up determination and focus, martial and valiant (fig. 195).[43] In this last case the 'look' is of restrained power; it is inconceivable without self-mastery. The affects run the gamut from the bestial to the human, from the mindless to the mindful, from self-possession to dispossession; and in that regard these masks all embody the same fiction, the same definite sense of an acting-out. One of the most trenchant contemporary discourses to capture these looks, their range and radicalism especially, is that of the clerical critique of the jongleur, the mime, the actor – even the prostitute: types who, in virtue of their moral misuse or distortion of the face and body, were associated 'professionally', perhaps as here.[44] These are faces that consciously push out the borders of what it is to be human and sentient; by the same token, these are also faces that have something to say about infamy. The marginal had long been the sphere of the facially grotesque. The distinction at Reims between the dignified stoic detachment of the portals and this elevated and almost invisible histrionic masquerade is partly one of natural hierarchy and decorum, as it was understood around 1210 or 1220. But the fact that these new masks are where they are at this point in Reims's development may say something about the necessary subculture of all great artistic projects, that of a talented workforce cutting a dash, impressing itself with

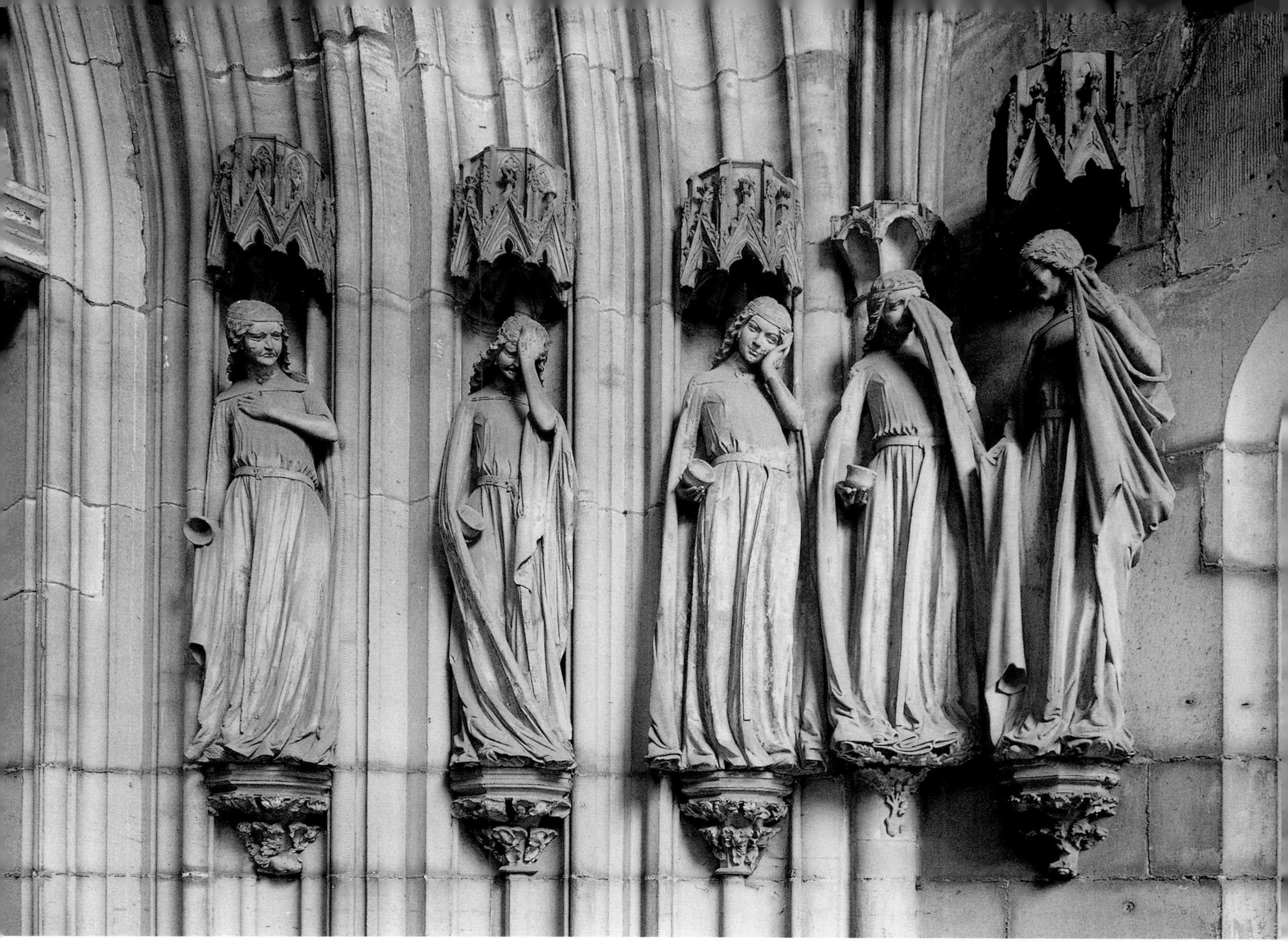

its own jocularity (its 'jongleuric' freedom), exerting its spare capacity and excess technique in ways that had no necessary relation to the project in hand, but lent ample scope for the flexing of creative muscle. (The term 'educated insolence' comes to mind, for reasons explained below.) Here then, competitive individualism is vaunted rather than uniformity – the same tension apparent in the morality of the performer in the choirstall in the great northern French cathedrals of the time.[45] The witty artistic insouciance of able competitive young men engaging in the in-house prank had been legitimized by Pliny; it was part of the heritage of Zeuxis and Apelles. Later, it was to be institutionalized by means of the art competition. The likelihood that the great Visitation group on the west front of the cathedral was based upon Roman models is generally recognized; Villard de Honnecourt plainly moved in this post-classical world. The masks here may be indebted in some way to the gamut of facial expressions, including 'unending felicity', found on Bacchic sarcophagi: had the famed *romanitas* of Reims also extended to the myths of its masons?[46]

But the key point is that it was at Reims that the aesthetic consequences of this, at first marginal, jocularity came to flood into the mainstream of sculpted religious representation. It is as if this mimicry – parodic, doubtless, and certainly natural to the culture of the professional circles of choral and artistic 'performers' of the period – were an initial stage in the progression towards the ethically more serious and so vulnerable centre of religious representation. The buttress-angels, more conservative in idiom than the masks, yet clearly if faintly smiling, are among the first signs of this rapprochement.

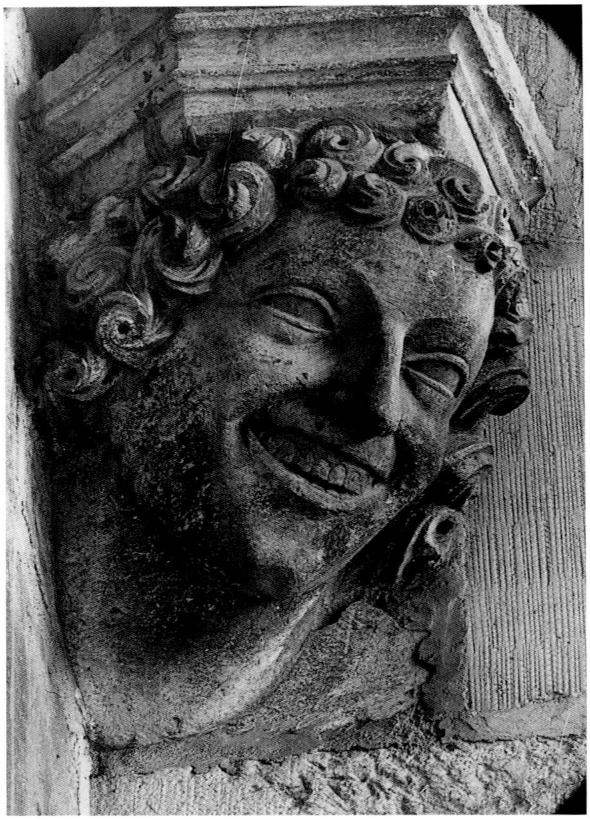
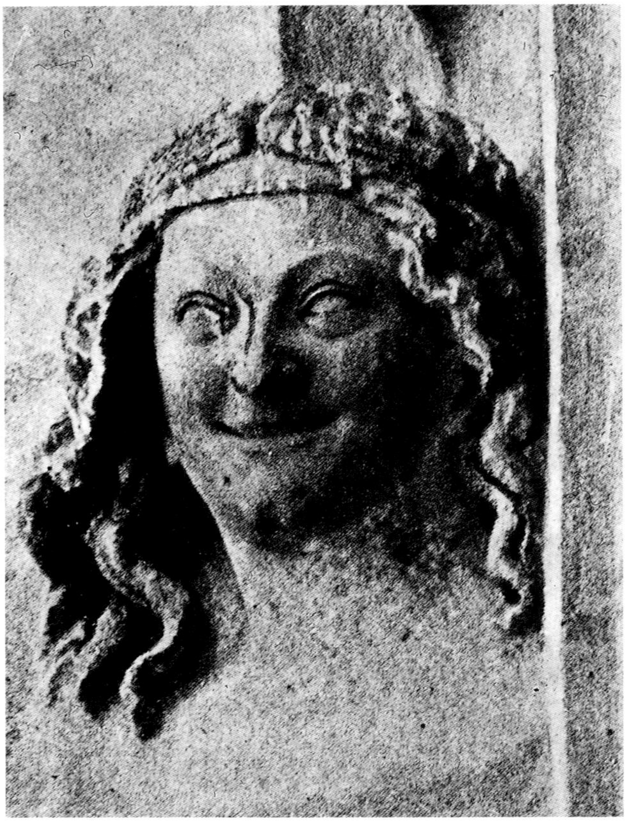
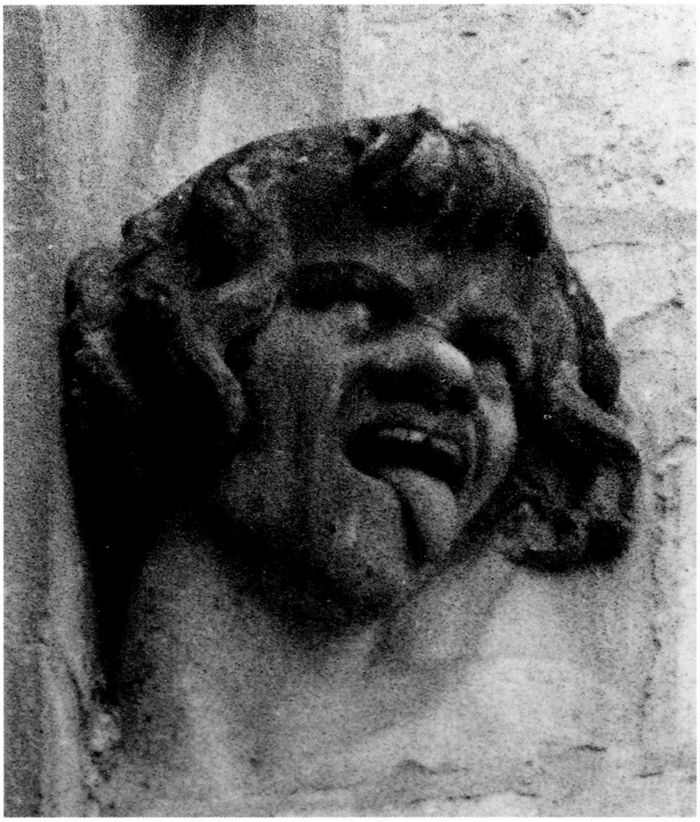
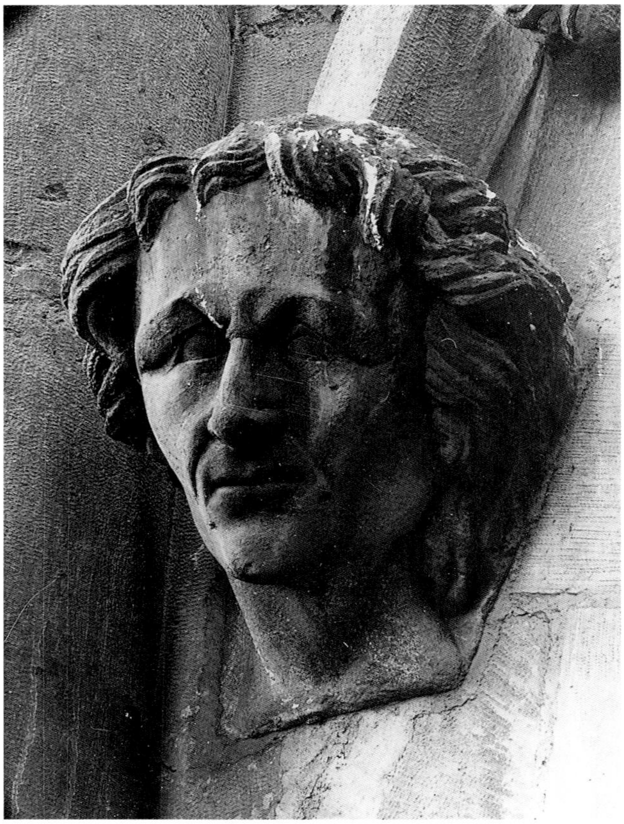

That one may fairly think of these blissful figures as smiling is suggested by the continuation of the angelic theme in the buttress-aedicules of the nave towards and after 1241, where the angels, now the product of teams whose practices accorded closely with the brisk elegant manners of contemporary Paris, beam out smiles broadly and emphatically (fig. 196), in order to harmonize with their forerunners clustered around the great chevet.[47] This was to be the style of the cathedral's west front begun after 1252, the style of the winsome smiling angels with St Denis, and of graceful Gabriel placed with the stolid Mary of the Annunciation (figs 197–8).[48] What was becoming permissible in the decades before 1240 had now become the positive hallmark of a new style of sculpted religious image at ground level, within the domain of ordinary human activity, perception and morality. For reasons explored below, the *imago agens* had taken another turn; and with it, the moment of danger at the frontier between the joyful and the jocular had apparently passed.

What matters for the present is how cleanly these radical developments at Reims dovetailed with those at the English court. Here, to reiterate, circumstances matter: human agency is critical. The key figure was the royal master mason whose career was in the ascendant at exactly this time, Henry of Reyns. Henry first emerged in charge of works at Windsor around 1240, and his authority was such that he began Henry III's reconstruction of Westminster Abbey in 1245.[49] Henry and his son Hugo seem to have used the tradename Reyns because of a professional association with the works at Reims. In Henry's case, this must have been formed before about 1240, since in that year a new royal chapel was begun at Windsor Castle for which Henry was rewarded in 1243, and in which he presumably had a large hand. The surviving parts of the Windsor building reveal French influence, and there is evidence that it may have been the first royal undertaking to have used

192 (FACING PAGE TOP LEFT) Grinning man. Reims Cathedral (Bildarchiv Foto Marburg).

193 (FACING PAGE TOP RIGHT) Grinning woman. Reims Cathedral (Bildarchiv Foto Marburg).

194 (FACING PAGE BOTTOM LEFT) Rude youth. Reims Cathedral (Bildarchiv Foto Marburg).

195 (FACING PAGE BOTTOM RIGHT) Self-possessed man. Reims Cathedral (Bildarchiv Foto Marburg).

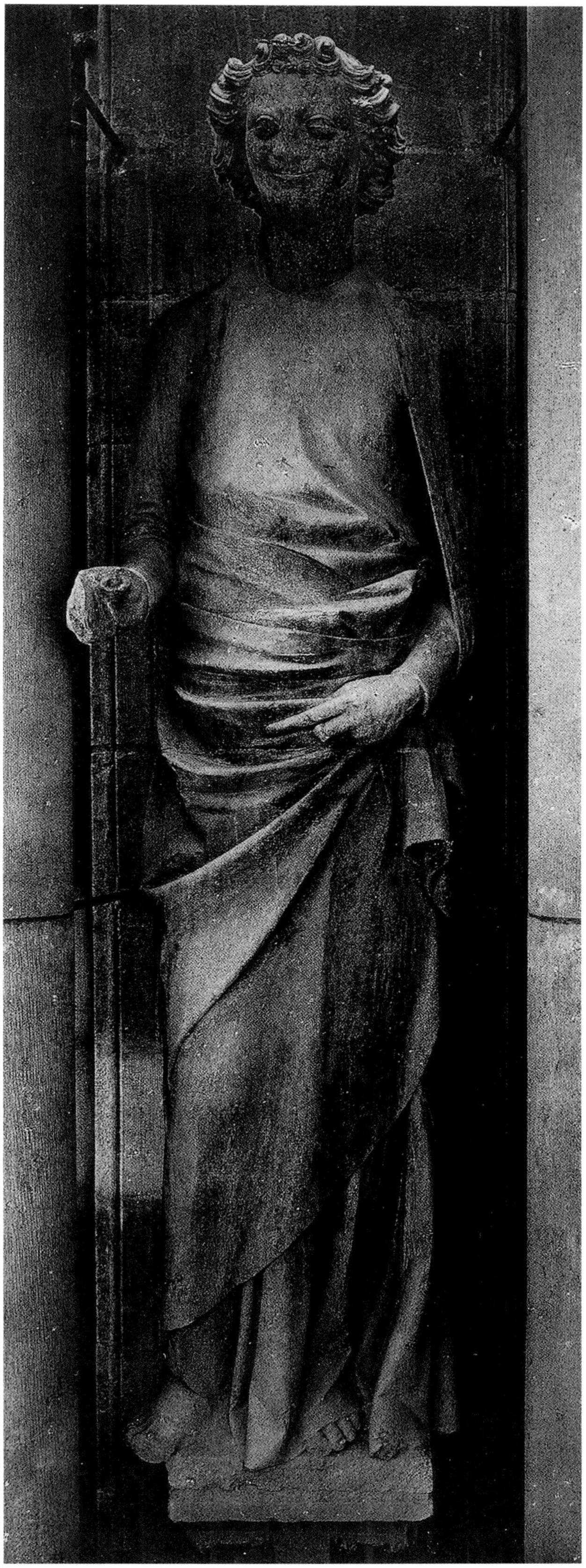

196 (RIGHT) Smiling angel (pre-1914–18). Reims Cathedral, nave buttress (Bildarchiv Foto Marburg).

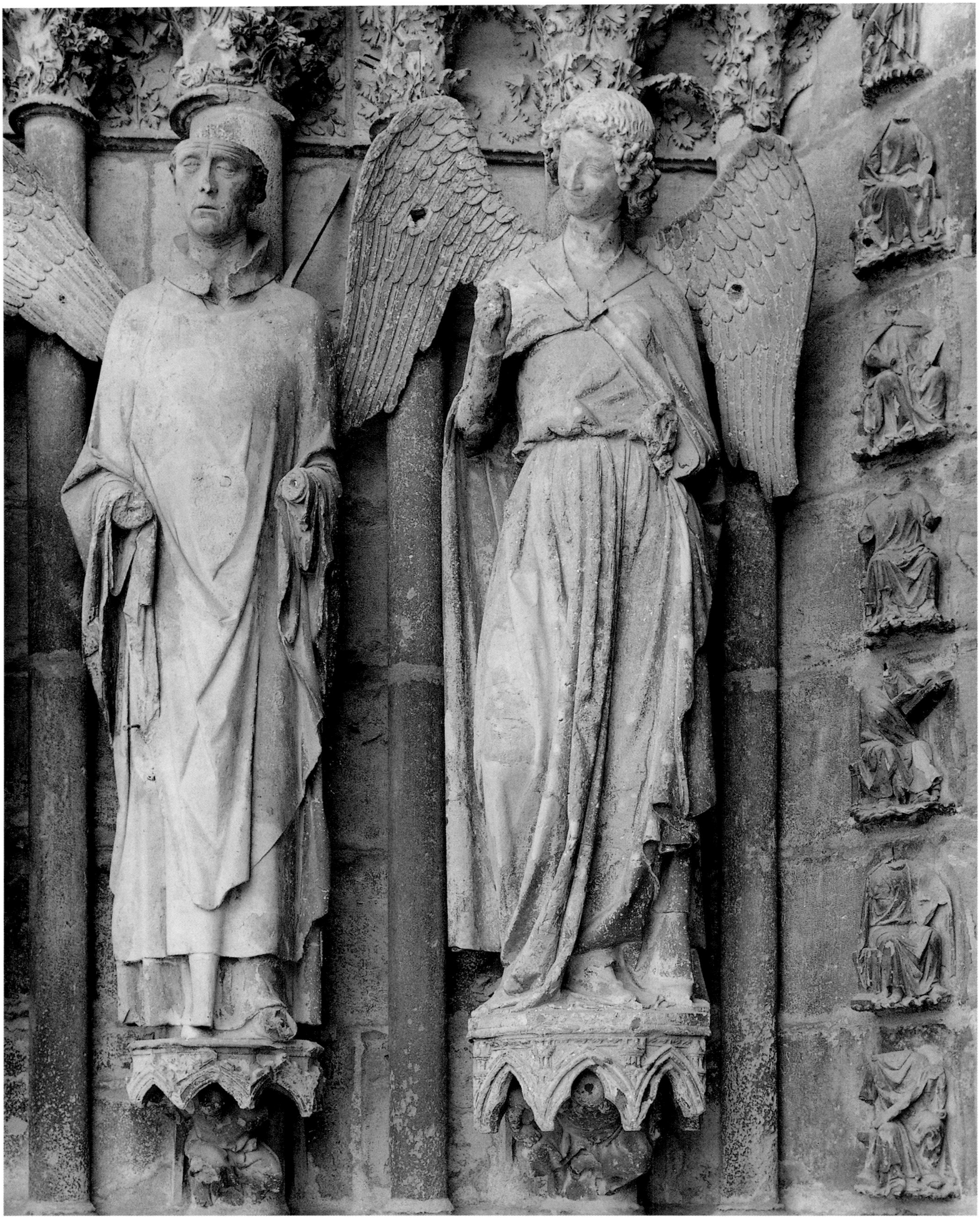

197 ?St Nicaise and smiling angel. Reims Cathedral, west facade, left portal (James Austin).

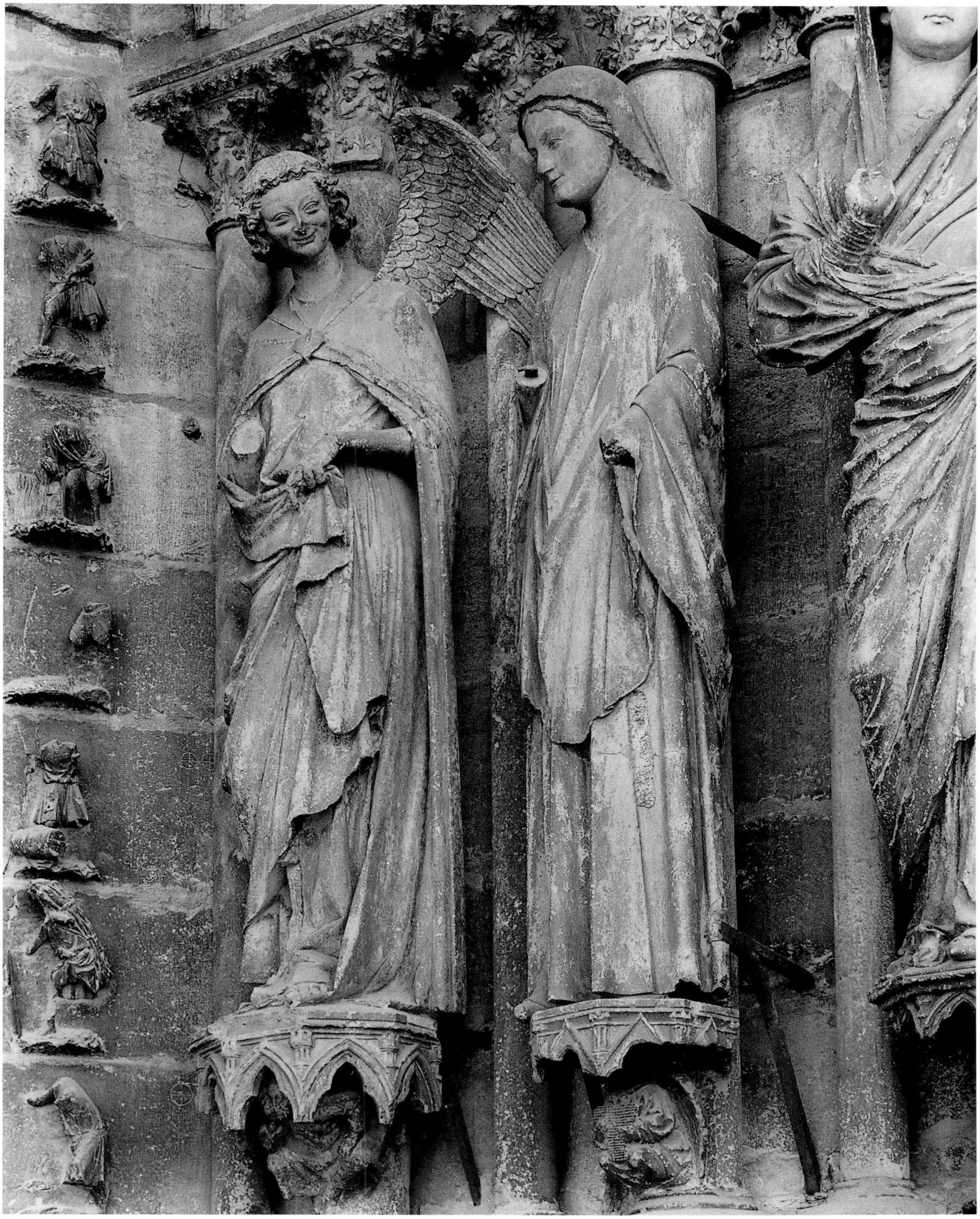

198 Gabriel and Virgin Mary. Reims Cathedral, west facade, centre portal (Conway Library, Courtauld Institute of Art).

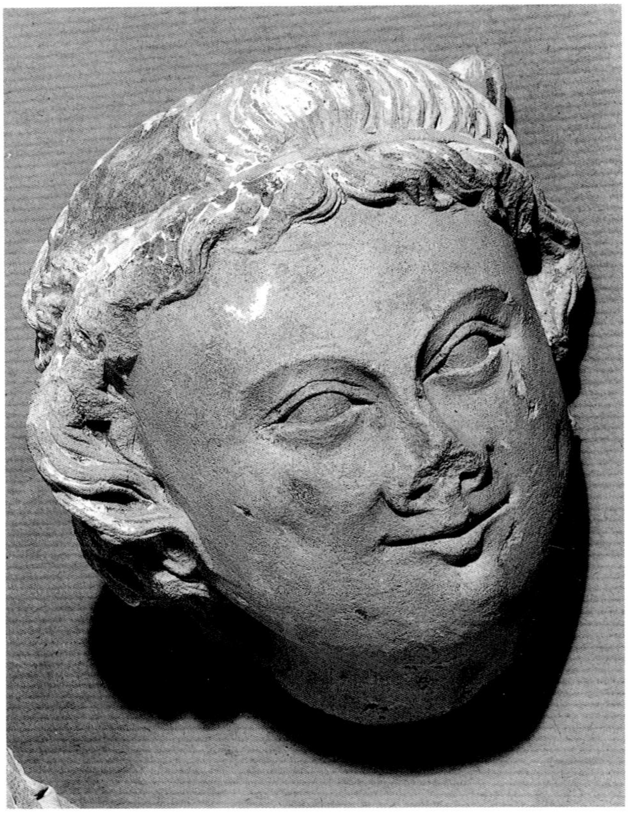

199 Head of angel from wall arcading, Westminster Abbey, east end, *c.* 1245–50 (Dean and Chapter of Westminster).

200 Pensive man, from triforium gallery, Westminster Abbey, *c.* 1250–55 (Dean and Chapter of Westminster).

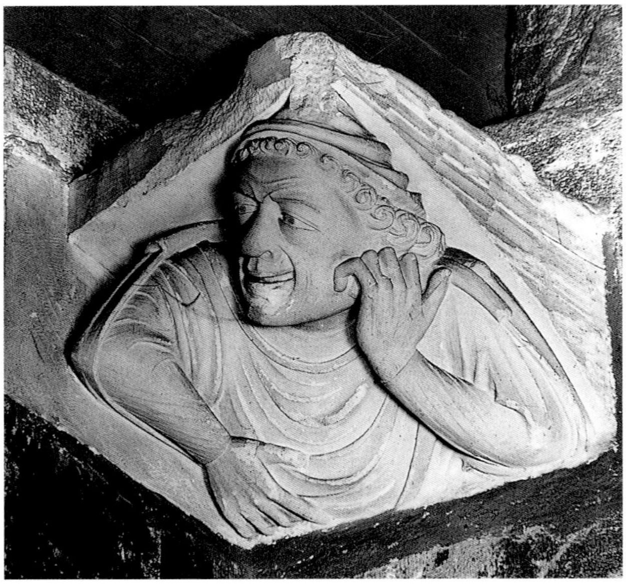

bar-window tracery, first developed at Reims. In view of its status as a coronation church, Reims was then adopted as the major paradigm for the plan and main elevations of Westminster Abbey in 1245.[50] This influence ran to the detailing: some of the better-preserved fragments of small-scale figurative sculpture from the apsidal chapels at Westminster set out around 1245-50 include a figure with gently smiling features (fig. 199), as well as the sort of vigorously naturalistic foliage explored since the second decade of the century by the Reims workshops; the abbey's tribune interior is decorated with character heads such as those on the exterior of Reims's choir (fig. 200).[51] Henry had begun the process of building up a portfolio on Reims which English royal master masons, notably Michael of Canterbury (who studied Reims's west facade, begun after 1252), continued to study and supplement until at least the 1290s.[52]

What was happening at Westminster in the early 1240s formed part of a distinct pattern of change in which the works at Reims played a major, arguably the major, role; and this pattern is equally observable within France itself, at Bourges, and well to the east of France, in sculpture commissioned at such centres as Bamberg, Naumburg, Magdeburg, Mainz and Meissen from the 1230s onwards.[53] A series of conduits for the new style had opened up; Villard de Honnecourt provided one well-documented one, Henry of Reyns another. In terms of the logic of fashion it is not difficult to explain why, by the end of 1240, it had become possible for the king to ask specifically for smiling angels to be sculpted for the Tower of London. The Last Judgement portal at Bourges and the great west front at Reims consolidated this grip (figs 204, 198). The seraphs and other angels that framed the Coronation of the Virgin high on the central gable of Reims's facade, complete in the 1260s, appear to have had radiant smiles.[54] To repeat: this achievement could manifest itself in painting, but its mimetic character was fundamentally that of sculpture, as evidenced by numerous instances from later thirteenth-century France.[55] The little seraphs from the stained glass of Reims's west rose window, put in later in the century, are glum and stoical.[56] St Edward is shown smiling in the illuminated French Life made in the 1250s (fig. 205). Small grinning heads support the shield strap of the arms of Simon de Montfort in the choir aisles of Westminster Abbey around 1260. The superb painted seraph from the ceiling of the King's Chamber at the nearby palace, executed in the 1260s, has the same broad tight-lipped curving smirk as the angels from the nave buttresses at Reims of the 1240s and 1250s (figs 189, 196).[57] It is exactly to the sphere of the new nave and facade workshops at Reims

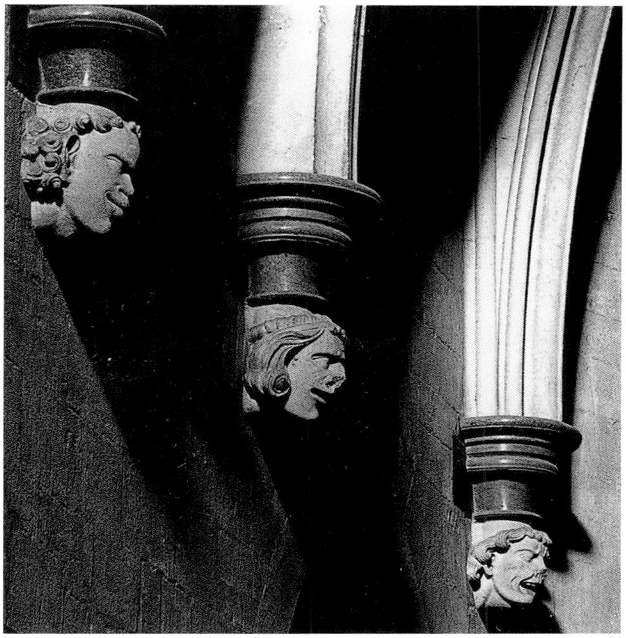

201 'Grinning for gladness': corbel heads addressing St Faith's altar, Westminster Abbey, *c.* 1245–50 (author).

that this painted figure, and its immediate neighbours in the great Douce Apocalypse, made for Eleanor of Castile or Edward I, belong: works that make increasingly confident use of a cheery *hilaritas* in the depiction of angels (fig. 237).[58] The Oscott Psalter made towards 1270 does the same for the Virgin Mary;[59] so too does the enigmatic Westminster Retable.[60] The Virgin and Child smile fetchingly on the magnificent mid-century ivory from the Sainte-Chapelle.[61] So too do the angels and Mary in the Angel Choir at Lincoln, going up in the 1260s (figs 224, 227); likewise the sly little heads from the rebuilt east end of Trondheim, which follow in the Reims-Lincoln path.[62] Cologne workshops still were turning to the nave at Reims around 1290.[63]

Joy, but not Mirth

Until around 1200 nothing could have been less expected than the breaking forth of a smile or the ringing out of a laugh in the religious art of northern Europe. Why this should have happened at all (let alone why it should have happened at Reims or at Westminster) is not clear. Traditionally, Christian ethics and metaphysics had been ambivalent towards the things that these physiognomic signs were thought to represent. For a millennium or more, the full expressive potential of the face – aside from the expression of grief or the stoic 'expressivity of the expressionless' – had correspondingly played no serious part in the art of most of Christian western Europe. On the contrary, precisely because a certain danger seemed to lie in the face, most of the burden of signification had been borne by the body, by its postures and gestures: and this was to remain the usual means by which the most important and most interesting aspects of morality and psychology could be demonstrated rhetorically.[64] This does not mean that the face did not matter: the medieval history of renovation of Italian panel paintings of the Virgin Mary, and of her face especially, indicates that her 'looks' mattered, though not necessarily for expressive reasons.[65] Before the period under discussion, and not always after it, to allow the face to express more than mourning was uncommon outside the sphere of the marginal or the grotesque. The still waters of inner *hilaritas* were not to be disturbed. The body was far freer. So, to extend to the face at the very centre of the field of religious representation that which had previously been allowed only to the body required something very like permission. Only then could the face and body together begin to register the gamut of signs of what it is to be fully human; and only then could the mask become legitimately implicated in the fiction that it might disclose not one, but a range, of thoughts, feelings, intentions, values, in ways familiar to the public domain, familiar to how such things are (and were) usually understood in all their human complexity and contingency.

To understand the extent of the change under way by about 1220 and in full flood by the 1240s, it serves only to imagine the semiotic devastation that would result if the famous smiling angels at Reims, or the extraordinary founder-figures in the choir at Naumburg, or the angels in the Angel Choir at Lincoln, were to be deprived of their heads. At Reims this actually happened during the First World War, as a result of artillery damage. The effect would be – indeed at Reims was – the virtual cancellation of the figures' most expressive, and arguably most symbolically telling, aspects. These lie principally in the dimpling of cheeks, the puckering of eyelids and in the tiniest painted details, such as the insertion of beautifully detailed and potentially mobile eyes, all of which create a 'look' (fig. 202): a 'look' that could be one of guardedness, or welcome, or of threat, of good humour, joy or

202 (FOLLOWING PAGE) Reglindis. Naumburg Cathedral, *c.* 1250–60 (Bildarchiv Foto Marburg).

203 (PAGE 249) Uta and Ekkehard. Naumburg Cathedral, *c.* 1250–60 (Bildarchiv Foto Marburg).

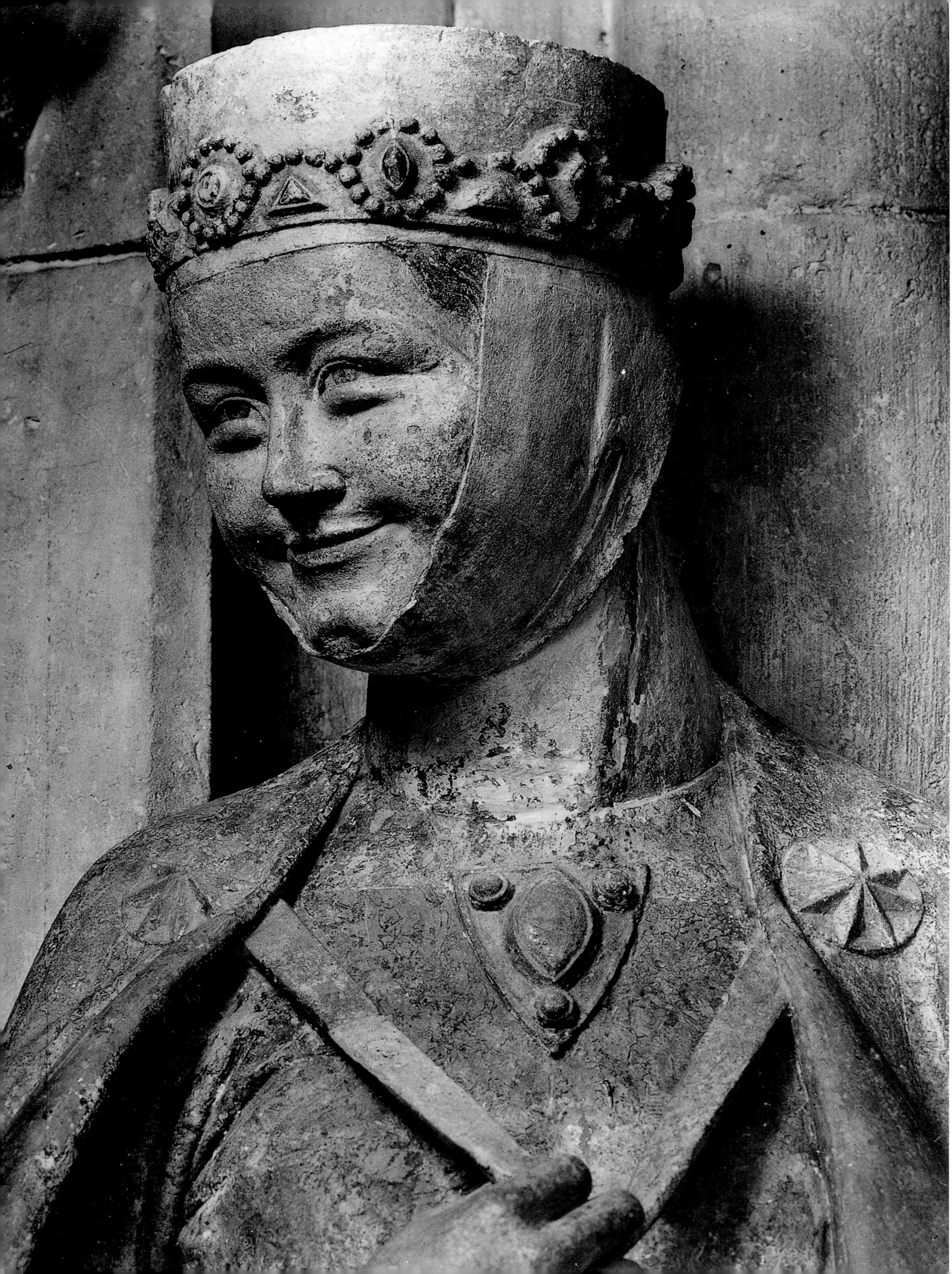

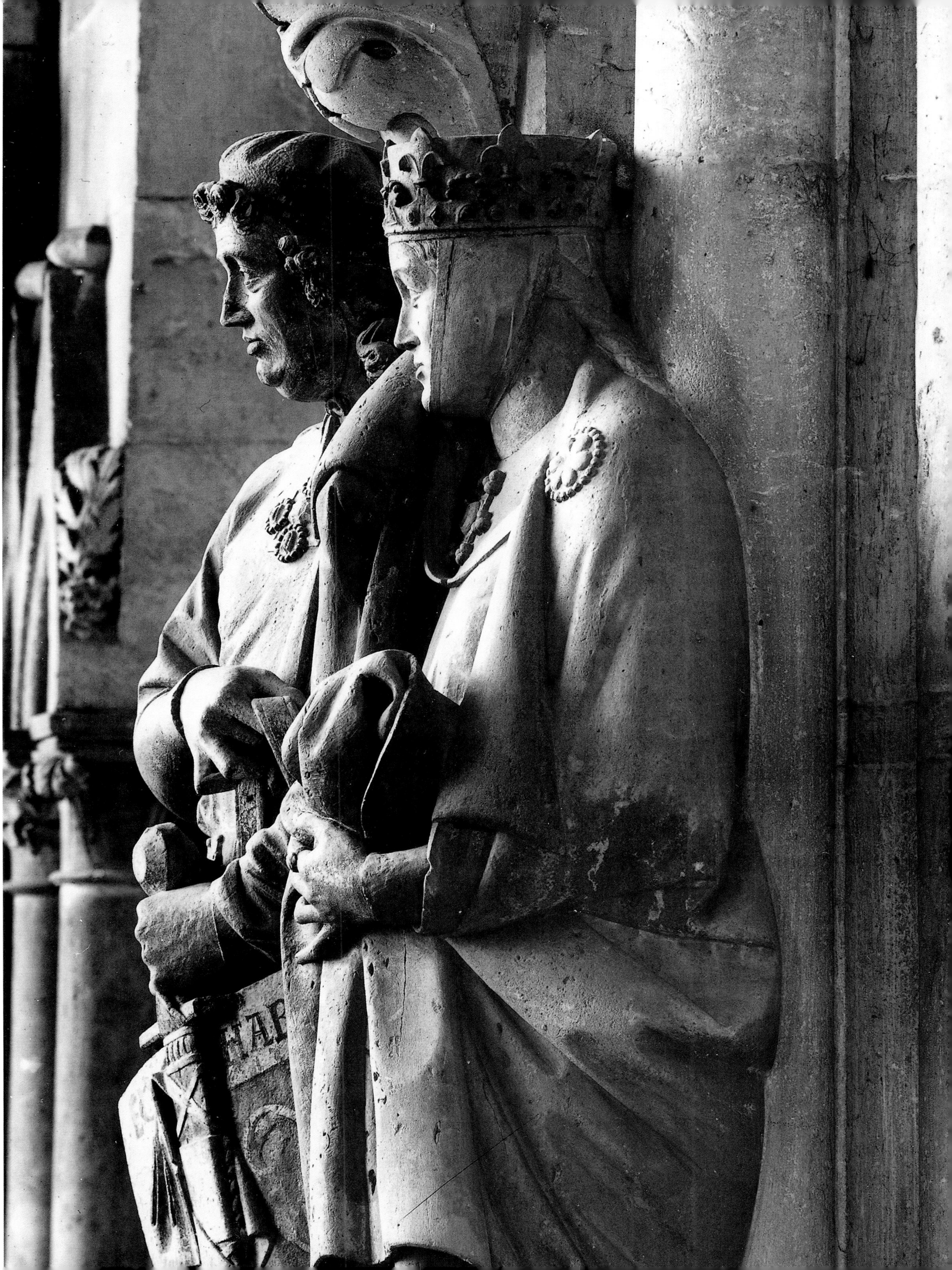

love. It also lies in the obvious differentiation of facial expressions. Such details and points of difference convey a sense of latency and audience-dependence quite absent in the work of previous generations of sculptors, no matter how noble or powerful. In stating what one thinks such faces mean, one can find various words appropriate to the task, even if one runs the very real risk of getting them at least slightly wrong. This is because the faces represent or 'express' emotion in a transitive sense (rather than being merely 'expressive' of nothing in particular): the expressions have predicates.[66] 'Transitive' expressivity in this sense was not new – the idea is not wholly irrelevant to Matthew Paris's heads, which arguably have expressive as well as ethical content. What was new was the sheer length of the scale along which ordinary social emotions were now being plotted. The face is now fundamental to the 'corporeal style' of the images. Expressive facial features are not (indeed cannot be) understood separately as signs from which expression can be 'inferred'. If an image smiles, that smile is part of its fundamental character as a representation: like the Cheshire cat, it 'is' the thing represented, as if by metonymy.[67] The bodies are 'expressive' too – they observe *la raison des gestes*, the 'rationale of human movement', in Schmitt's words.[68] Though Gothic figures are usually draped gracefully in such a way as to obscure the body, it still matters that the entire bodily frame, stance, even – perhaps especially – costume (because it can express an idea of *munditia*, elegance and neatness), should signify with a fair degree of coherence.[69] But their overall coherence in lexical terms is highly dependent on the faces. This may help to explain why in this new phase especially there are limits to a history of gesture alone, except in those cases, as in the iconography of the Passion, where gesture is very highly formalized indeed.

It is partly this feature that also explains why the most ambitious Gothic sculptures are never quite like classical Greek or Roman ones, and why they suffer damage in different ways. Panofsky's celebrated discussion of the emergence of the principle of liberation of Gothic sculpture on Greco-Roman lines is therefore problematical.[70] The insight is not totally misleading: the column-format disappears at exactly this time (1200–50), to be replaced by images set in niches or on corbels, or arranged in relation to one another within a shallow proscenium, as on the west front at Reims (figs 197–8). The images can and do swivel and react, as might automata, or persons. But the physical autonomy gained does not possess the moral autonomy, or total self-centredness, which for Panofsky defines 'intrinsic classicism'. His idea is deeply influenced by the Hegelian notion of classical deities being laws unto themselves. According to this, a classical statue of Venus completely embodies the idea of *venustas*: hence even the physical loss of her head or arms does not detract from her torso's capturing of, or bodying-forth, of her essence.[71] One might redeploy Hegel's views about the media and state that, on the contrary, this new Gothic autonomy is far more provisional, 'romantic' rather than 'classical'.[72] The plausibility of these images depends to an increasing extent on what they do in relation to one another: it matters whether the figures are from an Annunciation group (fig. 198) or from the Wise and Foolish Virgins (figs 191, 206), whether they are historical individuals or musician angels. Because they are relational and operate in clusters, such figures are not interchangeable. In fact the history of re-using slightly older portal figures in new contexts, apparent on the west centre and right portals of Reims, seems to have been stalled by this new context-dependence. In the same way, the relational context of viewing matters. Such images have a fixed 'arc of address', being in an important sense subject- or witness-dependent.[73] These sculptures can be seen as one might see any human being glimpsed at a particular moment, in a particular attitude, as in a cinema 'still' or a dramatic incident suddenly captured by flashlight. It follows that we also see (or are disposed to see) such figures not as objects, but as persons who can 'see' us back, or who may appear to be absorbed somewhere else altogether in a way which suggests the operation of will (fig. 203). The fact that many of these figures have beautifully painted eyes (fig. 202) is not irrelevant to this potential. Yet this style of looking at the image, and of being looked back at, is clearly different from the contemplative relationship discussed above in the context of Matthew Paris's drawings, where the gaze of the image is as it were deliberately sought out. In the new images, the subject-object relationship is far more contingent; indeed, contingency defines the image.

It will be obvious that such effects, such apparent contingencies, were not gained without effort on the part of artists and viewers. The level of technical accomplishment is of course astonishing. But it is clear that though the effects are wonderful (and were perhaps consciously conceived as such) they did not cancel thought or reflection. On the contrary: with them in fact came new demands and responsibilities which cast doubt on the idea that they were premised upon the development of a readily accessible popular, jongleuric or vernacular 'mode', enjoying a certain freedom.[74] To function, these sculpted ensembles were premised upon a high level of artistic determination, and also upon a style of viewing which entailed a certain urbanity. Such images required some understanding of why the representation of particular mental states would be appropriate to context, which in turn implies a grasp of genre and a feeling for decorum, or tact. These contingencies are not simply matters of ordinary common sense. To see these figures as persons is automatically to bring them into the orbit of a certain style of social and ethical reasoning. To understand why it is right to smile or frown in specific contexts involves the moral sense that comes from a rational and acculturated disposition. If morality informs action, if moral sense teaches one what to do – *Moralis docet quid agas* – action is also the mirror of morality. So it is one thing to identify an Annunciation group, another to start to ask why the angel might smile at Mary, what the smile might signify. The Annunciation is 'told', but something is also said about it, or 'shown'. The Annunciation now possesses predicates: the 'smile' is of a certain type, proper to this topic, but not necessarily to another.[75] If there was a new freedom here, its guarantor was discipline, and its character lay as much in a strategic narrowing of the range of articulate possibilities. It was the product of a certain authoritarianism. In being more highly determined, the art became less susceptible to the style of affective looking and ponderation discussed above in relation to Matthew Paris. The images have taken much more responsibility because they declare emotions (in the plural) to be an aspect of the surface of the image and not something lying beyond it.[76] By virtue of this efficiency, what they have to say can be taken in relatively more quickly. In so far as anything is left to the viewer, it is now a matter of judging the 'rightness' of this or that 'look'. Such judgement of course entails enquiry, educated guesswork, assessment (Jacques Le Goff refers not unhelpfully in this context to a medieval 'casuistry of laughter').[77] Room is left for mistakes, provided they are civilized ones. In the language of ethical theory, such judgement is a stochastic exercise, involving reasonable estimation of what is being aimed at by the representation.[78] This was the price to be paid by disturbing the old tranquil equilibrium of the face in the name of a new prompt ethical specificity; the 'absolute' expression had now been relativized. Two conclusions follow from this: first, that the issue of the face was a fully aesthetic one; second, that in this new regime the image was not something through which scrutiny passed, as by means of an icon, but something onto which scrutiny fixed. In this process the morally aware viewer was not in some sense dissolved into the image, but on the contrary actually separated from it. It is in this sense that one can think of these images as provoking a completely different, essentially reciprocal, social style of self-examination from that implied by Matthew's icons.

These very general points may be clarified by turning to details – not only eyes, but the representation of the mouth and teeth, targets of social regulation within the sphere of later medieval courtesy manuals quite as much as the activity of the eye and 'lewd looking'.[79] It is generally the case that representations of the face from around 1200 onwards distinguish between expressions that tally with laughing or grinning – in which cases the mouth is fairly or very wide open and the teeth clearly exposed – and smiling, in which case the lips are closed or only very slightly parted and the teeth invisible or mostly concealed. Of the actions, outright laughter is the hardest to identify, grinning amusement easier and the smile the most carefully deployed. Distinguishing in this way is a matter of nuance that can be understood only within the context of the general look of the face and the character and purpose of the image itself. One would not (and those with a knowledge of Christian iconography could not) conclude from the slight visibility of the teeth of Giotto's Ognissanti Madonna or of Gabriel on the west front at Reims (fig. 198), for example, that these faces were intended to be signs of appetite or bestiality, or of the demoniac. Yet in other contexts that is exactly what a full display of grinning and parted teeth commonly signified.[80] 'Placing' these looks correctly, or at least within a coherent horizon of interpretation, for there are frequently ambivalences, is thus necessarily an exercise in interpretative tact. Very often too the issue will be so extreme that tact of this type is not necessary. The rictus of insanity or demonic possession is noted in the *Magna vita* of St Hugh of Lincoln:[81] in terms of conventional decorum, facial distortion, like immoderate gesticulation, was a sign of inconstancy and the open mouth a symptom of ill discipline.[82] The *Ancrene Wisse* – echoing the clerical critique of the jongleuresque – sees the devil's work in the jester's screwed-up face, wiggling ears, scowls and twisted mouth (fig. 194).[83] *Þe Wohunge of ure Laverd* sees the tormentors of the virtuous Christian as grinning for 'gladness' at each other 'like wolves joyful of their prey', a prelude to the bestial derision of Christ in his Passion, as in Psalm 21: 8, and an almost epic image deliberately contrasted with Christ's measured beauty.[84] A predatory vulpine grinning for gladness exactly describes the look of many of the carved masks and corbels from Reims (fig. 192), Westminster (fig. 201) or Trondheim, or the flushed, cruel and intemperate look of the tormentors of Christ in numerous illuminated Gospel sequences from the middle of the century onwards, as in the Huth Psalter (fig. 180). Viewed in context, the denotation is explicitly negative.

The same generally holds true of laughter. Readers will recall the derisive character of the laughter (*cachin-*

natio) directed at the ludicrous remains of Abbot John's failed west front at St Albans, in the *Gesta abbatum*.[85] There is an episode in *Handlyng Synne* in which a deacon burst out laughing while reading the Gospel at Mass, and on being reprimanded by the priest explained that he had seen near him two chattering or jangling women, behind whom a fiend with pen and parchment was writing down their gossip; the women's chatter was such a gush that the demon had run out of space on his parchment, and had tried to lengthen it by pulling at it with his teeth, whereupon it ripped apart, sending his head slamming backwards against the wall.[86] Note the reference to teeth. It is important to this tale that the priest laughs loudly (*He logh a gret laghter an hy*) and was accordingly accounted a fool (*Held hym a fole þat coude no gode*). The mouth is the source of gossip and vice, worthy of reproof: demons left the possessed through the mouth; confession, as the *Ancrene Wisse* states elsewhere, was a form of vomiting.[87]

The story is funny enough, but the sense of humour or pretext for laughing in such cases – and there are many – is of a specific sort. Essentially it is Aristotelian, for it was Aristotle's theory of laughter as set out in his *Rhetoric* and *Ethics* (and presumable also in his lost thoughts on comedy in the second book of the *Poetics*) that formed part of the bedrock of medieval and Renaissance attitudes to the question.[88] In this model, laughter is natural to man as *homo risibilis*: far from being a sign of innocent joy or humour, however, it is the product of scorn or derision; in a sense, laughter is no laughing matter. It cannot be assimilated to some uncomplicated notion of innocent humour. It is in the light of this moral artifice that the unpleasant looks of the Reims masks may be understood. The ethical purpose, especially in regard to the manners of the young, to whom the jocular is natural, is to express not benevolence, but a joyful moral superiority, typically with regard to the ridiculous, the deformed or the indecorous.[89] This 'superiority' theory prevailed well into the post-medieval period, as in Thomas Hobbes's definition of laughter proffered at the head of this chapter, as 'sudden glory' arising from the conception of one's moral eminence in relation to the failings of others, or of oneself. Laughter is incompatible with pity. Instead, in its tempered and most constructive form, it takes the form of what Aristotle called 'witty contumely' or 'educated insolence' – that form of urbanity which had been formulated by Roman writers such as Cicero.[90] This notion of the risible – and of the fine line between *ridere* and *deridere* – accordingly forms part of the rhetorical theory of Cicero and Quintilian, in which laughter is a weapon of debate.[91] Grosseteste noted its use exactly in such a context, namely the scholastic disputation.[92] Even though there was a fine line between laughter and derision, the fact that it could be drawn in this way, and with reference to a positive and authoritative sense of decorum, creates a fatal obstacle to the view that Gothic art promoted a demotic or 'low' style, the *stilus humilis* (referred to earlier in the context of the crucifixion and the 'abject') in which, to quote Roland Recht, 'le comique, l'obscène, le laid occupent une position équivalente à celle du beau'.[93]

The Christian tradition had a particular place for this sort of sub-Aristotelian urbanity or jesting – *facetia* or witty speech – in relation to things spiritual: it was either proscribed or suppressed. This is traceable not later than Ambrose, whose use and transmission of Cicero was extensive. Ambrose, seeing virtue in physical grace, regarded such speech as absolutely improper for men of the Church: not only fulsome jokes (*jocos*), but all alike are to be rejected.[94] Precisely the same doctrine regarding the abhorrence of *facetia* is found in Aquinas, and here the source is surely Aristotle quite as much as Cicero: Aquinas bans joking in church.[95] The tale of the jangling women and the demon in *Handlyng Synne* is thus clearly patristic or Thomist in nature: there was a fine but identifiable line between joy and mirth. Though some medieval Christian writers, such as Alan of Lille in his *Anticlaudianus*, could promote the more constructive aspects of Aristotle's theory of laughter, this very natural human activity was the object of persistent, traditional, suspicion: biblical laughter (*subsannare*, *deridere*) is more often scornful than joyful; laughter had occurred at the foot of the cross.[96]

It is for this reason that grinning and contemptuous laughing in the art of this period were often segregated from smiling, for within the Christian (and indeed Renaissance) dispensation, smiling came to occupy a different frame of reference from laughing. In contrast to the appetitive wolfish grin or to the raucous belly laugh, the smile was the product of self-control and delicacy of sentiment.[97] The matter was not absolutely categorical: Philippe Ménard very properly pointed to the numerous semantic difficulties which arise in attempting to separate medieval usage of the terms *subridere* and *ridere* (*sourire* and *rire* in courtly French) before the thirteenth century in secular vernacular literature: to smile was an aspect of joyful (though not contemptuous) laughing, and it tended to carry with it the notion of secrecy or dissimulation: laughing up one's sleeve.[98] But in the religious domain, the smile was the particular focus of tact. It was above all the sign of bliss, joy, love and innocence, the sign of the saintly and sublime attribute of *hilaritas*.[99] Its character was thus as much

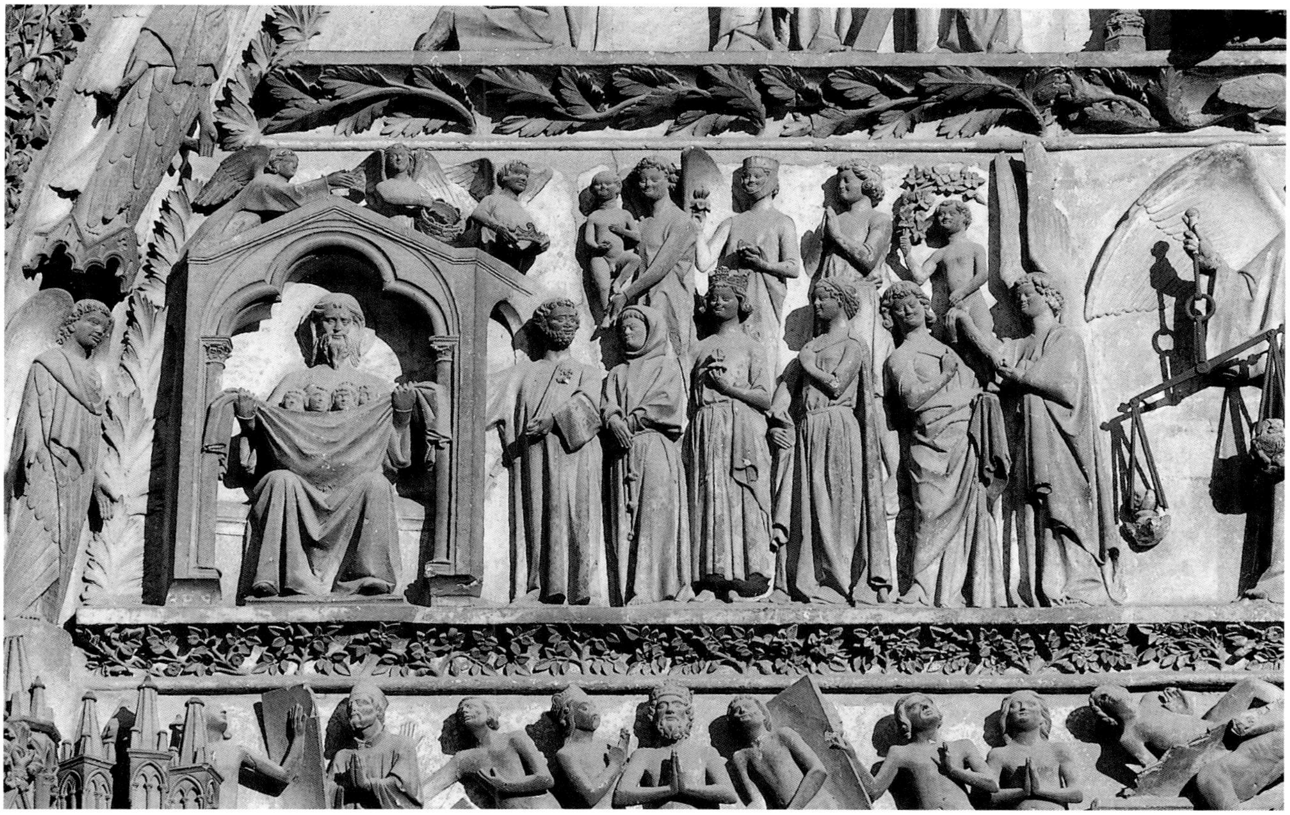

204 The blessed received into Abraham's Bosom. Bourges Cathedral, west facade, *c.* 1250 (Conway Library, Courtauld Institute of Art).

metaphysical as ethical. While it was inconceivable that Christ had laughed (for this would signal emotions and thoughts improper to him), it was possible that he had smiled, because this would be a positive sign of his humanity.[100] The smile as a sign of the divinization (or at least angelization) of the human evolved principally from the Neoplatonic language of Christian joy, particularly angelic joy, set out in the Pseudo-Dionysius's *Celestial Hierarchy* and in the liturgy of the Church, as in *Vere dignum*.[101] It is exactly this understanding of joy, the joy of the resurrected at the reunification of soul with body, and admission to Paradise, that illuminates the faces of the blessed at the cathedrals of Bourges (fig. 204) and Bamberg,[102] or a few tomb-effigies of the period made in England, France and Germany which show gently smiling females.[103] Blissful *hilaritas*, the reward of martyrdom, is the correct designation of the shining angelic smile of St Stephen on the Adamsportal at Bamberg.[104] As John Gage has shown, this notion of a smile literally illuminating the features is found in French and Italian romance literature, and in the 'flashing out' (*corruscazione*) of the soul's delight in Dante's *Convivio* – an idea already developed by St Bernard in his commentaries on Canticles.[105] The same associations provided contemporary artistic metaphors, such as that of 'smiling' colour – found in Alan of Lille and Dante, and the near-synonymous use of *riant* for *cler*.[106] In important respects too it is the attribute of angels and women, of the 'feminization' of loving discourse: Gabriel's somewhat androgynous smile at the Virgin Annunciate at Reims (fig. 198) is not only a loving smile, but the look of one who banishes fear: *ne timeas Maria* (Luke 1: 30). The smile wards off other affects.

Hilaritas was not a new human capacity, any more than the smile in the ordinary social sense was an invention of the period. Even in the desolate Fenland world of Felix's eighth-century Life of St Guthlac, one learns that the saint's inner understanding of spiritual events was greeted by a joyful countenance (*hilari vultu*) and a fleeting smile (*parumper subridens*).[107] This discretion or secrecy is important: it represents once again the notion that religious experience is ultimately internal; a view which St Bernard was later to stress in his sermons on Canticles following Isaiah 24: 16, *secretum meum mihi, secretum meum mihi*: my secret is mine, my secret is mine.[108] If the character of knowledge or, better, wisdom, is hidden, the fact of its possession is revealed by a lighting-up of the face, even if what is imparted is less obvious. It is in part from this Christian sapiential tradition that the 'mystery' of the smile of Leonardo's *La Gioconda* is derived.[109] This discretion is opposed to the moral psychology of the laugh as I have sketched it in here. For one thing, the most horrible way of breaking the silence in monastic communal *mores* was the rude guffaw; and the same sense of etiquette led to the banning of immoderate laughing and grinning in later courtesy literature.[110]

To illustrate these points, it will be useful to consider one important English instance of the way in which smiling and laughing were increasingly distinguished in the twelfth and thirteenth centuries, which is provided by the evolution of the hagiography of St Edward the Confessor. This brings me back to a point made earlier in this study: precisely because it had a pastoral character and was invested in pastoral texts and images, sainthood could provide concrete instances of good conduct, in this case the transformation of sudden and loud laughter into the more measured smile of saintly *hilaritas*. In this process one can see monastic and royal virtue being shaped by ideals of temperance.[111] It was with this in mind that the Cistercian Aelred of Rievaulx gently edited earlier writing on St Edward in the preparation of his post-canonization Life of the saint of the 1160s. In doing so he 'civilized' the image of St Edward proposed earlier in the twelfth century by the Benedictine hagiographer Osbert of Clare. Two episodes point to this editing: the account of Edward's vision of his old enemy, the King of Denmark, drowning, and his vision of the Seven Sleepers of Ephesus. While at Mass at Westminster, Edward has a vision of the downfall of the King of Denmark by drowning. At this moment of revelation, Osbert describes how the king erupted into immoderate laughter (*in cachinnum rex gloriosus erupit immoderatum*) to the great astonishment of those in his presence.[112] Aelred's version of the event tempers this *cachinnatio*, a style of laughter lacking in virtue: the king's face now shows *hilaritas* and a moderated or quiet laughter (*risum modicum*).[113] During a feast at Westminster, Edward has a vision of the Seven Sleepers of Ephesus. Osbert's version says that at this, Edward was suddenly moved to laugh out so loudly (*vocem suam subito promovit in risu*) that everyone in the hall was suddenly brought to silence by its immoderacy.[114] Aelred's version however maintains a virtuous silence: Edward's internal happiness produced no more than lips turned into a smile (*labia solvebat in risum*).[115] This produces puzzlement in his companions, but not the shock of silence: a dignified (and monastic) *taciturnitas* has been preserved. Aelred's view of private enlightenment was explicitly Bernardine: Edward's smile is the shining-out of his secret knowledge, but its character is tempered by *mediocritas* in such a way that it cannot be understood as foolish happiness or a sign of pride.[116] Understandably, in view of his sympathy with Cistercian styles of affective spirituality, Matthew Paris preserved this reading in his French verse version of Aelred's Life, the *Estoire* of 1236–45: at these visions, Edward smiles as if in a trance, or quietly to himself.[117]

Part II of this book describes how attributes of this type were in no sense restricted to kings: they formed the basis of the ethical character of aristocratic sanctity more generally. The mythology of the greatest pastoral bishop-saints of the era shared and sustained them. It was unthinkable that such scholars and ascetics as St Edmund of Abingdon or St Richard should abound in *facetia*.[118] On the contrary, their manner was more tempered. To repeat: St Edmund's decorous affability rendered him always joyous and cheerful (*semper gaudens et hilaris*);[119] St Richard's name was derived from his being cheerful, affectionate and sweet, *ri*dens, *car*us et *dul*cis (p. 126 above). These outward attributes of behaviour could exist only in virtue of the discipline of personal *mores*. Indeed the hagiography makes it clear that in each case they are framed by the (Aristotelian, Ciceronian and Thomist) notion that outward behaviour is the simulacrum of inner disposition (p. 126). Aelred of Rievaulx's quite deliberate literary tempering of St Edward's laughter into a civilized or courtly smile is based precisely upon such a notion. Aelred's 'taming' of boorish conduct is noted in one episode about him in his own Life.[120] His vision of conduct lay at the intersection of Christian monastic and classical ethical values. St Bernard's example is not far behind, not least in sanctioning Aelred's attack, in his *Speculum caritatis* of the 1140s, on the admission to churches of things suited only to the theatre, such as the histrionic display of ridiculous facial expressions and bodily movements during the performance of liturgical music, all symptoms of vanity and of the evils of the senses.[121] The basis of this ascetic viewpoint is clearly as much classical and patristic as Bernardine.[122] But it was not solely monastic: it was an aspect too of the ethics of the masters, of the men of the cathedral chapters. Indeed, in view of the ascetic doctrine regarding architecture discussed in Part I, it is not entirely surprising to find a generically similar view of decorum in the writings of Hugh of Saint-Victor for novices (as quoted in the second epigraph to this chapter) and in Peter the Chanter's writings on prayer: both Hugh's and Peter's views of human conduct assume rules not unlike those

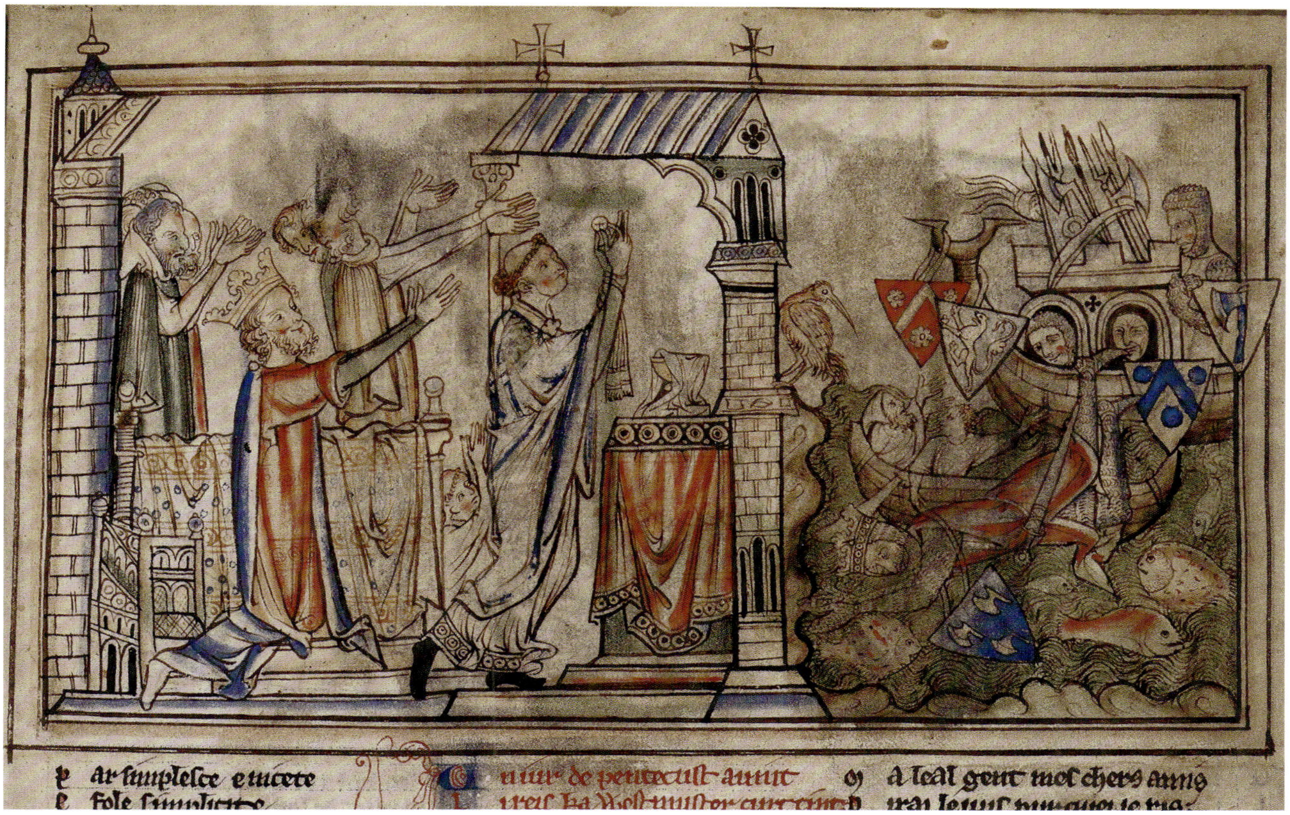

205 Vision of the King of Denmark drowning seen by St Edward at Mass. *La Estoire de Seint Aedward le Rei*, CUL MS Ee. 3. 59, fol. 12, *c.* 1255 (by permission of the Syndics of Cambridge University Library).

implicit in Aelred; bodily deportment is an index of devotion, and the face is a mirror of morality.[123]

At work in Aelred's and Matthew Paris's texts are therefore two related, but extremely important, processes: a process of tempering, in the course of which the concept of St Edward's erudite and moderated courtliness is forged; and a transmission of ideas from monastic Latin into pastoral courtly French. The outcome, finally, is the admission of the newly refined discourse of saintly *hilaritas* into the domain of representation itself, as on folio 12 of the *Estoire*, where Edward smiles at the vision of the death of his enemy the King of Denmark (fig. 205). This is the earliest surviving morally unambivalent smile in English art; the illuminator showed the smile because it embodies the pastoral objectives of the text. *Hilaritas* is now exposed on the surface – but only because it is the virtuous sign of a virtuous royal body, the character of which is now tempered. The positive artistic representation of a smiling king is inseparable from the representation of St Edward as one whose 'body was illuminated by his inner holiness', in whose face was visible an unusual mildness, and whose nature was instructive, *erudiens*.[124] Nor was it separable from that vision of Edward's courtly pedagogy – his court being the school of courtesy and moderation (*afaitment*, *mesure*) – developed finally by Matthew Paris (p. 142 above). This particular picture was an intelligent reaction to the text of the *Estoire* on the part of a court-employed artist working in the circle of those who were transforming the expressions of angels and other figures for the benefit of Henry III. As already mentioned, the poem is dedicated to Eleanor of Provence. But it would be hasty to conclude that Edward is shown smiling in the *Estoire* merely because of the stimulus of the new Gothic arts of Reims or Westminster, and in response to a French text. In St Edward's case the Latin text of Aelred had accomplished a taming of the laugh rather earlier than the widespread emergence of the notion of the 'secret' smile in vernacular romance literature, in which it is a dissimulative aspect of laughter.[125] The smile may well have become an increasingly common and distinct feature of the vernacular romance sensibility in the thirteenth century at the same time as its emergence in sculpture: the ideas were fashionable; the latest

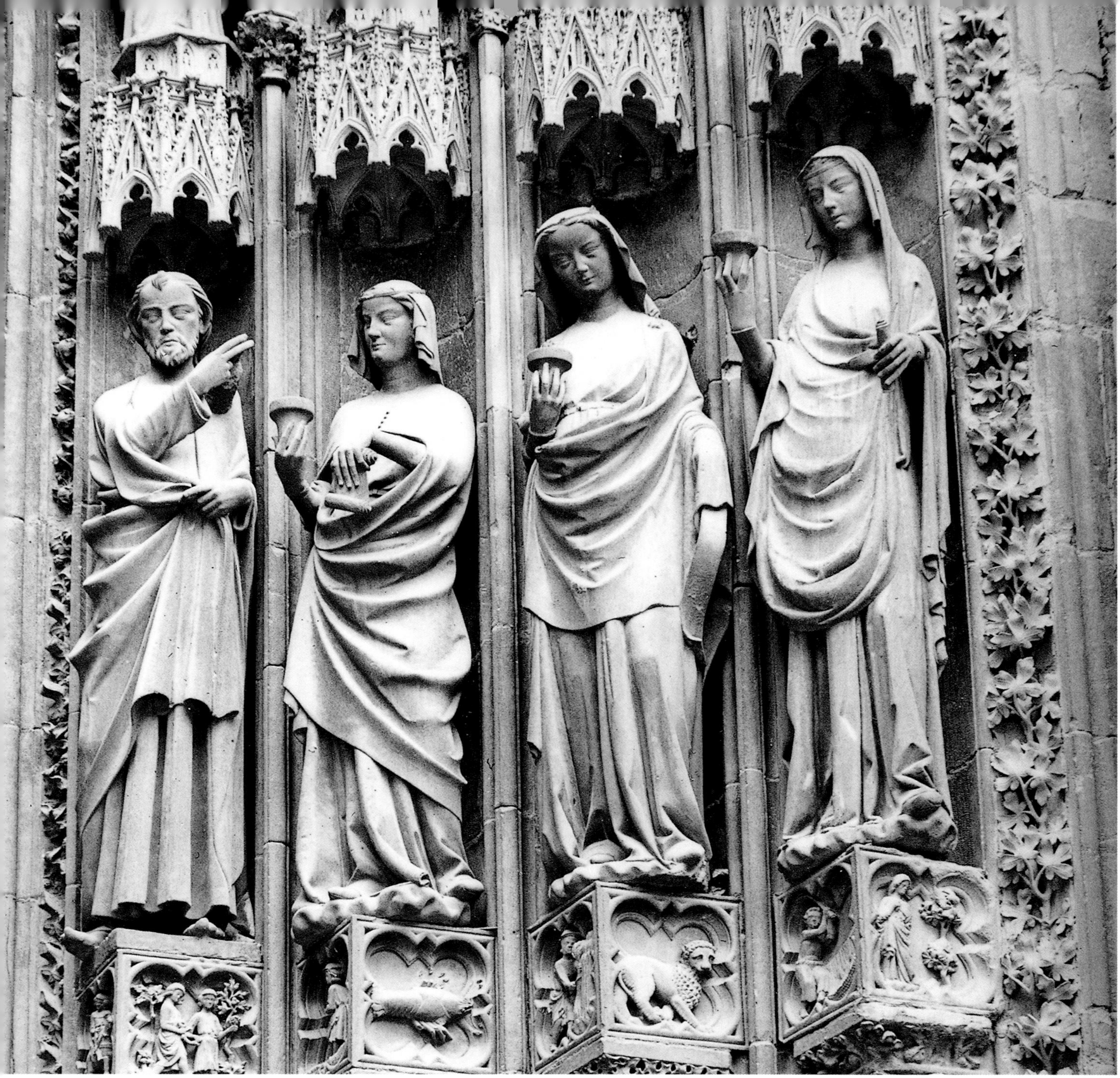

206 (ABOVE AND FACING PAGE) Wise and Foolish Virgins. Strasbourg Cathedral, west facade, late thirteenth century (Conway Library, Courtauld Institute of Art).

technical and artistic means were stupendous; and, above all, the nature of the audiences was changing.[126] But the foundations which lent this affectivity real human coherence were also older and deeper. In part they were textual: the groundwork had been done in twelfth-century monastic Latin, not thirteenth-century courtly French. In part they were artistic: the smile emerged at Reims and centres like it because it was at these sites that exceptionally talented workforces were prepared to take risks, perhaps even extrapolating intelligently from the remnants of classical tradition. In part they were both textual and artistic: the smile, one might say, was the tactful product of a particular moral, political and aesthetic regime.

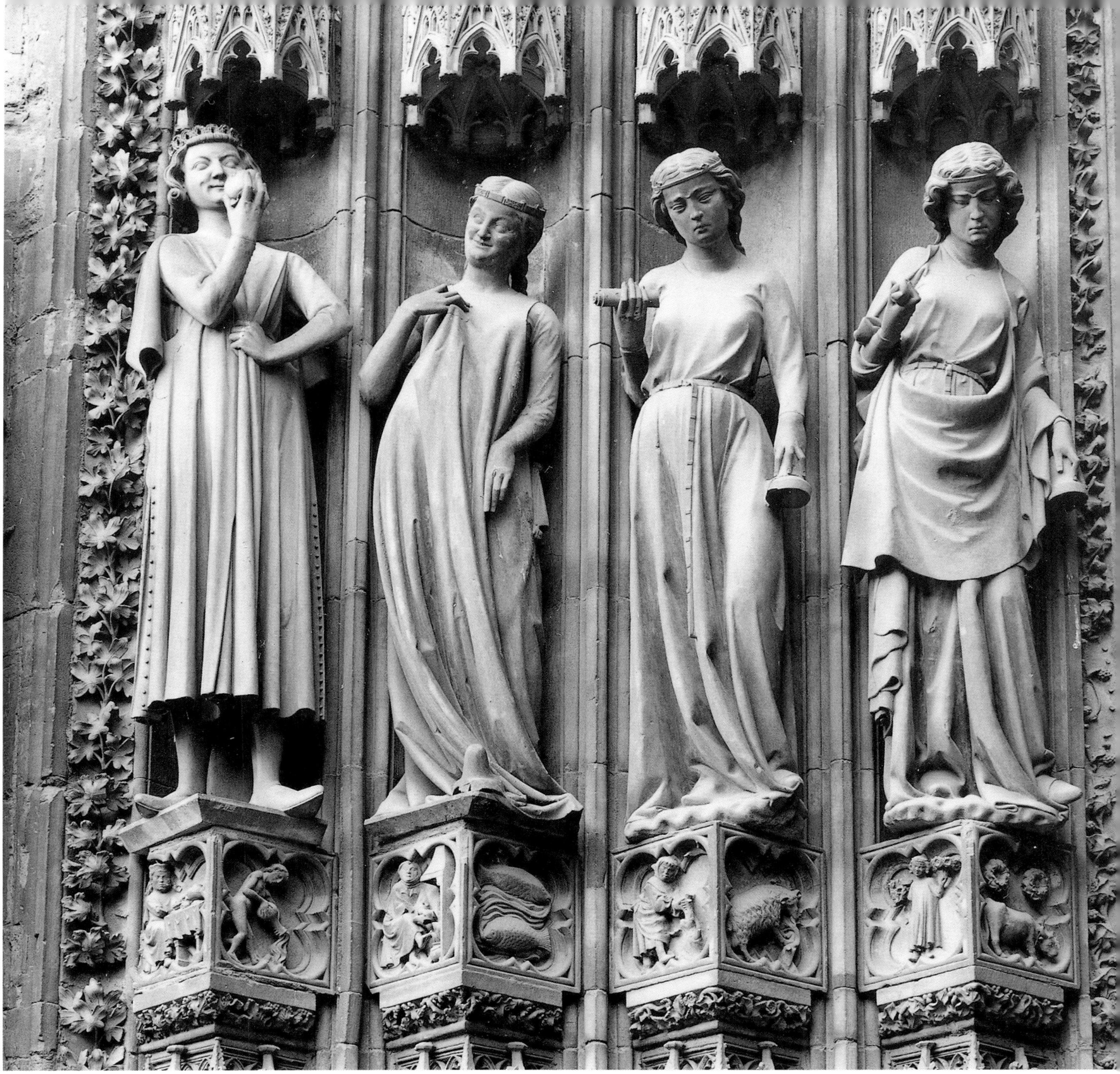

The Envy of Angels?

Of all recent commentators on this issue (and there have been few), C. Stephen Jaeger has provided much the most stimulating groundwork in an appendix to his study *The Envy of Angels*, in which he discusses the bodily and facial demeanour of the sculpted Wise and Foolish Virgins at Strasbourg Cathedral (fig. 206), dating to the last decades of the thirteenth century, in relation to his account of the origins of courtliness.[127] Jaeger argues that these sculptures represent the infusion into art of what he calls the *cultus virtutum* (the moral discipline of the cathedral schools that had developed over centuries on the basis principally of Roman models), and also that this infusion occurred only after the *cultus virtutum* itself had ceased to be an important preoccupation in theory or practice. The evidence of art is the evidence of an aestheticization of bygone social practices and moral discourses.[128] For Jaeger, the key feature of the Wise and Foolish Virgins is what he calls their 'moral transparency', the fact that the faces and bodies now carry meanings that would previously have been borne by figures carrying attributes or symbols, whose features were 'isocephalic': not only indistinguishable, but also blank.[129] Thus 'the mode of representation has shifted from abstract signalizing to incarnation', the Wise Virgins being 'realizations of virtue made visible': they are embodiments of tropology. The fact that they can look this way reflects the moral discipline of the cathedral schools and the acceptance of the 'simulacrum' theory of mind, ethos and body outlined in various ways in this study, not least in relation to the thought of such figures as St Bernard and Peter the Chanter, monks and schoolmen.

Jaeger also points to the smile, and to the casuistry involved in its interpretation, as a sign of this moral transparency.[130] In some regards his account is incomplete, or conceals aesthetic opinion. Isocephalic 'blankness' of features found in the period up to around 1220 may itself be the transitive sign of a stoical view of the emotions, rather than of an intransitive 'expressivity' or a species of post-classical inadequacy. It possesses an incarnational dimension; what it deliberately does not possess is range. Again, when it does emerge, the smile does not occur or work in the same way in the various groups of the Wise and Foolish Virgins sculpted in the Holy Roman Empire: at Magdeburg, the Wise Virgins smile broadly and openly while the Foolish ones are blatantly woeful; at Strasbourg the Wise Virgins are in comparison serious but serene beings, and a smile shines only from the single Foolish Virgin attracted by the Tempter. These permutations indicate significantly different didactic strategies, and the absolute necessity of context-dependent readings. So the fatuous grin of the tempted Foolish Virgin at Strasbourg (fig. 206, left), theoretically a sign of indiscipline and vanity, cannot convey the same ethos as the not wholly dissimilar smile of the foundress Reglindis at Naumburg (fig. 202), partly because the Foolish Virgin's entire deportment towards the Tempter, her sexy hipshot sway towards him especially, differs from the dignified frame of Reglindis, and partly because the contexts are incommensurate. What in one context might signal silly wantonness might in another advertise courtly benevolence. Hence (and for reasons I pointed out earlier in discussing Panofsky's Hegelian view of the 'autonomy' of classicizing sculpture, which Jaeger's humanistic account implicitly echoes) these new sorts of image do not fully or unambiguously embody in themselves virtues or dispositions. They appear to do so only by creating a very dense cluster of signs.

Nevertheless the outcome is sufficiently similar for the point to have some general validity: in the ethical content of these images lies, if not polemic, then at least a certain ideology. For Jaeger the relationship between the moral discipline of the schools and the practical tropology of these sculptures is not one merely of reciprocal illumination, but causality: 'It seems very unlikely that the sculptor's art [. . .] developed independently and in ignorance of this discipline'.[131] Despite my caveats, this general conclusion is highly likely to be correct, not least because this tropology seems to have begun in, and emanated from, the cathedral centres where such visual ideas were also developed. The dependence of the court at Westminster on the achievements of the archdiocesan chapter of Reims is a fair symbol of the order of events. What Jaeger claims not to be able to understand is the fact that sculpture came to such ideas so late, post-dating the death of instruction in moral discipline in the schools. His solution – that the sculptors were engaging in a 'nostalgic reconstruction of an ideal still mouthed and formulated by the sculptor's contemporaries but seldom attained in reality' – will not entirely convince, even though it captures the sense in which great programmes of cathedral sculpture such as that at Strasbourg were now enjoying their swansong. Whether or not the ideal was actually attained in social reality is not the point. Throughout this book I stress the importance of ideals of conduct and belief, whose purpose was to symbolize the mythologies or ideologies of a class, and to inform in an absolutely practical way the widespread pastoral and reforming mission of the Church. The role of art, as of the shaping of conduct, was profoundly implicated in this entire issue, and from a traditionally Gregorian viewpoint. The tropology of the image (the *imago agens* especially), its moral transparency, was an aspect of the demonstrative rhetoric of images, of their participation in the construction of moral awareness that the universal Church had now proposed (for better or worse) as one of its central tasks. The two substantially new and extremely widespread forces of the period after 1200 – the post-ecumenical reformist programme of mass education for the clergy and laity, and the increasingly Aristotelian tenor of the ethos of this programme (neither of which is discussed by Jaeger) – were not only contemporary with the emergence of these ideals at (say) Reims around 1220, but found in them an almost total outlet. There was no question of nostalgia, of 'the envy of angels' for a lost Golden Age of real yet ideal conduct – for in the Apocalyptic and reformist dispensation of the times, that world had yet to come. This was something that the cathedral chapters of north-western Europe, and the culture of the masters, continued to recognize and aspire to, and of which the angels were to be a prime symbol.

For this general outlook on the continuing utility of the image, there is one small but telling piece of evidence. My final witness is one such master, an Englishman working in mid-thirteenth-century Paris who fully participated in the culture of the schools and its discipline of *mores*: John of Garland. John was an Oxford-educated man born in the late twelfth century, who lived in Paris on the left bank of the Seine while the highest Parisian Gothic style was manifesting its extraordinary technical and artistic accomplishments. His work as a scholar embraced the so-called *ars poetria*, texts on the mysteries of the Church and the justifiability of the Crusades (*De triumphis ecclesiae*), and the *Morale scolarium*, a pedagogic intervention on the morality of young men composed in the early 1240s.[132] The *Morale scolarium* is the work of someone eager to complement some of his more outstanding English contemporaries, notably Fulk Bassett, Bishop of London, and John Blund, Chancellor of York.[133] It is heir to the wordly and satirical culture of the English clerks rising to fame at the time of Becket. Gerald of Wales and Walter Map would have appreciated it.[134] But its reputation resides principally in its character as an early manual of courtesy, a genre that became more familiar in the later Middle Ages.[135] The reader will be acquainted with its themes by now. Morality is contrasted with faults, urbanity with rusticity. The old values of the stoic ascetics of the twelfth century are reiterated: dislike of the lucrative arts, suspicion of subtlety in disputation. Table manners – the tempered manners of the hall of the great man discussed above in relation to Becket's conduct – sustain more than one chapter.[136] Senecan probity, 'the good old Roman morality', is commended: modesty, tact, self-denial – the excellent bishop quietly suffers his hair shirt; Aristotelian wit is recommended, for laughter at faults is one of the laws of satire.[137] But it is chapter 30 on student conduct that is startling, for in reiterating the norms of decent clerical behaviour set out in the ecumenical councils of the period, John provides their exemplar in a simple couplet:[138]

> Templi sculpturas morum dic esse figuras
> Vivas picturas in te gere non perituras

> Declare our churches' sculptures models of civility,
> Living pictures, to be borne in mind indelibly.

Not just a saint, not just a king, not just a noble man or woman, but images too are to be a model. By this John of Garland's couplet means nothing so banal as that images were to be courtesy books. Nor does it entail any necessary connection between *mores* and particular styles of deportment in representation: presumably figures could be models of stiff rectitude, or of 'courtly' grace. What it does suggest is the possibility that representations might be open to moral as well as symbolic scrutiny, and hence a part of ethical discourse. The claim was wide, and it had a formidable heritage. It stemmed ultimately from classical rhetoric, and from the notion of edification by example set out in Pope Gregory the Great's second letter to Serenus of Marseilles.[139] Gregory, cited in canon law, legitimized the pastoral use of the image. It remained for men such as Alan of Lille and Hugh of Saint-Victor to reintroduce to this function tropological weight, ethical substance, seeing in the 'eminences' of sculpture the 'eminence' of great men, the saints especially (p. 133 above).[140] In the same vein, Peter the Chanter regarded the body as an image in his work on prayer.[141] This style of thought was current among the masters and students of thirteenth-century Paris. In England, Stephen Langton, Edmund of Abingdon and Robert Grosseteste would have recognized it – and understood its wider value for the pastoral mission of the Church, to which it lent new vitality. The *antiqui*, so to speak, still had much to teach the *moderni*.[142] As Christopher Page has shown, the idea persists in England into the fourteenth century in the musical treatise *Quatuor principalia*, in which 'uprightness' of bodily carriage in performance is to be modelled on the painted image, *veluti ymago depicta*.[143] The Church had entered into a creative pact with the latest moral technology, art; art, in virtue of its utility, was in turn drawn into the Church's disciplinary ethos and regulatory framework. Music, the technologies of which were also developing rapidly in this period, was to follow. Jaeger's fundamental instincts are correct; and the next chapter starts to draw the central threads of my book together.

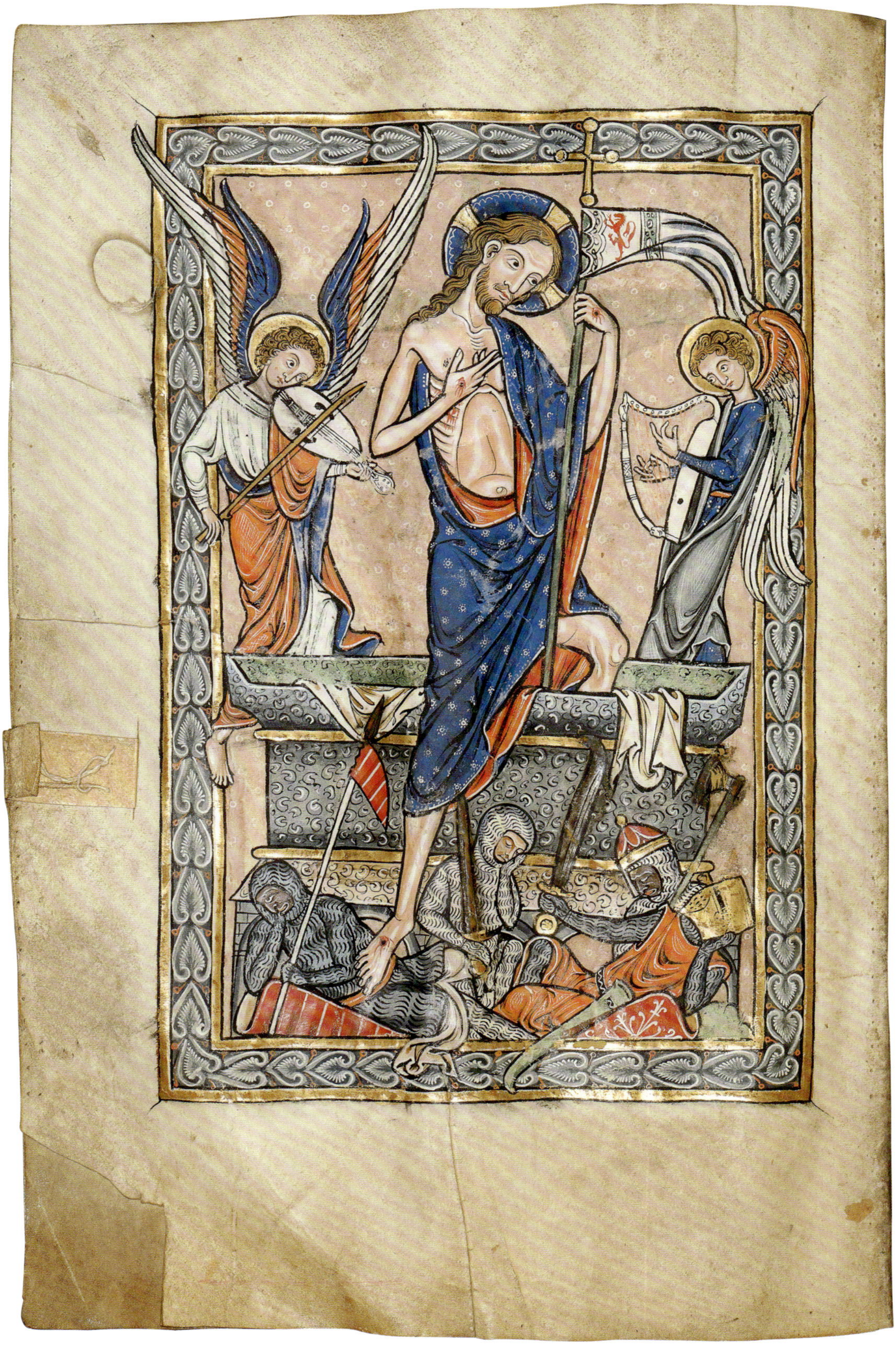

207 ‘Awake up my glory, awake psaltery and harp: I myself will awake early’ (Psalm 56). Resurrection, Missal of Henry of Chichester, Manchester, John Rylands Library MS Lat. 24, fol. 152v, *c.* 1250 (reproduced by courtesy of the Director and Librarian, the John Rylands University Library of Manchester).

Chapter 11

MUSIC AND THE ANGELIC

It is known that those who used to perform tragedies in theatres, represented to people the actions of conflicting forces by means of gestures. Thus too, our tragedian (the priest), represents to Christian folk by means of his gestures the combat of Christ in the theatre of the Church, and brings home to them the triumph of His redemption.

Honorius of Autun, *Gemma animae*

While all this [musical performance] is going on, the common people standing trembling and astonished nearby admire the sound of the organs [. . .] but look at the lascivious gesticulation of the singers in a way not without derisive laughter; so that someone might very well think that they had come not to a place of prayer but to a theatre, and not to pray, but to gawp.

Aelred of Rievaulx, *Speculum caritatis*

Theophilus's Pact

Reference in such works as *Morale scolarium* and *Quatuor principalia* to the moral utility of visual images brings me to my last question: how and to what extent the Church came to terms with developments that had traditionally posed ethical problems, not least in the sphere of what was acceptable within the conduct of the liturgy. As well as being a moralist, John of Garland was a music theorist: *Quatuor principalia* offered advice to musicians. Both have in common an established view of utility and excess: student behaviour is to be temperate, conforming to the old Roman morality; musical performers in church should not adopt absurd postures, stretching and bending themselves this way and that as if afflicted with an ague, or trying to catch the eye of the audience.[1] The reference to illness echoes the familiar moralist's connection between superfluity in building and madness – *quanta dementia* (p. 45 above), for excess indicates malaise. The new visual and ethical culture of the expressive body traced in the previous chapter, a culture which pushed significance to the surface, deployed ostensive form to affective ends and relativized expression, posed problems for these older, rather absolute, standards. It is as if different forms of consciousness were now co-existing, forms which in their 'ancient' guise emphasized the sublime certainties of common form, and in their 'modern' guise the urbane hazards of individuality. One might pursue a musical figure: the stoical suppression of the self in the name of humility, equality, the discipline of the community, is the 'placid unison' of plainsong, which is now confronted by the performative ego of many stranded polyphony, the domain of a 'modern' individuality: the sober Owl is displaced by the showy Nightingale.[2]

The musical figure is intended as a form of 'reciprocal illumination' or analogy. Yet its basis in hard historical realities – the new polyphonic chants in the liturgy, and the new subtleties of jongleuric performance in the great households and cities of the late twelfth and the thirteenth century – is undeniable. For twentieth-century art historians such as Meyer Schapiro, the picaresque world of the 'jongleuric' was the true domain of artistic reality, autonomy, originality and authenticity – the modern virtues of the marginal.[3] But from the viewpoint of an assertive and reformist medieval Church militant, newly conscious of enemies without and within, it signified ancient vice. The aesthetic and moral excesses of the jongleurs, mimes and actors smacked of pagan Roman mischief.[4] Their subtle and woven arts had been identified as the sites of decadence even by the ancient moralists, satirists and Church Fathers. To the ascetics of the twelfth century they were even more worth persecuting, not as heretics of belief, but of behaviour. The performers were to be brought under the same surveillance as architects, tradesmen and prostitutes: the performers and prostitutes especially dealt in commodities besmirched by lucre, and what they did with their bodies was ugly, monstrous, abusive. They belonged outside the canons of the normal and beautiful; they were an affront to the regime.

The problem of course was that the regime itself was doing much to open Pandora's box. As shown in the first epigraph to this chapter, a citation from Honorius of Autun's perfectly respectable meditational treatise *Gemma animae*, the church-theatre analogy, the *theatrum ecclesiae*, was not unknown to contemporaries.[5] Nor, deployed sensitively, is it absurd. As Jody Enders has shown, the type of theory embodied in Honorius's idea of the priest as tragic impersonator, and the Mass as a dramatic *agon*, stemmed ultimately from forms of dramatic representation in classical legal or forensic oratory.[6] It is not difficult to see how ultimately rhetorical techniques could influence a general conception of spectacle and aesthetic effect within the domain of the liturgy. The rational strategies which, as suggested earlier (p. 156), governed the early thirteenth-century reformers' attitude to *ornamenta* in church – the conduct of priests in regard to clear diction and gestures, the development of liturgical colours, adequate illumination, images, vestments, use of bells and fragrances – involved techniques. These techniques helped to ensure the proper efficacy of the sacraments, the completeness as well as the dignity of the rites; but their concerted character and their reliance on the senses were also intended to grip and hold the attention of the congregation: in turn, the congregation, itself 'regulated' in regard to conduct, could now be regarded as an audience, a public.[7] As Enders has put it, 'Audience participation, audience adaptation, and theatricalization are linked'.[8] Liturgical or para-liturgical 'props' in rituals of the Church year (liturgical automata, cribs, the *palmesel*, moving crucifixes, effigies of Christ) had the same ends; so too did *mirabilia*, things to be wondered at: clocks, stentorian bells and organs.[9] Such techniques and technologies formed part of the Gothic fantasy-imagery of the temple.[10] Sarah Beckwith is justified in pointing out the possibility that 'the theatrical resources of the priesthood' were 'not completely separable from the resources of the theatre' and that the Mass was 'a spectacular form of theatre', its character being dramatic, even if its form and purpose were not those of a drama.[11] The most discriminating patrons and legislators were being implicated in the 'theatricalization' of the Church. To repeat: the idea remains a figure, for the Church was not literally a theatre, but theatre-like. Contemporary English miracle collections deliberately oppose theatre and the truly miraculous; yet in doing so the connection of ideas is still present, even inadvertently reinforced. The miracles of St John of Beverley make the point well. One summer, perhaps in the early thirteenth century, a performance of a play about the Resurrection of Christ was put on in the churchyard on the north side of Beverley Minster. It drew a large crowd, attracted either by a thirst for spectacle or by a need to have devotion fired up. But many in the crowd, especially the shorter ones, could not see what was going on properly. So instead they went into the great church to pray, look at the paintings (*picturas inspicere*) or pass the time with other sorts of amusement (*aliquod genus recreationis*). One of them, a boy, climbed up to the top of the building to gain a better view, but tumbled down horribly to the ground, only to be brought back to life by St John. Thus a true miracle of resurrection inside is apposed to a theatrical sign of the Resurrection outside.[12] Yet a price is also paid, for despite itself the narrative still draws the Church into the domain of the theatrical and the curious. The predicament was not unusual for the times, but its symbolic interest here is considerable.

One reason for this is that the church-theatre analogy provided a useful admonitory idea for the moralists, whose accounts of performance have much in common with their views on superfluity in architecture. St Jerome, following the Roman satirists, had linked actors and demons;[13] for St Bernard, the monastic life was to have nothing of the theatre about it: *non est de theatro*.[14] Following patristic writing and St Bernard, Aelred of Rievaulx (quoted in the second epigraph to this chapter) engaged in a splendid tirade against certain forms of musical performance in church in his *Speculum caritatis* of the 1150s, seeing the lascivious gesticulation of singers as a proper object of derisive laughter (*cachinnatio*) – a theme that can now be better understood in the light of his 'taming' of the laughter of St Edward – and regarding such performance as the preserve of the *theatrum* not *oratorium*. Why, he asks,

> does the Church have so many organs and musical instruments [. . .] what is the point of that contraction and inflection of the human voice? This man sings bass, this one tenor, another treble, a fourth divides and as it were splits certain middle notes. [. . .] Sometimes, shame to say, [the voice] is forced into a horse's neighing, sometimes, masculine vigour

> laid aside, it is sharpened into a woman's shrillness. [. . .] Sometimes you may see a man with open mouth, as if not to sing but to breathe his last gasp. [. . .] Meanwhile the whole body pumps up and down with theatrical gestures, the lips curl, the eyes swivel, the shoulders hunch, and waggling fingers point out every note. And this absurd dissolution is called religion![15]

The method is essentially that of St Bernard's *Apologia*, deploying the device of ridicule at the start of Horace's *Ars poetica* to denounce the monstrous, in this case not grotesque or curious sculpture in the cloister, but grotesque and curious conduct.[16] Other Cistercian commentaries extend Bernard's anti-Cluniac polemic to the domain of music: thus the Cistercian in Idung of Prüfening's *Dialogue* of the 1150s claims that the Cluny monks kept their voices shrill with liquorice juice and had bells so heavy that the monks herniated themselves while trying to ring them.[17] Cistercian legislation limited the size of bells to those that could be rung by one man only.[18] Aelred's main targets were clearly the curiosity of a public wondering at the organ's bellow-blast, and the inutility and vanity of polyphonic singing which destroyed the tempered Cistercian notion of living according to one *caritas*, one rule.[19] He might have borrowed his attack on femininity and 'whorish' singing in music from Boethius, though the fear of effeminate theatrical excess stems ultimately from classical rhetoric.[20] The legacy of his critique may be traced subsequently in Franciscan and Wycliffite commentary, and in the anti-theatrical polemic of the English seventeenth century, in which it was quoted.[21] Yet no matter how dazzling such rhetorically honed assaults were, in practice by the fourteenth century a Cistercian church such as that at Meaux in Yorkshire could perfectly well possess not one but even two organs, as well as painted altarpieces and sculpted crucifixions following the beautiful form of the male body (p. 229 above). Three- and four-part polyphony in the secular manner and contrary to Bernardine *mediocritas* had been heard at Abbey Dore and Tintern as early as 1217.[22] Even by 1200 the advanced heavy technologies were starting to make headway even among the Cistercians, not least in the construction of stone-vaulted churches which presumably created ideal acoustics for plainchant.[23]

This pattern of critique and accommodation was true much more generally of the secular church, since the fundamental issues – the irresistible rise of extraordinary new technologies and methods of persuasion within and without the Church – were common to religious institutions of all types and ranks. How were the new forms of knowledge to be assimilated to the Christian *habitus*? The humanists and secular canons of the twelfth century were no less concerned. John of Salisbury, a man not untouched by ideas of stoic virtue, had already attacked church singers who outstripped nightingales and parrots in virtuosity.[24] In *De claustro animae* (see p. 45) Hugues de Fouilly proceeded on lines similar to those set out by the Cistercians in reproving over-elaborate and ornamented singing: care should be taken that the Church should not be turned into a theatre; abuse of singing signalled not only superfluity but also disruption of the uniformity, *aequalitas*, of the hearts of the brethren.[25] Hugh of Saint-Victor and, later, Gilbert of Tournai, set out ideals of decorous bodily conduct strikingly reminiscent of those implied by Aelred's account of facial and bodily distortion by singers.[26]

As one might expect, however, the most sophisticated and most comprehensive discourse on this issue came from the moral theologians and penitentialists in the circle of Peter the Chanter, including the Englishmen Robert of Courçon and Thomas of Chobham. Peter's thought concerned itself with the issue at its broadest because, in taking a moral view of professions – exactly the professions associated with the new light and heavy technologies – it had to consider both ecclesiastical and secular musicians, and the interface between the two. Peter's fundamental thinking on the infamy of jongleurs, actors, mimes and buffoons was clearly in line with patristic tradition and canon law.[27] Canon law itself had long imposed legal disabilities on actors, and ecumenical and synodal legislation strengthened, or aimed to strengthen, the boundaries between clergy and entertainers: canon 16 of Lateran IV was the classic statement.[28] The English legislators had long guarded against such taints and in the early post-ecumenical phase followed Lateran IV readily.[29]

Yet the contribution of these men generally was in fact markedly more subtle. Notwithstanding the marked streak of intolerance in the thinking of Peter the Chanter and his circle, he had nevertheless to confront the practical reality that prelates and clerks were involved in entertainment as patrons and professionals – the moral reality of the urban culture of Paris. Many in this sphere (not least at Peter's Notre-Dame) were themselves masters of organum, i.e. specialists in church polyphony and the very embodiments of urbane musical modernity. Professional entertainments were widely sanctioned by the episcopal households; the schools and the choirstalls provided recruiting grounds for able entertainers.[30] This obviated blanket condemnation; and the product of this typically pragmatic attitude to the secular by the masters was a sort of casuistical bowing to the inevitable. Subtle distinctions might be drawn between various types of actors in an attempt to comprehend what J. W. Baldwin called the 'social complexities' of the urban milieu.[31] The practical attitude of the moral theologians to secular music, instrumental music especially, softened markedly.[32] And within this practical casuistry, music discovered utility, not least with regard to pastoral objectives. Indeed the pastoral utility of both images and certain sorts of professional music is explicit in Peter the Chanter, who argued that painters were required who 'depict instructive narrative scenes, not vanities. Players of musical instruments are also necessary so that boredom and depression may be relieved by them, and in order that devotion, not wantonness, may be inspired by them'.[33]

Again, techniques of the musical, like those of the theatrical or the pictorial, were permissible in the light of the common objective of the excitation of faith. Organum was legitimate, as Robert of Courçon explained, if it was suitably masculine in tone: the issue was not the absolute standing of the method, but its style, or decorum.[34] Instrumental music was acceptable if, as Thomas of Chobham claimed, it offered rational solace and edification to men: indeed if the 'sanctioned' jongleur sang of the deeds of princes or the lives of the saints, he might hope for exoneration.[35] The profession of music was to an extent redeemed by the example of King David.[36] The issue had become less absolute: circumstances mattered, exceptions could be made.

It is of interest that some of the most prominent exponents of this new casuistry of music, Thomas of Chobham, Robert of Courçon and the Franciscan Thomas Docking, were English.[37] Their work is mentioned above in the context of *pastoralia*, the curricular literature of penance and the confessional which carried the thinking of the schoolmen out into the secular church more generally. There are a few pieces of evidence that something of this pastoral dispensation found its way into contemporary English visual culture, though the picture is very mixed. The canonical view that jongleurs might be subject to legal restraint or disability may have been a factor in the decision to include the very unusual image of a musician with his legs in stocks, playing or tuning a fiddle or lute, in a portal devoted probably to Mary at her church at Higham Ferrers of about 1260.[38] The great painted ceiling at Peterborough Abbey of the 1230s or 1240s, though radically compromised by repaintings, includes musical imagery in illustration of the Liberal Arts, a musical angel and other 'positive' musicians, as well as classicizing musical antics including Boethius's Ass and Harp in a way that suggests no great anxiety about musical morality among the Benedictines, except in so far as it insinuated that poor singing in choir was little better than the asinine antics on the ceiling.[39] However, much the most knowing contemporary illustrations of clerical musical activity – images which tend to echo the critics – are those found in illuminated initials to the Psalms which tended to attract musical imagery, especially Psalm 1, *Beatus vir*, Psalm 80, *Exultate Deo*, and Psalm 97, *Cantate Domino canticum novum*. Psalm 97 for matins on Saturdays, a Marian Psalm, is of particular interest in often representing groups of monks or clerks singing from a score on a lectern. The initial to *Cantate Domino* in the Benedictine Psalter from Worcester of *c.* 1220–30 (Oxford, Magdalen College MS 100, fol. 114; fig. 208) is a fine exemplification of monastic concord, the tonsured monks facing unanimously in one direction, their leader indicating strictly with his right hand the phrase 'his right hand and his holy arm hath gotten him the victory'.[40] Later Psalters volunteer a contrasting style of commentary. In them, as Christopher Page has noted, the *canticum novum* or 'new song' of Psalm 97 is identified quite clearly as polyphony, not least because a few include the polyphonic motet *Zelo tui langueo*.[41] The initials in such works as the Howard, Gorleston and Vaux Psalters (fig. 209) and in Queen Isabella's Psalter are distinctive in showing the performative habits of the clerks, swaying effeminately, turning hither and thither often away from the music, histrionically cupping their hands to their ears as proof of their efforts to keep in tune, or allowing their glances to slither round to fix on and catch the eye of the viewer – in short perfectly exemplifying the narcissistic posing and camp manners criticized in the traditions of bodily deportment extending from Aelred and Peter the Chanter to *Quatuor principalia*.[42] Sensitivities about the feminization of singing also revealed anxieties about homosexuality which, as Bruce W. Holsinger has argued, expose the 'erotic implications' of polyphonic perversity.[43] These nicely observed points are reinforced in the Psalm initials by the clerks' superbly rich and differentiated vestments executed in costly and perhaps even foreign-looking textiles – 'dear, fair and strange' clothing in the words of a contemporary Pseudo-Aristotelian treatise on royal conduct and habits; the terms 'strange' and 'new' – *moult etranges* and *moult nouviaus* – were applied by Guillaume de Machaut to many-stranded polyphony.[44] Not all initials to Psalm 97 have these features; but in some the woven arts of the performer clearly indicated special skills, and also special vices. What is interesting is that they could be represented at all.

The knowing tenor of these initials should not distract from the real and well-known role the Psalter itself had in providing a defence of music, instrumental music

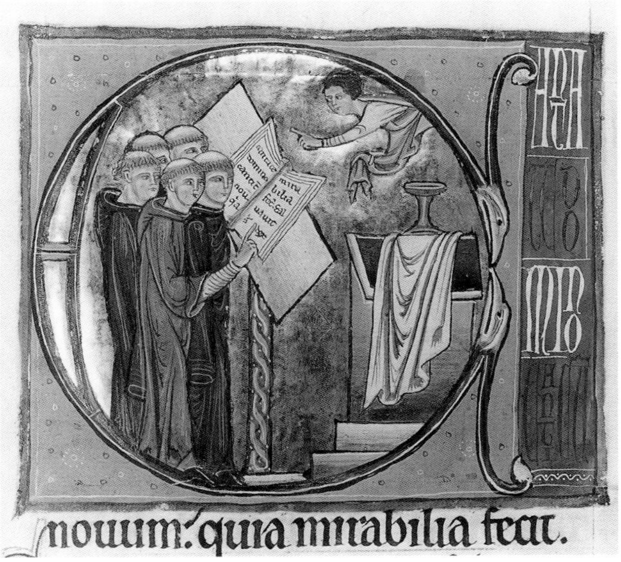

208 Singing clerks, Psalm 97. Oxford, Magdalen College MS 100, fol. 114, *c.* 1220 (The President and Fellows of Magdalen College, Oxford).

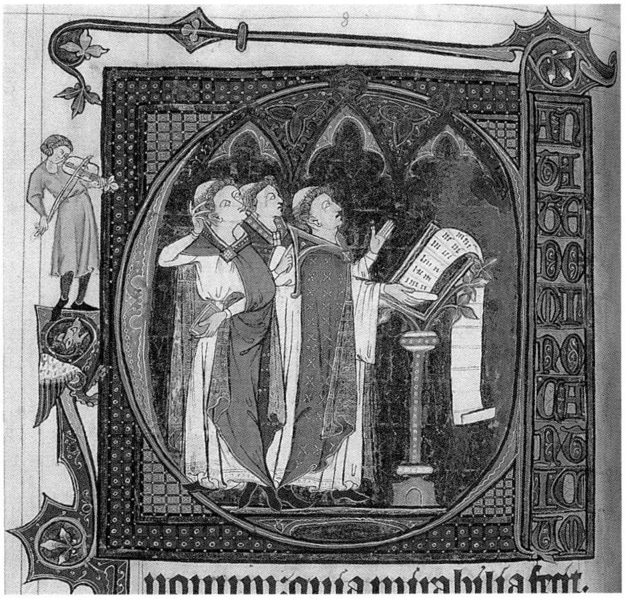

209 Singing clerks, Psalm 97. Vaux Psalter, Lambeth Palace Library MS 233, fol. 145v, *c.* 1310–20 (Lambeth Palace Library).

especially, for those who sought it.[45] The Psalms were important in virtue of their role in the daily liturgy and their highly developed and influential patristic and medieval commentaries, especially those of Augustine, Jerome and Cassiodorus, the Fathers aiming to volunteer essentially allegorical accounts of what they found in the Psalm texts.[46] Because the substantial tradition of musical iconography in Psalm illustrations was framed by this tradition of essentially allegorical commentary, there is some doubt as to the extent to which illuminations such as that on folio 115 of the late thirteenth-century English Marciana Psalter, showing a hooded and obviously secular fiddler accompanying singing clerks at Psalm 97 (fig. 210), can reveal anything positive about actual accompanimental practices in churches.[47] Here the point might specifically be that clerks do not, or should not, play instruments in the liturgy: but one cannot be sure. Yet the Psalms tended in practice to vindicate an informal relationship of secular and religious music-making until well into the period: hence perhaps the appearance of the two side by side on the ceiling at Peterborough and the proximity of secular musicians to angels on the thirteenth-century church tower at Raunds.[48] The clerical casuists naturally lighted on this angle of the Psalms in their exploration of the morality of instrumental performance. The salutary and rational role of music in calming, offering solace and healing was noted by Thomas of Chobham, Thomas Docking and the canonists.[49] Robert of Courçon cites the example of King David and others who dignified organs and plucked instruments especially.[50] The text of Revelation 14 linked harps to heaven. The citations in

210 Fiddler and singing clerks, Psalm 97. Marciana Psalter, Venice, Biblioteca Marciana MS lat. I. 77, fol. 115, *c.* 1280 (Conway Library, Courtauld Institute of Art).

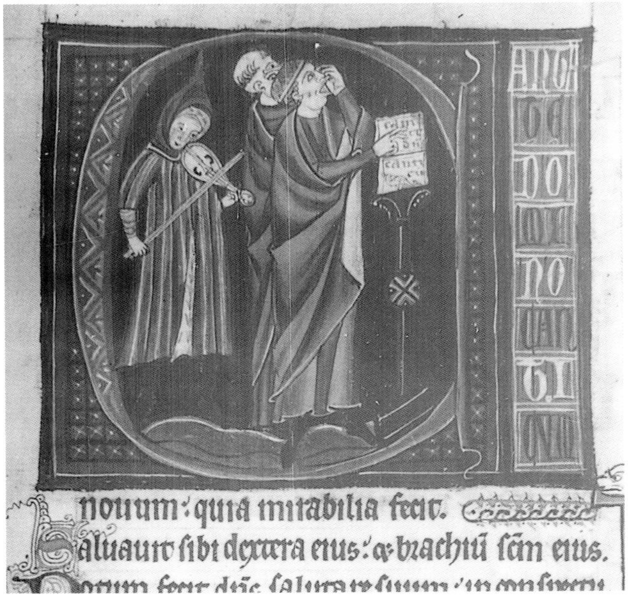

pastoralia of David's example as the harpist who by his cunning exorcized Saul (I Samuel 16: 14–23) doubtless help to explain the well-known passage in *Handlyng Synne*, composed by Robert Mannyng of Brunne from around 1303, in which Robert Grosseteste blessed harp music by having a harpist perform day and night in a nearby chamber to bring solace to the great scholar, the harp being likened to the Cross of Christ, and reminding Robert of the last Psalms of David.[51] These thoughts and associations are also very like those in Cassiodorus's comments made to Boethius on the subject of the harp, as well as his commentary on Psalm 56: 9, and doubtless stem from this same substantial allegorical tradition of reading.[52]

The great days of Robert Grosseteste's own commentaries on the Psalms pre-dated his busy episcopate.[53] His method of exegesis, informed in part by reading Greek and Hebrew versions of the Psalms and also by the methods of scientific enquiry he acquired from his reading of Aristotle, offered an approach different from the traditional allegorizing method, not least in exploring the 'naturalistic' basis of biblical imagery and allegory, and the ways that it could, or could not, be reconciled with a coherent theology.[54] Robert's work was at least in part fired by a patristic desire to locate authentic meaning in scripture. Yet his Aristotelianism, and his insistence on the centrality of the biblical text itself, provided a way of fleshing out and revitalizing allegory, not least because, by attending to the Greek and Hebrew texts, it was possible to take a more vivid and nuanced view of the literal properties of biblical instruments. Page has stressed the importance of the Aristotelian dimension of new attitudes to musical instruments on the part of Franciscan and Dominican commentators, some of them in the circle of Grosseteste, from the middle of the thirteenth century.[55] Aristotle's views on education were imported to underline the biblically sanctioned validity of plucked or string instruments, especially for the education of the young.[56] The decline of traditional allegorical *lectio* and the rise of a 'naturalistic' approach to the letter of the Bible as the sensible manifestation of its meaning under the influence of Aristotle is placed at the very centre of Beryl Smalley's account of development in contemporary study among the leading Franciscan and Dominican thinkers.[57] Smalley was not alone in regarding this push of meaning to the surface as central to a nominalist reading of the World, as of text: indeed, Nikolaus Pevsner had developed the same style of account concerning 'naturalistic' botanical representation in late thirteenth-century England.[58] In this regard attitudes to the representation of plants, as of musical instruments, belonged to the same general dispensation. In the light of this it is not unfair to ask whether the increased adoption of the most substantial musical technologies of the period in churches, organs especially, was not sanctioned by an increasingly literal attitude to what the Psalms and their commentaries had to say about jubilation and praise.[59]

Of course, Aristotelianism can be overplayed as a general explanatory principle, and there were other ways in which the use and representation of musical, and especially instrumental, performance could be sanctioned within the Church. English church legislators of the period are entirely silent about the legitimacy of instrumental music in the liturgy, and in this they followed the lead of the ecumenical councils in which attitudes to music generally are at best implicit in reservations about clerical contact with the 'jongleuric'. Provisions for excluding all but socially privileged laity from the chancel would anyway have had the effect of limiting performance on instruments to the clergy – for which last notion there is no positive evidence at all. The Psalms offered traditional allegorical, and more modern and increasingly literal, justifications, but actual practice was more restricted. Despite what Aelred and his ilk had to say, however, the organ was an exception. It is viewed neutrally or favourably in the commentaries of Augustine, Jerome and Cassiodorus, the latter likening the instrument to a tower or castle (*organum [. . .] est quasi turris*) and so implicitly connecting it to positive tower- or castle-imagery in the Bible (e.g. Canticles 4: 4, Psalms 17: 3, 60: 3, 90: 2).[60] In Psalter representations it is one of King David's chosen instruments (fig. 211).[61] And the organ in particular was lent legitimacy as the favoured liturgical instrument by the example of the saints, for although there is no sign that the newer English saints of the thirteenth century showed any interest in music, it is significant that the commissioning of fine organs recurs as a theme in the documented works of the great Anglo-Saxon reformer-saints between 950 and 1000. This may have mattered to the reformist ethos of the thirteenth century. William of Malmesbury attributes the spread of organs throughout England to St Dunstan, and notes the bells and organ built by him at Malmesbury and dedicated to St Aldhelm; and the greatest account of a pre-Conquest organ, at Winchester – an instrument of prodigious and improbable size – is to be found in a panegyric to St Alphege in the prologue to the Life of Swithun.[62] Again in such cases myth and expectation, not reality, are what matter. The use of organs at feast days, and of dedicating bells to patron or protector saints, belongs to this tradition.[63] Organs, like clocks and bells, were classed as wonders to be deployed on special occasions: so according to Matthew Paris, great pipes called

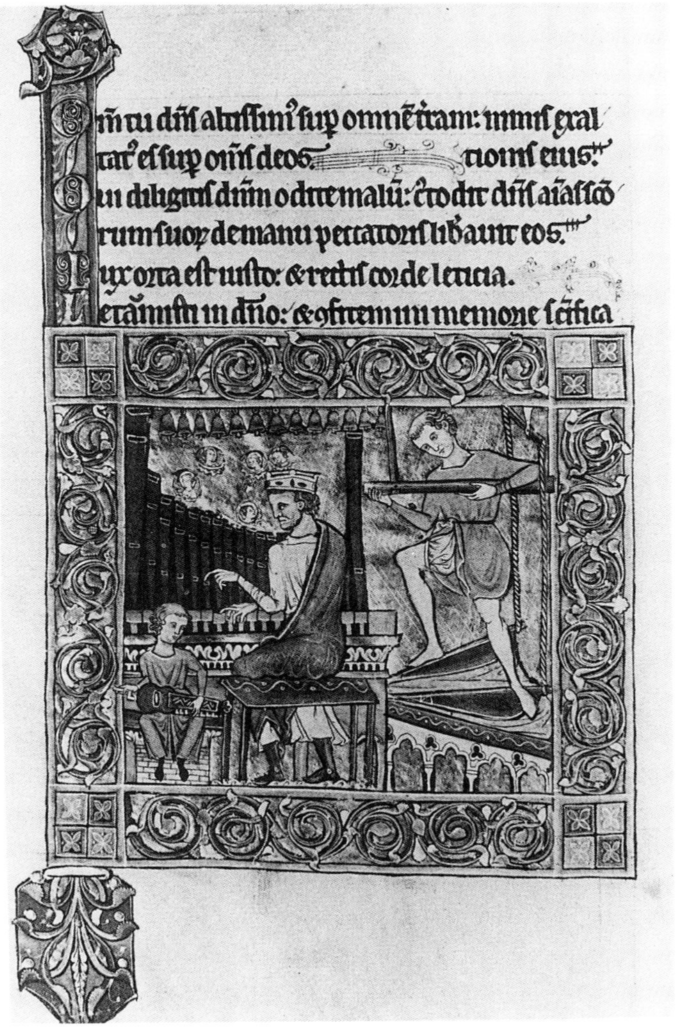

211 King David at the organ. Rutland Psalter, BL Add. MS 62925, fol. 97v, *c.* 1260 (by permission of the British Library).

'mules' (*bordones*) were blasted together with the singing of the *Te Deum*, the ringing of bells and the sounding of a clock at the presentation of John of Hertford as abbot-elect to St Alban in 1235.[64] Technologically (not least in view of the nature of their sliders or keyboards) organs dating to the early thirteenth century seem to have been incapable of the fiddly rapidity of playing, feminine trilling, which, in their masculinist ethos, the monastic and secular critics found uncongenial. Unlike most instruments depicted at this time, the volume and low tessitura of the organ was the one most suited not only to the solemn support of voices, but to apocalyptic eruptions of sound.[65] The organ required no unruly gang of trade musicians to work it. In being sanctioned by the saints, sublimely masculine, and easily controlled, the automaton-like organ was the ideal instrument for a clerical culture obsessed with centralized regulation and hidden levers.

All cultures find distinctive ways of symbolizing and fleshing out their most important desires, and in thirteenth-century England the wondrous large-scale technologies of sanctioned sound and music, and the miraculously concealed nature of its production, answered to particular imaginative needs. In the same way, cultures discover narratives which help to negotiate and reconcile difference. Throughout this study, I have shown how the new practical technologies of the period, whether superb (and equally miraculous) stone vaults, giant musical instruments and other *mirabilia*, had begun to be harnessed by the Church to pastoral ends, even though many continued to harbour doubts about them not least because they could easily be exposed as prideful. This harnessing implied a pragmatic and tolerant acceptance of the inevitable. And, as a sort of pact was formed with technological progress and all its difficulty and ambivalence, so too was it immediately redeemed and lent authority by the intellectual and spiritual means of the day: by those who produced the commentaries, by the casuists, and by the ever-present example of the saints. The redemption of technology – and of the classes that permitted the use of that technology – mattered to a practical and pragmatic pastoral church, because technology was persuasive, and thus useful. It is perhaps not surprising that one of the most popular Marian legends of the day concerned the tale

212 Theophilus performs homage to the Devil and hands him the charter. Hours of W. de Brailes, BL Add. MS 49999, fol. 34, *c.* 1240 (Conway Library, Courtauld Institute of Art).

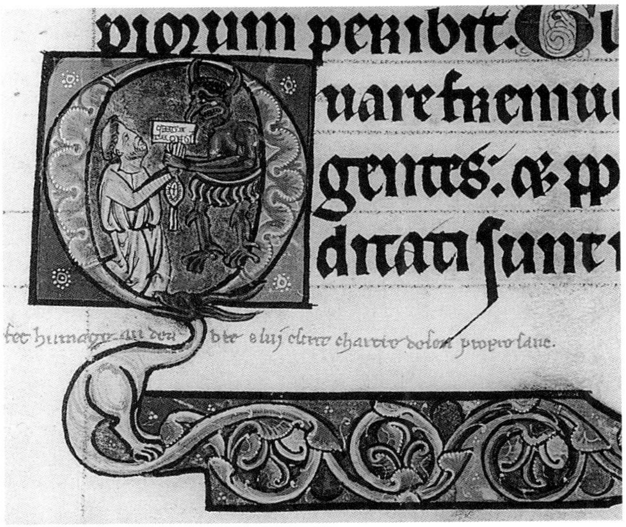

of an ambitious clerk called Theophilus who, having declined an episcopal see, immediately relented and in his vanity sold his soul to the devil in exchange for the world. This Faustian agreement, a parable about pride, was illustrated in a Book of Hours (p. 186 above) by the Oxford illuminator W. de Brailes, himself in minor orders, by showing Theophilus's pact in the form of a sealed charter (fig. 212).[66] Theophilus, plunged into despair, pleads for and is granted the intercession of the Virgin Mary who, biffing the devil on the nose, redeems the charter and so Theophilus's soul. In the Hours, De Brailes juxtaposes his own image as artist and supplicant, his face touched by the hand of God, with the scene of the charter being burnt; better it should go up in flames than he.[67] Many of the most spectacular aesthetic and technological accomplishments of the day were redeemed by association with Mary *mediatrix*. But Mary was not alone, for she was accompanied by the company of heaven, notably by the angels. In the angels, and in the 'angelization' of ideas, the Church was to find one its most vivid and durable vehicles of corporate self-understanding: and at Lincoln, where Mary and the angels preside over the sanctuaries, it found one of its most eloquent expressions.

Angelization and Seduction: The Angel Choir at Lincoln

Angels are such a stock device of thirteenth-century Gothic art in England, as cherubs are in the Baroque, that their mounting importance in being 'good to think with' can be overlooked. As mentioned above, in regard to their surface appearance the angels began by mid-century to reflect and participate in ordinary sublunary human emotional life. But if the product of this familiarization could be a certain androgyny, it entailed no serious loss of the types of power usually attributed to them. Pre-Conquest interest in the theme of the fall of the rebel angels survived well into the period.[68] Angels could still stand as dazzling, swift, powerful intelligences: witness the great trumpeting angel originally on the arch of the Fürstenportal at Bamberg, the elevation of colossal smiling angels around the choir at Reims (fig. 190) and the tremendous angels standing for the suffragan churches of Reims in its choir glass.[69] This celebration of the angel as a medieval *genius loci* was known in England well before the advent of Gothic: Canterbury Cathedral's main tower had been topped by a mighty cherub.[70] What strikes now is their multiplicity. The great west front at Wells is protected by vigilant angels secreted within its nooks like the Dove in the Rock (fig. 91); the churches in Revelation 2–3 are frequently shown in English Apocalypse manuscripts as impressive individual structures guarded from within by their resident angels, to whom St John writes. Strong angels standing confidently on colonettes crown the sainted kings of England at the start of *La Estoire de Seint Aedward le Rei* (fig. 103). This heroic, protective mode was particularly important to the symbolism of death and the commendation of the soul: burial at altars dedicated to St Michael, or in tombs accompanied by the image of St Michael and the angels, was a notable trait among bishops and archbishops, for example Nigel at Ely (d. 1169), Langton at Canterbury (d. 1228), De Gray at York (d. 1255) and possibly Des Roches at Winchester (d. 1238).[71]

It is also characteristic of the sociability of Gothic art that these presences multiply in number and range of ministry, liturgical action especially: the angels act as acolytes, deacons, chanters in bringing to the church lights, incense, music and other provocations of the senses. This specular role stemmed from the traditional Dionysian theory of hierarchy, which was known in the medieval period in a variety of forms: via patristic writing and the *Sentences* of Peter Lombard, as well as via the corpus of Dionysian writing itself.[72] Indeed a form of 'vulgar Dionysianism' was now widespread. Serious study was again burgeoning, for interest in the Pseudo-Dionysius, once the preserve of the tiny intellectual communities of twelfth-century Canterbury or Saint-Denis (p. 12 above), was undergoing a real revival.[73] Grosseteste's research into the writings of St Denis was among the most distinguished of the period.[74] The properties and ministries of the angels were part of the encyclopaedic brief: some of the most powerful drawings of such angels as Gabriel and Raphael in thirteenth-century England (fig. 213) are to be found in a compilation including a bestiary, Alan of Lille's (or more probably Clement of Llanthony's) *De sex alis* and extracts from Hugh of Saint-Victor's *De sacramentis* (CUL MS Kk. 4. 25, fols 39, 47v–51).[75] Versions of St Denis's thinking found their way into concise vernacular epitomes produced by the great pastoral bishops. For example, the Franciscan Archbishop of Canterbury, John Pecham (d. 1292), in his role as a royal confessor, produced a French 'moralized' epitome of Denis's hierarchy at the request of Queen Eleanor of Castile, in a text now bound up with a copy of the *Somme le Roi*.[76] Pecham's pastoral text explains the main attributes of the angelic hierarchy by deploying an analogy between the hierarchy of the celestial court and the royal court and its officers. St Denis was now invoked to help understand and account for political order. In order that this could happen, it was necessary that his obscure and elevated thought should

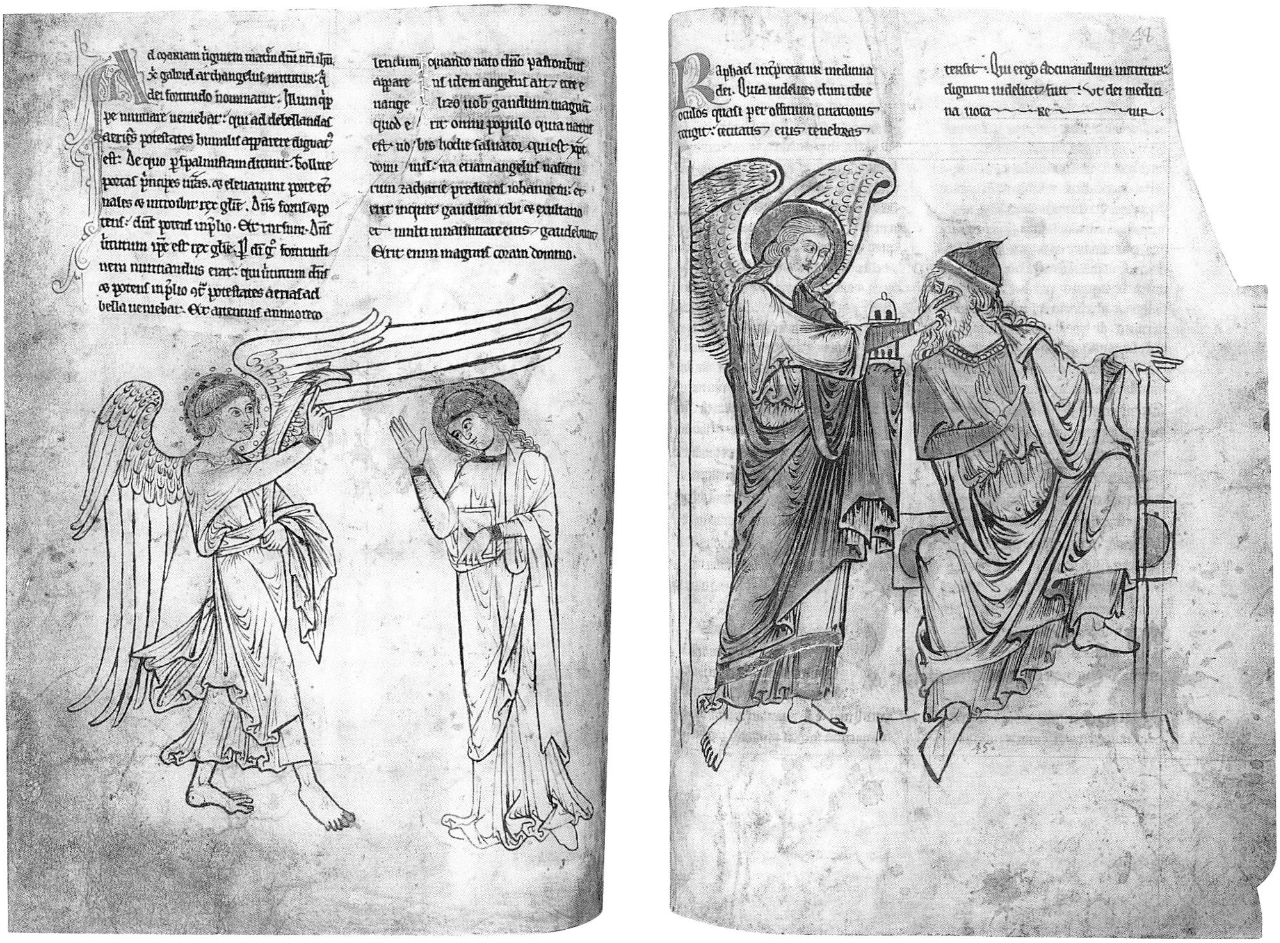

213a and b Gabriel and Raphael. CUL MS Kk. 4. 25, fols 47v, 48, mid-thirteenth century (by permission of the Syndics of Cambridge University Library).

be simplified and brought down to earth. This approach had begun with such figures as Alan of Lille and William of Auvergne: the mortal domain of politics was 'celestialized' and the celestial domain of the heavenly court 'politicized' as itself a place of law and government.[77] Not all commentators (notably Aquinas) agreed wholeheartedly with this smooth co-ordination of man and angel, but the idea was sufficiently widespread for me to posit the idea that the almost routine role of angels as ministers in this period acknowledged the possibility of a celestial commentary on mundane affairs. The angels provided a parallel text for human concerns: what they did not do was merely reflect them.

In its various forms Dionysian thought no more provides an absolute key to the period than does Aristotle. It was simply one important factor among many, not least in its more positive, or exoteric, guise as found in scholastic thinking of the thirteenth century which may, as John Gage suggested, have had aesthetic consequences in regard especially to attitudes to light and luminosity.[78] The great Angel Choir at Lincoln is, in this expansive sense, a monument to the plasticity and versatility of current ideas (fig. 214). Its angelic images are broadly Dionysian or Augustinian, its sheer luminosity an aspect of 'the re-evaluation of the role of light itself' that stemmed not only from high-level thinking but also from the practical introduction of very large multi-light traceried windows modelled on northern French examples.[79] It is also, in virtue of the *hilaritas* of its angels and their buoyant musicality, an expressive and uplifting achievement, which, in arriving at a considered and harmonious view of all the techniques at the disposal of the late thirteenth-century Church, discloses something not without theatre. It is the last major ensemble to be considered here, because it provides a practical *summa* of some of this book's main preoccupations.

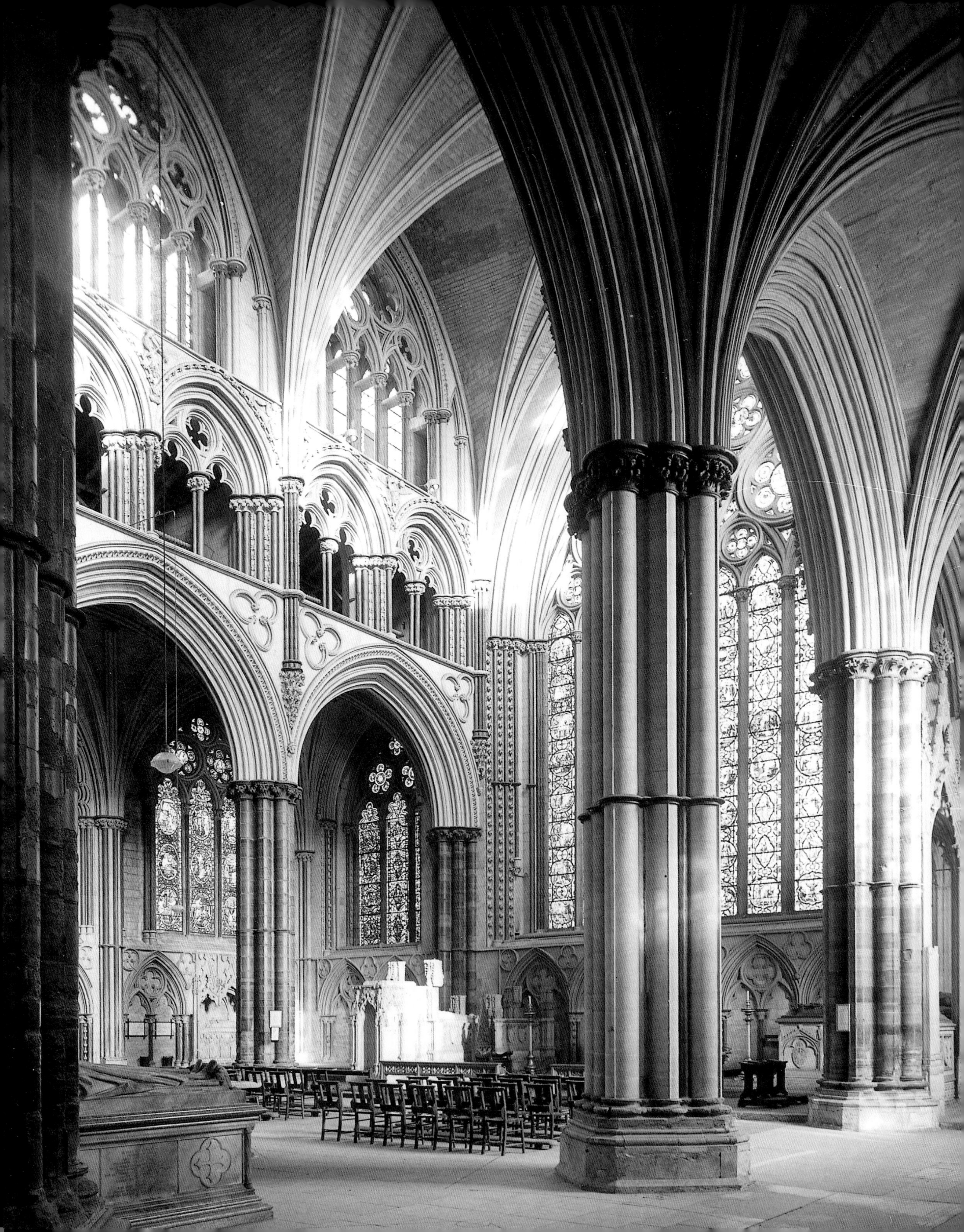

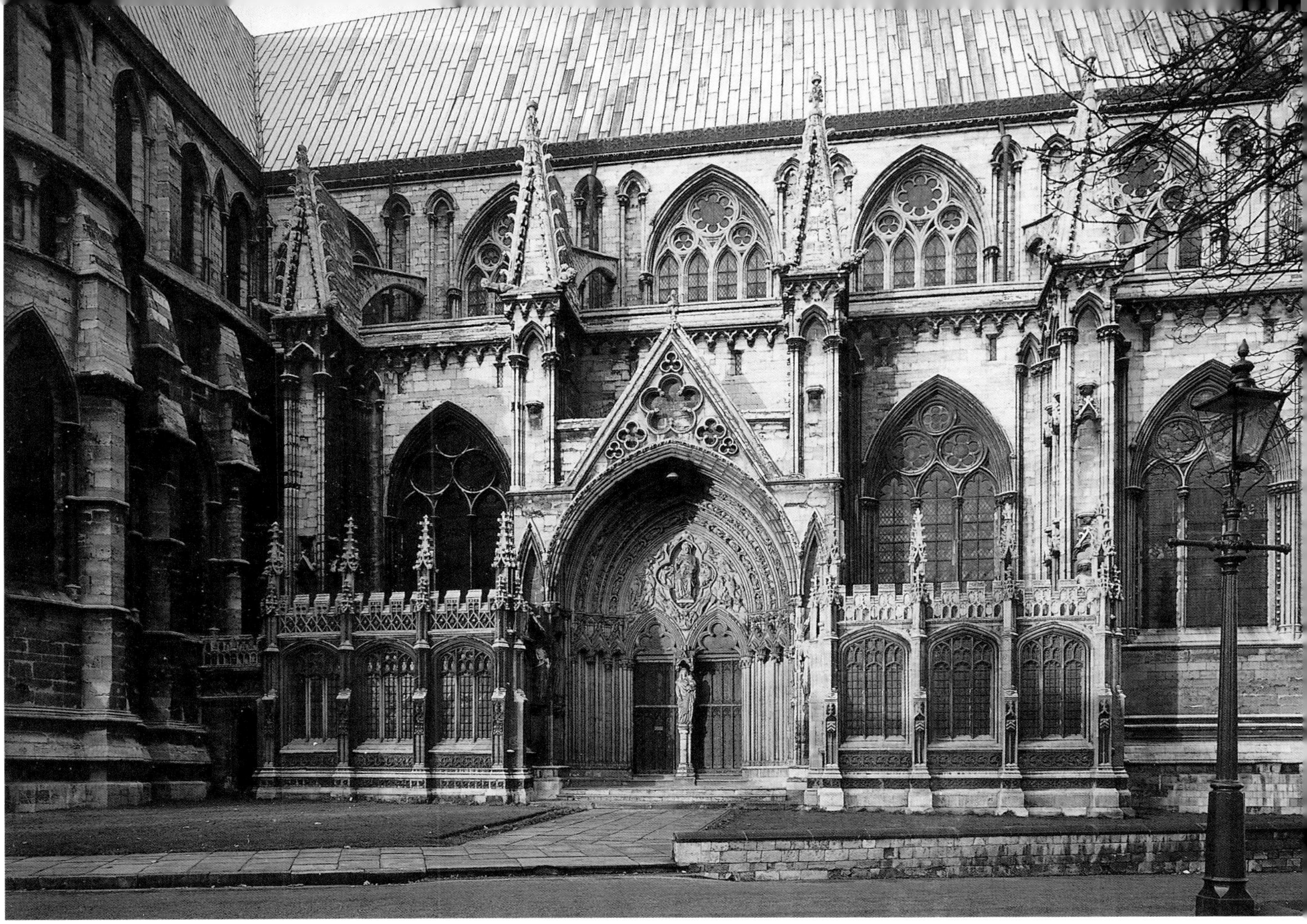

215 Lincoln Cathedral, Angel Choir, south porch (reproduced by permission of English Heritage. NMR).

The history of the Angel Choir needs only itself brief recapitulation here. The building replaced the late twelfth-century wedge-shaped apse begun by St Hugh, with a longer, five-bay and square-ended aisled presbytery and retrochoir enclosing the high altar and major shrines.[80] Access to it was gained not only from the choir and transepts but also via portals on the north and south sides, the south portal being elaborately furnished with sculptures of the Last Judgement, the north portal being a utilitarian exit. Though the proportions and lavish internal finish perpetuated features of the old building, the new plan was clearly a substantial critique of it, not least in pushing the principle shrine of St Hugh well to the east, greatly improving circulation and offering much improved scope for illumination by large traceried windows facilitated by the squaring-off of the east end. The new scheme first emerged under Bishop Henry of Lexington and Dean Richard of Gravesend in November 1255, when the king was petitioned by the dean and chapter to permit a breach of the city wall of Lincoln in order that the church might be extended eastwards, assent being granted in July 1256.[81] The times for such magnificence were propitious. There were new exemplars: the cathedral chapter could ponder the outcome of Hugh of Northwold's new works for St Etheldreda at Ely completed in 1252; the presbytery at Ely (fig. 62) is of generally similar form and, as noted above, shares with Lincoln an eastern-English tradition of rich internal elaboration. The cavernous new transepts at York Minster might have provided a yardstick of ambition. Again, the implications of Henry of Reyn's use of French bar tracery and relatively large-scale internal figurative sculpture at Westminster Abbey from 1245 were starting to become apparent (fig. 234).[82] In addition there were also new cults: St Hugh of Lincoln had been canonized in 1220; Robert Grosseteste had died in 1253 framed by the signs of sanctity; and from 1255 Hugh, a boy from Lincoln reputedly crucified by the city's Jews, was becoming the object of strident (and presumably remunerative) local veneration.[83] In the course of the new

214 Lincoln Cathedral, Angel Choir, looking north-east (reproduced by permission of English Heritage. NMR).

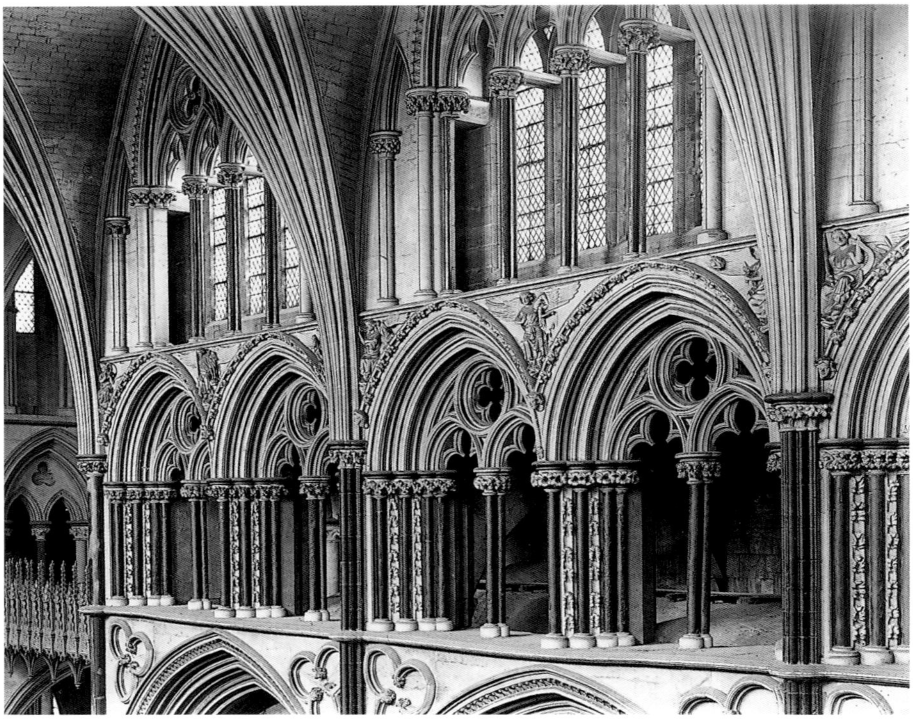

216 Lincoln Cathedral, Angel Choir, north gallery (Conway Library, Courtauld Institute of Art).

building's construction between 1256 and 1280 only the cult of St Hugh himself was to survive, the others proving ephemeral. The great age of formal canonization of the English saints was ending. But the shrines of Lincoln were only one factor in what was a multi-functional space. Despite its name, the Angel Choir was not strictly a choir at all, for the stalls lay to the west of the eastern transepts. Sheer corporate ambition dictated that the new presbytery should be a restatement in bolder terms of the function of the eastern arm as a separate church for the chapter, to which public access was granted if suitably managed. The walled-off sanctuary and high altar created a thoroughly elitist *cordon sanitaire* between the daily offices in the choir, and the shrines and procession-routes.

Yet over these functional highways and byways was set an overarching scheme of sculpture which, like the building itself, enjoys internal logic and coherence.[84] The scheme was inaugurated by the south portal Last Judgement (fig. 215); Ecclesia, Synagoga (the two being reversed in a pattern not uncommon in eastern and northern England),[85] kings and queens, the Wise and Foolish Virgins and apostles are gathered round the doorway and executed with exquisite detail, the voussoir figures being seated beneath canopies or enclosed in foliage bowers.[86] The sequence of construction entails that this entrance was planned and executed not long after 1255–6. Yet the portal's sculptors had little to do with the internal sculpted finish of the building, which started with the aisle wall arcades and bosses around 1260 and the high elevations around 1265–75: almost all this work was in the hands of another team.[87] The south aisle has a scheme of ten very fine figurated vault bosses; higher up within the main vessel, the gallery has thirty main subjects filling its spandrels, including Christ showing his wounds, Mary the church's patron interceding with Christ, and a very diverse array of thirty angels which give the 'choir' its name (fig. 216). This style has a physicality, amplitude and expressive directness lacking in the delicate work around the south entrance: indeed, it marks one important moment in the reception of the new idioms developed at Reims and Paris in the third quarter of the century (pp. 246–7 above). Here to a much greater extent surfaces are simplified to select general effects, and detail is dramatically sharpened and concentrated to enhance texture: the aim of the style is an increased sense of presence. In quality and receptivity to outside stimuli, Lincoln's interior sculpture is quite as avant-garde as any contemporary work at Westminster. Yet its bold resourcefulness also recalls the situation in St Hugh's choir around 1200 where, aside from odd but promising innovations like the crocket piers, the masons introduced witty conceits such as shrine-like busts projecting from the aisle arcades, or figure-corbels propping up the eastern transept vaults (fig. 53), motifs that suggested the language of contemporary metalwork shrines, but that also pointed to a neo-antique taste for dramatizing the relationship of figure to architecture.[88] Though the masons of the Angel Choir worked to much higher technical standards, their integrative approach is basically the same. In their case, however, the dynamic relationship of figure to building was lent added impetus and shape by a string of developments, typically in southern or south-western England, in the period 1225–50: the extensive use of sculpted angels on the west front at Wells, on the choir triforium at Worcester and on the pulpitum at Salisbury (fig. 217); the painted vaults of the eastern transepts at Salisbury (fig. 52); and the interior transept elevations and apsidal chapels at Westminster (fig. 234), itself certainly influenced by the Sainte-Chapelle in Paris, where angels figure in the arcades of the upper chapel (fig. 218).[89] The notion that angels could be imported on a large scale to adorn a major choir elevation had also been sanctioned by the exterior sculpture (fig. 190) and the glass of the choir at Reims. The repertory of possible effects had expanded almost exponentially, just as it had in the arena of bar window tracery at Reims, Amiens, Paris and Westminster. Lincoln delved deep into all these possibilities, and in doing so reinforced its long-standing influential role for projects (Grantham, Crowland, Raunds) sited along the great oolitic limestone belt running to the south and west. The masons at Trondheim Cathedral, the nave of which can only have been produced in knowledge of the Angel Choir itself, were also still alert to this church.[90]

Yet the specific thinking behind the choice of subjects at Lincoln is quite unlike any of these projects, for in no other major church of the period is the arena of the high altar and area behind it surrounded by so concerted a display of figurative sculpture. Nor is the Angel Choir simply juggling with received opinion, for its deeper thematic logic is not easy to discover. The remarkable bosses of the south aisle are a case in point.[91] In the area of the aisle that opens out to the west and leads to the eastern transept and choir aisle are five bosses showing men and monsters wrestling (fig. 219); the five bosses going eastwards in the opposite direction show biblical scenes of disputation (fig. 220), the Coronation of the Virgin (fig. 221), a Tree of Jesse with David tuning his harp (fig. 222) and a crowned female petting a lapdog with a youth in her presence, a masterpiece (fig. 223).

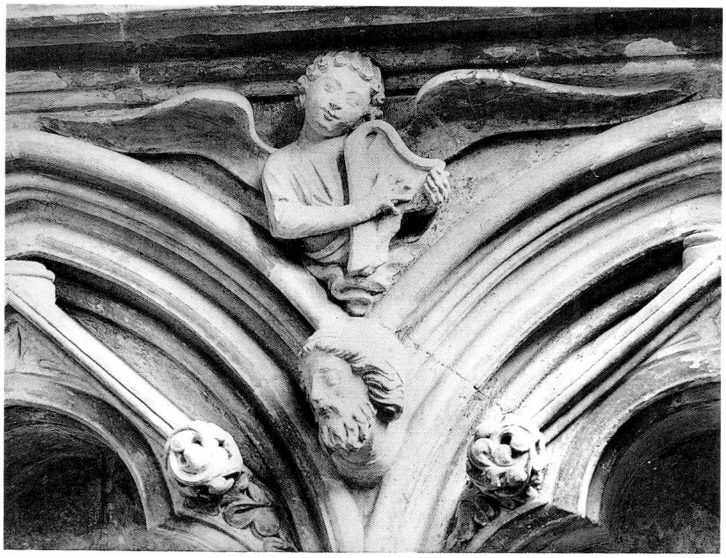

217 Salisbury Cathedral, pulpitum, detail (Conway Library, Courtauld Institute of Art).

218 Paris, Sainte-Chapelle, detail arcade, upper chapel (Bildarchiv Foto Marburg).

Why this last subject should have been placed easternmost and not the Tree of Jesse or the Coronation of the Virgin (both topics for altarpieces) is obscure. The east-west distinction may stem from the reversal of Ecclesia and Synagoga on the porch outside, in such a way that Ecclesia, usually to Christ's right, is placed 'higher up' than the Old Law.[92] But it cannot have held consistently for the east end, since it is hard to square with the rum-

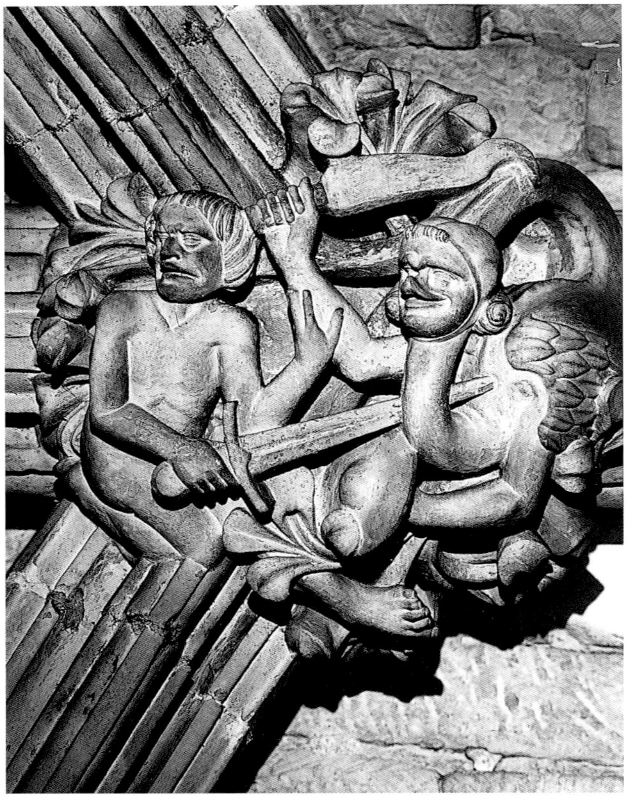

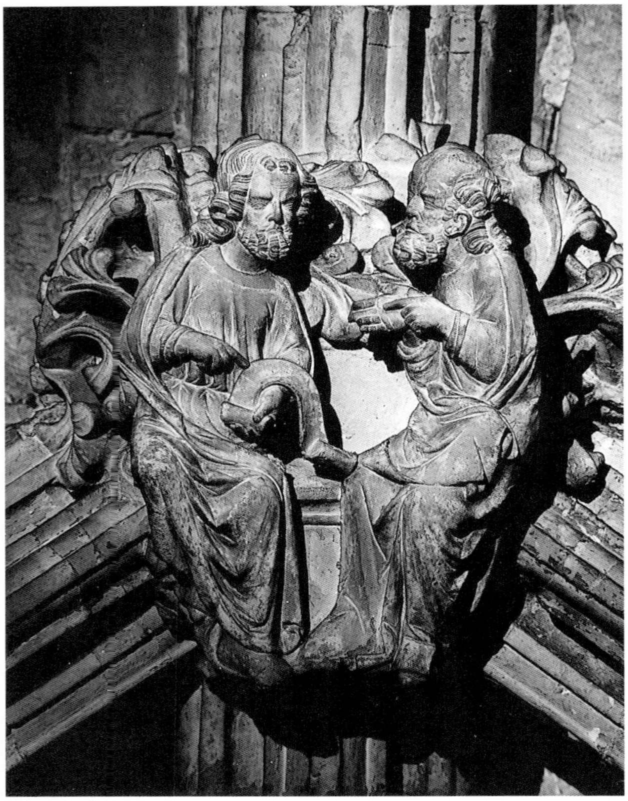

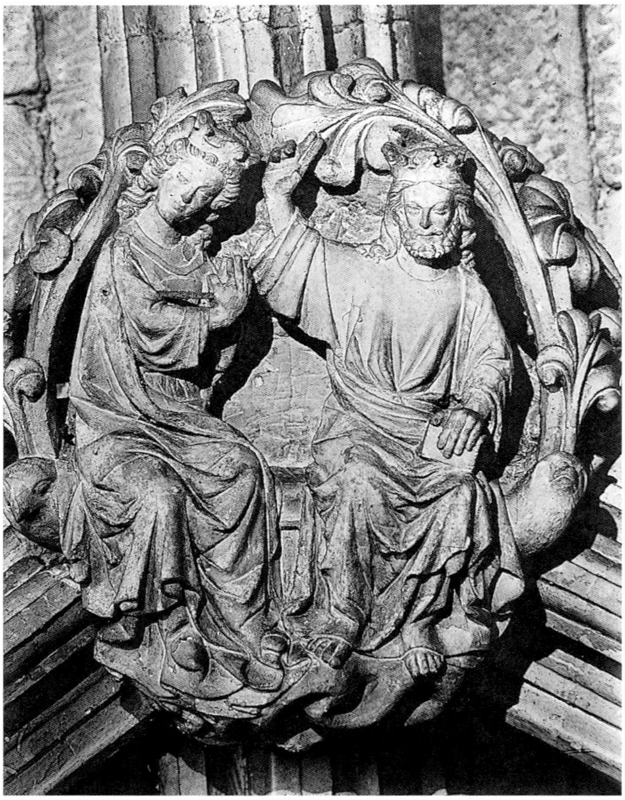

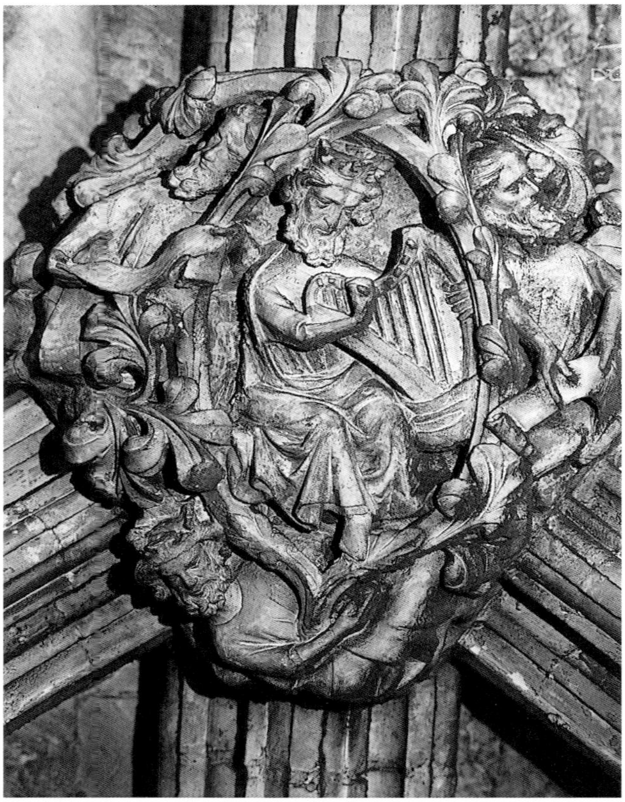

219, 220, 221, 222 Lincoln Cathedral, Angel Choir, bosses in south aisle (reproduced by permission of English Heritage. NMR): contention of man and beast (TOP LEFT); disputation among prophets (TOP RIGHT); Coronation of the Virgin (ABOVE LEFT); Tree of Jesse, with David tuning his harp (ABOVE RIGHT).

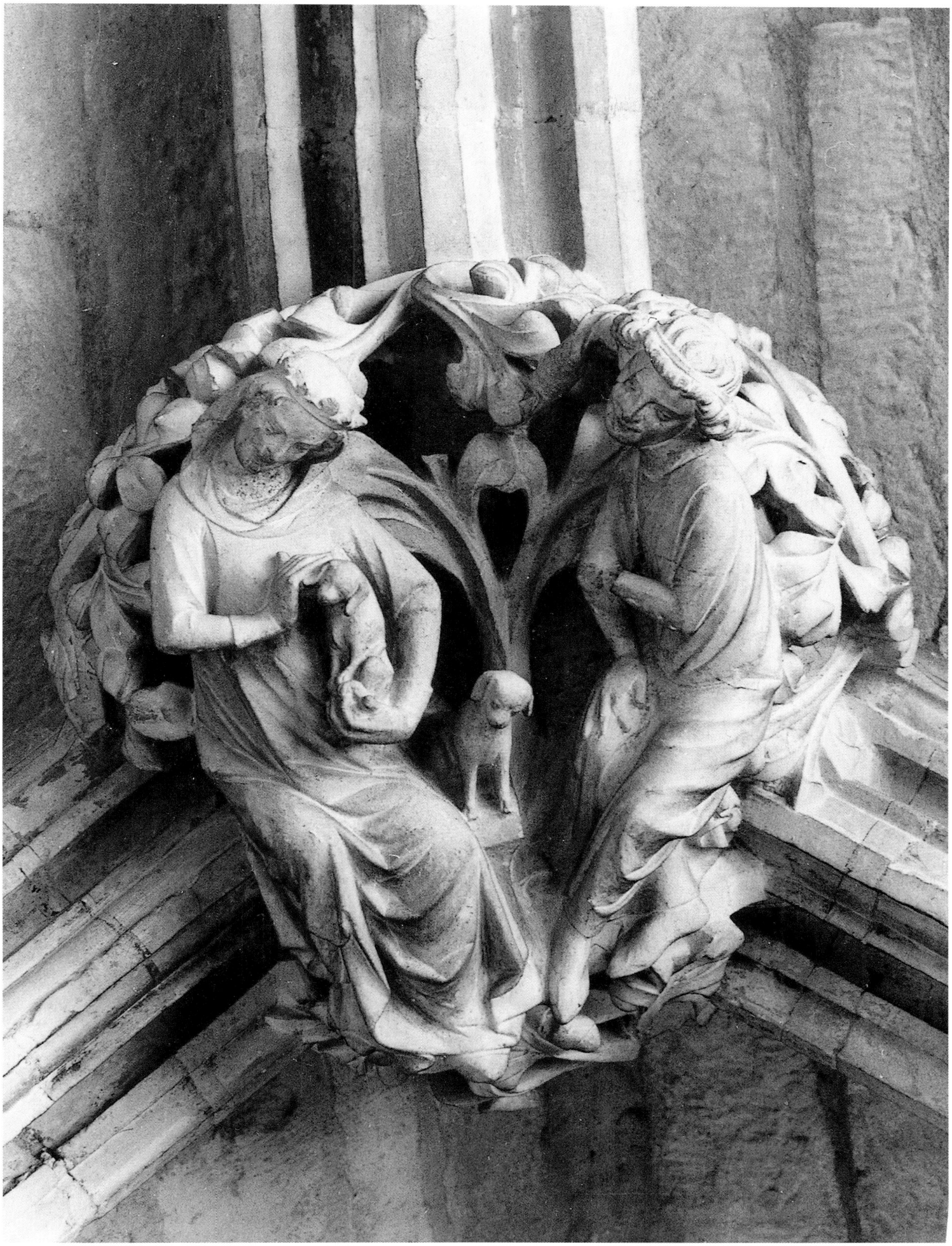

223 Bathsheba. Lincoln Cathedral, Angel Choir, boss in south aisle (Conway Library, Courtauld Institute of Art).

bustious and licentious topics in the north aisle opposite. The south aisle seems altogether more considered. To the west, as in the north aisle, are depictions of physical contention, bodily and bestial struggle; to the east, intellectual and spiritual contention in the form of disputation between representatives of the Old and New Law, king and prophet. If, as T. A. Heslop suggests, the scene of the crowned female and the youth (fig. 223) depicts the summoning of Bathsheba by David's servants (II Samuel 11: 3), things start to fall into place.[93] The *Bible moralisée* in Vienna (Österreichische Nationalbibliothek Cod.Vin. 2554) helps to explain the allegory: just as King David saw and fell in love with Bathsheba as she purified herself, so Christ saw Holy Church, Ecclesia, and held her dear.[94] This allegory is 'revealed' in the Coronation of the Virgin. The leafy bowers enclosing Bathsheba and the Coronation pick up the sponsorial garden image, the *hortus conclusus*, in Canticles 4: 12 and 5: 1, first developed for the small figures on the portal outside. Bower or arbours of the sort prompted by the imagery of Canticles were becoming as important to sculpted bosses as they were to the decorative repertory of contemporary and later liturgical *Opus anglicanum* such as the Steeple Aston and Butler Bowdon copes.[95] Here, detail matters to the smallest degree. In the Tree of Jesse boss (fig. 222) King David is not just playing his harp, but tuning it, as found quite commonly in illuminated initials to Psalm 1. By this means David calms the discord of contention and produces an Orphic concord of the two Testaments, the harp signifying the moment of reconciliation itself, the Crucifixion, and the Coronation the fulfilment of Holy Church.[96] David's well-tempered music thus reveals the *carmen intellectuale* of the Divine Musician, resounding through leafy Paradise.

The south aisle bosses are important not because they possess empty cheerfulness, but precisely because they provoke a certain amount of speculation. They suggest the importance of music and gardens not just as charming courtly conceits, but as vehicles of much more traditional religious signification of the type explored above in the case of Ely's *viriditas*. Music and gardens, or the products of gardens, were connected to the bringing of spiritual health in a *questio* for discussion at Paris in 1287 by the English theologian Richard of Middleton. Richard posed the question 'whether herbs or harmonies are capable of preventing a demon from afflicting mankind'.[97] The reply given by the Angel Choir to this question is affirmative, at least to the extent that the rather insistent undertow of demonic imagery sculpted on its interior appears to be played off against the cleansing or conciliatory properties of music. Richard's answer was more negative: since demons have no bodies they cannot properly be acted upon by music – therefore only the person possessed may be affected. But his way of framing the question at least points to the prophylactic associations of the imagery of the Angel Choir, to the health-bringing properties of plants, and the capacity of music to soothe the troubled breast. Cassiodorus, and following him such encyclopaedists as Bartholomaeus Anglicus, linked the harmony of the cord, *chorda*, with the 'heartstrings'.[98]

Lincoln, far from being lightheartedly secular in tone, is textually rather dense and opulent, as bedecked or festooned with meaning as its surfaces. The same may be said about the spandrels of the gallery. Again, from one viewpoint Lincoln conforms to common English practice in emphasizing decoratively the middle stage of a major elevation. However, to do this with relatively large-scale figurative material was more unusual: only Worcester and the transepts at Westminster (fig. 234) provided important precedents before the 1250s. Westminster is the obvious model in regard to its combination of large censing angels in spandrels with nearby expanses of French-style window tracery of a type also used at Lincoln, and because the soffits of its north transept entrance wall have a scheme of bust-length musical angels. But Lincoln takes these effects much further, deploying them as an organizing principle for the imagery of the whole of the main eastern limb. In creating a decorative continuum extending the length of all five bays, the designers were committed to either a repetitive or a supple programme, and, in choosing the latter, seem to have been guided by the two main known quantities of the plan: the location of the high altar, and the great east window. The presence of St Hugh's shrine behind the altar is perhaps acknowledged only by the two angels on its north side holding crowns and a palm as token of heavenly victory. In contrast to Westminster, where St Edward himself is included in the gallery sculptures, or to both Worcester and Ely (fig. 75), where the saints adorn the main vault bosses, St Hugh is very much not present at Lincoln, and the scheme discloses no important discursive links with his hagiography.

In keeping with the two main stresses just mentioned, the programme divides gently into two thematic phrases, one sacramental and intercessory, and the other jubilant and psalmodic. The first is the preserve of the images in the two bays between the high altar and the crossing, framing the sanctuary and high altar. In the spandrels on the north side reading from the west are: an angel bearing the Crown of Thorns (fig. 224); the frowning angel of the Expulsion (Genesis 3: 24) shoving Adam and Eve from Paradise with a sword (fig. 225); an angel bearing the spear and nails (held in a cloth); Christ

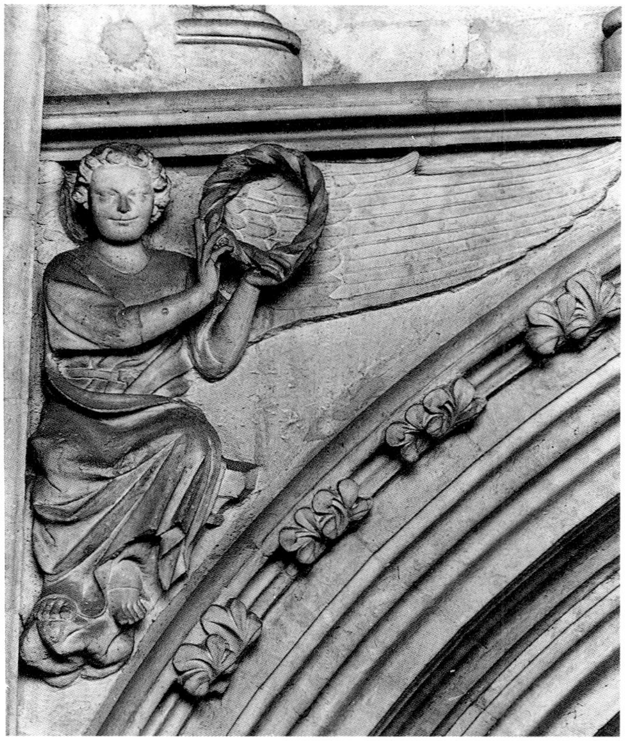

224 Angel with Crown of Thorns. Lincoln Cathedral, Angel Choir (Conway Library, Courtauld Institute of Art).

showing his wounded side (fig. 226); and St Michael with the scales and a censing angel. Opposite them, also from the west, are the cathedral's patron the Virgin Mary, revealing her breast to the Christ Child standing on her lap and with the serpent at her feet (fig. 227); an angel bearing a soul in her direction; angels with a book and a scroll; an angel with a bird of prey (fig. 228); and another angel with a scroll. The topics entail something like the following train of thought: the Fall of Man designates the moment at which the sacraments of the Church were inaugurated as acts of restoration; Mary, the new Eve, intercedes for mortals before her merciful son by bearing her breast; Christ, the new Adam, redeems sinners by his suffering and death, of which his wounds and Instruments of Passion are triumphant signs. Caedmon could have been a help here, or Hugh of Saint-Victor, or for that matter Milton.[99] Christ revealing his side wound, smiling almost as broadly as the mask on his footrest, and turning towards the high altar, pours his loving blood and water down to his Church, in the same dramatic and tender way as the great Christ on folio 6 of the Lisbon Apocalypse.[100] This is eucharistic theatre to vie with the bleeding rood, directly beneath which entrants must pass to gain admission to the *Westchor* at Naumburg.[101] As such it is primarily a commentary on the act of redemption commemorated at the high altar. The individual elements also have many points in common with the Gothic repertory of Last Judgement representations: Christ's revealed side wound is anticipated on the south portal, and the Instruments of the Passion are ostended in the manner of Gothic Judgement portals in France. The bearing of souls by angels on either side of the sanctuary occurs on the apex of the Judgement tympanum at Saint-Denis showing the granting of the beatific vision of the Trinity.[102] By about 1260 the image of Christ revealing his wound had found its way into English tomb iconography.[103] At Lincoln, however, the stresses have shifted towards physical signs of mercy and spiritual nourishment, to Mary's exposed breast and Christ's exposed side, now common topics of Gothic affective piety.[104]

And of course the angels as bearers of signs have gained hugely in importance. Like Mary and Christ, himself an extremely jovial figure, the angels possess a sort of bustling jollity, bursting with strength and vitality. Many of them smile; each is differentiated by look and posture from its neighbour; some are slim and lithe, others squat, and one so fat as to seem incapable of flight. No Gothic Judgement porch of the period possesses quite this level of zest: here, the *sacrum convivium* celebrates Paradise regained. The sentiment is conventionally Dionysian: in his *Celestial Hierarchy* the Pseudo-Dionysius explains that the qualities of this, the ninth, order of angels embrace the unspeakable joy (*gaudium*) of the heavenly ranks referred to in Luke 15: 7–10, which involve a participation in divine joy at the finding of the lost, a divine sense of well-being at the providence and

225 Angel of Expulsion. Lincoln Cathedral, Angel Choir (Conway Library, Courtauld Institute of Art).

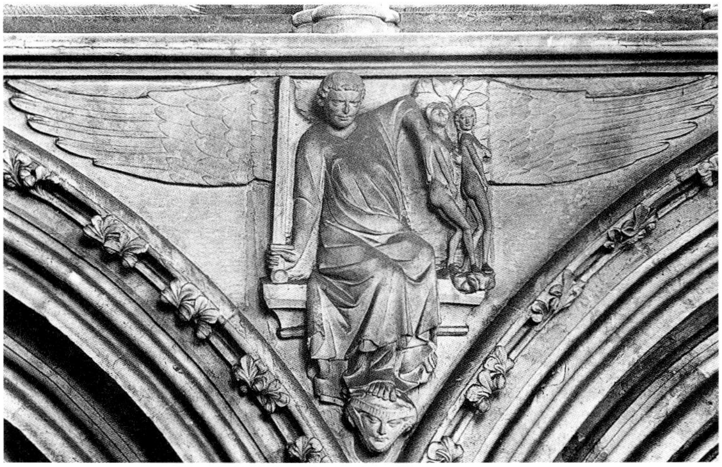

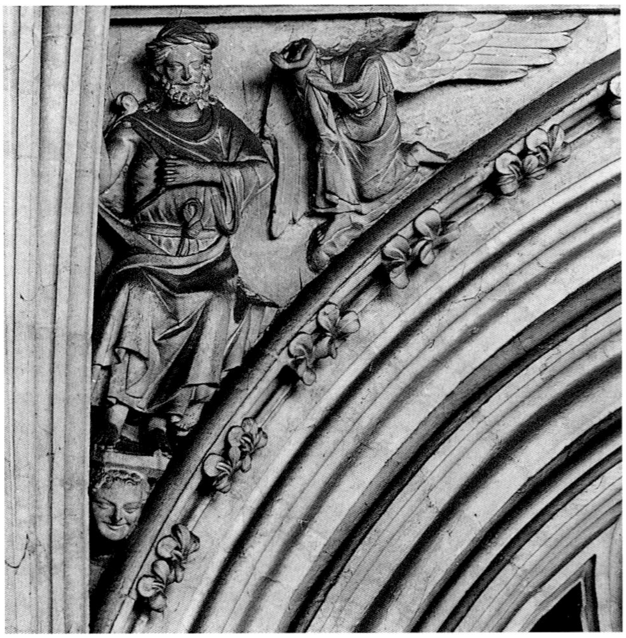

226 Christ the merciful Judge. Lincoln Cathedral, Angel Choir (Conway Library, Courtauld Institute of Art).

salvation of those who are returned to God.[105] The 'return' is of course effected by the sacraments, just as it is represented by the souls carried by the angels into the presence of Christ and the Church. It might also be signalled by the angel with hawk, lure and gauntlets just to the south of the high altar (fig. 228), a reference both to the fowls which gather at the supper of the great God in Revelation 19: 17, and to the allegorical role of the hawk which, like the soul, is lured back by the prospect of eating broken flesh at the altar of God.[106]

The notion of collective joy (for angels could smile singly, as in the case of St Guthlac's complacently smiling guardian angel on the Lincoln-influenced facade at Crowland) is embodied above all in music.[107] In the aisle, King David produces concord from discord by tuning his harp. In the retrochoir triforium between the high altar and east window, David reappears with his harp (fig. 229) and a band of musician angels playing plucked or bowed instruments on the north (lute, viol, harp) and wind instruments (pipes or trumpets) on the south (figs 230–31), a distinction which attends to Augustine's category of sounds (voice, wind and plucked, *vox*, *flatus*, *pulsu*) in his *Ennaratio in psalmos* commonly cited in the Middle Ages.[108] The Psalms and their commentaries must be especially relevant in this part of the choir because the attributes of the angels – sun and moon, palms and crowns for the saints, wind and string instruments – are specifically those of the final Psalms of praise, Psalms 145–50. Similar selections of angelic attributes occur more discreetly in the choir at Worcester, the south-east transept vault at Salisbury, the north transept at Westminster Abbey and the north porch at Lichfield.[109] The theme was increasingly common. Yet it entailed no reflection of liturgical custom with regard to the use of instruments: to assume as much would be an error, confusing the use of musical symbols as vehicles for enriching familiar doctrines with social practice.[110] It is known that at Lincoln plainsong was joined in the liturgy by polyphony in the period in which the Angel Choir was being built, and that the cathedral had an organ by 1310 at the latest.[111] But for the liturgical use of the sorts of instrument depicted in the Angel Choir there is no evidence at all; when viols were first recorded at Lincoln, after the Reformation, they were for the use of the cathedral school.[112] The tessitura of the smallish string instruments and pipes held by the angels was not suited to the support of chanting, and surely indicates that angelic sounds were thought of as high, distant and

227 *Virgo lactans*. Lincoln Cathedral, Angel Choir (Conway Library, Courtauld Institute of Art).

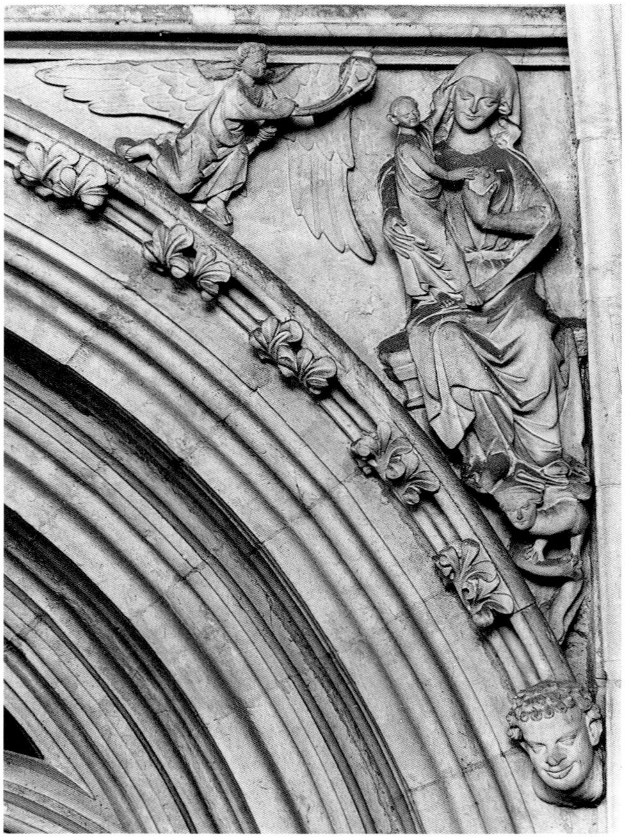

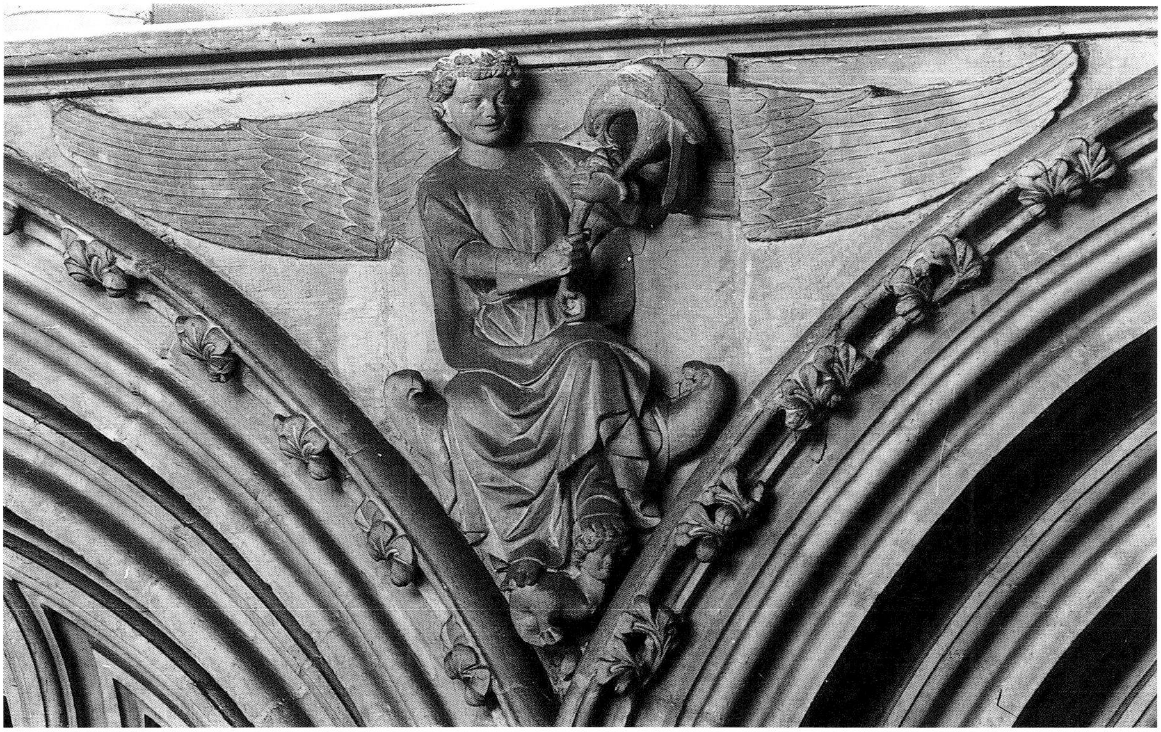

228 Angel with lure and hawk. Lincoln Cathedral, Angel Choir (Conway Library, Courtauld Institute of Art).

229 King David. Lincoln Cathedral, Angel Choir (Conway Library, Courtauld Institute of Art).

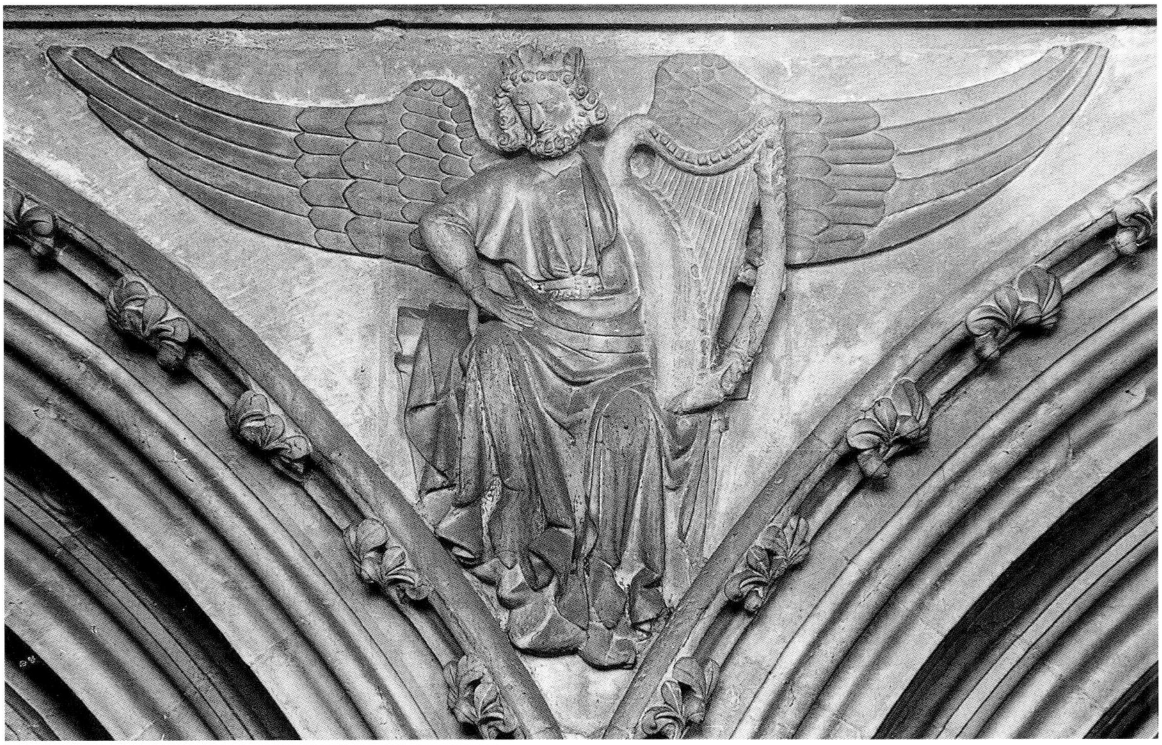

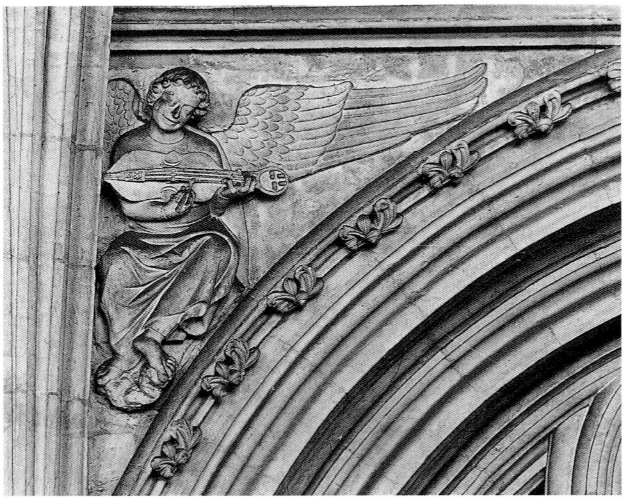

230 Angel and viol. Lincoln Cathedral, Angel Choir (Conway Library, Courtauld Institute of Art).

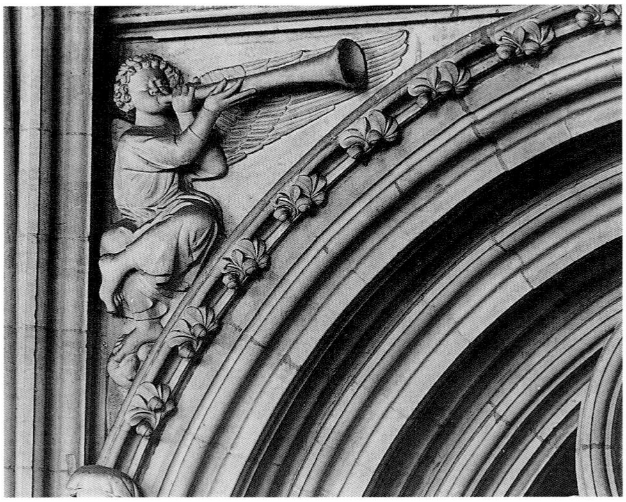

231 Angel and trump. Lincoln Cathedral, Angel Choir (Conway Library, Courtauld Institute of Art).

somewhat thin. Because the angelic was dissociated from the human, its detachment accorded it value as commentary: the angelic was a sublimation of that which could not be said at the mundane level. So, as motifs, musician angels cannot be conscripted to the social history of musical practice, but belong instead to the constant reinvigoration of symbolizing practices in medieval art: their role sheds some light on the networks of symbolism and action in liturgy, yet their character is not so much liturgical as para-liturgical.

To investigate this one needs to look more closely at a particular member of the angelic choir: King David, in the middle of the eastern bay on the south side, 'angelized' by the spectacular attribute of outspread wings (fig. 229). David is not tuning or strumming his harp; he has either stopped playing or is about to start; his head is turned pensively eastwards, and somewhat downwards, towards the east window. This assimilation of David to the angelic is specifically textual. One cue might have been the image of the psalmist assuming the 'wings of the morning' (*pinnas diluculo*) in Psalm 138: 9, for it was this text that provides one of the very few contemporary representations of King David with wings, in a *Bible moralisée* (BN MS lat. 11560).[113] The other was surely II Samuel 14: 17, 20, in which David is likened to an angel: *sicut enim angelus Dei sic est dominus meus rex*. Reference to exactly this passage is made in the *Magna vita* of St Hugh, in which the saint is likened to an angel.[114] *Handlyng Synne*, like the *Magna vita* a local compilation, also reminds readers that the harp was thought to bring to mind the last Psalms of David.[115] Lincoln was evidently in some way turning towards the end of David's life, and to his last words, the *verba novissima*, as set out specifically in II Samuel 23 and, of course, in the very last Psalms of praise, whose attributes are given to the nearby angels. This is real coherence, and it is a pattern encountered in earlier thirteenth-century Psalter illustration, as in the great Munich Psalter. In this manuscript the final Psalms of praise are illustrated together with the Last Judgement after the text of Psalm 150 (fols 146–8), David is shown as psalmist on folio 148v, the sequence ending on both sides of folio 149 with scenes from the end of David's life following II Samuel 24.[116]

In II Samuel 23 David the sweet psalmist is raised up, and shall be like the light of dawn at sunrise (*sicut lux aurorae oriente sole mane*). The *verba novissima* accordingly suggest one way in which viewers might understand David's angelic wings and elevated position near the east window, as it were the window of dawn. The daily offices suggest another, since David's last Psalms of praise were sung specifically during the dawn office of Lauds.[117] Finally, there are the words of the Easter Psalm 56: 9, *exsurge, gloria mea; exsurge, psalterium et cithara; exsurgam diluculo* – 'awake up my glory, awake psaltery and harp: I myself will awake early'. This text was traditionally associated with the Resurrection of Christ, and must explain why the image of the Resurrection on folio 152v of the Missal of Henry of Chichester shows Christ arising from his tomb to the accompaniment of angels playing a viol and harp (Manchester, John Rylands Library MS Lat. 24; fig. 207).[118] Taking all this into account, one can see that literal readings of the Psalms and Psalm commentaries are woven directly into the fabric of the building in a way that suggests not only the

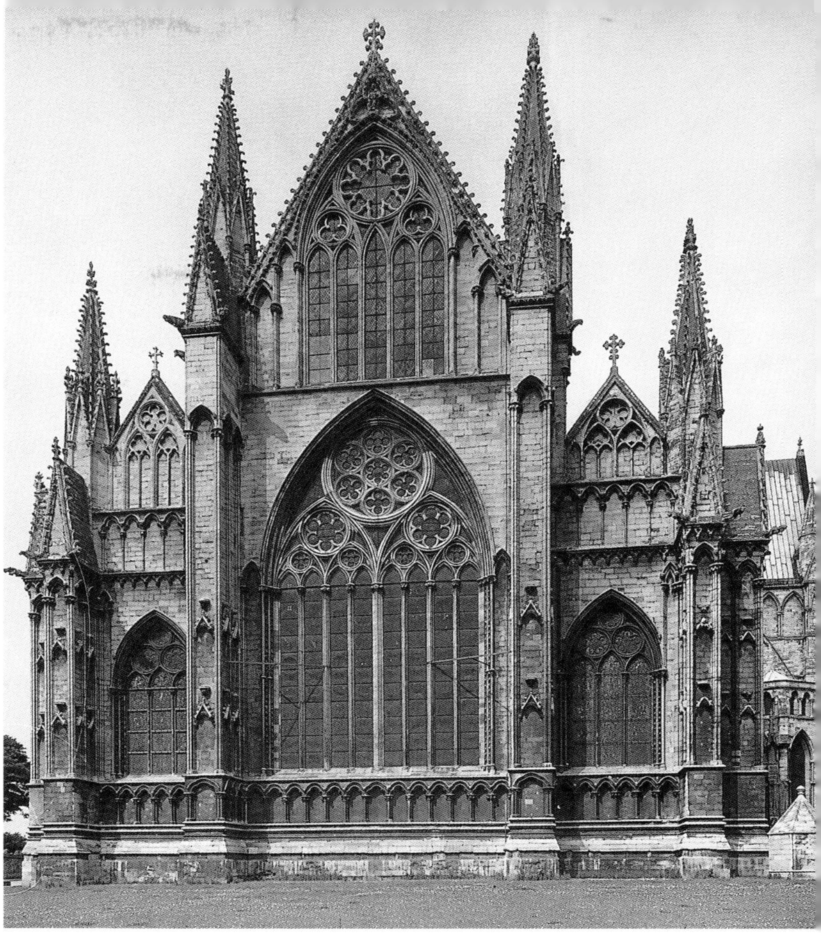

233 Lincoln Cathedral, Angel Choir, east window (reproduced by permission of English Heritage. NMR).

workings of a witty imagination, but also a rhapsodic, even theatrical, sensibility, the singing of the office of Lauds as it were rewarded by the progressive illumination of the psalmist and the angels during the early morning services, in summer especially.

This investment of conventional doctrinal and christological readings of the Psalms in architecture might at first appear old-fashioned, but it also suggests the many ways in which Gothic art and architecture continued to manifest a living Church. The means were of course changing significantly. The style of allegorical commentary that might have entailed thought about columnar imagery or fine materials in the late twelfth century now attached itself to the figuration of surfaces, and to the emergent technology of window tracery, and so in effect to the handling of light itself. The Angel Choir at Lincoln is a well-lit building, and there is no reason to believe that its gorgeously sculpted and coloured integument was ever obscured by anything more than relatively pale grisaille and some coloured glass. The contrast with one of its exemplars, the crepuscular east end of Ely, will be apparent; Ely itself was subject to substantial modification in the fourteenth century when the fenestration of the retrochoir was progressively altered to cast much more light on the shrine area and ambulatories.[119] This newly strategic attitude to the positive and revelatory character of light is manifest in numerous ways throughout the thirteenth century: in the huge expansion in window sizes and adoption of increasing quantities of luminous white glass in greater and lesser churches;[120] in the fairly frequent comments about inadequately lit sanctuaries in visitation records; and even in the emergence of a much more literal and self-conscious imagery of the daily hours of the offices in such works as the Egerton Hours of around 1260–70 (BL Egerton MS 1151), where the routines of the day include the welcoming of the sun at Prime (fig. 232).[121]

These factors suggest that at Lincoln the pivot of the Angel Choir was less the portal on its south side than its giant eight-light east window, designed in the 1250s and stretching across the width of the central vessel of the retrochoir (figs 214, 233). The geometry of the window is northern French in derivation, and shares sources in common with Westminster Abbey.[122] Its size and capacity to reorganize totally the main elevation points to the importance of large-scale fenestration as a force for innovation at the time.[123] The fact that it is also allied with relatively prominent figurative sculpture in the nearby gallery spandrels suggests that the abbey's transepts were known and admired by the designers.

232 The rising of the sun at Prime. Egerton Hours, BL Egerton MS 1151, fol. 38, *c.* 1270 (by permission of the British Library).

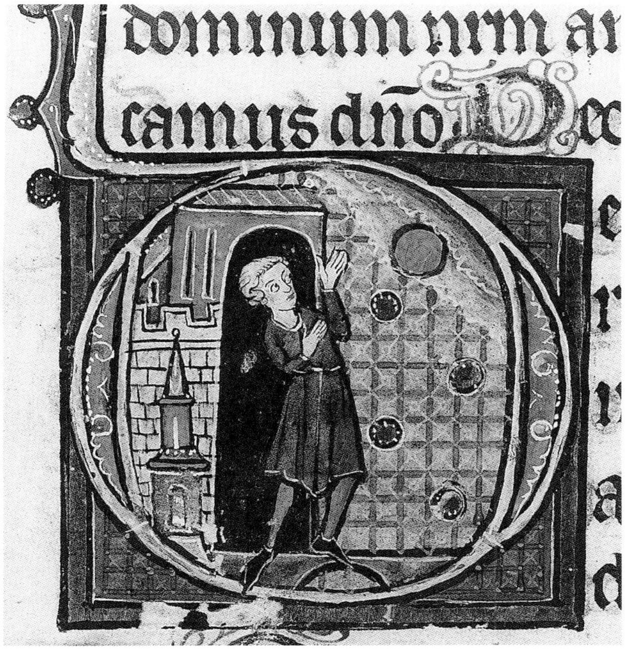

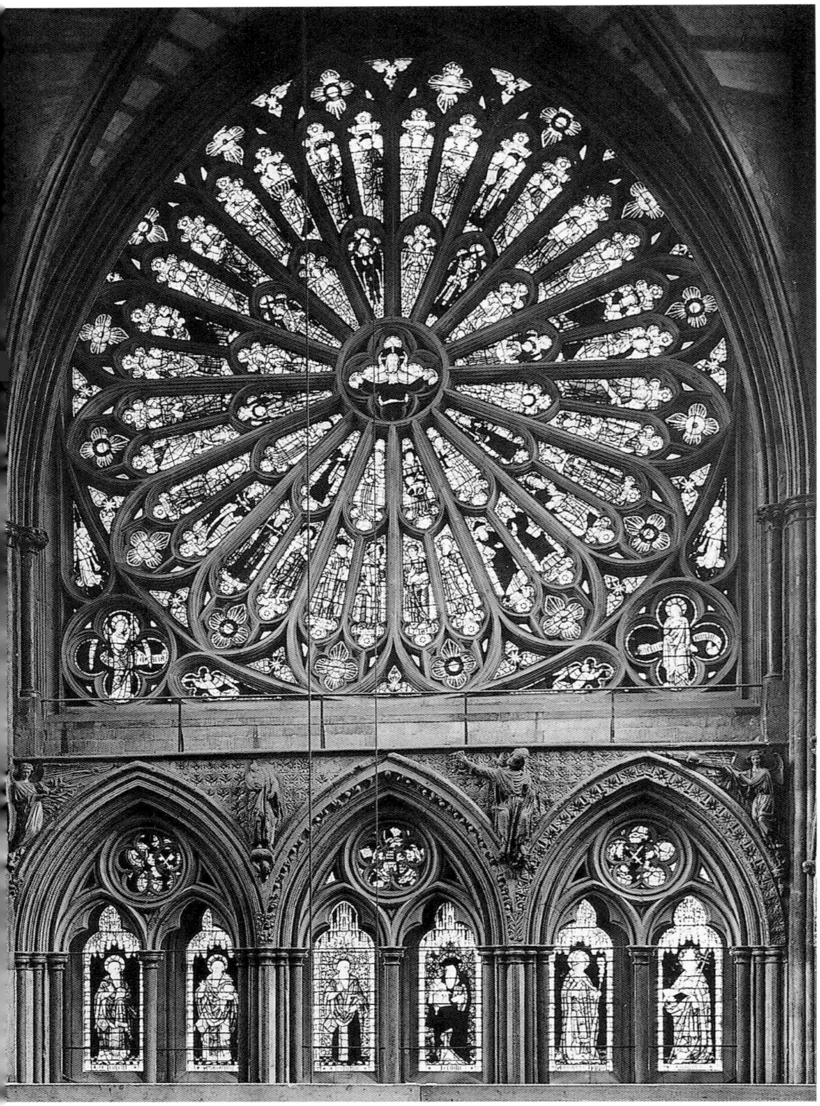

234 Westminster Abbey, south transept window (reproduced by permission of English Heritage. NMR).

At Westminster, the Parisian-looking rose windows opening out across the width of the transepts are expressly associated with sculpted imagery, including censing angels and images of the local saints beneath (fig. 234).[124] This looks very much like a paraphrase of the relationship of parts in the upper chapel of the Sainte-Chapelle.[125] As a great church effect, however, the co-ordination of large spreading windows, pyrotechnical tracery and rather eloquent sculpture were new. Its importance for subsequent generations of masons and church-planners was to be huge. In the 1250s what it served to do was underline in new formal terms the tendency in England for architecture to mesh with representation in a discursive fashion. In 1220 or so, as in the Metrical Life of St Hugh, this meshing would have taken the form of bodily allegories: understanding the round windows of the transepts as the surveillant eyes of the clergy, for example.[126] By 1260 the tendency is more frankly literal and theatrical, less austerely didactic: the sculptures now have a contingent relationship to the main architectural features, 'greeting' the dawn for example, and permitting an extension of chains of association leading into the traditional imagery of the Psalms. This is a *coup de théâtre* – but it is not theatre for its own sake so much as a theatre of traditional allegorical and exegetical associations, galvanized by Gothic rhapsody. The Angel Choir was a paradigm of one form of modernity, but this modernity, while founded on increasingly rational calculation, did not entail a loss or depletion of signification so much as the provision of new means whereby one might be seduced by it. Viewed in the long term, the mature Gothic art of Lincoln as a revelation of faith imagined in the years towards 1280 was quite as metaphorically dense and exegetically suggestive as that of the Gothic of Canterbury a century earlier, though the means or techniques differed. Both monuments, whether Canterbury's allegorical columns or Lincoln's theatre of paradise, celebrated a form of 'real presence', which made the finest and oddest art of the time both memorable and resistant to modern categorization.

Epilogue

Towards 1300: Virtuosity and Strangeness

As an ensemble (and here the notion of 'ensemble' seems perfectly appropriate)[1] the Angel Choir of Lincoln is fully in the tradition of great church magnificence, finished as it is with marble and sculpted detail of a very high order. It stands as a mature statement of many of the themes considered in this book. The keynote at Lincoln is, above all, assurance: an absolute belief in the potential of technique to serve simple yet great effects. With this assurance came tremendous accomplishment. At its best, the figurative and foliage sculpture at Lincoln has an energy and focus lacking in Westminster court work of the 1240s and 1250s, some of which seems aloof and sapless in comparison. The natural analogies to Lincoln at court are provided instead by a later generation of artists rising to prominence in the 1260s, whose priorities differed somewhat from the classicizing trends of the middle of the century. Of these, the most astonishing was the group of illuminators and painters linked to the court at the end of Henry III's reign and the start of that of Edward I, and most brilliantly represented by the Douce Apocalypse (fig. 235) and its satellite manuscript in Paris of around 1270 (BN MS lat. 10474).[2] The resemblance is not so much literal as essential, for it lies in a tendency to select and simplify certain forms while radically sharpening focus on others, to fill out and strengthen physiques, to explore the representation of complex movement, to deploy the expressive face, even caricature, and to revel in the consonance and dissonance of the human form related directly to the formal armature of architecture. In the Douce Apocalypse and its sister manuscript, weighty ample figures, angels especially, are rotated and disposed in extraordinary positions denoting power and poise, traced from the very core of their being out to their nimble and peculiar, though beautifully observed, fingertips. T. A. Heslop's analogy between the great angels in Douce and oriental dance conveys exactly the relationship between expressive freedom and control (or freedom through control) implicit in this choreography.[3] Tempting as it is to see in such dazzling displays of studied ingenuity the emergence of a vanguard, the truth is that, as at Lincoln, mature pretension of this order tends to come at the end, not at the start, of artistic 'movements'.

Though this style is now most vividly represented by a tiny group of court illuminators, its character is not solely painterly, for it owes much to ways of conceiving the human body and the curved nature of its movement that are by nature sculptural. In it is also to be found a powerful and absolutely self-conscious virtuosity. The roots of this new mode lay, as I have shown, in radical developments in sculpture, and then painting, in the Paris-Reims sphere before about 1260. In regard to the Douce style, one may be certain that something very significant in the field of polychrome sculpture has been lost from the London end of the London-Paris-Reims triangle, whose presence can also be sensed indirectly at Lincoln. Large active cathedral and court projects of the sort examined above at Reims and Westminster provided precisely the right experimental and ideological context for artists to engage in bravura display of 'difficulty'. What one sees in Douce is likely to have arisen from a situation in which some illuminators were also highly talented and quite possibly literate generalists, who also produced sculpture, panel and wall painting; who were in effect virtuoso *imagiers* in the broadest sense of the word. This casts serious doubt on the common assumption that design as such became a valuable commodity only a century or so later in northern Europe. In fact during the third quarter of the thirteenth century there was a flowering of *varietas* in the advanced visual cultures of cathedral workshops and courts, and a voracious appetite for novelty and surprising juxtapositions. Even antique and medieval Roman art could form part of the equation. The mosaic arts of Westminster Abbey are one instance, the sculptures of the facade at Auxerre Cathedral another, the two having in common a renewed fas-

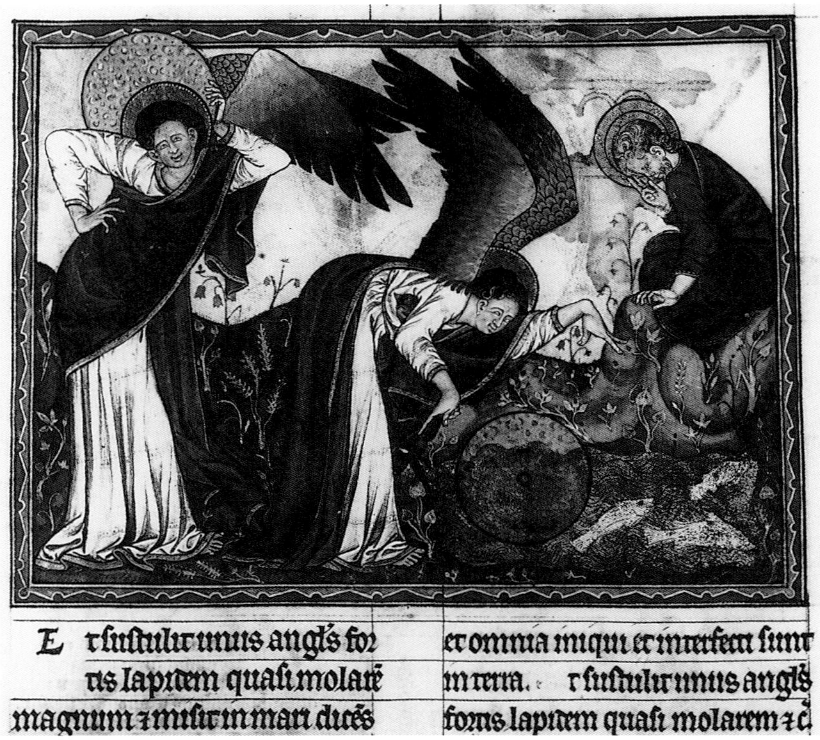

235 Angel and the Millstone. Douce Apocalypse, Oxford, Bodleian Library MS Douce 180, p. 77, *c.* 1270 (Conway Library, Courtauld Institute of Art/The Bodleian Library, University of Oxford).

cination for the richness and distinguished complexity of Roman art: *romanitas* was not the sole preserve of the generation of 1200.[4] It is also unlikely to be coincidence that there is at least one important document of English art of around 1400, the Pepysian 'sketchbook', which shows a particular interest in this period of English or Anglo-French inventiveness in reproducing figure designs not unlike those from the circle of the Douce workshop: like was looking upon like.[5] So, to some extent this virtuosity was the product of a particular elitism, of a culture of mastery that revelled in the difficult and the (occasionally) disconcerting and positively alien. Of it one might echo Guillaume de Machaut and say that its representations were *moult etranges* and *moult nouviaus*. Such cultures can require reining in: it may not be coincidental that it was during this period that some of the first serious efforts took place to regulate and codify, perhaps even to civilize, artistic and technological practices in such cities as Paris, a process that may owe at least something to the serious reflection on the ethical character and autonomy of professions at large typical of the moral theologians.[6]

Nor can one overlook an extremely important dimension of the new virtuoso mode which returns one to the sphere of religious imagination, and which challenges the idea that virtuosity was an uncomplicated token of artistic modernity. The genius of works such as the Douce Apocalypse (or indeed the Angel Choir) lies in their unorthodox harmonization of form and content, their cunning deployment of the most radical artistic techniques in the service of the unchanging discourse of the Bible. Seduction becomes rapture. The sheer energy of Douce is in one sense an amplification of what Wolfgang Kemp has diagnosed as the over-strung 'hyperactivity' of English narrative illustration of the mid-century.[7] It was not, however, simply the product of a style of narration given over to the circumstantial and the matter-of-fact. One should also think of this strange idiom of physical exaltation as an embodiment of the spiritual predicament of Revelation itself, of the rapture of St John carried away in the spirit – so brilliantly and so typically realized in Douce and its sister manuscript by the device of St John being carried aloft pick-a-back by a mighty angel (Revelation 21:9–10), athleticism con-

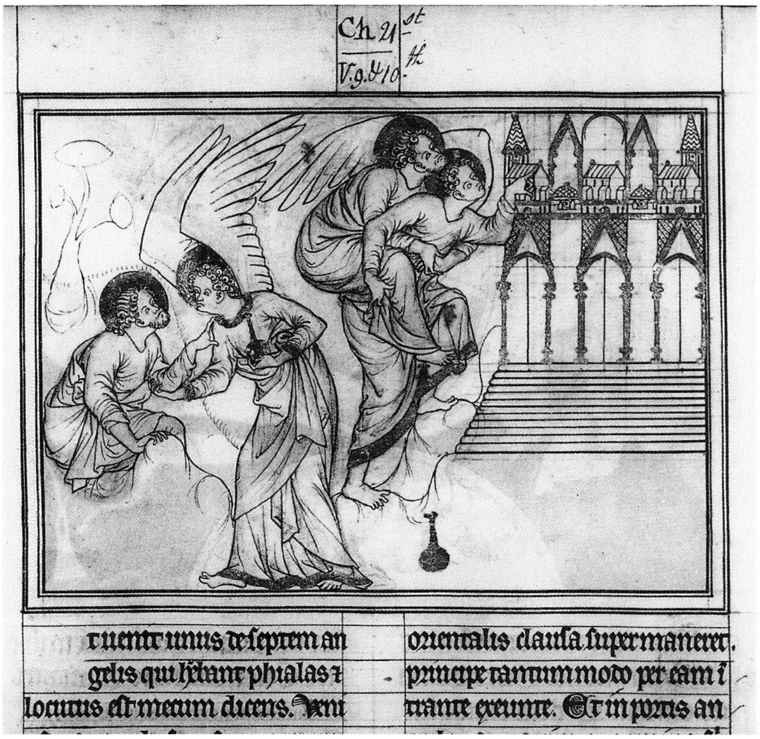

236 St John carried up to the New Jerusalem. Douce Apocalypse, Oxford, Bodleian Library MS Douce 180, p. 92, *c.* 1270 (Conway Library, Courtauld Institute of Art/The Bodleian Library, University of Oxford).

237 Angel whose face was the sun. Douce Apocalypse, Oxford, Bodleian Library MS Douce 180, p. 32, *c.* 1270 (Conway Library, Courtauld Institute of Art/The Bodleian Library, University of Oxford).

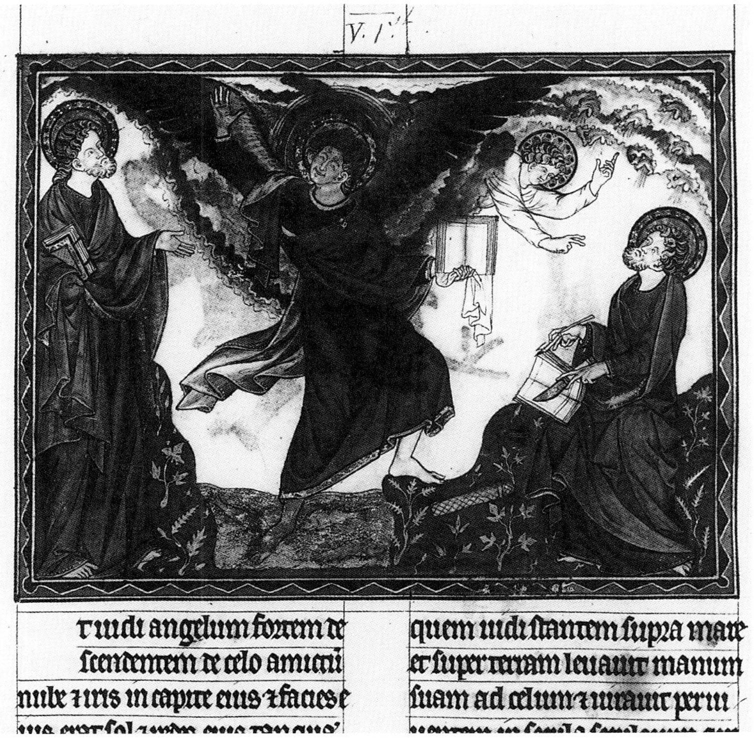

veying not only a rejoicing in artistic technique but also, and more importantly, the physical and spiritual dynamism of glorified bodies (fig. 236). It is hard to find a more witty or telling exemplification of the body as a sign of the spirit in European art of the period. In Douce, meaning shifts repeatedly onto bodily signs. Note, for instance, the exultant stance and broad grin of the angel whose 'face was the sun' in illustration of Revelation 10: 1–7 (fig. 237) – a perfect demonstration of the smile as a shining-out of the soul.[8] The physical energy, speed of movement and rotation of angelic figures in Douce creates an extremely sophisticated disequilibrium in the service of the metaphysical notion of transport: glimpsed views, lost profiles, figures facing away from the viewer and so on, are created not in the service of a contingent 'naturalism' but in order literally to flesh out the *velatio-revelatio* theme prominent in religious and aesthetic speculation since the previous century.[9] Such poses and gesticulations are not spent but are in a state of becoming, latent, full of imaginative and exegetical potential. This latency has indeed given rise to Helga Sciurie's valuable suggestion that the common posture of Synagoga turned away from Ecclesia, beautifully exemplified by the sculptures of the south transept at Strasbourg Cathedral, may signal not only defeat but the possibility of turning back: *revertere, revertere Sulamitis* (Canticles 6: 12), the body indicating the possibility of conversion.[10]

This trait was not in fact restricted to the elite cultures of the courts and cathedral chapters. In his work on female spirituality in Flanders and the Rhineland, Jeffrey Hamburger has stressed the use of ecstatic postures among the illustrations of the Adoration of the Lamb and the Wise and Foolish Virgins in the remarkable Rothschild Canticles (New Haven, Yale Univer-sity, Beinecke Rare Books and Manuscript Library MS 404, fols 13, 30) produced in Flanders around 1300.[11] This manuscript manifests an intensification of interest in Dionysian speculation, though of a more sophisticated sort than the positive version to which I alluded earlier in discussing the angelic: here the allegiance is to the new mysticism of the Rhineland. What matters here is that the compilation includes a pictorial commentary on the bride mysticism of Canticles by making extensive use of decidedly idiosyncratic *velatio-revelatio*, dancing, turning, climbing and athletic motifs. It is unclear exactly how gender-specific the intended patronage of the Canticles manuscript actually was; yet its strongly somatic imagery of rapture may well bear some relationship to contemporary accounts of excessive physical exertion and religious rapture among male and especially female religious of the thirteenth century in the Rhineland and Low Countries, and elsewhere.[12] As Walter Simons has put it 'ambiguity loomed large when the body ventured into the world of rapture. Harmony gave way to disorder, proportion to disorder'.[13] The spinning of the angels called virtues in the Passionale of Kunigunde (made around 1321 for the abbess of the imperial monastery of Prague) shows too that this new spirituality was not without an angelic aspect.[14] What defined order and proportion, in contrast, was the clerical discourse of moderation, whose formulation and application to various spheres of the official Church are explored throughout this study. Between the two there was inevitably a certain antagonism: the new athletes of Christ went beyond the bounds of normality in their strange mysticism of the body, their breach of an ultimately aristocratic canon of temperate behaviour.[15]

Though the Rothschild Canticles manuscript reveals no signs of ascetic and penitential spirituality, the Netherlandish and Rhenish culture for which it was made was close to that which also produced the horrors of the Conyhope cross, an extreme and abnormal sign. In that case, as shown above, a strange image bore the brunt of official clerical disapprobation. Yet there was no question of a work like the Douce Apocalypse meeting the same fate, for although it was not untouched by the new ethos of disequilibrium, it was also shielded by the status of its patronage and by the fact that it contested nothing: unlike the Y-cross, it remained within the bounds of the acceptable and the fashionable, and held no dangers. Again one is struck by the diversity, the polyphony, of the urban milieu towards 1300 in regard to the representation of the natural and the supernatural, and also by the common elements, notably the new imaginative use of the human body to convey what was metaphysically extraordinary, as well as what was ethically appropriate. The common elements had arisen from a much more fundamental re-evaluation of the relationship between the human and the divine, by means of which the divinity of Christ was now anchored to the historical facts of his incarnation and suffering and, conversely, ordinary and extraordinary mortals were not merely 'angelized', but divinized. As André Vauchez expressed it in his remarkable survey of the relationship between the natural and supernatural in sainthood, 'The identification of the human body with the glorious body, even the body of Christ, led, paradoxically, to a new form of marvel: physiological marvellousness'.[16]

This insight may help to explain why something is missing from efforts to understand the most remarkable achievements in the representation of the human body in the thirteenth century in terms of the extremely problematical categories of the 'natural' and the unmetaphorical, as opposed to the artificial and the metaphorical. The *locus classicus* of the 'naturalistic' interpretation is Nikolaus Pevsner's *The Leaves of Southwell* (1945), in which the fashion for botanically accurate leaf carving in France and England in the thirteenth century was explained by a 'balance between science and revelation or between experience and authority such as Europe had not known since the days of Aristotle' in the thought of such men as Albertus Magnus: what Erwin Panofsky a few years later heralded as the 'victory of Aristotelianism'.[17] The conceits of nominalism, if that is what they were, produced a dazzling integument of wonders (figs 238–9). Later work on the religious culture of the period, however, has exposed the difficulties arising from this exclusively nominalist or empiricist reading, not least because it has drawn attention to the facts that the body, whether divinized or angelized, is not a plant, that few signs of human culture are absolutely natural, and that, to quote Caroline Walker Bynum, it was not so much the Aristotelians like Aquinas, as 'the more conservative, more Augustinian-Platonic thinkers [. . .] who made the body "real" in a commonsense way'.[18] Again and again throughout this study, I have stressed the importance of this very diverse strain of thought for the formation of 'Gothic' sensibilities, sensibilities which, in the figurative arts at least, owe much less to the hard dialectics, the confrontation of opposites, of scholasticism than they do to the older, more peaceful and contemplative drawing out of meaning and affect.

This last point leads me to a degree of scepticism about another influential view of 'naturalism' and contemporary medieval culture, according to which there was some relation between the rise in literature of vernacular language and the new capacity of the visual arts in the thirteenth century to create 'naturalistic' pictorial fictions. These fictions are held to have reflected a shift from formulaic and metaphorical representation in the twelfth century to concrete, particular and unmetaphorical representation in the thirteenth: F. H. Bäuml called this process 'demetaphorization'.[19] As he put it, 'The characterization of medieval pictorial communication as essentially textual [. . .] becomes less applicable after the thirteenth century.'[20] This shift is further allied in the minds of other critics to another view, based ultimately on classical hierarchies of style, according to which Gothic represented a more accessible or 'low' style: a visual vernacular of 'simple sights for simple folk'.[21] The conclusions of the present study obviously point in a very different direction. Little of what has been set out in this book can satisfactorily be shoe-horned into the spaces provided by such binary (and frequently rationalistic) oppositions as high and low, latinate and vernacular, religious and secular, metaphorical and non-metaphorical, or unnaturalistic and naturalistic – it is the second in each pair of these terms that has dominated recent discussions of Gothic art. In considering the Crucifixion, and bodily expressivity more generally, I have argued for caution in the use of the notion of the demotic – the *stilus humilis* – as if it guaranteed a deeper total understanding of Gothic art at this phase of its development, as opposed to offering an important *aperçu*. Nor, as shown in my consideration of the relationship, theoretical and practical, between ethos and affect, is there a lack of evidence for the actual reinforcement of some (but not all) classically derived norms of decorum, as opposed to their dissolution in the service of a populist late medieval realism. The occasionally voiced idea that the mimetic arts of the thirteenth century were an 'exaltation of the trivial and contingent' and represented a currency of the 'bland and banal' – that Gothic 'naturalism' was either empty, or the product of the admission of 'the low narrative mode' – is not without (modernist) opinion about the perceived relative decline of Gothic art from the intellectual, spiritual and moral heights of the twelfth century.[22] It entails a questionable aesthetic judgement as well as a potentially damaging philosophical dualism. One should be wary of it: the arts of this period were not necessarily signs *avant la lettre* of late medieval 'decline' and nor should they be judged by the standards of the late Middle Ages. The Gothic of this era owed too much to the thought of previous generations to be annexed in this way.

In similar anti-teleological vein, I have also challenged the idea that the public and 'official' latinate culture of the thirteenth-century Church was the site of conservative retrenchment, as opposed to the realism, freedom (and modernism?) of private, unofficial vernacular religious culture. This idea is founded in part upon a questionable public-private antinomy, and in part upon the characterization of Latin, as opposed to vernacular languages, as elite and formulaic, or inherently anti-natural.[23] Against it and its attendant assumptions, I have found evidence that the public sphere of the Church witnessed – indeed sanctioned and encouraged – innovation not solely in the service of the pastoral reform of the laity, but, equally importantly, the reform of itself: its endeavours, though indisputably top-down in character, were aimed quite as much at the clerical literate (i.e. latinate) as the lay members of society, technically the illiterate. While it is true that Latin was the principal language of public power rather than public culture as a whole, it was also the language of the Bible and of the scholarly, scientific and (perhaps more importantly)

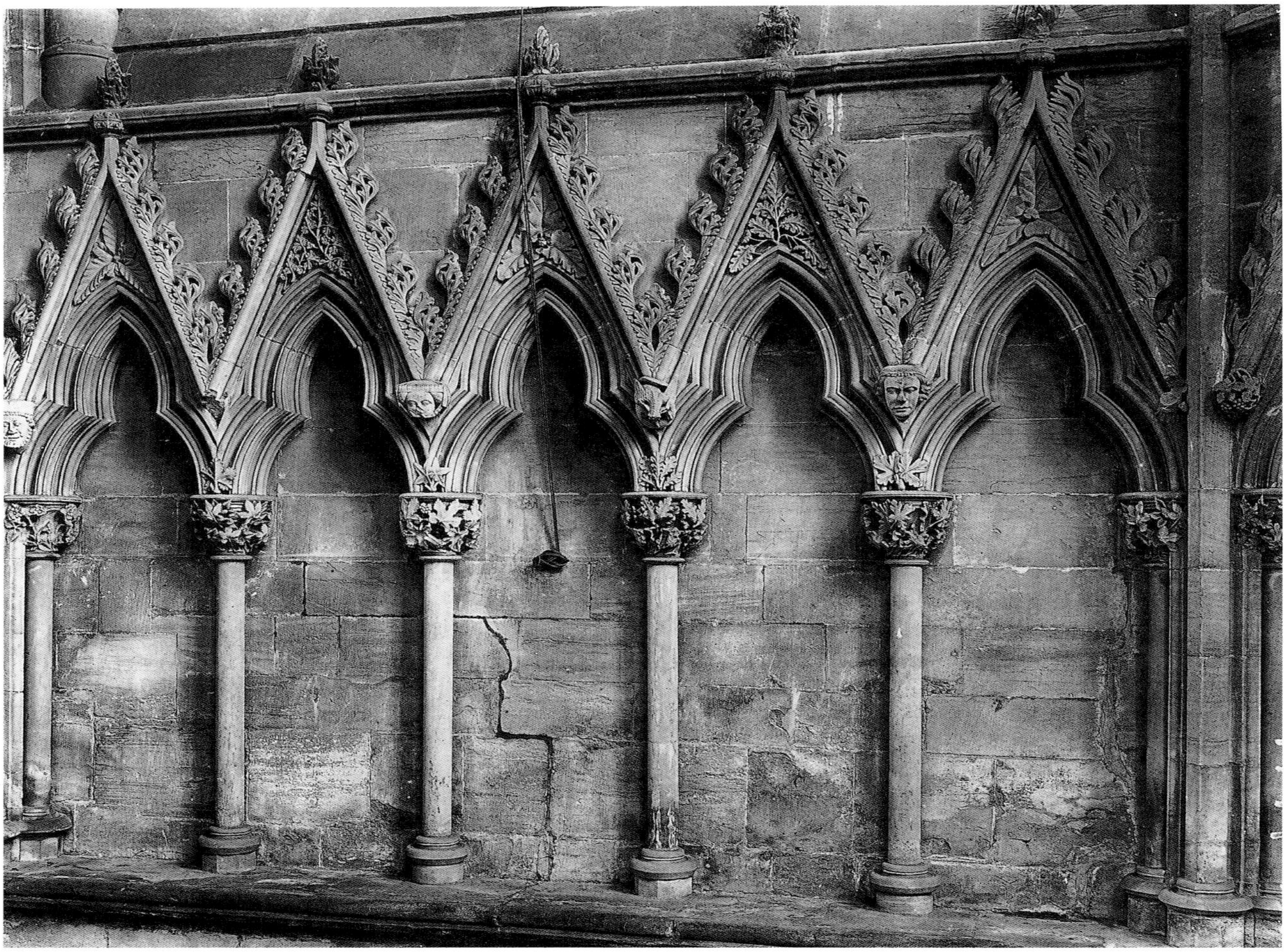

238 Arcading, Southwell Minster chapter house (Conway Library, Courtauld Institute of Art).

ethical and rhetorical discourse of the very regime that produced most of the images discussed in this book. Latin was itself versatile and adaptable. There are formidable objections to the assumption that it was not the site of individuality or self-consciousness in this period.[24] A very large number of the expressive, devotional and exegetical ideas pondered in this study can be, and were, expressed perfectly adequately within the diverse framework of the Latin language for the duration of the period covered here. Indeed, I contend that without this framework, the art of the period would be incomprehensible. The possibilities of a solely populist or vernacularist explanation of the things discussed above are hedged about by distinct limitations.

In considering Gothic, I have aimed constantly to alert the reader to its sustained exegetical and textual density, its ethical sophistication, its urbanity, its unconventional thinking – in short to its metaphorical as well as its stylistic virtuosity. Virtually nothing examined in this book favours the idea that thirteenth-century art as a whole was gradually divested of textual, symbolic or metaphorical potential in the service of a popular visual language. Depletion of meaning was not the corollary of the new techniques: these techniques, as I have suggested in relation to the expressivity of the Cross of Christ, or of the face, or of the body, actually preceded and revitalized meaning. As George Henderson concluded of the profoundly somatic art of the Douce Apocalypse, the 'deepening of the visual content' of this artist is exactly what gives his work 'intellectual dimension'.[25] In emphasizing the demotic character of Gothic art, one runs the risk of losing sight of the extent to which it remained conventional, discursive, difficult and authoritarian: and this may be precisely why, in England and northern France and Flanders especially, it came to support a prodigious but complementary and collusive sphere of the marginal.[26] It remains to be ascertained whether the sharpening language and practice of official Church control evident in some of the sources for the second half of the thirteenth century enjoyed some deeper, perhaps causal, relationship to the concurrent explosion of the sphere of the marginal. Finally – and this must be a fatal objection to the rather conventional evolutionary art-historical assumptions of the vernacularist argument – Gothic art had no straightforward linear progression towards an ever-increasing 'nominalist' realism in tandem with the consolidation of literary and state vernaculars. After 1300, indeed, many of the traits considered in the last part of this book stalled or went wholly into reverse. With the emergence of English as a serious literary and governmental language in the fourteenth century, the smile faded from the face, and the great age of botanical naturalism ceased: figures and plants tended to withdraw into the elegant, the self-referential and the schematic. The objectives of these arts also remained profoundly religious: and it is for this reason that I have tried to focus on patient and practical interpretation, on a case-by-case basis, of images and forms in relation to the texts most known and most frequently deployed by contemporaries.

It is also true that, from the time of the generation of 1300 or so, English architecture especially entered a renewed period of fertile inventiveness identified with what is now known as the Decorated Style and the emergence of the Perpendicular Style.[27] Both are conspicuously successful manifestations of the culture of virtuosity, involving a self-conscious professional quest for formal variety and innovation. Though it would be misleading to see these styles as a fulfilment of the major architectural movements of the thirteenth century in England and France, there can be no serious doubt that this is where their roots lay both formally, practically and imaginatively. The new styles were developed at least in part for projects that adapted or replaced work of previous generations, and that accordingly tended to adhere to their general standards of display, as well as to their pre-existing physical limitations. Even where largely new works were begun in their entirety, as at Exeter Cathedral, the older forms of the great church, understood broadly, were adhered to. A factor in this must have been a settled acknowledgement that the aesthetic of magnificence of the great church was now beyond serious question. It had survived the era of reform because it had become useful to it. Suspicion of the Promethean powers of the new church technologies, and of the Daedelan ingenuity of artists and masons, had not prevailed in the face of the Church's pragmatic recognition that virtuosity of one type or another had pastoral utility. In the Decorated Style, perhaps, *curiositas* had found a legitimate harbour and outlet. Of course, such continuities cannot account for styles understood as specific detailed formal procedures, any more than they can account for striking zestful deviations from what went before. The fourteenth-century works undertaken by the cathedral priory at Ely in replacing its old crossing tower with a giant octagon (fig. 60) and erecting a Lady Chapel of unprecedented sculptural richness are testimony to an aesthetic of the prodigious and the surprising; for such an aesthetic to be developed, institutional wealth and the ethical acceptance of magnificent architectural display were necessary, but not sufficient, conditions. Some such understanding pre-

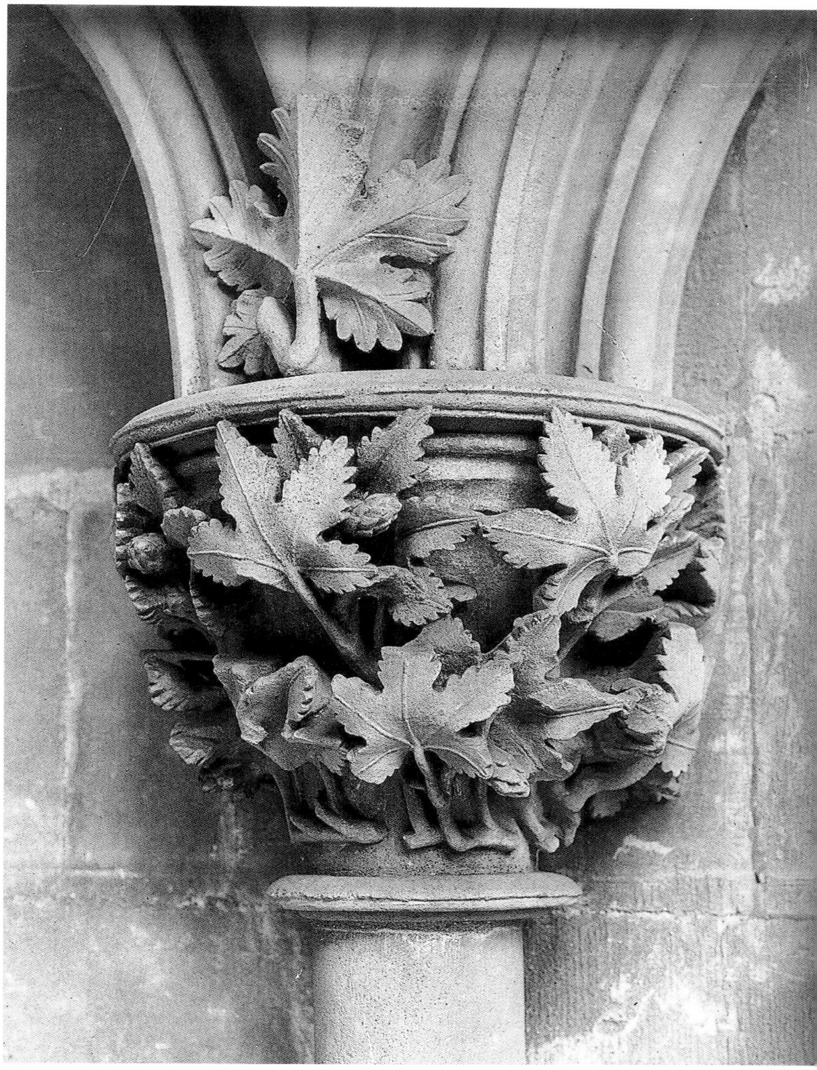

239 Detail, arcading, Southwell Minster chapter house (Conway Library, Courtauld Institute of Art).

sumably accounted for the relative neglect of human and cultural circumstances apparent in Jean Bony's formalist account of the origins and development of the Decorated Style. However, it is impossible at this stage of my enquiry to consider further this most interesting and important aspect of English visual culture at the dawn of the later Middle Ages. Quite clearly the great age of architectural display did not end with the passing of the most fertile period of clerical thought on the *habitus*, or of the formal canonization of the English saints. Churches with spires, octagons, magnificent ranks of windows and gorgeously furnished interiors continued to embody the powers of the Gothic style and the inventiveness of its artists. What their 'imaginative universe' consisted of is, however, a matter for further study.

Abbreviations

AoC	*Age of Chivalry: Art in Plantagenet England 1200–1400*, eds J. Alexander and P. Binski, London 1987
AL	*Annales Londinienses*, in W. Stubbs, ed., *Chronicles of the Reigns of Edward I and Edward II*, I, RS 76, London 1882
AM	*Annales Monastici*, ed. H. R. Luard, 5 vols, RS 36, London 1864–9
AS	*Anglia Sacra*, ed. H. Wharton, 2 vols, London 1691
BAACT	*British Archaeological Association Conference Transactions*
BL	British Library, London
BN	Bibliothèque Nationale, Paris
CCR	Calendar of the Close Rolls
CLR	Calendar of the Liberate Rolls
CDS	*Charters and Documents Illustrating the History of the Cathedral, City, and Diocese of Salisbury*, eds W. H. R. Jones and W. D. Macray, RS 97, London 1891
CM	Matthew Paris, *Chronica majora*, ed. H.R. Luard, 7 vols, RS 57, London 1872–83
CMA	*Chronica monasterii S. Albani*, V/II, ed. H. T. Riley, RS 28, London 1871
CMM	*Chronica monasterii de Melsa*, III, ed. E.A. Bond, RS 43, London 1868
CPL	Calendar of Papal Letters
CPR	Calendar of the Patent Rolls
C&S I	*Councils & Synods*, I: *A.D. 871–1204. Part II, 1066–1204*, eds D.M. Whitelock, M. Brett, and C.N.L. Brooke, Oxford 1981
C&S II	*Councils & Synods*, II: *A.D. 1205–1313. Part I, 1205–1265. Part II, 1265–1313*, eds F.M. Powicke and C.R. Cheney, 2 vols (continuously paginated), Oxford 1964
CUL	Cambridge University Library
CVMA	Corpus Vitrearum Medii Aevi
DNR	Alexander Neckam, *De naturis rerum*, ed. T. Wright, RS 34, London 1863
EETS	Early English Text Society
EpC	*Epistolae Cantuarienses: The Letters of the Prior and Convent of Christ Church, Canterbury, from A.D. 1187 to A.D. 1199*, in *Chronicles and Memorials of the Reign of Richard I*, II, ed. W. Stubbs, RS 38, London 1865
Fasti	*Fasti ecclesiae anglicanae 1066–1300*, ed. J. le Neve et al., London 1968–
FH	*Flores historiarum*, ed. H. R. Luard, 3 vols, RS 95, London 1890
GA	*Gesta abbatum monasterii Sancti Albani*, ed. H. T. Riley, 3 vols, RS 28, London 1867–9
GC	*Historical Works of Gervase of Canterbury*, ed. W. Stubbs, 2 vols, RS 73, London 1879–80
GPA	William of Malmesbury, *De gestis pontificum anglorum*, ed. N.E.S.A. Hamilton, RS 52, London 1870
GRA	William of Malmesbury, *Gesta regum anglorum*, eds R.A.B. Mynors, R. M. Thomson and M. Winterbottom, 2 vols, Oxford 1998–9
GW	Giraldus Cambrensis, *Opera omnia*, eds J.S. Brewer, J. F. Dimock and G. F. Warner, 8 vols, RS 21, London 1861–91
HA	Matthew Paris, *Historia anglorum*, ed. F. Madden, 3 vols, RS 44, London 1866–9
JBAA	*Journal of the British Archaeological Association*
JSAH	*Journal of the Society of Architectural Historians*
JWCI	*Journal of the Warburg and Courtauld Institutes*
L-B	Lehmann-Brockhaus, O., *Lateinische Schriftquellen zur Kunst in England, Wales und Schottland vom Jahre 901 bis zum Jahre 1307*, 5 vols, Munich 1955–60
LEC	*Lives of Edward the Confessor*, ed. H.R. Luard, RS 3, London 1858
Mats	*Materials for the History of Thomas Becket, Archbishop of Canterbury*, eds J.C. Robertson and J. B. Sheppard, 7 vols, RS 67, London 1875–85
MGL	*Monumenta Gildhallae Londiniensis*, ed. H.T. Riley, 4 vols, RS 12, London 1859–62
MLH	*The Metrical Life of St Hugh*, ed. and trans. C. Garton, Lincoln 1986
MV	*Magna Vita Sancti Hugonis/The Life of St Hugh of Lincoln*, ed. and trans. D.L. Douie and D.H. Farmer, 2 vols, London and Oxford 1961–2
NMR	National Monuments Record
PL	*Patrologia Latina: Cursus completus*, ed. J.-P. Migne, 221 vols, Paris 1844–64
RCHM	Royal Commission on Historical Monuments
RGE	Roberti Grosseteste, *Epistolae*, ed. H.R. Luard, RS 25, London 1861
RIBA	Royal Institute of British Architects
RS	Rolls Series
TRHS	*Transactions of the Royal Historical Society*
V&A	Victoria and Albert Museum, London
VCH	The Victoria History of the Counties of England
VRS	*Vetus registrum Sarisberiense: The Register of S. Osmund*, ed. W.H.R. Jones, 2 vols, RS 78, London 1883–4

Psalms are numbered according to the Vulgate (*Gallicanum*)

Notes

PROLOGUE

1 Sauerländer in Raguin, Brush and Draper, eds, 1995, 15.
2 Jaeger 1985, xii.
3 Brieger 1957, v.
4 Jaeger 1985, 3–16; Elias, trans. Jephcott 1994.
5 Panofsky 1951.
6 Smalley 1973, Vauchez, trans. Birrell 1997.
7 Helmholz 1996, 397–8.
8 Cheney 1960, 1961b, 1968, 1982; *C&S* II.
9 Bynum 1982.
10 Duffy 1992, 30.
11 Schmitt 1990.

CHAPTER 1

1 Suetonius, Life of Augustus, ch. 28, trans. Graves 1979, 69; Mortet 1911, 38, 128; Greenhalgh 1989, 121–2; Schneider 2001.
2 Curtius, trans. Trask 1953, 48–54; Roberts 1968, 101; in general Hunt 1991.
3 Virgil, *Aeneid*, VII, lines 170–71, in Christie and Fordyce, eds, 1977, 6: *Tectum augustum, ingens, centum sublime columnis orbe fuit summa*; Statius, *Silvae*, IV/2, lines 18–31, ed. and trans. Coleman 1988, 8–11; Sidonius, *Carmina*, XXII, lines 136–41, ed. and trans. Anderson 1956, 272–3: *Ipsa autem quantis, quibus aut sunt fulta columnis*; Ovid, *Metamorphoses*, II, lines 1–5, ed. and trans. Hill 1985, 48–9: *Regia Solis erat sublimibus alta columnis*; also Greenhalgh 1989, 131; Schneider 2001, 8.
4 Gregory of Tours, 2/14 and 16, trans. Thorpe 1974, 130–31; Isidore of Seville, ed. Lindsay 1911, XIX: xiii; also Greenhalgh 1989, 119–21, 131.
5 *GC* I, 3–29; Davidson-Cragoe, 2001.
6 *GC* I, 27: *In capitellis veteribus opus erat planum, in novis sculptura subtilis . . . Ibi columpna nulla marmorea, hic innumerae*; Willis 1845, 59.
7 *GC* I, 6; Willis 1845, 35.
8 *GC* I, 6–7, 27–8; Willis 1845, 36, 58–61; Stansbury-O'Donnell 1990, I, 1–3, cf. Vitruvius 1.3.2, trans. Morgan 1914, 17. The tripartite division in Isidore of Seville fits slightly less well: ed. Lindsay 1911, XIX: ix (*dispositio*), x (*constructio*) and xi (*venustas*).
9 Curtius, trans. Trask 1953, 159–63; Greenhalgh 1989, 119–22.
10 Gransden 1972, 36–7, 38–40; Gransden 1974, 129–42; also for Eadmer, Southern 1990, 404–36.
11 *GC* I, 7, 8; Willis 1845, 11, 20–31; Gem 1983, 1–7.
12 For the *Mappa*, see *GC* I, xxviii–xxix, *GC* II, 414. For Gervase, see also *GC* I, ix–xlix and 51; Willis 1845, 51; Gransden 1972, 36–7, 39–40 and n. 58; Gransden 1974, 253–60; Woodman 1981, 88, 93; Woodman in Gibson, Heslop and Pfaff, eds, 1992, 177.
13 Deér 1959; Greenhalgh 1989, 131–3; Schneider 2001, 7–8; Norton 2002, 12.
14 Greenhalgh 1989, 121, 126–7; [Master Gregorius], trans. Osborne 1987, 27 no. 15, and 34 no. 29; Schneider 2001, 6.
15 Onians 1988, 70–73.
16 Fernie 1983, 35–6 and fig. 13.
17 Gibson, Heslop and Pfaff, eds, 1992, 189; Henderson 1999, 59–73.
18 Dronke 1972, 54.
19 Gage 1993, 25–7; Gage 1999, 71–3.
20 For another account of Gervase's various deficiencies, see Kidson 1993.
21 *GC* I, 28–9; Willis 1845, 61.
22 *GC* I, 28–9; Willis 1845, 61.
23 Kidson 1993, 990 incorrectly asserts that the columns are monoliths.
24 *GC* I, 29; Willis 1845, 62.
25 For the proposed translation, see *Mats* VII, 581–2; Foreville 1958, 5; for the shrine base, Mason 1920, 112–13 notes the representations of the shrine with pink columns in the Becket windows at Canterbury; Urry 1975, 198 and 204–5 esp. no. 2; Tatton-Brown 1981, 51–4; Stratford, Tudor-Craig and Muthesius 1982, 76; Draper 1997, 199–201; Tatton-Brown 1998a, 53–8; Tatton Brown 2002, 96 and n. 22.
26 *GC* I, 7: *In adquirendis igitur lapidibus transmarinis opera data est.*
27 Bony 1949, 8–11; Severens 1970, 310–12; Woodman 1981, 109, 113–15; Mair 1982; Bony 1983, 158–66, 161; Wilson 1990, 86–9; Kahn 1991, 143.
28 Mortet 1911, 173; Bony 1949, 8–11; Sauerländer 1985, 40 (for St-Remi at Reims); Zarnecki 1986, 168; Greenhalgh 1989, 131–5; Kahn 1991, 95–137, 143–4, ill. 183; Clark 1997 for Paris.
29 Kidson 1993, 981–91.
30 Recht 1999, 217.

31 O'Reilly 1981, 305; Dronke 1972, 79; Henderson 1999, 126–7.
32 *Mats* I, 1–2. For the martyrdom, Barlow 1986, 225–50; Urry 1999, 127–49.
33 Abbott 1898, I, 38, 54, 89, 96, 114–15, 183, 205–6; Mason 1920, 84–5, 117; O'Reilly 1981, 308; O'Reilly 1985, 191–7; also Caviness 1977, 149–50; A. Duggan 1982, 33. For John of Salisbury, see *Mats* II, 318–19; Smalley 1973, 196; Millor and Brooke, eds, 1979, 726–31. For the *Quadrilogus*, see *Mats* IV, 266–430; also VII, 464–5.
34 O'Reilly 1985, 195; Gameson 2002, 53–9.
35 *Mats* II, 43; O'Reilly 1985, 196; Cave 1948, fig. 60; Gameson 2002, 58–9.
36 O'Reilly 1985, *passim*, quote on 236.
37 *Mats* II, 437–8, III, 143.
38 Abbott 1898, I, 185; O'Reilly 1981, 303. The biographers are William fitz Stephen, Edward Grim, Garnier, 'Anonymous IV' and 'Anonymous X'.
39 Dronke 1972, 89.
40 O'Reilly 1981, 304–5.
41 Abbott 1898, I, 149; O'Reilly 1981, 305–6.
42 Procter and Wordsworth, eds, 1879–86, I, col. cclviii; see also *Mats* II, 42–3 for water, 189–91 for blood and *Mats* I, 354–7 for milk; also *Mats* III, 150 for the phials of water. The topic is anticipated at Canterbury by St Dunstan's miraculous water, in which his staff had rested. Also O'Reilly, 1981, 306–9; Ward 1982, 101–3.
43 Bynum 1982, 123, 132–3.
44 Magnússon 1875–83, I, 549; O'Reilly 1981, 306–7 after Guernes de Pont-Sainte-Maxence, ed. Walberg 1936, 173–4, lines 5636–40; also Shirley, trans., 1996, 149.
45 O'Reilly 1985, 197.
46 O'Reilly 1981, 310–12; for purple, see also *Mats* II, 357–8.
47 A. Duggan 1982, 34, after Procter and Wordsworth, eds, 1879–86, I, ccxlviii–cclviii; Eales 1993, 137 after P. B. Roberts 1973, ed. 1980, 1989.
48 P. B. Roberts 1973, ed. 1980, 53–64 at 56–8, 1992, 36–7; also A. Duggan 1982, 40–41.
49 Conti in *PL* 217, cols 774, 799–802, bk I, cap. 65: *Hinc sponsa dicit in Canticis: Dilectus meus candidus et rubicundus, electus ex millibus. Candidus in confessoribus et virginibus, rubicundus in martyribus et apostolis. Hi et illi sunt flores rosarum et lilia convallium.* Cf. Durandus, eds Davril and Thibodeau 1995–8, I, 224–9; Gardner 1994, 7, n. 9; Guest, commentary, 1995, 81 for the *Bible moralisée*.
50 For the *eruditi*, see *Mats* III, 206–7, 523–31.
51 Wilson 1990, 90.
52 Astell 1990, 8, 17–18.
53 Geertz 1966, 5.
54 Cf. Panofsky 1951; Draper 1996.
55 Recht 1999, 160: 'l'architecture ne se fait pas a l'aide de concepts'.
56 Onians 1988, 59–90, esp. 69–76.
57 Cf. Hoey 1986.
58 Panofsky, ed., 2/1979, 104–5.
59 *GC* I, 27.
60 Deshman 1986, 261–2, 275–7; Deshman 1995, 138, 181–3.
61 *De universo*, *PL* 111, cols 9–614; *Diadema*, *PL* 102, cols 594–690. Mortet 1911, 26–7 for Saint Bénigne at Dijon: *Quoniam multa in eo videntur mystico sensu facta*; also 159–60 n. 3. Reudenbach 1980; Deshman 1986, 276, 282 n. 46 for CUL MS Ff. 4. 43 containing the *Diadema*, attributed to tenth-century Christ Church; Onians 1988, 70–90, 74–5, 86.
62 For Honorius, *PL* 172, col. 586; Mortet and Deschamps 1929, 14–18 (Honorius) and 183–8 (Peter of Roissy); Kennedy 1943, 7, 21–2; Falletti 1953, col. 1057; Durandus, ed. Davril and Thibodeau 1995–8, I, 11–28.
63 Smalley 1973, 196–200 and n. 44: *quasi columpna maxima et fortissima ad sublevandum fabricam*; Smalley 3/1984, 109–10; Orme 1966; A. Duggan 1982, 25; Gameson 2002, 80.
64 *Mats* II, 301.
65 Procter and Wordsworth, eds, 1879–86, III, cols 447–8, *lectio* vi: *Beatus martyr est lapis ille quem reprobaverunt aedificantes: qui et factus est in caput anguli*; Ladner 1942.
66 Foreville 1958, 89–95.
67 Foreville 1958, 90; P. B. Roberts 1973, ed. 1980, 65–94 at 72, 85, 1989, 1992, 22–3 and n. 39.
68 Mortet 1911, 159–60 and n. 3; Onians 1988, 86.
69 Legg and Hope, eds, 1902, 30.
70 *Mats* II, 437: *et summitate coronae, quam sancti chrismatis unctio dicaverat Deo, abrasa.*
71 *Mats* II, 17–18, III, 507; Smalley 1973, 194. Also Procter and Wordsworth, eds, 1879–86, I, col. ccliii, *lectio* v: *consecratam capitis coronam funestis gladiis amputaverunt*. See also the *Liber poenitentialis* of Robert of Flamborough, ed. Firth 1971, 116: *corona monstrat clericos spiritualiter esse regnum Dei*. For the tonsure, Bock 1952; Cox 1959, 30–38. The symbolism of the corona was discussed along these lines by Martin Aurell at a conference in Cambridge in 2001.
72 Roberts 1992, 35, 91 (no. 38), 93 (no. 40).
73 Borenius 1932, 36–7.
74 Millor and Brooke, eds, 1979, 724–59 no. 305; *Mats* I, 133; II, 320, 437; III, 141, 499; IV, 77, 131; VII, 466; Abbott 1898, I, 29, 39, 102–3, 159; Walberg 1929, xciv; Procter and Wordsworth, eds, 1879–86, I, col. ccliii, *lectio* vi; Luscombe 1985, 142.
75 O'Reilly 1981, 193–4; Gameson 2002, 80.
76 Legg and Hope, eds, 1902, *passim*; Southern 1990, 327 fig. 1 (III); Tatton-Brown 2002, fig. 1.
77 Caviness 1977, 139; cf. Morgan 1983, 12.
78 *Mats* I, 304–5; Walberg 1929, xciv; Guernes de Pont-Saint-Maxence, ed. Walberg 1936, 116, line 3759, 123, line 4012, 172 line 5578; Luscombe 1985, 142; Shirley, trans., 1996, 100, 107, 148.
79 *Mats* I, 304: *Permiserat hunc theologus Ariopagita Dionisius, dum symbolicis et anagogicis demonstrationibus vacat, coelestes hierarchias considerans*; Smalley 1973, 191.
80 Luscombe 1985, 138, 140.
81 Smalley 1973, 211–12; Luscombe 1985, 140–41.
82 *Mats* III, 58; Smalley 1973, 59–86; Smalley 3/1984, 186–95.
83 Smalley 1973, 61–2.
84 Smalley 1973, 63–4, 71–2; Barlow 1986, 141.
85 Smalley 1973, 75.
86 Smalley 1973, 75–6.

87 *Mats* III, 210–11, 217–18; *Mats* III, 213–15 for Anselm; also O'Reilly 1985, 202, 229–30; in general Southern 1990, esp. 91–112.
88 *Mats* III, 214; cf. Panofsky, ed., 2/1979, 64–6.
89 *Mats* III, 217; Smalley 1973, 80; Luscombe 1985, 142 n. 102.
90 *GC* I, 393.
91 Smalley 3/1984, 186–95.
92 Smalley 1973, 81–3; Smalley 3/1984, 189; Châtillon 1975; Fassler 1993, 257.
93 Dodwell 1954, 98–113; De Hamel 1984, 38–54; Nilgen 1986, 150–54.
94 Fassler 1993, 137–8.
95 Kidson 1993, 979–80.
96 Nilgen 1980, 1986; Hoey 1995a.
97 Knowles 2/1963, 320; *GC* I, 332: *Subverterant enim quidam clerici seculares ipsius simplicitatem, fabricantes continua suggestione de litteratura ejus arma malitiae et nequitiae.*
98 For internal machinations, see Draper 1983, 245; Hearn 1994, 47–52; Kidson 1993, 969–81; Draper 1997, 194–201.
99 Fernie 1982; Kahn 1991, 35–6; O'Reilly 1985, 186; Ridyard 1986, 200–04; Southern 1990, 106–9; Heslop 2002.
100 Woodman 1981, 120; cf. the various solutions in Kidson 1993 and Hearn 1994, reviewed sceptically in Hoey 1995a; the solution in Draper 1997 is the most satisfactory.
101 *GC* I, 16; Willis 1845, 46–7; *Mats* II, 81–3; Urry 1975, 196–7; Crook 2000, 242–81.
102 *Mats* II, 81: *duas in utroque laterum habens fenestras, quibus advenientes capitibus immissis ad osculum sarcophagi pervenire valerent.*
103 Crook 2000, 16, 30–31, 76, 168–9, 208–9.
104 Wilson 1977, 12, 25 n. 36; Crook 2000, 30–31, 76, 163–4, 168–9, 217.
105 Woodruff 1932; Hearn 1994, 51.
106 Abbott 1898, II, 14.
107 *GC* I, 256, 262.
108 Cf. Bony 1949, 7; Severens 1970; Kidson 1993.
109 Cf. Kidson 1969; Draper 1983, 428; Kidson 1993, 979–80; Hearn 1994, 51.
110 Clark 1997.
111 Bony 1986, 132, 136.
112 Roberts, ed., 1980, 72–3; Roberts 1989.
113 Roberts, ed., 1980, 90–94 (sections 38–40, after Luke 11: 38); Crook 2000, 32–4.
114 Esposito, ed., 1960, 26–7.
115 *Mats* II, 27–8; Mason 1920, 110–11; Caviness 1981, 187; Ward 1982, 90.
116 Cf. Panofsky, ed., 2/1979; Rudolph 1990a; Kidson 1987a; McGinn 1995.
117 Kidson 1987a.
118 Caviness 1977, 1981; cf. Grodecki 1961; Gerson, ed., 1986.
119 Kemp 1948, 82–106; Vauchez, trans. Birrell 1997, 13.
120 Kemp 1948, 86–9.
121 O'Reilly 1985, 218–35.
122 *Mats* I, 150–51; Abbott 1898, I, 4–5, II, 6–7; Kemp 1948, 88–9; Ward 1982, 104.
123 Borenius 1932; Foreville, ed., 1975, 211–71; O'Reilly 1985, 225; Gameson 2002, 75, 78, pl. 17.
124 Meyer, ed., 1885, viii; Backhouse and de Hamel 1988; Morgan 1982, no. 61; Morgan 1988b.
125 Meyer, ed., 1885, 10: *soli pauperes benedictionem ejus petunt*; cf. the antiphon for St Thomas at Vespers in the Sarum Breviary, Procter and Wordsworth, eds, 1879–86, I, col. cclx: *robur Ecclesiae, plebis amor, cleri deliciae.*
126 *Mats* IV, 143; Abbott 1898, I, 21; Walberg 1929, 143; Vauchez, trans. Birrell 1997, 142 n. 2.
127 Boureau 1992.
128 Graboïs 1975; Boureau 1992.
129 *GC* II, 285; Mason 1984; Mason 1990, 281.
130 Rollason 1983; Binski 1990.
131 Borenius 1932, 10; Smalley 1973, 191–2; Foreville, ed., 1975; Foreville 1981; A. Duggan 1982, 24–9; Gameson 2002, 48–52.
132 Smalley 1973, 206–8; De Laborde 1911–27, I, pls 17, 141, IV, pls 678–9, 758; Caviness 1979, 50.
133 A. Duggan 1982, 36.
134 Smalley 1973, 194; *HA* II, 242.
135 Bony 1983, 153–66.
136 Thomson 1983; Bony 1983, 178–9; Wilson 1990, 94–6.
137 *GC* I, 7, 8; Greenhalgh 1989, 124–6; Brooks 1984, 37–59; also Brooks in Collinson, Ramsay and Sparks, eds, 1995, 33–7.
138 Fernie 1980, 1982, 31; Gem 1983, 1–7; Kahn 1991, 75–9; Heslop 2002, 156–7.
139 *GC* I, 13; Mortet 1911, 217, 226; Greenhalgh 1989, 142.
140 Brooks in Collinson, Ramsay and Sparks, eds, 1995, 3, 7–8; Gibson in Gibson, Heslop and Pfaff, eds, 1992, 137, 189, 212.
141 Grabar 1946, I, 580; Cheney 1951–2, 22–3; Bony 1983, 64; Colvin 1991, 115, 128; Kidson 1993, 988; Crook 2000, 135–60; Draper 2001.
142 Kemp 1948, 83; Nilgen 1980, 363; O'Reilly 1985, 221–2.
143 Shirley, trans., 1996, 14.
144 E.g. *Mats* II, 19, 299–300, 436, III, 145, 429–30, 479; Abbott 1898, I, 182; Roberts, ed., 1980, 57 section 5; Roberts 1992, 21, 82 (no. 82); Procter and Wordsworth, eds, 1879–86, I, cols ccliii, cclvi; O'Reilly 1985, 192–3.
145 Heslop 2002, 163.
146 Caviness 1977, 77; Caviness 1987; cf. Pfaff 1984.
147 Norton 2002, 11–16.
148 *GPA*, 137–8: *in marmorei pavimenti nitore*; for *nitens*, cf. Statius, *Silvae* IV/2, line 27, ed. and trans. Coleman 1988, 8–9; Norton 2002, 11; for onyx, Kahn 1991, 111, 195 n. 29, ill. 183; Greenhalgh 1989, 121.
149 *Mats* III, 147; Norton 2002, 15; Tatton-Brown 2002, 91–3.
150 Tatton-Brown 1981; Eames 1982; Tatton-Brown 1998a, 53–8; Norton 2002, 11–16.
151 Caviness 1974, 70; Norton 2002, 15.
152 Caviness 1973; Sauerländer 1985; Bony 1983, 36; Clark 1995, 1997; Grant 1998, 255, 261.
153 Panofsky, ed., 2/1979, 46–7.
154 Panofsky, ed., 2/1979, 64–5.

155 Panofsky, ed., 2/1979, 90–97.
156 Panofsky, ed., 2/1979, 169, 230–31 n. 90; Binski 2002.
157 Bloch 1982; Cowdrey 1983, 12–17; Greenhalgh 1989, 127–8, 135; Grant 1998, 33–5; Grant 2000, 50–51, 52; Schneider 2001, 6.
158 Greenhalgh 1989, 127, Pliny, *Historia naturalis*, XXXVI/14, trans. Eichholz 1962, 55; Curtius, trans. Trask, 1953, 167–82; Grant 2000, 51–2. For Gregory's Life, De Vogüé and Antin 1978–80, II, 170.
159 Greenhalgh 1989, 127; Binski 2002, 120.
160 *GPA*, 371–3; Greenhalgh 1989, 129.
161 L-B, no. 1399; Greenhalgh 1989, 129.
162 Mortet 1911, 38 and cf. also 66; Berland 1968.
163 Mortet 1911, 128; Greenhalgh 1989, 121–2.
164 Fernie 1995, 89; Gem 1987.
165 Kitzinger 1972; Caviness 1973; Kitzinger 1982; Bony 1986; Grant 1998, 255–60.
166 *GC* I, 293: *Magister Alanus ante paucos annos Beneventanae ecclesiae canonicus, sed natione Anglus*; Caviness 1977, 152; Bloch 1982; Bony 1986, 136 n. 19; Greenhalgh 1989, 51, 126; Draper 1997, 199–201; Draper 2001, 175.
167 Foreville 1958, 3 n. 4.
168 Caviness 1973.
169 Sauerländer 1985; Onians 1988, 74–90.
170 Draper 2001.
171 Kitzinger 1972, 99; Sauerländer 1982.
172 Curtius, trans. Trask 1953, 254–5.
173 Clanchy 1975, 676; Le Goff 2001.
174 Southern 1970; Thomson 1983; Coleman 1992; cf. Dodwell 1954, 98; Caviness 1977, 152.

CHAPTER 2

1 See among others Bony 1949; Webb 1956, 72–116; Bony 1983, 178–9, fig. 173, 334–5; Draper 1986b; Kidson 1986; Kidson 1994; Wilson 1990, 72–90, 160–78; Grant 1991.
2 Southern 1970, 159; cf. Thomson 1983.
3 Kidson 1986.
4 See for example Oakeshott 1972, 1981.
5 Thomson 1983, 4.
6 In general, Smalley 1973.
7 Baldwin 1982, 156–7; Thomson 1983.
8 Thomson 1983, 18–19.
9 Barrow 1989.
10 Baldwin 1982, 149–50; Smalley 3/1984, 368–9.
11 Baldwin 1982, 155.
12 Knowles 2/1963, 315–16, 662–77; Baldwin 1970, I, 175–204; Southern 1970; Smalley 1973; Murray 1978, 213–314; Thomson 1983; Smalley 3/1984, 244–5; Moore 1987.
13 Woods and Copeland 1999, 378–89.
14 Smalley 1973, 13; Moore 1987, 135–40.
15 Smalley 1975, 126; also Murray 1978; Moore 1987, 124–40, 128 n. 8.
16 Smalley 1973, 216–34.
17 Smalley 1973, 215.
18 *Mats* III, 527.
19 *GC* I, xxxiii–xxxvi; Smalley 1973, 221–8; Barlow 1986, 42, 78–9; *Fasti*, V (Chichester), 58.
20 Smalley 1973, 227–8.
21 Gervase of Chichester, BL Royal MS 3 B. X, fols 16 col. b–16v col. a; Smalley 1973, 224–6.
22 Wiesen 1964, 35, 59.
23 *Fasti*, V (Chichester), 3 for Seffrid II; Tatton-Brown 1994.
24 Webb 1956, pls 96–7.
25 On plasticity and classicism at Laon, Bony 1983, 145, 169–72; see also Woodman 1981, 109–15; Hoey 1986; Grant 1991, 118.
26 Hoey 1986, 52, pl. XXIb.
27 Rudolph 1990b, 278, line 13: *sumptuosas depolitiones.*
28 *Mats* III, 526–7; *Fasti*, V (Chichester), 8.
29 Fischer 1965, II, 566; Österlin 1995, 28–35.
30 Fischer 1965, II, 565–6; also I, 135.
31 Fischer 1965, II, 565–86; Liden 1981, 69–84.
32 Fischer 1965, II 567–8; Kidson 1993, 988; Hearn 1994, 39–40; Wilson, ed., 1983, 97.
33 Kidson 1986; Alexander 1995.
34 Fischer 1965, II, 569–70; in general, Grabar 1946.
35 Borenius 1932, 20–21, 38; A. Duggan 1982, 24–5; Österlin 1995, 32–5; Gameson 2002, 50.
36 Österlin 1995, 32–3.
37 A. Duggan 1982, 24; Duggan, ed. and trans., 2000, II, 1004 no. 233 and n. 4, 1368 (Appendix I). For aspects of Trondheim liturgy, see Iverson 2000.
38 Châtillon 1975; Fassler 1993, 256–7.
39 Vauchez, trans. Birrell 1997, 70 n. 29, 171.
40 Smalley 1973, 240.
41 Cheney 1967, 5.
42 E.g. *GW* IV, 75–81; Moorman 1945, 294–307; Knowles 2/1963, 313.
43 Knowles 2/1963, 322–30.
44 Smalley 1973, 216–17.
45 *GC* I, xvi–xix; 36; Knowles 2/1963, 318.
46 *GC* I, 332.
47 *GC* I, 337–8.
48 *GC* I, 338–42; also *MV* I, 122; Cheney 1967, 137; Smalley 1973, 216–17; great emphasis is placed on this by Kidson 1993, 972–81, but cf. Hoey 1995a.
49 Knowles 2/1963, 316–26; Gibson in Collinson, Ramsay and Sparks, eds, 1995, 66–7.
50 Kidson 1993, 972–3.
51 *GC* I, 483–4; Gibson in Collinson, Ramsay and Sparks, eds, 1995, 67; Tatton-Brown 2000, 19–20; Tatton-Brown 2001.
52 *GC* II, 407–10; Cheney 1967, 38, 135–57; Tatton-Brown 2000, 22.
53 Cheney 1967, 41, 154–5.
54 Cheney 1967, 137–8.
55 *GC* II, 412; Cheney 1989; Davidson Cragoe 2001.
56 Cheney 1956, 27.
57 Cheney 1967, 16–19, 88–114; Clanchy 1979, 48–53, 122–3.
58 Cheney 1967, 4–5, 106; *GC* II, 411–12.
59 Cheney 1967, 58, 85, 117, 181; Clanchy 1979, 180; Moore 1987, 137.
60 Cheney 1967, 51–2, also 182–3.
61 Cheney 1967, 64–8; *GC* II, 410.
62 Cheney 1967, 66; for the canons, *C&S* I, 1053–74, no. 182.

63 Cheney 1967, 66–7, 121.
64 Cheney 1967, 68; *C&S* II, 23–36.
65 Cheney 1967, 76–7, 97–8, 124.
66 Tatton-Brown 2000, 23; Tatton-Brown 2001, 209.
67 Cheney 1967, 39–48.
68 Cheney 1967, 115–34; 140; Tatton-Brown 2000, 20; Tatton-Brown 2001, 209.
69 *GC* I, 552–4.
70 Caviness 1977, figs 19, 21, also figs 186, 195, 207 and appendix figs 1–2.
71 Dodwell 1954, 98–9, 102; Morgan 1982, no. 1; Henderson 1999, pl. 34; in general Gibson, Heslop and Pfaff, eds, 1992.
72 Caviness 1977, 78–9, figs 161–2; as at San Clemente, Demus, trans. Whittall 1970, 299–300, figs 48–9.
73 *EpC*, 499; *GC* II, 410–14; Caviness 1974, 69 and n. 6.
74 Cheney 1967, 135–6; *GC* II, 93, 410.
75 Phillips 1949, 26–7; Reeve 2003.
76 Cheney 1967, 160–61; Stratford, Tudor-Craig and Muthesius 1982; Wilson 1995, 456 n. 14.
77 Caviness 1974, 70; Caviness 1977, 87–8 and appendix fig. 2c.
78 Ellis 1986, 67 no. M631, pl. 13.
79 Heslop 1982, 98, pl. XXIXc.
80 Panofsky 1960, 59, 60, fig. 24; Stratford, Tudor-Craig and Muthesius 1982, 71–80 and figs 1A–B; Wilson 1995, 454–8. Dr Lindy Grant has suggested to me that the Lisieux tomb commemorates not Arnulf de Lisieux (d. 1181) but Ralph de Warneville, Chancellor of England (d. 1191).
81 Stratford, Tudor-Craig and Muthesius 1982, 87–93, but cf. Henig 1983, 56; for Hubert Walter's legacies to Christ Church, Cheney 1967, 174–7; *GC* II, 413–14.
82 *GC* II, 410–11: *Adeo dapsilis erat archiepiscopus, liberalis et largus in hospitum et pauperum refectione*; Cheney 1967, 178–9.
83 Cheney 1967, 178.
84 Cheney 1967, 179.
85 *GC* II, 410–11: *in aedificiis magnis et honestis constructione mirabilis.*
86 *GC* II, 412; Tatton-Brown 1982; Rady, Tatton-Brown and Bowen 1991, 6–10.
87 *AM* III, 58: *quale visum non credimus a tempore Salamonis.*
88 Liebermann, ed., 1879, 329 (also L-B, no. 864): *in palacio estimabili* [. . .] *quod consumavit archiepiscopus.*
89 *GA* I, 314.
90 Krautheimer 1980, 203–6.
91 Birch 1887, 159 no. 1187; D'Esneval 1975.
92 O'Reilly 1985.
93 *Mats* III, 17.
94 Jaeger 1994, 298.
95 Henig 1983, 58–9; Nilgen 1986, 146, pl. xlib.
96 *Mats* III, 176; Jaeger 1994, 299.
97 *Mats* III, 176.
98 Jaeger 1994, 297–308.
99 Jaeger 1994, 301–7; *Mats* III, 226–38.
100 *GW* IV, 39–40; Gerald of Wales, trans. Loomis 1985, xxii.
101 *Mats* III, 218–19.
102 *Mats* III, 226–32.
103 *Mats* III, 230.
104 *Mats* III, 226.
105 Jaeger 1994, 306.
106 Jaeger 1994, 306–8.
107 Henry of Avranches, eds Russell and Heironimus 1935, 75–8, 76 lines 190–98; Townsend and Rigg 1987, 360 no. 2.
108 Jaeger 1994, 297; *Mats* III, 156.
109 Smalley 1973, 15; Moore 1987, 128 n. 8.
110 Cf. Crossley 2001.
111 Pantin in Callus, ed., 1955, 204–5; Gieben 1967; Oschinsky 1971, 192–3, 399–409; Southern 1986, 318–19.
112 CCR 1242–7, 23: *cum finestris et verinis ad modum aule Cant'.*
113 Tuve 1963, 268–70, 276–88; for the tradition see Colish 1985, I, 85–7, 126–52; for access to Seneca, Reynolds 1965, 104–24.
114 Wiesen 1964, 32–3; Colish 1985, I, 223–4.
115 Onians 1988, 112–13.
116 Panofsky, ed., 2/1979; cf. Rudolph 1990a and b.
117 Wilson 1991, 191.
118 Fassler 1993, 137–8.
119 Fassler 1993, 211; cf. Trachtenberg 2000.
120 Fassler 1993, 213–14.
121 Fassler 1993, 248–9.
122 As in Fassler 1993, 215 and n. 24, after Esmeijer 1978, 56.
123 Norton and Park, eds, 1986, 332, 340.
124 Bernard of Clairvaux, *Apologia*, XII 28, in Rudolph 1990b, 278; cf. Aelred of Rievaulx in *PL* 195, col. 572.
125 Rudolph 1990b, 80.
126 *PL* 182, cols 812–13: *Honorificabitis autem non cultu vestium, non equorum fastu, non amplis aedificiis*; Mortet 1913, 107–9; Vauchez, trans. Birrell 1997, 287–8.
127 Holdsworth 1986, 43, 55.
128 *PL* 176, col. 1019; Mortet 1913, 109–16; De Clercq 1963; Viller, Cavallera and De Guibert, 1969, cols 880–86; Baldwin 1970, I, 67; Carruthers 1990, 239–42; Rudolph 1990b, 85, 94–5 and n. 286.
129 *PL* 176, cols 1019–20: *Episcopi domos non impares ecclesiis magnitudine construunt, pictos delectantur habere thalamos* [. . .]. *Ornant praetoria columnis, fores domibus anteponunt.*
130 *PL* 176, col. 1053; Mortet 1913, 112–14: *Ut aedificatio fratris* [. . .] *sit modesta; Aedificia fratrum non superflua sint, sed humilia; non voluptuosa, sed honesta. Utilis est lapis in structura, sed quid prodest in lapide caelatura*? Cf. Gervase of Chichester in n. 21 above.
131 *PL* 176, col. 1089: *Quod politur, aequale efficitur*; cf. Rudolph 1990b, 122–3; for Bernard's *sumptuosas depolitiones*, Rudolph 1990b, 278, line 13.
132 *PL* 205, cols 255–9; Mortet 1913, 116; Baldwin 1970, I, 3–16, 67–8 and for the textual tradition, II, 246–65.
133 Reynolds 1965, 118.
134 Wiesen 1964, 20–21.
135 *PL* 205, cols 256–7; Rudolph 1990b, 95–7.
136 Wiesen 1964, 97.
137 *PL* 205, cols 257–8; Wiesen 1964, 35.
138 Baldwin 1970, I, 68 and n. 31.
139 Caesarius of Heisterbach, trans. Von Scott and Swinton Bland 1929, 119–20; Baldwin 1970, I, 65–6; Rudolph 1990b, 96–7.

140 Baldwin 1970, I, 69–72; Smalley 1973, 226 and n. 21 above.
141 *PL* 205, 253; Talbot 1986, 63.
142 Talbot 1986, 63, n. 31.
143 *DNR*; Mortet 1913, 119; Hunt and Gibson 1984.
144 *DNR*, x, 503; Baldwin 1970, I, 77; Hunt and Gibson 1984, 1–18.
145 *DNR*, 503; Baldwin 1970, I, 77; Hunt and Gibson 1984, 4–7.
146 *DNR*, 240–48.
147 *DNR*, 281–3.
148 *DNR*, 351.
149 *O curiositas! O vanitas! O vana curiositas! O curiosa vanitas!* Cf. Bernard of Clairvaux, *Apologia*, XII: 28: *O vanitas vanitatum, sed non vanior quam insanior*! or *mira quidam deformis formositas ac formosa deformitas*!; also Rudolph 1990b, 280, lines 24–5, 282, line 15.
150 Clanchy 1975, 678; Baldwin 1970, I, 82; Smalley 1975, 126.
151 Clanchy 1975, 677–8; for Peter of Blois and Seneca, Reynolds 1965, 118, 120.
152 *DNR*, 193–4; for webs and subtlety see also *GPA*, 288.
153 Clanchy 1975, 679.
154 Hunt and Gibson 1984, 10.
155 Hunt and Gibson 1984, 10.
156 Hunt and Gibson 1984, 7.
157 *DNR*, xiii–xiv; Hunt and Gibson 1984, 118–24.
158 Morgan 1982, no. 84, ills 280–81; Hunt and Gibson 1984, 118–19.
159 Hunt and Gibson 1984, 134–6 at 135; Thomson 1982, 93–4 no. 24.
160 *GA* I; Vaughan 1958, 86–7, 182–9; Paris, ed. and trans. Vaughan 1984; also Gransden 1974, 372–7.
161 *GA* I, 217–53; Vaughan 1958, 185.
162 Knowles 2/1963, 502–3; Thomson 1982, 63–9, 70.
163 *GA* I, 232; Paris, ed. and trans. Vaughan 1984, 24.
164 Carruthers 1990, 18–19.
165 Carruthers 1990, 35; *GC* I, 227 refers to Becket's *cella memorialis*.
166 *GA* I, 217; Paris, ed. and trans. Vaughan 1984, 14.
167 *GA* I, 218–20; Paris, ed. and trans. Vaughan 1984, 14–16.
168 Binski 1992; Hoey 2001, 184.
169 *CM* III, 391.
170 *GA* I, 219; Pairs, ed. and trans. Vaughan 1984, 15.
171 *GA* I, 251–3.
172 Moorman 1945, 294–307; Knowles 2/1963, 303–4, 310–11; Gransden 1974, 375–6.
173 *GA* I, 221–4; Paris, ed. and trans. Vaughan 1984, 16–18.
174 Muratova 1986.
175 Harrison 2001, 178; Hoey 2001, 184–90.
176 Ovid, ed. and trans. Hill 1992, 112–13, line 215.
177 *GC* I, 20: *In solum magistrum vel Dei vindicta, vel diaboli desaevit invidia*. Cf. Peter the Chanter in *PL* 205, col. 258: *Non assimileris arte Daedalo in aedificando domo, non gigantibus altitudine*.
178 *GA* I, 366–8.
179 *CM* IV: 279–80; Thomson 1977.
180 *GA* I, 314.

CHAPTER 3

1 Hoey 2001, 184, 189–90.
2 The source for the date 1192, seldom given, is an Irish chronicle continued to 1274 which contains a number of references to Lincoln: Smith, ed., 1842, 11: *Jacitur fundamentum ecclesie Lincolniae*. However, the dates in the chronicle are of variable accuracy, often within two years: the *terremotus* of 1185 is dated to 1184, the consecration of Hugh as bishop to 1185, the death of Hugh to 1199. By these criteria the date for the laying of the foundations might be *c*. 1193–4; see Dimock 1867, 197, and Owen, ed., 1994, 120–21 'the work of rebuilding seems to have been begun about 1193/4'.
3 Kidson 1986, 1994, 26–33; Foot, Litton and Simpson 1986, 56–7; Stocker 1987; Baily 1991; Alexander 1995.
4 Baily 1991, 29–33; Alexander 1995.
5 Kidson 1986, 1994, 26–33; Wilson 1990, 160–65; Baily 1991.
6 *MV* I, vii–xliv; Farmer 1985a; Mayr-Harting, ed., 1987.
7 Cheney 1967, 97–8; Farmer 1985a; Leyser 1987.
8 *MV* for Aelfric, Ridyard 1988, 54.
9 *MV* II, 189.
10 *MV* II, 140–41; cf. Duggan 1989; Kessler 1989; Chazelle 1990.
11 *MV* II, 99; Gerald of Wales, trans. Loomis 1985, 29–31; Heslop 2000, 71.
12 Gerald of Wales, trans. Loomis 1985, xlv; *MLH*.
13 *GW* VII, xi–xii, 3–80, esp. 39–42.
14 *GW* VII, 43–80.
15 *GW* VII, 4, 6–7, 80; for the lamp image, see also Crook 2000, 34.
16 *GW* VII, 28–9, 30–31.
17 Scott and Martin, eds, 1978, 243.
18 *GW* VII, 40–41.
19 *GW* VII, xii–xiii, 83–147; Gerald of Wales, trans. Loomis 1985.
20 *MV* I, xxviii n. 2; Gerald of Wales, trans. Loomis 1985, xiii, 18–19.
21 Gerald of Wales, trans. Loomis 1985, 115–16.
22 *MV* I, 110.
23 Gerald of Wales, trans. Loomis 1985, xiii; Heslop 1998, 132–5; Gardner 2000, 76–7.
24 Greenhalgh 1989, 130–31; Crook 2000, 77–8.
25 Clanchy 1975, 678.
26 Sanford 1945; Baldwin 1970, I, 41–3; Gerald of Wales, trans. Hagen 1979.
27 *MLH*.
28 Henry of Avranches, ed. Russell and Heironimus 1935, 5, 79–80 no. 95; Townsend and Rigg 1987; Binkley 1990; *MLH*.
29 Gerald of Wales, trans. Loomis 1985, xliv.
30 See the remarks on *Toposforschung* in D'Avray 1985, 243–4; also Heslop 2000, 60–61. Contrast Wilson 1990, 10.
31 *MLH*, 8–9; for other heroic imagery, Henry of Avranches, ed. Russell and Heironimus 1935, 108 no. 19; Henderson 1985, 87–8.
32 *MLH*, 12–13.

33 *MLH*, 18–21.
34 *MLH*, 46–7.
35 *MLH*, 52–61.
36 Heslop 2000, 63.
37 Farmer 1955–6, 88, 94, 97–8 no. ii.
38 Heslop 2000, 65.
39 Heslop 2000, 66.
40 E.g. *HA* II, 242: *artificio materiam superante*; Branner 1965, 57–8; Heslop 2000, 65–6.
41 Heslop 2000, 64–5; for Brieger 1957, 27 the motif is 'Greek in spirit'.
42 Statius, *Silvae*, IV/2, ed. and trans. Coleman 1988.
43 Heslop 2000, 64.
44 Dronke 1972, 54–5.
45 Master Gregorius, trans. Osborne 1987, 4, 29–30; Chibnall, ed., 1956, 78–80, 90–4.
46 *MLH*, 60–61.
47 *MLH*, 56–61; Heslop 2000, 64; also Rudolph 1990b, 60 n. 171.
48 *MLH*, 56–7, cf. Gerald of Wales, trans. Loomis 1985, 93.
49 Deshman 1986, 268, 272.
50 *PL* 159, cols 995–1004; Kauffmann 1975, no. 102, though making no mention of this figure; Corti 1979, 342–4; Gwynn 1992, 125–9; Constable 1995, 261–2; for variations of opinion on the relationship of MS Ff. 1. 27 to Cambridge, Corpus Christi College MS 66, see Meehan 1994, 442–6, Norton 1998.
51 Gwynn 1992, 123–4.
52 Gwynn 1992, 125–9.
53 Constable 1995, 251–341.
54 Norton 1998, 79, 94–5, 103–4.
55 Norton 1998, 79–80, 98, pls 18, 24.
56 *PL* 159, col. 997; the idea is also found in Rupert of Deutz (d. 1129), *Epistola ad Liezelinum canonicum*, in *PL* 170, cols 636–8; Smalley 1985, 52.
57 For Normandy, Grant 1991, 120.
58 Wilson 1991, 189 n. 37; D. H. Heslop 1995, fig. 27.
59 Nordström 1955, 253–72; it is difficult to improve on the riposte to Nordström by Kidson 1994, 31; Baily 1991, 8–10.
60 Carruthers 1998.
61 Panofsky 1951, 27–48.
62 Carruthers 1990, 43.
63 Hugh of Saint-Victor, ed. and trans. Taylor repr. 1991, 135, 138, 140–42.
64 Hugh of Saint-Victor, ed. and trans. Taylor repr. 1991, 138–9.
65 Smalley 3/1984, 95–6; Carruthers 1990, 43–5; Zinn 1992; Fassler 1993, 211–40; Sicard 1993.
66 Smalley 3/1984, 95–7, 107; Carruthers 1990, 231–9; Zinn 1992; Fassler 1993, 227–40.
67 Cahn 1994.
68 Norton 1998, 103–4.
69 Fassler 1993, 236.
70 Bynum 1982, 36–43, 99.
71 De Clercq 1963; Carruthers 1990, 239–42.
72 *PL* 176, col. 1121.
73 *PL* 176, cols 1121–2.
74 Carruthers 1990, 242; Carruthers 1998.
75 For Honorius, *PL* 172, col. 586; also Mortet and Deschamps 1929, 14–18 (Honorius) and 183–8 (Peter of Roissy); Kennedy 1943, 7, 21–2; Falletti 1953, col. 1057; Durandus, eds Davril and Thibodeau 1995–8, I, 11–28.
76 Heslop 2000, 71.
77 *MV* I, xxviii; Gerald of Wales, trans. Loomis 1985, xv; Heslop 2000, 69–70.
78 Baldwin 1982, 155.
79 Goering 1992.
80 Scammell 1956, 69–70; *MV* I, xxviii–xxxiii; Kuttner and Rathbone 1949–51, 326–7; Emden 1959, 1704; Owen 1994, 126–7; also Heslop 2000, 69–71.
81 Smalley 3/1984, 186–96.
82 Sanford 1945.
83 Rudolph 1990b, 32–4.
84 Brieger 1957, 3.
85 Brieger 1957, 2.
86 Powicke 1928, 154.
87 Powicke 1928, 75–101, 129–61; Vincent 1996, 165, 195.
88 *VRS* II, 14; *AM* III, 58; Powicke 1928, 144; Eales 1993.
89 Cocke and Kidson 1993, 43.
90 Jansen 1985; Draper in *AoC*, 83–91; Draper 1996, Jansen 1996.
91 Powicke 1928, 31, 48, but cf. Powicke 1933, 554.
92 Powicke 1928, 34–8 and in general 23–74; Baldwin 1970, I, 25–9; Smalley 3/1984, 196–263; De Hamel 1984; De Hamel 1986, 116–17.
93 Gibbs and Lang 1934, 25–7, 116–17; Cheney 1960, 16–17; Cheney 1968, 51–89; *C&S* II, 57–96; Baldwin 1970, I, 31, 54.
94 Procter and Wordsworth, eds, 1879–86; Frere, ed., 1894; Frere, ed., 1898–1901; Wordsworth 1901; Wordsworth and Macleane 1915; Legg, ed., 1916; Morgan 2001; also VCH Wiltshire III, 159–69, VI, 51–79; Cocke and Kidson 1993, 3–4, 37–62.
95 *VRS* II, 2; also *CDS*, 266–70, and *VRS* II, cii–cvi; Cocke and Kidson 1993, 3, 37, 40.
96 *VRS* II, 3; Cocke and Kidson 1993, 3; Tatton-Brown 2000, 23.
97 *VRS* II, lxxx 3; VCH Wiltshire III, 165; Cheney 1967, 32, 39–48; cf. Tatton-Brown 2001, 209 n. 40.
98 Bliss, ed., 1893, 46; *VRS* II, 5–6.
99 Bliss, ed., 1893, 53; *VRS* II, 7–9.
100 *VRS* II, 12–13; Blair 1975; Tatton-Brown 1998b.
101 *VRS* II, 37–40.
102 *VRS* II, 55; Stroud 1983.
103 Blum 1991, 14–15; Cocke and Kidson 1993, 4, 42–3.
104 Henry of Avranches, eds Russell and Heironimus 1935, 6–11 and 110–16 no. 20; Malden 1898–9; Torrance 1959; *CM* III, 190, 391: *Rex largitur opes, fert praesul opem, lapicidae/ Dant operam, tribus his est opus, ut stet opus.* The citations occur in reference to the consecration of Roger Bingham (1229) and the death of Richard Poore (1237); Townsend and Rigg 1987, 370 no. 20, 386–7, 389–90 are cautious on the point of attribution; for the version in BL Cotton MS Vespasian D.v., fols 159–62, see Binkley 1990, 237–8 no. 19, and for attribution, 248–54.
105 Binkley 1990, 237–8, see *VRS* II, 11–12.
106 As in Torrance 1959.

107 *VRS* II, ciii, cv–cvi; *CDS*, 267.
108 Southern 1970, 105–32, at 107, 122.
109 *PL* 207, cols 326–7; noted VCH Wiltshire III, 165.
110 Bliss, ed., 1893, 46, 53; VCH Wiltshire III, 164.
111 Foreville 1958, 10, 90, 94–5; Henry of Avranches, eds Russell and Heironimus 1935, 77 line 252.
112 VCH Wiltshire III, 156–69, VI, 51–79; Draper in *AoC*, 83–91; Draper 1996.
113 Cocke and Kidson 1993, 62, 88–9.
114 Whittingham 2/1979; Brown 1999, 175 and figs 137–8.
115 *VRS* I, xxxii; Cocke and Kidson 1993, 5–6, pl. 11.
116 Cocke and Kidson 1993, 43, 88.
117 Stalley 1971, 71–81; Wilson 1990, 174–7; Cocke and Kidson 1993, 50–62, 82–91; Draper 1996, 21, 27.
118 Jansen 1985, 97; Cocke and Kidson 1993, 75; Draper 1996, 22–3, 24; Jansen 1996, 33.
119 Wilson 1990, 174; Cocke and Kidson 1993, 88; Draper 1996, 21, 23.
120 Cocke and Kidson 1993, 83; Gransden 1982, 25–8; Rodwell 2001, I, 128–31.
121 Cocke and Kidson 1993, 43–6, 82–91; Jansen 1996; Draper 1996, 21.
122 Wilson 1990, 174; for 'modernity', Trachtenberg 2000.
123 Smalley 1975, 114.
124 Jansen 1985, 98–9.
125 Jansen 1985, 98–9.
126 Jansen 1996, 36; also 1985, 98–9.
127 Draper 1996, 29–30.
128 Draper 1996, 29.
129 Panofsky 1951, 1, 36.
130 Pickering 1970, 7–12 at 9 is useful on this style of reasoning. Cf. also the direct and almost immediate critique of Panofsky's use of analogy by Schapiro 1953, at 305–6.
131 *Mats* II, 435: *non decet orationis domum [. . .] turrem facere.*
132 Cocke and Kidson 1993, 7.
133 Evans 1982, 20.
134 Ayers, ed., 2000, 81.
135 Jansen 1985, 96.
136 Brown 1999, 161–6 and figs 125–7; cf. Binski 2003.
137 Ayers, ed., 2000; Brown 1999, 175–8, col. pl. 1, figs 139–41.
138 Webber 1992, 116–23.
139 *PL* 207, cols 326–8; Southern 1970, 124; Cahn 1994.
140 Powicke 1928, 15, 56–62; Powicke 1933, 554: 'The traditional view, which I accepted, that he was the pupil of Peter the Chanter must be surrendered, and, indeed, the tone of Langton's references to the Chanter in his commentary of the Epistles of St Paul makes it improbable that the Chanter was his master' (following Lacombe 1930, 107); cf. Jansen 1985, 99. For alternative opinions, see Veal 1955 and Quinto 1994, 12–13.
141 Powicke 1928, 29–30, 49–74; Lacombe and Smalley 1930, 8; Veal 1955; Baldwin 1970, I, 18, 20, 25–31; Smalley 1973, 204; Smalley 3/1984, 197.
142 Powicke 1928, 15–17, for usury, 25 n. 2, 88–9; Baldwin 1970, I, 85–6, 296–311.
143 Kennedy 1944, 135–8.
144 Powicke 1928, 49–74, 177–204; Lacombe 1929; Lacombe and Landgraf 1929; Lacombe 1930; Smalley 1933, 128. See also Quinto 1994.
145 Cf. Jansen 1996, 35–6.
146 *CM* III, 391.
147 *VRS* II, cv–cvi: *In dominio suo proprio.*
148 Toulmin Smith, ed., 1907, 263; Cocke and Kidson 1993, 61.
149 *C&S* II, 201; Draper 1996.
150 VCH Wiltshire III, 163.
151 *VRS* II, 11–12; Cocke and Kidson 1993, 50, 52; Kemp, ed., 2000, no. 356.
152 Cocke and Kidson 1993, 46.
153 McGlashan and Sandell 1974, 86; VCH Wiltshire VII, 211–12.
154 Dean 1986, 94–5; also Hoey 1995b, 67–8 for Canterbury.
155 VCH Wiltshire III, 156.
156 *C&S* II, 552–3 no. 2.
157 Wilson 1990, 9: 'the functions and architectural forms of the Gothic great churches showed remarkably little interaction'; Cocke and Kidson 1993, 6.
158 Klukas 1981; cf. Morgan 2001.
159 Morgan 2001, 183.
160 Toulmin Smith, ed., 1907, 266 following Leland: *Helias de Derham Canon' Sarum qui a prima fundacione Rector fuit novae fabricae Eccl. Sarum 25 annis.*
161 See principally Major 1933, 542–5; A. H. Thompson 1941–2; Colvin, ed., 1963, I, 99–101; Hastings 1997; Cocke and Kidson 1993, 51–2; Vincent 2002a.
162 *VRS* II, 70; Hastings 1997, 12; Vincent 2002a, 145, 147.
163 Vincent 2002a, 140–44.
164 *HA* II, 241–2; Hastings 1997, 11; Vincent 2002a, 142–3, 151–2, 153.
165 Hastings 1997, 8, 10, 17–18; Holt 1964, 86–7; Vincent 2002a, 141.
166 *CM* IV, 418.
167 *CDS*, 203; Vincent 2002a, 144–6, 155–8.
168 Hastings 1997, 12–13.
169 CLR 1226–40, 219; Colvin 1963, I, 93, II, 858–9, 861.
170 *VRS* II, cxxv, 21; Dayman and Jones 1883, 13–17.
171 *CDS*, 203–5; Wordsworth 1917, 440–41; Hastings 1997, 12; Vincent 2002a, 145; cf. Jansen 1996, 36.
172 Hastings 1997, 11–12; Ayers, ed., 2000, 79.
173 Jansen 1985, 98 n. 12; Tatton-Brown 2000, 29–32; Vincent 2002a, 158.
174 Major 1933.
175 Hastings 1997, 16–17; Vincent 2002a, 148–51.
176 Lawrence 1960, 141–2; Lawrence, ed., 1996, 59–60; Vincent 2002a, 151.
177 Vincent 2002a, 156–8, at 157.
178 Jansen 1985, 95; Jansen 1996, 33–4.
179 Colvin, ed., 1963, I, 94.
180 *CDS*, 203–5; Wordsworth 1917, 440–42; VCH Wiltshire VI, 76; Hastings 1997, 12, 25; Vincent 2002a, 145.
181 Dixon-Smith 1999.
182 Murray 1978, 319–20.
183 Green 1968, 151, 153–4, pls 50a, b; Binski 1986, 33–45.
184 Binski 1986, 35.
185 Aristotle, *Ethics*, Book 2: 1106b9–1109b15–26; 3:

1117b28–1119a20, trans. Thomson et al., rev. 1976, 101–10, 135–9; Callus, ed., 1955, 62–5; Lawrence 1960, 110–24; Gauthier 1975; Southern 1986, 287–9.

186 Torrance 1959, 246, line 201: *Delicias dulces facit experiencia pene conditurque bonum cognitione mali.*

187 Ward 1903, 53–4; cf. Aristotle, *Ethics*, Book 4: 1119b22–1123a11, trans. Thomson et al., rev. 1976, 142–52; Cicero, *De Officiis*, Book 2: XVIII, esp. sec. 64, trans. Miller 1913, 233–9; Lawrence 1960, 47–9, 188, 191; Lawrence, ed., 1996, 17, 39; Hastings 1997, 14.

188 Blum 1991, 15; Cocke and Kidson 1993, 43; Draper 1996, 23.

189 Binski 1995a, 11.

190 Binski 1995a, 33–51.

191 Binski 1986, 33–45; Dixon-Smith 1999.

192 Murray 1989, 161 no. 11: *in choro recens extructo mirae altitudinis et amplitudinis.*

193 Vincent 2002a, 156.

CHAPTER 4

1 *CM* V, 192.

2 *CM* IV, 378, V, 195.

3 *CM* V, 195; *HA* III, 318; Vaughan 1958, 5.

4 *HA* III, 318.

5 *HA* III, 318.

6 Spurrell 2000.

7 Vauchez, trans. Birrell 1997, 158–83.

8 Ridyard 1988, 3.

9 Rollason 1983; Ridyard 1988; Hayward 1993.

10 Elkins 1988; Thompson 1991; Bolton 1999; Wogan-Browne 2001.

11 Ward 1982, 82–8, 106–8; Blair 1987, 1990; Wogan-Browne 2001.

12 Grundmann 1935; Bynum 1982, 14; Bynum 1987; Elkins 1988; Rubin 1991, 164–76; Dor, Johnson and Wogan-Browne, eds, 1999, 2–17.

13 Dobson 1976, 1–3.

14 Bynum 1982, 14–16, 170–262; Elkins 1988, 162; Tanner, ed., 1990, 242; Vauchez, trans. Birrell 1997, 369–86; Bolton 1999.

15 Finucane 1974; Ward 1982, 76–82, 106–8.

16 For saints' relics, see Thomas 1974, also Rollason 1978; for parishioners, Cheney 1967, 2.

17 Ridyard 1988, 176–52.

18 Lawrence 1960, 88, 276; Lawrence, ed., 1996, 160; for an earlier instance, Crook 2000, 187–8.

19 Nilson 1998, 9.

20 Binski 1995a, 10, 53, 55–6.

21 Rollason 1978.

22 Cheney 1961a, 135–47, 138 no. 5 for London.

23 Russell 1929; Geertz 1966, 2; Rollason 1983, 22.

24 Elkins 1988, 125–44; Vauchez, trans. Birrell 1997, 40, 41 n. 38.

25 Kemp 1948; Ridyard 1986; Whatley, ed., 1989, 41–5; Vauchez, trans. Birrell 1997.

26 Kemp 1948, 82–106; Vauchez, trans. Birrell 1997, 22–32.

27 Darlington, ed., 1928, xlvii–xlviii; Vauchez, trans. Birrell 1997, 39.

28 Vauchez, trans. Birrell 1997, 27–8.

29 Vauchez, trans. Birrell 1997, 29.

30 Vauchez, trans. Birrell 1997, 32; see Nilson 1998 and Crook 2000.

31 Vauchez, trans. Birrell 1997, 61, 64–7.

32 Morgan 2001.

33 Kemp 1948, 82–124; Vauchez, trans. Birrell 1997, 33–57.

34 Vauchez, trans. Birrell 1997, 36.

35 Tanner, ed., 1990, 263.

36 Kemp 1948, 104; Lawrence 1960, 11–14; Elkins 1988, 126–30; Vauchez, trans. Birrell 1997, 38–40.

37 Lawrence 1960, 7–30, 17; Bynum 1982, 16–17; Whatley 1989, 45–56; Vauchez, trans. Birrell 1997, 54.

38 Moore 1987, 134–5.

39 Gardner 1990, 213.

40 Jaeger 1994, 189–90.

41 Lawrence 1960, 68; Vauchez, trans. Birrell 1997, 179.

42 Crook 2000, 218–33; Draper 1979; Draper 1986a.

43 Blake, ed., 1962, 237–41; Ridyard 1988, 200.

44 Vauchez, trans. Birrell 1997, 176, 180.

45 Vauchez, trans. Birrell 1997, 177.

46 Ridyard 1988, 50–61, 176–210; Blake, ed., 1962, 6–62.

47 Bede, ed. Colgrave and Minors 1969, 390–93; Ridyard 1988, 53–61, 82–92.

48 Blake, ed., 1962, 78–9, 120–23, 145, 230–31; Elkins 1988; Ridyard 1988, 177–8; Wogan-Browne 2001.

49 Crook 2000, 169.

50 Miller 1951; Ridyard 1988, 186–92.

51 Blake, ed., 1962, 33; Vaughan 1958, 198–204.

52 Ridyard 1986; Ridyard 1988, 206–10; Blake, ed., 1962, 263–76.

53 Blake, ed., 1962, 264.

54 *AS* I, 644: *illa tamen pulchra et magna fabrica eminens supra sanctarum virginum sepulcra, protegente Deo et meritis suae deliciae virginis Etheldredae, ut speratur, ab omni laesione salvata est et fractura.*

55 Draper 1979, 10, 11 n. 16, 18 n. 60 cf. Grabar 1946; Cheney 1951–2; cf. however Nilson 1998, 15–20, 63–91.

56 Blake, ed., 1962, 289–90.

57 Draper 1979, 26–7.

58 Draper 1979, 14–15.

59 Draper 1979, 13–15; cf. Roberts 1988, 82–4.

60 Farmer 1955–6, 90–93.

61 Sparke 1723, 119, 121; Ridyard 1988, 60, 242–3; Binski 2003, 45–6.

62 *GA* I, 253–305, esp. 279–93; Vaughan 1958, 198–204; Binski 1992.

63 Blake, ed., 1962, 274; Ridyard 1988, 208.

64 *CM* V, 454–5; also *AS* I, 635–6. For Hugh's disputed election as abbot of Bury in 1215 see Thomson, ed. and trans., 1974, xxv–xlvii, 193–5; Draper 1979, 26–7; Maddison 2000, 58.

65 Gibbs and Lang 1934, 1–10; Vincent 1996, 165–7.

66 *CM* V, 454–5.

67 Thomson, ed. and trans., 1974, xxv–xlvii; Maddison 2000, 47.

68 Hoey 1986.

69 Sauerländer, trans. Sondheimer 1972, pl. 136; Nicolai 2002, 118–21, figs 4, 13.

70 Deuchler and Hoffmann 1970, I, 96 no. 102; Lasko 1972, 223–5; 245; Kidson 1986, 41.
71 Caviness 1977, fig. 75.
72 Ladner 1961b; Zarnecki 1988, 93–6; Heslop 1994, 39; Heslop 2000, 73.
73 Fernie 1984; Wilson 1991, 184 n. 15.
74 Fischer 1965, I, 164–7, 171, II, 228–9, 571.
75 For the Ely spring, see Blake, ed., 1962, 48, 365–8; see also Hayward 1993, 86; Maddison 2000, 66.
76 Caviness 1977, 118, 126, 131–2, 137–8, 174, fig. 137; Morgan 1983, 28–30.
77 Heslop 2000, 73.
78 Bynum 1995, 169; Guest, commentary, 1995, 91, fol. 32v.
79 Heslop 2000, 73; Heslop 2001, 300–01.
80 Heslop 2000, 72; also O'Reilly 1987; cf. Branner 1977, fig. 121.
81 *GW* VII, 4, 31; *MV* II, 174; *MLH*, 10–11; Heslop 2000, 72–3.
82 Draper 1979, 10.
83 Blake, ed., 1962, 29–30.
84 Maddison 2000, 50.
85 Geertz 1966, 5.
86 Ridyard 1988, 82–92; Deshman 1995, 121–4, 184–5; cf. Aldhelm, *De Virginitate*, trans. Lapidge and Herren 1979, 87–8, 127, 131 (caps. 28–9, 57, 60); Wogan-Browne 2001.
87 Draper 1979, 14.
88 Duffy 1990.
89 Blake, ed., 1962, 49; Bede, ed. Colgrave and Minors 1969, 390–401 at 398–9; Deshman 1995, 121–4.
90 Lindley 1986, 77, 81; Vauchez, trans. Birrell 1997, 179.
91 Heslop 1994.
92 Heslop 1981; Zarnecki et al. 1984, 78, 361 no. 360; Zarnecki 1988, 77; Heslop 2000, 72.
93 Heslop 1994.
94 Marquet de Vasselot 1941, no. 94, cf. also no. 78, 108–9; Deuchler and Hoffmann 1970, I, 83 no. 91; also Taralon 1966, 261 fig. 1, 283 fig. 32.
95 *GPA*, 384–5.
96 Mason 1984.
97 Ridyard 1986, 184–5.
98 Blake, ed., 1962, 231–2; Crook 2000, 194, 210–11.
99 Draper 1979, 13; Roberts 1988, 83, fig. 17.
100 Blake, ed., 1962, 44–7 at 46; Bede, ed. Colgrave and Minors 1969, 394–7.
101 *GPA* 371–3.
102 Blake, ed., 1962, 43–4; Bede, ed. Colgrave and Minors 1969, 392–5; Ridyard 1988, 179; Greenhalgh 1989, 130; Crook 2000, 77–8.
103 Blake, ed., 1962, 289.
104 Kimpel and Suckale, trans. Neu, 1990, 143, fig. 136.
105 *MLH* 32–3; Heslop 2000, 62–3.
106 Dronke 1972, 77–88.
107 Dronke 1972, 77–80.
108 Ridyard 1988, 181–96; Deshman 1995, 172.
109 Blake, ed., 1962, 78–9, 120–23, 230–31; Crook 2000, 167. The post-Conquest shrine is described in Blake, ed., 1962, 288.
110 Blake, ed., 1962, 78–9: *fecit namque beatarum virginum imagines easque auro et argento gemmisque pretiosissime texuit et iuxta altare maius duas a dextris et duas a sinistris statuit*; Ridyard 1988, 185, n. 45; Deshman 1995, 121 n. 81.
111 *GC* I, 13; Wilson 1980, 102 n. 16.
112 Deshman 1995, 121–4, 146–57, 181–3, col. pls 1–7, 3 (left) for Etheldreda.
113 Deshman 1995, 184–5, col. pls 28–9.
114 Deshman 1995, 122 n. 86.
115 Wormald, ed. Alexander et al., 1984, 85–6.
116 VCH Cambridgeshire IV, 69–72 for shrine; *AS* I, 636 note: *sepultus est in ecclesia Eliensi versus orientem juxta feretrum S. Etheldredae*; James 1895, 181; Roberts 1988.
117 Deshman 1995, 122.
118 Bloomfield 1952, 249; Green 1968, 152.
119 Roberts 1988, figs 13–15.
120 Roberts 1988, 79.
121 Henderson 1985, 88.
122 Roberts 1988, figs 5–7.
123 Heslop 1998, 132–5.
124 Wormald, ed. Alexander et al., 1984, 153–68; Morgan 1982, no. 22.
125 Cf. Draper 1979, 16–21.
126 Vincent 1996, 244–7.

CHAPTER 5

1 Cheney 1956, 121; Knowles 2/1963, 313.
2 For what follows, Hunter, ed., 1840, 3–28; Rodwell 1982; Gransden 1982, 24–35; Draper 1995; Rodwell 2001, I, 123–60.
3 Gransden 1982, 27–8 and 47 n. 21; cf. Rodwell 2001, I, 127 for the contrary view.
4 Robinson 1928, 2–7; Bilson 1928; Colchester and Harvey 1974, 200–03; Wilson 1990, 78; Draper 1995, 120–22.
5 For Wells and Glastonbury, Draper 1995.
6 Robinson 1921, 145–7, 149.
7 CPL I, 70.
8 Clanchy 1979, 26, 124.
9 Robinson 1928, 11.
10 Robinson 1928, 16–17.
11 Gransden 1976, 347.
12 Robinson 1921, 1–25; Gransden 1976, 339 n. 4, 344–5; Brown 1989.
13 Gransden 1976, 347–58, 350.
14 Gransden 1976, 353–5.
15 Hunter, ed., 1840, 3–41; cf. Palmer 1924, 54–6; Gransden 1982, 28, 33–4.
16 Hunter, ed., 1840, 16: *privilegium Apostolicae auctoritatis*.
17 Hunter, ed., 1840, 25: *in curia Romana, et in registris, et scriptis a curia missis, Pontifices Fontanensis dicerentur*.
18 CPL I, 70.
19 Cf. Gransden 1982, 28, 33–4 who argues that the *Historiola* gives no hint that the canons 'aspired to the church's restoration as a cathedral', and for a date for it of after 1206; cf. Rodwell 2001, I, 127.
20 Robinson 1913–14 for the fullest discussion; Prior and Gardner 1912, 296–7; Stone 1972, 106–7; Rodwell 1982,

17–21; Lindley 1995, 115–17; Rodwell 2001, I, 146–7; Reeve 1998.
21 Prior and Gardner 1912, 568–77; Brown 1999, 113–15; Draper 1995, 121–2.
22 Robinson 1913–14, 107–8; Reeve 1998, 237–9.
23 Robinson 1928, 5; Rodwell 1982, 21; Rodwell 2001, I, 145–6; Reeve 1998.
24 Robinson 1913–14; Rodwell 1982, 21–2, fig. 12.
25 Palmer, ed., 1924, 59; cf. Robinson 1913–14, 104, 109–10, pl. XII, fig. 13.
26 Gransden 1976, 347–58, 350; Gransden 1982, 33–4.
27 Lindley 1986, 86; Crook 2000, 218–33.
28 Palmer, ed., 1924, 65: *in medio chori ecclesie Wellensis honorifice sepelitur*.
29 Robinson 1913–14, 107.
30 Robinson 1913–14, 109–10; Wright 1974; Lindley 1995.
31 Reeve 1998, 236–7.
32 Sampson 1998, 11–28, 133–49.
33 McAleer 1988; Sampson 1998, 45, 133–49, fig. on 146.
34 Robinson 1928, 16–17; Sampson 1998, 113–32.
35 Palmer, ed., 1924, 55: *ipsamque ecclesiam a parte occidentali pro majore parte erexit*; Robinson 1928, 12.
36 Hope and Lethaby 1904, 148; William Worcestre, ed. Harvey 1969, 288–91; Sampson 1998, 150.
37 Shearman 1992.
38 Ayres, ed., 2000, 37–8; Maddison 1993, 78–80.
39 Bony 1979, 43.
40 McAleer 1988, 149.
41 Webb 1956, 104; Brieger 1957, 34–5; Sampson 1998, 18; Ayres, ed., 2000, 77–8.
42 *PL* 159, col. 997; Wilson 1990, caption to fig. 126.
43 Hope and Lethaby 1904, 181–3; Stone 1972, 108–9; Tudor-Craig 1982, 111–14.
44 Robinson 1928, 13; Robinson 1921, 154; cf. Brieger 1957, 33–4.
45 Webb 1956, 105.
46 Sauerländer, trans. Sondheimer 1972, 160, 172–3.
47 Lasko 1972, fig. 296.
48 Caviness 1977, 107–15.
49 Morgan 1982, no. 32.
50 Wormald, ed. Alexander et al., 1984, 123–37, fig. 153.
51 Rodwell 2001, I, 131–3, fig. 111B.
52 Kahn 1991, 139–71.
53 Heslop 1982; Ellis 1986, 18 no. M166, pl. 17; *AoC*, no. 461; Ayers, ed., 2000, fig. 21, pl. IVa.
54 Ellis 1986, 67 no. M631, pl. 13; Harvey and McGuiness 1996, 103 fig. 99.
55 *AoC*, no. 462.
56 Kahn 1991, 139–71; Brown 1999, 175–8; cf. also VCH Cambridgeshire IV, 72 and fig. on 71.
57 Hope 1916–17; Brieger 1957, 35 n. 1; Williamson 1995, 181–4, fig. 273.
58 As also at Higham Ferrers, Henderson 1988, 246 n. 35.
59 Bishop 1918, 276–300; Wooley, ed., 1917, 26; Knowles 2/1963, 545; Shortt 1970, 4; Tudor-Craig 1982, 116–18; Blum 1986; McAleer 1988, 147–9; Deshman 1995, 79; Sampson 1998, 168–76; Ayers, ed., 2000, 37, 75.
60 E.g. Heslop 1998, 132.
61 Page 1989; Williams 1993.
62 Knowles 2/1963, 559–60; Williams 1993, 94–134, also 312 for organs being provided in 1310 at Wells; Sampson 1998, 135–6.
63 Williams 1993, 187–203, 188.
64 Legg and Hope, eds, 1902, 44.
65 Hope and Lethaby 1904; Colchester 5/1976; Sampson 1998, 150–81.
66 Robinson 1921, 149; Robinson 1928, 9; Draper 1990, 141.
67 Robinson 1921, 157.
68 Ayers, ed., 2000, 39–43.
69 Brieger 1957, 41, cf. Hope and Lethaby 1904, 174–7, 178–80.
70 Hope and Lethaby 1904, 153–4.
71 M. Roberts 1973, 14; Morgan 1988a, no. 179; Sampson 1998, 250–51 no. 280.
72 Sampson 1998, 248–9 no. 275; Rickert 1954, pl. 98; Brieger 1957, 36.
73 Sampson 1998, 165–6.
74 Buschhausen 1980.
75 Cf. Sampson 1998, 189.
76 Hope and Lethaby 1904, 145 state that the Christ figure is thirteenth century; Sampson 1998, 40, 159, 167; cf. Morgan 1982, fig. 87.
77 Hope and Lethaby 1904; Colchester 5/1976; Sampson 1998, 150–59 and catalogue entries on 182–270.
78 Reynolds 1881, 101–3; Robinson 1927; Wormald, ed., 1934, 99–111; Morgan 2001, 184.
79 Hope and Lethaby 1904, 151–2; Sampson 1998, 153–4, 157.
80 Hope and Lethaby 1904, 158, 171–2; Rollason 1983; Hayward 1993; Sampson 1998, 154, 158–9.
81 Hope and Lethaby 1904, 155–6, 170–71.
82 Deshman 1995, 121–4, 146–57, 181–3, col. pls 1–7.
83 Wormald, ed. Alexander et al., 1984, 79, 91–3.
84 Liebermann, ed., 1889; Rollason 1978; Ridyard 1988, 241–7.
85 Rollason 1978, 69–72.
86 *CMV*, 617–18.
87 Hunter, ed., 1840, 15; Sampson 1998, 160, 216 no. 151, 218 no. 160.
88 Morgan 1982, no. 22.
89 Binski 2003.
90 Binski 2003, 47–50.
91 Binski 2003, 49.
92 Brieger 1957, 41–2.
93 St Bernard, ed. Leclercq, Talbot and Rochais 1957, 154–61.
94 Summerson 1963.
95 St Bernard, ed. Leclercq, Talbot and Rochais 1957, 156 (II.2, 8–9): *Delectatur admodem istiusmodi caverni Deus e quibus sibi vox resonat gratiarum actionis vox admirationis et laudis*.
96 Bynum 1982, 119–23.
97 Hamburger 2000b, 373–4, n. 78.
98 Webb 1956, 90–92; Wilson 1990, 78–80.
99 Wilson 1991, 191.

CHAPTER 6

1 *CMV*, 336–7.
2 Personal (i.e. face-to-face) knowledge is implied by the sentiments in Jones 1995, 84, 162.
3 Lawrence 1960, 87, after Plehn 1897.
4 James 1920, 1924; Paris, ed. and trans. Vaughan 1958, 170; for other examples of composite volumes, Lawrence 1960, 49–50 nos 1, 4; Henderson 1967b, 79; Morgan 1982, no. 85; Morgan 1988a, no. 123; Binski 1990.
5 *CMA*, 303: *vitas sanctorum Albani, Amphibali, Thomae, et Edmundi Archiepiscoporum Cantuariae conscripsit et depinxit elegantissime*; Paris, ed. and trans. Vaughan 1958, 19, 161–8, 170; Lawrence 1960, 70–100, 222–89; Henderson 1967b, 78–9; Paris, ed. Lawrence 1996.
6 *CMV*, 369–70; Baker 1929, 337–8.
7 Baker 1929, 337–42; Lawrence 1960, 75, 96–100 for date.
8 Baker 1929, 343 lines 28–32 for Isabel, 374 line 1692 for 'Maheu'.
9 Wogan-Browne 2001, 151–88 for a thorough account of this neglected figure, at 155–6 for Wymondham; for Alban, James 1924; Morgan 1982, no. 85.
10 Baker 1929, 379 lines 1983–4.
11 Jones 1995, 83–245; St Richard, ed. Russell 1995, 1, 12.
12 Wogan Browne 2001.
13 Jones 1995, 84–5, 162–3: *Unde et inter specula scripture sacre et vite sanctorum, que penes vos copiose habentur in unum, ad decorum domus Dei et edificationem animarum*; Baker 1929, 338–40; Jacob 1956, 174–5; Wogan-Browne 2001, 151–88.
14 *CDS*, 130: *frequenter domestico idiomate sane inculcent*; Cheney 1968, 51, 62–89, 150; Jankofsky 1977; Samson 1986; Heffernan 1988, 255–9.
15 St Richard, ed. Russell 1995, 13.
16 Binski 1990, 339–40.
17 Meyer, ed., 1885; Henderson 1967b, 79; Paris, ed. and trans. Vaughan 1958, 168–81; Morgan 1982, no. 61; Morgan 1988b; Backhouse and De Hamel 1988.
18 Vauchez, trans. Birrell 1997, 167–73.
19 Nilson 1998, 9–10.
20 A. Duggan 1982, 24–5; Vauchez, trans. Birrell 1997, 219–25.
21 Vauchez, trans. Birrell 1997, 168 n. 37, table on 257.
22 Gibbs and Lang 1934, 25–50.
23 Vauchez, trans. Birrell 1997, 169–77, 292; Murray 1978, 405–12.
24 Leyser 1987, 57.
25 Barlow 1986, 10–23.
26 Lawrence 1960, 108–9, 222; Jones 1995, 88, 166; Paris, ed. Lawrence 1996, 63.
27 Powicke 1928, 3–8; for Grosseteste, *HA* II, 376: *ex humillima stirpe procreatus*; Southern 1986, 63 n. 1.
28 Murray 1978, 319–20; also Schulte 1922.
29 Jacob 1956, 183.
30 Murray 1978, 354.
31 E.g. *Ancrene Wisse*, ed. Dobson 1972, 129; trans. Savage and Watson 1991, 110.
32 Vauchez, trans. Birrell 1997, 303–4, and above chapter 3, n. 187; Jones 1995, 104–7, 180–84.
33 Vauchez, trans. Birrell 1997, 169 n. 40, 304.
34 Gibbs and Lang 1934, 187, 211; Ramm et al. 1971, 104–6; Wilson 1977; Paris, ed. Lawrence 1996, 20–21.
35 Johnstone 1929; Binski 1986, 35; Dixon-Smith 1999.
36 Vauchez, trans. Birrell 1997, 288–90, 285–310.
37 Vauchez, trans. Birrell 1997, 285–6.
38 Dronke 1984, 186–7, 190; in general, see Jaeger 1985, 1994; also Wogan-Browne 2001, 181–2.
39 Felix, ed. and trans. Colgrave 1956, 84–5, cap. XXI.
40 Jaeger 1994, 108.
41 Trexler 1987, 38–9.
42 Leyser 1987, 58.
43 Jaeger 1994, 297–9.
44 Lawrence 1960, 215: *affabilis omnibus* [. . .] *cum debita maturitate semper gaudens et hilaris*.
45 Jones 1995, 88–9, 167.
46 Jones 1995, 88, 166 and 109, 185: *Gestus vero ejus exterior, interioris hominis simulacrum, mentis compositionem indicabat*.
47 Jones 1995, 108–10, 184–6; as also his diocesan statutes, cf. Jones 1995, 65, 67.
48 Cicero, *De Officiis*, Book 1: XXXIV–XXXV, 126–32, trans. Miller 1913, 125–31; Peter the Chanter, see Trexler 1987, 208 lines 1394–5: *Gestus vero corporis est argumentum et probatio mentalis devotionis. Status autem exterioris hominis instruit nos de humilitate et affectu interioris*; Aquinas, *Summa Theologiae*: 2a.2ae. *Quest*. 168.1, trans. Gilby 1972, 211–27, esp. 212–13: *motus exteriores sunt quaedam signa interioris dispositionis*. See also Schmitt 1990; Simons 1994, 14.
49 Murray 1978, 355–62.
50 Deshman 1986; Crook 2000, 163–6.
51 Gibbs and Lang 1934, 3, 5–10, 185.
52 Vauchez, trans. Birrell 1997, 287–92; O'Reilly 1985, 201–2.
53 Murray 1981, 317–18.
54 O'Reilly 1985, 185, 199.
55 O'Reilly 1985, 197–213.
56 *Mats* III, 156.
57 *Mats* III, 37: *intus omnia dissimilia*.
58 O'Reilly 1985, 201–2, 208; Southern 1990, 439.
59 *Mats* III, 357; Powicke 1928, 75–6; Lawrence 1956; Lawrence 1960, 14.
60 Lawrence 1960, 242; Paris, ed. Lawrence 1996, 134.
61 Wallace 1893, 168–9; Lawrence 1960, 212, 244–6; Paris, ed. Lawrence 1996, 135–6.
62 Jones 1995, 95, 171–2; Tristram 1955, 230.
63 Vauchez, trans. Birrell 1997, 397.
64 Moore 1987, 135–40.
65 Murray 1978, 213–57; Vauchez, trans. Birrell 1997, 138, 397–400.
66 Lawrence 1960, 215; Jones 1995, 104, 180; Vauchez, trans. Birrell 1997, 399.
67 Gibbs and Lang 1934, 196; Roberts 1983, 573–83; S. Lewis 1985.
68 Henig 1983, 58–9; Southern 1986, 318–19; for pedagogy in general, see Jaeger 1994; for Grosseteste, Gieben 1967; for St Richard, Jones 1995, 193–4, 118: *moribus quoque ornatos suos esse voluit discipulos*.
69 Southern 1986, 238.

70 Russell 1929.
71 Powicke 1928, 2, 41; Vaughan 1958, 159–61; Roberts 1968, 17–18; for the poetry, Henry of Avranches, ed. Russell and Heironimus 1935, 54 no. 44; Townsend and Rigg 1987; Binkley 1990.
72 Liebermann, ed., 1879, 318–29; Powicke 1928, 2, 134; Vaughan 1958, 159–61; Newman 1999.
73 Powicke 1928, 128–61; *C&S* II, 100–25.
74 *VRS* II, 14; *AM* III, 58; Powicke 1928, 144–5; Eales 1993; Vincent 1996, 195–6.
75 Powicke 1928, 145; Henry of Avranches, ed. Russell and Heironimus 1935, 71–8 no. 2; Foreville 1958, 7–11, 89–91 for the translation liturgy in the Sarum Breviary, also 94–5; A. Duggan 1982, 33–41; P. B. Roberts 1968, 1973, ed. 1980, 1989, 1992; Eales 1993.
76 P. B. Roberts 1973, 38–9, 41; Roberts, ed., 1980, 65–94; Roberts 1989, 1992; Eales 1993, 137.
77 Roberts 1968, 127.
78 O'Reilly 1985, 235–6; Eales 1993, 135–9, 138.
79 Jankofsky 1977, 713–14.
80 Roberts, ed., 1980, no. III, 53–64; Roberts 1992.
81 Talbot 1986, 63 n. 31.
82 Henry of Avranches, ed. Russell and Heironimus 1935, 54 no. 44; D'Esneval 1975.
83 Lawrence 1960, 76, 238–9.
84 *GW* VII, 43–80.
85 *AoC*, no. 29; A. Duggan 1982, 43–4.
86 RCHM City of Oxford, pl. 209; Marks 1993, 143, fig. 115.
87 Lawrence 1960, 110–82, 155, 164–8; Paris, ed. Lawrence 1996; Dobson in Collinson, Ramsay and Sparks, eds, 1995, 69–75.
88 Lawrence 1960, 5.
89 Lawrence 1960, 7–30, 118–19; Paris, ed. Lawrence 1996, 90–99; Vauchez, trans. Birrell 1997, 125.
90 Baker 1929, 342; cf. Powicke 1928, 75–6; Wogan-Browne 2001, 168.
91 *CM* IV, 631–2, 646–7; Paris, ed. Lawrence 1996, 97–9.
92 Lawrence 1960, 4, 18, 168–72.
93 Constable 1995, 213.
94 Bynum 2001, 51–3, also Constable 1995, 169, 173–4.
95 Constable 1995, 169–93; Vauchez, trans. Birrell 1997, 388.
96 Lawrence 1960, 225–6; Paris, ed. Lawrence 1996, 120–21.
97 Lawrence 1960, 226, 252; Paris, ed. Lawrence 1996, 142; *CM* VI, 384.
98 Lawrence 1960, 229–30, 250–51; Paris, ed. Lawrence 1996, 123–4, 140.
99 Heslop 1982, 96, pl. XXIXB.
100 Barlow 1986, 39.
101 Birch 1887, 159 no. 1187, 160 no. 1196, 161 nos 1201–2, 162 no. 1205; Powicke 1928, frontispiece.
102 *CM* IV, 248; Lewis 1987, 88–9.
103 Lawrence 1960, 260; Paris, ed. Lawrence 1996, 148–9.
104 Bynum 1982, 98 n. 36.
105 Constable 1995, 192 n. 289, 214; generally, 194–217.
106 Bynum 1982, 97–8, 105; Carruthers 1990, 16–32, 71; Schmitt 1990, 173–205; Jaeger 1994, 10–11, 108–9, 244–68 at 258–9; Fulton 2002, 254–65.
107 Jaeger 1994, 258–9, 461 n. 73; for the influence of the Victorines on Edmund, see Forshaw 1972.
108 Hamburger 2000a, 58–9; Hamburger 2002, 77, 132–40, 181, 197–8.
109 Vauchez 1968; Constable 1995, 194–217; Vauchez, trans. Birrell 1997, 427–43.
110 *C&S* II, 100, 105–6; Constable 1995, 213–17.
111 Lawrence 1960, 226–7, 242; Paris, ed. Lawrence 1996, 121, 134; John of Salisbury, ed. Millor and Brooke 1979, nos 305, 724–39, 728–9.
112 Murray 1981, 317–18.
113 Edmund of Abingdon, ed. Forshaw 1973, 37; Edmund of Abingdon, ed. Wilshere 1982, 10–11.
114 *Mats* II, 292–3.
115 Morgan 1982, no. 72(a); Donovan 1991, 81–8, 86 fig. 53; Henderson 1991a, 682–3.
116 Aelred of Rievaulx, trans. Hoste and Dubois 1958; Lawrence 1960, 224–5, Paris, ed. Lawrence 1996, 119–20.
117 *Mats* II, 297–8.
118 *CM* IV, 324; Lawrence 1960, 270; Paris, ed. Lawrence 1996, 156, 162.
119 L-B, no. 5878.
120 James 1951; Rudolph 1990b, 107–10.
121 Morgan 1988a, no. 126; Morgan 1990, 49–71; Lewis 1995, 272–96, 289–90.
122 Morgan 1990, 58; cf. Lewis 1995, 289–92.
123 Constable 1995, 204–8, 207, 211; Paris, ed. Lawrence 1996, 6–7.
124 Lawrence 1960, 269; Paris, ed. Lawrence 1996, 155.
125 Bynum 1982, 110–69; Southern 1990, 153–4; Constable 1995, 203; for the *Ancrene Wisse*, ed. Dobson 1972, 108–9, or trans. Savage and Watson 1991, 99.
126 Lawrence 1960, 25, 36.
127 Jones 1995, 137, 214; Wogan-Browne 2001, 178.
128 *CM* V, 369: *cujus vestigia sequi nitebatur pedetentim.*
129 Jacob 1956; Jones 1983, 1995.
130 Jacob 1956, 178.
131 *C&S* II, 451–67; Jones 1983; Jones 1995, 54–65.
132 Jones 1995, 93, 170.
133 Jones 1995, 125–6, 202 and 129–30, 206.
134 Lawrence 1960, 146–7; Jones 1995, 93, 170.
135 Jacob 1956, 179–80.
136 Jacob 1956, 187; Jones 1983; Jones 1995, 138–9, 214 and for his will, 67.
137 Jacob 1956, 180; Jones 1995, 93, 170.
138 Gilson, trans. Downes 1940, 8–13; Ailred of Rievaulx, trans. Laker 1977, 29–30; Jaeger 1994, 103–6, 279–80; for Anselm on friendship, Southern 1990, 138–65.
139 Jones 1995, 136, 213; for the kiss, Wallace 1893, 334. On kissing and Anselmian spirituality, see Southern 1990, 153–4.
140 Bynum 1982, 36–43.
141 Powicke 1928, 143–4; Vincent 1996, 243–4.
142 Vincent 1996, 243.
143 Powicke 1928, 143–4; Henry of Avranches, eds Russell and Heironimus 1935, 123–5 no. 23; *C&S* II, 127–8 no. 10; Townsend 1994, 317; Vincent 1996, 21, 244–7; for Birinus's relics, Crook 2000, 219 n. 47.
144 Gransden 1974, 67–91.
145 Gransden 1978; Singleton 1978; Vincent 1996, 153, 246; Crook 2000, 165–6; in general, Engel 2000.
146 Robinson 1913–14, 107–8; Singleton 1978, 109–10.

147 Mason 1990, 254–85.
148 Powicke 1928, 85–8; William of Malmesbury, ed. Darlington 1928; Draper 1984, 46–9; Mason 1984; Mason 1990, 281–4; Eales 1993, 134–5.
149 Binski 1995a, 3; Vincent 1996, 246.
150 Vincent 1996, 154, 208.
151 Binski 1991, also 1995a, 56.
152 *LEC*; James 1920; Binski 1990, 1991, 1995a, 57–63.
153 *LEC*, 25–8; Jones 1995, 83, 161.
154 Russell 1929; Binski 1990, 339–49; Binski 1995a, 61.
155 *GC* II, 130.
156 *LEC*, 25, 179 lines 1–15.
157 Rollason 1983; Hayward 1993, 87–8.
158 *LEC*, 28, 182 lines 97–101.
159 *LEC*, 131, 133, 285 lines 3766–76, 286 lines 3805–58.
160 *HA* I, 9.
161 *Mats* III, 261–4.
162 *LEC*, 26, 180 line 29.
163 *LEC*, 60, 214 lines 1249–50.
164 Jones 1995, 83, 161; Wogan-Browne 2001, 152, 169.
165 Ridyard 1994.
166 *LEC*, 61, 214 lines 1240–46, 215 line 1271.
167 *LEC*, 126, 280 lines 3587–90.
168 Binski 1986, 33–45; Dixon-Smith 1999.
169 *LEC*, 50–51, 204–5 lines 894–907.
170 Wogan-Browne 2001, 183.
171 Wogan-Browne 2001, 181.
172 *LEC*, 96–7, 251 lines 2514–73.
173 *MV* II, 85–9; Lawrence 1960, 225–6; Paris, ed. Lawrence 1996, 120–21; Rubin 1991, 108–29, esp. 118 n. 219; Constable 1995, 204–8, 207; Binski 1995a, 146.
174 Binski 1995a, 141–4; Vincent 2001.
175 Binski 1995a, 142, fig. 190; Wogan-Browne 2001, 187–8.
176 *LEC*, 122–5, 276–9 lines 3453–570; Binski 1995a, 49, 66.
177 Lawrence 1960, 224–5; Paris, ed. Lawrence 1996, 119–20; Jones 1995, 107–8, 184 and 102–3, 179; Wogan-Browne 2001, 177.
178 Binski 1995a, figs 67–8, 77, 86, 90, 106–7; Binski 2002, esp. 126–31.
179 Gardner 1990, 211–14; Binski 1995a, 104; Nilson 1998, 4.
180 Binski 1995a, 99–100; Binski 2002, 129–30.
181 Binski 1986, 14 and fig. 2, 35–40, pls I, II, col. pl. 1.
182 Jaeger 1994, 313.
183 Jones 1995, 133, 209.
184 Binski 1995a, 3; *CMV*, 297: *quem rex diligit specialiter*; also caption shown in Lewis 1987, col. pl. VII, lower right.
185 Aquinas, *Summa Theologiae*: 1a.2ae. *Quest.* 28.1–6, esp. 2, trans. D'Arcy 1963, 88–107, esp. 93–4.
186 *De Officiis*, Book 1: XXXVII, trans. Miller 1913, 58: *ut unus fiat ex pluribus*; also Gilson, trans. Downes 1940, 12–13.

CHAPTER 7

1 Barratt 1984, 413.
2 Morgan 2001, 2003 for aspects of the calendar and Use.
3 *C&S* II, 552–3 no. 2.
4 Tentler 1977; Moore 1987, 140; for the ordeal, see Baldwin 1970, I, 323–32; Baldwin 1998.
5 Murray 1978; Moore 1987, 131, 134–5.
6 Bolton 1999, 150; Dobson, ed., 1972, 66, fol. 33v; Dobson 1976; trans. Savage and Watson 1991, 78–9.
7 For Lateran III: Alberigo, ed., 1973, 205–25; Tanner 1990, 205–25; for Lateran IV: Alberigo, ed., 1973, 227–71; Tanner, ed., 1990, 227–71; in general, Foreville 1965; for the summons, *C&S* II, 47–9.
8 Lewis 1987, 122–5.
9 *GA* I, 261–2; Gibbs and Lang 1934, 102.
10 Tentler 1977, 345; Foucault, trans. Hurley 1990, 58; Kemp, trans. Saltzwedel 1997, 132.
11 Moore 1987, 6–11, 66, 124–40; see the useful overview in Biller and Minnis, eds, 1998, 30–31.
12 Macy 1984, 1994; for pluralism, Leclercq 1982.
13 Broomfield, ed., 1968, xl–xliii; Tanner, ed., 1990, 230–31, 245, also Moore 1987, 93.
14 *C&S* II, 57, 72 no. 38, cf. 32 no. 43.
15 Baldwin 1970, I, 17–59, 315–43 at 343; D'Avray 1985, 26.
16 Foreville 1965, 392; Thomson 1983, 4.
17 Cheney 1956, 46, 175.
18 Webber 1992, 113–42; Baldwin 1970, I, 49.
19 Cheney 1956, 121; Cheney 1960, 14–16; Cheney 1967, 64–8, 121; *C&S* I, 1055–74.
20 Cheney 1967, 66.
21 *C&S* II, 23–36; Cheney 1967, 68.
22 Cheney 1960, 29; also Cheney 1956, 175–6.
23 Friedberg, ed., 1881; Gibbs and Lang 1934, 104.
24 Gibbs and Lang 1934, 105.
25 Gibbs and Lang 1934, 113; Tanner, ed., 1990, 236–7.
26 Gibbs and Lang 1934, 143–7.
27 Gibbs and Lang 1934, 122–3; *C&S* II, 61 nos 4, 7, 77 no. 55, also 371 no. 15.
28 Powicke 1928, 151–2; *C&S* II, 106.
29 Cheney 1960, 29 n. 1; *C&S* II, 125 no. 60: *et in synodis episcoporum constitutiones illius concilii una cum istis prout videbitur expedire volumus recitari*; see also *C&S* II, 366; also Winchester 1224, *C&S* II, 126 no. 1.
30 *C&S* II, 100.
31 Gibbs and Lang 1934, 106; *C&S* II, 48.
32 *C&S* II, 254 no. 20: *De archidiaconis*; 321 no. 102, 426–7 no. 17.
33 Simpson 1895a, 1895b; Moorman 1945, 144–5; Cheney 1968, 143; cf. Graves 1989, 303–5.
34 Collected in *C&S* II.
35 Gibbs and Lang 1934, 122, also 104; Shaw 1985, 47.
36 Gibbs and Lang 1934, 129–30, 174–7.
37 Powicke 1928, 151.
38 Cf. Cheney 1956, 173.
39 Friedberg, ed., 1881, cols 633, 642.
40 Gardner 1994, 6–7.
41 Graves 1989, 303.
42 Tanner, ed., 1990, 230–31.
43 Tanner, ed., 1990, 244–5, 263–4.
44 Macy 1984, 1994.
45 Camille 1989, 215–17; Recht 1999, 97–145, 393–409.
46 Van Os 1988, 13, 17: 'The year 1215 marked a watershed in the development of the liturgy'; cf. Binski 1995b.
47 Jungmann, trans. Brunner 1986, II, 206–7; Kennedy 1943, 1944, 1946.

48 Kennedy 1944, 149; on joining of hands as part of history of prayer, Ladner 1961a; Trexler 1987.
49 Kennedy 1944, 135–7.
50 Kennedy 1944, 121–2.
51 In general Dumoutet 1926, 1942; also Kennedy 1943, 123; Kennedy 1946, 93–4.
52 Tanner, ed., 1990, 244.
53 *C&S* I, 1063, 1071 no. 2; cf. also 1049.
54 Tanner, ed., 1990, 244, 263–4.
55 King 1965, 67–8; Broomfield, ed., 1968, lv; *C&S* II, 352 no. 45, 412 no. 62, 622 no. 74, 1044 no. 48.
56 *C&S* II, 27 no. 14, cf. 78–9 no. 56.
57 *C&S* II, 115 no. 29; cf. 894–5 no. 1: *De custodia eukaristie: et ut in qualibet ecclesia parochiali fiat tabernaculum cum clausura*. See also Sekules 1986, Sheingorn 1987.
58 Worcester 1229 and 1240, Salisbury 1238–44: *C&S* II, 171 no. 2, 296 no. 2, 378 no. 29.
59 Gauthier 1972, 1978, 37; Boehm 1996, 44.
60 *C&S* II, 1411 index for 'children'; Gillespie 1980.
61 *C&S* II, 512–3 no. 8.
62 Hope 1990, 536.
63 Hills 1990.
64 Gardner 1994, 1997.
65 *C&S* II, 172 no. 7, 245–6 no. 1; 296–7 no. 3, 367 nos 1, 3, 1004, no. 10; Gardner 1994, 9–11; Binski 1995b.
66 *C&S* II, 29 no. 18, 268–9 no. 4, 346 no. 4, 405 no. 7, 426–7 no. 17; Gardner 1997, 33–4 n. 35 for a different interpretation of the term 'superaltar'.
67 *RGE*, 156.
68 *PL* 217, cols 765–916; Gardner 1994, 6–7 and n. 9.
69 *PL* 204, cols 642–774; Leclercq et al. 1963; Smalley 1973, 218–19; Bynum 1982, 192–3.
70 Kennedy 1943, 6–7, 8–9.
71 *PL* 217, col. 774; Gardner 1994, 7.
72 *PL* 217, cols 799–802; cf. also Durandus, eds Davril and Thibodeau 1995–8, I, 224–9; Gage 1993, 60, 84; Gage 1999, 53, 70.
73 Tanner, ed., 1990, 243.
74 *C&S* II, 63–4 no. 11.
75 *C&S* II, 296 no. 2.
76 Dendy 1959, 25.
77 Borg 1985, 85–7.
78 Norton and Park, eds, 1986, 331.
79 *PL* 217, col. 811; Dendy 1959, 48; Gardner 1994, 7.
80 Durandus, eds Davril and Thibodeau 1995–8, I, 43; Dendy 1959, 49; Gardner 1994, 7–9.
81 *C&S* II, 144 no. 25.
82 *C&S* II, 126 no. 6: *Numquam celebret sacerdos nisi cruce ante se posita*.
83 *C&S* II, 378 no. 29; also 372 no. 16: *cum propter hoc excitetur devotio fidelium*; cf. also 143 no. 19, 296 no. 2, 453–4 no. 13, 592–3 no. 5, 990 no. 4.
84 Goering and Mantello, eds, 1984, 63.
85 *C&S* II, 72 no. 38, 460 no. 41; see also *C&S* I, 1060 no. 1.
86 *C&S* II, 460 no. 41: *ita quod ex festinatione nimia verba non precidantur vel sincopentur*.
87 Trexler 1987, 32–3, 206 line 1325.
88 Schmitt 1990, 321–55.
89 CCR 1253–4, 165.
90 *LEC*, 136, 290 lines 3961–4.
91 *C&S* II, esp. 171 no. 2, 296 no. 2, 379 no. 29.
92 Binski 1995b, 51–2; see the discussion in Gardner 1988, 44–5.
93 *C&S* II, 33 no. 45, 79 no. 59, 210–11 no. 3, 299–300 no. 14, 372 no. 16, 593–4 no. 5, 990–91 no. 4.
94 Sandler 1983, 131; Trexler 1987.
95 Carruthers 1990, 78–9, 229–30; Carruthers 1998, 207; Recht 1999, 290–307.
96 In general Jungmann, trans. Brunner 1986, I, 103–27; Waddell 1982, 96–7.
97 Harper 1991.
98 Baxandall 1980, 64.
99 Berthelé and Valmary, eds, 1900–07, 3, 107: *Precipimus ut in unaquaque ecclesia ante vel post vel supra quodlibet altare sit ymago vel sculptura seu pictura vel scriptura expresse designans et cuilibet intuenti manifestans in cujus sancti nomen et honorem sit ipsum altare constructum*; Durandus, eds Davril and Thibodeau 1995–8, I, 40; Braun 1924, II, 280; Binski 1987, 171–2 n. 44; Gardner 1994, 6; Binski 1995b, 52–3.
100 Hope 1990, 537–8; cf. Lane 1984.
101 *C&S* II, 1006 no. 12: *sit* [. . .] *ymago beate virginis et sancti loci eiusdem*.
102 Binski 1995b, 54; cf. Belting, trans. Jephcott 1994, 443–53; also Wilson 1980 for the reredos.
103 Binski 1995b, 53–4.
104 *C&S* II, 1005 no. 12.
105 Cheney 1961b; *C&S* II, 1386–7 no. III.
106 Hager 1962; Fuchß 1999; Gardner 1994, 1997.
107 Lasko 1972, 171–2; Andersson et al. 1984, 98–9; Blake, ed., 1962, 289–90 for a frontal at Ely, also with a Majesty and Sun and Moon.
108 Thompson 1902–4, I, 374, 382, II, 55–6; numerous examples in L-B, e.g. nos 501, 525, 720, 1552, 1638, 1853, 3454, 3458, 3566, 3713, 3723, 3760, 3839, 3890, 4053, 4765; and cf. L-B, V, 410–12 under 'tabula'.
109 L-B, nos 13, 525, 3458.
110 Lasko 1972, 170–71, pl. 179.
111 Bishop 1918, 20–38; Braun 1924, II, 277–647; Lasko 1972, 192, pl. 208; cf. Garrison 1949, section XXIV, nos 417–22; Gauthier 1978; Fuchß 1999.
112 L-B, nos 13–14; cf. also no. 541.
113 Guérard, ed., 1850, 146: *tabula aurea ante majus altare*; Van Os 1988, 12–17; Binski 1995b, 47–8.
114 Formigé 1960, 120–48, figs 99–101, 106, 108, 112, 116, 118, 122; Belting, trans. Jephcott 1994, 446, fig. 270; Fuchß 1999, 77–118, 180–83, figs 417–19.
115 Braun 1924, II, 302–18; Hager 1962 ; Martindale 1995; Gardner 1997.
116 Sureda 1981; Morgan 1998.
117 Binski 1987; Binski and Freestone 1995; Plahter 1983.
118 Thorpe, ed., 1769, 123; L-B, no. 3762; Greatrex 1997, 609–10: before 1214.
119 L-B, no. 4091: *tabula depicta cum ymaginibus*.
120 L-B, no. 109: *tabula picta satis conveniens super altare*.
121 L-B, no. 3425: *tabula cum ymagine s. Mariae ibidem super altare*.

122 Simpson 1895a, 1895b; L-B, nos 90, 109, 157–8, 294, 414, 933, 1271, 1656, 1793, 2123–5, 2155, 2221, 2223, 2457, 2933, 3052, 3111, 3178, 3510, 3890–91, 3905, 4091, 4242, 4353, 4406, 4408–9, 4496, 4609–10, 4441–2, 4497–8, 4594.
123 Andersson 1949; Andersson et al., 1964–80; Malmanger et al., eds 1995.
124 Norton and Park, eds, 1986, 374, also 378.
125 As the Winchester Bible, Kauffmann 1975, nos 83–4; Oakeshott 1972, 1981; see also Morgan 1982, nos 1, 2, 3; for glass, Caviness 1977; Gibson, Heslop and Pfaff, eds, 1992; for Winchester and Canterbury wall paintings, Demus, trans. Whittall 1970, 120–25; Park 1983; for Canterbury, Nilgen 1980.
126 Wormald 1973, 87–90; Kauffmann 1975, no. 78.
127 CLR 1226–40, 261.
128 Belting, trans. Jephcott 1994, 228–9, 323–9, 498–9.
129 Powicke 1962, 74, 451; *C&S* II, 238; Gregorius, trans. Osborne 1987, 14–15.
130 Binski 1995a, 142–3.
131 Tristram 1950, 529, 548–9, 553, 556, 573, 579, 585, 610–11, 623, 630; Colvin, ed., 1963, I, 157, II, 952; Binski 1995a, 152–67; Binski 1995b, 49.
132 See in general Binski 1986.
133 Martindale 1995, 38.
134 Blume 1983, 9–21; Krüger 1992, 101–47; Belting, trans. Jephcott 1994, 377–84; Duffy 1997b, 202–13.
135 Garrison 1949, nos 357, 360, 361, 363, 365–8, 371–6, 390–412; Duffy 1997b, 204–5, 'it seems certain that Francis was the first saint, in the West at any rate, to have his life and miracles painted in this way'.
136 Blume 1983; Krüger 1992, 101–47.
137 Vauchez, trans. Birrell 1997, 158–87.
138 Duffy 1997b, 202–3.
139 *CM* IV, 324.
140 Borenius 1932, 9–10.
141 Borenius 1932; A. Duggan 1982, 24–9; Gameson 2002.
142 Borenius 1932, 10–11, 109–11.
143 Borenius 1932, 10, 13–14, pl. II/1; Kitzinger 1960, 18–19, pl. 96; Urry 1999, 46–7.
144 Morgan 1982, no. 5.
145 Foreville, ed., 1975, 211–71; Foreville 1981; Gameson 2002; Little 2002.
146 Borenius 1932, 18, pl. II/3; Tristram 1950, 552, pl. 208.
147 Trollope 1866, 248–51; Borenius 1932, 57, pl. XVII/1; Tristram 1950, 602.
148 *MV* I, 104–9, 122, II, 38.
149 Belting, trans. Jephcott 1994, 377.
150 Lowden 1997, 367–8, ill. 227; Ševčenko 1999. The early Catalonian frontals have seated, not standing, figures: Sureda 1981, nos 73, 76, 77; Morgan 1998.
151 Urry 1975, 198.
152 *GA* I, 233.
153 Borenius 1932, 56–7.
154 Morgan 1995, 20, pl. 11.
155 Magnússon 1875–83, II, xxiv–xxxii; Borenius 1932, 38; Orme 1966; A. Duggan 1982, 24–5.
156 Borenius 1932, 20–21; Morgan 1995, 19, pl. 10.
157 Lindblom 1953.
158 Morgan 1995, 20.
159 Tristram 1950, 497–500; Binski 1992.
160 Binski 1992, 249–52; cf. Lethaby 1916, 190.
161 See the admirable appreciations in Henderson 1967b, 71–85; Lewis 1987, 1–33.
162 VCH Hertfordshire II, 483–507; Coldstream 1990; Binski 1992, 252–6; Harrison 2001; Hoey 2001.
163 Knowles 2/1963, 417–22.
164 *GA* I, 83–7.
165 *GA* I, 232–3, 279–80.
166 Thomson 1982, 71–2.
167 *GA* I, 232–3; Lethaby 1916, 1917b.
168 *GA* I, 279–81; *CM* III, 59–60; *CM* VI, 278; *HA* II, 241–2.
169 Ovid, *Metamorphoses*, II, 5, ed. and trans. Hill 1985, 48–9; cf. *HA* II, 242: *artificio materiam superante*; Branner 1965, 57–8; Rudolph 1990b, 60–61, nn. 169, 171.
170 Muratova 1986, 63, 65.
171 Henderson 1967b, 74–5, n. 16; *GA* I, 394–5.
172 Grant 1998, 35–6.
173 Gransden 1974, 372–7; *CM* V, 244.
174 Lewis 1987, 45, 72–3, 143, 420; cf. however Lewis 1995, 295.
175 Morgan 1982, no. 85.
176 James 1924, 16; Binski 1991, 90, 94, 100 n. 87.
177 Vaughan 1958, 4–7.
178 Vaughan 1958, 6–7, 18.
179 Vaughan 1958, 19.
180 Lindblom 1916, 40–41, 128–32, pl. 7; Lethaby 1917a, 48 fig. 6, 51; Vaughan 1958, 205–7, 228–9; *AoC*, no. 311.
181 Omont 1927, pl. 8.
182 Andersson 1949, 190–91 for a crucifix from Fåberg.
183 *GA* I, 283; Jocelin of Brakelond, ed. and trans. Butler 1949, 107–8; *GC* I, 13; Thomson 1982, 72; Binski 1987, 116; Binski 1992, 264.
184 The literature is very extensive: see for example Formigé 1960, figs 111–13, 123; Keller 1965, 125–6; Gauthier 1978, 36–9; Wilson 1980, 93–4; Ehresmann 1982; Tångeberg 1986, 18–49; Krüger 1992; Belting, trans. Jephcott 1994, 443–53; Binski 1995a, 167–74; Legner 1995, 172–98; Scharff 1995, 85, pl. 52a; Kobler 1997, 52, pls 12–13; Fuchß 1999, 119–204; Ehresmann 2001, 32–3.
185 *GA* I, 233.
186 *GA* I, 281–2; Thomson 1982, 72; Spurrell 2000, 70–71.
187 *GA* I, 284.
188 *GA* I, 284–6; Draper 1990, 140–41.
189 *GA* I, 285; Coldstream 1990, 147–9; Hoey 2001, 192.
190 *GA* I, 286–7.
191 *GA* I, 287: *ad laicorum et omnium illuc adventantium aedificationem et consolationem saecularium*.
192 Duggan 1989; Kessler 1989; Chazelle 1990.
193 Binski 1992, 259–61.
194 Tristram 1950, 499.
195 Binski 1992, 252–63.
196 Binski 1992, 256–9, pls 3, 4.
197 *GA* I, 287.
198 Binski 1992, 259, pls 5–6, 261, pl. 9.
199 Binski 1992, 271–2.
200 Hills 1990, 40.
201 Binski 1992, 256–63; Hoey 2001, 185–91.

202 Binski 1992, 266–71.
203 Moorman 1945, 22; Franklin 1992; Blair 1998, 281–2.
204 Binski 1992, 274.
205 Binski 1992, 274; Franklin 1992.
206 Binski 1992, 274–5.
207 Franklin 1992, 192–4.
208 Draper 1990; Coldstream 1990.
209 Franklin 1992, 178–82; Binski 1992, 278.
210 Hope 1916–17, 43; Vallance 1947; Brooke 1971; Waddell 1982, 95.
211 Graves 1989 overstates the case; cf. Beckwith 1993, 42–4.
212 Oliver 1846, 270 no. 43, 271 no. 49.
213 Murray 1978, 237–44.
214 Panofsky 1951, 27–35.
215 Boyle 1982, 188.
216 In general, Freedberg 1989.
217 As suggested broadly by Belting, trans. Jephcott 1994, 409–19; see also Ringbom 1965, 30–39.
218 Hamburger 1998, 111–48 at 131; Marks 2001, 428–37: see the discussion in Ringbom 1965, 52–8; cf. Belting, trans. Jephcott 1994, 409–57; also Van Os, trans. Hoyle 1994.
219 Duffy 1992, 11–87.
220 Ringbom 1965, 23–30; F. Lewis 1985, 1992.
221 Beckwith 1993, 42–4.
222 Boyle 1982, 187–8; Hope 1990, 537–8.
223 Boyle 1982, 190; cf. however Graves 1989, 318.
224 Moorman 1945, 140–44; Drew 1954; Mason 1976.
225 *C&S* II, 174 no. 23, cf. 297 no. 4.
226 *C&S* II, 128 no. 11, 512–13 no. 8, 600 no. 16; see also Shinners and Dohar, eds, 1998, 224–5 no. 88; *C&S* II, 367 no. 2; Drew 1954, 8–9; Cheney 1956, 155 n. 2; Mason 1976, 23; Blair 1998, 293 n. 52.
227 *C&S* II, 1002–4 no. 9, 1005–8 no. 12.
228 Cf. Graves 1989, 301; cf. Marks 2001, 436.
229 *C&S* II, 1005–6.
230 *C&S* II, 1118, 1122–3 no. VII; Cheney 1961b.
231 *C&S* II, 1385–8 nos II–IV; Cheney 1961b; Shinners and Dohar, eds, 1998, 219–20 no. 86.
232 Cheney 1956, 155–77, 160.
233 Moorman 1945, 38–51; Blair and Pyrah, eds, 1996, 63–84; Lawrence 2001, 651.
234 Blair 1998, 279–80.
235 *C&S* II, 1006 no. 12; Drew 1954, 10.
236 *C&S* II, 1002–4 no.9; Drew 1954, 14–15.
237 Drew 1954, 19; Le Goff, trans. Goldhammer 1984, 284–6.
238 *C&S* II, 1008; Drew 1954, 6–7; Mason 1976, 26.
239 Drew 1954, 13.
240 Cf. Graves 1989, 305.
241 Duffy 1992, 133.

CHAPTER 8

1 In general, see Baldwin 1970.
2 Owst 1926, 277; Young 1936; McNeill and Gamer 1938; Arnould 1940; Robertson 1945; Laird 1946; Robertson 1949; Bloomfield 1952, 105–55; Pantin 1955, 189–243; Michaud-Quantin 1962; Broomfield, ed., 1968; Roberts 1968; Wenzel 1970; Firth, ed., 1971; Tentler 1977; Goering 1978; Bloomfield, et al., 1979; Gillespie 1980; Boyle 1981; Murray 1981; Boyle 1982; Evans 1982; Braswell 1983; Barratt 1984; Goering and Mantello, eds, 1984; Boyle 1985, 1986; Bennett 1990; Biller and Minnis, eds, 1998; Shinners and Dohar, eds, 1998, 121–211; Woods and Copeland 1999.
3 Broomfield, ed., 1968, xxiii.
4 Baldwin 1970; Trexler 1987.
5 Trexler 1987, 15.
6 Trexler 1987, 17, 28.
7 Trexler 1987, 43.
8 Trexler 1987, 38–9; Schmitt 1990, 303–9.
9 Murray 1981, 279; Woods and Copeland 1999, 392–3.
10 Baldwin 1970, I, 14–59; Boyle 1985, 1986; Biller and Minnis, eds, 1998, 3–33 for an overview.
11 Pantin 1955, 189–243; Cheney 1960, 12–13; Broomfield, ed., 1968, xi–xxv; lxix–lxxv.
12 Webber 1992, 113–39; Baldwin 1970, I, 17–18, 25–31.
13 Pawicke 1928, 45; Morgan 1990, 59.
14 Broomfield, ed., 1968, xx; Baldwin 1970, I, 18, 32–4; Robert of Flamborough, ed. Firth 1971, 1–20; Boyle 1986, 54.
15 Broomfield, ed., 1968; Baldwin 1970, I, 34–6; Goering 1978.
16 Goering 1992; Woods and Copeland 1999, 385–6.
17 Boyle 1985, 1986, 46–7; Broomfield, ed., 1968, xx.
18 Tanner, ed., 1990, 245.
19 Robertson 1946; e.g. Dobson, ed., 1972, 235–8, trans. Savage and Watson 1991, 165–6; *C&S* I, 1062 no. 4.
20 *C&S* II, 31 no. 34.
21 Cheney 1960; Baldwin 1970, I, 31.
22 *C&S* II, 57, 72 no. 38, cf. 32 no. 43.
23 *C&S* II, 61 nos 4, 7, 77 no. 55, also 371 no. 15.
24 *C&S* II, 65 no. 15.
25 *C&S* II, 96 no. 114.
26 Shaw 1985, 47–8.
27 *C&S* II, 214–26; Pantin 1955, 191–5.
28 *C&S* II, 172 no. 8.
29 *C&S* II, 304–5 nos 34, 35 and n. 1, 320, 321 no. 102; Arnould 1940; Robertson 1945; Robertson 1949, 380–81; Pantin 1955, 192; Shinners and Dohar, eds, 1998, 37; Graves's conclusion, 1989, 318 that such texts 'did not circulate from central ecclesiastical administration' is surely incorrect.
30 *C&S* II, 1059–77 nos 1–38.
31 *C&S* II, 900–05 no. 9.
32 Pantin 1955, 211–12.
33 Robertson 1949; Douie 1952, 133–42; Pantin 1955, 193–4; Duffy 1992, 53–5; Thompson 2002, 8, 12.
34 Kemp in Callus, ed., 1955, 241–6; Southern 1986.
35 *C&S* II, 261–5; *RGE*, 154–64; *C&S* II, 265–78.
36 *C&S* II, 268 no. 1, cf. also 304 no. 34, 345 no. 1.
37 Murray 1918; Sajavaara 1967, 43–8 for the date; Southern 1986, 222 n. 27, 25–30.
38 Brentano 1935, 49–50; Pantin in Callus, ed., 1955, 204–5; Gieben 1967; Oschinsky 1971, 192–3, 399–409; Gillespie 1980; Southern 1986, 318–19.
39 Southern 1986, 226 n. 32.
40 Sajavaara 1967, 50–51; Constable 1995, 9; Fulton 2002, 259–61.
41 Sajavaara 1967, 282–4.

42 Wormald, ed. Alexander et al. 1988, 61–9.
43 Evans 1982, 20, 31–2; cf. Smalley 3/1984, 276–7.
44 Evans 1982, 20–21; Morgan 1982, no. 80; see also Woolf 1968, 46–55; Morgan 1990, 64.
45 Lewis 1987, 195, fig. 113a.
46 Dobson, ed., 1972, 286–8 fols 182–3, trans. Savage and Watson 1991, 191–2.
47 Dobson 1976, 1–3.
48 Evans 1982, 22–4, 27–8, pls 3, 4c, 5a, 5b, 6b; cf. however Southern 1986, 178; S. Lewis 1987, 194–7, figs 113–15; S. Lewis 1995, 287, 292–3; F. Lewis 1996, 217–23; Morgan 1990, 62–5 n. 63 cites Morgan 1982, no. 43(b) as an early instance of the combination of a triangular diagram of the Trinity plus the Crucifixion.
49 Gardner 2000, 87–9.
50 In general Bony 1979; Binski 1995a, 76–83.
51 Keen 1984, 44–63; also Hopkins 1990.
52 Taylor in Colvin, ed., 1963, I, 370 after Ellis and Lloyd, trans., 1929, 135–8.
53 Baldwin 1970, I, 261–95; Lawrence 2001, 665; cf. however D'Avray 1985, 204–25.
54 Goering and Mantello, eds, 1984; Boyle 1981, 10–11 gives a later date, 1239–46; for Grosseteste's 'edificatory' imagery, Smalley 3/1984, 276–7.
55 Robert of Flamborough, ed. Firth 1971; Goering and Mantello, eds, 1984, 4–6.
56 Evans 1982, 43–5; Morgan 1982, no. 80.
57 Boyle 1981, 46 n. 27.
58 *C&S* II, 268 nos 1, 8.
59 Broomfield, ed., 1968; Shinners and Dohar, eds, 1998, 123.
60 Boyle 1981, 10.
61 Goering and Mantello, eds, 1984, 51–3.
62 Goering and Mantello, eds, 1984, 52.
63 Aristotle, *Ethics*, Book 2: 1106a20–1109b26 (trans. Thomson et al., rev. 1976, 99–110).
64 Pantin 1955, 193; Boyle 1981, 11; Murray 1981, 312–13; Goering and Mantello, eds, 1984, 4–6.
65 Murray 1981, 317–18; Wenzel 1970.
66 Oschinsky 1971, 409 no. xxiv.
67 Edmund of Abingdon, ed. Forshaw 1973, 37 no. 8; Edmund of Abingdon, ed. Wilshere 1982, 10–11.
68 Dondaine 1948; Murray 1981, 308.
69 Robertson 1946; Murray 1981, 320.
70 Clanchy 1979, 175–201.
71 Cf. Denton 2002.
72 *C&S* II, 115 no. 29.
73 For a range of views, see Moorman 1945, 90–109, 230–32; Boyle 1981; Shinners and Dohar, eds, 1998, 37; Lawrence 2001, 652, 661–6; Denton 2002.
74 *Mats* II, 293–5; Morgan 1982, no. 73; Donovan 1991; Borenius 1932, 42.
75 Donovan 1991, 81–94.
76 *C&S* II, 61 no. 3, 69 no. 23; *C&S* II, 172 no. 8, also 214 no. 26, 452 no. 2, 721 no. 95; Boyle 1985, 35.
77 Gillespie 1980.
78 Tanner, ed., 1990, 239–40; see also Caplan 1933; Robertson 1949; Baldwin 1970, I, 36–9; D'Avray 1985, 13–63; Boyle 1986, 47.
79 Roberts 1968, 1980.
80 Boyle 1985, 34–5, also chart on 38; Lewis 1995, 272–3.
81 Arnould 1940; Laird 1946; Pantin 1955, 224–5; Bennett 1990.
82 Bennett 1990, 170–71.
83 Bennett 1990, 166–7.
84 Jones 1995, 84, 162.
85 Sullens, ed., 1983, xii–xviii; Robertson 1947.
86 Millar 1953; Pantin 1955, 225–6; Millar 1959; Tuve 1964, 42–52; Turner 1968; Kosmer 1973; Gaborit-Chopin et al., 1998, no. 183.
87 Tuve 1964, 42–52.
88 Green 1968; Cocke and Kidson 1993, frontispiece, 8–10; Brown 1999, 28–30.
89 Green 1968, 153–4, 158.
90 Ayers, ed., 2000, 39–44; also Binski 1995a, 185–6; for York, Brown 2003, 71–2, fig. 2.33.
91 Green 1968, 152 n. 31; Tuve 1964, 59–60; Brown 1999, 28 appears not to take account of this possibility.
92 Evans 1982, 22–3, 27–8; Morgan 1988a, no. 126; Morgan 1990, 49–71, esp. 59–65; Lewis 1995, 272–96.
93 Morgan 1982, no. 72 (a); Henderson 1991a.
94 Morgan 1982, no. 86; Binski 1991, 94; Lewis 1995, 295.
95 Sandler 1983.
96 Sandler 1983, 23–7.
97 Sandler 1983, 12.
98 Sandler 2002.
99 Hanna 1996.
100 Gillespie 1980, 42; Goering and Mantello, eds, 1984, 9.
101 D'Avray 1985, 205–6, 242; cf. Kemp, trans. Saltzwedel 1997, 154–9.
102 D'Avray 1985, 244–8; Colish 1985, I, 191.
103 Binski 1999, 15–17.
104 Tristram 1950, 1955; Pantin 1955, 239–43; Kemp, trans. Saltzwedel 1997.
105 Tristram 1955; Binski 1986, Dixon-Smith 1999; for tropology and life lived, Esmeijer 1978, 27–9, 97–128.
106 Edmund of Abingdon, ed. Forshaw 1973, 15–16 for the early texts. See Forshaw 1964, 1971, 1972; also Bloomfield 1952, 142; Pantin 1955, 222–4; Paris ed. Lawrence 1996, 28–36; for the *Mirour*, Edmund of Abingdon, ed. Wilshere 1982.
107 Forshaw 1971, 1972; also Edmund of Abingdon, ed. Forshaw 1973, 18–24.
108 Hamburger 2000b.
109 *C&S* II, 904 n. 3; Robertson 1949, 385.
110 Edmund of Abingdon, ed. Forshaw 1973, 19–20, 109–10 cap. 30.
111 Edmund of Abingdon, ed. Forshaw 1973, 35 no. 6.
112 Bynum 1982, 16.
113 Forshaw 1964; Woolf 1968, 25–6; Bestul 1986; Constable 1995, 205–6.
114 Forshaw 1964, 47–9.
115 Donovan 1991; Higgitt 2000, 165–93.
116 Cf. Stephen of Sawley's meditations on the gradual psalms, ed. and trans. Lackner and O'Sullivan 1984, 5–24, 25–62.
117 Forshaw 1964, 56; Forshaw 1972, 19; Ragusa and Green, eds, 1961.

118 *Debes cogitare diligenter tempus, locum et horam*: Edmund of Abingdon, ed. Forshaw 1973, 83, 85; also Forshaw 1972, 29.
119 Bennett 2001, 4–5.
120 Turner 1968, 58–64; Greenhill 1986; Simmons 1994; Bennett 1997; in general Higgitt 2000, esp. 116–18; cf. the Vernon Psalter, Sandler 1986, no. 53.
121 Simmons 1994, reviewed by Bennett 1997.
122 Bennett 1997, 272.
123 Simmons 1994, pls xviii–xxxi; Greenhill (i.e. Simmons) 1986, 89–93 at first attributed this sequence to the impact of the Bonaventure *Meditations*, but see also Greenhill 1986, 96–9 (intervention by Nigel Morgan), points largely accepted by Simmons 1994, 16–22.
124 Simmons 1994, 22, pl. xxxix; cf. Edmund of Abingdon, ed. Forshaw 1973, 19–20, 105–9, cap. 29; also cf. Stephen of Sawley, ed. and trans. Lackner and O'Sullivan 1984, 25–62; Bennett 1997, 273 notes that the gender forms used in the collects do not point exclusively to female ownership; for *anima* as 'everyman', see Matter 1990, 141.
125 Forshaw 1971, 13; Forshaw 1972, 12; Edmund of Abingdon, ed. Forshaw 1973, 49 cap. 7 no. 25.
126 St Anselm, trans. Ward 1973, 96–7.
127 Hunt and Gibson 1984, 107; Bestul 1986, 17.
128 Bestul 1986, 17; Woolf 1968, 30–33; Constable 1995, 210.
129 Edmund of Abingdon, ed. Forshaw 1973, 85, 91–2.
130 Cf. Woolf 1968, 11–12: 'medieval meditation is concerned with only one of the five senses, that of sight'.
131 Edmund of Abingdon, ed. Forshaw 1973, 83 no. 90, 85 no. 93, 87 no. 96, 91 nos 102, 103.
132 Constable 1995, 203; cf. Woolf 1968, 11–12; Hamburger 2000b, 382.
133 Summers 1987, 312.
134 Forshaw 1972, 30.
135 Bynum 1982, 7–8.
136 Boyle 1985, 35–6.
137 Tanner, ed., 1990, 328.
138 Edmund of Abingdon, ed. Forshaw 1973, 57 no. 44.
139 Mannyng, ed. Sullens 1983, 231–3; Sekules 1995, 51.
140 *AoC*, no. 557; also no. 561; Tristram 1955, 108–12, 111–12 suggests that the mirror is a host and so a symbol of desecration; and for jangling, Simmons, ed., 1879, 4 (text B), 169–70; Moorman 1945, 70; Owst 1926, 172–8.
141 Kennedy 1944, 149; Ladner 1961a, 266.
142 *C&S* II, 991 no. 4.
143 Simmons, ed., 1879.
144 Wormald 1966–8; Sandler 1986, no. 58; Schmitt 1990, 289–355 at 350–55, pls 29–40.
145 Sandler 1986, no. 60.
146 Sandler 1986, no. 65.
147 Waddell 1982, 98.
148 *C&S* II, 894.
149 Edmund of Abingdon, ed. Wilshere 1982.
150 Wormald 1966–8, 41; cf. Edmund of Abingdon, ed. Wilshere 1982, 58, 59, and ed. Forshaw 1973, 83 no. 92.
151 Trexler 1987.
152 Ladner 1961a.
153 Trexler 1987, 24, 43, 49–53.
154 Schmitt 1990, 330–55 at 350–53.
155 Cf. e.g. Dix 1945, 598–612; Waddell 1982, 95–9; Jungmann, trans. Brunner 1986, I, 103–27; Macy 1984. On the communitarian aspects of the Mass, see Bossy 1983; Duffy 1992, 91–130, 92, 111.
156 Duffy 1992, 6–7, 11–52.
157 Aston 1990.
158 Cheney 1956, 155, 157; *C&S* II, 275 no. 45, 297 no. 4.
159 *C&S* II, 1007–8 no. 12; Trexler 1987, 40–41.
160 Southern 1986, 180–81.
161 *C&S* II, 100, 105–6, *CM* III, 71; Constable 1995, 216; Vauchez, trans. Birrell 1997, 440 n. 51.
162 Vincent 1996, 84–5; *MV* II, 201.
163 *C&S* II, 303 no. 30, 622 no. 74; also Shinners, ed., 1997, 463–5 no. 68; for early cults, Hayward 1993, 86.
164 Tanner, ed., 1990, 323 no. 17.
165 Binski 2001.
166 *AL*, 136; Heslop in *AoC*, 26.
167 Fowler 1911, 19; Coulton 1919, 473–4; Berliner 1945, 282 n. 69 for reading adopted here.
168 Newcourt 1708, 550–51; Stow, ed. Strype 1720, 33; *MGL*, 229; Milbourn 1872, 3–5; Barron 1985, 15.
169 Berliner 1945; see also Gilbert 1985.
170 Lucas of Tuy 1612, 90–107 (Book 2 caps 9–11); Coulton 1919, 474–6; Berliner 1945, 278–9; Gilbert 1985, 130–31.
171 Lucas of Tuy 1612, 94, 95–107.
172 Ladner 1955, 88–95; Pickering 1970, 253–63; for the sign of the cross, *C&S* II, e.g. 269 no. 8, 346 no. 7; cf. also Peter the Chanter's prayer mode 2 *ad modum atque similitudinem crucis*, Trexler 1987, 183–4.
173 Kjølbye-Biddle 2001; see also BL MS Cotton Nero C VI. as in O'Reilly 1987, 154; Wormald, ed. Alexander et al., 1988, 123–38.
174 Berliner 1945, 282; Huffman 1998; also Liebermann 1910.
175 I am grateful to Professor Alison Stones for drawing this to my attention.
176 Esposito, ed., 1960, 26–7; the Lombards were also blamed for 'shouting'.
177 Strucken 1928; Vavalà 1929, 714, figs 25, 458; De Francovich 1938; Berliner 1945, 282 n. 70; Garrison 1949, nos 155, 243; Thoby 1959–63, 178–9; Mühlberg 1960; Lisner 1970, figs 6, 7, 9, 17, 20, 76; Von Alemann-Schwartz 1976; White 1987, 140.
178 Simpson, ed., 1873, lxvi, 91.
179 Rastall 1970–71, 87.
180 Barron 2003, 126–32.
181 Barron 2003, 130.
182 Rubin 1991, 164–212.
183 Rubin 1991, 176–85.
184 Rubin 1991, 199–204.
185 Rubin 1991, 180.
186 Simpson, ed., 1873, 141; Sekules 1986, 121, 129 n. 45, 131 n. 52.
187 Mühlberg 1960, 78.
188 Shinners, ed., 1997, 463–5 no. 68 for rural errors.
189 Huffman 1998.
190 Bolton 1999, 150.
191 Bolton 1999, 135–6, 150–51.
192 *C&S* II, 1285–90, 1349.
193 *FH* III, 213–4.

CHAPTER 9

1 Bynum 1982, 1–21; Jaeger 1994, 9–10; Constable 1995.
2 Fortenbaugh 1975; see also Carruthers 1990.
3 Fortenbaugh 1975, 17.
4 Carruthers 1990, 68.
5 Pickering 1970, 223–307; 1980, 31–45.
6 Pickering 1970, 251.
7 Pickering 1970, 233.
8 Pickering 1970, 223–4 (emphasis in original).
9 Pickering 1970, 244.
10 Newman, ed. Kerr 1985, 31–68.
11 Marrow 1979, 7–27, 190–205.
12 Hamburger 2000b.
13 Passarge 1924; Panofsky 1927; Mühlberg 1960; Krönig 1962; Woolf 1968, 389–94; Büttner 1983; Belting, trans. Bartusis and Meyer 1990; Hamburger 1997b; Ridderbos 1998; Recht 1999, 252–69.
14 Gilbert 2001, 11–12.
15 Gage 1973; Colish 1985, I, 198–202; Duggan 1989; Kessler 1989; Carruthers 1990, 17; Gilbert 2001.
16 Gilson, trans. Downes 1940, 78–81; Shepherd, ed., 1959, lv–lvi; Woolf 1968, 19–26.
17 Berliner 1945.
18 Constable 1995.
19 Swarzenski 2/1974, pl. 18, fig. 40; O'Reilly 1987, 154.
20 Lasko 1972, 36–7, 46, pl. 29, also frontispiece; O'Reilly 1987, 154.
21 Pickering 1970, 255–6, 276; O'Reilly 1987, 153; O'Reilly 1992, 170–80; generally, Raw 1990.
22 O'Reilly 1987, 153, pl. 5.
23 O'Reilly 1987, 153; Raw 1990, 197–8, 151–5, pl. 12b.
24 O'Reilly 1987, 153–4; O'Reilly 1992, 184–5.
25 Zarnecki et al. 1984, nos 207–8; Parker and Little 1994, 48–52.
26 Morgan 1982, no. 23, figs 82–3.
27 Morgan 1982, nos 45, 47, figs 147, 157.
28 O'Reilly 1987, 157; cf. Woolf 1968, 9–11.
29 Bradley, ed., 1982, 158–63.
30 O'Reilly 1987, 157.
31 Bradley, ed., 1982, 367–9, 375–6.
32 Morgan 1988a, no. 101 fig. 29, no. 111 fig. 67; O'Reilly 1992, 186.
33 Andersson 1949, 190–91, also figs 90–91, 96–7, 131, 134, 148, 154–5; Anker 1981, 232 fig. 2.88, 245 fig. 2.95; also Blindheim 1998.
34 Gardner 1995.
35 Gransden 1998, 262. I am grateful to Antonia Gransden for drawing this image to my attention.
36 Lewis 1986, 549; Morgan 1988a, no. 128; Moleiro, ed., 2002, 135, 226, 299.
37 Hildburgh 1923–4, 209–10, figs 1–2, pl. 47; Scott 1996, I, no. 4; II, fig. 29; O'Reilly 1981, 305.
38 O'Reilly 1992, 193–201.
39 Thoby 1959–63; Haussherr 1963; O'Reilly 1987; Belting, trans. Bartusis and Meyer 1990, 144, 254 n. 37; Raw 1990; Constable 1995, 179–83, 181 n. 222; Chazelle 2001.
40 Henderson 1968, 106–8.
41 Thoby 1959–63, I, 129–58.
42 Morgan 1982, no. 23 figs 81–2, no. 18 fig. 57.
43 Butler 1990, 139–41; the fundamental model is that of 'body techniques', Mauss 1935.
44 Thoby 1959–63, I, 133 wrongly sees this as an English innovation; Wirth 1953 is fundamental, and is discussed in Cames 1966; Roth 1967, 26–32; Verdier 1970; for the 'ternary logical model' see *inter alia* Le Goff, trans. Goldhammer 1984, 7, 220–27.
45 Cames 1966, 201–2.
46 Verdier 1970.
47 Panofsky 2/1979, 56–7.
48 Cames 1966, 186, fig. 2.
49 *PL* 198, col. 1631: *tres tantum claves.*
50 *PL* 158, cols 761–2; cf. *PL* 159 cols 282–3; Roth 1967, 29; Pickering 1970, 237.
51 Pickering 1970, 243.
52 Dobson, ed., 1972, 286–7 fol. 182, trans. Savage and Watson 1991, 191–2, n. 15.
53 Cames 1966, 185; Roth 1967, 31.
54 Ragusa and Green, eds, 1961, 333–4; Pickering 1970, 241–2.
55 Lucas of Tuy 1612, II, caps 9–11, 90–107.
56 Lucas of Tuy 1612, 94; cf. Coulton 1919, 474.
57 Lucas of Tuy 1612, 94; cf. Coulton 1919, 475.
58 Lucas of Tuy 1612, 104 (my translation); Berliner 1945, 278–9 n. 54; Gilbert 1985, 132–3 for *Haec et huius modi illis quasi rationabiliter asserentibus.*
59 Lucas of Tuy 1612, 95–107; cf. *PL* 217 cols 609–14 at 612; Cames 1966, 185. For a copy of the *volto santo* at Bury, James 1895, 139; Gransden 1973, 115.
60 Constable 1995, 208–17.
61 *Nam [. . .] mater satietatis est identitas*: Trexler 1987, 43, 227 lines 2102–3.
62 Carruthers 1990, 68; cf. Trexler 1987, 38; Jaeger 1994, 11; Bennett 2001, 3.
63 Taubert and Taubert 1969; Tripps 1998, 121–8.
64 Bräm 1997; Stones 1997.
65 Constable 1995, 181, 221; Christie 1938, 130–33, frontispiece, pls 81–4.
66 Cames 1966, 195–6.
67 Morgan 1988a, no.137; Henry 1990.
68 Henry 1990, 122–4, 159; Lewis 1995, 323.
69 Pickering 1970, 254, 260–62; O'Reilly 1992, 180–86.
70 Lewis 1995, 323.
71 Pickering 1970, 264, 276–9; Pickering 1980, 13–14.
72 Roth 1967; Morgan 1988a, no. 126; Morgan 1990, 65–7; Lewis 1995, 286–9; Morgan 1995, 14–15.
73 Pickering 1970, 240–42; Pickering 1980, 7–8.
74 Kemp, trans. Saltzwedel 1997, 112–13.
75 Morgan 1988a, no. 167, fig. 337.
76 Screech 1997.
77 Strucken 1928; De Francovich 1938; Mühlberg 1960; Von Alemann-Schwartz 1976.
78 Sandler 1986, no. 97.
79 Wormald, ed. Alexander et al., 1984, 166–7.
80 Woolf 1968, 183–238 for the later era.
81 *PL* 176, col. 954; Woolf 1968, 58.
82 *PL* 158, cols 761–2.
83 Edmund of Abingdon, ed. Forshaw 1973, 83 no. 90, 85 no. 93, 87 no. 96, 91–2 nos 102, 103; Constable 1995, 205.
84 Woolf 1968, 63–4.

85 Thompson, ed., 1958; Woolf 1968, 32–3, 46–8; 58–66; Dobson, ed., 1972; Dobson 1976, 114–73; Savage and Watson, trans., 1991 1991; Innes-Parker 1995; Lewis 1996, 217–23.
86 Woolf 1968, 53–66; Dobson, ed., 1972, 285, 288; Savage and Watson, trans., 1991, 191–2; Innes-Parker 1995, 141–6.
87 Dobson, ed., 1972, 291–2; Savage and Watson, trans., 1991, 194.
88 Thompson, ed., 1958; Savage and Watson, trans., 1991, 245–57.
89 Thompson, ed., 1958, 20, 43; Savage and Watson, trans., 1991, 247–8, 419 n. 3.
90 Thompson, ed., 1958, 20–27; Savage and Watson, trans., 1991, 248–51; Innes-Parker 1995, 139–42.
91 Binski 1986, 41–2, 43 for *Deboneretė* in other contexts.
92 Woolf 1968, 19, 67–74.
93 Woolf 1968, 22–3.
94 Lewis 1996.
95 Dobson 1976, 2–4; Trexler 1987, 47–8.
96 Woolf 1968, 28–33.
97 Morgan 1988a, no. 100.
98 Von Simson 1953; Morgan 1991, 94–5.
99 Ringbom 1965; F. Lewis 1985, 1992; S. Lewis 1995, 293–4; Hamburger 1998, 317–82.
100 *CMM*, 35–6.
101 Norton and Park, eds, 1986, 324: *sculpturas nusquam, picturas tantum licet habere in crucibus*, cf. also 356; for Meaux's paintings, ibid., 141, 158, 208–9; Rudolph 1990b, 180–91, esp. 185–6.
102 VCH Yorkshire III, 146–9, 147.
103 Recht 1999, 256.
104 Gilson, trans. Downes 1940, 78–81; Woolf 1968, 22–3, 184; Rudolph 1990b, 107–10.
105 Constable 1995, 199.
106 Woolf 1968, 60.
107 Sandler 1986, no. 120; Wormald, ed. Alexander et al., 1988, 88–102. I owe this observation to Christopher Moule.
108 Wormald, ed. Alexander et al., 1988, 88–90.
109 Bony 1979, 19–22.
110 Auerbach, tans. Trask 1953; see Cameron 1992, 33–4; Hamburger 1997b, esp. 19–23; cf. also Kemp, trans. Saltzwedel 1997, 102–14; Recht 1999, 394–6.
111 Knox and Carelis 1979, xl–l.

CHAPTER 10

1 Morgan 1982, no. 92; Lewis 1987, 423–4.
2 Temple 1976, no. 11.
3 Temple 1976, no. 64, fig. 210; Raw 1997, 168, pl. XVa; Henderson 1992, 243.
4 Morgan 1991, 93–4.
5 *O felicia oscula lactentis labris impressa, cum inter crebra indicia reptantis infancie utpote verus ex te filius tibi matri alluderet; cum verus ex Patre Deus Dei unigenitus imperaret*. Cf. *PL* 39, col. 2131; variants in *PL* 30, col. 144, 57, col. 866, 101 col. 1303; also St Bernard, *PL* 183, col. 416; cf. *PL* 96, col. 272.
6 *MV* II, 14–15; Hunt and Gibson 1984, 107.
7 Cf. Lewis 1987, 420–23.
8 For the Veronica, Ringbom 1965, 23–30; F. Lewis 1985; S. Lewis 1987, 126–31, 421–2; Morgan 1990, 67–70, n. 89; S. Lewis 1995, 293–4; New 2002, 57–9. For the Man of Sorrows, Ringbom 1965, 70; Belting, trans. Bartusis and Meyer 1990, 132, but cf. F. Lewis 1985, 102.
9 Ringbom 1965; Belting, trans. Bartusis and Meyer 1990.
10 *PL* 206, cols 378–9; see Bell 1977a, 1977b, 1978; also Constable, 1995, 168, 191–2. See also my paper 'The Faces of Christ in Matthew Paris's *Chronica majora*', forthcoming in the festschrift for Professor J. Marrow.
11 Henderson 1967b, 100–01: cf. e.g. *AoC*, no. 263.
12 Bennett 2001.
13 Nodelman 1975.
14 Baxandall 1972, 46–7.
15 Sartre, trans. Mairet 1962, 56–94 at 57, 63; Casey 1990, 114–28.
16 In general, Lewis 1995.
17 Belting, trans. Jephcott 1994, 261–96, fig. 218.
18 Shearman 1992, 5–6, also 46.
19 Cf. Camille 2000.
20 In general, Lewis 1987.
21 Bayley 1821, 118–19 note b: *et duos scherumbinos, stantes a dextris et a sinistris magni patibuli, pulcros fieri faciatis in praedicta ecclesia, cum hyllari vultu et jocoso*; CLR 1240–45, 14–15.
22 Haussherr 1977; Morgan 1988a, no. 159.
23 Binski 1995a, 151, fig. 199.
24 *GC* I, 9–10.
25 De Wald 1932, pl. xci.
26 Haussherr 1977, 150, 152, 156.
27 Jaeger 1985, 168–75.
28 Keck 1998, 105–9.
29 CLR 1226–40, 444.
30 CCR 1237–42, 514.
31 Kemp, trans. Saltzwedel 1997; Jung 2000; Recht 1999.
32 Svanberg 1993, 361–2; Binski 1997a, 354–5.
33 Branner 1961; Ravaux 1979; Kurmann 1987, 20–22; Kimpel and Suckale, trans. Neu 1990, 288–90.
34 Sauerländer 1972, 457, 468–9, pls 157, 179.
35 Sauerländer 1976, 1977; Bony 1983, 266–75; Suckale 1987; Schuller et al. 1993.
36 Hahnloser 2/1972.
37 Kurmann 1987; Williamson 1995, 59–65; for a useful summary see Frankl, rev. Crossley 2000, 322–3 n. 13a.
38 Sauerländer 1976.
39 Sauerländer, trans. Sondheimer 1972, pls 236–53; Hamann-Mac Lean and Schüssler 1996, II/5; Recht 1999, 311–16; Clark 2000.
40 Frodl-Kraft 1972.
41 Sauerländer, trans. Sondheimer 1972, pl 255; Hamann-Mac Lean and Schüssler 1996, II/8, nos 3019, 3027, 3032, 3036, 3045, 3048.
42 Sauerländer, trans. Sondheimer 1972, pl. 262; Hamann-Mac Lean and Schüssler 1996, II/8, nos 3381–7.
43 Sauerländer, trans. Sondheimer 1972, pl 257; Hamann-Mac Lean and Schüssler 1996, II/8, nos 3460, 3474–5, 3496–9, 3542–5, 3563, 3572–5, 3689–90, 3724–6, 3730–32; Recht 1999, 314–15.

44 Schmitt 1990, 33–55, 253–88; Kemp, trans. Saltzwedel 1997, 146; Baldwin 1997, 639.
45 Page 1989, 8–41, 134–7.
46 Williamson 1995, 62–3; Panofsky 1964, 33–4, fig. 105. For more recent revisions to the notion of *romanitas* at Reims, see Sauerländer 2003.
47 Hamann-Mac Lean and Schüssler 1996, II/8, nos 3060, 3072, 3088–92.
48 Sauerländer, trans. Sondheimer 1972, pls 193, 198, 200, 206, 211; Ravaux 1979; Kurmann 1987; Williamson 1995, 156–60; Hamann-Mac Lean and Schüssler 1996, II/6, nos 586, 645–50.
49 Colvin, ed., 1963, I, 104–5.
50 Wilson et al. 1986, 26–8, 7–9, 59; Wilson in *AoC*, 75–7; Binski 1995a, 13–29, 33–43.
51 *AoC*, no. 294; Binski 1995a, figs 179–80; Williamson 1995, 201–2.
52 Binski 1995a, 116; Wilson 1995, 459–64, 461 n. 38.
53 Sauerländer 1976, 1977; Bony 1983, 266–75; Suckale 1987; Schuller et al. 1993; Williamson 1995, 91–8, 155, 174–86; Recht 1999, 313.
54 Hamann-Mac Lean and Schüssler 1996, II/6, nos 1714–33.
55 Gaborit-Chopin et al. 1998, nos 19–23, 25–6.
56 Michael 2002, 14–15 no. 2.
57 Liversidge, Binski and Lynn 1995; Hamann-Mac Lean and Schüssler 1996, II/8, nos 3088–92.
58 Morgan 1988a, no. 153; Binski 1995a, 165; Binski 1997a, 366–9.
59 Morgan 1988a, no. 151, fol. 9v.
60 Binski 1995a, fig. 207.
61 Williamson 1995, 149–50, fig 223; cf. Barnet, ed., 1997, figs 1–4, nos 2, 4, 5; Gaborit-Chopin et al. 1998, no. 109.
62 Binski 1997a; for Trondheim, see Anker 1981, 159–85; *AoC*, nos 299–306; Williamson 1995, 221.
63 Legner 1991, 219 fig. 153; cf. Hamann-Mac Lean and Schüssler 1996, II/8, nos 3091–2.
64 Von Simson 1953; Barasch 1976; Schmitt 1990, 1991; Svanberg 1993; Recht 1999, 307–19.
65 Hoeniger 1995, 21–42.
66 Wittgenstein 1958, 177–85; Wollheim 1980, 93–6 section 41; for another sense of transitivity, Shearman 1992, 27, 33.
67 Gombrich 3/1978.
68 Schmitt 1990.
69 Cf. Recht 1976, 183; Recht 1999, 316–19.
70 Panofsky 1960, 55–63.
71 Hegel, trans. Knox 1975, I, 517–51, II, 788–887; Knox and Karelis 1979, xxxii–xxxvii.
72 Knox and Karelis 1979, xl–l, lx–lxxiii.
73 Again, Hegel: Knox and Karelis 1979, lxv–lxvi; for application, see Baxandall 1980, 166–8; cf. Riegl's (Hegelian) concept of exterior unity: Podro 1982, 81–95; Shearman 1992, 10–58; Recht 1999, 315–16.
74 For the issue of vernacular 'modes' see for example Bäuml 1980; Kemp, trans. Saltzwedel 1997; Jung 2000; cf. however Camille 1985, 37–44; Camille in *AoC*, 36.
75 Ménard 1969.
76 Recht 1999, 402: 'il n'y a rien "derrière" les formes visibles'.
77 Le Goff 1997, 50.
78 Fortenbaugh 1975, 73.
79 Sekules 1995.
80 Loux 1981.
81 *MV* II, 125.
82 Schmitt 1990, 30–31, 33–55; Jaeger 1994, 112, 255.
83 Dobson, ed., 1972, 156; Savage and Watson, trans., 1991, 126.
84 Thompson, ed., 1958, 28; Savage and Watson, trans., 1991, 251–5.
85 *GA* I, 219; Vaughan 1984, 15.
86 Mannyng, ed. Sullens 1983, 231–3 lines 9264, 9270, 9273; cf. Wright, ed., 1868, 41–2.
87 Dobson, ed., 1972, 153; Savage and Watson, trans., 1992, 124; cf. Biller and Minnis, eds, 1998, 95.
88 Aristotle, *Rhetoric*, 1389b (trans. Lawson-Tancred 1991, 174); *Ethics*, Book 4: 1127b–1128b (trans. Thomson et al., rev. 1976, 167–9); *Poetics*, 3. 4 (trans. Heath 1996, 9); also Fortenbaugh 1975, 20–21; Screech 1997, 1–5; Skinner 2002.
89 Skinner 2002, 151–2.
90 Jaeger 1985, 113–26; 143–7.
91 Graf 1997; Skinner 2002, 153–4.
92 Southern 1986, 114–15. Cf. the courtesy text *Stans puer ad mensam* attributed to Grosseteste, *nec coram domino debes monstrare cachinno*: Gieben 1967, 57 line 9.
93 Recht 1999, 395; cf. Kemp, trans. Saltzwedel 1997, 102–14.
94 Brentano 1935, 8–13; Jaeger 1985, 162–3, also 138–9, 147–8; Jaeger 1994, 32, 109–10; Le Goff 1997, 43–6; cf. Curtius, trans. Trask 1953, 417–35.
95 Aquinas, *Summa Theologiae* (trans. Gilby 1972, 212–13, 218–19), *quaest.* 168, 1–2: *motus exteriores sunt quadam signa interioris dispositionis, secundum illud* (*Ecclesiasticus* 19: 27), *Amictus corporis, et risus dentium, et igressus hominis enuntiant de illo. [. . .] Licet interdum honesta joca ac suavia sint, tamen ab ecclesiastica abhorrent regula; quoniam quae in Scripturis sanctis non reperimus, ea quemadmodum usurpare possumus?*
96 Le Goff 1997, 46–9; Screech 1997, 4 and *passim*.
97 Jaeger 1985, 127–75.
98 Ménard 1969, 28–31, 419–62; Le Goff 1997, 48.
99 Jaeger 1985, 168–75; Jaeger 1994, 102–3; Le Goff 1997, 50–51; Skinner 2002, 149–51.
100 Screech 1997; Skinner 2002, 150.
101 Pseudo-Dionysius, trans. Luibheid 1987, 190; Binski 1997a.
102 Bynum 1992, 256–7.
103 Coss 1998, fig 36; Williamson 1995, 173 fig 257, 191–2 fig 286.
104 Suckale 1987, figs 51, 55; Williamson 1995, 94–5.
105 Gage 1986, 34; Schmitt 1990, 153–4; Svanberg 1993, 360; Jaeger 1994, 110–11, 269–77.
106 Gage 1986, 34; Gage 1993, 77–8.
107 Felix, ed. and trans. Colgrave 1956, 126–7, 134–5.
108 Morris repr. 1987, 155–6.
109 Shearman 1992, 121–4.
110 Le Goff 1997, 45; Brentano 1935, 95–6.
111 Schmitt 1990, 33–55.
112 Bloch 1923, 75, cap. 5.

113 *PL* 195, cols 748–9.
114 Bloch 1923, 98, cap. 18.
115 *PL* 195, col. 767.
116 Schmitt 1990, 152–5; Jaeger 1994, 343–4.
117 *LEC*, 61, 215 lines 1291–2; cf. *PL* 195, col. 749; *LEC* 120, 274 line 3370; cf. *PL* 195, col. 767.
118 Jaeger 1985, 161–8.
119 Lawrence 1960, 215.
120 Jaeger 1985, 38–9.
121 *PL* 195, cols. 571–4.
122 Williams 1993, 217–18.
123 Brentano 1935, 8–13; Trexler 1987, 38–9, 197 lines 982–4, 208 lines 1394–5; cf. Schmitt 1990, 179–84; Elias, trans. Jephcott 1994, 48–56; Jaeger 1994, 10–13, 244–68.
124 *PL* 195, cols 745–6.
125 Ménard 1969, 446–7.
126 Ménard 1969, 426–47.
127 Jaeger 1994, 331–48; cf. Jaeger 1985; cf. also Recht 1999, 307–19.
128 Jaeger 1994, 1–17 at 7–9; for *cultus virtutum*, 76–117.
129 Jaeger 1994, 331, 339.
130 Jaeger 1994, 342–4.
131 Jaeger 1994, 346.
132 John of Garland, ed. and trans. Paetow 1927; 1928; Wright, ed., 1856.
133 John of Garland, ed. and trans. Paetow 1927, 157, 177.
134 Cf. Gerald of Wales on the monks of Canterbury, in *GW* IV, 39–40.
135 Brentano 1935; Elias, trans. Jephcott 1994.
136 John of Garland, ed. and trans. Paetow 1927, 159–60, 168–9.
137 John of Garland, ed. and trans. Paetow 1927, 161, 168, 170, 174.
138 John of Garland, ed. and trans. Paetow 1927, 174, 243–4.
139 Enders 1992, 48–9; Chazelle 1990, 139–40, 143, 150.
140 Jaeger 1994, 258–9, 284–91.
141 Trexler 1987, 49–53.
142 Contrast however the relationship between (Lotharingian) *antiqui* and (Parisian) *moderni* proposed in Sauerländer 2003.
143 Page 1997, 21.

CHAPTER 11

1 Page 1997, 12.
2 Page 1989, 3, 134–5, 157.
3 Schapiro 1977, 42–6; cf. Kemp, trans. Saltzwedel 1997, 136–59.
4 Greenhalgh 1989, 106–7; Williams 1993, 363.
5 Young 1933, I, 82–3, also 549; Marshall 1950, 471.
6 Enders 1992, 54–68.
7 Schmitt 1990, 321–55, esp. 333–5.
8 Enders 1992, 111.
9 Williams 1993; Tripps 1998; Recht 1999, 269–76; for 'wonder', Bynum 2001.
10 Williams 1993, 222; Timmermann 2000.
11 Beckwith 1992, 75–81; cf. Young 1933, I, 79–111; see also Gibson 1989; Kemp, trans. Saltzwedel 1997, 145–53.
12 L-B, no. 339: Kemp, trans. Saltzwedel 1997, 148–9.
13 Baldwin 1970, I, 198–9; Page 1989, 19; Baldwin 1997, 639–40.
14 In general Rudolph 1990b, 104–26; Williams 1993, 217
15 *PL* 195, cols 571–2.
16 Gage 1973, 359; Rudolph 1990b, 106 n. 322.
17 Chadd 1986, 300–01.
18 Norton and Park, eds, 1986, 329, 331, 349.
19 Chadd 1986, 299, 304–6.
20 Chadd 1986, 305; Baldwin 1997, 645; Enders 1992, 123–4; Holsinger 2001, 137–87 at 160–61.
21 Prynne 1974, 279–81; Williams 1993, 219; Page 1997, 8; Holsinger 2001, 157–8.
22 Chadd 1986, 305.
23 Williams 1993, 218–19, n. 39.
24 Reynolds 1965, 118; Page 1989, 4, 134–5; Holsinger 2001, 157–60.
25 Page 1989, 135 after *PL* 176, cols 1080–82, 1089.
26 Schmitt 1990, 174–205; Jaeger 1994, 244–68; Kemp, trans. Saltzwedel 1997, 145–6.
27 Baldwin 1970, I, 198–204, 200, II, 139 n. 194, 140 n. 196; Page 1989, 19–33, 134–7, 144–54; Schmitt 1990, 269–70; Baldwin 1997, 639.
28 Baldwin 1970, I, 199; Tanner, ed., 1990, 243; Baldwin 1997, 640–41.
29 *C&S* I, 984–5 no. 2; *C&S* II, 26 nos 6–8; *C&S* II, 63–4 no. 11.
30 Baldwin 1970, I, 198; Baldwin 1997, 640, 644.
31 Baldwin 1970, I, 199–200; Baldwin 1997, 642–3.
32 Page 1987, 50–76 at 53; Baldwin 1997, 643–8.
33 *Historias, non vana, depingentes; artifices etiam instrumentorum musicorum, ut eis tristitia et taedium amoveatur, devotio non lascivia excitetur*: *PL* 205, col. 253; Baldwin 1970, I, 202–4; Page 1989, 20.
34 Page 1989, 145–6; Baldwin 1997, 645.
35 Baldwin 1997, 643.
36 Baldwin 1970, I, 203.
37 Page 1989, 20.
38 Henderson 1991b; Lawson 1991.
39 Holsinger 2001, 138–40; Binski 2003.
40 Morgan 1982, no. 49; Page 1997, 14, fig. 14.
41 Page 1997.
42 Sandler 1986, nos 30, 50, 51, 110; Page 1997, 12, figs 1–3, 8, 12; Holsinger 2001, 153–4.
43 Holsinger 2001, 137–87.
44 Steele, ed., 1898, 12, 55–6; Page 1997, 9.
45 Bowles 1957; Harrison 1967; McKinnon 1968; Rastall 1970–71; Seebass 1973; Foster 1977; Rastall 1992, 115–16; Williams 1993, 297–301, 363; Page 1997.
46 McKinnon 1968, 4–10.
47 McKinnon 1968, 14–20; Morgan 1988a, no. 166.
48 Henderson 1991b, 135.
49 Page 1989, 28–9; Baldwin 1997, 643–4.
50 Baldwin 1970, I, 203; Page 1989, 26.
51 Mannyng, ed. Sullens 1983, 119–20; Foster 1977, 29; cf. Pickering 1970, 285–307.
52 McKinnon 1968, 4–10; Pickering 1970, 286–99; in general, Van Schaik 1992.
53 Southern 1986, 113–19.

54 Smalley 3/1984, 336–7, 343; Southern 1986, 176–81, 230–31.
55 Page 1987, 52–61, 255 n. 10.
56 Page 1987, 58–61.
57 Smalley 3/1984, 281–328; cf. Esmeijer 1978, 127–8.
58 Pevsner 1945; cf. Smalley 3/1984, 371.
59 Williams 1993, 363.
60 Williams 1993, 297–301.
61 Williams 1993, 165–86.
62 Williams 1993, 187–203, 228–31, 354; Bicknell 1996, 13–16.
63 Williams 1993, 94–102, 200, 124; for bell founding, Blair and Ramsay, eds, 1991, 89–93.
64 *GA* I, 520, discussed Williams 1993, 301–3, and for clocks 216, 331–5; cf. Rastall 1970–71, 93.
65 Williams 1993, 70–93.
66 Donovan 1991, 69–81, figs 38–41, 43–6, 49.
67 Donovan 1991, fig. 46.
68 Morgan 1982, nos 32, 43b, 63, 71–2.
69 Williamson 1995, 93, fig. 141; Frodl-Kraft 1972.
70 *GC* I, 9; cf. Heslop 1982, pl. xxviie.
71 For Langton, Wilson 1995, 458–9, n. 23; for De Gray, Ramm et al. 1971, 104. The exact whereabouts of the burial at Winchester of Peter des Roches is unknown, but the paintings in the so-called Chapel of the Guardian Angels (St Michael and All Angels?) date to the period of his death: Demus, trans. Whittall 1970, 509–10; Park 1993, 129–30, figs 10.5–6.
72 Pseudo-Dionysius, trans. Luibheid 1987; Rorem 1993, 73–83; Keck 1998, 174–9.
73 Luscombe 1985.
74 Callus, ed., 1955, 56–62; Southern 1986, 200–03.
75 Morgan 1982, no. 53.
76 Legge 1941.
77 Vallentin 1908; Luscombe 1979; Rorem 1993, 30–36.
78 Gage 1982, 46–9.
79 Gage 1982, 46; Binski 1997a.
80 Venables 1883; Webb 1956, 117–19; Dean 1986; Kidson 1986, Heslop 1990; Wilson 1990, 183–4; Kidson 1994, Alexander 1995; Binski 1997a, 357.
81 CPR 1247–58, 506; Foster, ed., 1931, 184–5.
82 Binski 1995a.
83 *CMV*, 407–9; Callus, ed., 1955, 241–6; Stocker 1985, 1986, 1987; Alexander 1995.
84 Lethaby 1907; Gardner 1960; Stone 1972, 125–7, 130–31; Glenn 1986; Heslop 1990; Williamson 1995, 207–10; Binski 1997a.
85 Heslop 1990, 152; cf. also Crowland, Henderson 1985, 92–4; York Minster Chapter House vault, *AoC*, no. 344; Huth Psalter, fol. 119v, Morgan 1988a, no. 167.
86 Lethaby 1907, 83–8; Stone 1972, 125–7; Williamson 1995, 207–9.
87 Foot, Litton and Simpson 1986, 61 for the date.
88 Kidson 1986, 41–2; Heslop 2000, 68–9.
89 In general Hammerstein 1962, esp. 218–38; Glenn 1986; Binski 1995a, 71–3, figs 96–7; Brown 1999, 161–6, fig. 127; Engel 2000, 112–70.
90 For the Lincoln-related buildings, Dean 1986; for Trondheim, Fischer 1965, I, 324–40, II, 580.
91 Cave 1948, figs 121–33.
92 Heslop 1990, 152.
93 Heslop 1990, 154.
94 Guest, commentary, 1995, 123, fol. 45.
95 Christie 1938, 161–5, 167–71 nos 87, 90.
96 Pickering 1970, 285–99; Foster 1977, 29; Jaeger 1994, 139–72; Van Schaik 1992, 38–61, esp. 44–51, also 97–101. My thanks to Laura Williams for discussing these points with me.
97 Page 1989, 160.
98 Pickering 1970, 287; Trevisa, ed. Seymour 1975, II, 1391–2; Page 1987, 193.
99 Rudolph 1990a, 42–3, after *PL* 176, cols 183–4, 317–19; Lethaby 1907, 388–90.
100 Lewis 1995, 210, figs 175, 371, nn. 31–3; for a different reading, cf. Roberts 1985.
101 Williamson 1995, pl. 274; Jung 2000.
102 Lethaby 1907, 388–90; Sauerländer, trans. Sondheimer 1972, pl. 1; Gerson 1986, 192–4, fig. 11.
103 Roberts 1983, 582, figs 42–3.
104 Bynum 1982; Roberts 1985; Bynum 1987; Hamburger 1990, 72–7; Constable 1995, 204–5; Hamburger 1998, 111–48; Lewis 1997; Bennett 2001; for the Holy Blood, Vincent 2001.
105 Pseudo-Dionysius, trans. Luibheid 1987, 190.
106 Heslop 1990, 155; Anderson 1963, 1–2.
107 Henderson 1985, 94, fig. 13.
108 *PL* 37, cols 1960–66; cf. also *PL* 176, col. 1081.
109 Engel 2000, 112–70; Brown 1999, 161–6, fig. 127; Binski 1995a, 71–3, figs 96–7; Lethaby 1907, 389.
110 Hammerstein 1962. For debate, see Bowles 1957; McKinnon 1968; Rastall 1970–71; Seebass 1973; Foster 1977; Harrison 2/1978, 319–35 at 321, 328; also *AoC*, no. 608; Rose 2001.
111 Bowers 1994, 52–3.
112 Bowers 1994, 69; for strings, see Page 1987, 60.
113 De Laborde 1911–27, II, pl. 260.
114 *MV* II, 70.
115 Mannyng, ed. Sullens 1983, 119–20.
116 Morgan 1982, no. 23; Henderson 1991a, 682–6.
117 Harper 1991, 70, 93, 95, 258–9, 270–71; for the Lincoln Use, Bradshaw and Wordsworth, eds, 1892, 62–81, 125–9, 364–96 at 387; additionally see Wickenden 1883, 215–24. The extent to which the Use differed from Sarum prompts disagreement: Bowers 1994, 47–8; cf. Morgan 2001, 183 who stresses the fundamental similarities.
118 Morgan 1988a, no. 100; Pickering 1970, 288–98.
119 Draper 1979, 8–9.
120 Gage 1982, 46–9.
121 Morgan 1988a, no. 161; cf. also Donovan 1991, 136–40.
122 Dean 1986, 91–2.
123 Bony 1979, 5–6.
124 Binski 1995a, 28–9, 74–6.
125 Binski 1995a, 39–42.
126 *MLH*, 56, 58.

EPILOGUE

1 In general see Raguin, Brush and Draper, eds, 1995.
2 Morgan 1988a, nos 153–4.
3 Heslop 1988, 160–61.
4 Binski 2002, 121.
5 Sandler 1986; Heslop 1988, 159–61.
6 Sears 1997, 19–37.
7 Kemp, trans. Saltzwedel 1997, 112–13.
8 Gage 1993, 77–8.
9 Binski 1997a, 367.
10 Sciurie 1993–4; Nicolai 2002, 117–18.
11 Hamburger 1990, 45–69 at 52, 57–9, figs 10, 12, 21.
12 Schmitt 1990, 316–20; Bynum 1992, 181–238; Simons 1994; Elliott 1997.
13 Simons 1994, 20.
14 Keck 1998, 107, fig. 11.
15 Schmitt 1990, 319–20; Simons 1994, 13–15; Vauchez, trans. Birrell 1997, 427–43.
16 Vauchez, trans. Birrell 1997, 443; in general Bynum 2001, 37–75.
17 Pevsner 1945, 53; Panofsky 1951, 6.
18 Bynum 1992, 259, 256; for an uncritical use of Aristotle, see Caviness 1991; cf. also Hamburger 2000b, 395.
19 Bäuml 1980, esp. 258–65.
20 Bäuml 1980, 259.
21 Kemp, trans. Saltzwedel 1997, 102–28; Jung 2000, 645–50 at 649. Jung 2003 however appears to put forward a view more congenial to the present argument.
22 Henderson 1967a, 88–93; Kidson 1987b, 143; Kemp, trans. Saltzwedel 1997, 103–4.
23 Bäuml 1980; Kemp, trans. Saltzwedel 1997, 115–16.
24 Dronke 1970.
25 Henderson 1968, 120.
26 Camille 1992.
27 Bony 1979; Coldstream 1994; Wilson in Marks and Williamson, eds, 2003, 98–119.

Bibliography

Abbott, E. A., *St Thomas of Canterbury: His Death and Miracles*. 2 vols, London 1898

Abou-El-Haj, B., 'Bury St Edmunds Abbey between 1070 and 1124: A History of Property, Privilege, and Monastic Art Production', *Art History*, 6: 1983, 1–29

Aelred of Rievaulx, trans. A. Hoste and J. Dubois, *Quand Jésus eut douze ans*, Sources chrétiennes, 60, Paris 1958

——, trans. M. E. Laker, *Spiritual Friendship*, Cistercian Fathers Series, 5, Kalamazoo 1977

Alberigo, G., ed., *Conciliorum oecumenicorum decreta*, Bologna 1973

Aldhelm, trans. M. Lapidge and M. Herren, *The Prose Works*, Ipswich 1979

Alexander, J. S., 'The Angel Choir of Lincoln Cathedral and the Shrines of St Hugh', *JBAA*, 148: 1995, 137–47

Anderson, M. D., *Drama and Imagery in English Medieval Churches*, Cambridge 1963

Andersson, A., *English Influence in Norwegian and Swedish Figuresculpture in Wood 1220–1270*, Stockholm 1949

——, et al., *Medieval Wooden Sculpture in Sweden*, 5 vols, Stockholm 1964–80

——, et al., *Treasures of Early Sweden*, Stockholm 1984

Anker, P., 'Høymiddelalderens skulptur i stein og tre', *Norges kunsthistorie*, 2: *Høymiddelalderen og Hansa-tid*, Oslo 1981, 126–251

St Anselm, trans. B. Ward, *The Prayers and Meditations of St Anselm*, Harmondsworth 1973

Aquinas, St Thomas, trans. E. D'Arcy *Summa Theologiae*, Blackfriars edn, 19, London and New York 1963

——, trans. T. Gilby, *Summa Theologiae*, Blackfriars edn, 44, London and New York 1972

Aristotle, trans. J. A. K. Thomson et al., *Ethics*, Harmondsworth, rev. 1976

——, trans. H. C. Lawson-Tancred, *The Art of Rhetoric*, London 1991

——, trans. M. Heath, *Poetics*, London 1996

Arnould, E. J., *Le Manuel des Péchés*, Paris 1940

Astell, A. W., *The Song of Songs in the Middle Ages*, Ithaca and London 1990

Aston, M., 'Segregation in Churches', in W. J. Sheils and D. Wood, eds, *Women in the Church*, Studies in Church History, 27: 1990, 237–94

Auerbach, E., trans. W. R. Trask, *Mimesis: The Representation of Reality in Western Literature*, Princeton 1953

Ayers, T., ed., *Salisbury Cathedral, the West Front: A History and Study in Conservation*, Chichester 2000

Backhouse, J., and C. de Hamel, *The Becket Leaves*, London 1988

Bailey, T., *The Processions of Sarum and the Western Church*, Toronto 1971

Baily, J., 'St Hugh's Church at Lincoln', *Architectural History*, 34: 1991, 1–35

Baker, A. T., 'La Vie de Saint Edmond Archevêque de Cantorbéry', *Romania*, 55: 1929, 332–81

Baldwin, J. W., *Masters, Princes and Merchants: The Social Views of Peter the Chanter and his Circle*, 2 vols, Princeton 1970

——, 'Masters at Paris from 1179 to 1215: A Social Perspective', in Benson and Constable eds, 1982, 138–72

——, 'The Image of the Jongleur in Northern France around 1200', *Speculum*, 72: 1997, 635–63

——, 'From Ordeal to Confession: In Search of Lay Religion in Early Thirteenth-Century France', in Biller and Minnis eds, 1998, 191–209

Barasch, M., *Gestures of Despair in Medieval and Early Renaissance Art*, New York 1976

Barlow, F., *Thomas Becket*, London 1986

Barnet, P., ed., *Images in Ivory: Precious Objects of the Gothic Age*, Detroit and Princeton 1997

Barratt, A., 'Works of Religious Instruction', in A. S. G. Edwards, ed., *Middle English Prose: A Critical Guide to Major Authors and Genres*, New Brunswick 1984, 413–29

Barron, C. M., 'The Parish Fraternities of Medieval London', in C. M. Barron and C. Harper-Bill, eds, *The Church in Pre-Reformation Society: Essays in Honour of F. R. H. Du Boulay*, Woodbridge 1985, 13–37

——, 'London and St Paul's Cathedral in the Later Middle Ages', in J. Backhouse ed., *The Medieval English Cathedral: Papers in Honour of Pamela Tudor-Craig*, Harlaxton Medieval Studies, 10, Stamford 2003, 126–49

Barrow, J., 'Education and the Recruitment of Cathedral Canons in England and Germany 1100–1225', *Viator*, 20: 1989, 117–38

Baschet, J., and J.-C. Schmitt, eds, *L'Image: Fonctions et usages des images dans l'occident medieval*, Paris 1996

Bäuml, F. H., 'Varieties and Consequences of Medieval Literacy and Illiteracy', *Speculum*, 55: 1980, 237–65

Baxandall, M., *Painting and Experience in Fifteenth Century Italy: A Primer in the Social History of Pictorial Style*, Oxford 1972

——, *The Limewood Sculptors of Renaissance Germany*, New Haven and London 1980
Baxter, R., *Bestiaries and Their Users in the Middle Ages*, Stroud 1998
Bayley, J., *The History and Antiquities of the Tower of London*, London 1821
Beckwith, S., 'Ritual, Church and Theatre: Medieval Dramas of the Sacramental Body', in D. Aers, ed., *Culture and History 1350–1600: Essays on English Communities, Identities and Writing*, Hemel Hempstead 1992, 65–89
——, *Christ's Body: Identity, Culture and Society in Late Medieval Writings*, London and New York 1993
Bede, ed. B. Colgrave and R. A. B. Minors, *Bede's Ecclesiastical History of the English People*, Oxford 1969
Bell, D. N., 'The Commentary on the Song of Songs of Thomas the Cistercian and His Conception of the Image of God', *Cîteaux*, 28: 1977a, 5–25
——, 'Love and Charity in the Commentary on the Song of Songs of Thomas the Cistercian', *Cîteaux*, 28: 1977b, 249–67
——, 'Contemplation and the Vision of God in the Commentary on the Song of Songs of Thomas the Cistercian', *Cîteaux*, 29: 1978, 207–27
Belting, H., trans. M. Bartusis and R. Meyer, *The Image and Its Public in the Middle Ages: Form and Function of Early Paintings of the Passion*, New Rochelle 1990
——, trans. E. Jephcott, *Likeness and Presence: A History of the Image before the Era of Art*, Chicago and London 1994
Bennett, A., 'A Book Designed for a Noblewoman: An Illustrated *Manuel des Péchés* of the Thirteenth Century', in L. L. Brownrigg, ed., *Medieval Book Production: Assessing the Evidence*, Los Altos Hills 1990, 163–81
——, Review of Simmons 1994, in *Studies in Iconography*, 18: 1997, 269–74
Bennett, Jill, 'Stigmata and Sense Memory: St Francis and the Affective Image', *Art History*, 24: 2001, 1–16
Benson, R. L., and G. Constable, eds, *Renaissance and Renewal in the Twelfth Century*, Oxford 1982
Berland, J.-M., 'Le Pavement du chouer de Saint-Benoît-sur-Loire', *Cahiers de civilisation médiévale, Xᵉ–XIIᵉ siècles*, 11: 1968, 211–19
Berliner, R., 'The Freedom of Medieval Art', *Gazette des beaux-arts*, 28: 1945, 263–88
[St Bernard], eds J. Leclercq, C. H. Talbot and H. M. Rochais, *Sermones Super Cantica Canticorum 1–35: S. Bernardi, Opera Omnia*, I, Rome 1957
Berthelé, J., and M., Valmary, eds, 'Les Instructions et constitutions de Guillaume Durand le Spéculateur, d'après le manuscrit de Cessenon', *Académie des sciences et lettres de Montpellier. Mémoires de la Section des lettres*, 2 ser., 3: 1900–07, 1–148
Bestul, T. H., 'Devotional Writing in England between Anselm and Richard Rolle', in V. M Lagorio, ed., *Mysticism Medieval and Modern*, Salzburg 1986, 12–28
Bicknell, S., *The History of the English Organ*, Cambridge 1996
Biller, P., and A. J. Minnis, eds, *Medieval Theology and the Natural Body*, York Studies in Medieval Theology, 1, York 1997
——, *Handling Sin: Confession in the Middle Ages*, York Studies in Medieval Theology, 2, York 1998
Bilson, J., 'Notes on the Earlier Architectural History of Wells Cathedral', *Archeological Journal*, 85: 1928, 23–68
Binkley, P., 'Medieval Latin Poetic Anthologies (VI): The Cotton Anthology of Henry of Avranches (B. L. Cotton Vespasian D.v., fols. 151–184)', *Mediaeval Studies*, 52: 1990, 221–54
Binski, P., *The Painted Chamber at Westminster*, Society of Antiquaries Occasional Papers, n.s. 9, London 1986
——, 'What was the Westminster Retable?', *JBAA*, 140: 1987, 152–74
——, 'Reflections on *La Estoire de Seint Aedward le Rei*: Hagiography and Kingship in Thirteenth-century England', *Journal of Medieval History*, 16: 1990, 333–50
——, 'Abbot Berkyng's Tapestries and Matthew Paris's Life of St Edward the Confessor', *Archaeologia*, 109: 1991, 85–100
——, 'The Murals in the Nave of St Albans Abbey', in D. Abulafia, M. Franklin and M. Rubin, eds, *Church and City 1000–1500: Essays in Honour of Christopher Brooke*, Cambridge 1992, 249–78
——, *Westminster Abbey and the Plantagenets: Kingship and the Representation of Power 1200–1400*, New Haven and London 1995a
——, 'The 13th-century English Altarpiece', in Malmanger et al., eds, 1995 (1995b), 47–57
——, 'The Angel Choir at Lincoln and the Poetics of the Gothic Smile', *Art History*, 20: 1997a, 350–74
——, 'A Survey of English Thirteenth-century Figurative Painting on Panel', in Emmerling and Ringer, eds, 1997 (1997b), 325–34
——, 'The English Parish Church and Its Art in the Later Middle Ages: A Review of the Problem', *Studies in Iconography*, 20: 1999, 1–25
——, 'The Crucifixion and the Censorship of Art Around 1300', in P. Linehan and J. Nelson, eds, *The Medieval World*, London and New York 2001, 342–60
——, 'The Cosmati and *Romanitas* in England: An Overview', in L. Grant and R. Mortimer, eds, *Westminster Abbey: The Cosmati Pavements*, Courtauld Research Papers, 3, Aldershot 2002, 116–34
——, 'The Painted Nave Ceiling of Peterborough Abbey', in J. Backhouse, ed., *The Medieval English Cathedral: Papers in Honour of Pamela Tudor-Craig*, Harlaxton Medieval Studies, 10, Stamford 2003, 41–62
—— and I. Freestone, 'The Technique of the Westminster Retable: A Preliminary Report with an Analysis of the Glass Components', in Malmanger et al., eds, 1995, 59–71
Birch, W. de G., *Catalogue of Seals in the Department of Manuscripts*, I, London 1887
Bishop, E., *Liturgica Historica*, Oxford 1918
Blair, W. J., 'The Consecration-cross Indents of Salisbury Cathedral', *Transactions of the Monumental Brass Society*, 12: 1975, 16–20
——, 'Saint Frideswide Reconsidered', *Oxoniensia*, 52: 1987, 71–127
——, *St Fridewide's Monastery at Oxford: Archaeological and Architectural Studies*, Stroud 1990
——, 'Clerical Communities and Parochial Space: The Planning of Urban Mother Churches in the Twelfth and Thirteenth Centuries', in T. R. Slater and G. Rosser,

eds, *The Church in the Medieval Town*, Aldershot 1998, 272–93
—— and C. Pyrah, eds, *Church Archaeology: Research Directions for the Future*, CBA Research Report, 104, York 1996
—— and N. Ramsay, eds, *English Medieval Industries: Craftsmen, Techniques, Products*, London 1991
Blake, E. O., ed., *Liber Eliensis*, Camden Society, 3rd ser., 92, London 1962
Blindheim, M., *Painted Wooden Sculpture in Norway c. 1100–1250*, Oslo 1998
Bliss, W. H., ed., *Calendar of Entries in the Papal Registers relating to Great Britain and Ireland. I (1198–1304)*, London 1893
Bloch, H., 'The New Fascination with Ancient Rome', in Benson and Constable, eds, 1982, 615–36
Bloch, M., 'La Vie de S. Edouard le Confesseur par Osbert de Clare', *Analecta bollandiana*, 41: 1923, 5–131
Bloomfield, M. W., *The Seven Deadly Sins*, East Lansing 1952
——, et al., *Incipits of Latin Works on the Virtues and Vices, 1100–1500 A.D.*, Cambridge Mass. 1979
Blum, P. Z., 'Liturgical Influences on the Design of the West Front at Wells and Salisbury', *Gesta*, 25: 1986, 145–50
——, 'The Sequence of the Building Campaigns at Salisbury', *Art Bulletin*, 73: 1991, 6–38
Blume, D., *Wandmalerei als Ordenspropaganda: Bildprogramme im Chorbereich franziskanischer Konvente Italiens bis zur Mitte des 14. Jahrhunderts*, Worms 1983
Bock, C., 'Tonsure monastique et tonsure cléricale', *Revue de droit canonique*, 2: 1952, 373–406
Boehm, B. D., 'Opus Lemovicense: The Taste for and Diffusion of Limousin Enamels', in J. P. O'Neill and T. Egan, eds, *Enamels of Limoges 1100–1350*, Metropolitan Museum of Art, New York 1996, 40–47
Bolton, B., 'Thirteenth-century Religious Women: Further Reflections on the Low Countries "Special Case"', in Dor, Johnson and Wogan-Browne, eds, 1999, 129–57
Bond, F., *Screens and Galleries in English Churches*, London 1908
——, *The Chancel of English Churches*, Oxford 1916
—— and W. Watkins, 'Notes on the Architectural History of Lincoln Minster from 1192 to 1255', *RIBA Journal*, 18: 1911, 33–50, 84–97
Bony, J., 'French Influences on the Origins of English Gothic Architecture', *JWCI*, 12: 1949, 1–15
——, *The English Decorated Style: Gothic Architecture Transformed 1250–1350*, Oxford 1979
——, *French Gothic Architecture of the 12th & 13th Centuries*, Berkeley 1983
——, 'What Possible Sources for the Chevet of Saint-Denis?', in Gerson, ed., 1986, 131–42
Borenius, T., *St Thomas Becket in Art*, London 1932
——, 'The Cycle of Images in the Palaces and Castles of Henry III', *JWCI*, 6: 1943, 40–50
Borg, A., 'The Gloucester Candlestick', *BAACT*, 7: 1985, 84–92
Bossy, J., 'The Mass as a Social Institution 1200–1700', *Past and Present*, 100: 1983, 29–61
Boureau, A., 'L'Adage *Vox Populi, vox Dei* et l'invention de la nation Anglaise (VIIIe–XIIe siècle)', *Annales ESC*, 4/5: 1992, 1071–89
Bowers, R., 'Music and Worship to 1640', in Owen, ed., 1994, 47–76
Bowles, E. A., 'Were Musical Instruments used in the Liturgical Service during the Middle Ages?', *Galpin Society Journal*, 10: 1957, 40–84
Boyle, L. E., 'Robert Grosseteste and the Pastoral Care', in *Pastoral Care, Clerical Education and Canon Law, 1200–1400*, London 1981, 3–51
——, 'Popular Piety in the Middle Ages: What is Popular?', *Florilegium*, 4: 1982, 184–93
——, 'The Fourth Lateran Council and Manuals of Popular Theology', in T. J. Heffernan, ed., *The Popular Literature of Medieval England*, Tennessee Studies in Literature, 28, Knoxville 1985, 30–43
——, 'The Inter-Conciliar Period 1179–1215 and the Beginnings of Pastoral Manuals', in F. Liotta, ed., *Miscellanea Rolando Bandinelli, Papa Alessandro III*, Siena 1986, 45–56
Bradley, S. A. J., ed., *Anglo-Saxon Poetry*, London 1982
Bradshaw, H., and C. Wordsworth, eds, *Statutes of Lincoln Cathedral*, I, Cambridge 1892
Bräm, A., *Das Andachtsbuch der Marie de Gavre*, Wiesbaden 1997
Branner, R., 'Historical Aspects of the Reconstruction of Reims Cathedral, 1210–1241', *Speculum*, 36: 1961, 23–37
——, *St Louis and the Court Style in Gothic Architecture*, London 1965
——, *Manuscript Painting in Paris during the Reign of Saint Louis*, Berkeley 1977
Braswell, M. F., *The Medieval Sinner: Characterization and Confession in the Literature of the Early Middle Ages*, London 1983
Braun, J., *Der christliche Altar in seiner geschichtlichen Entwicklung*, 2 vols, Munich 1924
Brentano, M. T., 'Relationship of the Latin *Facetus* Literature to the Medieval English Courtesy Poems', *University of Kansas Humanistic Studies*, 5: 1935 (whole volume)
Brentano, R., *Two Churches: England and Italy in the Thirteenth Century*, Berkeley 1968
Brieger, P., *English Art 1216–1307*, Oxford 1957
—— and P. Verdier, *Art and the Courts: France and England from 1259 to 1328*, 2 vols, Ottawa 1972
Brooke, C. N. L., 'Religious Sentiment and Church Design in the Later Middle Ages', in his *Medieval Church and Society: Collected Essays*, London 1971, 162–82
Brooks, N., *The Early History of the Church of Canterbury: Christ Church from 597 to 1066*, London and New York 1984
Browe, P., *Die Verehrung der Eucharistie im Mittelalter*, Munich 1933
——, *Die Eucharistischen Wunder des Mittelalters*, Breslauer Studien zur historischen Theologie, 4, Breslau 1938
Brown, A. D., *Popular Piety in Late Medieval England: The Diocese of Salisbury 1250–1550*, Oxford 1995
Brown, R. A., 'William of Malmesbury as an Architectural Historian', in his *Castles, Conquests and Charters: Collected Papers*, Woodbridge 1989, 227–34
Brown, S., *Sumptuous and Richly Adorn'd: The Decoration of Salisbury Cathedral*, London 1999
——, *'Our Magnificent Fabric': York Minster, An Architectural History c. 1220–1500*, Swindon 2003
Bunjes, H., *Die steinernen Altaraufsatze der hohen Gotik und der stand der gotischen Plastik in der Ile de France um 1300*, diss., Marburg 1937

Buschhausen, H., *Der Verduner Altar: Das Emailwerk des Nikolaus von Verdun im Stift Klosterneuburg*, Vienna 1980
Busse, W. G., 'Bishops' Courts as Cultural Centres: The Case of the Harley Lyrics', *Anglistentag 1995 Greifswald: Proceedings of the Conference of the German Association of University Teachers of English*, 27: 1995, 285–95
Butler, J., *Gender Trouble: Feminism and the Subversion of Identity*, New York and London 1990
Büttner, F. O., *Imitatio pietatis: Motive der christlichen Ikonographie als Modelle zur Verähnlichung*, Berlin 1983
Bynum, C. W., *Jesus as Mother: Studies in the Spirituality of the High Middle Ages*, Berkeley and Los Angeles 1982
——, *Holy Feast and Holy Fast: The Religious Significance of Food to Medieval Women*, Berkeley and Los Angeles 1987
——, *Fragmentation and Redemption: Essays on Gender and the Human Body in Medieval Religion*, New York 1992
——, *The Resurrection of the Body in Western Christianity, 200–1336*, New York 1995
——, *Metamorphosis and Identity*, New York 2001
Caesarius of Heisterbach, trans. H. Von Scott, and C. C. Swinton Bland, *The Dialogue on Miracles*, I, London 1929
Cahn, W., 'Architecture and Exegesis: Richard of St.-Victor's Ezekiel Commentary and Its Illustrations', *Art Bulletin*, 76: 1994, 53–68
Callus, D. A., ed., *Robert Grosseteste, Scholar and Bishop*, Oxford 1955
Cameron, A., 'The Language of Images: The Rise of Icons and Christian Representation', in D. Wood, ed., *The Church and the Arts*, Studies in Church History, 28, Oxford 1992, 1–42
Cames, G., 'Recherches sur les Origines du Crucifix à Trois Clous', *Cahiers archéologiques*, 16: 1966, 185–202
Camille, M., 'Seeing and Reading: Some Visual Implications of Medieval Literacy and Illiteracy', *Art History*, 8: 1985, 26–49
——, 'The Language of Images in Medieval England, 1200–1400', in *AoC*, 33–40
——, *The Gothic Idol: Ideology and Image-making in Medieval Art*, Cambridge 1989
——, *Image on the Edge: The Margins of Medieval Art*, London 1992
——, 'Mimetic Identification and Passion Devotion in the Later Middle Ages: A Double-sided Panel by Meister Francke', in A. A. MacDonald, H. N. B. Ridderbos and R. M. Schlusemann, eds, *The Broken Body: Passion Devotion in Late-Medieval Culture*, Mediaevalia Groningana, 21, Groningen 1998, 183–210
——, 'Before the Gaze: The Internal Senses and Late Medieval Practices of Seeing', in R. S. Nelson, *Visuality Before and Beyond the Renaissance: Seeing as Others Saw*, Cambridge 2000, 197–223
Caplan, H., 'Classical Rhetoric and Mediaeval Theory of Preaching', *Classical Philology*, 28: 1933, 73–96
Carruthers, M. J., *The Book of Memory: A Study of Memory in Medieval Culture*, Cambridge 1990
——, *The Craft of Thought: Meditation, Rhetoric and the Making of Images, 400–1200*, Cambridge 1998
Casey, J., *Pagan Virtue: An Essay in Ethics*, Oxford 1990
Cave, C. J. P., *Roof Bosses in Medieval Churches*, Cambridge 1948
Caviness, M. H., '"De convenientia et cohaerentia antiqui et novi operis": Medieval Conservation, Restoration, Pastiche and Forgery', in P. Bloch, ed., *Intuition und Kunstwissenschaft: Festschrift für Hanns Swarzenski*, Berlin 1973, 205–21
——, 'A Lost Cycle of Canterbury Paintings of 1220', *Antiquaries Journal*, 54: 1974, 65–74
——, *The Early Stained Glass of Canterbury Cathedral, Circa 1175–1220*, Princeton 1977
——, 'Conflicts between *Regnum* and *Sacerdotium* as Reflected in a Canterbury Psalter of ca. 1215', *Art Bulletin*, 61: 1979, 38–58
——, *The Windows of Christ Church Cathedral Canterbury*, CVMA Great Britain, 2, London 1981
——, 'Canterbury Cathedral Clerestory: The Glazing Programme in Relation to the Campaigns of Construction', *BAACT*, 5: 1982, 46–55
——, 'Romanesque "Belles verrières" in Canterbury?', in Stratford, ed., 1987, 35–8
——, '"The Simple Perception of Matter" and the Representation of Narrative ca. 1180–1280', *Gesta*, 30: 1991, 48–64
Chadd, D. F. L., 'Liturgy and Liturgical Music: the Limits of Uniformity', in Norton and Park, eds, 1986, 299–314
Châtillon, J., 'Thomas Becket et les Victorines', in Foreville, ed., 1975, 89–101
Chazelle, C. M., 'Pictures, Books and the Illiterate: Pope Gregory I's Letters to Serenus of Marseilles', *Word & Image*, 6: 1990, 138–53
——, *The Crucified God in the Carolingian Era: Theology and Art of Christ's Passion*, Cambridge 2001
Cheney, C. R., 'Church-building in the Middle Ages', *Bulletin of the John Rylands Library*, 34: 1951–2, 20–36
——, *From Becket to Langton: English Church Government 1170–1223*, Manchester 1956
——, 'The Earliest English Diocesan Statutes', *English Historical Review*, 75: 1960, 1–29
——, 'Rules for the Observance of Feast-days in Medieval England', *Bulletin of the Institute of Historical Research*, 34: 1961a, 117–47
——, 'The So-called Statutes of John Pecham and Robert Winchelsey for the Province of Canterbury', *Journal of Ecclesiastical History*, 12: 1961b, 14–34
——, *Hubert Walter*, London 1967
——, *English Synodalia of the Thirteenth Century*, Oxford 1968
——, *Pope Innocent III and England*, Stuttgart 1976
——, *The English Church and Its Laws 12th–14th centuries*, London 1982
——, 'The Settlement between Archbishop Hubert Walter and Christ Church, Canterbury in 1200: A Study in Diplomatic', in E. C. Viola, ed., *Medievalia Christiana XIe–XIIIe siècles: Hommage à Raymonde Foreville*, Tournai 1989, 136–51
Chibnall, M., ed., *Historia Pontificalis*, London 1956
Christie, A. G. I., *English Medieval Embroidery*, Oxford 1938
Cicero, Marcus Tullius, trans. W. Miller, *De Officiis*, Loeb Classical Library, 30, Cambridge Mass. and London 1913
Clanchy, M. T., '*Moderni* in Education and Government in England', *Speculum*, 50: 1975, 671–88
——, *From Memory to Written Record: England 1066–1307*, London 1979
——, *England and Its Rulers 1066–1272*, Oxford 2/1998
Clark, W. W., '"The Recollection of the Past is the Promise of

the Future". Continuity and Contextuality: Saint-Denis, Merovingians, Capetians, and Paris', in Raguin, Brush and Draper, eds, 1995, 92–113
——, 'Defining National Historical Memory in Parisian Architecture (1130–1160)', in N. Gauthier and H. Galinié, eds, *Grégoire de Tours et l'espace gaulois: Actes du congrès international, Tours*, Révue Archéologique du Centre de la France, 13th supplement, Tours 1997, 341–58
——, 'Reading Reims, I: The Sculptures on the Chapel Buttresses', *Gesta*, 39: 2000, 135–45
Cocke, T., and P. Kidson, *Salisbury Cathedral: Perspectives on the Architectural History*, London 1993
Cockerell, C. R., *Iconography of the West Front of Wells Cathedral*, London 1851
Colchester, L. S., *The West Front of Wells Cathedral*. Wells 5/1976
——, ed., *Wells Cathedral: A History*, Shepton Mallet 1982
—— and J. H. Harvey, 'Wells Cathedral', *Archaeological Journal*, 131: 1974, 200–14
Coldstream, N., 'English Decorated Shrine Bases', *JBAA*, 129: 1976, 15–34
——, '"Cui Bono?" The Saint, the Clergy and the New Work at St Albans', in E. Fernie and P. Crossley, eds, *Medieval Architecture and Its Intellectual Context: Studies in Honour of Peter Kidson*, London 1990, 143–9
——, *The Decorated Style: Architecture and Ornament 1240–1360*, London 1994
Coleman, J., *Ancient and Medieval Memories: Studies in the Reconstruction of the Past*, Cambridge 1992
Colish, M. L., *The Stoic Tradition from Antiquity to the Early Medieval Ages*, 2 vols, Leiden 1985
Collinson, P., N. Ramsay and M. Sparks, eds, *A History of Canterbury Cathedral*, Oxford 1995
Colvin, H. M., *Architecture and the After-Life*, New Haven and London 1991
——, ed., *The History of the King's Works: The Middle Ages*, 2 vols, London 1963
——, ed., *Building Accounts of King Henry III*, Oxford 1971
Constable, G., *Three Studies in Medieval Religious Life and Thought*, Cambridge 1995
——, *The Reformation of the Twelfth Century*, Cambridge 1996
Corti, M., 'Models and Antimodels in Medieval Culture', *New Literary History*, 10: 1979, 339–66
Coss, C., *The Lady in Medieval England 1000–1500*, Stroud 1998
Coulton, G. G., *Social Life in Britain from the Conquest to the Reformation*, Cambridge 1919
Cowdrey, H. E. J., *The Age of Abbot Desiderius*, Oxford 1983
Cox, R. J., *A Study of the Juridic Status of Laymen in the Writing of the Medieval Canonists*, Catholic University of America, Canon Law Studies, 395, Washington 1959
Crook, J., *The Architectural Setting of the Cult of Saints in the Early Christian West c.300–1200*, Oxford 2000
——, ed., *Winchester Cathedral: Nine Hundred Years, 1093–1993*, Chichester and Winchester 1993
Crossley, P., 'The Nave of Stone Church in Kent', *Architectural History*, 44: 2001, 195–211
Curtius, E. R., trans. W. R. Trask, *European Literature and the Latin Middle Ages*, Bollingen Series, 36, Princeton 1953
Davidson Cragoe, C., 'Reading and Rereading Gervase of Canterbury', *JBAA*, 154: 2001, 40–53
D'Avray, D. L., *The Preaching of the Friars: Sermons Diffused from Paris before 1300*, Oxford 1985
Dayman, E. A., and W. H. R. Jones, *Statutes of the Cathedral Church of Sarum*, Bath 1883
Dean, M. A., 'Architecture at Peterborough in the Thirteenth Century', *JBAA*, 137: 1984, 114–29
——, 'The Angel Choir and Its Local Influence', *BAACT*, 8: 1986, 90–101
De Clercq, C., 'Hugues de Fouilloy, imagier de ses propres oeuvres?', *Revue du Nord (Université de Lille)*, 45: 1963, 31–42
Deér, J., *The Dynastic Porphyry Tombs of the Norman Period in Sicily*, Dumbarton Oaks Studies, 5. Washington 1959
De Francovich, G., 'L'Origine e la diffusione del crocifisso gotico doloroso', *Römisches Jahrbuch für Kunstgeschichte*, 2: 1938, 143–261
De Hamel, C., *Glossed Books of the Bible and the Origins of the Paris Booktrade*, Woodbridge 1984
——, *A History of Illuminated Manuscripts*, Oxford 1986
De Laborde, A., *La Bible Moralisée illustrée*, 5 vols, Paris 1911–27
Demus, O., trans. M. Whittall, *Romanesque Mural Painting*, London 1970
Dendy, D. R., *The Use of Lights in Christian Worship*, Alcuin Club Collections, 41, London 1959
Denton, J. H., 'The Competence of the Parish Clergy in Thirteenth-century England', in C. M. Barron and J. Stratford, eds, *The Church and Learning in Later Medieval Society: Essays in Honour of R. B. Dobson*, Harlaxton Medieval Studies, 11, Stamford 2002, 273–85
Deshman, R., 'The Imagery of the Living Ecclesia and the English Monastic Reform', in P. E. Szarmach, ed., *Sources of Anglo-Saxon Culture*, Studies in Medieval Culture, 20, Kalamazoo 1986, 261–82
——, *The Benedictional of St Aethelwold*, Princeton 1995
D'Esneval, A., 'La Survivance de saint Thomas Becket a travers son quatrième successeur, Etienne Langton', in Foreville, ed., 1975, 111–14
Deuchler, F., and K. Hoffmann, *The Year 1200*, 2 vols, New York 1970
De Wald, E. T., *The Illustrations of the Utrecht Psalter*, Princeton 1932
Dimock, J. F., 'Recorded History of Lincoln Cathedral', *Associated Architectural Societies' Reports and Papers*, 9: 1867, 190–201
Dix, G., *The Shape of the Liturgy*, London 1945
Dixon-Smith, S., 'The Image and Reality of Alms-giving in the Great Halls of Henry III', *JBAA*, 152: 1999, 79–96
Dobson, E. J., *The Origins of Ancrene Wisse*, Oxford 1976
——, ed., *The English Text of the Ancrene Riwle: Edited from B. M. Cotton MS. Cleopatra C.VI*, EETS, 267, Oxford 1972
Dodwell, C. R., *The Canterbury School of Illumination 1066–1200*, Cambridge 1954
——, 'The Meaning of "Sculptor" in the Romanesque Period', in Stratford, ed., I, 49–59
Dondaine, A., 'Guillaume Peyraut: Vie et ouevres', *Archivum Fratrum Praedicatorum*, 18: 1948, 162–236
Donovan, C., *The de Brailes Hours: Shaping the Book of Hours in Thirteenth-century Oxford*, London 1991
Dor, J., L. Johnson and J. Wogan-Browne, eds, *New Trends in*

Feminine Spirituality: The Holy Women of Liège and Their Impact, Turnhout 1999
Douie, D. L., *Archbishop Pecham*, Oxford 1952
Draper, P., 'Bishop Northwold and the Cult of Saint Etheldreda', *BAACT*, 2: 1979, 8–27
——, 'The Nine Altars at Durham and Fountains', *BAACT*, 3: 1980, 74–86
——, 'The Sequence and Dating of the Decorated Work at Wells', *BAACT*, 4: 1981, 18–29
——, 'William of Sens and the Original Design of the Choir Termination of Canterbury Cathedral 1175–1179', *Journal of the Society of Architectural Historians*, 42: 1983, 238–48
——, 'King John and St Wulfstan', *Journal of Medieval History*, 10: 1984, 41–50
——, 'The Retrochoir of Winchester Cathedral: Evidence and Interpretation', *JBAA*, 139, 1986a, 68–74
——, 'Recherches récentes sur l'architecture dans les isles Britanniques à la fin de l'époque Romane et au début du Gothique', *Bulletin monumental*, 144: 1986b, 305–38
——, 'Architecture and Liturgy', in *AoC*, 83–91
——, 'Seeing that it was Done in all the Noble Churches in England', in E. Fernie and P. Crossley, eds, *Medieval Architecture and Its Intellectual Context: Studies in Honour of Peter Kidson*, London 1990, 137–42
——, 'Interpreting the Architecture of Wells Cathedral' in Raguin, Brush and Draper, eds, 1995, 114–30
——, 'Salisbury Cathedral: Paradigm or Maverick?', *BAACT*, 17: 1996, 21–39
——, 'Interpretations of the Rebuilding of Canterbury Cathedral, 1174–1186: Archaeological and Historical Evidence', *Journal of the Society of Architectural Historians*, 56: 1997, 184–203
——, 'Canterbury Cathedral: Classical Columns in the Trinity Chapel?', *Architectural History*, 44: 2001, 172–8
Drew, C., *Early Parochial Organization in England: The Origins of the Office of Churchwarden*, London 1954
Dronke, P., *Poetic Individuality in the Middle Ages: New Departures in Poetry 1000–1150*, Oxford 1970
——, 'Tradition and Innovation in Western Colour Imagery', *Eranos-Jahrbuch*, 41: 1972, 51–106
——, *Women Writers of the Middle Ages*, Cambridge 1984
Duffy, E., 'Holy Maydens, Holy Wyfes: The Cult of Women Saints in Fifteenth- and Sixteenth-Century England', in W. J. Sheils and D. Wood, eds, *Women in the Church*, Studies in Church History, 27, Oxford 1990, 175–96
——, *The Stripping of the Altars: Traditional Religion in England c.1400–c.1580*, New Haven and London 1992
——, 'The Parish, Piety, and Patronage in Late Medieval East Anglia: The Evidence of Rood Screens', in K. L. French, G. G. Gibbs and B. A. Kümin, eds, *The Parish in English Life, 1400–1600*, Manchester 1997a, 133–62
——, 'Finding St Francis: Early Images, Early Lives', in Biller and Minnis, eds, 1997 (1997b), 193–236
Duggan, A., 'The Cult of St Thomas Becket in the Thirteenth Century', in Jancey, ed., 1982, 21–44
——, ed. and trans., *The Correspondence of Thomas Becket, Archbishop of Canterbury 1162–1170*, 2 vols, Oxford 2000
Duggan, C., *Canon Law in Medieval England: The Becket Dispute and Decretal Collections*, London 1982
Duggan, L. D., 'Was art really the "book of the illiterate?"', *Word & Image*, 5: 1989, 227–51
Dumoutet, E., *Le Désir de voir l'hostie et les origines de la dévotion au saint sacrament*, Paris 1926
——, *Corpus domini: Aux sources de la piété eucharistique médiévale*, Paris 1942
[Durandus], ed. A. Davril and T. M. Thibodeau, *Guillelmi Duranti: Rationale divinorum officiorum*, 2 vols, Turnhout 1995–8
Eales, R., 'The Political Setting of the Becket Translation of 1220', in D. Wood, ed., *Martyrs and Martyrologies*, Studies in Church History, 30, Oxford 1993, 127–39
Eames, E., 'Notes on the Decorated Stone Roundels in the Corona and Trinity Chapel in Canterbury Cathedral', *BAACT*, 5: 1982, 67–70
Edmund of Abingdon, ed. H. P. Forshaw, *Speculum Religiosorum and Speculum Ecclesie*, Auctores Britannici Medii Aevi, III, Oxford 1973
——, ed. A. D. Wilshere, *Mirour de Seinte Eglise (St Edmund of Abingdon's Speculum Ecclesiae)*, Anglo-Norman Text Society, 40, London 1982
Edwards, K., *The English Secular Cathedrals in the Middle Ages*, Manchester 1949
Ehresmann, D. L., 'Some Observations on the Role of Liturgy in the Early Winged Altarpiece', *Art Bulletin*, 64: 1982, 359–69
——, 'The Iconography of the Cismar Altarpiece and the Role of Relics in the Early Winged Altarpiece', *Zeitschrift für Kunstgeschichte*, 64: 2001, 1–36
Elias, N., trans. E. Jephcott, *The Civilizing Process: The History of Manners and State Formation and Civilization*, Oxford 1994
Elkins, S. K., *Holy Women of Twelfth-Century England*, Chapel Hill and London 1988
Elliott, D., 'The Physiology of Rapture and Female Spirituality', in Biller and Minnis, eds, 1997, 141–73
Ellis, R. H., *Catalogue of Seals in the Public Record Office: Monastic Seals*, I, London 1986
Ellis, T. P., and J. Lloyd, trans., *The Mabinogion*, I, Oxford 1929
Emden, A. B., *A Biographical Register of the University of Oxford to A.D. 1500*, III, Oxford 1959
Emmerling, E., and C. Ringer, eds, *Das Aschaffenburger Tafelbild: Studien zur Tafelmalerei des 13. Jahrhunderts*, Arbeitshefte des Bayerischen Landesamtes für Denkmalpflege, 89, Munich 1997
Enders, J., *Rhetoric and the Origins of Medieval Drama*, Ithaca and London 1992
Engel, U., *Die Kathedrale von Worcester*, Berlin 2000
Esmeijer, A. C., *Divina Quaternitas: A Preliminary Study in the Method and Application of Visual Exegesis*, Assen 1978
Esposito, M., ed., *Itinerarium Symonis Semeonis ab Hybernia ad Terram Sanctam*, Scriptores Latini Hiberniae, IV, Dublin 1960
Evans, M. W., 'An Illustrated Fragment of Peraldus's *Summa* of Vice: Harleian MS 3244', *JWCI*, 45: 1982, 14–46
Falletti, L., 'Durand', in R. Naz, ed., *Dictionnaire de droit canonique*, 7 vols, Paris 1935–65, V, cols 1014–75
Farmer, D. H., 'The Canonization of St Hugh of Lincoln', *Lincolnshire Architectural and Archaeological Society Reports and Papers*, 6: 1955–6, 86–117
——, *Saint Hugh of Lincoln*, London 1985a

——, 'Some Saints of East Anglia', *Reading Medieval Studies*, 11: 1985b, 31–49
——, 'The Cult and Canonization of St Hugh', in Mayr-Harting, ed., 1987, 75–87
Fassler, M., *Gothic Song: Victorine Sequences and Augustinian Reform in Twelfth-century Paris*, Cambridge 1993
[Felix], ed. and trans. B. Colgrave, *Felix's Life of Saint Guthlac*, Cambridge 1956
Fernie, E. C., 'Observations of the Norman Plan of Ely Cathedral', *BAACT*, 2: 1979, 1–7
——, 'The Spiral Piers of Durham Cathedral', *BAACT*, 2: 1980, 49–58
——, 'St Anselm's Crypt', *BAACT*, 5: 1982, 27–38
——, *The Architecture of the Anglo-Saxons*, London 1983
——, 'The Use of Varied Nave Supports in Romanesque and Early Gothic Churches', *Gesta*, 23: 1984, 107–17
——, 'Suger's "Completion" of Saint-Denis', in Raguin, Brush and Draper, eds, 1995, 84–91
Ferruolo, S. C., 'The Twelfth-Century Renaissance', in W. Treadgold, ed., *Renaissances before the Renaissance: Cultural Revivals of Late Antiquity and the Middle Ages*, Stanford 1984, 114–43
Finucane, R. C., 'The Posthumous Miracles of St Godric of Finchale', *Transactions of the Architectural and Archaeological Society of Durham*, n.s. 3: 1974, 47–50
——, *Miracles and Pilgrims: Popular Beliefs in Medieval England*, Totowa N. J. 1977
Fischer, G., *Domkirken I Trondheim*, Oslo 1965
Foot, N. D. J., C. D. Litton and W. G. Simpson, 'The High Roofs of the East End of Lincoln Cathedral', *BAACT*, 8: 1986, 47–74
Foreville, R., *Le Jubilé de Saint Thomas Becket, du XIIIe au XVe siècle (1220–1470)*, Paris 1958
——, *Latran I, II, III et Latran IV*. Histoire des conciles oecuméniques, 6, Paris 1965
——, *Thomas Becket dans la tradition historique et hagiographique*, London 1981
——, ed., *Thomas Becket*, Actes du colloque international de Sédières, 1973, Paris 1975
Formigé, J., *L'Abbaye royale de Saint-Denis*, Paris 1960
Forshaw, H. P. [Mary Philomena], 'St Edmund of Abingdon's Meditations before the Canonical Hours', *Ephemerides Liturgicae*, 78: 1964, 33–57
——, 'New Light on the Speculum Ecclesie of St Edmund of Abingdon', *Archives d'histoire doctrinale et littéraire du Moyen Age*, 38: 1971, 7–33
——, 'St Edmund's *Speculum*: A Classic of Victorine Spirituality', *Archives d'histoire doctrinale et littéraire du Moyen Age*, 39: 1972, 7–40
Fortenbaugh, W. W., *Aristotle on Emotion*, London 1975
Foster, C. W., ed., *The Registrum Antiquissimum of the Cathedral Church of Lincoln*, Lincoln Record Society, 27, Hereford 1931
Foster, G., *The Iconology of Musical Instruments and Musical Performance in Thirteenth-century French Manuscript Illuminations*, PhD diss., City University of New York 1977
Foucault, M., trans. R. Hurley, *The History of Sexuality*, I, Harmondsworth 1990
Fowler, R. C., *Registrum Radulphi Baldock*, Canterbury and York Society, 7, London 1911
Frankl, P., rev. P. Crossley, *Gothic Architecture*, New Haven and London 2000
Franklin, M. J., 'The Cathedral as Parish Church: The Case of Southern England', in D. Abulafia, M. Franklin and M. Rubin, eds, *Church and City 1000–1500: Essays in Honour of Christopher Brooke*, Cambridge 1992, 173–98
Freedberg, D., *The Power of Images: Studies in the History and Theory of Response*, Chicago and London 1989
Frere, W. H., ed., *Graduale Sarisburiense*, London 1894
——, *The Use of Sarum*, 2 vols, Cambridge 1898–1901
Friedberg, E., ed., *Corpus Iuris Canonici*, II, Leipzig 1881
Frodl-Kraft, E., 'Zu den Kirchenschaubildern in den Hochchorfenstern von Reims – Abbildung und Abstraktion', *Wiener Jahrbuch für Kunstgeschichte*, 35: 1972, 53–86
Fuchß, V., *Das Altarensemble*, Weimar 1999
Fulton, R., *From Judgment to Passion: Devotion to Christ and the Virgin Mary, 800–1200*, New York 2002
Gaborit-Chopin, D., et al., *L'Art au temps des rois maudits: Philippe le Bel et ses fils 1285–1328*, Paris 1998
Gage, J., 'Horatian Reminiscences in Two Twelfth-century Art Critics', *JWCI*, 36: 1973, 359–60
——, 'Gothic Glass: Two Aspects of a Dionysian Aesthetic', *Art History*, 5: 1982, 36–58
——, '*Lumen, Alluminar, Riant*: Three Related Concepts in Gothic Aesthetics', in E. Liskar, ed., *Europäische Kunst um 1300*, Acts of the 25th International Congress of the History of Art, VI, Vienna 1986, 31–7
——, *Colour and Culture: Practice and Meaning from Antiquity to Abstraction*, London 1993
——, *Colour and Meaning: Art, Science and Symbolism*, London 1999
Gameson, R., 'The Early Imagery of Becket', in Morris and Roberts, eds, 2002, 46–89
Gardner, A., *A Handbook of English Medieval Sculpture*, Cambridge 1937
——, *The Lincoln Angels*, Lincoln Minster Pamphlets, 1st ser., no. 6, 1960
Gardner, J., 'A Princess among Prelates: A Fourteenth-Century Neapolitan Tomb and Its Northern Relations', *Römisches Jahrbuch für Kunstgeschichte*, 23–4: 1988, 29–60
——, 'The Cosmati at Westminster: Some Anglo-Italian Reflections', in J. Garms and A. M. Romanini, eds, *Skulptur und Grabmal des Spätmittelalters in Rome und Italien*, Vienna 1990, 201–15
——, 'Altars, Altarpieces, and Art History: Legislation and Usage', in E. Borsook and F. S. Gioffredi, eds, *Italian Altarpieces 1250–1550: Function and Design*, Oxford 1994, 5–19
——, 'The Tomb of Bishop Peter of Aquablanca in Hereford Cathedral', *BAACT*, 15: 1995, 105–10
——, '. . . Ante et Super Altare . . . : From Antependium to Altarpiece', in Emmerling and Ringer, eds, 1997, 25–40
——, 'Legates, Cardinals, and Kings: England and Italy in the Thirteenth Century', in M. Seidel, ed., *L'Europa e l'arte italiana*, Collana del kunsthistorisches Institut in Florenz, 3, Venice 2000, 73–93
Garrison, E. B., *Italian Romanesque Panel Painting: An Illustrated Index*, Florence 1949
Gauthier, M.-M., *Emaux du moyen âge occidental*, Fribourg 1972
——, 'Du tabernacle au rétable: Une innovation limousine vers 1230', *Revue de l'art*, 40–41: 1978, 23–42

Gauthier, R., 'Le Cours sur *l'Ethica nova* d'un maître ès arts de Paris (1235–1240)', *Archives d'histoire doctrinale et littéraire du moyen age*, 42: 1975, 71–141
Geertz, C., 'Religion as a Cultural System', in M. Banton, ed., *Anthropological Approaches to the Study of Religion*, London 1966, 1–46
——, *The Interpretation of Cultures*, New York 1973
Gem, R. D. H., 'The Anglo-Saxon Cathedral Church at Canterbury: A Further Contribution', *Archaeological Journal*, 127: 1970, 196–201
——, 'Towards an Iconography of Anglo-Saxon Architecture', *JWCI*, 46: 1983, 1–18
——, 'Lincoln Minster: Ecclesia Pulchra, Ecclesia Fortis', *BAACT*, 8: 1986, 9–28
——, 'Canterbury and the Cushion Capital: A Commentary on Passages from Goscelin's De Miraculis Sancti Augustini', in Stratford, ed., 1987, 83–97
Gerald of Wales [Giraldus Cambrensis], eds A. B. Scott and F. X. Martin, *Expugnatio Hibernica/The Conquest of Ireland* Dublin 1978
——, trans. J. J. Hagen, *The Jewel of the Church: A Translation of Gemma Ecclesiastica by Giraldus Cambrensis*, Davis Medieval Texts and Studies, 2, Leiden 1979
——, trans. R. M. Loomis, *The Life of St. Hugh of Avalon, Bishop of Lincoln 1186–1200*, Garland Library of Medieval Literature, 31 ser. A, New York and London 1985
Gerson, P. L., 'Suger as Iconographer: The Central Portal of the West Facade of Saint-Denis', in *Abbot Suger and Saint-Denis: A Sympsium*, ed. Gerson, New York 1986, 183–98
Gibbs, M., and J. Lang, *Bishops and Reform, 1215–72: With Special Reference to the Lateran Council of 1215*, Oxford 1934
Gibson, G. McM., *The Theatre of Devotion: East Anglian Drama and Society in the Late Middle Ages*, Chicago and London 1989
Gibson, M., T. A. Heslop and R. W. Pfaff, eds, *The Eadwine Psalter: Text, Image, and Monastic Culture in Twelfth-century Canterbury*, London and University Park 1992
Gieben, S., 'Robert Grosseteste and Medieval Courtesy-Books', *Vivarium*, 5: 1967, 47–74
Gilbert, C., 'A Statement of the Aesthetic Attitude around 1230', *Hebrew University Studies in Literature and the Arts*, 13: 1985, 125–52
——, *The Saints' Three Reasons for Paintings in Churches*, Ithaca 2001
Giles, K., 'Marking Time? A 15th-century Liturgical Calendar in the Wall Paintings of Pickering Parish Church', *Church Archaeology*, 4: 2000, 42–51
Gillespie, V., '*Doctrina* and *Predicatio*: The Design and Function of some Pastoral Manuals', *Leeds Studies in English*, 11: 1980, 36–50
Gilson, E., trans. A. H. C. Downes, *The Mystical Theology of Saint Bernard*, London 1940
Glass, D. F., *Romanesque Sculpture in Campania: Patrons, Programs, and Style*, University Park 1991
Glenn, V., 'The Sculpture of the Angel Choir at Lincoln', *BAACT*, 8: 1986, 102–8
Goering, J., 'The *Summa* of Master Serlo and Thirteenth-century Penitential Literature', *Mediaeval Studies*, 40: 1978, 290–311
——, *William de Montibus (c. 1140–1213): The Schools and the Literature of Pastoral Care*, Toronto 1992
Gombrich, E. H., 'Moment and Movement in Art', *JWCI*, 27: 1964, 293–306
——, 'On Physiognomic Perception', in his *Meditations on a Hobby Horse*, London 3/1978, 45–55
Grabar, A., *Martyrium*, 2 vols, Paris 1946
Graboïs, A., 'L'Idéal de la royauté biblique dans la pensée de Thomas Becket', in Foreville, ed., 1975
Graf, F., 'Cicero, Plautus and Roman Laughter', in J. Bremmer and H. Roodenburg, eds, *A Cultural History of Humour: From Antiquity to the Present Day*, Cambridge 1997, 29–39
Gransden, A., 'Realistic Observation in Twelfth-century England', *Speculum*, 47: 1972, 29–51
——, *The Customary of the Benedictine Abbey of Bury St Edmunds in Suffolk*, Henry Bradshaw Society, 99, Chichester 1973
——, *Historical Writing in England c.550–c.1307*, London 1974
——, 'The Growth of the Glastonbury Traditions and Legends in the Twelfth Century', *Journal of Ecclesiastical History*, 27: 1976, 337–58
——, 'Cultural Transition at Worcester in the Anglo-Norman Period', *BAACT*, 1: 1978, 1–14
——, 'The History of Wells Cathedral, *c*.1090–1547', in Colchester, ed., 1982, 24–51
——, 'Some Manuscripts in Cambridge from Bury St Edmunds Abbey: Exhibition Catalogue', *BAACT*, 20: 1998, 228–85
Grant, L., 'Gothic Architecture in Southern England and the French Connection in the Early Thirteenth Century', in P. R. Coss and S. D. Lloyd, eds, *Thirteenth Century England, 3*, Proceedings of the Newcastle upon Tyne Conference, Woodbridge 1991, 113–26
——, *Abbot Suger of St-Denis: Church and State in Early Twelfth-century France*, London and New York 1998
——, 'Naming of Parts: Describing Architecture in the High Middle Ages', in G. Clarke and P. Crossley, eds, *Architecture and Language: Constructing Identity in European Architecture, c.1000–c.1650*, Cambridge 2000, 46–57
Graves, P., 'Social Space in the English Medieval Parish Church', *Economy and Society*, 18: 1989, 297–322
Greatrex, J., *Biographical Register of the English Cathedral Priories of the Province of Canterbury c. 1066 to 1540*, Oxford 1997
Green, R. B., 'Virtues and Vices in the Chapter House Vestibule in Salisbury', *JWCI*, 31: 1968, 148–58
Greenhalgh, M., *The Survival of Roman Antiquities in the Middle Ages*, London 1989
Greenhill, E., 'Ms. Solger 4°.4, Nuremberg: Its Pictorial Cycle', in E. Liskar, ed., *Europäische Kunst um 1300*, Acts of the 25th International Congress of the History of Art, Vienna 1983, VI, Vienna 1986, 89–99
[Gregorius, Master], trans. J. Osborne, *The Marvels of Rome*, Mediaeval Sources in Translation, 31, Toronto 1987
Gregory the Great, eds A. de Vogüé and P. Antin, *Dialogues*, Sources chrétiennes, 251, 260, 265, Paris 1978–80
Gregory of Tours, trans. L. Thorpe, *History of the Franks*, Harmondsworth 1974
Grodecki, L., 'Les Vitraux allégoriques de Saint-Denis', *Art de France*, 1: 1961, 19–46
Grosseteste, Robert, eds J. Goering and F. A. C. Mantello, *Templum Dei: Edited from MS. 27 of Emmanuel College, Cambridge*, Toronto 1984

Grundmann, G., *Religiöse Bewegungen im Mittelalter*, Berlin 1935
Guérard, B., ed., *Cartulaire de l'eglise Notre-Dame de Paris, IV*, Collections des cartulaires de France, 7, Paris 1850
Guernes de Pont-Sainte-Maxence, ed. E. Walberg, *La Vie de Saint Thomas Becket*, Les Classiques Français du Moyen Age, 77, Paris 1936
Guest, G. B., commentary, *Bible moralisée: Codex Vindobonensis 2554, Vienna, Österreichische Nationalbibliothek*, London 1995
Gwynn, A., *The Irish Church in the Eleventh and Twelfth Centuries*, Dublin 1992
Hager, H., *Die Anfänge des italienischen Altarbildes*, Munich 1962
Hahnloser, H. R., *Villard de Honnecourt: Kritische Gesamtausgabe des Bauhüttenbuches ms. fr 19093 der Pariser Nationalbibliothek*, Graz 2/1972
Hamann-Mac Lean, R., and I. Schüssler, *Die Kathedrale von Reims*, II: *Die Skulpturen*, Stuttgart 1996
Hamburger, J. F., *The Rothschild Canticles: Art and Mysticism in Flanders and the Rhineland circa 1300*, New Haven and London 1990
——, *Nuns as Artists: The Visual Culture of a Medieval Convent*, Berkeley 1997a
——, '"To make women weep": Ugly Art as "Feminine" and the Origins of Modern Aesthetics', *Res*, 31: 1997b, 9–34
——, *The Visual and the Visionary: Art and Female Spirituality in Late Medieval Germany*, New York 1998
——, 'Seeing and Believing: The Suspicion of Sight and the Authentication of Vision in Late Medieval Art and Devotion', in K. Krüger and A. Nova, eds, *Imagination und Wirklichkeit: Zum Verhältnis von mentalen und realen Bildern in der Kunst der frühen Neuzeit*, Mainz 2000a, 47–69
——, 'Speculations on Speculation: Vision and Perception in the Theory and Practice of Mystical Devotion', in W. Haug and W. Schneider-Lastin, eds, *Deutsche Mystik im abendländischen Zusammenhang*, Tübingen 2000b, 353–408
——, *St John the Divine: The Deified Evangelist in Medieval Art and Theology*, Berkeley 2002
Hammerstein, R., *Die Musik der Engel*, Bonn and Munich 1962
Hanna, R., 'Miscellaneity and Vernacularity: Conditions of Literary Production in Late Medieval England', in S. G. Nichols and S. Wenzel, eds, *The Whole Book: Cultural Perspectives on the Medieval Miscellany*, Ann Arbor 1996, 36–51
Harper, J., *The Forms and Orders of Western Liturgy from the Tenth to the Eighteenth Century*, Oxford 1991
Harrison, F. L., 'Tradition and Innovation in Instrumental Usage 1100–1450', in J. LaRue, ed., *Aspects of Medieval and Renaissance Music: A Birthday Offering to Gustave Reese*, New York, 2/1978, 319–35
Harrison, S., 'The Thirteenth-century West Front of St Albans Abbey', *BAACT*, 24: 2001, 176–91
Harvey, J. H., 'The Building of Wells Cathedral, I: 1175–1307', in Colchester, ed., 1982, 52–75
Harvey, P. D. A., and A. McGuinness, *A Guide to British Medieval Seals*, London 1996
Hassall, W. O., *The Holkham Bible Picture Book*, London 1954
Hastings, A., *Elias of Dereham: Architect of Salisbury Cathedral*, Much Wenlock 1997
Haussherr, R., *Der tote Christus am Kreuz: Zur Ikonographie des Gerokreuzes*, PhD diss., Bonn 1963
——, 'Triumphkreuzgruppen der Stauferzeit', in R. Haussherr and C. Väterlein, eds, *Die Zeit der Staufer: Geschichte, Kunst, Kultur*, 5, Stuttgart 1977, 131–68
Hayward, P. A., 'The Idea of Innocent Martyrdom in Late Tenth- and Eleventh-century English Hagiology', in D. Wood, ed., *Martyrs and Martyrologies*, Studies in Church History, 30, Oxford 1993, 81–92
Hearn, M. F., 'The Rectangular Ambulatory in English Medieval Architecture', *Journal of the Society of Architectural Historians*, 30: 1971, 187–208
Hearn, M. F., 'Canterbury Cathedral and the Cult of Becket', *Art Bulletin*, 76: 1994, 19–52
Heffernan, T. J., *Sacred Biography: Saints and Their Biographers in the Middle Ages*, Oxford 1988
Hegel, G. W. F., trans. T. M. Knox, *Aesthetics: Lectures on Fine Art*, 2 vols, Oxford 1975
Helmholz, R. M., *The Spirit of Classical Canon Law*, Athens and London 1996
Henderson, G. D. S., *Gothic*, Harmondsworth 1967a
——, 'Studies in English Manuscript Illumination', *JWCI*, 30: 1967b, 71–137
——, 'Studies in English Manuscript Illumination', *JWCI*, 31: 1968, 103–47
——, 'The Imagery of St Guthlac of Crowland', in Ormrod, ed., 1985, 76–94
——, 'The West Portal in the Porch at Higham Ferrers: A Problem of Interpretation', *Antiquaries Journal*, 68: 1988, 238–47
——, 'The Meaning of Leaf 5 of Fitzwilliam MS 330', *Burlington Magazine*, 133: 1991a, 682–6
——, 'The Musician in the Stocks at Higham Ferrers, Northamptonshire', in Ormrod, ed., 1991 (1991b), 135–47
——, 'The Idiosyncracy of Late Anglo-Saxon Religious Imagery', in C. Hicks, ed., *England in the Eleventh Century*, Harlaxton Medieval Studies, 2, Stamford 1992, 239–49
——, *Vision and Image in Early Christian England*, Cambridge 1999
Henig, M., 'Archbishop Hubert Walter's Gems', *JBAA*, 136: 1983, 56–61
Henry, A., *The Eton Roundels*, Aldershot 1990
Henry of Avranches, eds J. C. Russell and J. P. Heironimus, *The Shorter Latin Poems of Master Henry of Avranches Relating to England*, Medieval Academy of America, Studies and Documents no. 1, Cambridge Mass. 1935
Heslop, D. H., 'Excavation within the Church at the Augustinian Priory of Gisborough, Cleveland 1985–6', *Yorkshire Archaeological Journal*, 67: 1995, 51–126
Heslop, T. A., 'The Virgin Mary's Regalia and 12th Century English Seals', in A. Borg and A. Martindale, eds, *The Vanishing Past: Studies of Medieval Art, Liturgy and Metrology Presented to Christopher Hohler*, BAR International Series, 111, 1981, 53–62
——, 'The Conventual Seals of Canterbury Cathedral 1066–1232', *BAACT*, 5: 1982, 94–100
——, 'Attitudes to the Visual Arts: The Evidence from Written Sources', in *AoC*, 26–32
——, 'The Visual Arts and Crafts', in B. Ford, ed., *The Cambridge Guide to the Arts in Britain*, 2: *The Middle Ages*, Cambridge 1988, 155–99
——, 'The Iconography of the Angel Choir at Lincoln Cathe-

dral', in E. Fernie and P. Crossley, eds, *Medieval Architecture and Its Intellectual Context: Studies in Honour of Peter Kidson*, London 1990, 151–8

——, 'Towards an Iconology of Croziers', in D. Buckton and T. A. Heslop, eds, *Studies in Medieval Art and Architecture Presented to Peter Lasko*, Stroud 1994, 36–45

——, 'Late Twelfth-century Writing about Art, and Aesthetic Relativity', in G. R. Owen-Crocker and T. Graham, eds, *Medieval Art: Recent Perspectives. A Memorial Tribute to C. R. Dodwell*, Manchester 1998, 129–41

——, 'Art, Nature and St Hugh's Choir at Lincoln', in J. Mitchell and M. Moran, eds, *England and the Continent in the Middle Ages: Studies in Memory of Andrew Martindale*, Harlaxton Medieval Studies, 8, Stamford 2000, 60–74

——, 'Worcester Cathedral Chapterhouse and the Harmony of the Testaments', in P. Binski and W. Noel, eds, *New Offerings, Ancient Treasures: Studies in Medieval Art for George Henderson*, Stroud 2001, 280–311

——, 'Contemplating Chimera in Medieval Imagination: St Anselm's Crypt at Canterbury', in L. Golden, ed., *Raising the Eyebrow: John Onians and World Art Studies*, BAR International Series, 996, 2002, 153–68

Higgitt, J., *The Murthly Hours: Devotion, Literacy and Luxury in Paris, England and the Gaelic West*, London and Toronto 2000

Higgonet, E. C., 'Spiritual Ideas in the Letters of Peter of Blois', *Speculum*, 100: 1975, 218–44

Hildburgh, W. L., 'An Alabaster Table of the Annunciation with the Crucifix: A Study in English Iconography', *Archaeologia*, 74: 1923–4, 203–32

Hills, P., 'The Renaissance Altarpiece: A Valid Category?', in P. Humfrey and M. Kemp, eds, *The Altarpiece in the Renaissance*, Cambridge 1990, 34–48

Hoeniger, C., *The Renovation of Paintings in Tuscany, 1250–1500*, Cambridge 1995

Hoey, L., 'Pier Alternation in Early English Gothic Architecture', *JBAA*, 139: 1986, 45–67

——, 'New Studies on Canterbury Cathedral', *Avista Forum*, 9: 1995a, 6–9

——, 'Style, Patronage and Artistic Creativity in Kent Parish Church Architecture: *c.*1180–1260', *Archaeologia Cantiana*, 115: 1995b, 45–70

——, 'The Gothic Reconstruction of the Nave and Presbytery of St Albans Abbey', *BAACT*, 24: 2001, 182–203

Holdsworth, C. J., 'John of Ford and English Cistercian Writing, 1167–1214', *TRHS*, 5th ser., 11: 1961, 117–36

——, 'The Chronology and Character of Early Cistercian Legislation on Art and Architecture', in Norton and Park, eds, 1986, 40–55

Holsinger, B. W., *Music, Body, and Desire in Medieval Culture: Hildegard of Bingen to Chaucer*, Stanford 2001

Holt, J. C., 'The St Albans Chroniclers and Magna Carta', *TRHS*, 5th ser., 14: 1964, 67–88

Hope, C., 'Altarpieces and the Requirements of Patrons', in T. Verdon and J. Henderson, eds, *Christianity and the Renaissance: Image and Religious Imagination in the Quattrocento*, Syracuse 1990, 535–71

Hope, W. H. St J., 'The Seals of English Bishops', *Proceedings of the Society of Antiquaries*, 11: 1885–7, 271–306

——, 'Quire Screens in English Churches, with Special Reference to the Twelfth-century Quire Screen formerly in the Cathedral Church of Ely', *Archaeologia*, 68: 1916–17, 43–110

——, 'The Sarum Consuetudinary and Its Relation to the Cathedral Church of Old Sarum', *Archaeologia*, 68: 1916–17, 111–26

——, and E. G. Atchley, *English Liturgical Colours*, London 1918

——, and W. R. Lethaby, 'The Imagery and Sculptures on the West Front of Wells Cathedral Church', *Archaeologia*, 59: 1904, 143–206

Hopkins, A., *The Sinful Knights: A Study of Middle English Penitential Romance*, Oxford 1990

Huffman, J., *Family, Commerce, and Religion in London and Cologne: Anglo-German Emigrants, c.1000–c.1300*, Cambridge 1998

Hugh of Saint-Victor, ed. and trans. J. Taylor, *The Didascalicon of Hugh of St Victor*, New York repr. 1991.

Hunt, R. W., and M. T. Gibson, *The Schools and the Cloister: The Life and Writings of Alexander Nequam (1157–1217)*. Oxford 1984

Hunt, T., *Teaching and Learning Latin in Thirteenth-century England*, 3 vols Woodbridge 1991

Hunter, H., ed., *Ecclesiastical Documents*, London 1840

Innes-Parker, C, '*Ancrene Wisse* and *þe Wohunge of Ure Lauerd*: The Thirteenth-century Female Reader and the Lover-Knight', in L. Smith and J. H. M. Taylor, eds, *Women, the Book and the Godly*, Woodbridge 1995, 137–47

Isidore of Seville, ed. W. M. Lindsay, *Isidori Hispalensis Episcopi: Etymologiarum sive Originum*, Libri XX, 2, Oxford 1991

Iverson, G., 'Transforming a Viking into a Saint: The Divine Office of St Olav', in M. E. Fassler and R. A. Baltzer, eds, *The Divine Office in the Latin Middle Ages*, Oxford 2000, 401–29

Jacob, E. F., 'St Richard of Chichester', *Journal of Ecclesiastical History*, 7: 1956, 174–88

Jaeger, C. S., *The Origins of Courtliness: Civilizing Trends and the Formation of Courtly Ideals 939–1210*, Philadelphia 1985

——, *The Envy of Angels: Cathedral Schools and Social Ideals in Medieval Europe, 950–1200*, Philadelphia 1994

James, M. R., *On the Abbey of St Edmund at Bury*, Cambridge Antiquarian Society, 28, Cambridge 1895

——, *La Estoire de Seint Aedward le Rei*, Roxburghe Club, Oxford 1920

——, *The Apocalypse in Latin and French*, Roxburghe Club, Oxford 1922

——, *Illustrations to the Life of St Alban*, Oxford 1924

——, *The Canterbury Psalter*, London 1935

——, 'Pictor in Carmine', *Archaeologia*, 94: 1951, 141–66

Jancey, M., ed., *St Thomas Cantilupe Bishop of Hereford: Essays in his Honour*, Hereford 1982

Jankofsky, K. P., 'Entertainment, Edification, and Popular Education in the *South English Legendary*', *Journal of Popular Culture*, 11: 1977, 706–17

Jansen, V., 'Lambeth Palace Chapel, the Temple Choir, and Southern English Gothic Architecture of c. 1215–1240', in Ormrod, ed., 1985, 95–9

——, 'Salisbury Cathedral and the Episcopal Style in the Early 13th Century', *BAACT*, 17: 1996, 32–9

Jocelin of Brakelond, ed. and trans. H. E. Butler, *The Chronicle of Jocelin of Brakelond*, London 1949

John of Garland [Johannis de Garlandia], ed. T. Wright, *De Triumphis Ecclesiae*, London 1856
——, ed. and trans. L. J. Paetow, 'Morale Scolarium of John of Garland,' *Memoirs of the University of California*, 4: 1927, 69–273
John of Salisbury, ed. W. J. Millor and C. N. L. Brooke, *The Letters of John of Salisbury*, II: *The Later Letters (1163–80)*, Oxford 1979.
Johnstone, H., 'Poor Relief in the Royal Households of Thirteenth-century England', *Speculum*, 4: 1929, 149–67
Jones, D., 'The Cult of St Richard of Chichester in the Middle Ages', *Sussex Archaeological Collections*, 121: 1983, 79–86
——, *Saint Richard of Chichester: The Sources for His Life*, Sussex Record Society, 79, Lewes 1995
Jones, W. H. R., ed., *Fasti Ecclesiae Sarisberiensis*, Salisbury 1879
Jung, J. E., 'Beyond the Barrier: The Unifying Role of the Choir Screen in Gothic Churches', *Art Bulletin*, 82: 2000, 622–57
——, 'Peasant's Meal or Lord's Feast? The Social Iconography of the Naumburg Last Supper', *Gesta*, 52: 2003, 39–61
Jungmann, J. A., trans. F. A. Brunner, *The Mass of the Roman Rite: Its Origins and Development*, 2 vols, Blackrock 1986
Kahn, D., *Canterbury Cathedral and Its Romanesque Sculpture*, Austin 1991
Kammerer-George, M., *Zur Rahmung der toskanischen Altarbilder im Trecento*, Strasbourg 1966
Kauffmann, C. M., *Romanesque Manuscripts 1066–1190*, A Survey of Manuscripts Illuminated in the British Isles, 3, London 1975
Keck, D., *Angels and Angelology in the Middle Ages*, Oxford 1998
Keen, M., *Chivalry*, New Haven and London 1984
Keller, H., 'Der Flügelaltar als Reliquienschrein', in K. Martin, ed., *Studien zur Geschichte der europäischen Plastik: Festschrift Theodor Müller*, Munich 1965, 125–44
Kemp, B. R., ed., *Salisbury 1217–1228*. English Episcopal Acta, 19, Oxford 2000
Kemp, E. W., *Canonization and Authority in the Western Church*, Oxford 1948, repr. 1980
Kemp, W., trans. C. D. Saltzwedel, *The Narratives of Gothic Stained Glass*, Cambridge 1997
Kennedy, V. L., 'The Handbook of Master Peter Chancellor of Chartres', *Mediaeval Studies*, 5: 1943, 1–38
——, 'The Moment of Consecration and the Elevation of the Host', *Mediaeval Studies*, 6: 1944, 121–50
——, 'Robert Courson on Penance', *Mediaeval Studies*, 7: 1945, 291–336
——, 'The Date of the Parisian Decree on the Elevation of the Host', *Mediaeval Studies*, 8: 1946, 87–96
Ker, N. R., ed., *Medieval Libraries of Great Britain: A List of Surviving Books*. London 2/1964
Kessler, H. L., 'Diction in the "Bibles of the Illiterate"', in I. Lavin, ed., *World Art: Themes of Unity in Diversity*, Acts of the 26th International Congress of the History of Art, II, University Park and London 1989, 297–304
—— and G. Wolf, eds, *The Holy Face and the Paradox of Representation*, Villa Spelman Colloquia, 6, Bologna 1998, 153–80
Kidson, P., 'Canterbury Cathedral, the Gothic Choir', *Archaeological Journal*, 126: 1969, 244–6
——, 'St Hugh's Choir', *BAACT*, 8: 1986, 29–42
——, 'Panofsky, Suger, and St-Denis', *JWCI*, 50: 1987a, 1–17
——, 'A Note on Naumburg', in Stratford, ed., 1987 (1987b), 143–6
——, 'Gervase, Becket, and William of Sens', *Speculum*, 68: 1993, 969–91
——, 'Architectural History', in Owen, ed., 1994, 14–46
Kimpel, D., and R. Suckale, trans. F. Neu, *L'Architecture Gothique en France 1130–1270*, Paris 1990
King, A. A., *Eucharistic Reservation in the Western Church*, London 1965
Kitzinger, E., *The Mosaics of Monreale*, Palermo 1960
——, 'The Gregorian Reform and the Visual Arts: A Problem of Method', *TRHS*, 5th ser., 22: 1972, 87–102
——, 'The Arts as Aspects of a Renaissance: Rome and Italy', in Benson and Constable, eds, 1982, 637–70
Kjølbye-Biddle, B., 'The Alban Cross', *BAACT*, 24: 2001, 85–110
Klukas, A. W., 'The *Liber Ruber* and the Rebuilding of the East End of Wells', *BAACT*, 4: 1981, 30–35
——, 'Durham Cathedral in the Gothic Era: Liturgy, Design, Ornament', in Raguin, Brush and Draper, eds, 1995, 69–83
Knowles, D., 'Archishop Thomas Becket: A Character Study', *Proceedings of the British Academy*, 35: 1949, 177–205
——, *The Monastic Order in England*, Cambridge 2/1963
Knox, T. M., and C. Karelis, *Hegel's Introduction to Aesthetics*, Oxford 1979
Kobler, F., 'Deutsche Tafelmalerei des 13. Jahrhunderts: Ein Überblick', in Emmerling and Ringer, eds, 1997, 41–72
Kosmer, E., *A Study of the Style and Iconography of a Thirteenth-century Somme le Roi (British Museum Ms.Add.54180)*, PhD diss., Yale 1973
Krautheimer, R., *Rome, Profile of a City, 312–1308*, Princeton 1980
Krönig, W., 'Rheinische Vesperbild aus Leder und ihr Umkreis', *Wallraf-Richartz-Jahrbuch*, 24: 1962, 97–142
Krüger, K., *Der frühe Bildkult des Franziskus in Italien: Gestalt- und Funktionswandel des Tafelbildes im 13. und 14. Jahrhundert*, Berlin 1992
Kurmann, P., *La Façade de la cathédrale de Reims: Architecture et sculpture des portails. Etude archéologique et stylistic*, 2 vols, Paris 1987
Kuttner, S., and E. Rathbone, 'Anglo-Norman Canonists of the Twelfth Century', *Traditio*, 7: 1949–51, 279–358
Lacombe, G., 'The Questiones of Cardinal Stephen Langton', *New Scholasticism*, 3: 1929, 1–18
——, 'The Authenticity of the Summa of Cardinal Stephen Langton', *New Scholasticism*, 4: 1930, 97–114
—— and A. Landgraf, 'The Questiones of Cardinal Stephen Langton (II)', *New Scholasticism*, 3: 1929, 113–58
—— and B. Smalley, 'Studies on the Commentaries of Cardinal Stephen Langton', *Archives d'histoire doctrinale et littéraire du Moyen Age*, 5: 1930, 5–220
Ladner, G. B., 'The Symbolism of the Biblical Corner Stone in the Mediaeval West', *Mediaeval Studies*, 4: 1942, 43–60
——, 'St Gregory of Nyssa and St Augustine on the Symbolism of the Cross', in K. Weitzmann, ed., *Late Classical and Medieval Studies in Honor of Albert Mathias Friend Jr.*, Princenton 1955, 88–95 (repr. Ladner 1983, I, 197–208)
——, 'The Gestures of Prayer in Papal Iconography of the

Thirteenth and Early Fourteenth Centuries', in S. Prete, ed., *Didascaliae: Studies in Honor of Anselm M. Albareda*, New York 1961a, 245–75 (repr. Ladner 1983, I, 209–37)
——, 'Vegetation Symbolism and the Concept of Renaissance', in M. Meiss, ed., *De Artibus Opuscula XL: Essays in Honor of Erwin Panofsky*, 2 vols, New York 1961b, I, 303–22 (repr. Ladner 1983, II, 727–63)
——, *Images and Ideas in the Middle Ages: Selected Studies in History and Art*, Storia e Letteratura, Raccolta di Studi e Testi, 155–6, 2 vols, Rome 1983
Laird, C., 'Character and Growth of the Manuel des Pechiez', *Traditio*, 4: 1946, 253–306
Lane, B., *The Altar and the Altarpiece: Sacramental Themes in Early Netherlandish Painting*, New York 1984
Lasko, P., *Ars Sacra: 800–1200*, Harmondsworth 1972
—— and N. J. Morgan, eds, *Medieval Art in East Anglia 1300–1520*, Norwich 1973
Lawrence, C. H., 'The Alleged Exile of Archbishop Edmund', *Journal of Ecclesiastical History*, 7: 1956, 160–73
——, *St Edmund of Abingdon: A Study in Hagiography and History*, Oxford 1960
Lawrence, C. H., 'The English Parish and Its Clergy in the Thirteenth Century', in P. Linehan and J. Nelson, eds, *The Medieval World*, London and New York 2001, 648–70
——, ed., *The English Church and the Papacy in the Middle Ages*. Stroud 1999
Lawson, G., 'The Musician in the Stocks at Higham Ferrers, Northamptonshire: An Archaeological Postscript', in Ormrod, ed., 1991, 149–54
Le Goff, J., 'Laughter in the Middle Ages', in J. Bremmer and H. Roodenburg, eds, *A Cultural History of Humour: From Antiquity to the Present Day*, Cambridge 1997, 40–53
——, 'What did the Twelfth-century Renaissance *Mean*?', in P. Linehan and J. Nelson, eds, *The Medieval World*, London and New York 2001, 635–47
——, trans. A. Goldhammer, *The Birth of Purgatory*, Chicago 1984
Leclercq, J., 'The Renewal of Theology', in Benson and Constable, eds, 1982, 68–87
——, et al., *Baudouin de Ford: Le sacrement de l'autel*, Sources chrétiennes, 93–4, 2 vols, Paris 1963
Legg, J. W., *Tracts on the Mass*, Henry Bradshaw Society, 27, London 1904
——, ed., *The Sarum Missal*, Oxford 1916
—— and W. H. St J. Hope, eds, *Inventories of Christchurch Canterbury*, Westminster 1902
Legge, M. D., 'John Pecham's *Jerarchie*', *Medium Aevum*, 10: 1941, 77–84
Legner, A., *Rheinische Kunst und das Kölner Schnütgen-Museum*, Cologne 1991
——, *Reliquien in Kunst und Kult: Zwischen Antike und Aufklärung*, Darmstadt 1995
Lethaby, W. R., 'Notes on Sculptures in Lincoln Minster: The Judgement Porch and the Angel Choir', *Archaeologia*, 60: 1907, 379–90
——, 'English Primitives – I', *Burlington Magazine*, 29: 1916, 189–96
——, 'English Primitives – V', *Burlington Magazine*, 31: 1917a, 45–52
——, 'English Primitives – VI', *Burlington Magazine*, 31: 1917b, 97–98,
——, 'English Primitives – VII', *Burlington Magazine*, 31: 1917c, 192–3
Lewis, F., 'The Veronica: Image, Legend and Viewer', in Ormrod, ed., 1985, 100–06
——, 'Rewarding Devotion: Indulgences and the Promotion of Images', in D. Wood, ed., *The Church and the Arts*, Studies in Church History, 28, Oxford 1992, 179–94
——, 'The Wound in Christ's Side and the Instruments of the Passion: Gendered Experience and Response', in J. H. M. Taylor and L. Smith, eds, *Women and the Book: Assessing the Visual Evidence*, London 1996, 204–29
Lewis, S., 'Giles de Bridport and the Abingdon Apocalypse', in Ormrod, ed., 1985, 107–19
——, '*Tractatus adversus Judaeos* in the Gulbenkian Apocalypse', *Art Bulletin*, 68: 1986, 543–66
——, *The Art of Matthew Paris in the Chronica Majora*, Berkeley 1987
——, *Reading Medieval Images: Narrative Discourse and Reception in the Thirteenth Century Illuminated Apocalypse*, Cambridge 1995
Leyser, K. J., 'The Angevin Kings and the Holy Man' in Mayr-Harting, ed., 1987, 49–73
Liden, H. E., 'Middelalderens steinarkitektur i Norge', *Norges kunsthistorie, 2: Høymiddelalderen og Hansa-tid*, Oslo 1981, 7–125
Liebermann, F., 'Ein deutsches Bildhauer in London 1306', *Repertorium für Kunstwissenschaft*, 33: 1910, 550
——, ed., *Ungedruckte anglo-normannische Geschichstquellen*, Strassburg 1879
——, ed., *Die Heiligen Englands*, Hannover 1889
Lindblom, A., *La Peinture Gothique en Suède et en Norvège*, Stockholm 1916
——, *Björsätersmålningarna: The Legends of St. Thomas Becket and of the Holy Cross Painted in a Swedish Church*, Stockholm 1953
Lindley, P., 'The Imagery of the Octagon at Ely', *JBAA*, 139: 1986, 75–99
——, 'Retrospective Effigies, the Past and Lies', *BAACT*, 15: 1995, 111–21
Lisner, M., *Holzkruzifixe in Florenz und in der Toskana*, Munich 1970
Little, C., 'The Road to Glory: New Early Images of Thomas Becket's Life', in E. S. Sears and T. K. Thomas, eds, *Reading Medieval Images: The Art Historian and the Object*, Michigan 2002, 201–11
Liversidge, M., and P. Binski (appendix by J. Lynn), 'Two Ceiling Fragments from the Painted Chamber at Westminster Palace', *Burlington Magazine*, 137: 1995, 491–501
Loux, F., *L'Ogre et le dent: Pratiques et savoirs populaires relatifs aux dents*, Paris 1981
Lowden, J., *Early Christian & Byzantine Art*, London 1997
Lucas of Tuy [Lucas Tudensis Episcopus], *De Altera Vita*, Ingolstad 1612
Luscombe, D. E., 'Conceptions of Hierarchy before the Thirteenth Century', in A. Zimmermann, ed., *Soziale Ordnungen im Selbstverständnis des Mittelalters*, Miscellanea Mediaevalia, 12, Berlin and New York 1979, 1–19
——, 'The Reception of the Writings of Denis the Pseudo-

Areopagite into England', in D. Greenway et al., eds, *Tradition and Change: Essays in Honour of Marjorie Chibnall*, Cambridge 1985, 115–43
Macy, G., *The Theologies of the Eucharist in the Early Scholastic Period*, Oxford 1984
——, 'The Dogma of Transubstantiation in the Middle Ages', *Journal of Ecclesiastical History*, 45: 1994, 11–41
Maddison, J., 'Building at Lichfield Cathedral during the Episcopate of Walter Langton (1296–1321)', *BAACT*, 13: 1993, 65–84
——, *Ely Cathedral, Design and Meaning*, Ely 2000
Magnússon, E., *Thómas Saga Erkibyskups*, 2 vols, RS, 65, London, 1875–83
Mair, R., 'The Choir Capitals of Canterbury Cathedral 1174–84', *BAACT*, 5: 1982, 56–66
Major, K., 'The 'Familia' of Archbishop Stephen Langton', *English Historical Review*, 48: 1933, 529–53
Malden, A. R., 'A Contemporary Poem on the Translation of the Cathedral from Old to New Sarum', *Wiltshire Archaeological and Natural History Magazine*, 30: 1898–9, 210–17
Malmanger, M., L. Berczelly and S. Fuglesang, eds, *Norwegian Medieval Altar Frontals and Related Materials*, Acta, Institutum Romanum Norvegiae, 11, Rome 1995
Mannyng, Robert [of Brunne], ed. I. Sullens, *Handlyng Synne*, Binghamton 1983
Marks, R., *Stained Glass in England during the Middle Ages*, Toronto 1993
——, 'Altarpiece, Image and Devotion: Fourteenth-century Sculpture at Cobham, Kent', in P. Binski and W. Noel, eds, *New Offerings, Ancient Treasures: Studies in Medieval Art for George Henderson*, Stroud 2001, 417–44
—— and N. J. Morgan, *The Golden Age of English Manuscript Painting 1200–1500*, London 1981
—— and P. Williamson, eds, *Gothic: Art for England 1400–1547*, London 2003
Marquet de Vasselot, J. J., *Les Crosses limousines du XIIIe siècle*, Paris 1941
Marrow, J. H., *Passion Iconography in Northern European Art of the Late Middle Ages and Early Renaissance*, Kortrijk 1979
Marshall, M. H., 'Boethius' Definition of Persona and Mediaeval Understanding of the Roman Theater', *Speculum*, 25: 1950, 471–82
Martindale, A., 'Altarpieces in Italy during the 13th Century', in Malmanger et al., eds, 1995, 37–45
Mason, A. J., *What Became of the Bones of St Thomas?*, Cambridge 1920
Mason, E., 'The Role of the English Parishioner, 1100–1500', *Journal of Ecclesiastical History*, 27: 1976, 17–29
——, 'St Wulfstan's Staff: A Legend and Its Uses', *Medium Aevum*, 53: 1984, 157–79
——, *St Wulfstan of Worcester c. 1008–1095*, Oxford 1990
Matter, E. A., *The Voice of My Beloved: The Song of Songs in Western Medieval Christianity*, Philadelphia 1990
Mauss, M., 'Les Techniques du corps', *Journal de psychologie normale et pathologique*, 39: 1935, 271–93
Mayr-Harting, H., ed., *St Hugh of Lincoln*, Oxford 1987
McAleer, J. P., 'Particularly English? Screen Facades of the Type of Salisbury and Wells Cathedrals', *JBAA*, 141: 1988, 124–58
McGinn, B., 'From Admirable Tabernacle to the House of God: Some Theological Reflections on Medieval Architectural Integration', in Raguin, Brush and Draper, eds, 1995, 41–56
McGlashan, N. D., and R. E. Sandell, 'The Bishop of Salisbury's House at His Manor of Potterne', *Wiltshire Archaeological and Natural History Magazine*, 69: 1974, 85–96
McKinnon, J. W., 'Musical Instruments in Medieval Psalm Commentaries and Psalters', *Journal of the American Musicological Society*, 21: 1968, 3–20
McNeill, J. T., and H. M. Gamer, *Medieval Handbooks of Penance*, New York 1938
Meehan, B., 'Durham Twelfth-century Manuscripts in Cistercian Houses', in D. Rollason et al., eds., *Anglo-Norman Durham 1093–1193*, Woodbridge 1994, 439–49
Ménard, P., *Le Rire et le sourire dans le roman courtois en France au Moyen Âge (1150–1250)*, Geneva 1969
Merback, M. B., *The Thief, the Cross and the Wheel: Pain and the Spectacle of Punishment in Medieval and Renaissance Europe*, London 1999
Meyer, P., ed., *Fragments d'une vie de Saint Thomas de Cantorbéry*, Société des Anciens Textes Français, Paris 1885
Michael, M. A., *Images in Light: Stained Glass 1200–1550*, London 2002
Michaud-Quantin, P., *Sommes de casuistique et manuels de confession au Moyen Âge (XII – XVI siècles)*, Analecta Mediaevalia Namurcensia, 13, Louvain 1962
Milbourn, T., *The History of the Church of St Mildred the Virgin, Poultry, in the City of London*, London 1872
Millar, E. G., *An Illuminated Manuscript of La Somme le Roy, Attributed to the Parisian Miniaturist Honoré*, Oxford 1953
——, *The Parisian Miniaturist Honoré*, London 1959
Miller, E., *The Abbey & Bishopric of Ely*, Cambridge 1951
Minet-Mahy, V., 'Etude des métaphors végétales dans trois commentaires sur le Cantique de cantique (Origène, Apponius, Bernard de Clairvaux)', *Cahiers de civilisation médiévales, Xe–XIIe siècles*, 46: 2003, 159–89
Moleiro, M., ed., *Apocalipsis Gulbenkian*, Barcelona 2002
Moore, R. I., *The Formation of a Persecuting Society*, Oxford 1987
Moorman, J. R. H., *Church Life in England in the Thirteenth Century*, Cambridge 1945
Morgan, N. J., *Early Gothic Manuscripts (I), 1190–1250*, A Survey of Manuscripts Illuminated in the British Isles, 4, London 1982
——, *The Medieval Painted Glass of Lincoln Cathedral*, CVMA, Occasional Papers, 3, London 1983
——, *Early Gothic Manuscripts (II), 1250–1285*. A Survey of Manuscripts Illuminated in the British Isles, 4, London 1988a
——, 'Matthew Paris, St Albans, London, and the Leaves of the 'Life of St Thomas Becket', *Burlington Magazine*, 130: 1988b, 85–96
——, *The Lambeth Apocalypse*, London 1990
——, 'Texts and Images of Marian Devotion in Thirteenth-century England', in Ormrod, ed., 1991, 69–104
——, 'Texts and Images of Marian Devotion in Fourteenth-century England', in N. Rogers, ed., *England in the Fourteenth Century*, Harlaxton Medieval Studies, 3, Stamford 1993, 34–57

——, 'Western Norwegian Panel Painting 1250–1350: Problems of Dating, Styles and Workshops', in Malmanger et al., eds, 1995, 9–23
——, 'Devotional Aspects of the Catalan Altar Frontals c. 1100–1350: A Consideration of Their Iconographical Programmes', in R. Archer and E. Martinell, eds, *Proceedings of the First Symposium on Catalonia in Australia (1996)*, Barcelona 1998, 101–22
——, 'The Introduction of the Sarum Calendar into the Dioceses of England in the Thirteenth Century', in M. Prestwich, R. Britnell and R. Frame, eds, *Thirteenth Century England, 7*, Proceedings of the Durham Conference, Woodbridge 2001, 179–206
——, 'Marian Liturgy in Salisbury Cathedral', in J. Backhouse, ed., *The Medieval English Cathedral: Papers in Honour of Pamela Tudor-Craig*, Harlaxton Medieval Studies, 10, Stamford 2003, 89–111
Morris, C., *The Discovery of the Individual 1050–1200*, Toronto repr. 1987
—— and P. Roberts, eds, *Pilgrimage: The English Experience from Becket to Bunyan*, Cambridge 2002
Mortet, V., *Recueil de textes relatifs à l'histoire de l'architecture et à la condition des architectes en France, au Moyen Âge, XIe–XIIe siècles*, Paris 1911
——, 'Hugue de Fouilloi, Pierre le Chantre, Alexandre Neckam et les critiques dirigées au douzième siècle contre le luxe des constructions', in *Mélanges d'histoire offertes à M. Charles Bémont*, Paris 1913, 105–37
—— and P. Deschamps, *Recueil de textes relatifs à l'histoire de l'architecture et à la condition des architectes en France, au Moyen Âge, XIIe–XIIIe siècles*, Paris 1929
Mühlberg, F., 'Crucifixus dolorosus: Uber Bedeutung und Herkunft des gotischen Gabelkruzifixes', *Wallraf-Richartz-Jahrbuch*, 24: 1960, 69–86
Muratova, X., 'Vir quidem fallax et falisidicus, sed artifex praeelectus: Remarques sur l'image sociale et littéraire de l'artiste au Moyen Age', in X. Barral I Altet, ed., *Artistes, artisans et production artistique au Moyen Age*, I, Paris 1986, 53–72
——, 'Exeter and Italy: Assimilation and Adaptation of a Style: The Question of Italian Trecento Sources in the Sculptured Front of Exeter Cathedral (Fourteenth Century)', in I. Lavin, ed., *World Art: Themes of Unity in Diversity*, Acts of the 26th International Congress of the History of Art, II, University Park and London 1989, 117–32
Murray, A., *Reason and Society in the Middle Ages*, Oxford 1978
——, 'Confession as a Historical Source in the Thirteenth Century', in R. H. C. Davis and J. M. Wallace-Hadrill, eds, *The Writing of History in the Middle Ages: Essays Presented to Richard William Southern*, Oxford 1981, 275–322
Murray, J., *Le Château d'Amour de Robert Grosseteste êveque de Lincoln*, Paris 1918
Murray, S., *Beauvais Cathedral, Architecture of Transcendence*, Princeton 1989
New, E. A., 'Christological Personal Seals and Christocentric Devotion in Later Medieval England and Wales', *Antiquaries Journal*, 82: 2002, 47–68
Newcourt, R., *Repertorium Ecclesiasticum Parochiale Londiniense*, II, London 1708
Newman, J. H., ed. I. T. Kerr, *An Essay in Aid of a Grammar of Assent*, Oxford 1985
Newman, B., 'Devout Women and Demoniacs in the World of Thomas of Cantimpré', in Dor, Johnson and Wogan-Browne, eds, 1999, 35–60
Newton, S. M., *Fashion in the Age of the Black Prince: A Study of the Years 1340–1365*, Woodbridge 1980
Nicolai, B., 'Orders in Stone: Social Reality and the Artistic Approach: The Case of the Strasbourg South Portal', *Gesta*, 41: 2002, 111–28
Nilgen, U., 'Thomas Becket as a Patron of the Arts: The Wall Painting of St Anselm's Chapel at Canterbury Cathedral', *Art History*, 3: 1980, 357–74
——, 'Intellectuality and Splendour: Thomas Becket as a Patron of the Arts', in S. Macready and F. H. Thompson, eds, *Art and Patronage in the English Romanesque*, Society of Antiquaries Occasional Papers, 8, London 1986, 145–58
Nilson, B., *Cathedral Shrines of Medieval England*, Woodbridge 1998
Nodelman, S., 'How to Read a Roman Portrait', *Art in America*, 63: 1975, 26–33
Nordström, F., 'Peterborough, Lincoln, and the Science of Robert Grosseteste: A Study in Thirteenth Century Architecture and Iconography', *Art Bulletin*, 37: 1955, 241–72
Norton, E. C., 'History, Wisdom and Illumination', in D. Rollason, ed., *Symeon of Durham, Historian of Durham and the North*, Stamford 1998, 61–105
——, 'The Luxury Pavement in England before Westminster', in L. Grant and R. Mortimer, eds, *Westminster Abbey: The Cosmati Pavements*. Courtauld Research Papers, 3, Aldershot 2002, 7–27
—— and D. Park, eds, *Cistercian Art and Architecture in the British Isles*, Cambridge 1986
——, D. Park and P. Binski, *Dominican Painting in East Anglia: The Thornham Parva Retable and the Musée de Cluny Frontal*, Woodbridge 1987
Oakeshott, W., *Sigena: Romanesque Paintings in Spain and the Winchester Bible Artists*, London 1972
——, *The Two Winchester Bibles*, Oxford 1981
Oliver, G., *Monasticon Dioecesis Exoniensis*, London 1846
Omont, H., *Psautier illustré (XIIIe siècle)*, Paris 1927
Onians, J., *Bearers of Meaning: The Classical Orders in Antiquity, the Middle Ages, and the Renaissance*, Cambridge 1988
O'Reilly, J., '"Candidus et Rubicundus": An Image of Martyrdom in the "Lives" of Thomas Becket', *Analecta bollandiana*, 99: 1981, 303–14
——, 'The Double Martyrdom of Thomas Becket: Hagiography or History?', *Studies in Medieval and Renaissance History*, 7: 1985, 185–247
——, 'The Rough-hewn Cross in Anglo-Saxon Art', in M. Ryan, ed., *Ireland and Insular Art AD 500–1200*, Dublin 1987, 153–8
——, 'The Trees of Eden in Mediaeval Iconography', in P. Morris and D. Sawyer, eds, *A Walk in the Garden: Biblical, Iconographical and Literary Images of Eden*, Journal for the Study of the Old Testament, Supplement Series, 136, Sheffield 1992, 167–204
Orme, M., 'A Reconstruction of Robert of Cricklade's Vita et Miracula S. Thomae Cantuariensis', *Analecta bollandiana*, 84: 1966, 379–98
Ormrod, W. M., ed., *England in the Thirteenth Century*, Proceedings of the 1984 Harlaxton Symposium, Harlaxton 1985

——, *England in the Thirteenth Century*, Harlaxton Medieval Studies, 1, Stamford 1991 (1991b), 135–47
Oschinsky, D., *Walter of Henley and Other Treatises on Estate Management and Accounting*, Oxford 1971
Österlin, L., *Churches of Northern Europe in Profile: A Thousand Years of Anglo-Nordic Relations*. Norwich 1995
Ovid, ed. and trans. D. E. Hill, *Metamorphoses I–IV, V–VIII*, 2 vols, Warminster 1985–92
Owen, D., 'Historical Survey 1091–1450', in Owen, ed., *A History of Lincoln Minster*, Cambridge 1994, 112–63
Owst, G. R., *Preaching in Medieval England*, Cambridge 1926
——, *Literature and Pulpit in Medieval England*, Oxford 1933
Pächt, O., 'The Illustrations of St Anselm's Prayers and Meditations', *JWCI*, 19: 1956, 68–83
Paetow, L. J., 'The Crusading Ardor of John of Garland', in Paetow, ed., *The Crusades and Other Historical Essays Presented to D. C. Munro by his Former Students*, New York 1928, 207–22
Page, C., *Voices and Instruments of the Middle Ages: Instrumental Practice and Songs in France 1100–1300*, London 1987
——, *The Owl and the Nightingale: Musical Life and Ideas in France 1100–1300*, London 1989
——, 'An English Motet of the 14th Century in Performance: Two Contemporary Images', *Early Music*, 25: 1997, 7–32
Palmer, T. F., ed., *Collectanea*, I, Somerset Record Society, 39, London 1924
Panofsky, E., '*Imago pietatis*: Ein Beitrag zur Typengeschichte des "Schmerzenmanns" und der *Maria mediatrix*', in *Festschrift für Max J. Friedländer zum 60. Geburtstage*, Leipzig 1927, 261–308
——, *Gothic Architecture and Scholasticism*, Latrobe 1951
——, *Early Netherlandish Painting*, 2 vols Cambridge Mass. 1953
——, *Renaissance and Renascences in Western Art*, Stockholm 1960
——, *Tomb Sculpture: Four Lectures on Its Changing Aspects from Ancient Eqypt to Bernini*, New York 1964
——, ed., *Abbot Suger on the Abbey Church of St Denis and Its Art Treasures*, Princeton 2/1979
Pantin, W. A., *General and Provincial Chapters of the English Black Monks*, I, Camden Society, 3rd ser., 45, London 1931
——, *The English Church in the Fourteenth Century*, Cambridge 1955
Paris, Matthew, ed. and trans. R. Vaughan, *Chronicles of Matthew Paris: Monastic Life in the Thirteenth Century*, Gloucester and New York, 1984
——, ed. and trans. C. H. Lawrence, *The Life of St Edmund*, Stroud 1996
Park, D., 'The Wall Paintings of the Holy Sepulchre Chapel', *BAACT*, 6: 1983, 38–62
——, 'The Medieval Polychromy of Winchester Cathedral', in Crook, ed., 1993, 123–38
Parker, E. C., and C. T. Little, *The Cloisters Cross: Its Art and Meaning*, London 1994
Passarge, W., *Das deutsche Vesperbild im Mittelalter*, Cologne 1924
Peckham, J. L., *Archbishop Peckham as a Religious Educator*, New Haven 1934
Pevsner, N., *The Leaves of Southwell*, London 1945
—— and P. Metcalf, *The Cathedrals of England*, 2 vols, Harmondsworth 1985
Pfaff, R. W., 'Some Anglo-Saxon Sources for the "Theological Windows" at Canterbury Cathedral', *Mediaevalia*, 10: 1984, 49–62
Phillips, C. S., 'The Archbishop's Three Seats in Canterbury Cathedral', *Antiquaries Journal*, 29: 1949, 26–36
Pickering, F. P., *Literature and Art in the Middle Ages*, London 1970
——, *Essays on Medieval German Literature and Iconography*, Cambridge 1980
Plahter, U., 'Norwegian Easel Paintings from the Period 1250–1350', in H. W. Van Os and J. R. J. Van Asperen der Boer, eds, *La pittura nel XIV e XV secolo: Il contributo dell'analisi tecnica alla storia dell'arte*. Acts of the 24th International Congress of the History of Art, III, Bologna 1983, 73–89
Platt, C., *The Architecture of Medieval Britain*, New Haven and London 1990
Plehn, H., 'Der politische Charakter von Matheus Parisiensis', in G. Shmoller, ed., *Staats- und socialwissenschaftliche Forschungen*, 14/2, Leipzig 1897
Pliny, trans. D. E. Eichholz, *Natural History, X*, Cambridge Mass. 1962
Podro, M., *The Critical Historians of Art*, New Haven and London 1982
Powicke, F. M., *Stephen Langton*, London 1928
——, 'Bibliographical Note on Recent Work upon Stephen Langton', *English Historical Review*, 48: 1933, 554–7
——, *The Thirteenth Century, 1216–1307*, Oxford 1962
Prior, E. S., and A. Gardner, *An Account of Medieval Figure-Sculpture in England*, Cambridge 1912
Procter, F., and C. Wordsworth, eds, *Breviarium ad Usum Insignis Ecclesiae Sarum*, 3 vols, Cambridge 1879–86
Prynne, W., *Histriomastix*, New York and London 1974
Pseudo-Dionysius, trans. C. Luibheid, *The Complete Works*, New York 1987
Quinto, J., *'Doctor Nominatissimus': Stefano Langton (=1228) e la tradizione delle sue opere*, Münster 1994
Rady, J., T. Tatton-Brown and J. A. Bowen, 'The Archbishop's Palace, Canterbury', *JBAA*, 144: 1991, 1–60
Raguin, V. C., K. Brush and P. Draper, eds, *Artistic Integration in Gothic Buidings*, Toronto and London 1995
Ragusa, I., and R. B. Green, eds, *Meditations on the Life of Christ: An Illustrated Manuscript of the Fourteenth Century*, Princeton 1961
Ramm, H. G., et al., 'The Tombs of Archbishops Walter de Gray (1216–55) and Godfrey de Ludham (1258–65) in York Minster, and Their Contents', *Archaeologia*, 103: 1971, 101–47
Rastall, R., 'Minstrelsy, Church and Clergy in Medieval England', *Proceedings of the Royal Musical Association*, 97: 1970–71, 83–98
——, 'The Sounds of Hell', in C. Davidson and T. H. Seiler, eds, *The Iconography of Hell*, Early Drama, Art, and Music Monograph Series, 17, Kalamazoo 1992, 102–31
Ravaux, J.-P., 'Les Campagnes de construction de la cathédrale de Reims au XIIIe siècle', *Bulletin monumental*, 137: 1979, 7–66
Raw, B. C., *Anglo-Saxon Crucifixion Iconography and the Art of the Monastic Revival*, Cambridge Studies in Anglo-Saxon England, 1, Cambridge 1990

——, *Trinity and Incarnation in Anglo-Saxon Art and Thought*, Cambridge Studies in Anglo-Saxon England, 21, Cambridge 1997

Recht, R., 'Torsion et hanchement dans la sculpture gothique', *Gesta*, 15: 1976, 179–84

——, *Le Croire et le voire: L'Art des cathédrales (XIIe–XVe siècle)*, Paris 1999

Reeve, M. M., 'The Retrospective Effigies of Anglo-Saxon Bishops at Wells Cathedral: A Reassessment', *Somerset Archaeology and Natural History*, 142: 1998, 235–59

——, 'A Seat of Authority: The Archbishop's Throne at Canterbury Cathedral', *Gesta*, 42: 2003, 131–42

Reiners-Ernst, E., *Das freudvolle Vesperbild und die Anfänge der Pietà-Vorstellung*, Munich 1939

Reudenbach, B., 'Säule und Apostel: Überlegungen zum Verhältnis von Architektur und architekturexegetischer Literatur im Mittelalter', *Frühmittelalterliche Studien*, 14: 1980, 310–51

Reynolds, H. E., *Wells Cathedral: Its Foundations, Constitutional History, and Statutes*, Wells 1881

Reynolds, L. D., *The Medieval Tradition of Seneca's Letters*, Oxford 1965

Rickert, M., *Painting in Britain: The Middle Ages*, Harmondsworth 1954

Ridderbos, B., 'The Man of Sorrows: Pictorial Images and Metaphorical Statements', in A. A. MacDonald, H. N. B. Ridderbos and R. M. Schlusemann, eds, *The Broken Body: Passion Devotion in Late-Medieval Culture*, Mediaevalia Groningana, 21, Groningen 1998, 145–81

Ridyard, S. J., '*Condigna veneratio*: Post-Conquest Attitudes to the Saints of the Anglo-Saxons', *Anglo-Norman Studies*, 9: 1986, 179–206

——, *The Royal Saints of Anglo-Saxon England: A Study of West Saxon and East Anglian Cults*, Cambridge 1988

——, 'Monk-Kings and the Anglo-Saxon Hagiographic Tradition', *Haskins Society Journal*, 6: 1994, 13–27

Ringbom, S., *Icon to Narrative: The Rise of the Dramatic Close-up in Fifteenth-century Devotional Painting*, Acta Academiae Aboensis, ser. A, 31 no. 2, Åbo 1965

Robert of Flamborough, ed. J. J. F. Firth, *Liber poenitentialis*, Pontifical Institute of Medieval Studies, Studies and Texts, 18, Toronto 1971

Roberts, M., 'Noah's Ark', *Friends of Wells Cathedral: Annual Report*, 1973, 10–14

——, 'The Tomb of Giles de Bridport in Salisbury Cathedral', *Art Bulletin*, 65: 1983, 559–86

——, 'The Relic of the Holy Blood and the Iconography of the North Transept Portal of Westminster Abbey', in Ormrod, ed., 1985, 129–42

——, 'The Effigy of Bishop Hugh de Northwold in Ely Cathedral', *Burlington Magazine*, 130: 1988, 77–84

Roberts, P. B., *Stephanus de Lingua-Tonante: Studies in the Sermons of Stephen Langton*, Toronto 1968

——, 'Langton on Becket: A New Look and a New Text', *Mediaeval Studies*, 35: 1973, 38–48

——, ed., *Selected Sermons of Stephen Langton*, Toronto Medieval Latin Texts, 10, Toronto 1980

——, 'Archbishop Stephen Langton and His Preaching on Thomas Becket in 1220', in T. L. Amos, E. A. Green and B. Mayne Kienzle, eds, *De Ore Domini: Preacher and Word in the Middle Ages*, Kalamazoo 1989, 75–92

——, *Thomas Becket in the Medieval Latin Preaching Tradition*, Instrumenta Patristica, 25, The Hague 1992

Robertson, D. W., 'The *Manuel des péchés* and an English Episcopal Decree', *Modern Language Notes*, 60: 1945, 439–47

——, 'A Note on the Classical Origin of "Circumstances" in the Medieval Confessional', *Studies in Philology*, 43: 1946, 6–14

——, 'The Cultural Tradition of *Handlyng Synne*', *Speculum*, 22: 1947, 162–85

——, 'Frequency of Preaching in Thirteenth-century England', *Speculum*, 24: 1949, 376–88

Robinson, J. A., 'Effigies of Saxon Bishops at Wells', *Archaeologia*, 65: 1913–14, 95–112

——, *Somerset Historical Essays*, London 1921

——, 'An Essay on Somerset Mediaeval Calendars', *Somerset Record Society*, 42: 1927, 143–83

——, 'Documentary Evidence relating to the Building of the Cathedral Church of Wells (*c.*1186–1242)', *Archaeological Journal*, 85: 1928, 1–22

Rodwell, W., 'The Anglo-Saxon and Norman Churches at Wells', in Colchester, ed., 1982, 1–23

——, *Wells Cathedral: Excavations and Structural Studies, 1978–93*, English Heritage Archaeological Reports, 21, 2 vols, London 2001

Rollason, D. W., 'Lists of Saints' Resting-places in Anglo-Saxon England', *Anglo-Saxon England*, 7: 1978, 61–93

——, 'The Cults of Murdered Royal Saints in Anglo-Saxon England', *Anglo-Saxon England*, 11: 1983, 1–22

Rorem, P., *Pseudo-Dionysius: A Commentary on the Texts and an Introduction to Their Influence*, Oxford 1993

Rose, A., 'Angel Musicians in the Medieval Stained Glass of Norfolk Churches', *Early Music*, 29: 2001, 187–217

Roth, E., *Der volkreiche Kalvarienberg in Literatur und Bildkunst des Spätmittelalters*, Philologische Studien und Quellen, 2, Berlin 1967

Rouse, E. C., and A. Baker, 'The Wall-paintings at Longthorpe Tower near Peterborough, Northants', *Archaeologia*, 96: 1955, 1–57

Rubin, M., *Corpus Christi: The Eucharist in Late Medieval Culture*, Cambridge 1991

——, 'What did the Eucharist Mean to Thirteenth-century Villagers?', in P. R. Coss and S. D. Lloyd, eds, *Thirteenth Century England, 6*, Proceedings of the Newcastle upon Tyne Conference, Woodbridge 1992, 47–55

Rudolph, C., *Artistic Change at St-Denis: Abbot Suger's Program and the Early Twelfth-century Controversy over Art*, Princeton 1990a

——, *The 'Things of Greater Importance': Bernard of Clairvaux's Apologia and the Medieval Attitude toward Art*, Philadelphia 1990b

Russell, D. W., ed., *La Vie seint Richard, Evesque de Cycestre*, Anglo Norman Text Society, 51, London 1995

Russell, J. C., 'Master Henry of Avranches as an International Poet', *Speculum*, 3: 1928, 34–63

——, 'The Canonization of Opposition to the King in Angevin England', in C. H. Taylor, ed., *Anniversary Essays in*

Mediaeval History by Students of Charles Homer Haskins, New York 1929, 279–90
——, 'Some Thirteenth-century Anglo-Norman Writers', *Modern Philology*, 28: 1931, 257–69
Sajavaara, K., *The Middle English Translations of Robert Grosseteste's Chateau d'Amour*, Mémoires de la Société Néophilologique de Helsinki, 32, Helsinki 1967
Salu, M. B., trans., *The Ancrene Riwle*, London 1955
Sampson, J., *Wells Cathedral West Front: Construction, Sculpture and Conservation*, Stroud 1998
Samson, A., 'The South English Legendary: Constructing a Context', in P. R. Coss and S. D. Lloyd, eds, *Thirteenth Century England, 1*, Proceedings of the Newcastle upon Tyne Conference, Woodbridge 1986, 185–95
Sandler, L. F., *The Peterborough Psalter in Brussels and Other Fenland Manuscripts*, London 1974
——, *The Psalter of Robert de Lisle*, Oxford 1983
——, *Gothic Manuscripts 1285–1385*, A Survey of Manuscripts Illuminated in the British Isles, 5, 2 vols, Oxford 1986
——, 'John of Metz, the Tower of Wisdom', in M. Carruthers and J. Ziolkowski, eds, *The Medieval Craft of Memory: An Anthology of Texts and Pictures*, Philadelphia 2002, 215–25
Sanford, E. M., 'Giraldus Cambrensis' Debt to Petrus Cantor', *Medievalia et humanistica*, 3: 1945, 16–32
Sartre, J.-P., trans. H. E. Barnes, *Being and Nothingness: An Essay in Phenomenological Ontology*. London 1958
——, trans. P. Mairet, *Sketch for a Theory of the Emotions*, London 1962
Sauer, J., *Symbolik des Kirchengebaudes und seiner Ausstattung in der Auffassung des Mittelalters*, Freiburg im Breisgau 1924
Sauerländer, W., 'Reims und Bamberg: Zu Art und Umfang der Übernahmen', *Zeitschrift für Kunstgeschichte*, 39: 1976, 167–92
——, 'Die Naumburger Stifterfiguren: Rückblick und Fragen', in R. Haussherr and C. Väterlein, eds, *Die Zeit der Staufer: Geschichte, Kunst, Kultur*, 5, Stuttgart 1977, 169–245
——, 'Architecture and the Figurative Arts: The North', in Benson and Constable, eds, 1982, 671–710
——, '"Première Architecture gothique" or "Renaissance of the Twelfth Century"? Changing Perspectives of Evaluation in Architectural History', in B. King, ed., *Sewanee Medieval Colloquium Occasional Papers*, 2. Sewanee 1985, 25–43
——, '*Antiqui et moderni* at Reims', *Gesta*, 52: 2003, 19–37
——, trans. J. Sondheimer, *Gothic Sculpture in France 1140–1270*, London 1972
Savage, A., and N. Watson, trans., *Anchoritic Spirituality: Ancrene Wisse and Associated Works*, Mahwah 1991
Saxl, F., 'A Spiritual Encyclopedia of the Later Middle Ages', *JWCI*, 5: 1942, 82–134
Scammell, G. V., *Hugh du Puiset, Bishop of Durham*, Cambridge 1956
Schapiro, M., 'Style', in A. L. Kroeber, et al., *Anthropology Today: An Encyclopedic Inventory*, Chicago 1953, 287–312
——, *Romanesque Art*, London 1977
Scharff, M., 'The Altar Frontal from Løgum', in Malmanger et al., eds, 1995, 83–91
Schmitt, J.-C., *La Raison des gestes dans l'occident médiéval*, Paris 1990
——, 'The Rationale of Gestures in the West: Third to Thirteenth Centuries', in J. Bremmer and H. Roodenburg, eds, *A Cultural History of Gesture from Antiquity to the Present Day*, Oxford 1991, 59–83
Schneider, R. M., 'Coloured Marble: The Splendour and Power of Imperial Rome', *Apollo*, 154: 2001, 3–10
Schuller, M., et al., *Das Fürstenportal des Bamburger Domes*, Munich 1993
Schulte, A., *Der Adel und die deutsche Kirche im Mittelalter: Studien zur Sozial-, Rechts- und Kirchengeschichte*, Darmstadt 1922
Sciurie, H., 'Ecclesia und Synagoge an den Domen zu Strassburg, Bamberg, Magdeburg und Erfurt: Körpersprachliche Wandlungen im gestalterischen Kontext', *Wiener Jahrbuch für Kunstgeschichte*, 46–7: 1993–4, 679–87
Scott, K. L., *Later Gothic Manuscripts 1390–1490*, A Survey of Manuscripts Illuminated in the British Isles, 6, 2 vols, London 1996
Screech, M. A., *Laughter at the Foot of the Cross*. London 1997
Sears, E., 'Ivory and Ivory Workers in Medieval Paris', in Barnet, ed., 1997, 19–37
Seebass, T., *Musikdarstellung und Psalterillustration im frühen Mittelalter*, 2 vols, Berne 1973
Sekules, V., 'The Tomb of Christ at Lincoln and the Development of the Sacrament Shrine: Easter Sepulchres Reconsidered', *BAACT*, 8: 1986, 118–31
——, 'Beauty and the Beast: Ridicule and Orthodoxy in Architectural Marginalia in Early Fourteenth-century Lincolnshire', *Art History*, 18: 1995, 37–62
Ševčenko, N., 'The Vita Icon and the Painter as Hagiographer', *Dumbarton Oaks Papers*, 53: 1999, 149–65
Severens, K. W., 'William of Sens and the Double Columns at Sens and Canterbury', *JWCI*, 33: 1970, 307–13
Shaw, J., 'The Influence of Canonical and Episcopal Reform on Popular Books of Instruction', in T. J. Heffernan, ed., *The Popular Literature of Medieval England*, Tennessee Studies in Literature, 28, Knoxville 1985, 44–60
Shearman, J., *Only Connect . . . Art and the Spectator in the Italian Renaissance*, National Gallery of Art, Washington, Bollingen Series, XXXV: 37, Princeton 1992
Sheingorn, P., *The Easter Sepulchre in England*, Early Drama, Art and Music Reference Series, 5, Kalamazoo 1987
Shepherd, G., ed., *Ancrene Wisse: Parts Six and Seven*, London 1959
Shinners, J., ed., *Medieval Popular Religion 1000–1500: A Reader*, Peterborough Ontario, 1997
—— and W. J. Dohar, eds, *Pastors and the Care of Souls in Medieval England*, Notre Dame Indiana 1998
Shirley, J., trans., *Garnier's Becket*, Felinfach 1996
Shortt, H., *Salisbury Cathedral and Indications of the Sarum Use*, Salisbury 1970
Sicard, P., *Diagrammes médiévaux et exégèse visuelle: Le Libellus de formatione arche de Hugues de Saint-Victor*, Paris 1993
Sidonius, ed. and trans. W. B. Anderson, *Poems and Letters*, I, London and Cambridge Mass. 1956
Simmons, E., *Les Heures de Nuremberg*, Paris 1994
Simmons, T. F., ed., *The Lay Folks Mass Book*, London 1879
Simons, W., 'Reading a Saint's Body: Rapture and Bodily Movement in the *Vitae* of Thirteenth-century Beguines', in S. Kay and M. Rubin, eds, *Framing Medieval Bodies*, Manchester 1994, 10–23

Simpson, W. S., 'Visitations of Churches belonging to St Paul's Cathedral 1249–1252', *Camden Miscellany*, 9: 1895a (whole volume)

——, 'Visitations of Churches belonging to St Paul's Cathedral in 1297 and in 1458', *Camden Society*, n.s. 55: 1895b

——, ed., *Registrum statutorum et consuetudinum Ecclesiae Cathedralis Sancti Pauli Londonensis*, London 1873

Singleton, B., 'The Remodelling of the East End of Worcester Cathedral in the Earlier Part of the Thirteenth Century', *BAACT*, 1: 1978, 105–15

Skinner, Q., *Visions of Politics*, 3: *Hobbes and Civil Science*, Cambridge 2002

Smalley, B., 'Stephen Langton and the Four Senses of Scripture', *Speculum*, 6: 1931, 60–76

——, 'Exempla in the Commentaries of Stephen Langton', *Bulletin of the John Rylands Library*, 17: 1933, 121–9

——, *The Becket Conflict and the Schools: A Study of Intellectuals in Politics*, Oxford 1973

——, 'Ecclesiastical Attitudes to Novelty c.1100–c.1250', in D. Baker, ed., *Church, Society and Politics*, Studies in Church History, 12, Oxford 1975, 113–31

——, *The Study of the Bible in the Middle Ages*, Oxford 3/1984

——, 'Use of the "Spiritual" Senses of Scripture in Persuasion and Argument by Scholars in the Middle Ages', *Recherches de théologie ancienne et médiévale*, 52: 1985, 44–63

Smith, A., ed., *Annales de Monte Fernandi/Annals of Multifernan*, Tracts Relating to Ireland (Irish Archaeological Society), 2, Dublin 1842

Southern, R. W., *The Making of the Middle Ages*, London 1953

——, *Medieval Humanism and Other Studies*, Oxford 1970

——, *Robert Grosseteste: The Growth of an English Mind in Medieval Europe*, Oxford 1986

——, *St Anselm: A Portrait in a Landscape*, Cambridge 1990

Sparke, J., *Historiae Anglicanae Scriptores Varii*, London 1723

Spurrell, M., 'The Promotion and Demotion of Whole Relics', *Antiquaries Journal*, 80: 2000, 67–85

Stalley, R., 'A Twelfth-century Patron of Architecture: A Study of the Buildings Erected by Roger, Bishop of Salisbury 1102–1139', *JBAA*, 34: 1971, 62–83

Stanley, A. P., *Historical Memorials of Canterbury*, London 1855

Stansbury-O'Donnell, M. D., *The Shape of the Church: The Relationship of Architecture, Art, and Liturgy at the Cathedral of Trier*, PhD diss., Yale University 1990

Statius, ed. and trans. K. M. Coleman, *Silvae IV*, Oxford 1988

Staunton, M., trans., *The Lives of Thomas Becket*, Manchester 2001

Steele, R., ed., *Three Prose Versions of the Secreta Secretorum*, I: *Text and Glossary*, EETS, extra ser. 74, London 1898

Stephen of Sawley, ed. and trans. B. K. Lackner and J. F. O'Sullivan, *Treatises*, Cistercian Fathers Series, 36, Kalamazoo 1984

Stocker, D. A., 'The Tomb and Shrine of Bishop Grosseteste in Lincoln Cathedral', in Ormrod, ed., 1985, 143–8

——, 'The Shrine of Little St Hugh', *BAACT*, 8: 1986, 109–17

——, 'The Mystery of the Shrines of St Hugh', in Mayr-Harting, ed., 1987, 89–124

Stone, L., *Sculpture in Britain: The Middle Ages*, Har-mondsworth 1972

Stones, A., *Le Livre d'images de Madame Marie*, Paris 1997

Stow, J., ed. J. Strype, *A Survey of the Cities of London and Westminster*, 2 vols, London 1720

Stratford, N., P. Tudor-Craig and A. M. Muthesius, 'Archbishop Hubert Walter's Tomb and Its Furnishings', *BAACT*, 5: 1982, 71–93

Stratford, N., ed., *Romanesque and Gothic: Essays for George Zarnecki*, 2 vols, Woodbridge 1987

Stroud, D., 'The Cult and Tombs of St Osmund at Salisbury', *Wiltshire Archaeological and Natural History Magazine*, 78: 1983, 50–54

Strucken, M., *Literarische und künstleriche Quellen des Gabelkruzifixus*, PhD diss., Dusseldorf 1928

Suckale, R., 'Die Bamberger Domskulpturen', *Münchner Jahrbuch der bildenden Kunst*, 38: 1987, 27–82

Suetonius, trans. R. Graves, *The Twelve Caesars*, Harmondsworth 1979

Summers, D., *The Judgment of Sense: Renaissance Naturalism and the Rise of Aesthetics*, Cambridge 1987

Summerson, J., 'Heavenly Mansions: An Interpretation of Gothic', in *Heavenly Mansions and Other Essays on Architecture*, New York 1963, 1–28

Sureda, J., *La pintura románica en Cataluña*, Madrid 1981

Svanberg, J., 'The Gothic Smile', in T. W. Gaehtgens, ed., *Künstlerischer Austausch, Artistic Exchange*. Acts of the 28th International Congress of the History of Art, II, Berlin 1993, 357–70

Swarzenski, H., *Monuments of Romanesque Art*. London 2/1974

Talbot, C. H., 'The Cistercian Attitude towards Art: The Literary Evidence', in Norton and Park, eds, 1986, 56–64

Tammen, B. R., *Musik und Bild im Chorraum mittelalterlicher Kirchen 1100–1500*, Berlin 2000

Tångeberg, P., *Mittelalterliche Holzskulpturen und Altarschreine in Schweden*, Stockholm 1986

Tanner, N. P., ed., *Decrees of the Ecumenical Councils*, I, London and Washington 1990

Taralon, J., *Treasures of the Churches of France*, New York 1966

Tatton-Brown, T., 'The Trinity Chapel and Corona Floors', *Canterbury Cathedral Chronicle*, 75: 1981, 51–6

——, 'The Great Hall of the Archbishop's Palace', *BAACT*, 5: 1982, 112–19

——, 'The Medieval Fabric', in M. Hobbs, ed., *Chichester Cathedral: An Historical Survey*, Chichester 1994, 25–46

——-, 'The Two Great Marble Pavements in the Sanctuary and Shrine Areas of Canterbury Cathedral and Westminster Abbey', in J. Fawcett, ed., *Historic Floors: Their History and Conservation*, Oxford 1998a, 53–62

——, 'The Salisbury Cathedral Consecration Crosses', *Transactions of the Monumental Brass Society*, 16: 1998b, 113–16

——, *Lambeth Palace: A History of the Archbishops of Canterbury and Their Houses*, London 2000

——, 'The Beginnings of Lambeth Palace', *Anglo-Norman Studies*, 24: 2001, 203–14

——, 'Canterbury and the Architecture of Pilgrimage Shrines in England', in Morris and Roberts, eds, 2002, 90–107

Taubert, G., and J. Taubert, 'Mittelalterliche Kruzifixe mit schwenkbaren Armen: Ein Beitrag zur Verwendung von Bildwerken in der Liturgie', *Zeitschrift des Deutschen Vereins für Kunstwissenschaft*, 23: 1969, 79–121

Temple, E., *Anglo-Saxon Manuscripts 900–1066*. A Survey of Manuscripts Illuminated in the British Isles, 2, London 1976
Tentler, T. N., *Sin and Confession on the Eve of the Reformation*, Princeton 1977
Thielman, J., 'Political Canonization and Political Symbolism in Medieval England', *Journal of British Studies*, 29: 1990, 241–6
Thoby, P., *Le Crucifix des origines au Concile de Trente*, 2 vols, Nantes 1959–63
Thomas, I. G., *The Cult of Saints' Relics in Medieval England*, PhD diss., University of London 1974
Thomas of Chobham, ed. F. Broomfield, *Summa Confessorum*, Analecta Mediaevalia Namurcensia, 25, Louvain 1968
Thompson, A. H., 'Master Elias of Dereham and the King's Works', *Archaeological Journal*, 98: 1941–2, 1–35
——, *The English Clergy and Their Organisation in the Later Middle Ages*, London 1947
Thompson, B., 'The Academic and Active Vocations in the Medieval Church: Archbishop John Pecham', in C. M. Barron and J. Stratford, eds, *The Church and Learning in Later Medieval Society: Essays in Honour of R. B. Dobson*, Harlaxton Medieval Studies, 11, Stamford 2002, 1–24
Thompson, E. M., *Customary of the Benedictine Monasteries of Saint Augustine, Canterbury, and Saint Peter, Westminster*, 2 vols, London 1902–4
Thompson, S., *Women Religious: The Founding of English Nunneries after the Norman Conquest*, Oxford 1991
Thompson, W. M., ed., *Þe Wohunge of Ure Lauerd*, EETS, 241, Oxford 1958
Thomson, R. M., *Manuscripts from St Albans Abbey 1066–1235*, 2 vols, Woodbridge 1982
——, 'England and the Twelfth-century Renaissance', *Past and Present*, 101: 1983, 3–21
——, ed. and trans., *The Chronicle of the Election of Hugh Abbot of Bury St Edmunds and later Bishop of Ely*, Oxford 1974
Thomson, W. R., 'The Image of the Mendicants in the Chronicles of Matthew Paris', *Archivum Franciscanum Historicum*, 70: 1977, 3–34
Thorpe, J., ed., *Registrum Roffense*, London 1769
Thurlby, M., 'The West Front of Binham Priory, Norfolk, and the Beginnings of Bar Tracery in England', in Ormrod, ed., 1991, 155–65
Timmermann, A., 'Architectural Vision in Albrecht von Scharfenberg's *Jüngerer Titurel*', in G. Clarke and P. Crossley, eds, *Architecture and Language: Constructing Identity in European Architecture, c.1000–c.1650*, Cambridge 2000, 58–71
Torrance, W. J., 'A Contemporary Poem on the Removal of Salisbury Cathedral from Old Sarum', *Wiltshire Archaeological and Natural History Magazine*, 57: 1959, 242–6
Toulmin Smith, L., ed., *The Itinerary of John Leland in or about the Years 1535–43*, I, London 1907
Townsend, D., 'The Vita Sancti Birini of Henry of Avranches (*BHL* 1364)', *Analecta Bollandiana*, 112: 1994, 309–38
—— and A. G. Rigg, 'Medieval Latin Poetic Anthologies (V): Matthew Paris' Anthology of Henry of Avranches (Cambridge, University Library MS. Dd.11.78)', *Mediaeval Studies*, 49: 1987, 352–90
Trachtenberg, M., 'Suger's Miracles, Branner's Bourges: Reflections on "Gothic Architecture" as Medieval Modernism', *Gesta*, 39: 2000, 183–205
Trevisa, John, ed. M. C. Seymour, *On the Properties of Things: John Trevisa's Translation of Bartholomaeus Anglicus, De Proprietatibus Rerum. A Critical Text*, 2 vols, Oxford 1975
Trexler, R. C., *The Christian at Prayer: An Illustrated Prayer Manual Attributed to Peter the Chanter (d.1197)*, Medieval and Renaissance Texts and Studies, 44, Binghamton 1987
Tripps, J., *Das handelnde Bildwerk in der Gotik*, Berlin 1998
Tristram, E. W., *English Medieval Wall Painting: The Thirteenth Century*, 2 vols, Oxford 1950
——, *English Wall Painting of the Fourteenth Century*, London 1955
Trollope, E., 'Notes on Gainsborough', *Associated Architectural Societies' Reports and Papers*, 8: 1866, 213–54
Tudor-Craig, P., 'Wells Sculpture', in Colchester, ed., 1982, 102–31
Turner, D. H., 'The Development of Maître Honoré', *British Museum Quarterly*, 33: 1968, 53–65
——, 'The Customary of the Shrine of St Thomas Becket', *Canterbury Cathedral Chronicle*, 70: 1976, 16–22
Tuve, R., 'Notes on the Virtues and Vices', *JWCI*, 26: 1963, 264–303; 27: 1964, 42–72
Urry, W., 'Some Notes on the Two Resting Places of St Thomas Becket at Canterbury', in Foreville, ed., 1975, 195–209
——, *Thomas Becket: His Last Days*, Stroud 1999
Vale, M., *The Princely Court: Medieval Courts and Culture in North-West Europe 1270–1380*, Oxford 2001
Vallance, A., *English Church Screens*, London 1936
——, *Greater English Church Screens*, London 1947
Vallentin, B., 'Der Engelstaat: Zur mittelalterlichen Anschauung von Staate (bis auf Thomas von Aquino)', in K. Breysig et al., *Grundrisse und Bausteine zur Staats- und zur Geschichtslehre zusammengetragen zu den Ehren Gustav Schmollers*, Berlin 1908, 41–120
Van Os, H., *Sienese Altarpieces 1215–1460*, I, Groningen 1988
——, trans. M. Hoyle, *The Art of Devotion in the Late Middle Ages in Europe 1300–1500*, London and Amsterdam 1994
Van Schaik, M., *The Harp in the Middle Ages: The Symbolism of a Musical Instrument*, Amsterdam 1992
Vauchez, A., 'Les Stigmates de saint François et leurs détracteurs dans les derniers siècles du Moyen Âge', *Mélanges d'archéologie et d'histoire: Ecole française de Rome*, 80: 1968, 595–625
——, trans. J. Birrell, *Sainthood in the Later Middle Ages*, Cambridge 1997
Vaughan, R., *Matthew Paris*, Cambridge 1958
Vavalà, E., *La Croce Dipinta Italiana*, Verona 1929
Veal, J. F., *The Sacramental Theology of Stephen Langton and the Influence upon Him of Peter the Chanter*, Rome 1955
Venables, E., 'The Architectural History of Lincoln Cathedral', *Archaeological Journal*, 40: 1883, 377–418
Verdier, P., 'La Grande Croix de l'abbé Suger à Saint Denis', *Cahiers de civilisation médiévale, X^e–XIIe siècles*, 13: 1970, 1–26
Viller, M., F. Cavallera and J. De Guibert, eds, *Dictionnaire de spiritualité ascétique et mystique*, VII/1, Paris 1969
Vincent, N., *Peter des Roches*, Cambridge 1996
——, *The Holy Blood: King Henry III and the Westminster Blood Relic*, Cambridge 2001

——, 'Master Elias of Dereham (d.1245): A Reassessment', in C. M. Barron and J. Stratford, eds, *The Church and Learning in Later Medieval Society: Essays in Honour of R. B. Dobson*, Harlaxton Medieval Studies, 11, Stamford 2002a, 128–59
——, 'The Pilgrimage of the Angevin Kings of England', in Morris and Roberts, eds, 2002 (2002b), 12–45
Virgil, ed. J. D. Christie, commentary C. J. Fordyce, *P. Vergili Maronis Aeneidos, Libri VII–VIII*, Glasgow 1977
Vitruvius, trans. M. H. Morgan, *The Ten Books on Architecture*, Cambridge 1914
Von Alemann-Schwartz, M., *Crucifixus dolorosus: Beiträge zur Polychromie und Ikonographie der rheinischen Gablekruzifixe*, PhD diss., Bonn 1976
Von Dobschütz, E., *Christusbilder: Untersuchungen zur Christlichen Legende*, Texte und Untersuchungen zur Geschichte der Altchristlichen Literatur, 3, Leipzig 1899
Von Simson, O. G., '*Compassio* and *Co-redemptio* in Roger van der Weyden's *Descent from the Cross*', *Art Bulletin*, 35: 1953, 9–16
Waddell, C., 'The Reform of the Liturgy from a Renaissance Perspective', in Benson and Constable, eds, 1982, 88–109
Walberg, E., *La Tradition hagiographique de Saint Thomas Becket avant la fin du XIIe siècle: Etudes critiques*, Paris 1929
Wallace, A., *Life of St Edmund of Canterbury*, London 1893
Ward, B., *St. Edmund, Archbishop of Canterbury: His Life, as Told by Old English Writers*, London 1903
——, *Miracles and the Medieval Mind: Theory, Record and Event 1000–1215*, Aldershot 1982
Ward-Perkins, J. B., eds H. Dodge and B. Ward-Perkins, *Marble in Antiquity: Collected Papers of J. B. Ward-Perkins*, Archaeological Monographs of the British School at Rome, 6, London 1992
Webb, G., *Architecture in Britain: The Middle Ages*, Harmondsworth 1956
Webber, T., *Scribes and Scholars at Salisbury Cathedral c.1075–c.1125*, Oxford 1992
Wentzel, H., 'Portraits "à l'antique" on French Mediaeval Gems and Seals', *JWCI*, 16: 1953, 342–50
Wenzel, S., 'Robert Grosseteste's Treatise on Confession, "Deus Est"', *Franciscan Studies*, 30: 1970, 218–93
Whatley, E. G., ed., *The Saint of London: The Life and Miracles of St. Erkenwald*, Medieval & Renaissance Texts and Studies, 58, Binghamton 1989
White, J., *Art and Architecture in Italy 1250–1400*, Harmondsworth 1987
Whittingham, S., *A Thirteenth-century Portrait Gallery at Salisbury Cathedral*, Salisbury 2/1979
Wichstrøm, A. A., 'Maleriet i høymiddelalderen', *Norges kunsthistorie*, 2: *Høymiddelalderen og Hansa-tid*, Oslo 1981, 252–314
Wickenden, J. F., 'John de Dalderby, Bishop of Lincoln, 1300–20', *Archaeological Journal*, 40: 1883, 215–24
Wiesen, D. A., *St Jerome as a Satirist: A Study in Christian Latin Thought and Letters*, Ithaca 1964
William of Malmesbury, ed. R. R. Darlington, *The Vita Wulfstani of William of Malmesbury*, Camden Society, 3rd Series, 40, London 1928
William Worcestre, ed. J. H. Harvey, *Itineraries*, Oxford 1969
Williams, P., *The Organ in Western Culture 750–1250*, Cambridge 1993
Williamson, P., *Gothic Sculpture 1140–1300*. New Haven and London 1995
Willis, R., *The Architectural History of Canterbury Cathedral*. London 1845
——, *The Architectural History of the Conventual Buildings of the Monastery of Christ Church in Canterbury*, London 1869
Wilson, C., *The Shrines of St William of York*, York 1977
——, 'The Neville Screen', *BAACT*, 3: 1980, 90–104
——, 'Cistercians as "Missionaries of Gothic" in Northern England', in Norton and Park, eds, 1986, 86–116
——, *The Gothic Cathedral*, London 1990
——, 'The Early Thirteenth-century Architecture of Beverley Minster: Cathedral Splendours and Cistercian Austerities', in P. R. Coss and S. D. Lloyd, eds, *Thirteenth Century England, 3*, Proceedings of the Newcastle upon Tyne Conference, Woodbridge 1991, 181–95
——, 'The Medieval Monuments', in Collinson, Ramsay and Sparks, eds, 1995, 451–510
——, et al., *Westminster Abbey*, London 1986
Wilson, J. M., ed., *The Liber Albus of the Priory of Worcester*, London 1919
Wilson, S., ed., *Saints and Their Cults*, Cambridge 1983
Wirth, K. A., *Die Entstehung des Dreinagelkruzifixus*, diss., Frankfurt-am-Main 1953
Wittgenstein, L., *The Blue and Brown Books*, Oxford 1958
Wogan-Browne, J., *The Saints' Lives and Women's Literary Culture c.1150–1300: Virginity and Its Authorizations*, Oxford 2001
Wollheim, R., *Art and Its Objects*, Cambridge 1980
Woodman, F., *The Architectural History of Canterbury Cathedral*, London 1981
Woodruff, C. E., 'The Financial Aspect of the Cult of St Thomas of Canterbury', *Archaeologia Cantiana*, 44: 1932, 13–32
—— and W. Danks, *Memorials of the Cathedral & Priory of Christ in Canterbury*, London 1912
Woods, M. C., and R. Copeland, 'Classroom and Confession', in D. Wallace, ed., *The Cambridge History of Medieval English Literature*, Cambridge 1999, 376–406
Wooley, R. M., ed., *The Canterbury Benedictional*, Henry Bradshaw Society, 51, London 1917
Woolf, R., *The English Religious Lyric in the Middle Ages*, Oxford 1968
Wordsworth, C., *Ceremonies and Processions of the Cathedral Church of Salisbury*, Cambridge 1901
——, 'Elias de Derham's Leadenhall in Salisbury Close, 1226–1915', *Wiltshire Archaeological and Natural History Magazine*, 39: 1917, 433–44
—— and D. Macleane, *Statuta et Consuetudines Ecclesiae Cathedralis Beatae Mariae Virginis Sarisberiensis*, London 1915
Wormald, F., 'Some Pictures of the Mass in an English XIVth Century Manuscript', *Walpole Society*, 41: 1966–8, 39–45
——, *The Winchester Psalter*, London 1973
——, ed., *English Benedictine Kalendars before A.D. 1100*, I, Henry Bradshaw Society, 72, London 1934
——, ed. J. J. G. Alexander et al., *Collected Writings*, I: *Studies in Medieval Art from the Sixth to the Twelfth Centuries*; II: *Studies*

in English and Continental Art of the Later Middle Ages, Oxford 1984–8
Wright, G. S., 'A Royal Tomb Program in the Reign of St Louis', *Art Bulletin*, 56: 1974, 224–43
Wright, T., ed., *The Book of the Knight of La Tour-Landry*, EETS, 33, London 1868
Young, K., *The Drama of the Medieval Church*, 2 vols, Oxford 1933
——, 'Instructions for Parish Priests', *Speculum*, 11: 1936, 224–31
Zarnecki, G., 'Henry of Blois as a Patron of Sculpture', in S. Macready and F. H. Thompson, eds, *Art and Patronage in the English Romanesque*, Society of Antiquaries Occasional Papers, 8, London 1986, 159–72
——, *Romanesque Lincoln: The Sculpture of the Cathedral*, Lincoln 1988
——, et al., *English Romanesque Art 1066–1200*, London 1984
Zinn, G. A., 'Suger, Theology and the Pseudo-Dionysian Tradition', in Gerson, ed., 1986, 33–40
——, 'Hugh of St Victor, Isaiah's Vision, and *De Arca Noe*', in D. Wood, ed., *The Church and the Arts*, Studies in Church History, 28, Oxford 1992, 99–116

Index